EARLY DYNASTIC EGYPT

EARLY DYNASTIC EGYPT

—•—

Toby A.H. Wilkinson

London and New York

First published 1999
by Routledge
11 New Fetter Lane, London EC4P 4EE

Simultaneously published in the USA and Canada
by Routledge
29 West 35th Street, New York, NY 10001

Reprinted 2000 (twice)

Routledge is an imprint of the Taylor & Francis Group

© 1999 Toby A. H. Wilkinson
Typeset in Stempel Garamond by
The Florence Group, Stoodleigh, Devon

Printed and bound in Great Britain by
Biddles Ltd, Guildford and King's Lynn

British Library Cataloguing in Publication Data
A catalogue record for this book is available from the British Library.

Library of Congress Cataloguing in Publication Data
Wilkinson, Toby A. H.
Early Dynastic Egypt / Toby A. H. Wilkinson
p. cm.
Includes bibliographical references (p. 378) and index.
1. Egypt–History–To 332 B.C. I. Title
DT85.W49 1999
932´.012–dc21
98–35836
CIP

ISBN 0–415–18633–1

For Benjamin

CONTENTS

———— •◆• ————

PLATES

——— •◆• ———

FIGURES

———— •◆• ————

PROLOGUE

——— ·◆· ———

Ancient Egypt holds a unique fascination. No other civilisation of the ancient world has such popular appeal, none is as significant for the history of human society and its organisation. The valley of the River Nile witnessed the world's first example of that enduring and now omnipresent political structure, the nation state. Today, practically the entire land surface of the earth is divided among nation states, which number nearly two hundred. But the origins of this phenomenon go back five thousand years, to the formation of a unified territory and government in Egypt. Moreover, that government, centred on the royal court and the person of the king, succeeded in creating and promoting an élite culture which expressed itself on a grand scale. Hence, ancient Egyptian civilisation has left an unparalleled series of monuments to allure and intrigue countless generations of visitors.

The pyramids of the Old Kingdom are perhaps the most remarkable, and certainly the most captivating, of Egyptian monuments. Those at Giza were hailed as one of the wonders of the ancient world; to modern eyes they are perhaps the quintessential symbol of the ancient Egyptians' extraordinary creativity and craftsmanship. Yet the cultural and political developments which led to the construction of the pyramids have been comparatively neglected. Without central control of the economy, the royal court would not have had the resources to engage in monumental building projects. Without the ability to command the necessary manpower, the pyramids could not have been raised. Without the religious and ideological motivation, the construction of huge funerary monuments would, quite literally, never have got off the ground. All these prerequisites for pyramid-building have their roots in the Early Dynastic period. Hence to understand the most potent symbols of ancient Egypt, we must look at what went before. Five hundred years separate the birth of the Egyptian state and the erection of the pyramids. This half-millennium constitutes the formative period of civilisation in the Nile valley, when Egypt's early kings developed the mechanisms of rule and the élite culture that were to characterise their country for the next three thousand years. This crucially important formative stage is the subject of the current work.

The chapters that follow seek to explain not only the background to the formation of the Egyptian state, but also the means by which its early rulers controlled the people, the land and its resources. Central authority, however, is only one side of the coin. At all periods, Egypt's governing élite strove to convey the impression that the nation was unified politically and culturally, that all its institutions revolved around the king and took their lead from the royal court. The true picture is rather more complex: in reality, local and regional concerns were important, and often had a direct impact on the pace and direction of change. Egypt was never a monolithic state, despite the wishes and protestations of its rulers. The current work addresses this interesting question, examining the character of Early Dynastic Egypt at the provincial level.

The evidence for local and regional variation is by no means straightforward; but here, as elsewhere in the study of early Egypt, recent scholarship has led to major advances in understanding. Indeed, research into the formative period of ancient Egyptian civilisation has intensified exponentially over the past thirty years. The re-evaluation of material from old excavations has been accompanied by dramatic new discoveries. Record numbers of archaeological expeditions have been concentrating their efforts on illuminating the remotest periods of Egyptian history, and in particular the processes which led to the formation of the Egyptian state. As a result of this new information, a comprehensive study of the Early Dynastic period can now be attempted for the first time.

Early Dynastic Egypt has traditionally suffered from being squeezed between two, more obviously glamorous, neighbours. On the one hand, the prehistoric origins of ancient Egypt and the unification of the country at the beginning of the historic period have intrigued scholars, attracting much comment and debate. On the other hand, the glories of the pyramid age, combined with a wealth of artistic and written evidence, have given the Old Kingdom an undeniable appeal for professionals and public alike. While the Predynastic period and the Old Kingdom have been intensively studied, the intervening phase of Egyptian history – the Early Dynastic period – has been comparatively neglected. The current work seeks to redress the imbalance, giving the first three dynasties the attention they deserve as a period of great innovation and lasting importance, a period, moreover, which paved the way for the familiar glories of ancient Egypt.

This book is arranged in three parts. Part I forms an introduction to the study of Early Dynastic Egypt. The re-discovery of Egypt's remote past, although very much a feature of the last three decades, began more than a century ago. A long line of distinguished archaeologists and scholars have added pieces to the puzzle, although the picture is by no means complete. Chapter 1 tells the extraordinary story of how 'Egypt before the pyramids', once an obscure dark age, has emerged from the shadows into the spotlight of academic inquiry and popular interest.

The formation of a unified state marks the beginning of Egyptian history and this pivotal development is examined in detail in Chapter 2. The roots of the process lie far back in prehistory, in the period called

'Predynastic' (that is, before the dynasties). Southern (Upper) Egypt was the heartland of social change, since it was here that hierarchies and social divisions based upon inherited status first developed. During the second half of the fourth millennium BC, political and economic power came to be concentrated in the hands of a few ruling élites. Advances in technology and an intensification of trade benefited some centres more than others, and at these favoured sites the local rulers began to adopt the trappings of royalty. As these trends accelerated, Egypt was transformed and a nation was born.

The five centuries which followed comprise a fascinating period of Egypt's history, but one which is all too often glossed over in standard books on the subject. Chapter 3 presents the first ever, detailed, reign-by-reign account of the period, drawing on the results of the latest research by an international community of experts. The discussion includes an evaluation of the historical sources for the first three dynasties, and examines the splendid achievements of Egypt's early kings.

With Part I, the scene is thus set for an in-depth analysis of Early Dynastic Egypt.

The dominant themes of early Egyptian civilisation are examined in Part II, which forms the core of the book. Subtitled 'The establishment of authority', Part II analyses the various mechanisms by which Egypt's early rulers first developed and then exercised authority over a newly unified country. The word 'establishment' has been deliberately chosen for its dual meaning: the setting up of an ideology of rule, and the institutional structures by which this ideology was put into effect. The most obvious facet of the 'establishment' is the administration, the governmental apparatus which allowed the royal court to supervise and control Egypt and its resources. Very little has been written about early Egyptian administration, mainly because the source material is fragmentary and difficult to interpret. However, a close look at the surviving evidence for administrative practices indicates that – in ancient Egypt as in countries today – control of the economy lay at the heart of the government's activities. The court itself comprised a bewildering array of officials, and there are tantalising glimpses of how political power was exercised at this earliest period of Egyptian history. Of course, control of the national economy was dependent upon control of the various provinces; provincial government seems to have developed initially as an adjunct to economic supervision, later taking on a life of its own (as the history of the Old Kingdom demonstrates). Chapter 4 examines all these aspects of Early Dynastic administration, and seeks to draw a coherent picture of how early Egypt was governed.

Egypt was not alone in the ancient world. To the north and south were other lands and cultures, and contact with them was unavoidable. If the continued supply of commodities to the court lay at the heart of Egyptian administration, it also formed the backdrop to early Egypt's foreign relations. In its quest for raw materials and prestige goods, the royal court had to look beyond the Nile valley to the adjoining desert regions and other lands further afield. The desire to gain access to trade routes with Palestine and Nubia may have been a key factor in the process of state formation. Once Egypt had been unified, mere access to foreign imports was no longer sufficient: direct control of foreign trade or of the commodity sources themselves became both desirable and feasible. Economic interest provided grounds for political expansionism. There is evidence that Early Dynastic kings launched military campaigns against neighbouring lands, and the motive is likely to have been largely economic, even if such activities were dressed in a cloak of ideology. Egypt's foreign relations during the Early Dynastic period highlight both the concerns of the early state and the ways in which these affected, and were affected by, the geo-politics of the wider region. The complex interaction between the Nile valley, Egypt's desert margins, and neighbouring lands is discussed in Chapter 5.

In order to control Egypt and its people, the early kings followed a number of different strategies. Together with the overt political and economic control attested in administrative records, more subtle psychological means were deployed to ensure the loyalty and subservience of the population. Perhaps the most powerful and pervasive ideology in ancient Egyptian culture was the ideology of divine kingship: the belief that the king was the earthly incarnation of the supreme deity, a channel of communication between the divine and human spheres, and the unifying force that held Egypt together, without whom chaos would ensue. Such an ideology obviously suited the system of government since it ensured strong support for the status quo and made any return to the political fragmentation of the Predynastic period unthinkable. Divine kingship is often cited as the defining characteristic of ancient Egyptian civilisation. Yet its success and longevity as an ideology of rule owes much to the efforts of the Early Dynastic kings, who formulated and promoted it. The origins and early development of this most fundamental aspect of Egyptian culture are explored in Chapter 6. The nature of early kingship – how the rulers saw themselves and their office – can be gauged from a variety of sources, in particular the names and titles adopted by successive monarchs, and the activities deemed worthy of record in the royal annals. The means by which kingship ideology was promulgated are equally fascinating. They included a repertoire of symbols (iconography) which became indelibly associated with royal authority, and whose preponderance in official art constantly reinforced the message that Egypt depended on the king for its well-being. Ceremonies and rituals provided the early Egyptian kings with carefully controlled, symbolically charged occasions on which they could demonstrate their legitimacy and authority.

Finally, the potency of architecture to express ideas of status was appreciated from an early stage. Through the development of an explicitly royal architectural style the Early Dynastic kings sought to secure their position by appealing to the Egyptian psyche.

The concern to provide for life after death is one of the best known aspects of ancient Egyptian civilisation. To it is due such characteristic features as mummies and pyramids. The most impressive monuments to have survived from Early Dynastic Egypt are the funerary structures built for the kings and their relatives. The development of the royal tomb, leading eventually to the concept of the pyramid, is explored in Chapter 7. The changes in the form of the royal burial over the course of the Early Dynastic period reflect not only advances in architecture and building technology, but also changes in the concept of the afterlife. Moreover, as the most important project of a king's reign, the royal tomb can tell us much about the self-image and public portrayal of kingship.

Religion plays an important role in most societies and early Egypt was no exception. The bewildering array of cults so characteristic of pharaonic Egypt was a feature of religious life in the Nile valley from the beginning of Egyptian history. Numerous gods and goddesses are attested from Early Dynastic Egypt, together with religious festivals and other cultic activities. Chapter 8 presents the evidence for early Egyptian religion, and examines the way in which religion was manipulated by the royal court for its own ends. The concerns of the individual and those of the state rarely coincide where interaction with the divine sphere is involved. Nothing illustrates the divide between the early Egyptian state and its subjects better than temple building: whilst care was lavished on a few, nationally significant, temples, local shrines received little or no state attention. An analysis of religion in the first three dynasties highlights the tension between rulers and ruled: a tension that Egypt's first kings sought to contain, and which forms a central theme of the current work.

Tombs and temples are certainly impressive and informative, but they tell only part of the story. To get to the heart of Early Dynastic Egypt, to understand life in the Nile valley and how it developed, we must escape the alluring world-view promoted by the court and look instead at individual communities and regions. This is the focus of Part III, which seeks to provide a counterbalance to the court-centred culture so dominant in books about ancient Egypt. The growth of urban communities marks an important stage in the history of human society. The process of urbanisation in Egypt is particularly instructive as it seems to reflect local and regional factors more than centrally inspired policies. In recent years the number of settlements excavated in Egypt has increased markedly. Chapter 9 discusses the evidence for early urbanism, pointing out the factors which influenced the development of each community.

This leads on to the final chapter of the book, which stands back and takes a regional view of developments in Early Dynastic Egypt. Much of the history of Egypt is the history of its regions. Particular combinations of natural and strategic advantages favoured some parts of the country over others; the interplay between regions affected the development of Egyptian society as a whole. Chapter 10 seeks to explain why some areas prospered during the first three dynasties while others declined; for in the answers to such questions lies the history of Egypt's formative period.

ACKNOWLEDGEMENTS

————— •◆• —————

Plate 3.2 is reproduced with the kind permission of the Committee of the Egypt Exploration Society.

This book could not have been written without the assistance, support and encouragement of many individuals.

First and foremost, my thanks are due to Christ's College, Cambridge, which, in awarding me the Lady Wallis Budge Junior Research Fellowship in Egyptology, provided generous financial support for the four years of research and writing which went into this book. I should like to express my gratitude to the Managers of the Lady Wallis Budge Fund; to the Research Fund Managers and the College Council of Christ's College for further financial support; and not least to the late Sir Ernest Alfred Thompson Wallis Budge himself, one-time scholar of Christ's College, for the generosity and foresight which have so benefited British Egyptology in the six decades since his death. Christ's has also provided the perfect environment in which to live and work, for which everyone in the College – the Master, former Master, fellows, staff and students – deserves my heartfelt thanks.

My research into the early periods of ancient Egyptian civilisation has benefited greatly from discussions with a number of colleagues. For their unfailing interest in my work, their help and encouragement, I should like to thank Cambridge Egyptologists Barry Kemp, John Ray, Janine Bourriau, Dr Eleni Vassilika, Dr Kate Spence and Will Schenck. Kate Spence also drew the excellent illustrations which accompany the text. Other scholars have given generously of their time to provide advice and information: Barbara Adams, Nicole Alexanian, Professor John Baines, Dr Stan Hendrickx, David Jeffreys, Dr Christiana Köhler, Ian Mathieson, Dr Stephan Seidlmayer and Ana Tavares. Many distinguished experts were kind enough to read and comment on the first draft of this book: Dr Edwin van den Brink, Dr Stan Hendrickx, Barry Kemp, Dr Geraldine Pinch, Dr Stephen Quirke, Dr Kate Spence and Dr Jeffrey Spencer. I should like to express my profound thanks to all of them for their insightful comments and suggestions which have contributed immeasurably to the final form of the work. Any errors or omissions remain, of course, the author's sole responsibility.

Finally, I owe a great debt of gratitude to all my family and friends, without whose love, friendship and encouragement this book could not

PART I

INTRODUCTION

CHAPTER ONE

EGYPTOLOGY AND THE EARLY DYNASTIC PERIOD

———— •◆• ————

THE PIONEERS: 1894–1935

Abydos: Amélineau and Petrie

The history of Egypt began at Abydos. Here in **Upper Egypt**, on the low desert beneath the towering western escarpment (Plate 1.1), the **Predynastic** rulers of the region, and their descendants, the earliest kings of a united Egypt, were buried with their retainers and possessions. Amongst the tombs of the ancestral royal cemetery, a burial of unparalleled size was prepared around 3150 BC for a leader who may already have ruled over most, if not all, of Egypt. About a century later, another king was buried nearby: Narmer, who was apparently regarded by his immediate successors as the founder of the First Dynasty, and whose ceremonial **palette** recalls the **unification** of the Two Lands, in ritual if not in fact. The mortuary complex of Narmer's successor, Aha, was also constructed at Abydos. Aha's reign may mark the systematic keeping of **annals**, and it may thus be regarded as the beginning of Egyptian history in a strict sense of the word.

Egyptian history also began at Abydos in another sense: it was here, in the dying years of the nineteenth century and in the early years of the twentieth, that archaeologists first uncovered evidence of Egypt's remote past. The excavation and re-excavation of the royal cemetery at Abydos – which still continues after more than a century – has transformed our understanding of the earliest period of Egyptian history. Today, as a hundred years ago, each new discovery from the sands of Abydos enhances or modifies our picture of the Nile valley during the formative phase of ancient Egyptian civilisation. As we shall see, many other sites have contributed to the total picture, but none more so than Abydos. Abydos, above any other site, holds the key to Egypt's early dynasties.

Before the first excavations in the royal cemetery at Abydos, there was not a single object in the Egyptian Museum that could be dated securely to the First or Second Dynasty (de Morgan 1896: 181). Indeed, before excavators began unearthing the burials of the **Early Dynastic** kings, 'the history of Egypt only began with the Great Pyramid' (Petrie 1939: 160). The pyramids of the late Third/early Fourth Dynasty at Maidum and Dahshur were the oldest monuments known to scholars. The Step Pyramid

3

Plate 1.2   Mastaba K1 at Beit Khallaf, dating to the reign of Netjerikhet, Third Dynasty (author's photograph).

Discoveries further south: de Morgan, Quibell and Green

Whilst Amélineau and Petrie were arguing over the spoils of Abydos, discoveries in southern Upper Egypt were shedding important new light on Early Dynastic Egypt, its rulers and their achievements. Together with Abydos, two sites are of key significance for the process of state formation and for the early development of Egyptian civilisation, Naqada and Hierakonpolis, and it was at these two sites that excavations at the turn of the century yielded spectacular results. One of the outstanding achievements of Jacques Jean Marie de Morgan (1857–1924) was the discovery and excavation of the royal tomb at Naqada (de Morgan 1897). Identified at first as the tomb of the legendary **Menes** (Borchardt 1898), but subsequently as the burial of Queen Neith-hotep (probably the mother of Aha), this was the first substantial structure of the First Dynasty to be excavated in Egypt, and it demonstrated the scale of monumental architecture at the very beginning of Egyptian history. De Morgan also established the link between the Predynastic period and the early dynasties, thus implicitly recognising the Early Dynastic period as the culmination of a long sequence of cultural development.

In the same year as de Morgan's great discovery at Naqada, excavations began on the town mound at Hierakonpolis, the Kom el-Ahmar. They were directed by James Edward Quibell (1867–1935), who had excavated

CHAPTER ONE

EGYPTOLOGY AND THE EARLY DYNASTIC PERIOD

—— •◆• ——

THE PIONEERS: 1894–1935

Abydos: Amélineau and Petrie

The history of Egypt began at Abydos. Here in **Upper Egypt**, on the low desert beneath the towering western escarpment (Plate 1.1), the **Predynastic** rulers of the region, and their descendants, the earliest kings of a united Egypt, were buried with their retainers and possessions. Amongst the tombs of the ancestral royal cemetery, a burial of unparalleled size was prepared around 3150 BC for a leader who may already have ruled over most, if not all, of Egypt. About a century later, another king was buried nearby: Narmer, who was apparently regarded by his immediate successors as the founder of the First Dynasty, and whose ceremonial **palette** recalls the **unification** of the Two Lands, in ritual if not in fact. The mortuary complex of Narmer's successor, Aha, was also constructed at Abydos. Aha's reign may mark the systematic keeping of **annals**, and it may thus be regarded as the beginning of Egyptian history in a strict sense of the word.

Egyptian history also began at Abydos in another sense: it was here, in the dying years of the nineteenth century and in the early years of the twentieth, that archaeologists first uncovered evidence of Egypt's remote past. The excavation and re-excavation of the royal cemetery at Abydos – which still continues after more than a century – has transformed our understanding of the earliest period of Egyptian history. Today, as a hundred years ago, each new discovery from the sands of Abydos enhances or modifies our picture of the Nile valley during the formative phase of ancient Egyptian civilisation. As we shall see, many other sites have contributed to the total picture, but none more so than Abydos. Abydos, above any other site, holds the key to Egypt's early dynasties.

Before the first excavations in the royal cemetery at Abydos, there was not a single object in the Egyptian Museum that could be dated securely to the First or Second Dynasty (de Morgan 1896: 181). Indeed, before excavators began unearthing the burials of the **Early Dynastic** kings, 'the history of Egypt only began with the Great Pyramid' (Petrie 1939: 160). The pyramids of the late Third/early Fourth Dynasty at Maidum and Dahshur were the oldest monuments known to scholars. The Step Pyramid

Plate 1.1 The Umm el-Qaab at Abydos, burial ground of Egypt's early rulers (author's photograph).

complex at Saqqara had not yet been excavated from the drift sand. As for the kings of the first three dynasties recorded in the **king lists** of the New Kingdom and in Manetho's history, they were no more than names, legendary figures for whom no historical evidence existed.

Emile Clément Amélineau (1850–1915) was the first to clear the royal tombs of the First and late Second Dynasties in a systematic way, although Auguste Mariette (1821–81) had worked at the site some forty years before. Amélineau's excavations at Abydos from 1894 to 1898 yielded important results, but his unscientific methods drew criticism, especially from his great rival and successor at Abydos, Petrie. It is probably fair to say that the *Mission Amélineau* was driven more by the ambition of private collectors than by academic or scientific concerns for the culture of early Egypt. However, the same was undoubtedly true of many other excavations in the Nile valley at that time and later. Amélineau's contribution – in bringing the importance of Abydos to the attention of Egyptologists

– should not be dismissed, despite his obvious failings by modern standards. The objects he found in the royal tombs were published in four volumes (Amélineau 1899, 1902, 1904, 1905) and were sold at auction in Paris in 1904. Some entered museums, others ended up in private collections. Scholarly interest in Egypt's earliest historical period had now been well and truly awakened, and archaeologists were swift to follow in Amélineau's footsteps.

William Matthew Flinders Petrie (1853–1942), the founding father of Egyptian archaeology, had been interested in Egypt's formative period for some years. His pioneering mission to Coptos in 1893–4 revealed material of the late Predynastic and Early Dynastic periods for the first time – most famously the colossal statues of a fertility god – and effectively pushed back Egyptian history by some 400 years, from the beginning of the Old Kingdom to the beginning of the First Dynasty (Petrie 1896). Petrie's subsequent excavations at Naqada and Ballas in 1895 yielded extensive Predynastic material (Petrie and Quibell 1896) and led him to formulate his famous **sequence dating system**, the principle of which has been used by scholars ever since to date Predynastic contexts.

Petrie's 'discovery' of the Predynastic period was followed by new insights into the earliest dynasties, gained through his excavations at Abydos in 1899–1903. He rushed to the Early Dynastic royal cemetery following the departure of Amélineau and was able 'to rescue for historical study' (Petrie 1900: 2) what had been left behind. Petrie no doubt exaggerated Amélineau's failings and his own achievements, but there is no denying that Petrie's discoveries were of great significance, and dramatically enhanced understanding of Egypt's early history, not least by establishing the order of the First Dynasty kings (Petrie 1900, 1901). In the later seasons, Petrie turned his attention to the early town and temple of Abydos (Petrie 1902, 1903). His excavations uncovered a small cemetery of the early First Dynasty, a jumble of walls belonging to the Early Dynastic temple, and three deposits of **votive** objects.

At the same time as Petrie was re-excavating the royal tombs at Abydos, his colleague John Garstang (1876–1956) was investigating Predynastic and Early Dynastic sites a little to the north, in the vicinity of the villages of Mahasna, Reqaqna and Beit Khallaf. Near the first two he revealed a cemetery of Third Dynasty tombs (Garstang 1904), while on the low desert behind Beit Khallaf he excavated several huge **mastaba**s of mudbrick (Plate 1.2), also dated to the Third Dynasty (Garstang 1902). From the point of view of Early Dynastic history, the most important finds from Beit Khallaf were the seal-impressions. One of these, from mastaba K2, shows the name of King Sanakht opposite the lower end of a **cartouche**. This is the earliest attested occurrence of the frame used to enclose the royal name, and the sealing provides the sole evidence for equating the **Horus** name, Sanakht, with the cartouche name, Nebka.

Plate 1.2 Mastaba K1 at Beit Khallaf, dating to the reign of Netjerikhet, Third Dynasty (author's photograph).

Discoveries further south: de Morgan, Quibell and Green

Whilst Amélineau and Petrie were arguing over the spoils of Abydos, discoveries in southern Upper Egypt were shedding important new light on Early Dynastic Egypt, its rulers and their achievements. Together with Abydos, two sites are of key significance for the process of state formation and for the early development of Egyptian civilisation, Naqada and Hierakonpolis, and it was at these two sites that excavations at the turn of the century yielded spectacular results. One of the outstanding achievements of Jacques Jean Marie de Morgan (1857–1924) was the discovery and excavation of the royal tomb at Naqada (de Morgan 1897). Identified at first as the tomb of the legendary **Menes** (Borchardt 1898), but subsequently as the burial of Queen Neith-hotep (probably the mother of Aha), this was the first substantial structure of the First Dynasty to be excavated in Egypt, and it demonstrated the scale of monumental architecture at the very beginning of Egyptian history. De Morgan also established the link between the Predynastic period and the early dynasties, thus implicitly recognising the Early Dynastic period as the culmination of a long sequence of cultural development.

In the same year as de Morgan's great discovery at Naqada, excavations began on the town mound at Hierakonpolis, the Kom el-Ahmar. They were directed by James Edward Quibell (1867–1935), who had excavated with Petrie at Coptos in the pioneering season of 1893–4. Assisted by Frederick Green and Somers Clarke, he worked at Hierakonpolis from 1897 to 1898, before handing over to Green for the following season (Quibell 1900; Quibell and Green 1902). In the temple area of the town mound the archaeologists found a circular revetment belonging to the Early Dynastic temple and a crude limestone cylindrical statue similar to the colossi from Coptos. The temple also yielded spectacular objects of Old Kingdom date, including life-size copper statues of two Sixth Dynasty kings and a golden hawk head. Most significant for Early Dynastic studies was the discovery – in circumstances which remain unclear – of the so-called **'Main Deposit'**, a hoard of early votive objects including the famous Scorpion and Narmer **macehead**s and the Narmer palette. These provided the earliest images of Egyptian kings, bringing life to the otherwise obscure royal names attested at Abydos and Naqada. They also represent the earliest expression of the classic conventions of Egyptian artistic depiction, and indicate that these principles were formalised and canonised at the very beginning of the Egyptian state. The complex **iconography** of the palette reveals much about early conceptions of kingship, whilst the quality of workmanship gives an indication of the sophisticated taste of the early Egyptian court. Since its discovery, the Narmer palette has acquired something of the status of an icon of early Egypt. Today it is displayed in the entrance hall of the Egyptian Museum, where it serves as an admirable starting-point for the glories of Egyptian civilisation. The palette, together with the other Early Dynastic objects that had flooded into the museum since Amélineau's work at Abydos, was catalogued by Quibell in his capacity as a member of staff of the Antiquities Service. The two volumes of *Archaic objects* (Quibell 1904–5) represent the first published corpus of early material.

Excavation intensifies: Petrie and Quibell joined by Reisner, Junker and Firth

The first two decades of the twentieth century witnessed a substantial increase in the number of early sites excavated. Spurred on by the spectacular discoveries at Abydos and Hierakonpolis, archaeologists turned their attention to cemeteries throughout Egypt. The American interest in the early periods of Egyptian civilisation began in earnest with the Hearst Expedition to Egypt, directed by George Andrew Reisner (1867–1942). From 1901 to 1903, Reisner excavated the sequence of cemeteries at Naga ed-Deir, a site on the east bank of the Nile in the Abydos region, directly opposite the modern town of Girga. Assisted first by Green, fresh from his excavations at Hierakonpolis, and subsequently by Arthur Mace, Reisner uncovered graves of virtually every period at Naga ed-Deir, stretching from the early Predynastic period to modern times (Reisner 1908; Mace 1909).

The Early Dynastic period was particularly well-represented, with four cemeteries covering the period of the first three dynasties (Cemeteries 1500, 3000, 3500 and 500). By the standards of the time, Reisner's excavations were conducted in a thorough and professional manner. As well as providing a wealth of information on Early Dynastic burial practices and provincial culture, the Naga ed-Deir excavations yielded a few finds which indicated contacts between Egypt and other early civilisations of the Near East. Contacts of some form had already been suggested by the decoration of late Predynastic élite objects (palettes and knife handles) which included elements of Mesopotamian iconography. The discovery of **cylinder seals** – a class of object indisputably Mesopotamian in origin – in graves at Naga ed-Deir offered tangible evidence for trade between the two cultures.

In concentrating on the rich remains of Upper Egypt, Reisner was following the pioneering missions of the late nineteenth century. At the end of the first decade of the twentieth century a change of emphasis occurred, and sites in the **Memphite** area were investigated for the first time. Petrie (1907) excavated a series of Early Dynastic mastabas to the south of Giza, one of which had already been investigated by Daressy (1905) for the Cairo Museum. However, the pioneer of archaeological investigation in the Memphite area was Hermann Junker (1877–1962). He significantly enhanced the understanding of Early Dynastic Egypt by his work at Tura, a site on the east bank of the Nile about 10 kilometres south of central Cairo. It was Junker's first excavation in Egypt, and he certainly struck lucky. During the winter of 1909–10, a large cemetery of some 500 late Predynastic and Early Dynastic graves was revealed, together with a wealth of grave goods, particularly pottery (Junker 1912). This was the first time that early material had been discovered on the east bank of the Nile in the Memphite region, and it paved the way for later excavations in the vicinity by Brunton and Saad. What made the Tura cemetery so important for future studies was its linear growth over time: the earliest graves were located in the southern part of the site, the latest graves in the northern part. The contents of each grave were recorded in detail; this information, in conjunction with the cemetery plan, could therefore be used to chart the development of artefact assemblages over time, and the growth of the cemetery itself.

In 1911, responding to reports of looting by local villagers, Petrie turned his attention back to early Egypt and to the extensive cemetery on the desert edge behind the hamlet of Kafr Tarkhan (Plate 1.3), near the entrance to the Fayum (Petrie *et al.* 1913; Petrie 1914). In two seasons of excavation, from 1911 to 1913, Petrie uncovered many hundreds of tombs dating to the very beginning of Egyptian history, including several large mudbrick mastabas decorated with recessed niches, in the style exemplified by the royal tomb at Naqada. The wealth of grave goods shed considerable light on the accomplishments of the Early Dynastic Egyptians,

Plate 1.3   The Early Dynastic cemetery at Tarkhan (author's photograph).

particularly in the spheres of arts and crafts. A number of burials contained objects inscribed with early royal names. Analysis of the other objects in these graves enabled characteristic types of pottery and stone vessels to be associated with the reigns of particular kings. This provided useful comparative material to help with the dating of other tombs which did not contain any inscriptions. Just as important, Petrie's work at Tarkhan enabled him to extend his sequence dating system down to the Third Dynasty, thus linking the first three dynasties with the preceding Predynastic period in one continuous sequence of **ceramic** development. This built upon de Morgan's work at Naqada and firmly established the cultural and historical context of the Early Dynastic period.

Following his spectacularly productive excavations at Hierakonpolis, Quibell was appointed to the post of Chief Inspector at Saqqara. His attention turned to the myriad monuments of the Saqqara plateau, and he began by excavating two small areas of the Early Dynastic cemetery in the years 1912 to 1914. This marked the beginning of a period of intensive archaeological investigation in the cemeteries of Memphis, which was to continue for over forty years. Quibell uncovered many tombs, including that of Hesira, a high official in the reign of Djoser/Netjerikhet (Quibell 1913, 1923). The systematic excavation of Netjerikhet's Step Pyramid complex – perhaps the outstanding architectural achievement to have survived from Early Dynastic Egypt – occupied Quibell's later years (Firth and Quibell 1935). He directed work at the complex from 1931 until his death in 1935.

Plate 1.4   An élite First Dynasty tomb at North Saqqara (author's photograph).

The complex of buildings surrounding the Step Pyramid had been discovered by Cecil Mallaby Firth (1878–1931), who had succeeded Quibell as Inspector of Antiquities at Saqqara in 1923. Firth conducted excavations at the complex from 1924 to 1927, his results completely transforming theories about the origins of stone architecture in Egypt. Excavation and restoration of the Step Pyramid complex has continued ever since, yielding important information on many aspects of early Egypt, including material culture, architecture, kingship, the order of succession and, of course, funerary religion. After he handed control of the Step Pyramid excavations to Quibell, Firth turned his attention to the Early Dynastic cemetery at North Saqqara (Plate 1.4). The excavation of this site was to have been Firth's second major project, but fate cruelly intervened. He was about to start clearing the cemetery when he returned to England on leave in 1931. On the journey home he contracted pneumonia and within a few days he was dead. It was left to his young assistant, Emery, to carry out Firth's plans, with spectacular results.

THE CEMETERIES OF MEMPHIS: 1936–1956

Emery at North Saqqara

Walter Bryan Emery (1903–71) took over as director of excavations at North Saqqara in 1935, in succession to Firth. Rejecting the piecemeal approach to excavation pursued by his predecessors, Emery decided that only a systematic clearance of the entire cemetery would do the site justice and produce the best results. He was keenly aware of the importance of the cemetery for the early history of Egypt (Emery 1938: vii), and his first season of excavation did not disappoint. In 1936 he cleared the tomb of Hemaka, which Firth had partially excavated five years earlier (Emery 1938). The tomb's contents included several masterpieces of Egyptian craftsmanship, notably an inlaid gaming disk and the earliest roll of papyrus ever discovered. Although uninscribed, it proved that this writing medium – and therefore a **cursive** version of the Egyptian script for use on papyrus – already existed in the First Dynasty. In the following season of 1937–8, Emery and his team excavated the earliest tomb in the élite cemetery, number 3357, dated to the reign of Aha (Emery 1939). The Second World War interrupted work at Saqqara, but Emery returned to the site to re-commence excavations in 1946. Another break of three years followed from 1949 to 1952, before Emery was able to complete his work in the cemetery during the years 1952 to 1956. The years of excavation succeeded in revealing an entire sequence of large First Dynasty tombs, strung out along the edge of the escarpment (Emery 1949, 1954, 1958). Emery was particularly impressed by the size and splendour of the tombs, especially by comparison with the contemporary royal tombs at Abydos. He formed the belief that the Saqqara tombs were the true burial places of the First Dynasty kings, and that the Abydos monuments excavated by Petrie were merely **cenotaph**s. Thus began a long debate between Egyptologists, one which continues to this day. There can be no doubt that Emery's results at North Saqqara represented 'the most important contributions made to the history of the 1st Dynasty since ... Petrie's excavations at Abydos' (Lauer 1976: 89). The numerous seal-impressions and **label**s have added greatly to knowledge of Early Dynastic titles and kingship, whilst the artefacts of copper, stone, wood and ivory are some of the most impressive achievements of early Egyptian craftsmanship to have survived. Emery limited his excavation reports to 'the hard facts' (1949: iv); the interpretation of his finds was left for a later, semi-popular work (Emery 1961). Whilst some of the theories it expresses can no longer be substantiated, it none the less remains an important source-book for the Early Dynastic period, and in particular for Emery's own discoveries at North Saqqara.

In contrast to the important series of First Dynasty mastabas, the numerous minor tombs of the First Dynasty, plus the Second and Third

Dynasty burials excavated by Emery before and after the Second World War (1934–9 and 1945–7), were never published. This is much to the detriment of Early Dynastic studies, since the later tombs, in particular, yielded important evidence for the evolution of mortuary architecture in the latter half of the Early Dynastic period, providing a link between the First Dynasty élite tombs and the mastabas of the Old Kingdom.

Saad at Helwan

In his first five years at North Saqqara, up to the outbreak of the Second World War, Emery was assisted by Zaki Youssef Saad (1901–82). Saad was to make his own major contribution to Early Dynastic studies by excavating the huge **necropolis** across the river at el-Maasara (Plate 1.5) (Saad named the site 'Helwan' after the nearest large town). The excavations lasted from 1942 to 1954, and revealed in excess of 10,000 graves (Saad 1947, 1951, 1957, 1969). All but a handful dated to '**Dynasty 0**' and the Early Dynastic period. The necropolis must have served the city of Memphis, which lay directly opposite on the west bank of the Nile. The sheer size of the Helwan burial ground is staggering, and reflects the size of the capital's administrative class, even at the beginning of Egyptian history. Some of the tombs clearly belonged to individuals of considerable status (Wood 1987), almost equalling in size the contemporary

Plate 1.5 The Early Dynastic necropolis at Helwan/el-Maasara
(author's photograph).

mastabas at North Saqqara (Wilkinson 1996a). Unfortunately, to the great loss of Early Dynastic studies, the results of Saad's later seasons were never published (although some finds from the later seasons are discussed in Saad 1969), and the wealth of material that must have been uncovered in the years 1947 to 1954 remains inaccessible.

Montet at Abu Rawash

Jean Pierre Marie Montet (1885–1966), best known as the excavator of Tanis, directed work at Abu Rawash, at the northernmost end of the Memphite necropolis, in the late 1930s, at the same time that Emery was excavating at North Saqqara. Montet's discoveries on so-called Hill M – a prominent knoll close to the edge of the cultivation – paralleled those of Emery further south: élite mastaba tombs of mudbrick, their façades decorated with recessed niches, dating to the First Dynasty (Montet 1938, 1946). The cemetery at Abu Rawash seems to have been used exclusively during the reign of Den, and may have served as an 'overspill' burial ground from North Saqqara. As at the latter site, one of the large tombs at Abu Rawash was accompanied by two boat burials.

Lauer at the Step Pyramid complex

After two years of excavation at the Step Pyramid complex, it became clear to Firth that the skills of an architect were required to reassemble the mass of confusing fragments and reconstruct the original appearance of Netjerikhet's great funerary monument. So, in 1926, Firth called upon the services of the young Jean-Philippe Lauer, who has since devoted his entire life – in a career spanning the last seventy years – to the restoration of the complex. Most of the architectural elements that are visible today owe their appearance and restoration to Lauer's patience and insight. More than any other scholar, Lauer has been responsible for elucidating the history and symbolism of the Step Pyramid complex (Lauer 1936, 1939, 1962).

Discoveries of great importance were made by Lauer during the clearance of the galleries beneath the Step Pyramid. Particularly interesting is the hoard of stone vessels amassed by Netjerikhet to furnish his burial. The vessels seem to have been gathered together from the royal stores as they include many inscribed for earlier kings (Lacau and Lauer 1959). Nearly every king before Netjerikhet is attested, including some ephemeral rulers unknown from other sources. Some vessels are inscribed with the names of successive rulers, including a group of bowls bearing the names of the last four kings of the First Dynasty. The stone vessels from the Step Pyramid thus comprise one of the most important sources of historical information for the first two dynasties. Many vessels bear inscriptions not incised but written in ink (Lacau and Lauer 1965). These attest the use of cursive script as early as the First Dynasty – already suggested by the papyrus discovered by Emery in the tomb of Hemaka – and provide valuable insights into the workings of the Early Dynastic administration. They include the earliest known occurrence of the title of '**vizier**' (the executive head of the administration), and the earliest reference to an administrative division or **nome**. The inscriptions from the Step Pyramid complex form one of the largest bodies of early writing from Egypt.

Goneim at the Sekhemkhet complex

Zakaria Goneim (1911–59) was responsible for one of the most important and unexpected discoveries at Saqqara: the unfinished Step Pyramid complex of King Sekhemkhet, the successor of Netjerikhet whose own mortuary complex so dominates the Saqqara plateau. Goneim was appointed Keeper of the Saqqara necropolis in 1951 and almost immediately began excavations to the south-west of the pyramid of Unas. His discovery and excavation of an unknown mortuary complex built for a previously unknown king of the Third Dynasty caused something of a sensation (Goneim 1957). In some respects, the architecture of the Sekhemkhet complex is more developed than that of the Netjerikhet monument, illustrating a gradual refinement in the monumental use of stone. A pen holder from the chambers beneath the pyramid is inscribed with the second name of King Sekhemkhet, confirming his identification with the Djoserty of the New Kingdom lists. Goneim's discovery not only resolved one of the outstanding problems of Third Dynasty chronology, it also helped scholars to see the Step Pyramid complex of Netjerikhet in context: as part of a sequence of development in the sphere of royal mortuary architecture, rather than as a unique and unparalleled monument.

A change of perception

During the two decades of excavation in the Memphite necropolis, Early Dynastic studies struggled to keep up with the wealth of new evidence provided by archaeologists. However, despite the continuous flow of excavation reports, critical examination of some of the overriding issues did not cease altogether. An important transformation in the understanding and perception of Early Dynastic Egypt came with the publication of Emile Massoulard's book, *Préhistoire et protohistoire d'Egypte* (Massoulard 1949). He seems to have been the first scholar to recognise, or at least to articulate in print, that the civilisation of dynastic Egypt was largely an indigenous development, with its most fundamental roots in the culture of the Predynastic period (Massoulard 1949: 333). By contrast, the theory of the 'dynastic race' – a 'master race' of invaders from the east, thought to be responsible for imposing civilisation on the 'primitive' and unsophisticated indigenous Egyptians – had been articulated by Petrie only ten years before (Petrie 1939) and was still being espoused enthusiastically by scholars such as Emery (1961) and Edwards (1971) two decades after the publication of Massoulard's work. The recognition of the indigenous roots of classic Egyptian civilisation emphasised the continuities between Predynastic and Early Dynastic culture. The achievements of the First Dynasty, it was realised, were the result of a long period of cultural and political development, rather than a radically new order imposed from outside. This change of perception undoubtedly influenced the course of Early Dynastic scholarship, and has now totally replaced the discredited 'dynastic race' theory.

A TIME OF TRANSITION: 1957–76

The end of an era: Klasens and Emery in the Memphite necropolis

From 1953 until the break in excavations in 1956, Emery was assisted at North Saqqara by Adolf Klasens. The following year, Klasens took his own team to the northernmost site of the Memphite necropolis, Abu Rawash. Here, he directed three seasons of excavation for the Leiden Museum of Antiquities, from 1957 to 1959 (Klasens 1957, 1958, 1959, 1960, 1961). He re-investigated the élite cemetery excavated by Montet, uncovering several more mastabas of the First Dynasty (Klasens 1961). Immediately below Hill M, at the edge of the cultivation, Klasens revealed a sequence of four Early Dynastic cemeteries, spanning the period from 'Dynasty 0' to the late Second Dynasty. The graves yielded abundant quantities of stone vessels and pottery, including imported Syro-Palestinian jugs, providing concrete evidence for trade between Egypt and the Near East during the First Dynasty. One of the most significant objects was an ivory plaque, originally covered in gold foil, decorated in relief with the head of a cow goddess (Hathor or, more likely, Bat) between two 'thunderbolt' symbols of Min (Klasens, 1958: 50, fig. 20 (y) and 53, pl. XXV). This small object is an important piece of evidence for Early Dynastic religious iconography.

Emery resumed his excavations in the Early Dynastic necropolis in 1964, after an interval of nearly nine years. He directed his attention to the western part of the site, where he still hoped to locate the Asklepieion and the associated tomb of Imhotep (H.S. Smith 1971: 199). Emery uncovered several mastabas of the Third Dynasty, overlying cult places of the Late Period, and this gave him hope that the tomb of Imhotep lay nearby. The Early Dynastic tombs discovered in these seasons were published only as preliminary reports (Emery 1965, 1968, 1970); an analysis of Emery's field notebooks might be expected to reveal significant information about the development of mortuary architecture in the Third Dynasty.

Pointing the way: Kaiser, Kaplony and Kemp

Following the end of Klasens' excavations at Abu Rawash and the change in emphasis of Emery's work at North Saqqara, little archaeological interest was shown in Egypt's early periods throughout most of the 1960s. The Egyptological world was largely preoccupied with the campaign to record and salvage the monuments of Lower Nubia, threatened by the construction of the Aswan High Dam. Few scholars paid much attention to questions surrounding the origins of Egyptian civilisation, with two notable exceptions.

Werner Kaiser may be credited with the rebirth of interest in early Egypt. His article on the internal chronology of the **Naqada culture** (Kaiser 1957) revolutionised Predynastic studies, replacing Petrie's sequence dating system for establishing the relative date of Predynastic graves. A series of seminal articles in the late 1950s and early 1960s (Kaiser 1959, 1960, 1961a, 1964) reviewed the state of knowledge on early Egypt and investigated particular questions relevant to the birth of the dynastic state. Kaiser was particularly interested in the possibility that the legend of a line of kings ruling Egypt before Menes might have a basis in reality, and he explored the evidence for a degree of political unity prior to the beginning of the First Dynasty (Kaiser 1961a). In doing so, Kaiser made an important contribution to the problem of reconciling the later king lists with the names recorded on monuments of the Early Dynastic period, and he produced a valuable new reconstruction of the **Palermo Stone**, one of the key documents for early Egyptian history. Kaiser was the first Egyptologist to recognise the significance of early *serekh* marks, and the possibilities of arranging them in chronological order by reference to the types of pots on which they occurred. His analysis of the Tura cemetery led him to conclude that up to ten generations of kings had ruled a united Egypt before the reign of Aha (Kaiser 1964). Whilst this dramatic suggestion can no longer be entirely sustained, there is no doubt that state formation was well advanced before the beginning of the First Dynasty, and that the credit for developing this new picture of Egyptian origins belongs to Kaiser. He was also the first scholar to recognise the spread of Upper Egyptian cultural traits northwards during the late Predynastic period (Kaiser 1964), and this model of cultural development remains at the heart of present theories of state formation. Kaiser's interest in early Egypt was to have a profound impact on the direction taken by Egyptian archaeology in the 1970s and 1980s. As director of the German Archaeological Institute in Cairo, he was to launch major new projects at Abydos and

Buto, which continue to shed new light on the Predynastic and Early Dynastic periods. However, his influence was not restricted to the world of German Egyptology. Kaiser's work also had a pivotal role in reawakening interest in the site of Hierakonpolis, one of the key sites for the rise of the Egyptian state. He was the first scholar to re-examine the material excavated by Quibell and Green at the turn of the century, and to suggest an important role for Hierakonpolis in the process of state formation (Kaiser 1958). The publication of an extensive field survey of sites in Upper and **Middle Egypt** revealed the extent of early remains at Hierakonpolis, and the great potential of the site for further study (Kaiser 1961b). As a direct result of this information, the Hierakonpolis Project was launched in 1967 (see below).

Another scholar of Kaiser's generation is Peter Kaplony. His interest lies primarily in the fragmentary inscribed material to have survived from early Egypt, and his pioneering work unlocked some of the secrets of the earliest Egyptian script for the first time (Kaplony 1962, 1963, 1964, 1966). Much of what we know about Early Dynastic administration is based upon Kaplony's analysis of seal-impressions.

The late 1960s witnessed a revival of interest in the monuments of the first three dynasties, in particular the royal tombs and **funerary enclosure**s at Abydos. Since Emery's excavations at North Saqqara, the balance of scholarly opinion had shifted in favour of his firm belief that the First Dynasty royal tombs were located at Saqqara, the monuments of Abydos being no more than southern 'cenotaphs'. In two articles Barry Kemp re-examined the evidence in favour of Abydos as the true burial ground of Egypt's earliest kings (Kemp 1966, 1967). He established beyond all reasonable doubt the claim of Abydos to be the Early Dynastic royal necropolis, a view which is now shared by most Egyptologists. Kaiser picked up on Kemp's work and showed how the Step Pyramid complex of Netjerikhet, from the beginning of the Third Dynasty, was related, both architecturally and symbolically, to the late Second Dynasty enclosures of Peribsen and Khasekhemwy at Abydos (Kaiser 1969). Together, Kemp and Kaiser contributed enormously to our understanding of Early Dynastic royal mortuary complexes, and the process of development that led from mastabas to pyramids.

New beginnings in Upper Egypt: Hierakonpolis and Elephantine

The late 1960s also saw the launch of two important new projects in southern Upper Egypt, projects that continue to reveal important information about their respective sites. The Hierakonpolis Project, under the direction of Walter Fairservis (1921–94), began survey and excavation in 1967. Hierakonpolis had been visited sporadically by archaeologists since Quibell's and Green's pioneering excavations, but no systematic survey of the whole site had ever been attempted. The project was formed to examine the site from a regional perspective, establishing both the geographical and the chronological range of the surviving archaeological material. Fairservis was primarily interested in the Early Dynastic period, and he began by excavating on the Kom el-Gemuwia, the ancient town site of Nekhen. Preliminary results indicated that the site had great potential, and a full-scale expedition was launched. The early seasons of excavation yielded a spectacular discovery: a mudbrick gateway from a monumental building, decorated with an elaborate series of recessed niches in the '**palace-façade**' style (Weeks 1971–2). The context of the gateway indicated that the adjoining building probably served a secular purpose, and a royal residence seemed the most plausible explanation. This identification has been generally accepted, and the building confirms the suitability of the term 'palace-façade' to describe the style of recessed niche decoration common in the Early Dynastic period. The political situation in the Middle East forced the abandonment of the Hierakonpolis Project in 1971, to be resumed again seven years later.

In 1969, a joint German–Swiss mission, under Kaiser's overall direction, began excavations on the island of Elephantine, on ancient Egypt's southern border. Buildings of many periods have been investigated by the Elephantine mission, including important Early Dynastic structures. One of the most revealing sites is the small temple of Satet, a shrine serving the local community on the island and built initially in a natural niche between granite boulders (Dreyer 1986). Excavations between 1973 and 1976 revealed the walls of the earliest building, dating back to the Early Dynastic period, and a large number of early votive objects from the floor of the shrine. Together, the evidence forms an important source for provincial cults in early Egypt. Like the Hierakonpolis Project, the excavations at Elephantine were to yield more important results for the understanding of Early Dynastic Egypt in subsequent seasons.

EARLY EGYPT REDISCOVERED: 1977–90

The German revival

The reawakening of scholarly interest in Egypt's Predynastic and Early Dynastic periods was driven very largely by the activities of German archaeologists, particularly from the German Archaeological Institute in Cairo. With the easing of the Middle East political situation in 1977 and the resumption of foreign excavations, the resources of the German Archaeological Institute were directed towards exploring the problems of early Egypt through the excavation of key sites known to have played an important part in the process of state formation. The first such site, important since the very beginning of archaeological interest in Egypt's early history, was Abydos.

The Umm el-Qaab

Over seventy years after Petrie had worked on the **Umm el-Qaab**, a third re-excavation of the Early Dynastic royal tombs was launched in 1977, under Kaiser's direction. The stated aim of the mission was to investigate the construction of the tombs, illuminating changes in royal mortuary architecture over the course of the Early Dynastic period, a subject which had been dealt with only summarily in Petrie's publications. The early seasons of excavation concentrated on Petrie's Cemetery B, comprising the tombs of Aha, Narmer and their immediate predecessors of 'Dynasty 0'. The clearance of these tombs resulted in a much better understanding of the royal tomb's early development, and inscribed pottery from tomb complex B1/2 has suggested to some the possible existence of a late Predynastic king called *Iry-Hor. Kaiser made an important contribution to the history of early Egypt by suggesting an order of succession for Aha's predecessors based upon the early royal names incised on vessels. Clearance work in Cemetery B uncovered late Predynastic burials belonging to an adjacent cemetery, named Cemetery U. This seems to have been the burial ground of the **Thinite** rulers, ancestors of the First Dynasty kings. Systematic excavation of Cemetery U has revealed numerous tombs spanning almost the entire Predynastic period. Vessels from one of the late Predynastic brick-lined tombs, U-s, bear ink inscriptions which include some of the earliest *serekh* marks known from Egypt. They confirm the élite status of those buried in Cemetery U. The most dramatic discovery was made in 1988: an eight-chambered mudbrick tomb, designated U-j, which is by far the largest tomb of its date anywhere in Egypt. The tomb contained a massive collection of imported vessels, bone labels bearing the earliest writing yet attested in Egypt, and an ivory sceptre, symbol of kingship.

Concurrent with excavation of Cemetery U, clearance began of selected First Dynasty royal tombs, to record details of their construction. During clearance of the tomb of Den, an impression from the king's necropolis seal was discovered, which lists the first five kings of the First Dynasty (Narmer to Den) and also names the king's mother, Merneith. This is the first ancient document to confirm the order of succession in the first half of the First Dynasty, and it further suggests that Narmer was regarded in some way as a founder figure by his immediate successors. Further re-excavation of Den's tomb revealed the unique annex at the south-western corner, which seems to have housed a statue of the king (a statue which could act as a substitute for the king's body in providing a dwelling-place for his spirit or *ka*). In 1988 the south-west corner of Djet's tomb was investigated to clarify the original appearance of the superstructures of the royal tombs. These investigations discovered the vestiges of a 'hidden' **tumulus**, covering the burial chamber but completely enclosed within the larger superstructure, a fact which has dramatically enhanced our knowledge of early royal mortuary architecture and which raises important issues about its symbolic nature. Regular preliminary reports (Kaiser and Grossmann 1979; Kaiser and Dreyer 1982; Dreyer 1990, 1993a; Dreyer *et al.* 1996) have presented the findings from the ongoing excavations on the Umm el-Qaab.

Buto

In order to shed light on the role of the Delta in the process of state formation, the German Archaeological Institute launched a preliminary geological and archaeological survey of the area around Tell el-Fara'in (ancient Buto) in 1983 (Plate 1.6). The team, directed by Thomas von der Way, investigated the various settlement mounds (**tell**s) in the vicinity and carried out a number of drill cores to establish the whereabouts and depth of early occupational strata; full-scale excavations began in 1985. Aided by pumping equipment, which Hoffman had pioneered at Hierakonpolis, von der Way and his team were able to excavate far below the water

Plate 1.6 Tell el-Fara'in, the site of ancient Buto in the north-western Nile Delta (author's photograph). The tents in the distance are those of the German Archaeological Institute's expedition.

table, reaching strata dating back to the early Predynastic period (von der Way 1984, 1986, 1987, 1988, 1989, 1991; von der Way and Schmidt 1985). The results were spectacular: **sherd**s of spiral reserved slipware suggested contacts between Buto and northern Syria, whilst imported Palestinian vessels indicated trade with areas further south. The excavation of a second area, a little to the north, from 1987 to 1990, revealed a large building of the Early Dynastic period comprising a series of interconnected corridor-like rooms leading to two central chambers; it may have served a cultic purpose, perhaps connected with divine kingship. Seal-impressions from the building dated its later phase of occupation to the Second Dynasty. An earlier building in an adjacent location may also have had a religious significance, perhaps associated with the cult of a divine bull kept at Buto. Careful analysis of the pottery from the complete **stratigraphic** sequence at Buto revealed a 'transition layer', where pottery manufactured in the indigenous, Lower Egyptian tradition was superseded by pottery made according to the more advanced ceramic technology of Upper Egypt (Köhler 1992). This discovery was hailed as proof of an Upper Egyptian expansion believed to have characterised the process of state formation (von der Way 1991, 1992). Although the interpretation of the transition layer has since been revised (Köhler 1995), there is no doubt that Buto provides unique evidence for the technological and social changes which accompanied the rise of the Egyptian state. Excavations resumed at Buto in 1993 under the direction of Dina Faltings; to date, these have concentrated on the Predynastic settlement levels (Faltings and Köhler 1996).

Minshat Abu Omar

During the 1960s a number of late Predynastic and Early Dynastic objects, said to have come from the north-eastern Delta, had appeared on the international antiquities market. Some were bought by the Staatliche Sammlung Ägyptischer Kunst in Munich, which subsequently launched an exploratory survey of the Delta to try and locate the source of the objects. As early as 1966, the site of Minshat Abu Omar was identified for future excavation by the frequency of early pottery and stone vessels on the surface. The Munich East Delta Expedition was launched in 1977 and excavations at Minshat Abu Omar began in 1978, continuing until 1991, under the direction of Dietrich Wildung and Karla Kroeper (Kroeper and Wildung 1985, 1994; Kroeper 1988, 1992, 1996). A cemetery spanning the late Predynastic and First Dynasty periods was revealed, comprising some 420 graves. Close contacts with southern Palestine were indicated by imported vessels in some of the tombs. The richest grave in the entire cemetery was further distinguished by a unique architectural feature: signs of recessed niche decoration on the *inner* faces of three walls. The use of 'palace-façade' decoration in a location which would have been invisible after the burial illustrates the strength of the symbolism inherent in this style of architecture. Moreover, the identification of the tomb owner as a child of nine has important implications for the social structure of the local community, which seems to have been characterised by hereditary status even after the foundation of the Egyptian state.

Intensive excavation throughout Egypt

The north-eastern Delta

The success of the Munich East Delta Expedition proved that good results could be obtained from excavating in the Delta, and prompted other archaeological missions to investigate the region for early sites. An expedition of Amsterdam University, directed by Edwin van den Brink, conducted four seasons of geo-archaeological survey in the north-eastern Delta between 1984 and 1987, identifying eight Early Dynastic sites (van den Brink 1989). Soundings at Tell el-Iswid South revealed a settlement spanning the transition between the late Predynastic and Early Dynastic periods, whilst contemporary cemetery and settlement material was excavated at the nearby site of Tell Ibrahim Awad in three seasons from 1988 to 1990. The level dating to the period of state formation yielded several sherds incised with early royal names, including the *serekh*s of 'Ka' and Narmer. An Italian mission conducted small-scale excavations at nearby Tell el-Farkha in 1988 and 1989, revealing mudbrick buildings of the Early Dynastic and Old Kingdom periods, whilst excavations by the University of Zagazig at Ezbet et-Tell/Kufur Nigm in the late 1980s uncovered a substantial cemetery of the early First Dynasty. The upsurge of interest in the archaeology of the Delta – particularly in the early periods – was marked by a symposium held at the Dutch Institute in Cairo in 1986. The publication of the proceedings from this meeting (van den Brink 1988) sparked further interest in the potential of the Delta to reveal important information about the process of state formation, a potential which is increasingly being realised.

Abydos

Whilst the German Archaeological Institute has been excavating on the Umm el-Qaab, an American team under the overall direction of David O'Connor has concentrated on the accompanying funerary enclosures on the low desert nearer the cultivation. A new clearance of the area in 1988 yielded firm evidence of a built structure within the enclosure of Djer, previously demarcated only by a rectangle of subsidiary tombs (O'Connor 1989). This discovery links the enclosures of the early First Dynasty with their later counterparts, and enhances our understanding of Early Dynastic royal mortuary architecture. Even more striking was another discovery made in the same season. Excavations within the funerary enclosure of Khasekhemwy (the **Shunet ez-Zebib**) revealed the lower courses of a mud-brick mound in the centre of the enclosure. Reconstructed as a substantial massif with sloping sides, this feature has been dubbed a 'proto-pyramid' (O'Connor 1991, 1995). The funerary enclosure of Khasekhemwy seems, therefore, to have foreshadowed in many ways the architecture of the Step Pyramid complex, built in the following reign. The recent discoveries at Abydos have highlighted the step-by-step development of royal mortuary architecture during the Early Dynastic period, and the striking links between the late Second and early Third Dynasties.

Hierakonpolis

Archaeological work resumed at Hierakonpolis in 1978 with the excavation of the temple area of the early town. The complex stratigraphy of the temple, published in a rather confusing manner by Quibell and Green, was clarified, proving beyond doubt that the circular stone revetment identified as the early temple platform did indeed date back to the beginning of the Early Dynastic period. Fairservis returned to Hierakonpolis in 1981 for a final season of excavation as director, concentrating on the Early Dynastic buildings east of the niched gateway. Other commitments forced him to hand over direction of the entire project to Michael Hoffman (1944–90), who subsequently followed his own particular interests and sought to illuminate the diverse Predynastic activity in the Hierakonpolis region. One of the most important sites investigated by Hoffman's Predynastic Research Team is the élite cemetery at Locality 6. Between 1979 and 1985, excavations revealed high-status burials from Naqada I and the period of state formation. Hoffman even speculated that the largest tomb, numbered 1, may have been the burial of King 'Scorpion', whose ceremonial macehead was found in the 'Main Deposit' at Hierakonpolis at the turn of the century.

Elephantine

Excavations at Elephantine from 1981 to 1988 revealed the extent and development of the Early Dynastic town, providing an important picture of provincial life early in the history of the Egyptian state. Equally significant was the discovery of a substantial fortress, built on the eastern edge of the island at the very beginning of the First Dynasty (Ziermann 1993). The fortress clearly represents a state-sponsored project to secure Egypt's southern frontier and provide a base from which to launch punitive expeditions against Lower Nubia. The construction and subsequent strengthening of the fortress had a major impact on the life of the local community and provides a striking illustration of the realities of power in the Early Dynastic period: namely, the absolute authority of the central government from the earliest times, and its blatant disregard for local sensibilities if these threatened to impede court initiatives (Seidlmayer 1996b).

AN INTERNATIONAL EFFORT:
THE 1990s AND BEYOND

A century after the discovery of Early Dynastic Egypt, scholarly interest in the formative period of Egyptian civilisation is probably stronger than at any time over the last one hundred years. An unprecedented number of archaeological missions from a wide variety of countries are excavating throughout Egypt at sites with Predynastic and/or Early Dynastic material. Following the success of the missions to Minshat Abu Omar and Buto, a particular focus in the late 1980s and 1990s has been the archaeology of the Delta. This interest was reflected in an international conference held at the Netherlands Institute in Cairo in 1990, devoted specifically to the topic of the Nile Delta during the period of state formation. The published proceedings (van den Brink 1992) included reports from excavations conducted some time ago, such as the Egyptian Antiquities Organisation excavations at Beni Amir carried out in the late 1960s and the 1970s, as well as the results of recent or ongoing missions. Thus, a large body of new and important information concerning **Lower Egypt** in the late Predynastic and Early Dynastic periods has been made available to scholars. A particular focus of the meeting and published proceedings was the evidence for connections between Egypt and southern Palestine. The results of Israeli excavations at sites such as Tel Erani and En Besor indicate substantial Egyptian activity in southern Palestine during the late Predynastic to Early Dynastic transition, possibly extending to an Egyptian presence at the two sites. This evidence has necessitated a reassessment of Egypt's early foreign relations, and suggests that the phenomenon of core and periphery associated with the rise of other early states was also a feature of state formation in Egypt. Excavations at Early Bronze Age sites in southern Palestine, particularly in the Negev Desert, continue to yield evidence for contacts with Egypt, as illustrated by the discovery of a sherd bearing the *serekh* of Narmer at Nahal Tillah in 1995 (Levy *et al.* 1995).

The growing interest in early Egypt was also marked in 1993 by the opening of a new gallery at the British Museum in London especially dedicated to the formative period of Egyptian civilisation (Spencer 1993), and by the holding of an international conference there on the same theme (Spencer

1996). As archaeological missions in Egypt make increasing use of special-ist expertise – from **ceramicist**s to archaeo-botanists, geologists to palaeo-pathologists – the level of detailed information gained from excavations increases accordingly. Specific aspects of early Egyptian culture and society are now far more amenable to investigation than ever before. Yet some major problems remain to be solved, not least the chronology of the Second and Third Dynasties. As the study of Early Dynastic Egypt enters its second century, excavations both long-established and new continue to yield exciting new information. The most significant of these projects are described briefly below.

Two separate missions promise to shed new light on Egypt's first capital, Memphis, and its main cemetery, Saqqara, in the Early Dynastic period. The Egypt Exploration Society's ongoing Survey of Memphis, directed by David Jeffreys, has established the probable course of the Nile in the Early Dynastic period, considerably further west than its present course. Extensive drill cores have succeeded in pin-pointing the most probable location for the Early Dynastic city which, it is hoped, may be revealed by future excavations. The National Museums of Scotland Saqqara Survey Project, directed by Ian Mathieson, has used sophisticated remote sensing techniques, including **magnetometry** and **resistivity**, to map structures on the Saqqara plateau which lie hidden beneath deep accumulations of drift sand. A survey of this type and limited test excavations have been conducted at the mysterious 'Great Enclosure', or Gisr el-Mudir, in the desert to the west of the Step Pyramid complex. They have confirmed that the enclosure is not an unfinished step pyramid complex of the Third Dynasty, but rather a structure reminiscent of the First Dynasty funerary enclosures at Abydos. Furthermore, the construction of the Great Enclosure suggests that it pre-dates the Step Pyramid complex, and is probably the oldest substantial stone building in Egypt. The identity of its owner is still a mystery, but may be solved by future excavation.

Further important and unexpected discoveries have been made in the vicinity of the Abydos funerary enclosures. Clearance of the area adjacent to Khasekhemwy's enclosure (the Shunet ez-Zebib) in 1991 revealed a fleet of twelve boat burials, moored alongside the western wall of the enclosure. The date of these unparalleled structures remains uncertain: their location would suggest a date contemporary with the Shunet ez-Zebib, but they may be earlier (O'Connor 1995). First Dynasty élite burials at Abu Rawash, Saqqara and Helwan were occasionally accom-panied by boat burials, but such features have not previously been found in association with the mortuary complexes of kings. Once again, new material has forced a rethink of Early Dynastic beliefs and practices.

A short distance away on the Umm el-Qaab, the re-excavation of Khasekhemwy's tomb promises to clarify the design of the royal tomb at the end of the Second Dynasty, on the threshold of the pyramid age.

Seal-impressions from the tomb entrance, discovered in 1996, seem to indicate that Netjerikhet/Djoser was Khasekhemwy's immediate successor, confirming previous suspicions and solving one of the principal problems of Early Dynastic chronology. Another important contribution was made by discoveries in the tomb of Qaa, cleared in 1991 and 1992. An impression from the necropolis seal of Qaa lists all eight kings of the First Dynasty in their expected order, confirming the results of painstaking research over decades, and emphasising Narmer's position at the head of the First Dynasty. Seal-impressions of Hetepsekhemwy from chambers near the tomb entrance clarify the succession at the end of the First Dynasty, but do not explain why the kings of the Second Dynasty chose to move the royal necropolis north to Saqqara. Finally, the sifting of Petrie's spoil-dumps from the tombs in Cemetery B has yielded some significant finds, including a **year label** of Narmer identified by the same event as is depicted on the king's famous palette.

With these latest results from the royal tombs at Abydos, the discovery of Early Dynastic Egypt has come full circle. Archaeologists working at the end of the twentieth century at a site first excavated a century before continue to shed new light on the earliest period of Egyptian history. The chapters that follow seek to make sense of the wealth of evidence about early Egypt now available to scholars, and to present it in a coherent and accessible fashion. Whilst the most recent discoveries from the Nile valley have been utilised in this exploration of Early Dynastic Egypt, there is little doubt that our understanding of early Egyptian society will continue to develop in the light of fresh evidence.

Approximate Date BC	Period	Dynasty	Rulers	Significant developments
3200	LATE PREDYNASTIC		Owner of Abydos U-j	Process of state formation ('the Unification')
3100		'Dynasty 0'	King A King B 'Ka' 'Scorpion'	Expeditions to deserts; military raids into Nubia
3000	EARLY DYNASTIC	First Dynasty	Narmer Aha Djer Djet (Merneith) Den Anedjib Semerkhet Qaa Sneferka Ba	Egyptian presence in southern Palestine Advances in architecture, crafts, administration Imposing royal tomb and enclosure at Abydos
2900				
2800		Second Dynasty	Hetepsekhemwy Nebra Ninetjer Weneg Nubnefer Sened Peribsen Sekhemib Khasekhem(wy)	Saqqara adopted as royal necropolis Possible political fragmentation Royal tombs located once again at Abydos; Shunet ez-Zebib built
2700				
2600		Third Dynasty	Netjerikhet Sekhemkhet Khaba Sanakht Huni	Step Pyramids at Saqqara Mining expeditions to Sinai
2500				

Chronological chart of the late Predynastic and Early Dynastic periods.

CHAPTER TWO

BIRTH OF A NATION STATE

—— •◆• ——

INEQUALITY IN LIFE AND DEATH

Ancient Egypt gives the impression of having been obsessed with status. From the **hierarchical scaling** seen in relief decoration to the sentiments expressed in 'wisdom literature', Egyptian civilisation made constant reference to rank, and the inhabitants of the Nile valley seem to have been acutely conscious of their relative position within the pyramidal structure of society. The formation of the Egyptian state at the end of the fourth millennium BC crystallised social distinctions in a particularly marked way, placing the king at the apex of the pyramid, almost removed from the human sphere. Beneath him the ruling élite, minor officials and peasant farmers occupied progressively lower and larger tiers. Above all, therefore, it was the socio-economic dynamic within Predynastic Egyptian society which led ultimately to the birth of Egypt as a nation state. The structure of Egyptian society in the historic period may be seen as an extreme manifestation of inequality, but the roots of the phenomenon go back to the earliest settled cultures of the Nile valley.

For most of the Predynastic period, society in Lower Egypt seems to have been relatively egalitarian. There is little mortuary evidence for status differentiation (Rizkana and Seeher 1989: 80) so if social hierarchies did exist they were not reflected in burial practices. An exception to this general picture is a grave (A35) from the site of el-Omari, dated by radiocarbon to *c.* 4600–4400 BC (Debono and Mortensen 1990: 81), but perhaps somewhat later, closer to *c.* 4100 BC (F.A. Hassan 1995: 674). The burial of an adult male contained a carved wooden staff (Debono and Mortensen 1990: 67, pls 28.1 and 43.2) which is generally interpreted as a symbol of office (Hoffman 1980: 196; F.A. Hassan 1995: 674; for a more cautious view see Debono and Mortensen 1990: 75), although the other grave goods do not seem to indicate particular wealth or status. However, despite the greater propensity for display at el-Omari than in other Lower Egyptian communities (reflected in the frequency of imported ornaments), the settlement material indicates an egalitarian social structure based on the family unit (Hoffman 1980: 195). It is likely that the man buried with a staff was someone with special power and prestige, though not necessarily of a political or economic nature.

In contrast to Lower Egypt, Upper Egyptian society seems to have been characterised by hierarchies as far back as the Badarian period (*c.* 4500–*c.* 3800 BC). Badarian graves show variation in their size and wealth, indicating that different levels of status were accorded to the deceased (Anderson 1992). Mortuary practices generally reflect aspects of living society (but note the reservations expressed by R. Friedman 1994: 2), and we may assume that within Badarian communities certain individuals enjoyed greater status and the preferential access to resources which went with it. The presence of local élites is even more apparent in the mortuary record of the Naqada I period. The differentiation of graves in terms of size and number of grave goods is marked, and some graves were furnished with luxury or imported items. For example, a Naqada I grave at Matmar (number 3075) contained no less than 18 pottery vessels, the largest number of any contemporary burial in the local cemetery (Wilkinson 1996b: 75). In addition, the contents included an ivory tag, bracelets and an ostrich eggshell (Brunton 1948: pl. X). At several sites in Upper Egypt, particular graves were furnished with distinctive artefacts which may be termed 'badges of status'. Most common are maceheads, found in five Naqada I graves at Mahasna (numbers 6, 23, 29, 39 and 41) and one at el-Amra (number 144); but a grave of the same date at Matmar (number 3131) contained a fine axe, one of the earliest examples of advanced metalworking from Egypt (Brunton 1948: pl. XVI.47). Such a rare object would undoubtedly have conferred great prestige and reflects the status of its owner within the local Predynastic community. The stratified nature of Upper Egyptian society in the Naqada I period is also highlighted by the presence, in certain graves, of objects which seem to indicate a special role for the tomb owner, though not necessarily a position of political power. Two burials at Mahasna (numbers 33 and 42) each contained a female figurine made from clay (Ayrton and Loat 1911: 13–14). These almost certainly possessed some magical or religious significance, and their inclusion amongst a deceased person's grave goods probably indicates special status. Significantly, one of the graves (number 33) also yielded a vessel of Petrie's black-incised ware, a rare class of pottery probably imported from Nubia (Needler 1984: 224; but cf. Bourriau 1981: 23).

Within any community, élite status may be conferred on an individual in one of two ways. It may either be achieved – that is, gained by an individual as a result of his or her actions – or inherited, that is ascribed from birth as a result of descent (Renfrew and Bahn 1991: 176). In general, inherited status is considered to be a characteristic of more complex societies in which the heredity principle operates to the benefit of a restricted élite (Bard 1988: 52). The change from achieved to inherited status as the primary means of distinguishing a privileged class marks an important stage in socio-economic development. In the Egyptian case, kingship – that hallmark of Egyptian civilisation – would not have existed without the heredity principle. If the Predynastic period is seen as a precursor to dynastic Egypt, a long trajectory with the end-point being the codification of certain cultural traits, then the earliest evidence of inherited status is an important milestone. Burials of the Badarian period show no signs of inherited status, in marked contrast to the mortuary record of the following Naqada I period. A grave at Mahasna (number 41) belonged to a family group, consisting of a man, a woman and a child. The whole family obviously enjoyed a privileged position in the local community, since the grave goods included a female figurine, several ivory objects, gold and silver beads, and a **diorite** macehead (Ayrton and Loat 1911: 16). Elaborate child burials are the clearest evidence of inherited status, since for there to be greater expenditure of time and resources on the burial of a child than of an adult must indicate that the child occupied an exalted position within the local community, and this could only have come about through descent. The largest Naqada I grave at Armant (number 1461) was identified as belonging to a child (Mond and Myers 1937: 28), and the status of the deceased is also reflected in the grave goods, which included two ivory wands. The Predynastic community buried at Armant seems to have been a small, undistinguished farming village, removed from the growing centres of political power at sites like Hierakonpolis and This/Abydos. None the less, status was clearly inherited by some members of the community, as early as the Naqada I period.

In the following Naqada II period (*c.* 3500–*c.* 3200 BC), social differentiation becomes even more apparent in the mortuary record of Upper Egypt. Badges of status continued to be buried with important individuals. For example, a large grave of Naqada IIb (*c.* 3500–*c.* 3400 BC) at Matmar (number 3129) contained a macehead made from **travertine** as well as two stone vessels (Brunton 1948: pls X, XIII.31–2), rare at such an early date. A contemporary burial at Armant (number 1466) was furnished with a number of unusual artefacts, including a gazelle skull, three painted objects made of plaster and a bed. A second grave in the same cemetery also contained a bed and it has been suggested that both burials may have belonged to leaders of the local village (Bard 1988: 52). Country-wide, the wealth of burials increases in the Naqada II period, both in terms of the number of objects interred with the deceased and their costliness (Bard 1988; Seidlmayer 1988; Wilkinson 1996b). Thus, in the Predynastic cemetery at el-Amra south of Abydos (Randall-MacIver and Mace 1902), graves of Naqada II were commonly furnished with palettes, jewellery and items made from prestige materials such as ivory, lapis lazuli, copper, silver and gold (Wilkinson 1993a: 183). Again, elaborate child burials point to a ranked society with inherited status. The wealthiest early grave (number 66) in the 'Fort' cemetery at Hierakonpolis – a cemetery representing the local population from which the élite had already been separated, to be buried in discrete areas – was identified as belonging to a child. The artefacts in the grave included 24 pottery vessels, palettes and copper objects (B. Adams 1987: 67–8). As Egypt progressed on the path to statehood, social distinctions became greater and these became increasingly explicit in the mortuary record. By the end of the Predynastic period, local élites – now royal families in every sense – had successfully monopolised the economic resources in their territories to such an extent that they were able to command sufficient labour to construct monumental tombs. Moreover, they could call upon the services of professional administrators to obtain prestige goods from abroad by long-distance trade, and employed skilled craftsmen to manufacture further elaborate grave goods. The birth of the Egyptian state with its rigid hierarchies can therefore be charted in the growing differentiation and elaboration of mortuary provision.

THE ICONOGRAPHY AND IDEOLOGY OF RULE

Power can be expressed in many ways, both explicit and subtle. One of the most effective ways of appealing to people's deeper feelings is through art. A repertoire of distinctive symbols, employed in a consistent and highly symbolic way (iconography) was a feature of Egyptian kingship from the earliest times. The series of carved stone palettes and ivory knife handles from the late Predynastic period are well known examples of royal iconography (Williams and Logan 1987; Davis 1989, esp. 141–9, figs 6.9–14; Cialowicz 1991). Some motifs are borrowed from contemporary Mesopotamian iconography (Boehmer 1974; Teissier 1987; H.S. Smith 1992 plus references), but the total compositions reflect a peculiarly Egyptian view of rule. The king is presented in animal form, emphasising both his coercive power and the concentration of the powers of nature in his person. By the end of the Predynastic period, many of the characteristics of Egyptian art had already been canonised, including the conventions of representation, the hierarchical scaling of figures, the use of **register**s to order the composition, and the attributes of kingship. However, the roots of royal iconography – and of the ideology it expresses – go back much further.

At the end of the Naqada I period (*c*. 3500 BC) we have the first indications that an ideology of power was being formulated by the ruling lineages of Upper Egypt. Iconography is the articulation of beliefs through the medium of art, and the earliest example of royal iconography – recognisable as such from later parallels – marks the beginning of a phase of rapid social change which, with accelerating speed, led to the emergence of classic kingship ideology within the space of some two hundred years. Recent excavations in the earliest part of the Predynastic Cemetery U at

Abydos have revealed some astonishing examples of Naqada I crafts-manship, in graves which clearly belonged to persons of high status. The burial of a premature baby (U-502) was furnished with an elaborate pottery vessel of unique appearance: eight female figurines, modelled in clay, are arranged around the rim of the bowl, holding hands; each figure is distinctive, and traces of bitumen wigs survived. Three larger, male figurines found in the same grave may once have decorated a similar bowl (Dreyer 1996). Most striking of all, however, was a vessel from another, contemporary grave. On a red background, the decoration in off-white paint included a scene of pregnant women, and a male figure wearing a tail and with a feather on his head, holding a mace in the classic smiting pose of later royal iconography (Dreyer 1995a). It is hard to interpret this latter motif as anything other than the depiction of a ruler, so close are the parallels with royal scenes on monuments from the period of state formation. To date, the Abydos vessel is the earliest example of the ruler figure in Egyptian art. It highlights not only the high standard of crafts-manship available to Upper Egyptian rulers, but also the ideological sophistication of the miniature courts that must have surrounded such individuals.

The most extensive example of early royal iconography is the series of scenes painted on the internal walls of an élite tomb at Hierakonpolis, numbered by its excavators tomb 100 and dubbed 'the painted tomb' (Quibell and Green 1902: pls LXXV–LXXIX; Case and Payne 1962; Payne 1973; Kemp 1973). Situated in a Naqada II cemetery south of the pre-historic town of Hierakonpolis and close to the cultivation, the painted tomb was one of a number of high-status burials in the cemetery, but was apparently unique in having painted decoration. The scenes covered one long wall and a cross wall half the width of the tomb. The scenes have been illustrated and reproduced many times since their discovery (for example, W.S. Smith 1949: 124, fig. 43; 1981: 31, fig. 9; Spencer 1993: 36–7, fig. 20), and their importance lies not only in the royal nature of much of the iconography but also in the Mesopotamian influence apparent in some of the motifs. The Predynastic rulers of Upper Egypt, when formulating a distinctive iconography of rule, seem to have borrowed various elements from contemporary Mesopotamian culture. Motifs such as the 'master of the beasts' – a hero figure standing between and reconciling two opposing wild animals, usually lions – are found on other royal artefacts from late Predynastic Egypt, but this particular motif makes its first appearance in Egyptian art in the Hierakonpolis painted tomb, which has been dated by its pottery to Naqada IIc (*c.* 3400 BC) (Case and Payne 1962). The main scene on the long wall shows a procession of boats, one of which is provided with an awning amidships, sheltering a figure who is probably the ruler and the person for whom the tomb was built. A more explicit indication of royalty is the motif of the ruler smiting a group of bound captives, clearly already established in Egyptian iconography as the expression of kingship *par excellence*. The Hierakonpolis painted tomb illustrates the extent of socio-political development in Upper Egypt since the end of the Naqada I period (when the Abydos painted vessel was made for a local ruler of This). Different artistic motifs depicting the ruler engaged in various activities – including a ritual water-borne procession, perhaps an ancestor of some of the later festivals of kingship – were being woven into a more highly developed iconographic repertoire which sought to express the multiple roles of the king in relation to his people and the supernatural realm. What is striking about the scenes in the Hierakonpolis painted tomb is the number of features characteristic of classic Egyptian art in the historic period that are already present some three hundred years before the beginning of the First Dynasty.

A similar set of scenes and motifs, with at least one important addition, is depicted on a painted cloth from a broadly contemporary élite grave at Gebelein (Galassi 1955: 5–42, pl. I; Aldred 1965: 39, fig. 28). The grave has never been published in detail, and only fragments of the painted cloth now survive (in the Egyptian Museum, Turin), but it is clear that it must have belonged to an individual of considerable status, probably a local ruler. A procession of boats and a ritual dance formed major parts of the original decorative scheme, while a detached fragment of cloth shows a hippopotamus being harpooned (Galassi 1955: 10, fig. 5, pl. I [top]; Behrmann 1989: Dok. 34). In historic times, the hunting of the hippopotamus was imbued with great religious significance, and there are several references to the activity from the reign of Den in the middle of the First Dynasty. It would appear that, in early times at least, hippopotamus hunting had a special connection with kingship. The Gebelein painted cloth is one of the earliest attested depictions of this event, and further emphasises the likely royal status of the object's original owner.

Both the Hierakonpolis painted tomb and the Gebelein painted cloth show close stylistic similarities to a contemporary class of Upper Egyptian pottery produced by specialist potters. This is Petrie's decorated ware, comprising closed vessels of **marl clay**, fired to a pale buff colour and decorated on the outside with scenes painted in red ochre (Bourriau 1981: 26–9; Needler 1984: 202–11). The earliest decorated ware appears in graves at the beginning of Naqada II (*c.* 3500 BC) and remains a distinctive feature of the Upper Egyptian funerary ceramic repertoire until early Naqada III (*c.* 3200 BC). Some examples are decorated with patterns of dots or spirals, in imitation of stone vessels. Others bear figurative decoration: flora, fauna (principally birds, but also animals such as crocodiles), and more complex ritual scenes involving human figures in distinctive postures and ships with many oars. This latter type of decoration – probably the output of a few specialist workshops – is rich in symbolism and must have conveyed some ideological meaning both to those who created the vessels and those who received them. We cannot be certain of their precise significance, but they seem to hint at the relationship between the human, natural and supernatural spheres. This theme was also explored in the emergent ideology of divine kingship being formulated in Naqada II Upper Egypt.

TECHNOLOGY AND SOCIAL CHANGE

As well as illustrating developments in iconography and ideology, decorated ware is an important indicator of another sphere where profound changes were taking place in the courts of Upper Egypt: technology. The rise of local élites, attested from early Predynastic times, accompanied increasing **social stratification** and craft specialisation. Élites require prestige objects with which to display their social and economic status, which in turn requires dedicated, full-time specialists to make such objects. As the economic influence of certain individuals within a community increased, so did their power of patronage. A local ruler, with more agricultural produce at his disposal than was necessary for mere subsistence, could afford to employ craftsmen on a permanent basis, providing for them out of his surplus income. The release of a growing number of people from agricultural production and their engagement in specialist production brought with it major technological advances, as new skills were developed and old ones passed down from generation to generation. The development of early metalworking and the unsurpassed ability of the early Egyptians to fashion elaborate vessels from some of the hardest stones were the result of Predynastic socio-economic trends which facilitated craft specialisation.

Pottery is abundant in Predynastic contexts. Hence, the technological development which is the easiest to trace in the archaeological record is the one that occurred in the sphere of ceramic production. During the transition from Naqada I to Naqada II (*c.* 3550–*c.* 3450 BC), hand-made pottery with a high degree of variation was swiftly replaced in Upper Egyptian settlements by Petrie's rough ware, its greater uniformity and rapid domination of the ceramic repertoire being signs of mass production (R. Friedman 1992: 204, n. 8 and 1994; Adams and Friedman 1992: 327). This fundamental change marks the beginning of a process that was eventually to take hold throughout Egypt, bringing with it important socio-economic developments. Until the beginning of the Naqada II period, pottery in the Nile valley was made exclusively from alluvial clays. These have the advantage of being easy to work, shape and fire, requiring only primitive technology available at the household level. Most of the pottery from Badarian and Naqada I sites was probably made in this small-scale way. There is evidence from Hierakonpolis of specialist pottery production as early as the Naqada I period (R. Friedman 1994: 401), but this is unusual, reflecting the advanced state of social stratification and craft specialisation at Hierakonpolis. The output of the Hierakonpolis kilns seems to have been intended primarily for funerary consumption, probably grave goods for the local élite buried in large tombs at Locality 6 (Hoffman 1982; B. Adams 1996). This type of specialist workshop became much more common from the beginning of Naqada II, and was marked by the advent of a more complex ceramic technology, producing vessels of a new and distinctive type. Pots made from desert or marl clays require much more controlled firing conditions than vessels made from alluvial clays. The kiln must also reach a far higher temperature for the process to be successful. The appearance of decorated ware – made from marl clay – in the ceramic repertoire of Upper Egypt represents a major technological advance, one which seems to have been made possible by the increasing activity of specialist potters.

The production of pottery for a market by professional workshops had a profound impact upon methods of distribution and exchange in Predynastic Egypt. In the archaeological record, one of the most striking phenomena is the spread of Upper Egyptian ceramic technology north-wards during the latter part of the Naqada II period (Kaiser 1956, 1990; Kemp 1995: 682). By Naqada IIc (*c.* 3400–*c.* 3300 BC), pottery made in classic Upper Egyptian fashion appears in graves at sites such as Haraga and Girza, near the entrance to the Fayum; whilst by Naqada IId2 (*c.* 3300–*c.* 3200 BC) it has spread to sites in the extremities of the Delta like Buto and Minshat Abu Omar. This phenomenon has been interpreted as a broader 'cultural superposition', reflecting a northward expansion of Upper Egyptian cultural characteristics, if not people (von der Way 1991). However, this may be an over-ambitious reading of the evidence, which merely attests the gradual displacement of indigenous, Lower Egyptian patterns of ceramic production, distribution and exchange by patterns developed in Upper Egypt (Köhler 1993: 253–4 and 1995; cf. Kemp 1995: 683). Three factors may be at work in this process. First, the technological superiority of Upper Egyptian pottery, which must have made it attractive to the inhabitants of Lower Egypt. Second, the marl clays used to make decorated ware and other specialist ceramics, such as the class of wavy-handled jars imitating imported Palestinian forms, were probably restricted to Upper Egypt where the advanced firing technology required to make marl pottery was first developed. Third, we may speculate that the specialist pottery workshops of Upper Egypt were keen to seek out new markets for their products, and the thriving communities of the Delta seem to have provided them. Certainly, the Predynastic graves at Minshat Abu Omar in the north-eastern Delta were furnished with pottery almost entirely in the Upper Egyptian style, giving rise to the theory that Minshat was an Upper Egyptian 'colony site' (Kemp 1995: 687; cf. Kaiser 1987), perhaps established to conduct trade with Palestine. Vessels made from marl clay probably represent imports from Upper Egypt.

The spread of Upper Egyptian patterns of ceramic production, distribution and exchange northwards during late Naqada II accompanied other socio-economic developments which fundamentally changed the character of Lower Egyptian society. For the whole of the Predynastic period prior to late Naqada II, Lower Egypt seems to have been characterised by a generally egalitarian social structure. From the period before the advent of Upper Egyptian cultural characteristics, four substantial cemeteries have been excavated in Lower Egypt: at Heliopolis south (Debono and Mortensen 1988), Maadi and Wadi Digla (Rizkana and Seeher 1990), and es-Saff (Habachi and Kaiser 1985). The individual burials vary little in their size or wealth, and in general were furnished with few grave goods. There are certainly none of the prestige artefacts commonly found in contemporary Upper Egyptian graves. From the beginning of Naqada III (*c.* 3200 BC), however, this picture changes. At Minshat Abu Omar, the orientation of burials alters, bodies being laid on their left side rather than their right side (Kroeper 1988: 12–13). A simultaneous change in the pottery repertoire reinforces the division between earlier and later phases, indicating perhaps a change in the nature of funerary beliefs. Settlements excavated in the Delta also show a marked change, lightweight structures of timber and matting giving way to mudbrick architecture (van den Brink 1989). In Upper Egypt, the appearance of mudbrick architecture – in both domestic and funerary contexts – seems to be connected with the rise of élites, and it may indicate a similar process in Lower Egypt at the beginning of Naqada III (Wilkinson 1996b: 95). Several prestige artefacts, notably carved stone palettes, have been found at sites in the north-eastern Delta (Leclant 1952; Fischer 1958, 1963; Kroeper 1989), apparently confirming the existence of local élites in the area during the last phase of the Predynastic period. All the evidence seems to point towards the incorporation of the Delta into the socio-economic pattern characteristic of Predynastic Upper Egypt: local élites enjoying differential access to resources, expressing their status in the conspicuous consumption of prestige materials and in the wealth of their burials. In short, by the beginning of the Naqada III period, Upper and Lower Egypt shared the same material culture, and were increasingly characterised by the same social structure (von der Way 1993: 96). The stage was set for the process of state formation to begin in earnest.

EARLY CENTRES OF KINGSHIP

The heartland of the technological, social, ideological, economic and political changes that led Egypt to statehood was the southern part of the Nile valley. Here, in the narrow floodplain of Upper Egypt, the conditions seem to have been most favourable for the rise of early élites (Bard 1987). Basin irrigation could be practised with little difficulty, the fertile alluvial land producing more food than was necessary for mere subsistence. At a number of key locations, **wadis** gave access to the mineral resources of the western and eastern deserts, providing communities with the prestige materials required by their leaders for conspicuous consumption. Control of trade routes, whether overland or by river, gave certain sites a further advantage, allowing local élites to dominate economic exchange over a wider area than their immediate hinterlands. The combined effect of these factors was to give rise to a number of flourishing Predynastic communities ruled by highly developed élites displaying some of the features later associated with kingship (Kaiser and Dreyer 1982: 242–5). Four sites in particular seem to have played a major part in the concentration of political and economic power that was to characterise the formation of the Egyptian state (Figure 2.1).

The site of Naqada has given its name to the Predynastic material culture of Upper Egypt as a whole, and to the chronological divisions which modern archaeologists impose on the development of that culture. On the west bank of the Nile, opposite the entrance to the Wadi Hammamat that gives access to the mineral-rich Red Sea Hills, a large settlement grew up in early Predynastic times, accompanied by extensive cemeteries on the desert edge (Kemp 1989: 36, fig. 9). Since the name for Naqada in historic times was Nubt, 'city of gold', it is possible that the site's early prosperity was founded on this precious commodity, available at various sites in the eastern desert and no doubt traded throughout Predynastic Egypt (Trigger *et al.* 1983: 39). Certainly, by the Naqada II period, the local ruling class had grown wealthy and differentiated themselves increasingly from the general population. This is most noticeable in the mortuary sphere, élite burials being located in a separate cemetery (which, however, continued to include less wealthy interments as well). Cemetery T, as it is known, contained a number of large brick-lined tombs, furnished with abundant grave goods, many of them in prestige materials (Kemp 1973: 38–43, 1989: 35–7, esp. 36, fig. 9). Judging from the size and splendour of their burials, the Predynastic rulers of Naqada seem to have controlled a territory of some size, perhaps amounting to a 'kingdom'. The importance of Naqada and its ruling family in the process of state formation is highlighted by the construction of two royal tombs to the south of the Predynastic necropolis at the very beginning of the First Dynasty (Kemp 1967: 24–5, footnote). One of these belonged to Queen Neith-hotep (de Morgan 1897), probably the wife of Narmer, who may have been a descendant of the Predynastic rulers of Naqada. Moreover, the local god of Naqada, Seth, was closely associated with the kingship in Early Dynastic times, being one of the two deities embodied in the person of the king. Hence, a title borne

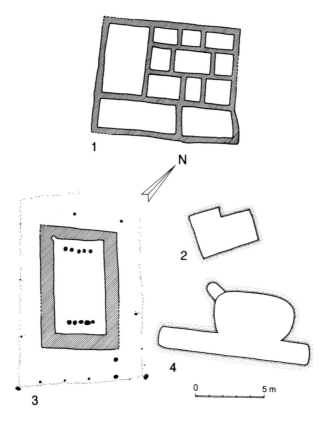

Figure 2.1 Early centres of kingship. Tombs of late Predynastic rulers: (1) Abydos tomb U-j (after Dreyer 1993: 33, fig. 4); (2) Naqada tomb T5 (after Kemp 1989: 36, fig. 9); (3) Hierakonpolis Locality 6 tomb 1 (after Hoffman 1982: 44, fig. I.13); (4) Qustul tomb L24 (after Williams 1986: 358, fig. 170).

by First Dynasty queens was 'she who sees Horus-and-Seth', whilst the Second Dynasty king Peribsen chose to emphasise Seth as his protector deity in preference to Horus. As we shall see, Naqada may have played a key role in the political consolidation of Upper Egypt that preceded the unification of the whole country (Kemp 1989: 35–7).

A large Predynastic settlement, extensive cemeteries and a concentration of élite burials in one cemetery are also features of another Upper Egyptian site, Hierakonpolis (B. Adams 1987, 1995, 1996; Hoffman 1982; Kemp 1989: 37–41, esp. 40, fig. 11). The area covered by the Predynastic town exceeds any other contemporary settlement in Egypt, marking Hierakonpolis out as perhaps the dominant centre in the fourth millennium BC (Kemp 1989: 44). Like Naqada, Hierakonpolis benefited from access to the mineral resources of the eastern desert, via the Wadi Abbad.

Close contacts with Lower Nubia may have given the rulers of Hierakonpolis control of, or at least access to, lucrative trade routes connecting Egypt and sub-Saharan Africa, whilst a broad expanse of cultivable land provided the necessary base for a growing population and an expanding sector of non-productive specialists. As early as Naqada I, members of the local élite were buried in a remote spot out in the desert, designated Locality 6 (B. Adams 1996). Their successors of the Naqada II period chose a cemetery closer to the cultivation, and it was here that the famous painted tomb was discovered. During the final phase of the Predynastic period, Naqada III, the local élite moved its burial ground back to Locality 6, constructing massive rock-cut tombs with offering places. Tombs are not the only sign of the important role played by Hierakonpolis in the late Predynastic period. A large ceremonial centre excavated on the low desert and dating back to the early Naqada II period has been interpreted as a temple, closely resembling shrines depicted on First Dynasty seal-impressions (R. Friedman 1996). At the end of Naqada II, the main focus of local religious activity was apparently relocated to the walled town of Nekhen, where a circular stone revetment and an adjoining paved area represent the earliest temple on the town mound (Quibell and Green 1902: pls LXV, LXXII; Hoffman 1980: 131–2). It was here that Egypt's first historic kings ('Scorpion' and Narmer) dedicated votive palettes and maceheads, to honour the local god, Horus of Nekhen. Although Narmer was probably descended from the Predynastic rulers of This, King 'Scorpion' may have been a member of the ruling family of Hierakonpolis (Trigger, in Trigger *et al.* 1983: 50). In common with Seth of Naqada, the close identification of Horus of Nekhen with divine kingship emphasises the important role played by Hierakonpolis and its rulers in the process of state formation, and in the formulation of kingship ideology (R. Friedman 1994: 17), a role already attested in the decoration of the painted tomb.

One of the earliest examples of classic kingship iconography is a decorated incense burner from the Naqada III royal cemetery at Qustul in Lower Nubia (Williams 1986: pls 34 and 38). So many motifs are presented together – including the ruler wearing the **white crown**, the god Horus, and a niched building similar to early *serekh*s – that the cemetery's excavator argued in favour of a Lower Nubian origin for Egyptian kingship (Williams 1986: 163–90, 1987). Whilst earlier Egyptian examples of royal iconography (for example, the Abydos vessel and the Hierakonpolis painted tomb) make such a theory unlikely (W.Y. Adams 1985; Baines 1995: 104–5), there is no doubt that the rulers buried in Qustul Cemetery L had adopted much of the symbolism of rule developed by their Upper Egyptian counterparts. Cattle burials are a feature of the Qustul royal cemetery and are also attested at Hierakonpolis Locality 6 (Hoffman 1982: 55–6; Williams 1986: 176). Together with the iconographic evidence, this seems to indicate significant cultural exchange between these two late Predynastic kingdoms on the Upper Nile. The size and wealth of the Qustul royal tombs make it likely that their owners were powerful rulers, perhaps exercising authority over much, if not all, of Lower Nubia. The basis of their economic and political power seems to have been the trade between Egypt and sub-Saharan Africa in which the rulers of Qustul would have acted as middlemen. As we shall see, access to and control of trade routes were key factors in the process of state formation.

The fourth centre of early kingship is the site where that institution is first attested iconographically, Abydos. Cemetery U, the site of high-status burials since Naqada I, continued to be used by the local rulers and their associates throughout the Predynastic period, although graves dating to Naqada II are rather scarce, perhaps suggesting that high-status tombs were located elsewhere in this period. In the final phase of the Predynastic, Cemetery U clearly underwent a transformation into a burial ground reserved for the rulers of the Thinite region. Whereas in Naqada I élite burials were intermingled with simple sand-cut pits, the Naqada III tombs are exclusively high status (cf. Dreyer 1993a; Dreyer *et al.* 1996). This demarcation of a separate élite cemetery, paralleled at the other three sites discussed above, is one of the key indications of political consolidation and incipient kingship (Baines 1995: 109). The earliest town levels at Abydos also date to the Naqada III period (Petrie 1902: 22; Kemp 1977: 189; Wilkinson 1993a: 218–19), demonstrating a link between the concentration of political power and the beginnings of urbanism. If some of the votive objects from three deposits are to be dated to the late Predynastic and Early Dynastic periods, as seems plausible, then Abydos, like Hierakonpolis, appears to have been the site of an early shrine (for further examples, at less prestigious sites, see Chapter 8). Unlike the situation at Naqada and Hierakonpolis, there is no evidence at Abydos for significant Predynastic settlement. The regional capital – and presumably the residence of the rulers buried at Abydos – was This, an ancient site which has not been located but which probably lies beneath the modern city of Girga. As at Naqada and Hierakonpolis, we would expect evidence of substantial late Predynastic construction at This as well. In the absence of such evidence, it is impossible to compare the three Upper Egyptian sites directly, but the mortuary record certainly indicates the primacy of This/Abydos towards the very end of the Predynastic period. The Naqada III tombs in Cemetery U are large, brick-lined structures, several of them with multiple chambers (Dreyer 1993a: 32–6, pls 4.d and 5). The most lavish burial, tomb U-j (*c.* 3150 BC), comprises eight chambers, some of them linked by small slits which probably symbolise doorways. The tomb as a whole may represent the royal palace in microcosm (Dreyer 1992b: 295), in which case it would be the earliest example of palace symbolism in Early Dynastic mortuary architecture (Baines 1995: 107). The provision of an arena for the ritual of kingship, modelled on the courts and buildings of the royal residence, was a key component of the royal mortuary complex in the first three dynasties. Tomb U-j may allow us to trace this aspect of royal mortuary architecture and ideology back into the Naqada III period, once again emphasising the Predynastic origins of Egyptian kingship. One of the objects recovered from tomb U-j was an ivory *heqa*-sceptre in the form of a shepherd's crook (Dreyer 1993a: pl. 7.a, 1993b: 11). This remained one of the essential elements of royal regalia throughout Egyptian history, and its presence among the grave goods of tomb U-j leaves no doubt as to the royal status of the occupant. Moreover, the tomb is by far the largest of its date anywhere in Egypt, suggesting the strong possibility that its owner exercised rule or at least hegemony over much, if not all, of the Nile valley. The extent of his influence is highlighted by the other grave goods with which tomb U-j was furnished.

TRADE, OWNERSHIP AND POWER

Perhaps the most striking categories of object from Abydos tomb U-j are those which illustrate the economic and administrative apparatus at the ruler's command (Figure 2.2). Dozens of inscribed bone labels constitute the earliest corpus of writing yet found in Egypt (Dreyer 1992b: pls 6.1–4, 1993a: pl. 7.c–j). The short inscriptions, comprising no more than two or three individual signs, refer to places which presumably supplied the ruler's court with commodities. The labels themselves would originally have been attached to these consignments, recording their quantity and provenance. Localities mentioned on the labels include Delta towns such as Bubastis (Dreyer 1992b: 297, pl. 6.4, 1993a: pl. 7.i). Either the Thinite king already ruled Lower Egypt or he possessed sufficient status to command supplies from the Delta. There is no doubt that his court engaged in large-scale trade with the Near East: the tomb contained over 400 imported vessels from **Syria-Palestine** (Hartung, in Dreyer 1993a: 49–56, pl. 9). (Note that the word 'trade' as used here refers to the exchange of commodities without the profit motive that characterises trade in the modern world.) Many types are previously unattested in Egypt, and petrographic analyses have led to the conclusion that some of the vessels may have come from as far afield as northern Israel and the Lebanon (van den Brink, personal communication). The closed forms indicate that the pots were used as containers for liquids; the residues which have survived inside some vessels suggest wine as one of the principal commodities (Dreyer 1992b: 297). We do not know what Egyptian products passed in the other direction, but the sheer number of pots illustrates the scale of trade conducted between Upper Egypt and the Near East in the late Predynastic period.

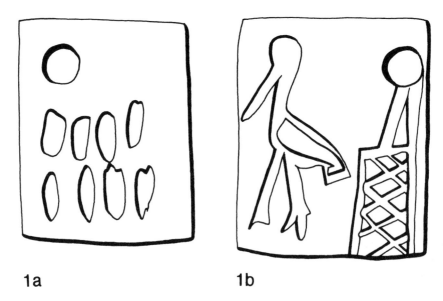

1a   1b

Figure 2.2 Trade, ownership and power. Objects from Abydos tomb U-j: (1) Bone labels (enlarged), originally attached to commodities. The short inscriptions record the quantity or provenance of the goods: (a) the number eight; (b) Bubastis (ancient Egypt *B3st*) in the north-eastern Delta (after Dreyer 1993: pl. 7.d, i). (2) Some of the hundreds of imported vessels found in the tomb; petrographic analysis suggests many of the vessels were manufactured in northern Israel, and may have contained wine (author's photograph).

Long-distance trade in high-status goods had been practised by Egyptians from early Predynastic times. Lapis lazuli from the mountains of Badakhshan (present-day Afghanistan) is attested in graves of the Naqada I period (Matmar 3005: Brunton 1948: pl. LXX); imported vessels from Syria-Palestine and even Mesopotamia turn up sporadically in burials from this time onwards (Kantor 1965: 6–14, figures 3–4), whilst Nubian hand-made bowls are a rare, but characteristic, type of pottery in graves of early Naqada II. As the élites of Upper Egypt grew increasingly powerful during the second half of the fourth millennium BC, they came to require prestige goods to demonstrate and reinforce their exalted social status. A particular type of Palestinian vessel – a jar with wavy ledge handles – was evidently so sought after that it inspired Egyptian potters to copy it, giving rise to a whole class of Naqada II Egyptian pottery known as wavy-handled jars (Bourriau 1981: 130–3; Needler 1984: 212–17). Demand for genuine imports grew, and with it the intensity of foreign trade practised by middlemen such as the Predynastic inhabitants of Minshat Abu Omar. The frequency of Palestinian pottery in the Predynastic graves at Minshat indicates that the community maintained close contacts with its neighbours to the north-east (Kroeper and Wildung 1985: 97–8). At the other end of the Nile valley, the Lower Nubian rulers buried at Qustul undoubtedly derived their power and influence from their ability to control Egyptian access to goods from sub-Saharan Africa, such as ebony, ivory and ostrich eggs. Qustul seems to have been at the hub of an extensive long-distance trade network, since some of the royal tombs were furnished with imported vessels from both Upper Egypt and Syria-Palestine (Williams 1986: pls 17–24 and pl. 25, respectively). With communities (and their rulers) on the frontiers of Egypt growing rich and powerful from trade, it is perhaps not surprising that the jealous eyes of the most influential Upper Egyptian rulers should have turned to trade routes. As we shall see, gaining direct access to imported commodities seems to have been one of the main motives behind the process of political unification.

The mass of foreign vessels from Abydos tomb U-j illustrates the commodities imported by Egypt from the Near East, but the other side of the trading relationship is less well attested. Gold may have been an important export for Predynastic Egypt; it was highly valued throughout the ancient world and, as we have seen, the early importance of at least one major Upper Egyptian centre, Naqada, may have been based upon exploitation of this precious metal. Egypt may also have exported cereal crops, its fertility and agricultural potential the envy of other, less fortunate lands. Such exports would be difficult, if not impossible, to detect in the archaeological record, but a few indications of trade with Egypt have been found in the Near East. Pottery storage vessels (or sherds from vessels), made in Egypt and incised before firing with marks of the royal treasury, have turned up throughout northern Sinai and southern Palestine, at sites such as el-Beda, Rafiah, Tell Arad and Nahal Tillah (van den Brink, in preparation). Some of these sites may have been Egyptian 'colonies', established to exploit local economic resources directly (Brandl 1992; Porat 1992). Others, notably Tell Arad, are known to have been flourishing centres of the indigenous late **Chalcolithic**/Early Bronze Age Palestinian civilisation (Amiran 1978), and it comes as little surprise that they maintained active trade links with Egypt.

The identification of commodity consignments – both those destined for foreign markets and those traded within Egypt – by means of pot marks illustrates the growing obsession of the Upper Egyptian rulers with ownership, accounting and the detailed management of economic resources. The very development of Egyptian writing can be seen in this context (Postgate *et al.* 1995), and the bone labels from tomb U-j emphasise the link between economic activity (especially long-distance trade) and bureaucratic sophistication. Since their control of resources gave the rulers of Predynastic Upper Egypt their political authority, it was clearly of great importance to ensure that accurate records were kept of receipts and deliveries, and that property was easily identified. The *serekh* – a panelled rectangle representing a section of the façade of the royal palace – seems to have been chosen as a mark of royal ownership. A *serekh* incised or painted in ink on a vessel denoted that the contents were the produce and/or property of the royal court. At first, a simple *serekh* was enough to convey this message; later, the individual ruler incorporated his name within the panel to specify ownership more precisely (Müller 1938: 13–17; cf. Kaiser and Dreyer 1982: fig. 14). *Serekh*s incised or painted on pottery vessels for this purpose constitute our earliest corpus of royal names. The distribution of particular royal names gives an indication, albeit a rough one, of the extent of a king's economic influence or political power. Hence, it is possible in some degree to trace the rise of the Egyptian state. Whereas vessels bearing the names of some kings (such as 'Ka') are attested rather rarely, Narmer's name has been found incised on vessels from sites throughout Egypt and southern Palestine, emphasising that his rule probably extended over the entire Nile valley and beyond.

THE DYNAMICS OF STATE FORMATION

As we have seen, the various trends which led to the formation of the Egyptian state were gradual processes which began in the early Predynastic period. Increasing social stratification, the development and expression of an ideology of rule, the spread of Upper Egyptian technology and other cultural attributes throughout the country, the concentration of economic and political power in the hands of a few ruling families, the intensification of foreign trade, the invention of writing and the emergence of a literate bureaucracy: these were not sudden developments, although the pace of change seems to have accelerated during the last quarter of the fourth millennium BC. What is clear is that these processes did not affect all regions of the country to the same extent. Local and regional factors such as the economic resource base, topography, communications and distance from the centres of power affected to a considerable extent the pace of developments at individual sites (Malek 1986: 26; Wilkinson 1996b: 89–90). Those localities which already enjoyed economic and political influence continued to develop rapidly, whilst the quieter backwaters (for example, Middle Egypt) participated hardly at all in the momentous changes sweeping the country. Indeed, it is likely that many smaller farming communities were relatively unaffected by Egyptian unification and the advent of a national government, except that they now paid taxes to the central treasury rather than to local or regional élites. When considering state formation in Egypt, it is important to recognise this pattern of regional variation, and of local variation within regions. The process was not a monolithic one, and although its ultimate effects were felt throughout Egypt, certain localities played a much greater role in determining the outcome.

Although the characteristics of early states are broadly similar for different regions of the ancient world, the factors involved in state formation are likely to have varied according to particular circumstances (Cohen 1978). Different authors have postulated different 'prime movers', that is principal factors, for the emergence of the Egyptian state (Bard 1994: 1–5). These include population pressure (Carneiro 1970; Bard and Carneiro 1989), prompting Upper Egyptian rulers to annex the fertile fields of the Delta to support a growing population (F.A. Hassan 1988: 165–6); the influence of irrigation in the concentration of power (Wittfogel 1957); trade (Bard 1987); and ideology (Bard 1992; cf. Kemp 1989: 32 and 35). Although all these factors are likely to have played a part in the concentration of political and economic power, some can be rejected decisively as 'prime movers'.

For example, given the carrying capacity of agricultural land in Upper Egypt and the probable size of the ancient population, it seems unlikely that population pressure was a significant factor in the formation of the Egyptian state (F.A. Hassan 1988: 165; Kemp 1989: 31; contra Hoffman 1980: 309). Even though the strip of cultivable land is often very narrow in Upper Egypt, it seems always to have been sufficient to support the ancient population. None the less, the end of the **Neolithic subpluvial** and the accompanying desiccation of the savannahs probably caused an influx of desert pastoralists into the Nile valley in the late Predynastic period. Such a phenomenon seems to be attested at Hierakonpolis (Hoffman *et al.* 1986), and it may have played a part in the social processes which led to the formation of the state. The Scorpion macehead is an exception amongst early royal iconography which generally makes no reference to irrigation works. It is also unlikely that water management in the Nile valley was organised on a national scale in Early Dynastic times. The evidence from later periods of Egyptian history indicates that irrigation was not centrally controlled, nor would central control have been practicable: basin irrigation was the most efficient way of harnessing the floodwaters of the Nile, and this would have been most effectively managed at the local or regional level by communities, perhaps overseen by local governors. Hence, the control of irrigation on a nation-wide basis can probably be discounted as a major factor in Egyptian state formation (Janssen 1978: 217; Lamberg-Karlovsky and Sabloff 1979: 129; F.A. Hassan 1988: 165; cf. Hoffman 1980: 315–16). It has been argued that the need for ever more complex information processing was a key factor in Mesopotamian state formation (Wright and Johnson 1975). In Egypt, too, there is little doubt that the increasing centralisation of political and economic authority required sophisticated forms of administration – notably record-keeping and the invention of writing (Postgate *et al.* 1995). However, this seems to be a correlate or effect of state formation rather than a primary cause.

It is now generally accepted that a combination of factors was responsible in the Egyptian case (Lamberg-Karlovsky and Sabloff 1979: 207–11, 329–30; F.A. Hassan 1988: 164–6; Wilkinson 1996b: 90). The archaeological and iconographic record emphasises two factors, trade and ideology. In discussing them, an obvious danger arises: because these two factors were clearly at work in late Predynastic Egypt (more clearly, perhaps, than other factors mentioned above), it is all too easy to overstate their influence on the process of state formation as a whole. The emergence of the Egyptian state is best understood as having a 'multiplicity of causes' (F.A. Hassan 1988: 165).

Recent excavations at Abydos and in the Delta – at sites such as Buto and Minshat Abu Omar – have highlighted the important part played by foreign trade in the dynamics of state formation (contra Kemp 1989: 31). Of course, the increasing demand for prestige goods acquired by trade was a consequence, not a cause, of social inequality (F.A. Hassan 1988: 165). None the less, a strategic location for trade seems to have been the common factor in the rise of particular Predynastic centres. From Buto and Minshat Abu Omar in the Delta to This, Naqada and Hierakonpolis in Upper Egypt, and Qustul in Lower Nubia: all seem to have gained importance and power through access to, or control of, trade routes. The vast numbers of imported vessels buried in tomb U-j at Abydos demonstrate the importance of foreign commodities to the late Predynastic rulers of Upper Egypt, and the active part they played in long-distance trade.

It is probably no coincidence that the territory conquered by the kings of Upper Egypt to achieve political unification was that which gave them direct access to Near Eastern trade routes, via land and sea. The rapid demise of the indigenous Lower Nubian **A-Group** at the beginning of the First Dynasty can also be attributed to Egyptian expansionism, as the early kings sought to eliminate the middlemen in their trade with sub-Saharan Africa. The desire for direct access to foreign commodities is manifested in the phenomenon of 'core and periphery', attested for other early civilisations (Rowlands *et al.* 1987; Algaze 1993). In the process of political and economic consolidation, the kings of the late Predynastic period and early First Dynasty temporarily extended their power beyond the natural borders of Egypt, mounting raids into Lower Nubia to subdue the local population and establishing outposts in southern Palestine to exploit the local resources directly. The character of the Egyptian presence in southern Palestine has been understood only recently, and it underscores the central importance of trade in the state formation process.

A factor which must have played a part in the unification of Egypt is the 'generative power that works from the top downwards and from the centre outwards' (Kemp 1989: 7) or, to put it another way, political ambition and the charisma of particular rulers (Service 1975: 291; Wilkinson 1996b: 89). Although Hierakonpolis and its rulers appear to have been at the heart of the unification process, it was the royal family of This that ultimately seized the prize of kingship. The reasons behind this are not clear, but perhaps the character of the competing rulers played a part in the final outcome. Once a unified state had been forged, Egypt's early kings lost no time in promulgating an ideology of kingship which presented the unification of the country as the fulfilment of a predestined order. We cannot hope to know if a similar belief in the divine ordination of Egyptian unity inspired the late Predynastic rulers of Upper Egypt with the missionary zeal to annex the north and make Egyptian unity a political reality (Lamberg-Karlovsky and Sabloff 1979: 133; cf. Kemp 1989: 35). However, ideology is a powerful force for historical change and, as one leading scholar has pointed out, 'states are . . . built on the urge to rule and on visions of order' (Kemp 1989: 9; cf. Wenke 1991: 283–4). We must now examine the process of conquest and annexation that resulted in Egyptian unification, and attempt to reconstruct the course of events that led to the birth of Egypt as a nation state.

POLITICAL UNIFICATION: A HYPOTHESIS

The archaeological evidence makes it clear that, by the end of Naqada II (*c.* 3200 BC), the most powerful centres were This, Naqada and Hierakonpolis in Upper Egypt (Kemp 1989: 34, fig. 8). The regional traditions of pottery manufacture identified in Naqada I Upper Egypt may hint at the existence of incipient territories even earlier (R. Friedman 1994: 4–5); these 'social regions' may have formed the basis for the later political divisions (R. Friedman 1994: 569). There is an unbroken sequence of élite/royal tombs at Hierakonpolis from the Naqada I period to the very threshold of the First Dynasty. At Naqada, there is a slight hiatus between the sequence of élite tombs in Cemetery T – the latest of which (T36) dates to early Naqada III, even though a relatively poor grave (T33) in the same cemetery dates to the threshold of the First Dynasty (Hendrickx 1993; cf. Baumgartel 1970: LXIX) – and the royal tombs of the early First Dynasty. This break is probably significant, and suggests that Naqada was eclipsed by one of its neighbouring territories (either Abydos to the north or Hierakonpolis to the south) during the final stages of the state formation process. At Abydos, the First Dynasty royal tombs on the Umm el-Qaab are the direct successors of the Predynastic élite burials in Cemetery U which span the period between late Naqada I and the end of the Predynastic period, with an apparent, unexplained gap during the middle of Naqada II. Moreover, the size of tomb U-j may indicate that its occupant already ruled much of Egypt as early as Naqada III (*c.* 3150 BC). The process of political unification seems to have been well under way, if not already complete, by the time tomb U-j was constructed. Indeed, the wide geographic distribution of similar types of pottery by the end of Naqada II may suggest that a degree of political unity already existed several generations before tomb U-j was built (R. Friedman 1994: 435). The royal cemetery at Qustul attests the short-lived existence of a powerful Lower Nubian **polity** during the Naqada III period. The largest grave in Cemetery L – which contained the decorated incense burner mentioned earlier – is roughly contemporary with Abydos tomb U-j. Rock-cut inscriptions in the vicinity of the Second Cataract seem to record punitive expeditions mounted by Egyptian rulers against Lower Nubia, leading to the extirpation of the indigenous A-Group and the demise of the Qustul kingdom by the beginning of the First Dynasty. Hence, the evidence of tombs provides some clues about the dominant players in the final centuries of state formation.

Iconography and ideology may also be of some help. The later importance of Horus and Seth in the doctrine of divine kingship points to the significance of Hierakonpolis and Naqada in the process of unification (Kemp 1989: 37). The two crowns associated with the king from the very beginning of the First Dynasty may have originated at these two places. The **red crown** is shown in relief on a sherd from a large black-topped red ware vessel from Naqada (Payne 1993: 94, fig. 34.774; Baines 1995: 149, fig. 3.1). The vessel probably dates to late Naqada I (*c.* 3600 BC), making this by far the earliest occurrence of the red crown and suggesting that this item of royal regalia may have originated at Naqada, perhaps as the headgear worn by the local ruler. The white crown is first attested on two royal artefacts from the late Predynastic period, the carved ivory handle of a flint knife (Williams and Logan 1987, esp. 273, fig. 1) and the decorated incense burner from Qustul Cemetery L. The knife handle is unprovenanced but is likely to have come from somewhere in Upper Egypt. Given the evidence for cultural contacts between Qustul and Hierakonpolis in Naqada III, it is tempting to locate the origins of the white crown at Hierakonpolis. In this case, the red crown would have symbolised a northern power to the Predynastic kings of Hierakonpolis, just as in the historic period the red crown was transferred to symbolise Lower Egypt (cf. F.A. Hassan 1988: 174). The so-called 'monuments of unification' – the decorated ceremonial palettes and maceheads commissioned by rulers of the late Predynastic period and early First Dynasty – were traditionally interpreted as records of actual events in the process of state formation. The Narmer palette, in particular, was thought to represent the king's victory over a Lower Egyptian ruler. Even recently, it has been suggested that this latter ruler may have been based at Buto, and that he controlled a territory which may have included Memphis and Tarkhan. This line of argument leads to the romantic suggestion that Buto was the last, northernmost refuge of a Lower Egyptian dynasty contemporary with the late Predynastic kings of Upper Egypt, giving rise to the later myth about two competing kingdoms (von der Way 1993: 96). The argument against such hypotheses centres around the purpose and interpretation of artefacts like the Narmer palette. They may just as easily depict symbolic or ritual activities as actual events in the political consolidation of Egypt (Millet 1990; Fairservis 1991; Baines 1995: 117). Literal interpretations of the scenes are now generally regarded as old-fashioned (Shaw and Nicholson 1995: 197), and it is perhaps safer to ignore the palettes and maceheads as potential historical sources. (Note, however, that an historical interpretation of the Narmer palette may be given new weight by the recent discovery of a label of the same king which names the event depicted on his palette.)

Taking into account all the evidence, it is possible to suggest the following hypothetical reconstruction of events leading to the political unification of Egypt. As early as Naqada I, powerful centres had developed at This, Naqada and Hierakonpolis in Upper Egypt, whilst local élites at other sites exercised varying degrees of economic and political control over their respective territories. During the course of Naqada II (c. 3400 BC), powerful local rulers are attested at Abadiya (Kaiser and Dreyer 1982: 244; Williams 1986: 173) and Gebelein, but it was the three major centres and their ruling families that continued to dominate the processes associated with state formation. Towards the end of Naqada II, a flourishing polity arose in Lower Nubia, ruled by kings who shared the emergent iconography of rule with their counterparts in Upper Egypt. At some point early in Naqada III, the Predynastic kingdom of Naqada was probably incorporated – whether by political agreement or by military force cannot be established – into the territory of a neighbouring kingdom. The amalgamation of these two polities would then have preceded the unification of Upper Egypt as a whole (F.A. Hassan 1988: 165). The Cairo fragment of the Palermo Stone shows, in the top register, a line of kings wearing the **double crown** (hand copy by I.E.S. Edwards in the library of the Faculty of Oriental Studies, Cambridge University; cf. Trigger *et al.* 1983: 44 and 70). If the red and white crowns originated at Naqada and Hierakonpolis respectively, then these figures – often interpreted as kings of a united Egypt before the beginning of the First Dynasty – may represent rulers of an Upper Egyptian polity comprising the territories of Hierakonpolis and Naqada. Furthermore, the adoption of the local god of Hierakonpolis, Horus of Nekhen, as the supreme deity of kingship, and the special attention paid to the temple of Horus by early kings, suggests that it was the rulers of Hierakonpolis who made the first move in the game of power-play that was ultimately to lead to the unification of Egypt. The annexation of Naqada would explain the gap in the sequence of élite burials at the site at the end of Naqada III, a period which is marked at Hierakonpolis by the large tombs at Locality 6. Alternatively, Naqada may have been eclipsed by its northern rival: despite the undoubted importance of Hierakonpolis, the unparalleled size of Abydos tomb U-j (slightly earlier in date than the élite tombs at Hierakonpolis Locality 6) suggests that the kingdom of This was already dominant by early Naqada III, at least in the northern part of the Nile valley. Perhaps the ruler of This also exercised hegemony over Lower Egypt by this time, giving him access to the foreign trade which is so dramatically attested in the imported vessels buried in his tomb. Nevertheless, it is still possible that several rulers, each with his own regional power-base, continued to co-exist and to claim royal titles. This may account for a number of the royal names attested at the end of the Predynastic period.

It is not clear how politically advanced the Delta was in late Predynastic times. A more hierarchical social structure may have developed rapidly in the wake of Upper Egyptian cultural influences which permeated Lower Egypt in late Naqada II (von der Way 1993: 96). There were probably powerful local élites at several sites, notably Buto and Saïs. Some Lower Egyptian rulers may have adopted elements of early royal iconography, particularly the *serekh*, since many of the vessels incised with *serekh* marks have a Lower Egyptian provenance (Kaiser and Dreyer 1982: figs 14 and 15). It is quite likely that the Upper Egyptians who spearheaded the drive toward political unification had to overcome or accommodate local Lower Egyptian rulers. None the less, we cannot discount the possibility that the Delta had been incorporated into a larger polity centred on This by the Naqada III period (*c.* 3200 BC). Certainly it was the rulers of This who ultimately triumphed in the contest for political power and claimed the prize of kingship over the whole country, even though Hierakonpolis seems to have remained important until the very end of the Predynastic period. Control of Lower Egypt would undoubtedly have given the Thinite rulers a major advantage over their southern rivals.

Given that King 'Scorpion' dedicated his ceremonial macehead in the temple at Hierakonpolis, and that he is not attested at Abydos, the theory that he belonged to the royal house of Hierakonpolis is an attractive one. If this was the case, there may have been two rival polities governed from This and Hierakonpolis up to the very threshold of the First Dynasty. The reverence shown to Hierakonpolis by the Early Dynastic kings may reflect the site's importance during the final stages of state formation. The end of Scorpion's reign may have marked a decisive turning-point, the moment at which the king of This assumed an uncontested position as sovereign of all Egypt. During the peak of activity that accompanied political unification, Egyptian control was extended beyond the borders of Egypt proper into Lower Nubia, crushing the local kingdom centred at Qustul and leading to the rapid disappearance of the indigenous A-Group culture. Military raids by early Egyptian rulers are commemorated in two rock-cut inscriptions at Gebel Sheikh Suleiman in the Second Cataract region (Needler 1967; Murnane 1987). Egyptian 'colony sites' also seem to have been established in southern Palestine, suggesting a degree of political control, or at least influence, in the region. The final stages of state formation may have been accomplished quite quickly, within two or three generations, and Narmer may, after all, have been the first king to exercise authority throughout the country unchallenged. He seems to have been regarded by at least two of his successors as something of a founder figure (Shaw and Nicholson 1995: 18). It remains impossible to define the moment at which a single king ruled Egypt for the first time. From the evidence, this must have occurred at some point between the lifetime of the owner of Abydos tomb U-j (*c.* 3150 BC) and the reign of Narmer (*c.* 3000 BC) (cf. Malek 1986: 26). Many scholars favour an earlier rather than a later date for political unification, but the evidence is by no means unanimous.

The actual means by which the rulers of This ultimately gained control over the whole country is not known. Annexation of neighbouring territories must have involved negotiation and accommodation at the very least. It is not unlikely that more forceful tactics were required, and the possibility of military action cannot be ruled out, despite the difficulties involved in interpreting monuments like the Narmer Palette. The 'Libyan Palette' depicts attacks on a number of fortified cities (Petrie 1953: pl. G; Kemp 1989: 50, fig. 16; Spencer 1993: 53, fig. 33), but again the symbolism of the decoration may not be straightforward. However, the campaigns of Khasekhem against northern, perhaps Lower Egyptian, rebels at the end of the Second Dynasty may provide a later parallel for the sort of action that was required to subjugate the Delta.

KINGS BEFORE THE FIRST DYNASTY

As we have seen, there is convincing evidence for the emergence of at least three Upper Egyptian polities by the Naqada II period (c. 3500 BC). The sites of This (with its cemetery at Abydos), Naqada and Hierakonpolis appear to have stood at the centres of powerful territories, each ruled by an hereditary élite exercising authority on a regional basis. The rulers of the three territories – plus an individual buried at Gebelein, who may have controlled a smaller area – used recognisably royal iconography to express the ideological basis of their power, and may justifiably be called 'kings'. However, the respective owners of the Abydos vessel, the tombs in Naqada Cemetery T, the Hierakonpolis painted tomb and the Gebelein painted cloth are anonymous. Whilst their status is clear, they are quite literally prehistoric, having left no written evidence. It has been proposed that these kings exercising only regional authority might be grouped together as 'Dynasty 00' (van den Brink 1992a: vi and n. 1), recognising their royal status but emphasising their place in prehistory. The term is perhaps rather contrived, and has not won general acceptance. None the less, the place of these late Predynastic anonymous rulers at the head of the later dynastic tradition should be acknowledged.

History begins with the advent of written records, in Egypt's case the bone labels from Abydos tomb U-j. Despite the number of inscribed labels from the tomb, the name of the owner himself is not certain. Several pottery vessels from U-j were inscribed in ink with the figure of a scorpion (Dreyer 1992b: pl. 4), and this has been interpreted as the owner's name, not to be confused with the later King 'Scorpion' who commissioned the ceremonial macehead found at Hierakonpolis (Dreyer 1992b: 297 and n. 6, 1993a: 35 and n. 4). Other vessels from tomb U-j bear short ink inscriptions consisting of a combination of two signs (Dreyer 1995b: 53, fig. 3.a–d). Some of the inscriptions have one sign in common, interpreted by the excavator as a stylised tree, perhaps indicating 'estate'. It has been suggested that the accompanying sign in each case is a royal name, giving the sense 'estate of King X' (Dreyer 1992b: 297, 1993a: 35, 1995b: 52 and 54). This hypothesis is based upon later parallels which may not be appropriate to the Naqada III period, and the identification of a large number of new royal names on vessels from a single tomb may be questioned. However, many scholars accept the hypothesis, even if the existence of late Predynastic kings called 'Fish' and 'Red Sea shell' seems somewhat unlikely.

'Dynasty 0'

Subsequent kings of the Thinite royal family were interred in the same ancestral burial ground, those rulers prior to Djer being buried in the section known to modern scholars as Cemetery B. The name of at least one pre-First Dynasty king is known, whilst inscriptions on vessels and on rocks in the eastern and western deserts attest the existence of further named kings before the reign of Narmer (Figure 2.3). Other inscriptions which may or may not be kings' names have also come into the discussion. It is these rulers that collectively constitute 'Dynasty 0'. The term has caused some confusion, and it is rather unhelpful as the word 'Dynasty' suggests a single ruling line, moreover one which exercised control over the whole of Egypt. The various names undoubtedly represent rulers of various polities from different regions of the country, and it is practically impossible to establish which king was the first to rule over the whole of Egypt. However misleading it may be, the term 'Dynasty 0' has nevertheless come into general use and is unlikely to be discarded. A preferable and more neutral term might be 'late Predynastic kings'.

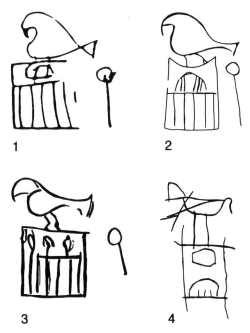

Figure 2.3 Kings before the First Dynasty. Royal names of four late Predynastic rulers, incised on pottery vessels to indicate royal ownership of the contents: (1) *serekh* of 'Scorpion' (after Kaiser and Dreyer 1982: 263, fig. 14.34); (2) *serekh* of 'Ka' (after Kaiser and Dreyer 1982: 263, fig. 14.23); (3) *serekh* of unidentified King A (after van den Brink 1996: pl. 30.a); (4) *serekh* of unidentified King B (after Wilkinson 1995: 206, fig. 1.b). Names not to same scale.

Several tall storage vessels from Tura and el-Beda (at the western end of the north Sinai coastal route) are incised with the motif of a *serekh* surmounted by two falcons (Junker 1912: 47, fig. 57.5; Clédat 1914; van den Brink 1996: table 1 nos 5–6, pl. 25.a). Some scholars have suggested that this represents the name of a particular late Predynastic ruler, perhaps based in Lower Egypt (von der Way 1993: 101). It could equally be a mark designating royal ownership without specifying the ruler in question.

The more famous of the two rock-cut inscriptions at Gebel Sheikh Suleiman in Lower Nubia shows an early *serekh* presiding over a scene which apparently records a punitive Egyptian raid into the Second Cataract region at the end of the Predynastic period. Once erroneously dated to the reign of Djer, the inscription has now been shown conclusively to date to the period of state formation (Murnane 1987; cf. Shaw and Nicholson 1995: 86). The *serekh* is empty and therefore anonymous, but we may hazard a guess that the ruler who ordered the inscription to be cut was an Upper Egyptian king, perhaps based at Hierakonpolis. The Gebel Sheikh Suleiman inscription proves that Egyptian military involvement in Lower Nubia – probably aimed at maintaining Egyptian access to sub-Saharan trade routes – began before the start of the First Dynasty. The process of Egyptian expansionism which led to the collapse of the Qustul kingdom and the disappearance of the indigenous A-Group culture may therefore have lasted several generations (cf. Williams 1986: 171).

Although the rulers buried at Qustul in Cemetery L adopted royal iconography, they do not seem to have recorded their names in recognisable form. An incised inscription on a pottery vessel from tomb L2 has been interpreted by the excavator as the name of an otherwise unattested Lower Nubian king, *Pe-Hor (Williams 1986: 149). However, once again, the inscription may not be a name at all, but rather a general mark of royal ownership.

Two pottery vessels from the Early Dynastic cemetery at Tura (Junker 1912: 47, fig. 57.3–4; van den Brink 1996: table 1 nos 7–8, pl. 25.b and d) are inscribed with a *serekh* which has been read as *Ny-Hor (Kaiser and Dreyer 1982: 264–8) but which may simply be a cursive rendering of the name of Narmer (Fischer 1963: 44–7), since abbreviated writings of this king's name are common (cf. Kaiser and Dreyer 1982: fig. 14.38). The same may be true of the *serekh* from Tarkhan (Petrie 1914: pls VI and XX.1; van den Brink 1996: table 1 no. 9, pl. 26.a), read by some scholars as *Hat-Hor (Kaiser and Dreyer 1982). However, in both cases, the vessels themselves suggest a date somewhat earlier than the reign of Narmer (van den Brink 1996), and the possibility that they record the names of earlier rulers cannot be excluded. The name written in ink on a vessel from tomb 412 at Tarkhan (Petrie *et al.* 1913: pl. XXXI.71) is unlikely to be royal (contra von der Way 1993: 100–1), as it is not written within a *serekh*. More probably the tomb owner was a member of the local or regional élite.

The owner of Abydos tomb B0/1/2

Many sherds and complete vessels from tomb B1/2 and the adjacent pit B0 at Abydos are inscribed with a device consisting of a falcon perching on a mouth-sign. This has been read as the name of a king and the presumed owner of the tomb, *Iry-Hor (Kaiser and Dreyer 1982: 212; cf. Petrie 1902: 4). There are problems with such an interpretation (Wilkinson 1993b; O'Brien 1996: 131–2), not least the fact that the 'name' is never found in a *serekh*, despite this device already having been in use for royal names prior to the construction of tomb B0/1/2 (von der Way 1993: 99, seeks to counteract this argument by citing the pot mark from Qustul Cemetery L discussed above). None the less, the existence of a King *Iry-Hor has gained wide acceptance (for example, van den Brink 1996). Whilst it is possible that the tomb belonged to a contemporary of Narmer's (Wilkinson 1993b), the recent re-excavation of chambers B1 and B2 and the discovery of an adjoining pit B0 (Dreyer *et al.* 1996) make it more likely that the whole complex belongs in the sequence of royal burials stretching back from the First Dynasty tombs in Abydos Cemetery B to their Predynastic forerunners in the adjacent Cemetery U. Moreover, the twin chambers closely resemble the tombs of kings 'Ka' and Narmer, and the location of B0/1/2 – if not the pottery – also suggests that the owner of the complex should be placed immediately before 'Ka' in the order of succession (Hendrickx, personal communication, contra Kaiser 1990: 289, fig. 1, who seems to place *Iry-Hor rather earlier, to account for the lack of a *serekh*).

King A

In contrast with some or all of the above cases, two royal names from the late Predynastic period almost certainly refer to particular kings. Because neither can be read as yet, they are designated here as King A and King B. The first is attested on a vessel from the eastern Delta. The inscription consists of a *serekh*, surmounted by a falcon, with three *ḥḏ* signs/maces in its upper part (Fischer 1963: 44, fig. 1, pl. VI.a and c; van den Brink 1996: pl. 30.a). Although the signs may be a writing of a royal name, it should be noted that maces and *serekhs* occur together on several other vessels dating to the threshold of the First Dynasty (van den Brink 1996: pls 26.a, 28, 30.b–c). Hence, the three maces on the eastern Delta jar may simply represent general symbols of royal authority, and the inscription as a whole could be 'an extended version of an anonymous *serekh*' (Hendrickx, personal communication). Two similar *serekhs* are attested on vessels from Tura (Junker 1912: 46 and 47, fig. 57.1 and 2), though both lack the Horus falcon. Moreover, in both cases the *ḥḏ* signs/maces occur in the lower part of the frame, replacing the more usual vertical strokes by which the palace façade is indicated, and three circles are shown beneath the *serekh* (van den Brink 1996: table 1 nos 18–19). Because of these differences, the Tura *serekh*s may not represent the ruler whose mark appears on the jar from the eastern Delta. If, on the other hand, the three inscriptions do signify one and the same king, the fact that he is unattested outside Lower Egypt may be significant (van den Brink 1996: 147), but it would be dangerous to reconstruct the extent of a ruler's authority on the basis of a few pot marks.

King B

Two rock-cut inscriptions in the western desert behind Armant show another royal name (Wilkinson 1996a). The **epigraphy** of the inscriptions, particularly the rendering of the falcon atop the *serekh*, confirms that the king in question reigned at the very end of the Predynastic period ('Dynasty 0', *c.* 3100 BC). Because of difficulties in deciphering early Egyptian script, a plausible reading of the name has not yet been proposed. Given the southerly location of the inscriptions, it is possible that the king was a member of the royal family of Hierakonpolis, which seems to have maintained control over the southernmost part of Upper Egypt until the threshold of the First Dynasty. The extent of King B's authority cannot be ascertained, but he was clearly in a position to mount expeditions into the western desert. The inscriptions highlight the extent of Egyptian interest in the peripheral areas prior to the First Dynasty. The *serekh* of King B may occur again, but without the falcon, on a rock-cut inscription in the eastern desert (Winkler 1938, I: 10 and 31). The site lies on the ancient Qena to Quseir route to the Red Sea coast, in an area visited regularly by Egyptian expeditions in late Predynastic and Early Dynastic times.

'Scorpion' and/or 'Crocodile'

One of the most striking royal monuments from the period immediately preceding the First Dynasty is the Scorpion macehead from Hierakonpolis. Despite the objection of some scholars (for example, Malek 1986: 29), the scorpion sign almost certainly records the name of the king, since it has been convincingly demonstrated that the **rosette/palmette** sign above the scorpion signified the ruler (H.S. Smith 1992: 244). In view of the close stylistic similarities between the Scorpion macehead and the monuments of Narmer, the two kings were probably near contemporaries (Kaiser 1990: 289, fig. 1). However, since no evidence of Scorpion has been found at Abydos – but note that the four-chambered tomb B50, devoid of any inscriptions, has been suggested as a possible burial place for Scorpion (Dreyer 1990: 71) – he may not fit into the Thinite dynastic sequence at all. Instead, he may have belonged to the royal house of Hierakonpolis (Trigger *et al.* 1983: 46), as suggested by the place he chose to dedicate his ceremonial macehead. In this case, he may have been at least partly contemporary with Narmer. The *serekh* of 'Scorpion' may occur on a wine jar from Minshat Abu Omar (Wildung 1981: 37, fig. 33; van den Brink 1996: pl. 28), although this inscription has also been read as the name of Aha (Wildung 1981: 35) Two *serekhs* written in ink on pottery vessels from Tarkhan (Petrie *et al.* 1913: pl. LX; Petrie 1914: pl. XL) have been read as 'Scorpion' (Kaplony 1963, II: 1090), although in the absence of any further comparable inscriptions a definitive reading remains impossible for the present.

A recent hypothesis assigns the Tarkhan inscriptions to another proposed king of 'Dynasty 0', the Horus 'Crocodile' (Dreyer 1992a). This reading is based upon new infra-red photographs of the inscriptions and their comparison with a seal-impression from a third tomb at Tarkhan, dated to the reign of Narmer. The sealing, which may have belonged to a governor of the Tarkhan region, shows a series of crocodiles above coils which probably represent water. On the basis of the inscribed vessels themselves and the form of the *serekhs*, the Horus 'Crocodile' is identified as a usurper or alternatively a king reigning concurrently with the main Thinite royal family, early in the reign of 'Ka'. Following this interpretation, the Minshat Abu Omar *serekh* mentioned above has now been attributed to 'Horus (Crocodile) the Subduer' (van den Brink 1996: 147). The proposed new reading of the three inscriptions and the existence of a King 'Crocodile' is not universally accepted. By contrast, the Scorpion macehead remains a powerful piece of evidence for the existence of a late Predynastic king of this name.

'Ka'

The horizontal stratigraphy of the royal burials at Abydos and the ceramic evidence – the types of pottery associated with the early royal names – make it fairly certain that Narmer was immediately preceded (as ruler of This, and perhaps as king of all Egypt) by the king whose Horus name shows a pair of arms, the hieroglyph later read as *k3*. King 'Ka', as he is generally known (but note Kaplony 1958), was buried in the double tomb B7/9, situated between the graves of his Predynastic forebears in Cemetery U and the tombs of his successors, the kings of the First Dynasty (Petrie 1901: pl. LIX). (The theory that the *serekhs* of 'Ka' from tomb B7/9 refer to the *ka*(-tomb) of Narmer [Baumgartel 1975: 31; repeated by O'Brien 1996: 132] would seem to be invalidated by the occurrences of the same *serekh* at sites other than Abydos.) Clay sealings from tomb B7/9 confirm its attribution (Petrie 1901: pls II.1 and XIII.89). 'Ka' is the best attested king before Narmer, his name having been found at sites from Tell

Ibrahim Awad in the north-eastern Delta (van den Brink 1992b: 53, n. 14) to Abydos in Upper Egypt. Two jars incised with the *serekh* of 'Ka' were found in graves at Helwan (Saad 1947: 111 and 112, figs 11–12), apparently indicating that the city of Memphis – which the Helwan necropolis served – was already in existence before the reign of Narmer. This is despite later tradition that Menes founded Egypt's new capital at the beginning of the First Dynasty. The *serekh* of 'Ka' also occurs on a **cylinder vessel** from Tarkhan (Petrie *et al.* 1913: pl. LXI). Here, and in the numerous inscriptions from the king's tomb at Abydos (Petrie 1902: 3, pls I–III), the accompanying signs refer to revenue received by the royal treasury. They illustrate the functioning of the centralised economy before the beginning of the First Dynasty, and they confirm that, from earliest times, tax collection was organised separately for Upper and Lower Egypt.

A NATION IS BORN

From the beginning of the First Dynasty, the Nile valley and Delta, from Elephantine to the Mediterranean coast, was under the control of a single government, presided over by a king from the Thinite royal family. Although the First Dynasty kings chose to be buried in their ancestral royal necropolis at Abydos, for at least part of the year they probably resided at and governed from a new capital city, located strategically at the junction of Upper and Lower Egypt, 'the balance of the two lands'. The foundation of Memphis as the national administrative centre really represents the culmination of the unification process. The earliest élite tomb at North Saqqara dates to the reign of Aha (*c.* 2950 BC), but burial activity at Helwan – which served as the capital's second cemetery – began at least as early as the reign of 'Ka' (cf. Saad 1947: 111 and 112, figs 11–12). It was 'Ka's' successor and Aha's predecessor, Narmer (probably the historical Menes), who became associated in later tradition with the foundation of Memphis, and he may have been the first king to establish his residence in the city.

Once the prize of national unity had been won, Egypt's early kings set about establishing mechanisms of rule that would maintain and bolster that unity, guaranteeing their own privileged position at the same time. The ideology of divine kingship, elements of which had been developed by Upper Egyptian rulers in Predynastic times, was promulgated vigorously through iconography, architecture, ritual and royal activities. The king was presented as the binding force of national unity and as the champion of Egypt and its people against the forces of chaos, embodied in Egypt's neighbours. Official xenophobia, nationalism and a strong sense of Egyptian identity were deliberately fostered by the early state as part of its propaganda of rule. In essence, the concept of the nation state, so dominant in world politics today, was the invention of Egypt's early rulers. The means they employed to promote this concept and the character of the state they moulded form the subjects of Parts II and III.

CHAPTER THREE

HISTORICAL OUTLINE

———— •◆• ————

THE EARLY DYNASTIC PERIOD: TERMINOLOGY AND DEFINITION

Ancient Egyptian civilisation – as defined by the use of monumental hiero-
glyphics and the institution of divine kingship – endured over a period of
some three millenniums. With such a long stretch of time to study,
Egyptologists have found it necessary to divide Egyptian history into
broader periods. These tend to follow the known pattern of internal
political developments, corresponding to eras of unified government and
the intervening periods of political fragmentation. The time-span that
concerns us here is the first such period, standing at the beginning of the
Egyptian historical sequence. The formative phase of Egyptian civilisation
is sometimes referred to as the '**Archaic**' period (Emery 1961). However,
the term 'archaic' implies a value-judgement based upon hindsight.
Moreover, it seems an unfair label to apply to the dynamic and sophisticated early culture of the Nile valley, and its use is waning amongst
Egyptologists who study the period (for example, Spencer 1993). Hence,
the more neutral and descriptive term, 'Early Dynastic', is preferred here.

For convenience, Egyptologists have adopted the finer division of
Egyptian history into dynasties drawn up by the third-century BC historian,
Manetho. Although based upon the ancient sources available to Manetho
at the time, in most cases the dynasties are not divisions which would
have been recognised by the ancient Egyptians themselves. The composition and demarcation of Manetho's dynasties have been continually
modified as scholarly understanding of Egyptian history has improved.

The pyramids of the Memphite necropolis have struck Egyptologists,
both ancient and modern, as the most characteristic, and awesome, ancient
Egyptian monuments. The construction of the first pyramid, under King
Netjerikhet/Djoser of the Third Dynasty, has therefore been regarded as
a major turning point in Egyptian history. For this reason, the Third
Dynasty is often assigned to the Pyramid Age, more usually termed the
Old Kingdom (for example, Trigger *et al.* 1983; Malek 1986: 124; Kemp
1989: 14). This view of the past – whereby the pyramids were seen as the
beginning of the first major flowering of Egyptian civilisation – relegated
Manetho's first two dynasties to a dimly known and poorly studied position at the beginning of the dynastic age. Dramatic advances in our understanding of early Egypt have taken place in the last half-century. No longer

is the formative phase of Egyptian civilisation a half-understood 'dark age'. Important though they are, the royal mortuary complexes (including the pyramids) no longer constitute the sole landmark or index of achievement from third millennium BC Egypt. Our appreciation of Egyptian culture in a broader sense continues to deepen and, as it does so, the similarities between the Third Dynasty and the preceding period become increasingly apparent. Despite the innovation of pyramid-building, Egyptian civilisation of the Third Dynasty shares more in common with the First and Second Dynasties than with the Fourth, Fifth and Sixth, the age of true pyramids. For this reason, a number of recent studies have placed the Third Dynasty in the Early Dynastic period, beginning the Old Kingdom with the Fourth Dynasty (for example, Quirke and Spencer 1992: 33 and 36; cf. Shaw and Nicholson 1995: 89). Although a scholarly convenience with little ancient relevance, this view seems to accord much better with the evidence for early Egyptian civilisation, and is adopted here.

Although, for our purposes, the end of the Early Dynastic period is fixed at the accession of King Sneferu – the first king of the Fourth Dynasty – the precise beginning of the period is, and is likely to remain, impossible to define. As we have seen, we now know of several kings who lived and reigned before the beginning of Manetho's First Dynasty. A new chronological term had to be found to describe these rulers, and logic dictated 'Dynasty 0'. Although this is a rather unsatisfactory term on many accounts, it has been widely adopted. It is fairly certain that at least some of the rulers assigned to 'Dynasty 0' exercised only regional power. Although a few of the kings at the end of the sequence – and therefore on the threshold of the First Dynasty – may have ruled over much or all of Egypt, it is as yet impossible to pin-point the exact moment at which the country was first unified politically under a single king. For this historical outline, the beginning of the First Dynasty, and more specifically the reign of Narmer, will be taken as a starting-point.

SOURCES

The source material for the history of the Early Dynastic period is diverse and often fragmentary, but with care it can be pieced together to provide a reliable picture of the first three dynasties. Sources can be divided into two broad categories, contemporary records and later accounts, each carrying its own inherent biases and problems. An understanding of the context in which particular inscriptions were produced is necessary before they can be used as historical sources.

Contemporary records

Obviously, contemporary records are more reliable as they present first-hand information about the activities of Egypt's early rulers. As we shall see in Chapter 6, contemporary sources such as year labels are by no means objective. They recorded only those events which the court considered significant and which presented the institution of kingship in the best light. None the less, they can be used, with care, to illuminate the time in which they were made. The same is true of royal monuments, comprising ceremonial palettes, maceheads, inscribed slabs, stelae and stone architectural elements from royal buildings. These present the iconography of early kingship, but in doing so may yield historical information, for example by recording the king's (inevitable) victory over his enemies in a military campaign. A number of rock-cut inscriptions from the eastern and western deserts and the Sinai provide valuable information about the extent of Early Dynastic activity in Egypt's peripheral regions, and the ability of the court to organise expeditions outside the Nile valley. Perhaps the most abundant inscriptions from the first three dynasties are the numerous seal-impressions from tombs and settlements. These are the main source for analysing the structure and functioning of the Early Dynastic administration, and the context of particular seal-impressions may afford important historical information, such as the order of succession. Here, two recent discoveries have made a significant impact. Excavations in the royal cemetery at Abydos have revealed impressions from the necropolis seals of Den and Qaa (Figure 3.1). The former lists in chronological order the kings of the First Dynasty from Narmer to Den, with the addition of the queen mother (and probable regent during Den's minority), Merneith. Qaa's seal lists all eight kings of the First Dynasty, confirming the order established by scholars from other, more fragmentary, sources. Finally, a large number of artefacts bearing royal inscriptions can be useful in filling in some of the gaps in our historical knowledge. In particular, the stone vessels amassed by Netjerikhet to furnish his Step Pyramid complex (Lacau and Lauer 1959) include many examples from earlier reigns, and these have proved invaluable in establishing the internal history of the Second Dynasty. Moreover, inscribed stone vessels provide the only evidence for a few ephemeral rulers. During the First Dynasty especially, large pottery vessels were often inscribed with the name of the king, sometimes accompanied by a short inscription detailing the contents.

Later accounts

Accounts of the first three dynasties written in later periods have clearly been filtered through a number of generations, and must therefore be treated with caution. In general, the later the account, the more prone it

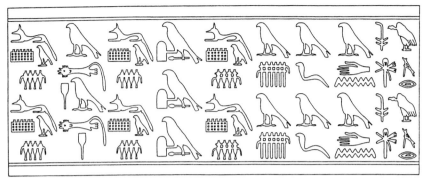

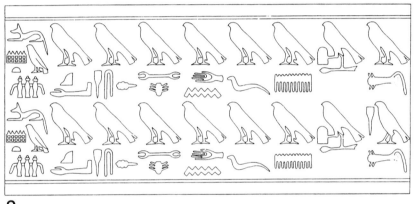

Figure 3.1 Rulers of the First Dynasty: contemporary lists. Reconstructed impressions from necropolis seals: (1) the seal of Den (after Dreyer 1987: 36, fig. 3); (2) the seal of Qaa (after Dreyer *et al.* 1996: 72, fig. 26).

will be to distortion. The various king lists of the New Kingdom (Redford 1986) offer a starting-point for reconstructing the Early Dynastic order of succession but, with the exception of the **Turin Canon**, they only record the kings who were viewed as legitimate in the eyes of the New Kingdom pharaohs. The Turin Canon (Gardiner 1959) does seem to have aimed at historical accuracy, and must have drawn upon temple archives for much of its information, but it remains doubtful whether the reign lengths given for kings who lived more than a millennium before the document was compiled can be treated as reliable. Even less reliable is the historical information gleaned by Herodotus in the fifth century BC – although some details have subsequently been corroborated by archaeological excavation – and that by Manetho a century-and-a-half later, the latter preserved only fragmentarily in the works of later writers. The accounts of Herodotus and Manetho were written at least two-and-a-half thousand years after the Early Dynastic events themselves. At such a distance, accuracy cannot be expected. As with all 'history', the material presented reflects the concerns of the chronicler's own period. Manetho's division of Egypt's rulers into dynasties has been adopted by Egyptologists and does seem partially to reflect historical circumstances. However, the royal names given by Manetho have proved notoriously difficult to equate with the names recorded in the Early Dynastic sources themselves; moreover, some of the more fantastic details about individual kings appear to stem from the realm of myth and cannot be taken as historically accurate. For these reasons, in the historical outline which follows, details provided by Manetho and Herodotus have been deemed too unreliable for inclusion (contra Emery 1961). The emphasis has been placed upon contemporary Early Dynastic sources, with one notable addition. The later source which has been used is not without its problems, but is generally accepted by scholars to present an accurate, if partial, view of Early Dynastic history. This is the Palermo Stone and its associated fragments which together comprise the royal annals.

The Palermo Stone is the name given to the main fragment of an annals stone which records the reigns of the kings of Egypt from before the First Dynasty to the Fifth Dynasty (Schäfer 1902; Helck 1982). The original stone, a large basalt slab, must have been considerably larger than the portion preserved in the Palermo Museum, and various attempts have been made to reconstruct its original dimensions and appearance (Daressy 1916; Borchardt 1917; Ricci 1917; Kaiser 1961a; Helck 1974; O'Mara 1979; Barta 1981). A second substantial, but heavily abraded piece from the same stone or a close copy is displayed in the Egyptian Museum in Cairo and is known as the Cairo fragment (Gauthier 1914; and see Figure 3.2). Several smaller fragments in Cairo and London fill in small gaps (Gauthier 1914; de Cénival 1965), although the authenticity of at least one of these fragments is questionable (O'Mara 1979). There is still some debate about the age of the Palermo Stone and the Cairo fragment. The entries on the Palermo Stone end in the Fifth Dynasty, and an Old Kingdom date has been proposed for the monument. However, it is also possible that the stone represents a later copy of an Old Kingdom original. Clearly, the later the monument, the greater the potential for inaccuracies, copying mistakes and invention. What makes the Palermo Stone and Cairo fragment so important are the registers which record the reigns of Early Dynastic kings. Each reign is divided into compartments, with one compartment for each year. Each year is identified by one or more significant events, recorded in very abbreviated form. Many of these **eponymous** events are concerned with the festivals and rituals of kingship, shedding light on the nature of that institution in the Early Dynastic period but providing very little information

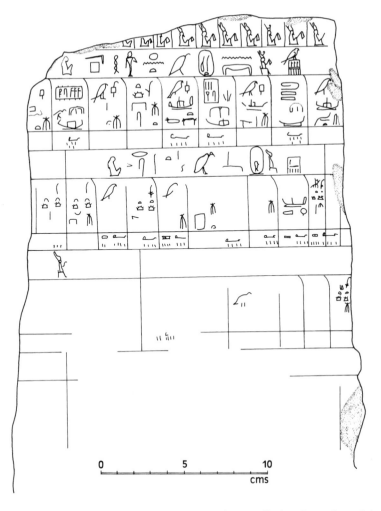

Figure 3.2 Royal annals. The Cairo fragment (new collation from the original).

for the writing of 'history'. Indeed, given the practicalities of administration, it seems very likely that each year of a king's reign would have had to be 'named' in advance. The events chosen would, therefore, necessarily have been of a predictable nature, such as pre-planned royal visits, recurrent festivals and the dedication of cult statues. From the middle of the First Dynasty, the compartments on the Palermo Stone also record the height of the annual **inundation** in palms and cubits. If accurate, these records are an invaluable source for climatic and ecological fluctuations over a period of some five-hundred years (Bell 1970). The topmost register of both fragments records, in more abbreviated form, a line of kings

65

who ruled before the beginning of the First Dynasty. It is impossible to say whether this reflects the historical reality of late Predynastic Egypt, or is simply an articulation of the later tradition of mythical rulers before Menes. The fact that some of the kings are shown wearing the double crown led to early speculation about the possible political unification of Egypt before the beginning of the First Dynasty, speculation which recent excavations have confirmed as having some foundation. Much of the historical value of the annals lies in their presumed original completeness, and many scholars have attempted reconstructions in order to establish both the Early Dynastic order of succession and the reign lengths of the early kings. None of the reconstructions to date can be treated as anything other than informed guesswork, and all assume that the annals began with the reign of Aha – a supposition which may be erroneous, in the light of the recent discovery of a year label of Aha's predecessor, Narmer (Giddy 1996: 30). We may have to admit that a totally convincing reconstruction of the royal annals is not achievable, unless further fragments of the same or similar stones come to light. None the less, the individual records contained in the surviving portions can yield significant information about the first three dynasties. Just as important, they tell us something about the Egyptians' own sense of history (O'Mara 1996).

THE FIRST DYNASTY

Ironically, it is the First Dynasty, the remotest sequence of kings in the Early Dynastic period, that is the best understood, in terms of the number of rulers and the order of their succession. The Abydos king list and Manetho agree in recording eight kings for the First Dynasty, and this number is confirmed by the recently discovered necropolis sealing of Qaa. Indeed, this sealing provides the best contemporary evidence for the historical accuracy of Manetho's First Dynasty. The original identification of Merneith as a king, rather than a queen regent (Petrie 1900: 5, chart opposite p. 1), caused some confusion, leading to Narmer's exclusion from the dynasty and a focus on Aha as the first king. There is no doubt that Aha's reign was marked by important innovations; none the less, first place in the sequence of eight kings properly belongs to Narmer (Lauer 1966: 169–70; Shaw and Nicholson 1995: 18 and 89; contra Baines 1995: 131), and the Den and Qaa necropolis sealings confirm that this was the belief of subsequent generations of Egyptians as well. The difficulties in correlating the names recorded in later king lists (usually the *nbty* names) with those attested on the monuments (usually the Horus names) have confused what should be a relatively straightforward picture. The debate about the true identity of Menes – first king of the First Dynasty according to the Abydos list and Manetho – has also muddied the waters (Emery

1961: 32–7). Those scholars who identify Menes with Aha posit the existence of an ephemeral King Athothis between Aha and Djer (Dreyer 1987: 39) in order to make up the required eight rulers for the dynasty as a whole, although no such ruler is attested on contemporary monuments or inscriptions. (The possible royal tomb at Abydos comprising the pit B40 with or without the adjacent tomb B50 has been attributed to 'Athothis' on the basis of its location and design [Dreyer 1990: 67–71], although there are no inscriptions to support this view, and the necropolis sealing of Qaa would seem to argue against the existence of an extra king between Aha and Djer.) Despite such difficulties, something of a consensus has been reached about the composition of the First Dynasty, greatly assisted by new discoveries, especially in the royal cemetery at Abydos. The duration of the First Dynasty cannot be estimated with any precision, since accurate historical records are, for the most part, absent from this early period. Estimates depend to a large extent on hypothetical reconstructions of the Palermo Stone and its associated fragments, together with a notional figure of twenty-five to thirty years for a generation. Various scholars have proposed figures ranging from two hundred to two-hundred-and-forty years for the eight kings of the First Dynasty (Lauer 1966: 184, especially n. 5), but such guesses are unlikely to be improved upon without new, more precise, historical evidence.

Narmer

Some time around 3000 BC the king whom we know as Narmer acceded to the throne of Egypt. The contemporary writings of his name – usually abbreviated to a single sign, the catfish (which had the phonetic value n^cr in later periods) – make it rather unlikely that his name was read as 'Narmer'; however, this name is universally used and will no doubt remain so until an acceptable alternative reading is proposed. According to Manetho, the First and Second Dynasty kings originated from Thinis (or This), the capital of the Abydos region, thought to lie near – or indeed under – the modern town of Girga. The presence of First and late Second Dynasty royal tombs at Abydos seems to confirm Manetho's account, since Abydos was the principal necropolis of the Thinite region. Whether or not Narmer had a royal residence at This, he clearly felt strong enough ties to the region and to his Predynastic forebears to maintain the tradition of being buried in the ancient ancestral necropolis. If Narmer is to be associated with the historical and/or legendary figure of Menes (Lloyd 1988: 10), he may have been the first King of Egypt to reside at Memphis. Herodotus recounts how Menes diverted the course of the Nile to found his new capital. However, it is noteworthy that, to date, no monument of Narmer has been found at Saqqara, the élite necropolis serving Memphis.

One of the most heated and protracted debates in Egyptology has raged over the identification of Menes: Narmer, Aha, a conflation of the two, or a mythical figure representing several rulers involved in the process of state formation? Dependent upon this argument is also the proper placement of Narmer: at the end of so-called 'Dynasty 0' or at the beginning of the First Dynasty? Although there is perhaps stronger evidence for the latter view (and for the identification of Menes as Narmer), the entire debate is actually rather anachronistic, since the dynasties were not invented until some two-and-a-half-thousand years after Narmer's lifetime. Nor did the Egyptians have the same sense of history as ourselves. What is of significance is the position held by Narmer in the eyes of his immediate successors, the kings of the First Dynasty. For at least two of them, Den and Qaa, Narmer seems to have been regarded as a founder figure, at least in the context of the royal burial ground at Abydos. In this context, it may also be significant that the earliest inscribed stone vessel from the hoard of thousands buried under the Step Pyramid at Saqqara dates from the reign of Narmer (Lacau and Lauer 1959: 9, pl. 1 no. 1). It has been suggested that the inscribed 'heirlooms' collected together by Netjerikhet to furnish his burial may have represented an attempt to harness the authority and legitimacy of the king's predecessors (F.D. Friedman 1995: 10).

It is tempting to interpret the significance of Narmer's reign in the light of his most famous monument, the ceremonial palette from the 'Main Deposit' at Hierakonpolis (Quibell 1898a: pls XII–XIII, 1900: pl. XXIX; Petrie 1953: pls J–K; Kemp 1989: 42, fig. 12). The scenes carved on this object are probably the best-known and most intensively studied from early Egypt. Whilst the symbolism of the scenes is clear – they convey Narmer's triumph and dominion over both Upper and Lower Egypt, particularly the latter – the occasion for which they were carved will never be known. A straightforward historical interpretation of the monument is now generally considered to be unsophisticated and old-fashioned. Instead, it is argued, the palette may commemorate the ritual re-enactment of an earlier military victory (the 'Unification of the Two Lands' was an integral component of early coronation rituals), or may belong entirely within the realm of myth and symbol, conveying the omnipotence of the king without alluding to any specific historical incident. However, a partially preserved year label of Narmer, found during the recent German excavations on the Umm el-Qaab, may offer support for the older, historical interpretation of the Narmer palette. The label apparently records the same event as the palette: it shows the catfish of the king's name smiting a bearded captive, identified by the papyrus plant on his head as an inhabitant (and leader?) of Lower Egypt.

Another important monument of Narmer's reign is the decorated macehead, also from the Hierakonpolis 'Main Deposit'. Like the palette, the macehead has been variously interpreted. An earlier generation of scholars believed it to commemorate Narmer's wedding to a northern princess. However, the (female?) figure in a carrying-chair shown before the enthroned king may represent a deity, and given the likely southern origin of Queen Neith-hotep there is no corroborative evidence that Narmer sealed the political unification of Egypt by marrying a northern heiress. None the less, a Lower Egyptian setting for whatever ceremony is depicted seems to be confirmed by the depiction of a shrine with a pitched roof, surmounted by a heron: this was the shrine of Djebaut, a district of Buto in the north-western Delta. A complicating factor is the wavy-walled enclosure shown beneath this shrine, which has been compared with the ceremonial centre recently excavated at Hierakonpolis (R. Friedman 1996: 33).

Compared to his known predecessors, Narmer is much more widely attested in archaeological contexts. His name has been found on sherds as far afield as Tel Erani (Ward 1969: 216, fig. 2), Tell Arad (Amiran 1974, 1976) and Nahal Tillah in Israel's northern Negev (Levy *et al.* 1995). Similar sherds have been excavated in the north-eastern Nile Delta (for example, van den Brink 1992b: 52, fig. 8.3; in preparation), suggesting active trade between Egypt and southern Palestine in Narmer's reign. It has been suggested that the Narmer Palette records a military campaign against Palestine (Yadin 1955; Weill 1961: 20), although this interpretation is disputed (Ward 1969). More convincing evidence for direct contact between Egyptians and **Asiatics** during the reign of Narmer is provided by a fragment of inscribed ivory from Narmer's tomb (B17) at Abydos. It shows a bearded man of Asiatic appearance in a stooping posture, perhaps paying homage to the Egyptian king (Petrie 1901: pl. IV.4–5). In the Delta, a complete vessel bearing Narmer's *serekh* was found in a grave at Minshat Abu Omar (Kroeper 1988: fig. 141) and a sherd incised with a damaged *serekh* which may be the name of Narmer was excavated at Buto (von der Way 1989: 293, fig. 11.7). Further objects bearing the name of Narmer have come to light at Zawiyet el-Aryan (Kaplony 1963, I: 65–6; II: nn. 252–3, 255; III: pl. 120, no. 721; Dunham 1978: 26, pl. XVIa), Tura (Junker 1912: 47, fig. 57.3–4; Fischer 1963: 46, fig. 3c–d, 47) and Helwan (Saad 1947: 165, fig. 13a) in the Memphite region; Tarkhan, near the entrance to the Fayum (Petrie *et al.* 1913: pl. LXI; Petrie 1914: pls VI, XX.1, XXXVIII; Fischer 1963: 44 and 45, fig. 2; Kaplony 1964: figs 1061–2); and Abydos (Petrie 1900: 5, pl. IV.2; 1901: pls II.3, 4, 6, 7, X.1, XIII.91–3, LII.359), Naqada (Spencer 1980: 64, pls 47, 52 [Cat. 454]) and Hierakonpolis (Quibell 1900: pl. XV.7 = Kaplony 1963, III: pl. 5, fig. 5; Garstang 1907: pl. III.1 = B. Adams 1995: 123–4) in Upper Egypt. Finally, there is a rock-cut inscription comprising the *serekh* of Narmer and a second, empty *serekh* at Site 18 in the Wadi Qash, half-way between the Nile valley and the Red Sea coast in the eastern desert (Winkler 1938:

10, pl. XI.1). Activity in Egypt's desert border regions is attested from Predynastic times, and the attractions of the eastern desert (principally its stone and mineral resources) clearly encouraged state-sponsored expeditions from the beginning of the First Dynasty.

Aha

There is little doubt that Narmer was succeeded by a king whose name is rendered as Hor-Aha, or more simply as Aha ('the fighter'). One of the most impressive monuments from the early First Dynasty was the royal tomb at Naqada (de Morgan 1897), now sadly lost through erosion. Identified originally as the tomb of Menes, it is now generally acknowledged to have been the burial place of a senior female member of the First Dynasty royal family named Neith-hotep (see de Morgan 1897: 167, figs 550–5; Spencer 1980: 63, pls 46 and 51 [Cats. 449, 450]; 1993: 61, fig. 41). The occurrence of several labels and sealings of Aha in the tomb probably indicates that the occupant died during the king's lifetime, and that he oversaw the burial. In this case, Neith-hotep is most plausibly identified as the mother of Aha. The location chosen for her tomb may indicate her provincial origins. Naqada is known to have been a major centre of political and economic influence in the Predynastic period, and it is not unlikely that Narmer – a member of the Thinite royal family – would have taken as his wife a member (perhaps the heiress?) of the ancient Naqada ruling family, to cement an important political alliance between two of the key centres of Upper Egyptian authority.

Aha seems to have made a decisive choice in favour of Memphis as the principal centre of government: the earliest élite mastaba tomb on the escarpment at North Saqqara – overlooking the site of ancient Memphis – dates to his reign (Emery 1939), and belonged to a senior figure in the national administration, perhaps a brother or other male relative of the king's. Aha himself maintained the tradition of his forebears, and was buried in the ancestral necropolis at Abydos (Petrie 1901). One of the accompanying **subsidiary burial**s yielded objects bearing the name Benerib (Petrie 1901: pls III.1, IIIA.13; Spencer 1993: 79, fig. 57) – literally 'sweet of heart' – and this may have been the name of Aha's wife. The design of the king's mortuary complex shows important new features; taken together with the Naqada and North Saqqara tombs, it marks out Aha's reign as a period of architectural innovation and sophistication. Craftsmanship, too, seems to have flourished under Aha. A few inscribed objects have survived to attest the skills which the king could command: two copper axe-heads; a fragment of an ivory box bearing the king's name and that of Benerib (Emery 1961: 53, fig. 13; Spencer 1993: 79, fig. 57); a fragment of a large vessel of **glazed composition** (faience), with the king's *serekh* inlaid in a darker glaze (Petrie 1903: 23, pls IV, V.32; Spencer 1993:

73); and two immaculately inscribed white marbles (Kaplony 1965: 6 and 7, fig. 4).

Although Aha's name has been found at several sites – Abu Rawash (Klasens 1959: 57, fig. 8, pl. XXVII.1), Zawiyet el-Aryan (Kaplony 1963, I: 66; II: n. 1592; Dunham 1978: 1, figs 1, 1a), Saqqara (Emery 1939: 20–5, figs 13–20; 1949: 76, fig. 38 and 78, fig. 39; Kaplony 1965: 9, pl. I fig. 14, pl. II fig. 15), Helwan (Kaplony 1965: 8 and 7, fig. 11), Abydos (Petrie 1901: pls III.2, 6, IIIA.5–6, XI.1–2, XIV) and Naqada (Emery 1961: 50, fig. 10) – he is not as widely attested as his predecessor, nor yet has his name been found outside the Nile valley. It is difficult to gain an accurate impression from the limited evidence, but a change in the nature of Egypt's relations with southern Palestine may have been the beginning of a long-term trend which saw reciprocal trade between Egypt and its neighbours ultimately replaced by more direct Egyptian exploitation of resources via outposts (such as the First Dynasty 'residency' at En Besor in southern Israel) or **entrepôts** (principally Byblos on the Lebanese coast). To date, only one fragment of Syro-Palestinian pottery has been found in a context datable to the reign of Aha: a sherd of combed ware from Abydos tomb B19 (Adams and Friedman 1992: 328, n. 9 [Ashmolean E4029]). Two ebony labels of Aha may record royal visits to the Delta (Petrie 1901: pl. IIIA.5–6), while another label from Abydos depicts a campaign against Ta-Sety (Petrie 1901: pl. III.2), the name given in later periods to Nubia. Whether the label records a real event or a symbolic activity, in a way the message remains the same: Egypt was now looking south with hostile intent, its eyes perhaps fixed on the lucrative trade in exotic goods which passed through the Nubian Nile valley.

Djer

Aha was succeeded by King Djer who, if the various reconstructions of the Palermo Stone are to be believed, must have reigned for a consider-able period. Nine years from Djer's reign are recorded on the main Cairo fragment of the royal annals. Apart from recording the biennial royal progress, 'the following of Horus', and the fashioning and/or dedication of a variety of cult statues, the Cairo fragment also mentions an expedition to a land named *S̲t̲t̲*. This is the name given later to Western Asia gener-ally, and it is difficult to be more precise about which locality is intended. The En Besor 'residency' seems to have been maintained well into the First Dynasty, and it is possible that the Cairo fragment refers to a trade or punitive expedition to southern Palestine. Other authors, however, have interpreted *S̲t̲t̲* as referring to the Sinai, and this must be a strong possi-bility. Either way, the royal annals seem to indicate renewed Egyptian interest or activity beyond Egypt's borders to the north-east. Fragments of at least a dozen vessels of Syro-Palestinian origin were found in Djer's tomb, demonstrating trade between Egypt and the Near East (Petrie 1902, pl. 8.2, 4–6; Bourriau 1981: 128 [Catalogue 253]; Serpico and White 1996).

It used to be thought that a rock-cut inscription at Gebel Sheikh Suleiman in Lower Nubia, recording a punitive expedition by Egyptian forces against the local inhabitants, bore the *serekh* of Djer (for example, Emery 1961: 60). It has been conclusively shown that this is not in fact the case; the *serekh* is anonymous, and the inscription dates to the late Predynastic period (Murnane 1987, following Helck 1970: 85; cf. Baines 1995: 102; Shaw and Nicholson 1995: 86).

Djer's burial on the Umm el-Qaab at Abydos (Petrie 1901) was accompanied by numerous subsidiary burials, some of which accommodated women of the royal harem. The short inscriptions – restricted to names and a few titles – on the private funerary stelae from these subsidiary burials provide some evidence for the composition of the royal court in the early First Dynasty, although some of the inscriptions are not easily understood (Amélineau 1899: pls XXXIV–XXXVII, 1904: pl. XVIII; Petrie 1901: pls XXVI–XXIXB). The layout of the royal mortuary complex shows important innovations, and for the first time the tomb on the Umm el-Qaab was accompanied by a separate funerary enclosure, itself surrounded by further subsidiary burials, on the low desert nearer the town and cultivation (Petrie 1925: pl. XVI; Kemp 1966; O'Connor 1989).

As in the previous reign, craftsmanship of a high quality was maintained under Djer. Among the most impressive artefacts to survive is a flint knife, the handle of which is covered in gold leaf embossed with the king's *serekh* (Needler 1956). Metalworking reached new levels of excellence, as attested by an impressive hoard of copper tools, weapons and vessels found in mastaba S3471 at North Saqqara, dated by inscriptions to the reign of Djer (Emery 1949). Even one of the subsidiary graves around the king's Abydos funerary enclosure yielded a copper adze incised with the royal *serekh* (Petrie 1925: 4, pls III.1, IV.8). Marbles similar to those of Aha have survived from Djer's reign (Kaplony 1965: 6 and 7, fig. 5), whilst another artefact probably represents the oldest known example of three dimensional royal statuary: a headless statuette of light-blue glazed composition from the Satet temple at Elephantine, showing a figure seated on a throne, bears a sign on one side which has been read as *Dr* (Dreyer 1981). Further objects bearing the name of Djer have been found at four sites: Saqqara (Quibell 1923: pls VIII.5, XI.2–3, 5, top; Emery 1938: 35, fig. 8, pls 17A, 18A; 1961: 59, fig. 21; 1939: 31, fig. 31; 1949: 13; 1954: 169, figs 225–7; 1958: 66, pl. 78.1; 1961: 60, fig. 23; Lacau and Lauer 1959: 9, pl. 1 nos 2–3, pl. 2 nos 4, 14), Tura (Kaiser 1964: 103, fig. 3), Helwan (Saad 1947: 165, fig. 13b), and Abydos (Petrie 1901: pls V.1–2, XV; 1925: 4, pls II.8, 14–15, XII.1; Spencer 1980: 64, pls 47, 53 [cat. 458]). An ivory label of Djer from Abydos seems to record a royal visit to Buto and Saïs in the Delta (Amélineau 1904: pl. XV.19; Emery 1961: 59, fig. 20), suggesting that Djer may have maintained his predecessor's policy of honouring important shrines. The institution of the biennial royal progress, first recorded in Djer's reign, may have been initiated for the same reason. Djer is not attested from outside Egypt, despite the tantalising reference to Setjet on the Cairo fragment of the royal annals.

Djet

The name of Djer's successor is rendered by modern scholars in a variety of forms: Djet is the most common, but Zet, Wadji and Uadji are also used by some authors. In fact, there is good evidence for an initial 'W' having formed part of the ancient pronunciation: a rock-cut inscription of the king in the western desert south of Edfu preserves a unique writing of the king's name, the *w3d* sign accompanying the usual *dt* sign in the *serekh* (Legrain 1903: 221, fig. 7; Porter and Moss 1937: 207). Wadjet or Wadji may, therefore, be a more accurate realisation of the king's name; but, as the most frequently used form, Djet will be retained here. The Horus-falcon in the rock-cut inscription just mentioned was reported as wearing the double crown. If so, it would be the earliest attested occurrence of this element of royal iconography, pre-dating the more famous Abydos label of Den by a generation.

The indications are that Djet did not enjoy a long reign. Sealings from the royal tombs at Abydos suggest that the career of one high official, Amka, began in the reign of Djer, spanned the entire reign of his successor and continued into the early part of Den's reign, when the country was under the regency of Queen Merneith (Petrie 1900: pls XIX.10, XX.12–15, 18; 1901: pl. XVI.121, 123). The implication is that Djet occupied the throne for a comparatively short period, probably less than twenty years. None the less, his reign has furnished us with one of the masterpieces of ancient Egyptian art, the king's magnificent funerary **stela** from Abydos, now in the Louvre (Vigneau 1935: 4; Emery 1961: 70, pl. 2b; Kemp 1989: 38, fig. 10).

In his mortuary provision, Djet followed the pattern established by his predecessor (Petrie 1900, 1901, 1925: pl. XVII; Kemp 1966). Other major funerary monuments dating from the reign of Djet include two large mastabas at Tarkhan, decorated with niches in the so-called 'palace façade' style (Petrie *et al.* 1913; Petrie 1914). They probably belonged to regional governors who were keen to demonstrate, by the architecture of their tombs, their functional and ideological proximity to the royal court (Wilkinson 1993a: 211). A niched mastaba of even larger proportions, labelled by its excavators mastaba V, was excavated near the village of Nazlet Batran, just south of Giza (Petrie 1907). Sealings of Djet (Petrie 1907: 5, pl. IIIA) have given rise to the suggestion that it was constructed for Djet's queen. An alternative explanation is that it belonged to Djet's mother, and therefore a wife of Djer's. Like the Naqada royal tomb, mastaba V may represent a lavish burial for the king's mother, constructed in the lifetime of her son. The name of the occupant is unknown, as are the reasons for the novel location of the tomb.

In addition to the fine funerary stela, other artefacts from Djet's reign include an ivory comb, engraved with the king's *serekh* and symbols with probable **cosmological** meaning (Petrie 1925: 4, pls II.6, XII.5; Malek 1986: 35; Quirke 1992: 21–2). Metalworking is represented by a massive copper axe and a large, copper adze, both from a subsidiary burial surrounding Djet's tomb at Abydos (Petrie 1925: pl. V.5, 7). A fragmentary limestone base from the town enclosure at Hierakonpolis may once have supported a statue of King Djet (Quibell and Green 1902: 48, pl. LIX.1). Trade with Syria-Palestine is attested by the pottery vessels of foreign origin found in tombs of Djet's reign at Saqqara (Emery 1954: 75), Tarkhan (Petrie *et al.* 1913: 16, pls XVI.1, XIX.24) and Abydos (Petrie 1925: pl. IV.9–10).

Merneith

One of the royal tombs excavated by Petrie at Abydos clearly belonged to an individual called Merneith (Petrie 1900): two large funerary stelae with this name in **raised relief** were discovered near the tomb (Petrie 1900: pl. LXIV.6; Emery 1961: 65, fig. 29; Spencer 1993: 82, fig. 60). Despite the fact that the name is not written in the customary *serekh*, Petrie at first believed Merneith to be a king, like the owners of the other tombs on the Umm el-Qaab. It has since been realised that the name belonged to a queen, more properly realised as Mer(t)neith, 'beloved of Neith'. From the many sealings of Den found in Merneith's tomb, Egyptologists surmised that Merneith must have been the king's mother. This has been confirmed by the recently discovered necropolis sealing from the tomb of Den, which ends with the signs denoting 'king's mother Mer(t)neith'. It is clear that Merneith must have occupied an unusually important position for her to have been granted the privilege of a tomb on the Umm el-Qaab. (Interestingly, the necropolis seal of Qaa, modelled closely on Den's, omits Merneith from the list of First Dynasty rulers; this may indicate that, after the reign of Den himself, Merneith was no longer accorded equal status to the *de jure* kings of the First Dynasty.) It seems virtually certain that Merneith acted as regent during Den's minority; Djet must therefore have died while Den was still a child. Merneith may have been the senior royal wife of Djet, although her influence seems to have derived from her position as the mother of the next king. Certainly, Den's name features prominently on the sealings from her tomb, even those which are thought to date to her own regency. One Egyptologist has speculated that she was also the daughter and heiress of Djer, and thus connected with three consecutive kings of Egypt (Lauer 1966: 175–7). This is an attractive theory, but one which cannot, at present, be proven.

The regency of Merneith is the first attested occasion in Egyptian history when a woman held the reins of power. As *de facto* ruler of Egypt, Merneith seems to have been accorded a full royal mortuary complex at Abydos. However, outside Abydos she is poorly attested. This is not surprising, since all official documents (including seals) drawn up during her regency would have borne the name of the reigning king, Den, despite his minority. An unprovenanced alabaster cylinder vessel bears Merneith's name in relief (Kaplony 1964: fig. 1075), and a further three vessel fragments from Saqqara show her name scratched on the surface (Emery 1954: 141 and 142, figs 205–6). The most notable object marked with the name of Merneith is a small ivory vessel from the Saqqara region (Kaplony 1964: fig. 1073).

Den

The name of Egypt's next ruler is usually rendered as Den, although this is unlikely to be an accurate realisation. The meaning of the name is as obscure as its proper pronunciation, despite the efforts of several scholars at decipherment (S. Schott 1956: 59; Kaplony 1958; Meltzer 1972; Godron 1990). Den has been called 'one of the most important rulers of the First Dynasty' (Lauer 1966: 177–8), his reign lauded as marking 'a significant stage in the cultural and material development of Early Dynastic Egypt' (Whitehouse 1987: 261). Without doubt, he is the best attested king of the First Dynasty.

His tomb at Abydos (Petrie 1901) – marked in traditional style by a pair of funerary stelae, of which only one survives (Amélineau 1899: pl. XLI; Balty *et al.* 1988: 15) – shows an important new feature in Egyptian mortuary architecture, an entrance stairway giving access to the burial chamber. This facilitated the provisioning of the tomb and the burial itself, and was swiftly adopted throughout Egypt in private as well as royal tombs. It highlights the reign of Den as a period of innovation; and this is reflected, too, in the king's **titulary**. The title *nswt-bity*, literally 'he of the reed and bee', and best translated as 'dual king', first appears in the reign of Den. It probably signifies a corresponding development in the ideology of divine kingship. The invention of the double crown – combining the older red and white crowns – is another innovation usually attributed to the reign of Den (Edwards 1971: 26); although, as we have seen, it may have already occurred in the preceding reign of Djet.

Den seems to have enjoyed a long reign, even taking into account his accession as a child. A recently discovered limestone vessel fragment from the south-west annex to Den's tomb mentions 'the second occasion of the Sed(-festival)' (Dreyer 1990: 80, fig. 9, pl. 26.d). This is the first indication that Den may have celebrated two such festivals (cf. Petrie 1900: pl. XIV.12), which would imply a long reign. (For the significance of the **Sed-festival**, see Chapter 6.) The number of élite tombs at North Saqqara is greater for Den's reign than for any other reign of the First or Second Dynasty. Moreover, insufficient space at this site seems to have necessitated the establishment of a new élite cemetery at Abu Rawash (Plate 3.1), on the northern edge of the Memphite necropolis (Montet 1938, 1946; Klasens 1961). Together with several large tombs at Abusir (Leclant and Clerc 1992: 242, 1994: 376, pls XV, XVI, figs 13, 14) and Helwan, the North Saqqara and Abu Rawash mastabas form a collection of well over 30 élite burials dated to Den's reign. Such a dramatic increase in the number of officials able to command a high-status tomb must reflect more than the mere length of Den's reign: it seems likely that changes were carried out in the structure of government. Institutional change is also suggested by the Palermo Stone entry for year x+4 of Den's reign, which records a 'census of all the people of the north, west and east' (Schäfer 1902: 19). It would not be surprising if an accurate assessment of the country's population and resources accompanied administrative reforms.

Other salient events of Den's reign are recorded on several contemporary year labels and in the third register of the Palermo Stone. The king seems to have taken a particular interest in Egypt's relations with her neighbours to the north-east: his second name (*Zmti* or *Ḥ3sti*), written with the sign for high desert/foreign land, may have been chosen to reflect

Plate 3.1 Abu Rawash: the élite First Dynasty cemetery on Hill M (author's photograph). The pyramids of Giza are visible on the horizon.

the king's particular preoccupation with Egypt's north-eastern frontier zone (Godron 1990). No fewer than five labels record military activity in southern Palestine, whether real or ritual (see Chapter 5). Possible sealings of Den from the First Dynasty Egyptian building at En Besor provide further evidence for Egyptian involvement in the area (Schulman 1980, 1983: 250). Year x+2 of Den's reign on the Palermo Stone records the smiting of the *'Iwnw*, a word indicating the nomads of the eastern or western desert. Eight years later, the annals record the destruction of an unidentified, possibly Asiatic, locality named *Wt-k3*. At least 76 complete examples of imported Syro-Palestinian vessels, plus countless fragments, have been excavated from contexts datable to the reign of Den, by far the largest number from any Early Dynastic reign. The impression they give is one of sustained and intensive contact between Egypt and the Near East during the middle of the First Dynasty.

Cultic activity, too, is well attested during Den's reign. Visits to important shrines, the foundation of a new temple called 'thrones of the gods', and the fashioning or dedication of divine images are all mentioned on the Palermo Stone. The fierce feline goddess Mafdet – probably a royal protectress – is unusually prominent, featuring both on the Palermo Stone and on an alabaster jar from Abydos (Petrie 1901: pl. VII.7). The running of the Apis bull – revered at Memphis – is recorded in the annals for year x+12, corroborated by a sealing from Saqqara (Emery 1938: 64, fig. 26). Particularly noteworthy are the references from Den's reign to rituals involving a hippopotamus (see Chapter 8). A group of graves near the Serapeum at Saqqara may once have delineated a cultic enclosure built for Den (Kaiser 1985a), although there are problems with this interpretation (see Chapter 7).

Finally, objects from Abydos and Saqqara highlight the extraordinary artistic achievements of Den's craftsmen. The lavish tomb of Hemaka (Emery 1938) – chancellor and perhaps the most important figure in the administration after the king himself – yielded a wealth of artefacts, ranging from inlaid gaming discs to a circular wooden box containing the oldest papyrus to survive from Egypt. A copper bowl inscribed with the name of Den was included as an heirloom in the tomb equipment of King Semerkhet, whilst an inscribed ivory was buried in the 'Main Deposit' at Hierakonpolis (Whitehouse 1987). Amongst the most remarkable products of Egyptian craftsmen from any period are the Early Dynastic stone vessels carved in a bewildering array of forms, ranging from imitations of reed baskets to flowers. Several complete examples have been excavated from graves dating to the reign of Den, including a three-lobed dish from the tomb of the king himself (Petrie 1901: pl. L). Many fragments from the same context (for example, Amélineau 1899: pls XXVII–XXVIII, 1904: pl. IX) are currently being studied, and show highly sophisticated designs. A number of simpler stone vessels inscribed with one or other of Den's names were among the hoard found in the galleries beneath the Step Pyramid at Saqqara (Lacau and Lauer 1959).

Anedjib

A series of inscribed stone vessels from this same hoard first allowed scholars to establish the sequence of kings from Den to the end of the First Dynasty (Lacau and Lauer 1959: pl. 4, nos 19–21; cf. Emery 1961: 73). More recently, the order has been confirmed by the necropolis sealing of Qaa from Abydos. There is thus no doubt that Den was followed by a king named Anedjib. In comparison with Den, little is known of his successor. He seems to have enjoyed a relatively long reign, since at least two stone vessel fragments, one from Saqqara (Quibell 1923: pl. XXXIII.5) and the other from Abydos (Petrie 1900: 20, pl. VII.6; Kaplony 1965), mention a Sed-festival. Anedjib's name has been found at only three sites in Egypt: Saqqara (Emery 1949: 82, fig. 45; Lacau and Lauer 1959: 10–11, pl. 5 nos 23–4, pl. 6 nos 26–7, 29, pl. 7 nos 30–3; Porter and Moss 1974: 443), Helwan (Saad 1951: 109, pl. LIIa) and Abydos (Amélineau 1899: pl. XXXIII (left middle), 1902: pl. XXI.4; Petrie 1900: pls VI.9–11, XXVI–XXVII, XLVI, 1901: pl. XLIV.7; Porter and Moss 1937: 82; Emery 1949: 82, fig. 47). His name may also occur on two sealings from the Egyptian building at En Besor (Schulman 1980, 1983: 250). The production of royal statuary is attested indirectly: several stone vessels with Anedjib's *serekh* show statues of the king in various guises. Otherwise, almost the only artefacts from his reign are two inscribed white marbles, unprovenanced and now in a private collection (Kaplony 1965: 6 and 7, fig. 8).

Like his predecessors, Anedjib was buried on the Umm el-Qaab at Abydos (Petrie 1900). However, the most important monument of his reign is the large mastaba S3038 at North Saqqara (Emery 1949: 82–94, pls 21–35), probably built for the highest official in the royal administration. What makes S3038 unique, and a landmark in the longer-term development of Egyptian mortuary architecture and symbolism, is the hidden tumulus covering the burial chamber. Entirely covered by the superstructure of the tomb, this tumulus is not a simple mound but rather a stepped construction. It seems to point the way to the design of the Step Pyramid adopted for royal tombs in the Third Dynasty (Emery 1961: 146, fig. 85). It is, of course, possible that earlier tombs at Saqqara may have contained forerunners of the mound which were not recognised at the time of excavation. Likewise, because of the poor state of preservation of the First Dynasty royal tombs at Abydos, we cannot be certain that the tomb of Den did not originally include a modified version of the hidden mound discovered in his predecessor's tomb (Hendrickx, personal communication). However, in the absence of such evidence, the reign of Anedjib remains most noteworthy, not for the achievements of the king himself, but for an architectural innovation in the tomb of one of his officials.

Semerkhet

Some doubts have been raised concerning the legitimacy of the next king, Semerkhet. His tomb at Abydos contained a number of stone vessels of his predecessor, reinscribed for Semerkhet. This suggested to some scholars that Semerkhet may have been a usurper (Emery 1961: 84; Lauer 1966: 178, n. 5). However, it has been rightly pointed out that the stone vessels from the Step Pyramid at Saqqara bearing a sequence of four royal names (Den–Anedjib–Semerkhet–Qaa) argue against such an interpretation (Lauer 1966: 178–9). Most recently, the necropolis sealing of Qaa seems to prove beyond doubt Semerkhet's legitimacy, at least in the eyes of his successor.

Semerkhet's reign was probably the shortest of the First Dynasty. The Cairo fragment of the annals preserves a complete record of his eight-and-a-half years on the throne of Egypt. Unfortunately, the events recorded on the annals are nothing more than the regular ceremonies of kingship (such as the biennial 'following of Horus' and the ritual 'appearances' of the king) and the fashioning or dedication of divine images. A year label of Semerkhet from the tomb of Qaa (Figure 3.3) records the planning of a building named *Ḥrw-ib-nṯrw*, perhaps Semerkhet's funerary

Figure 3.3 Year label of Semerkhet. The label was recently discovered during re-excavation of the tomb of his successor Qaa (after Dreyer *et al.* 1996: pl. 14.d).

enclosure at Abydos (Dreyer *et al.* 1996: 73, pl. 14.d). Trade with the Near East seems to have been maintained during his reign, albeit on a reduced scale compared with the middle of the First Dynasty. Fragments from 10 or 11 imported Syro-Palestinian vessels were found in Semerkhet's tomb (Petrie 1901: pl. LIV; Kantor 1965: figs 5B, 5E; Adams and Friedman 1992: 328, n. 9), and a contemporary grave at Abusir contained a painted, handled flask typical of Early Bronze Age vessels from Syria-Palestine (Bonnet 1928: 35–40, pl. 27; Kantor 1965: fig. 5F). The year label mentioned earlier was originally attached to a container of oil, described as 'first-quality choice oil from the *bš3*-plant'. It has been suggested that *bš3*-oil may have been imported from Libya (Dreyer *et al.* 1996: 74).

Semerkhet's is the only First Dynasty reign not represented among the élite tombs at North Saqqara. This is not surprising if he only reigned for eight years: the high official who served Semerkhet no doubt survived his royal master, and may have continued to serve in the government under Semerkhet's successor. Several élite tombs at North Saqqara are dated to the reign of Qaa, and one of these may well have belonged to a leading figure at Semerkhet's court. Indeed, an official named Henuka evidently served both Semerkhet and his successor Qaa, since Henuka's name appears on year labels of both kings from Abydos (Petrie 1900: pl. XVII.26, 28; Dreyer 1993b: 10; Spencer 1993: 67). Semerkhet's tomb shows a change of plan from previous generations (Petrie 1900). The subsidiary burials are arranged immediately adjacent to the main burial chamber, and would probably have been covered by the same superstructure. This implies that the occupants of the subsidiary burials – the king's retainers and perhaps women of the harem – were buried at the same time as the king, in turn suggesting retainer sacrifice. The architecture of Semerkhet's tomb complex may represent a deliberate attempt to emphasise the king's power of life and death over his subjects in a rather literal way. The only object of note to survive from Semerkhet's reign is a black granite funerary stela, one of a pair which originally stood in front of the king's tomb (Amélineau 1899: 245, fig. 65).

Qaa

Qaa was the builder of the last tomb and funerary enclosure at Abydos until the site was re-adopted as the royal burial ground towards the end of the Second Dynasty. Qaa's tomb on the Umm el-Qaab (Petrie 1900) follows the same plan as his predecessor's, suggesting a continuation of the practice of retainer sacrifice. The accompanying funerary enclosure has not been positively identified, but it is likely that the walled Coptic village of Deir Sitt Damiana incorporates the monument (Kaiser 1969: 2). Several large mastabas at North Saqqara are dated to the reign of Qaa, suggesting that it may have been a long one. This view is supported by a fragment of a **siltstone** bowl from Saqqara which mentions the king's second Sed-festival (Lacau and Lauer 1959: 12, pl. 8 no. 41). Moreover, the different building phases of his tomb at Abydos seem to have been separated by a significant period of time (Engel, in Dreyer *et al.* 1996: 57–71). The first year of his reign is recorded on the main Cairo fragment of the royal annals; the compartment lists the usual ceremonies associated with the accession of a new king. Several year labels discovered in the king's tomb at Abydos record events ranging from the royal progress ('the following of Horus') to the collection of timber for the royal workshops, from the foundation of a religious building (named *q3w-ntrw*) to the celebration of various cultic festivals. The running of the Apis bull and the festival of Sokar seem to have been celebrated periodically during Qaa's reign, whilst an obscure festival involving a divine or royal **bark** is also recorded (see Chapter 8).

In addition to sealings and labels from the three major Early Dynastic cemeteries – Saqqara (Emery 1949: 116 and 123, fig. 67B, 1954: 107, figs 123 and 127, fig. 200, 1958: 33, 97, 109, pls 28e, g, 37.1–5, 106.11, 124.1–2; Lacau and Lauer 1959: 12, pls 8 nos 40–1, 9 nos 44–6) and its northward extension at Abusir (Leclant and Clerc 1992: pl. XVI, figs 17, 18), Helwan (Saad 1951: 29 and 30, fig. 11, pl. XXIXa; Kaplony 1963, I: 149) and Abydos – Qaa is also attested in the deep south of Egypt, near Elkab. A rock-cut inscription in the Wadi Hellal shows the *serekh* of Qaa facing a figure of the local goddess, Nekhbet. In between are some less easily identifiable signs, perhaps an *ankh* and a *was*-sceptre. A similar rock-cut inscription, though without the additional signs, occurs near the small hamlet of Naga el-Oqbiya, about ten kilometres north of Elkab (Huyge 1984; Hendrickx, personal communication, has pointed out that Huyge erroneously located the inscription at es-Sibâ'îya). The nature of Qaa's activity in this region is unknown, but an expedition to exploit the desert's resources is a plausible suggestion. Contacts further afield are hinted at by an ivory gaming rod from the king's tomb (Petrie 1900: pl. XII.12–13, pl. XVII.30). One side shows the figure of a bound Asiatic captive, identified by the hieroglyph above his head as an inhabitant of *Stt*. The figure probably stands for Egypt's enemies in general, and cannot be taken as proof of punitive raids against southern Palestine in the reign of Qaa. None the less, the gaming rod does demonstrate Egyptian acquaintance with the inhabitants of Western Asia, and 18 imported Syro-Palestinian vessels from tombs at North Saqqara dating to the reign of Qaa point to continued trade between Egypt and its north-eastern neighbours. Craftsmanship from the reign of Qaa is represented by three copper bowls from his tomb at Abydos (Dreyer *et al.* 1996: 75–6, pl. 15.b). Two of them are inscribed with the king's *serekh* and an accompanying text mentioning court institutions including the royal palace.

'Ba' and Sneferka

The change of dynasty after the reign of Qaa is likely to have had a political ingredient. It may be no coincidence that two ephemeral Horus names are attested from the period. The first of these, written with a bird and possibly read as 'Ba', occurs only once, on a stone vessel fragment from the Step Pyramid (Lacau and Lauer 1959: pl. IV.7). The similarity of the accompanying text to known inscriptions of Qaa suggest that the vessel may originally have been inscribed for Qaa, and usurped by the Horus 'Ba' (Helck 1979: 124). The second name associated with the end of Qaa's reign is the Horus Sneferka. The name is attested twice: once on a fragment of a siltstone plate found in the surface debris of the North Saqqara élite cemetery (Emery 1958: pls 28a, 38.1); and once on a similar plate from the Step Pyramid galleries (Lacau and Lauer 1959: 15, pl. 17 no. 86). In both cases, the other sign groups in the inscription are associated elsewhere with the *serekh* of Qaa (Emery 1958: 31). On the plate from the Step Pyramid, the name Sneferka seems to be a later addition within the *serekh*. Neither 'Ba' nor Sneferka appears in later king lists. If they were usurpers, they are likely to have been viewed as illegitimate by their successors, and expunged from the historical record. Perhaps more plausible, at least in the case of Sneferka, is the suggestion that this was an alternative Horus name, adopted by Qaa for a short period. The discovery of sealings of Hetepsekhemwy in the tomb of Qaa seems to prove that there was a smooth transition between the First and Second Dynasties (see below).

THE SECOND DYNASTY

The kings who ruled Egypt between the death of Qaa and the accession of Netjerikhet/Djoser are some of the most shadowy figures from the entire span of Egyptian history (cf. Dodson 1996). The inscriptions and monuments from the period record a plethora of royal names, as do the surviving king lists. The names from these two sets of sources bear little relation to each other. It has proved difficult, if not impossible, to reconcile the varying lists and sequences, and scholars today are scarcely more confident about the internal history of the Second Dynasty than were their predecessors a generation ago. The identity and order of the first three kings is certain, thanks to an inscribed statue in the Cairo Museum. The contemporary monuments and the later king lists can be reconciled with reasonable certainty for the first five rulers of the dynasty, whilst Khasekhemwy is universally acknowledged as the last king of the dynasty. In contrast, the positions of the intervening rulers – and indeed the extent of their authority – are obscure. Internal tensions during the middle of the Second Dynasty are suggested by the appearance of Seth in the royal titulary under Peribsen, the very different king lists drawn up for the dynasty in later periods (whereas the king lists agree to a notable extent on the composition of the First Dynasty), and the references under Khasekhem to battles against northern enemies (Kaiser 1992: 184–5, n. 44). It is possible that, for a period in the middle of the dynasty, power was divided between kings in the north and south of the country. A study of Nile levels recorded on the Palermo Stone (Bell 1970) indicates that there was a significant drop in the average height of the annual inundation after the end of the First Dynasty. Hence, it is possible that ecological factors may have played a part in the apparent tensions (Hoffman 1980: 312). With considerable uncertainties surrounding the order and number of rulers, an accurate estimate for the length of the Second Dynasty is impossible. A figure of one hundred and twenty-one years has been proposed (Baines and Málek 1980: 36), but this is no more than an educated guess.

Hetepsekhemwy

We cannot be certain why the death of Qaa marked the end of a dynasty. The first king of the Second Dynasty seems to have legitimised his position by overseeing the burial of his predecessor, or at least by honouring his mortuary cult: sealings of Hetepsekhemwy have recently been discovered in the offering chambers nearest the entrance of Qaa's tomb (Dreyer 1993b: 11; Dreyer *et al.* 1996: 71–2, fig. 25, pl. 14.a). For his own burial, Hetepsekhemwy broke with tradition and abandoned the ancestral necropolis of Abydos in favour of a site adjacent to the capital. The relocation of the royal mortuary complex to Saqqara represents a fundamental change, and must have some historical significance, even if we are unable to be more specific. Furthermore, the design of the royal tomb at Saqqara was entirely new, necessitated, at least in part, by the different nature of the rock strata at Saqqara compared with Abydos (see Chapter 7).

The large gallery tomb at Saqqara was identified as Hetepsekhemwy's on the basis of numerous seal-impressions (Barsanti 1902; Maspero 1902). Apart from these sealings, the tomb was virtually empty. Objects bearing the name of Hetepsekhemwy have, however, come to light elsewhere. The best known is the pink granite statuette of Hetepdief, a priest who evidently served the mortuary cults of Hetepsekhemwy and his two successors (Fischer 1961: 46, fig. 1; Malek 1986: 32). In addition, an Early Dynastic grave at Badari contained an alabaster vessel fragment inscribed with the *serekh* of Hetepsekhemwy, the name of an estate, and the title of a mortuary priest (Brunton 1927: pl. XIX.25). A cup of black granite bearing the name of Hetepsekhemwy is unprovenanced (Kaplony 1965: 23, pl. IV, fig. 48), while a bone cylinder which probably formed the finial of a shaft or part of a piece of furniture is said to be from Helwan (Needler 1984: 375, 379, pl. 84, fig. 44). Two inscribed stone bowls were found in the pyramid complex of Menkaura at Giza (Reisner 1931: 102 and 186, fig. 57.37, pl. 70.c). Further examples of 'heirlooms' are the stone vessel fragments from the tombs of Peribsen (Petrie 1901: pl. VIII.8–11) and Khasekhemwy (Amélineau 1902: pl. XXI.6), and numerous inscribed stone vessels from the Step Pyramid complex (Lacau and Lauer 1959: pls 10–12). These latter formed part of the accumulated ritual material from the royal **magazine**s, collected together by Netjerikhet to furnish his burial. The inscriptions provide most of our meagre information on the reign of Hetepsekhemwy.

Nebra

Very little is known about Hetepsekhemwy's successor; there is even some dispute about the reading of his name. It used to be realised as 'Raneb', for *R*ᶜ-*nb*(.*i*), 'Ra is (my) lord' (for example, Baines and Málek 1980: 36; Trigger *et al.* 1983: 70); but recently, the favoured reading of the king's name reverses the two elements to give *Nb-r*ᶜ, 'lord of the sun'. According to this view, the word *r*ᶜ would simply be the name of the sun, not yet the name of the solar deity (Quirke 1990: 23–4).

Sealings of Nebra were found together with those of Hetepsekhemwy in the royal gallery tomb at Saqqara (Barsanti 1902; Maspero 1902), suggesting that Nebra oversaw the burial of his predecessor. Confirmation that Nebra succeeded Hetepsekhemwy is provided by a stone bowl from the Step Pyramid which shows the juxtaposed *serekh*s of the two kings (Lacau and Lauer 1959: pl. 11 no. 58), and by the statue of Hetepdief mentioned earlier. There is also a flint bowl of Hetepsekhemwy, reinscribed by Nebra, from the Menkaura pyramid complex (Reisner 1931: 102, pl. 70.c). The same practice was evidently continued by Nebra's successor, since a bowl with the *serekh* of Nebra, reused by Ninetjer, was found in the tomb of Peribsen at Abydos (Petrie 1901: pl. VIII.12). The most famous artefact created for Nebra is his fine funerary stela of pink granite (Fischer 1961). It is the first royal stela to come from a site other than Abydos, and lacks the raised border typical of First Dynasty funerary stelae. Although found at Mit Rahina, it seems certain that Nebra's stela once stood in front of his tomb, which must therefore be located at Saqqara. One possibility is that the gallery tomb constructed for Hetepsekhemwy was in fact appropriated by his successor. Alternatively, the galleries beneath the Western Massif and below the North Court of Netjerikhet's Step Pyramid complex may have been Second Dynasty royal tombs. Nebra is further attested only once: his *serekh* is cut on a rock at Site 34, behind Armant in the western desert (Winkler 1938, I: pl. XI.4; Emery 1961: 93, fig. 56). The site is close to an ancient trade route linking the Nile valley with the western oases, and the inscription suggests that Nebra mounted an expedition outside the Nile valley.

Ninetjer

By far the best attested king of the early Second Dynasty is Ninetjer, Nebra's successor. The position of his titulary on the Palermo Stone suggests that he must have been on the throne for at least thirty-five years (cf. Helck 1979: 128). Three high-status tombs in the élite cemetery at North Saqqara contained sealings of Ninetjer (S2171: Quibell 1923: pl. XV.3; Porter and Moss 1974: 436; S2302 (which probably belonged to the Overseer of Sculptors, *Ni-rw-3b*): Quibell 1923: 30, pl. XVII.3; Porter and Moss 1974: 437; S2498: Quibell 1923: 44–5; Porter and Moss 1974: 440), as did a tomb across the Nile in the Early Dynastic necropolis at Helwan (505 H.4: Saad 1951: 17, pls XII.a, b, XIII.a). Five different jar-sealings of the king were discovered in a large mastaba near Giza (Petrie 1907: 7, pl. VE). Further sealings of Ninetjer (S. Hassan 1938: 521; Porter and Moss 1974: 613) led to the identification of the king's own tomb at Saqqara. Located some 130 metres east of Hetepsekhemwy's (/Nebra's?) monument, Ninetjer's tomb follows a similar design (Kaiser 1992: 180, fig. 4d).

Much of what we know about Ninetjer's reign derives from the annals of the Palermo Stone. The whole of the fourth register of the stone comprises years from the early and middle parts of his reign, namely year 5 or 6 to year 20 or 21 (Schäfer 1902: 22–6, pl. I). The foundation of a chapel or estate, named *Hr-rn*, is recorded for year 7; but, otherwise, most of the eponymous events are the regular ritual appearances of the king and various religious festivals. The festival of Sokar seems to have been celebrated at intervals of six years, while the running of the Apis bull is recorded twice, in years 9 and 15. With the exception of a ceremony in year 19 associated with Nekhbet, goddess of the Elkab area, the festivals recorded for Ninetjer's reign are closely connected with the Memphite region. This may be significant: apart from stone vessels reused for the burials of Peribsen and Khasekhemwy at Abydos (Petrie 1901: pl. VIII.13; and Amélineau 1902: pl. XXI.5, respectively), Ninetjer is not attested outside the Memphite region. It is possible that court activity in the early Second Dynasty was largely, if not entirely, confined to Lower Egypt. This might account for the internal tensions – maybe amounting to civil war – which appear to have engulfed the country towards the end of Ninetjer's reign. The Palermo Stone hints at possible unrest in Ninetjer's year 13 (Schäfer 1902: 24). The entry reads 'first feast of *Dw3-Hr-pt*. Attacking the towns of *Šm-r'* and *H3*'. The name of the second locality means 'north land', and some have interpreted this entry as recording the suppression of a rebellion in Lower Egypt (Emery 1961: 93). Although the Palermo Stone breaks off after year 19, two further events which probably belong to the latter part of Ninetjer's reign are known from stone vessel inscriptions. The 'fourth occasion of the Sokar festival' (Lacau and Lauer 1965: 88, fig. 172 [no. 273]; Helck 1979: 128) probably took place in year

24, judging by the periodic nature of its celebration; the 'seventeenth occasion of the [biennial] census' (Lacau and Lauer 1965: 89, fig. 173 [no. 274]; Helck 1979: 128) will have occurred in year 34.

With so long a reign, it is likely that Ninetjer celebrated at least one Sed-festival. No contemporary inscriptions attest such an occasion, although the statuette of the king discussed below is certainly suggestive. The stock of stone vessels found in the Step Pyramid galleries may originally have been prepared for Ninetjer's Sed-festival (Helck 1979). According to this theory, the vessels remained in the magazine at Saqqara and were never distributed because internal unrest had already broken out, disrupting communications and weakening the authority of the central administration; the vessels were subsequently appropriated by kings of the late Second and early Third Dynasties. This hypothesis is certainly appealing and has received recent support from Buto (Faltings and Köhler 1996: 100 and n. 52): an analysis of the pottery from the Early Dynastic level V indicates a date not later than the reign of Peribsen; the same level also yielded seal-impressions naming Iy-en-khnum, one of the most prominent officials mentioned on stone vessels from the Step Pyramid galleries, and placed by Helck in the reign of Ninetjer.

The statuette of the mortuary priest Hetepdief indicates continuity between the first three kings of the Second Dynasty, their mortuary cults

Plate 3.2 King Ninetjer. Crude stone statuette of unknown provenance, now in the Georges Michailides Collection (photograph courtesy of the Egypt Exploration Society).

being served by one and the same individual. Ninetjer certainly maintained the mortuary cult of one predecessor: an inscribed stone vessel from the Step Pyramid juxtaposes the *serekh* of Ninetjer and the *ka*-chapel of Hetepsekhemwy (Lacau and Lauer 1959: pl. 15 no. 74). Apart from the numerous inscribed stone vessels (Lacau and Lauer 1959: pls 13–16), only two objects bearing the name of Ninetjer have survived. One is a small ivory vessel from the Saqqara region (Kaplony 1964: fig. 1074). The other is of far greater importance in the history of Egyptian art: an alabaster statuette of the king, enthroned and wearing the close-fitting robe associated with the Sed-festival (Simpson 1956). The statuette represents the earliest complete and identifiable example of three-dimensional royal statuary from Egypt.

Weneg

As we have seen, there are indications of a breakdown in central authority at the end of Ninetjer's reign. Before order was re-established towards the end of the Second Dynasty, the kingship seems to have been held by a number of ephemeral rulers who are only poorly attested in contemporary inscriptions (Figure 3.4). Ninetjer's immediate successor, at least in the north of Egypt, was a king whose *nswt-bity* name has been read as Weneg (Grdseloff 1944: 288–91). His Horus name remains unknown (cf. Wildung 1969b; Helck 1979: 131). An unpublished inscription of Weneg from a mastaba at North Saqqara (S3014: Lacau and Lauer 1959: 16,

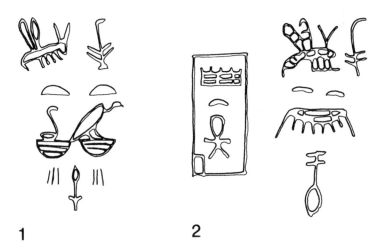

1   **2**

Figure 3.4 Ephemeral rulers, 1: Weneg (1) and Nubnefer (2). Both kings seem to have ruled in the middle of the Second Dynasty. The royal names were incised on stone vessels found in galleries beneath the Step Pyramid of Netjerikhet at Saqqara (after Lacau and Lauer 1959: planches V.4, VI.4).

n. 2) is very similar to an inscription of Ninetjer (Lacau and Lauer 1959: no. 68), suggesting that this may be another case of a king re-cutting one of his predecessor's stone vessels (Helck 1979: 124). A second stone vessel from the same Saqqara tomb names the two tutelary goddesses of Upper and Lower Egypt, Nekhbet and Wadjet (Kaplony 1965: 7, figs 6 and 8, 16 n. 6; Helck 1979: 131). However, Weneg is unattested outside Saqqara and there is no evidence to confirm that his rule extended into the south of the country. Twelve stone bowls from the Step Pyramid complex name Weneg (Lacau and Lauer 1959: pls 19 no. 105, 20 nos 101–7). Weneg's tomb has not been located. If, as is likely, it followed the pattern of earlier Second Dynasty tombs and comprised a set of subterranean galleries, then it may lie beneath the North Court of Netjerikhet's Step Pyramid complex. Alternatively, there is a possibility that other Second Dynasty royal tombs once stood to the south of the Hetepsekhemwy and Ninetjer galleries; this would explain the location of Sekhemkhet's step pyramid enclosure some distance to the west. The whole area was levelled by Unas for the construction of his pyramid and causeway.

Sened

According to later king lists, Ninetjer's second successor was a king with the *nswt-bity* name Sened (Helck 1984c). Unfortunately, there are no proven contemporary inscriptions of this ruler. The best piece of evidence is a block, inscribed with the words *nswt-bity Snd*, reused in the funerary temple of King Khafra at Giza (Steindorff, in U. Hölscher 1912: 106). It may be Second Dynasty, although the epigraphy of the inscription would tend to suggest a slightly later date. An undisputed Fourth Dynasty inscription, in the tomb of Shery, provides the second mention of a King Sened, and indicates that his mortuary cult was celebrated at Saqqara and was still current over one hundred years after his death (Grdseloff 1944: 294; Wildung 1969b: pl. III.2; Kaiser 1991). Shery's titles suggest a connection between the mortuary cults of Sened and Peribsen, a king of the Second Dynasty who is otherwise only attested in Upper Egypt. If Sened ruled only in the north of Egypt and Peribsen only in the south, the juxtaposition of their two mortuary cults at Saqqara may indicate that the territorial division of the country which is proposed after the reign of Ninetjer was amicable at first (Helck 1979: 132). The only other occurrence of Sened's name is on the belt of a Late Period bronze statuette of a king (Wildung 1969b: pl. IV.1). This suggests that, however obscure Sened may be to modern Egyptology, he was still remembered by his countrymen centuries after his death. As with Weneg, Sened's tomb has not been identified. Given the reference to his mortuary cult in the inscription of Shery, it must have been located somewhere in the Saqqara necropolis. It has been suggested, though without firm evidence, that the galleries beneath the Western Massif of the Step Pyramid complex may have been Sened's tomb, since the tomb of Shery (overseer of the king's mortuary priests) probably lay a short distance to the north (Dodson 1996: 24).

Nubnefer

This name is attested just twice, on stone vessels from the Step Pyramid (Lacau and Lauer 1959: pl. VI.3–4 [nos 99–100]). By a network of associations, we may conclude that Ninetjer and Nubnefer were near contemporaries (Helck 1979: 124). Nubnefer cannot easily be the *nswt-bity* name of Ninetjer, since this name is known (it is also Ninetjer). Nubnefer may, therefore, have been an ephemeral ruler who held the kingship briefly during the period of unrest which seems to have followed the death of Ninetjer. His exact place in the order of succession cannot be established.

Peribsen

Considerable uncertainty likewise surrounds another king from the middle of the Second Dynasty who, uniquely in Egyptian history, chose to replace the Horus-falcon surmounting the *serekh* with the **Seth-animal**. Just why Peribsen chose to break with custom and emphasise the latter god is a mystery. The change may have had 'real political implications', perhaps indicating a new development in the ideology of kingship (Hoffman 1980: 351). Some scholars have seen a connection between the change of title and two other aspects of Peribsen's reign: his decision to be buried in the First Dynasty royal cemetery at Abydos, and the fact that he is not attested by contemporary inscriptions outside Upper Egypt. It is possible that Peribsen ruled only in the southern part of the country; he may have been descended from the First Dynasty royal family, hence his decision to be buried at Abydos. Alternatively, if he was an Upper Egyptian usurper, the choice of the Umm el-Qaab as his burial place may have been intended to confer legitimacy, by association in death with the kings of the First Dynasty. The special features of Peribsen's reign easily lend themselves to speculative historical reconstructions, but caution should be exercised.

To judge from the tomb inscription of Shery, Peribsen's mortuary cult seems to have been celebrated at Saqqara despite the fact that his tomb (Petrie 1901: pl. LXI) and funerary enclosure (Ayrton *et al.* 1904: 1–5, pl. VII; Kemp 1966; sealings: Ayrton *et al.* 1904: pl. IX.1, 2) are located at Abydos. It is at the latter site that Peribsen is best attested. Some of the sealings from his tomb bear the **epithet** *inw S_tt*, 'tribute (or 'conqueror'?) of Setjet' (Petrie 1901: pl. XXII.181). The town determinative after Setjet seems to indicate that the locality lay within Egypt, rather than being the land of Syria-Palestine (also called Setjet by the Egyptians). The town has been plausibly identified as Sethroë in the north-eastern

Delta (Grdseloff 1944: 295–9), known to have been a cult centre of the god Seth in later times. It is possible, though not provable, that the town was incorporated into the Egyptian realm and a cult of Seth established during the reign of Peribsen. However, this would clearly require Peribsen to have ruled Lower Egypt as well as Upper Egypt.

Two funerary stelae were discovered in front of Peribsen's Abydos tomb (Fischer 1961: 52, fig. 7; BM 35597: Spencer 1980: 16, pls 8–9 [Cat. 15]). An official's sealing from the reign of Peribsen was recently discovered on the island of Elephantine, in the settlement area north of the Satet temple (Dreyer, in Kaiser *et al.* 1987: 107–8 and 109, fig. 13a, pl. 15a). The inscription names the 'seal(er) of all the things of Upper Egypt', and thus indicates the existence of state administrative structures on Elephantine from at least the late Second Dynasty (Pätznick, in Kaiser *et al.* 1995: 180). Mastaba K1 at Beit Khallaf, dated to the reign of Netjerikhet, none the less yielded a sealing of Peribsen (Garstang 1902: pl. X.8). An unprovenanced cylinder vessel of red limestone is decorated with the *serekh* of Peribsen in raised relief (Kaplony 1965: 24 and 26, fig. 51 [line drawing], pl. V fig. 51 [photograph]). Curiously, the name of Peribsen also occurs on a stone vessel fragment found by Petrie in the First Dynasty tomb of Merneith (Petrie 1900: pl. IV.7). The only possible explanation is that it represents later contamination of the tomb contents, perhaps from Amélineau's excavations.

Sekhemib-perenmaat

The final king whose identity and place in the succession are uncertain bore the two-part name Sekhemib-perenmaat. There are two main hypotheses concerning Sekhemib-perenmaat (Quirke 1990: 45): first, that he is one and the same king as Peribsen, in a different guise (for example, Grdseloff 1944: 295; Emery 1961: 95; Shaw and Nicholson 1995: 220; Dodson 1996: 25); second, that he was the successor of Peribsen (Kaplony 1963; Helck 1979: 132). For those who hold the first view, the occurrence of sealings bearing the name Sekhemib-perenmaat in both the tomb and funerary enclosure of Peribsen is significant (Petrie 1901: pl. XXI.164–72; and Ayrton *et al.* 1904: pl. IX.3, respectively). Moreover, on inscribed stone vessel fragments from the Step Pyramid complex (Lacau and Lauer 1959: pl. 18 nos 87–94), Sekhemib-perenmaat is given the epithet *inw ḫ3st*, 'tribute (or 'conqueror') of foreign land(s)' (Lacau and Lauer 1959: pl. 18 no. 93), reminiscent of the phrase *inw Stt*, discussed above, which appears on sealings of Peribsen from his Abydos tomb. Those who hold the second view point to the fact that the sealings from Peribsen's tomb bearing the name of Sekhemib-perenmaat were found in the entrance, a parallel situation to the sealing of Hetepsekhemwy found in the tomb of Qaa. On balance, the evidence seems to weigh slightly in favour of identifying Sekhemib-perenmaat as the same person as Peribsen, perhaps before he made the unusual move of adopting a Seth-name. The similarity of the two names, Sekhemib-perenmaat and Peribsen (both include the elements *ib* and *pr*), hint at a close connection. Apart from the instances already cited, the name Sekhemib-perenmaat is attested on a sealing from the debris of the Old Kingdom town at Elephantine (Leclant and Clerc 1993: 250), and on the inside of an unprovenanced alabaster bowl (Kaplony 1965: 24, pl. V fig. 52).

Khasekhem(wy)

The last king of the Second Dynasty is an important, and in many ways transitional, figure (cf. Hoffman 1980: 348–54). More is known about his reign than any other of the dynasty, and his surviving monuments are by far the most impressive of any Early Dynastic ruler before Netjerikhet. At the beginning of his reign, the last king of the Second Dynasty adopted the Horus name Khasekhem, 'the power has appeared'. Later, however, he added the Seth-animal to the top of his *serekh*, and changed his name accordingly to the dual form Khasekhemwy, 'the two powers have appeared', together with an additional epithet *nbwy ḥtp im=f*, 'the two lords are at peace in him'. The new name seems consciously to have been modelled on that of the dynasty's founder, Hetepsekhemwy. It may therefore have been intended to proclaim national renewal under Khasekhemwy (Kaiser 1992: 184–5, n. 44). It used to be thought that the two forms of the name belonged to two different kings (Emery 1961: 98); but it is now generally accepted that they were borne at different periods by one and the same monarch (for example, Quirke 1990: 46; Shaw and Nicholson 1995: 150).

In the early part of his reign, Khasekhem seems to have shown particular interest in, and reverence for, Hierakonpolis, the ancient Predynastic capital in the far south of the country. Indeed, Khasekhem is attested only once outside Hierakonpolis, on an inscribed diorite vessel from the Step Pyramid complex (Lacau and Lauer 1959: pl. 3 no. 18). Travertine and granite vessels of Khasekhem were discovered inside the temple of Horus at Hierakonpolis (Quibell 1900: pl. XXXVI). In all cases, the inscription shows the goddess Nekhbet standing on a ring containing the word *bš*, 'rebel'. The accompanying legend describes the scene as 'the year of fighting the northern enemy'. The Horus-falcon atop the king's *serekh* wears only the white crown, associated with Upper Egypt (Quibell 1900: pl. XXXVIII). Unless the scene represents nothing more than a traditional duty of kingship or a ritual, an historical interpretation would seem likely. It is probable that, when he acceded to the kingship, Khasekhem ruled only Upper Egypt. Campaigns against the rebellious north ultimately resulted in Khasekhem's victory, and he was able to reunite Egypt. To commemorate this achievement, he changed his name to the dual form, to demonstrate that peace and harmony had returned through his actions. In the absence of hard evidence, this reconstruction of events must remain speculative, though it does fit the available data well. In particular, two famous seated statues of Khasekhem from Hierakonpolis, one of limestone (Quibell 1900: pl. XXXIX), the other of siltstone (Quibell 1900: pl. XLI [left]), carry inscriptions which show defeated enemies in contorted positions, labelled as 'northern enemies 47,209' (Quibell 1900: pl. XL). These two statues clearly suggest hostile activity undertaken by Khasekhem against a northern foe, though a precise identification of the enemy is not possible. It has been suggested that the gap in the later sources, transmogrified into the name 'Hudjefa' by the New Kingdom scribes who compiled the Saqqara and Turin king lists, may once have contained the name of Khasekhem's opponent(s), later expunged from the record (Dodson 1996: 28). If a fragmentary stela from Hierakonpolis is to be interpreted at face value, Khasekhem may have preceded his attacks on the north by a campaign southwards into Nubia. The stela fragment shows part of a kneeling captive resting on a platform which ends in the head of a foreigner. This last is surmounted by a bow, the sign used to write the name applied to Nubia, Ta-Sety. Moreover, an inscription below the scene gives the *serekh* of Khasekhem and the phrase 'humbling the foreign land' (Quibell and Green 1902: pl. LVIII). The other known occurrence of Khasekhem's *serekh* is on an unprovenanced copper axehead in a private collection (Kaplony 1965: 24 and 29, fig. 55).

Under the later version of his name, Khasekhemwy, the king is much more widely attested, from Hierakonpolis in the far south of Egypt to Byblos on the Lebanese coast. A fragment of a **breccia** stone vessel was recovered from the Egyptian temple area at Byblos, incised with the phrase *Ḫ‘-shmwi di ‘nḫ*, 'Khasekhemwy, given life' (Montet 1928: 84, fig. 1). Unusually, the Seth-animal on top of the *serekh* appears to be wearing the red crown, whereas the Horus-falcon wears the usual double crown. This vessel may easily have reached Byblos through trade and/or at a later period. None the less, it seems likely that foreign relations reached a new level under Khasekhemwy, since a seal-impression of his reign gives the first occurrence of the title *imi-r3 ḫ3st*, 'overseer of foreign land(s)' (Kaplony 1963, III: pl. 72 fig. 269). It strongly suggests the imposition of Egyptian hegemony on foreign territory. This may be confirmed by a damaged stone block with a list of foreign countries from the temple area at Hierakonpolis (Quibell and Green 1902: pl. XXIII [bottom]). The inscription seems originally to have included numerals (some are partially preserved), and may therefore have recorded tribute or enemies slain in battle. Other inscriptions of Khasekhemwy have been found at Saqqara – in a private tomb (S3043: Kaplony 1963, I: 163), and in the Step Pyramid complex (Firth and Quibell 1935, I: 141, fig. 22; Lauer 1939: 21, pl. XIX.7–8; Lacau and Lauer 1959: pl. 19 no. 95) – and Abydos (Petrie

1901: pls XXIII–XXIV; Amélineau 1902: pls XXI, XXII; Ayrton *et al.* 1904: 3, pl. IX.9).

Khasekhemwy's mortuary constructions at Abydos are truly impressive. In their design and symbolism they point the way towards the Step Pyramid complex of Netjerikhet a generation later. The burial chamber of Khasekhemwy's tomb was lined with blocks of dressed limestone (Petrie 1901: pl. LVII.4–6), representing the largest-scale use of dressed stone to that date. His funerary enclosure, known today by its Arabic nickname, the Shunet ez-Zebib, is a mammoth structure of mudbrick (Ayrton *et al.* 1904: 1–5, pl. VI). A 'fleet' of funerary boats discovered adjacent to the enclosure may have formed part of the overall building programme (O'Connor 1991, 1995). Buildings inside the court of the enclosure foreshadow some of the elements of the Step Pyramid complex (Kemp 1989: 56, fig. 18; O'Connor 1995: 7). The Shunet ez-Zebib is still one of the most visible monuments at Abydos, its massively thick walls having withstood forty-five centuries. Despite its vast size and the investment of labour that it represents, the Shunet ez-Zebib is not the only such building attributable to Khasekhemwy. A parallel construction can be found on the northern side of the Great Wadi at Hierakonpolis (see Chapter 7). Why Khasekhemwy should have constructed two such funerary enclosures remains a mystery. In addition to the 'Fort', a granite door-jamb from the town site at Hierakonpolis may have belonged to a temple erected by Khasekhemwy (Quibell 1900: pl. II; Engelbach 1934). Two further blocks found nearby (Quibell and Green 1902: pls LIX.8, XXIII [bottom]) suggest a major building programme undertaken by Khasekhemwy at Hierakonpolis. Across the river at Elkab, a granite block with the king's *serekh* was discovered within the town enclosure, hinting at another large building (Sayce and Clarke 1905: 239). The Palermo Stone may provide further evidence for temple building, if the beginning of the fifth register comprises the last years of Khasekhemwy's reign. The entry for year 13 records the construction of a stone building called *Mn-nṯrt* (Schäfer 1902: 26). The reference to stone probably indicates a temple, since secular buildings of the Early Dynastic period were more usually made from mudbrick. If the Early Dynastic relief blocks from the temple of Hathor at Gebelein are also to be dated to the reign of Khasekhemwy (W.S. Smith 1949: 137–8), he would emerge as a major patron of temple construction in Upper Egypt, and by far the most prolific builder of the Early Dynastic period as a whole.

The achievements of Khasekhemwy's reign are not restricted, however, to architecture or administration. The objects from his tomb at Abydos are among the glories of Early Dynastic craftsmanship. They include a sceptre fashioned from the precious stone sard with bands of gold (Petrie 1901: pl. IX.1); **dolomite** limestone vases with sheet gold covers (Petrie 1901: pl. IX.2, 5–10; Spencer 1993: 86, fig. 65); and a ewer and basin of bronze (Petrie 1901: pl. IX.13–15; Spencer 1993: 88, fig. 68). Advanced metalworking is also indirectly attested by an entry on the Palermo Stone. The major event of year 15 was the fashioning of a copper statue called 'high is Khasekhemwy' (Schäfer 1902: 27; Sethe 1914). Life-size copper statues which would fit such a description have survived from the late Old Kingdom. The entry for year 15 may also contain a reference to shipbuilding. According to the Palermo Stone, the king whose reign is recorded at the beginning of the fifth register died in his sixteenth or seventeenth regnal year. However, on both the statues of Khasekhem from Hierakonpolis the king wears the close-fitting robe associated with the Sed-festival, usually – though not always – celebrated after a considerable period of time on the throne.

The reign of Khasekhemwy marks a turning point in Egyptian history and culture, linking the early development of dynastic civilisation during the First and Second Dynasties with the full flourishing of that civilisation from the beginning of the Third Dynasty. His mortuary constructions foreshadow the pyramid age, and his political achievements seem to have re-established the internal stability and prosperity needed for the great cultural achievements of his successors. A sealing from Khasekhemwy's tomb at Abydos demonstrates the family link between him and Netjerikhet. The sealing names the 'mother of the king's children, Ni-maat-hap' (Petrie 1901: pl. XXIV.210). This same personage is named, this time as 'mother of the dual king', on a sealing from mastaba K1 at Beit Khallaf (Garstang 1902: pl. X.7), dated by other sealings to the reign of Netjerikhet. In other words, Netjerikhet was Nimaathap's son, either by a second husband or, perhaps more likely (given the phraseology on the sealing from Khasekhemwy's tomb), by Khasekhemwy himself.

THE THIRD DYNASTY

The later king lists and the contemporary monuments are in rare agreement concerning the number of Third Dynasty kings. Both the Abydos king list and the Turin Canon record five rulers, whilst five Horus names are attested in Third Dynasty inscriptions. Unfortunately, the history of the dynasty is not without its problems. There remain difficulties in correlating the different royal names, and the order of the five kings is far from clear, as is the attribution of the royal funerary monuments at Zawiyet el-Aryan and Maidum. The archaeological evidence contradicts the Abydos and Turin lists by indicating that Netjerikhet succeeded Khasekhemwy directly. By contrast, the archaeological and historical sources agree concerning Netjerikhet's successor, now that the *nbty* name Djeserty has been irrefutably linked with the Horus Sekhemkhet. There is no doubt that the king known by his *nswt-bity* name Huni was the last ruler of the Third Dynasty, but the ordering of the remaining three Horus names (Sanakht, Khaba and Qahedjet) and one *nswt-bity* name (Nebka) is open to differing reconstructions. The duration of the Third Dynasty is also a matter of conjecture. The figures given for the five kings in the Turin Canon total seventy-four years, a comparatively short period. There is no independent means of checking these figures; we can only gauge how likely a particular reign-length is for a particular ruler, given the scale of his monuments or other known achievements. The end of the Third Dynasty has been plausibly placed at 2575 BC (Baines and Málek 1980: 36).

Netjerikhet

The weight of archaeological evidence favours Netjerikhet as Khasekhemwy's successor and thus the first king of the Third Dynasty. The sealings of Nimaathap, already mentioned, probably indicate that Netjerikhet was Khasekhemwy's son. Sealings of Netjerikhet found in the tomb of Khasekhemwy at Abydos (Petrie 1901: pl. XXIV.211; Kaplony 1963, II: 1187, 1190; III: figs 768, 798; Giddy 1996: 30, 1997: 29), and further examples from the Shunet ez-Zebib (Newberry 1909: pl. XXIII; Kaplony 1963, I: 164; III: pl. 131, figs 800–1), suggest that Netjerikhet, as son and heir, oversaw the burial of his predecessor. Moreover, the architectural and symbolic parallels between the funerary enclosure of Khasekhemwy (the Shunet ez-Zebib) and the Step Pyramid enclosure of Netjerikhet argue in favour of the close proximity of the two reigns (O'Connor 1991, 1995). The same store of ritual stone vessels seems to have supplied both kings' tombs, since both contained fragments with identical ink drawings of the god Min, clearly drawn from the same collection (Petrie 1901: pl. III.48; Lacau and Lauer 1965: pl. 15.1–5). Two sealings from mastaba K1 at Beit Khallaf bear an identical inscription – referring to the 'house of provisioning of the vineyards of Memphis' – except for the *serekh*, which is that of Khasekhemwy in one case (Weill 1908: 83) and that of Netjerikhet in the other (Weill 1908: 101). A plausible conclusion is that, after the death of Khasekhemwy, the original cylinder-seal was simply re-cut with the name of the new king. The archaeological evidence is supported by at least one historical source: the Saqqara king list names Djoser (Netjerikhet) as the immediate successor of Beby (a misreading of the name Khasekhemwy) (Weill 1908: 13).

Netjerikhet is better known by the name preserved in the later king lists, Djoser. Unfortunately, this name – presumably the king's *nbty* or *nswt-bity* name – does not appear on any contemporary monument or inscription, and the equation of Djoser and Netjerikhet (the king's Horus name) depends on the much later Sehel Famine Stela (Barguet 1953: esp. 14, pl. III). Since later tradition also revered Djoser as the king for whom the Step Pyramid complex was built (Grimal 1992: 65), there can be no doubt about the correctness of the identification. When the New Kingdom scribe drawing up the Turin Canon came to the name of Djoser, he changed the ink in his pen from black to red (Gardiner 1959: pl. II; Malek 1986: 37). By writing the name of Djoser in red ink, he was indicating the special place held by that king in the minds of later generations of Egyptians. Despite the continuities between the end of the Second and the beginning of the Third Dynasty, the scribe was justified in recording the accession of Netjerikhet/Djoser as a significant milestone in Egyptian history. The king made a decisive break with the past, by abandoning for good the traditional royal burial ground of Abydos in favour of a site overlooking the capital (cf. Shaw and Nicholson 1995: 149). This decision is likely to have been made for a variety of reasons. The rebellions in the north of the country recorded on the statue bases of Khasekhem may have been a factor. By siting the royal mortuary complex – the pre-eminent symbol of centralised authority – closer to Lower Egypt, the king may have been making a statement about royal control of the north. If the king now resided permanently at the capital, it would have been logical to site the royal tomb nearby. Furthermore, Netjerikhet may have had family ties with the Memphite area, since Manetho records that the Third Dynasty kings were from Memphis.

The mortuary complex of Netjerikhet at Saqqara is one of the most impressive monuments in the Memphite necropolis (Lauer 1936, 1939). It represents a staggering achievement, and remains one of the most important sources for Early Dynastic religion and kingship. The name of the king features most prominently on the six panels from the galleries beneath the pyramid and South Tomb (F.D. Friedman 1995). Lintels from the false doors framing the inscribed panels give the king's complete titulary (Firth and Quibell 1935, II: pls 16, 39, 43), whilst boundary stelae from the complex are inscribed with the names of the king and female members of his family (Firth and Quibell 1935, II: pl. 87; Porter and Moss 1974: 407; reconstructed by Lauer 1936: 187, fig. 209). Seal-impressions with Netjerikhet's *serekh* have also been found in the galleries beneath the North Court granaries (Firth and Quibell 1935, I: 141, figs 19–21) and beneath the pyramid itself (Lauer 1939: 74, pl. XIX.9). Recently, some unique decorated blocks thought to derive from a gateway in the complex have been published (Hawass 1994). They feature the king's *serekh* and a series of recumbent lions, the whole design framed by snakes.

The dominance of the Step Pyramid complex is something of a mixed blessing for ancient historians. It certainly highlights the reign of Netjerikhet as a period of great artistic, architectural and administrative innovation. However, it tends to obscure the king's other accomplishments and the evidence for his activities in other parts of Egypt. Only fragments now survive of a decorated shrine from Heliopolis (W.S. Smith 1949: 133–7, figs 48–53). The scenes in raised relief may be connected with the celebration of a Sed-festival and/or with the **ennead** (assembly of nine gods) worshipped at Heliopolis. Relief blocks from the temple of Hathor at Gebelein probably date to the reign of Khasekhemwy; however, it is possible that they date to the beginning of the Third Dynasty, if the 'archaic' style of decoration is due more to the provincial origin of the work (W.S. Smith 1949: 137). Although the royal burial ground at Abydos was abandoned after the death of Khasekhemwy, the region remained a location for high-status burials into the Third Dynasty. Mastaba K1 at Beit Khallaf (Garstang 1902) dwarfs even the Abydos and Hierakonpolis enclosures of Khasekhemwy. It yielded a large number of seal-impressions, most of them dating to the reign of Netjerikhet, including the sealing of Queen Nimaathap discussed above. One possibility is that mastaba K1 was her tomb. Other tombs were built at Beit Khallaf during the reign of Netjerikhet, though none of them equals K1 in size. A sealing of Netjerikhet was found in each of the mastabas K2, K3, K4 and K5 (Garstang 1902). These monuments may have belonged to minor members of Nimaathap's family, perhaps the descendants of the First Dynasty royal family who still exercised local authority as governors of the Thinite region. The only other site within Egypt where Netjerikhet is attested is Elephantine. Four jar-sealings have been excavated from the eastern area of the town (Dreyer, in Kaiser *et al.* 1987: 108 and 109, fig. 13c, pl. 15c). Each bears the king's *serekh*; one gives the titles of an official, 'controller of the cellar and assistant in the magazine of provisions . . . of Upper and Lower Egypt, follower of the king every day'. A further sealing has been found more recently in the Old Kingdom debris of the eastern and southern sectors of the town (Leclant and Clerc 1993: 250). At Saqqara, sealings of Netjerikhet have been found in three élite, private tombs (S2305 and S3518: Porter and Moss 1974: 437, 448, respectively; Emery 1970: 10, pl. XVII.1; G.T. Martin 1979: 18, pl. 19.5), including the tomb of Hesira (Quibell 1913: 3, pl. XXVIII.23), famous for its carved wooden panels.

By far the most significant development of Netjerikhet's reign, aside from the construction of his mortuary complex, was the instigation of regular Egyptian activity in the Wadi Maghara, the turquoise mining area of the south-western Sinai. Whilst there is evidence for sporadic Egyptian involvement in the Sinai from Predynastic times, centrally organised expeditions to exploit the area's mineral reserves, attested by rock-cut inscriptions, apparently began only in the early Third Dynasty (Gardiner and Peet 1952, 1955). It is possible that the administrative sophistication required to mount such long-distance enterprises was only developed as a result of the pyramid-building activity which characterised the Third Dynasty. Alternatively, state-sponsored activities outside the boundaries of Egypt proper may have been impossible during much of the Second Dynasty when the country seems to have been riven by internal tensions.

The Turin Canon gives Djoser a reign of just nineteen years. This seems rather brief, given the achievements of his reign. However, the Step Pyramid complex was left unfinished, and it is likely that the king died before his grand project could be completed.

Sekhemkhet

For once, the archaeological evidence and all the later king lists agree on the identity of Netjerikhet's successor (Figure 3.5). His Horus name was Sekhemkhet, his name given in the king lists, Djeserty. The correspondence of the two names was proven by the discovery of an ivory plaque in Sekhemkhet's step pyramid complex (Goneim 1957: pls LXV.B, LXVI). The plaque was engraved with the inscription *nbty Ḏsrti ʿnḫ.*

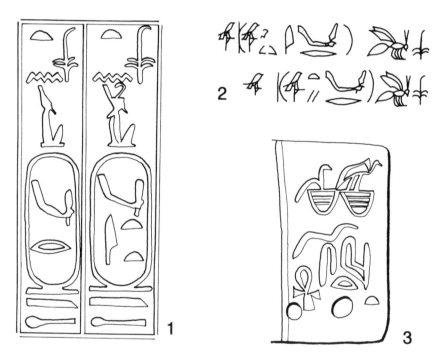

Figure 3.5 The Third Dynasty: a problem solved. A rare example of textual and archaeological sources in agreement: (1) cartouches of Djoser (Netjerikhet) and his successor 'Djoser-teti' from the king list in the tomb of Tjuneroy at Saqqara (after Gardiner, 1961: fig. 8); (2) corresponding entries from the Turin Royal Canon, naming Djoser's successor as 'Djoserty' (after Gardiner 1959: pl. III); (3) the royal name from an inscribed ivory plaque found in the unfinished step pyramid complex of Sekhemkhet at Saqqara, giving the king's 'Two Ladies' name Djesert(i)-ankh and thus confirming the identification of Sekhemkhet as Netjerikhet's immediate successor (after Goneim 1957: pl. LXVI). Not to same scale.

The king's mortuary complex is the principal monument to have survived from his reign (Goneim 1957). It seems that Imhotep, chancellor under Netjerikhet and fabled as the architect of his Step Pyramid complex, also had a hand in Sekhemkhet's mortuary complex: a graffito on the northern enclosure wall of the Sekhemkhet complex names Imhotep (Goneim 1957: 4, pl. XIII), although the context is unclear. The high quality of workmanship in Sekhemkhet's reign is eloquently attested by finds from his pyramid enclosure, particularly the set of gold jewellery discovered in the main corridor of the substructure (Goneim 1957: pls XXXI–XXXII *bis*).

Sekhemkhet continued the programme of expeditions to the Wadi Maghara instituted by his predecessor. A rock-cut inscription on a cliff above the valley shows the king smiting a Bedouin captive (Gardiner and Peet 1952: pl. I). (This inscription was once attributed to the First Dynasty king of a similar name, Semerkhet.) A seal-impression bearing the name of Sekhemkhet has been discovered recently in the Old Kingdom town at Elephantine (Leclant and Clerc 1993: 250; Pätznick, in Kaiser *et al.* 1995: 181 and 182, fig. 29a; Seidlmayer 1996b: 113). The sealing gives the titles of an official who was both 'overseer of Elephantine' and 'sealer of gold of Elephantine'. The seal represents the earliest known occurrence of the town's name (Egyptian *3bw*) (Seidlmayer 1996b: 113).

The Turin Canon assigns Djoser's successor a reign of just six years. Given the unfinished nature of Sekhemkhet's step pyramid complex – presumably the major construction project of his reign – and the paucity of other monuments dated to his reign, this figure seems reasonable (cf. Goedicke 1984).

Khaba

The Horus Khaba is attested at four, perhaps five, sites in Egypt. Eight stone bowls from a high-status mastaba at Zawiyet el-Aryan (Z500) in the Memphite necropolis are inscribed with the king's *serekh* (Arkell 1956; Kaplony 1965: 27, pl. VI, fig. 57; Dunham 1978: 34, pls XXV–XXVI). The mastaba is located in a cemetery adjacent to the so-called 'layer pyramid', an unfinished royal mortuary complex of the late Third Dynasty (Dunham 1978). There is no evidence from the pyramid itself to link it with Khaba, but it is generally attributed to him on the basis of the inscribed stone bowls found nearby (cf. Stadelmann 1984: 496; Edwards 1993: 64).

In Upper Egypt, the name of Khaba has been found on sealings from Hierakonpolis and Elephantine (Figure 3.6). The Hierakonpolis sealing came from the Early Dynastic town, either from houses or from the Early Dynastic stratum under the Old Kingdom temple of Horus (Quibell and Green 1902: pl. LXX.1). The Elephantine sealing was excavated from the eastern town, and shows a divine figure (possibly the god Ash, connected

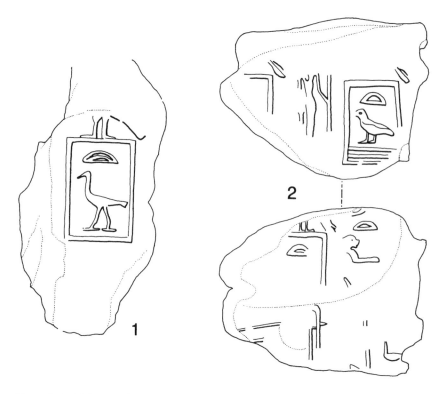

Figure 3.6 Ephemeral rulers, 2: Khaba. Sealings with the king's *serekh*: (1) from the early town at Hierakonpolis (after Quibell and Green 1902: pl. LXX.1); (2) from the early town at Elephantine (after Dreyer, in Kaiser *et al.* 1987: 109, fig. 13.b).

with royal estates) holding a long sceptre, flanked by *serekh*s of Khaba (Dreyer, in Kaiser *et al.* 1987: 108 and 109, fig. 13.b, pl. 15.b). The inscription on the other side of the sealing is almost illegible, but does include the title *ḥ3tï-ʿ*, 'mayor', one of the earliest references to this office. The *serekh* of Khaba is also inscribed on an unprovenanced diorite bowl in London's Petrie Museum (Arkell 1956) and on another diorite bowl in a private collection, said to have come from Dahshur (Arkell 1958).

We must admit that next to nothing is known for certain about the reign of Khaba. His *nswt-bïty* and *nbty* names are unknown. Even his position within the order of succession has not been established beyond doubt, though he clearly reigned in the latter part of the Third Dynasty. Many scholars identify him as the penultimate king of the dynasty (for example, Baines and Málek 1980: 36), though it has been suggested that Khaba was the Horus name of the last king, better known as Huni (Stadelmann 1984: 496). This is because stone bowls incised with the name of a king are common in the First and early Second Dynasties but, otherwise, are not attested again until the reign of Sneferu. This tends to suggest that Khaba preceded Sneferu by only a short period. Moreover, the sealings of Khaba come from two sites where Huni erected small step pyramids. The coincidence of the Khaba sealings and these monuments suggests at least the possibility that Khaba and Huni were one and the same king. None the less, the general consensus identifies Khaba as one of Huni's predecessors. In view of the evidence, discussed below, for the position of Sanakht within the Third Dynasty, and the close architectural similarity between Sekhemkhet's unfinished pyramid and the one at Zawiyet el-Aryan, Khaba may be most plausibly identified as Sekhemkhet's immediate successor, and thus the third king of the dynasty.

Sanakht and Nebka

The position of these two names in the order of succession remains to be firmly established (Seidlmayer 1996a: 198, n. 14). With a single exception, Sanakht is attested on contemporary monuments by his Horus name. His other names are not known for certain, although a fragmentary sealing from mastaba K2 at Beit Khallaf shows the king's *serekh* facing the lower portion of a cartouche (Garstang 1902: pl. XIX.7; Seidlmayer 1996b: pl. 23). Since the sign in the bottom of the cartouche resembles an archaic *ka*-sign, the name has been restored as Nebka, and this has been taken as the *nswt-bity* name of the Horus Sanakht. The fact that the *nswt-bity* name written in a cartouche did not come into regular use until the late Third Dynasty clearly argues in favour of Sanakht having reigned towards the end of the dynasty. Although the Abydos and Turin king lists record a King Nebka at the beginning of the Third Dynasty, between Khasekhemwy and Netjerikhet, this is contradicted by the archaeological evidence.

A number of further sealings from mastaba K2 at Beit Khallaf bear the Horus name of Sanakht (Garstang 1902: pl. XIX.2–6, 8). A seal-impression with the king's name was found in an Early Dynastic building on the island of Elephantine (Seidlmayer, in Kaiser *et al.* 1982: 303–6 and 304, fig. 15, pl. 65b; Pätznick, in Kaiser *et al.* 1995: 180; Seidlmayer 1996b: 121). The sealing gives a string of titles, translated as 'royal seal-bearer and judicial official connected with the royal estate'. The inscription suggests that an administrative building connected to a royal **domain** or estate was once located on the island, attached to the small step pyramid nearby. This monument, one of several similar structures throughout Egypt, has been dated to the last reign of the Third Dynasty (Seidlmayer 1996a, 1996b: 119–20). For this reason, the Elephantine sealing tends to favour a date for Sanakht towards the end of the dynasty. Seal-impressions of Sanakht from the Step Pyramid complex of Netjerikhet (Firth and Quibell 1935: 141, fig. 18; Lauer 1936: 5, fig. 3) do not help to resolve Sanakht's place in the Third Dynasty since they were found in a room in the north-east corner of the North Temple, a structure which post-dates the Step Pyramid itself. In the absence of any direct evidence to link the so-called 'brick pyramid' at Abu Rawash with Sanakht (Dodson 1996: 30, after Swelim), it must be admitted that no royal tomb can be assigned to this king. Although it is perhaps unlikely that Sanakht would have failed to start work on a funerary monument, it is possible that a fundamental reorganisation of economic and administrative structures in the late Third Dynasty disrupted temporarily the sequence of imposing royal tombs (Seidlmayer 1996a: 210–12).

The most significant monument attributable without doubt to the reign of Sanakht is a pair of rock-cut inscriptions in the Wadi Maghara, Sinai (Gardiner and Peet 1952: pls I, IV). One scene shows the king wearing the white crown, preceded by the standard of Wepwawet and a shrine surmounted by a falcon. In the other scene (BM 691: Spencer 1980: 16, pls 8–9 [Cat. 18], 1993: 101, fig. 77), the king wears the red crown and is shown in the pose of smiting a captive (now lost). A fragment of vertical inscription accompanying the scene contains the oldest known reference to turquoise (*mfk3t*), making clear the reason for the Egyptians' interest in the region.

The combination of sealings in mastaba K2 at Beit Khallaf suggests that Sanakht succeeded Netjerikhet (Sethe, in Garstang 1902: 25). However, it seems certain that Netjerikhet's immediate successor was Sekhemkhet, builder of the second step pyramid complex at Saqqara. Sanakht may therefore have been Netjerikhet's second successor, and he has been identified as such by a number of scholars (for example, Helck 1984a: 375). If this theory is correct, then the rock-cut inscriptions in the Wadi Maghara would have been made in three successive reigns, marking a period of intense Egyptian activity in the turquoise mining region. In the Turin Canon, Djeserty/Sekhemkhet's successor is named as Hudjefa; but, rather than being a name, this word probably indicates no more than a gap in the records from which the list was compiled (Goedicke 1956a). Given the epigraphy of the Beit Khallaf sealing, Sanakht was probably Huni's immediate predecessor, and thus the penultimate king of the dynasty. An unnamed king in this position is given just six years by the Turin Canon. This figure seems quite plausible, in view of the fact that Sanakht is so sparsely attested.

On the basis of the Beit Khallaf seal-impression, Sanakht is almost certainly to be identified with the king whose *nswt-bity* name, written in a cartouche, was Nebka (Seidlmayer 1996b: 121, pl. 23). Nebka is attested only indirectly: in the tomb of a late Third Dynasty priest at Saqqara (Weill 1908: 262–73, pls VI–VII; Porter and Moss 1974: 500) and in the Middle Kingdom 'Tales of Wonder' preserved in Papyrus Westcar (Erman 1890: 7). The earlier reference occurs in the autobiographical inscription from the tomb of Akhetaa, an official who, amongst other positions, was 'priest of King Nebka'. The position of Nebka within the Third Dynasty depends upon the precise interpretation of Akhetaa's title. If he was a priest serving the cult of the reigning king, then Nebka must be placed at the end of the Third Dynasty. However, if Akhetaa was a priest in the mortuary cult of Nebka, this king would probably have reigned somewhat earlier in the dynasty. The reference to Nebka in Papyrus Westcar may help to resolve the problem. The tale of wonder set in his reign comes after the tale set in the reign of Netjerikhet/Djoser and before a tale set in the reign of Huni. If the order of the tales is chronological then, as suggested here, Nebka will have reigned after Netjerikhet and preceded Huni on the throne. The Turin Canon places a King Nebka – with a reign of nineteen years – before Netjerikhet, but this is flatly contradicted by the archaeological evidence. The conclusion must be that Nebka reigned towards the end of the Third Dynasty, and this agrees with the available evidence for Sanakht.

Huni and Qahedjet

With the last king of the Third Dynasty, we stand on the threshold of the Old Kingdom. Just as the reign of Khasekhemwy at the end of the Second Dynasty marks something of a turning-point, so does the reign of Huni at the end of the Third Dynasty. Substantial construction projects and the possible restructuring of regional administration paved the way for the frenzy of pyramid building characteristic of the Fourth Dynasty. However, we still know comparatively little about the king who presided over these achievements. The Turin Canon records a reign-length of twenty-four years for Huni. A shorter reign would seem unlikely, given the scale of his completed building projects.

Huni is attested on contemporary monuments by his *nswt-bity* name, written in a cartouche. Alternative readings have been suggested (for example, Goedicke 1956b); but in the absence of an agreed **transliteration**, the name recorded in the later king lists, Huni, has been adopted by Egyptologists, even though it probably represents a corruption of the original. Huni's position as last king of the Third Dynasty and Sneferu's immediate predecessor is confirmed both by Papyrus Prisse (Jéquier 1911; Gardiner 1946) and by the autobiographical inscription in the tomb of Metjen at Saqqara (Goedicke 1966).

The most impressive monument which can be attributed to Huni directly is the small granite step pyramid on the island of Elephantine. This is now recognised as the provenance of a granite cone, bearing the inscription *sšd Ḥwni*, 'Diadem of Huni', followed by the determinative of a palace. The cone suggests that Huni built a palace or building associated with the royal cult on the island (Seidlmayer 1996a, 1996b). Other small step pyramids, similar in size and construction to the Elephantine monument, have been identified at sites throughout Egypt (Dreyer and Kaiser 1980; Edwards 1993): Seila in the Fayum (Lesko 1988); Zawiyet el-Meitin in Middle Egypt; south Abydos (Dreyer and Swelim 1982); Tukh near Naqada; el-Kula near Hierakonpolis; and south Edfu. On the basis of the Elephantine monument, all but the Seila pyramid have been dated to the reign of Huni; excavations have shown that the Seila pyramid was built by his successor, Sneferu (Edwards 1993: 69). The function of the small step pyramids has been hotly debated (Seidlmayer 1996a). It is probable that stone was reserved for royal building projects at this period, and the pyramids may have served as territorial markers, perhaps associated with cult places of the king or royal estates (there was an administrative building attached to the pyramid at Elephantine). The distribution of the monuments suggests that there was one pyramid for each nome, at least in southern Upper Egypt; and it is tempting to link their construction with the reorganisation of provincial government posited for Huni's reign.

The pyramid at Maidum has been attributed to Huni, despite Middle and New Kingdom graffiti from the site which credit Sneferu with its construction. It is possible that Sneferu only finished the monument, converting it into a true pyramid (but note Edwards 1993: 93). If the initial stage of the Maidum pyramid was not intended as Huni's funerary monument the location of his tomb remains a mystery. It may have been at Saqqara, but the only obvious location – the unexcavated Ptahhotep enclosure to the west of the Netjerikhet complex – lacks any substructure, making it highly unlikely that it represents an unfinished step pyramid complex. One suggestion is that the construction of a series of small step pyramids may, in some way, have lessened the importance attached to the principal royal monument, the king's tomb. According to this view, the absence of a pyramid securely datable to the reign of Huni may be no coincidence (Seidlmayer 1996a: 210–11). An estate of Huni is listed on the Palermo Stone in the reign of the Fifth Dynasty King Neferirkara (Schäfer 1902: 40); this indicates that the memory of Huni was still revered, and at least one of his foundations still in existence, a century-and-a-half after his death.

Until some thirty years ago, the four Horus names discussed above (Netjerikhet, Sekhemkhet, Sanakht and Khaba) were the only ones attested on monuments of the Third Dynasty. Then, in the late 1960s, an unprovenanced limestone stela was purchased by the Louvre, inscribed for a king with the previously unknown Horus name Qahedjet (Vandier 1968). The iconography of the stela is of great significance for Egyptian art history, since it shows the earliest representation of a god (in this case Horus) embracing the king. The style is very reminiscent of the relief panels from the Step Pyramid of Netjerikhet; on stylistic grounds, therefore, the stela may be placed close in time to the reign of Netjerikhet. However, the execution of the carving is superior to the Netjerikhet relief panels, and the more developed iconography of the Qahedjet stela tends to favour a date towards the end of the Third Dynasty. The precise identification of the Horus Qahedjet is impossible without further epigraphic evidence, but the scholar who published the Louvre stela favours Huni in preference to the shadowy Nebka (especially if the latter is equated with the Horus Sanakht).

Irrespective of whether the Qahedjet stela was carved for Huni or for one of his predecessors, the achievements of Huni's reign are impressive, and clearly set the scene for the great flourishing of Egyptian court culture in the Old Kingdom. The structure of provincial government recorded in the tomb of Metjen probably marks a decisive break from the Early Dynastic past, and presages the absolute central control of manpower and resources reflected in the pyramid building of the Fourth Dynasty. Thus, with the reign of Huni, the formative period of Egyptian civilisation comes to an end.

PART II

THE ESTABLISHMENT OF AUTHORITY

———•◆•———

CHAPTER FOUR

ADMINISTRATION

—— •◆• ——

INTRODUCTION

An analysis of Early Dynastic administration highlights the achievement of Egypt's early kings in fashioning a system of rule that was to survive for three thousand years. The word 'administration' can be used in two senses: the entirety of the state apparatus of government, and the more detailed system of recording and distribution employed by it (Husson and Valbelle 1992: 44). This chapter will seek to investigate both aspects, presenting the evidence for the various institutions of government, their organisation, operations and personnel. The section at the end of the chapter gives outlines of some individual careers of Early Dynastic high officials, in order to illustrate the possibilities of advancement within the ranks of the government.

While several authors have written about the administrative apparatus of the Old Kingdom and later periods (for example, Helck 1954; Strudwick 1985), to date 'no systematic analysis of the political organization of the Early Dynastic period has yet been attempted' (Trigger *et al.* 1983: 56). There are several reasons for this, primarily the difficulties in deciphering the earliest stage of the Egyptian script (Kahl 1994), coupled with the paucity and imbalance of the available evidence. Important contributions have been made to our understanding of early seal-impressions and the institutions and offices to which they refer (Kaplony 1963); autobiographical tomb inscriptions from the late Third Dynasty have likewise been analysed, shedding light on administrative organisation at the end of the Early Dynastic period (Junker 1939; Goedicke 1966); and individual studies have examined the origins of particular administrative mechanisms, such as **phyle**s (Roth 1991) and the nome system (Martin-Pardey 1976). But it seems no attempt has been made to combine all the evidence from the first three dynasties in a coherent account of the early development of Egyptian administration. As we shall see, the evidence is patchy and partial; but the administration itself may not have been thorough or all-embracing (Malek 1986: 35). By taking an inclusive approach to all the potential sources, something of the nature of Early Dynastic government, its structure and priorities, can be discerned. This is an important goal, for it was under the kings of the first three dynasties that the administrative mechanisms that were to characterise the Old Kingdom were first developed. The solutions adopted by Egypt's early rulers to the problems of political and economic control laid the foundations for the govern-mental apparatus of the mature Egyptian state.

The source material and its limitations

Any investigation into the structure of the Early Dynastic administration depends to a great extent upon the numerous seal-impressions recovered from royal and private tombs of the period. For the First Dynasty, these are supplemented by inscribed labels – of wood, bone or ivory – origi-nally attached to various commodities. Private stelae from First Dynasty graves at Abydos and Saqqara record the occasional official title, or longer sequences of titles in the case of two stelae from the reign of Qaa. Many of the stone vessels found beneath the Step Pyramid bear incised or painted inscriptions which convey significant information about adminis-trative activities. The majority of the inscribed vessels have been plausibly dated to the Second Dynasty, hence plugging what otherwise would be a serious gap in the evidence for early administration. From the very end of the Third Dynasty, the tomb inscriptions of Metjen, Akhetaa and Pehernefer provide detailed accounts of the careers of three professional administrators.

Although the different categories of source material span most of the Early Dynastic period, they are very uneven and give only partial insights into the administrative apparatus of the first three dynasties (Malek 1986: 35). Seal-impressions are an invaluable source of information about early Egypt. Indeed, without an analysis of the inscriptions they provide, no comprehensive history of the Early Dynastic period could be written (Kaplony 1963, I: 3). Nevertheless, they provide only a partial glimpse of government activities. Seal-impressions represent the surviving physical traces of administrative acts involving officials of the central government, so it is not surprising that indications of provincial administration are almost entirely lacking (Martin-Pardey 1976: 34). Instead, the seal-impressions from royal and élite tombs are primarily concerned with the provisioning of the tomb in question. Hence, most of the titles preserved on these sealings refer to the administration of royal estates and founda-tions (Martin-Pardey 1976: 35) – which provided the income for main-taining mortuary cults, in the form of agricultural produce – and of the various departments of the royal treasury, which was the central institution responsible for collecting and redistributing such produce. Much can be learned about the development and administration of economic institu-tions during the course of the first two dynasties; but seal-impressions afford almost no information about other branches of the administration. We are largely ignorant about the early development of the mechanisms of political (as opposed to economic) control (Trigger *et al.* 1983: 56). In particular, the surviving sources tell us nothing about military control, the specifically coercive face of political authority which was an important aspect of Egyptian government in later periods (cf. O'Connor, in Trigger *et al.* 1983: 215). As we shall see in Chapter 6, the iconography of early kingship stressed the coercive power of the ruler. Moreover, the message of early royal artefacts such as the Scorpion macehead seems to have been directed as much towards the subject population of Egypt (*rhyt*) as the king's foreign enemies. We may infer that the authority of the Early Dynastic state was bolstered by a degree of military might, but in the absence of any contemporary evidence this must remain no more than an educated guess.

The source material changes markedly in the Third Dynasty. Very few seal-impressions have survived from tombs constructed after the reign of Netjerikhet. The practice of furnishing burials with large numbers of sealed commodities seems to have died out early in the Third Dynasty. Instead, a tomb was provided with an offering-stela depicting the items considered necessary to sustain the deceased in the afterlife. Tombs of high officials began to be inscribed with biographical texts, several of which, from the end of the Third Dynasty, illuminate both economic and provincial administration. The private stelae of the Early Dynastic period usually bear few titles. Exceptions are two stelae from the reign of Qaa, inscribed for the high officials Sabef and Merka, which preserve a range of titles associated with the court. Taken together with occasional references on seal-impressions, these stelae provide much of our information about the structure of the royal household. The inscribed stone vessels from beneath the Step Pyramid comprise a rich and varied source of Early Dynastic titles, including religious, administrative and economic offices. Because they date mostly from the Second and Third Dynasties, they cannot be used reliably to illuminate the workings of the administration in earlier periods. This is a general problem with the source material for Early Dynastic administration: although the evidence as a whole covers many branches of government, the chronological spread is very uneven, making general trends in administrative development difficult to deduce. The following picture of the administration over the whole course of the Early Dynastic period therefore relies on a certain amount of extrapolation and informed guesswork, based upon the fragments of information available.

Origins

Some time around 3100 BC, Egyptians found themselves under the control of a single, unified government, presided over by a king claiming divine authority. The various political groupings of the Predynastic period had coalesced during the period of state formation, leaving the ruler of This as king of the Two Lands. Administration was now conducted on a national scale, bringing with it advantages as well as constraints. The burden of taxation imposed by the court may have exceeded that levied by provincial rulers, and **corvée labour** for royal building projects may have made increasing demands on the rural population. But in return, a centralised administration provided a stabilising influence and, critically, a guarantee of emergency relief in times of famine through the mainte-nance of central stocks of grain (O'Connor 1972: 99).

Though the impact of political decisions was now felt country-wide, the existence of a bureaucratic apparatus was by no means a new phenom-enon. The invention of writing in the late Predynastic period was undoubt-edly a result of the need for detailed accounting and record-keeping (Postgate *et al.* 1995), as the courts of Upper Egypt intensified their involvement in specialised craft production and foreign trade. The conti-nuities between late Predynastic and Early Dynastic Egypt in other spheres – such as material culture and kingship ideology – make it likely that at least some of the institutions of the Early Dynastic administration were inherited (Roth 1991: 1–2). Indeed, the sealings from Abydos tomb B2 and the accompanying pit B0 which mention the office of *nbi* (Kaiser and Dreyer 1982: 231 fig. 9; Dreyer *et al.* 1996: 49) – connected with managing the produce of royal domains – indicate that some of the char-acteristics of Early Dynastic administration were already in existence towards the end of the Predynastic period.

It has been suggested that the system of government, during the first two dynasties at least, 'kept many of its Predynastic trappings' (Hoffman 1980: 348). In particular, the composition of the court – the highest officials surrounding the king – is likely to have been based on family ties and bonds of kinship (Hoffman 1980: 325), reflecting the social organisation of the late Predynastic period (Roth 1991: 216). However, it must be admitted that there is little explicit evidence for the operation of a strongly kinship-based system in ancient Egypt. The mortuary record of the late Predynastic period suggests a society which was already highly structured (though not necessarily along kinship lines), and the evidence for kinship as a major factor in the government of Early Dynastic Egypt is largely architectural: the use of 'palace façade' decoration on the tombs of high officials at North Saqqara. It is generally assumed that in the First Dynasty many, if not all, of the most senior administrators were royal relatives, but this cannot be established beyond doubt.

The reign of Netjerikhet at the beginning of the Third Dynasty appears to have been marked by the establishment of a more structured admin-istration, comprising different departments each with its own bureau-cracy. For the first time, all the branches of government may have been brought together in one location, at Memphis (Helck 1954: 132). The reforms may have been designed to improve efficiency, not least in the area of levying taxation. An efficient bureaucracy and an uninterrupted flow of income into government coffers would certainly have been pre-requisites for the construction of the king's Step Pyramid complex which represented an unprecedented mobilisation of manpower and resources. The administrative changes brought about at this time are reflected, above all, in the appearance of the office of vizier. The vizier was in charge of the entire apparatus of government and was personally responsible to the king. To indicate his rank, the vizier adopted old courtly titles such as *iri-p't*. Indeed, titles which, in earlier periods, had distinguished the officials in the personal service of the king now became mere ranking titles.

The priorities of Early Dynastic administration

If we follow the modern assumption that all states are motivated, if not by self-interest then at least by an institutional instinct for self-survival, and apply this to the early Egyptian state, the priorities of Early Dynastic administration become clearer. As we have seen in Chapter 2, the very process of state formation seems to have been driven – at least in part – by the desire, on the part of Upper Egypt's rulers, to gain and then control access to trade routes with lands to the north and south. Prestige commodi-ties from Syria-Palestine – and, to a lesser extent, from Nubia – were not simply coveted by the princelings of Upper Egypt, they were necessary for the conspicuous consumption which proclaimed and maintained the power of the ruling élites. It seems to have been Lower Egypt's close contacts with the Near East, coupled perhaps with its abundant and fertile agricultural land, that made it the object of Upper Egyptian expansionism during the period of state formation. Once the rulers of the Thinite region had established themselves as sovereigns of the entire country – reigning as kings of the First Dynasty – their priorities need not have changed dramatically. With the trade networks and economic resources of the whole of Egypt now at their command, the opportunities for conspicuous consumption were greater than ever. The central theme of this book is the supreme achievement of Egypt's early rulers in creating mechanisms of rule which were to survive, virtually unchanged, for the next three thousand years. These mechanisms – economic, political and ideological – enabled the king and his court to go on doing what they had done before the unification of Egypt: exercising authority and commissioning grandiose projects to emphasise that authority. At its most basic level, political power depends upon economic control. A guaranteed income from taxation is also a prerequisite for supporting specialist craftsmen and undertaking major construction projects. The economy, then, emerges as the central concern of the Early Dynastic administration, for with-out adequate command of Egypt's economic resources, the state simply could not function. Hence, the annals make frequent reference to surveys of Egypt's resources, human, agricultural and mineral. An entry from the reign of Den apparently records a census of Egypt's population, and a regular occurrence from the early Second Dynasty onwards was the biennial cattle-count (*ṯnwt*). This operation would probably have recorded all the details of Egypt's agricultural base, including the size and location of herds, the productive capacity of fields, and so forth. A later entry on the Palermo Stone indicates a more general assessment of the country's wealth, referring as it does to the 'census of gold and fields'. Government concern for economic matters is reflected in the detailed records that were kept of the height of the annual inundation, a factor which had a direct impact on agricultural yields. From the reign of Djer, nearly every year in the annals records this measurement in cubits, palms and fingers.

The following analysis of Early Dynastic administration is divided into three sections for convenience, although all three spheres of activity are closely interrelated. As the driving force behind all administrative effort, the economy and the mechanisms employed to control it are examined first. The second section considers the activities of the court which were funded by taxation of Egypt's economic resources. In a way, economic management was simply a means to an end. The end was the ability to mount impressive projects to glorify the king and maintain the status of those around him. Inevitably, close control of the economy on a national scale required a regional approach. The administrative mechanisms introduced by the early state to exploit Egypt's resources and facilitate efficient taxation led to the development of a system of regional administration. At various periods of Egyptian history, when the power of the central government waned and the influence of the regions increased correspondingly, the administrative divisions imposed upon the country by its early rulers were transformed into political divisions. The Early Dynastic origins of provincial administration are thus of great importance for the later history of Egypt. Moreover, they illustrate how the self-interested ambitions of the court were translated into mechanisms of authority which were to characterise pharaonic civilisation.

Personnel

The word 'bureaucracy' has modern connotations of unnecessary complexity and overstaffing. It is not, perhaps, an altogether inappropriate term to describe ancient Egyptian administration, since the indications are that the government apparatus was multi-faceted and employed large numbers of people, even in the Early Dynastic period. The highest office-holders were probably royal kinsmen and members of the ruling élite, the *pˤt* (Malek 1986: 35). The lower ranks would have been open to persons of non-royal birth, though it is to be expected that many of the leading families of the Predynastic period retained some degree of influence in government, even after the unification of Egypt (Kemp, personal communication). The massive Early Dynastic necropolis at Helwan – which served as the burial ground for all but the highest officials of the Memphite court and comprised in excess of 10,000 graves – gives some idea of the size of the early administration (Wilkinson 1996a).

In discussing the composition of Egyptian administration at any period, it is important to be precise in our use of vocabulary, to avoid imposing on the ancient record modern distinctions which the ancient Egyptians themselves would not have recognised (Quirke, personal communication). Particular care must be taken with the use of the word 'title', since there is a tendency to describe any appellation of officialdom or administrative authority as a title. Strictly speaking, the word 'title' should be applied only to terms which indicate rank or distinction; by contrast, most of the 'titles' found in the Early Dynastic sources were probably mere descriptive terms, indicating membership of the ruling élite or a particular branch of the administration. (Compare, for example, the terms 'civil servant' and 'First Secretary', both used to designate members of the present-day British administration; strictly speaking, only the latter is a title.) However, in the absence of sufficient evidence to distinguish between the two categories, the word 'title' is applied in the following discussion to all appellations of office, except those few terms which were clearly used as general descriptive labels. A second point to bear in mind concerns Egyptologists' use of the term 'ranking title'. There has been a tendency to apply this label to terms whose significance is not properly understood, suggesting that they were used solely to designate relative status within the administrative hierarchy rather than particular offices. This may be misguided, reflecting more on our own imperfect understanding of the Egyptian language than on the ancient Egyptian administrative system. 'Titles' are well represented on the surviving Early Dynastic administrative documents, and they even allow the management structure of some government departments to be analysed. Specific titles relating to particular duties will be discussed under their appropriate heading. Here we will restrict ourselves to the more general designations of administrative competence.

At the most basic level, all officials employed by the administration would have required a certain degree of literacy. The use of writing as a means of political control has been described as 'the key factor in the administration of Early Dynastic Egypt' (Shaw and Nicholson 1995: 15). Moreover, the very origins of writing in Egypt can be linked to a nascent national administration. Supervision and control of the economy on a national scale required detailed accounting, which could only be achieved by means of the written record (Postgate *et al.* 1995). Hence, all administrators were scribes, and the designation 'scribe' (*zḫ*) seems to have been borne by certain individuals whose low rank in the government did not permit them the use of a grander title but who were, none the less, members of the literate élite. A good example is Metjen's father, Inpuemankh, who must have lived in the second-half of the Third Dynasty. He is described by two designations, *z3b* and *zh*, 'noble, official' and 'scribe' (Goedicke 1966). (The transliteration *zh* for 'scribe' is generally preferred by modern philologists; note, however, a late Second or early Third Dynasty seal-impression from the Shunet ez-Zebib which gives a phonetic spelling *zš* [Newberry 1909: pl. XXV.XVII].) The meaning of the first, not attested before the Third Dynasty, is not entirely clear. It probably indicated membership of the administrative class. The second term indicates Inpuemankh's status as a literate administrator, but does not tell us any more about his actual responsibilities. The designation 'scribe' is first attested at the end of the First Dynasty on a private stela from Abydos dating to the reign of Semerkhet or Qaa (Petrie 1900: pl. XXXI.43). Further examples of the term occur in the reigns of Peribsen and Netjerikhet (Petrie 1901: pl. XXII.189; Lacau and Lauer 1965: 60, no. 144, respectively). Other general administrative terms attested from the Early Dynastic period include *ind-hr*, 'counsellor' (Petrie 1900: pl. XXII.30; Emery 1958: pl. 106.4); *imi-hnt*, 'he who is at the front' (Lacau and Lauer 1965: 17, no. 23); and two connected but obscure terms from the reign of Netjerikhet, *wn-ʿ* and *hrp wn-ʿ*, perhaps meaning 'assistant' and 'controller of assistants' (Lacau and Lauer 1959: 9, 76). The designation *iri-ht*, 'functionary', attested on sealings of Hetepsekhemwy and Nebra (Kaplony 1963, III: figs 294, 295; Dreyer 1993b: 11; Dreyer *et al.* 1996: 72, fig. 25, pl. 14.a), appears more frequently in the form *iri-ht-nswt*, 'concerned with the king's property' (Weill 1908: 220, 226, 256, 257–9; Junker 1939; Goedicke 1966). The precise nature of the office is not clear (for the transliteration of the title see Wood 1978: 15; contra Junker 1939: 70; cf. Goedicke 1966: 62). The term may have designated someone with particular responsibility for palace income or property, or may simply have reflected access to the ultimate source of power.

THE ECONOMY

Two different spheres of economic administration are discernible in the Early Dynastic sources. The first involves the exploitation of Egypt's agricultural resources, achieved by means of an organised network of royal foundations throughout the country. These land-holdings seem to have acted both as primary producers of agricultural income for the court and as collection points for the taxation levied by the state on all production in Egypt. They were thus the structural backbone of the economic system. The second sphere was concerned with the processing of government revenue and its redistribution to the various state operations which were funded in this way. These operations were carried out by the treasury, the government department with overall responsibility for the management of the economy. We shall examine each of these two administrative spheres in turn.

Royal foundations

Ostensibly, a new royal foundation was established by each king to support his mortuary cult. Seal-impressions from the royal and élite tombs of the Early Dynastic period name many of these foundations, most of which can be linked to a particular ruler. Whilst each king seems to have established a new mortuary foundation, it is clear that the foundations of earlier kings were frequently maintained. Hence, an estate founded by Huni was maintained as late as the Fifth Dynasty, while Netjerikhet's foundation was still recognised in the Nineteenth Dynasty. As we have seen, the surviving sources for Early Dynastic administration are undoubtedly biased, and the emphasis they give to royal foundations should be regarded with caution. None the less, royal estates clearly played an important part in the apparatus of the early state, through their primary economic role in production and collection (Helck 1954: 131). The gradual increase in the number of royal foundations must have brought a larger swathe of agricultural land directly under court control. The income from these land-holdings would probably have exceeded what was required to maintain the royal cult, and any surplus could have been used to support other government activities. The ideological justification for the creation of royal foundations remained divine kingship and its central importance to Egyptian civilisation. Just as the governing Egyptians in New Kingdom Nubia used state temples as agents of economic exploitation, so in Early Dynastic Egypt the victorious kings of the First Dynasty and their successors used the royal cult in the same way (Seidlmayer 1996b: 124–6). This method of imposing effective economic management on the country is another example of the early state's adeptness in fashioning mechanisms of rule inextricably interwoven with ideology.

In the First and Second Dynasties, most, if not all, of the royal foundations may have been located in the Delta – where they were to form the backbone for the administration of the region as a whole – and more specifically in the western half. As well as being one of the most extensive fertile areas in Egypt, it is possible that the western Delta was less densely populated and politically developed than the eastern Delta in late Predynastic times. Hence, it may have been regarded by Egypt's new rulers as 'conquered territory', ripe for annexation and economic exploitation (Wilkinson 1996b: 96). Although the deity closely associated with royal foundations on Early Dynastic sealings is Ash, in later times a local god of the western desert oases, it is unlikely that royal estates would have been located in the oases themselves (contra Helck 1954: 83).

Towards the end of the Third Dynasty, royal land-holdings seem to have been distributed more widely. We may discern the beginnings of the Old Kingdom's nome-based economic system in the distribution of the small step pyramids – markers of the royal cult – erected by Huni and his successor throughout Egypt. 'Constructing these monuments throughout the country could have served to make explicit and intelligible the ideological background of the economic demands of the state on a local level' (Seidlmayer 1996b: 122). Recent excavations in the vicinity of one of these small pyramids, at Elephantine, have revealed an administrative building of the Third Dynasty (Seidlmayer 1996a; 1996b: 121–2). Seal-impressions from the site indicate that the building was connected with the administration of the **pr-nswt** (see below), and that it employed bureaucrats with the general titles 'scribe' (*zẖ*) and 'functionary' (*iri-ẖt*). The pottery assemblage is noteworthy for its huge numbers of bread moulds and beer jars, indicating that the complex prepared and distributed basic rations to a large number of people. Both the architecture of the building and its associated artefacts point to an economic role, and more specifically to involvement in the administration of the royal estate. The complex was ideally located for such a role, being close to the river – for the loading and unloading of commodities – and near an area of cultivable land which may have belonged to the *pr-nswt*.

In addition to the *pr-nswt*, which seems to have supported the royal household directly, the Early Dynastic sources distinguish two different types of land-holding associated with the maintenance of the royal cult. The first type is denoted by a crenellated oval frame enclosing the name of the foundation. The second type is indicated by a rectangular enclosure with a small building in one corner which forms the hieroglyph *ḥwt*. For convenience, these two types of foundation will be referred to as *domains* and *estates* respectively (Figures 4.1 and 4.2). The precise difference between the two is difficult to establish from the fragmentary sources, but there are some indications that domains and estates differed in both size and function, although both contributed income to support the royal cult and other state projects. Each *domain* was established by a particular king, above all to guarantee the maintenance of his mortuary cult. The oval frame probably represents the totality of the institution in question: its land, work-force and administrative apparatus. We may envisage domains as substantial, though not necessarily contiguous, areas of farming land in the Delta, each with its dependent communities and each served by its own bureaucracy. In contrast, an *estate* (*ḥwt*) seems to have designated a more specific institution, either a particular locality or a foundation supplying a particular commodity. To confuse matters, the royal palace and royal tomb also seem to have been denoted by the term *ḥwt*. As the larger and more general economic foundations, it is domains that are attested more frequently in the inscriptions.

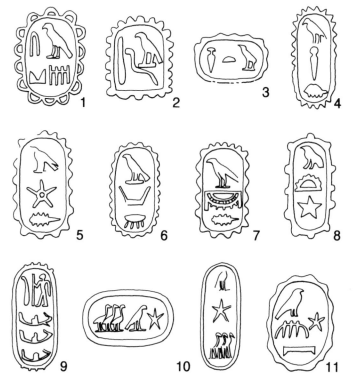

Figure 4.1 Royal domains. Names of royal foundations preserved on Early Dynastic seal-impressions from Abydos and Saqqara: (1) *Ḥr-shnti-dw* (after Petrie 1901: pl. XIX.153); (2) *W3d-Ḥr* (after Petrie 1900: pl. XVIII.5); (3) *tpi-t-w* (after Petrie 1900: pl. XXI.22); (4) *Ḥr-tpi-ḥt* (after Petrie 1901: pl. XVIII.139); (5) *Ḥr-sb3-ḥt* (after Petrie 1900: pl. XXVI.63); (6) *Ḥr-dsr-ḥt* (after Petrie 1900: pl. XXVIII.76); (7) *Ḥr-nbw-ḥt* (after Petrie 1900: pl. XXIX.84); (8) *Ḥr-ḥʿ-sb3* (after Kaplony 1963, III: fig. 281); (9) *wi3w-iti*(?) (after Petrie 1901: pl. XXII.179); (10) two writings of *Ḥr-sb3-b3w* (after Kaplony 1963, III: fig. 303; and Petrie 1901: pl. XXIII.200); (11) *Ḥr-sb3-ḥnti-pt* (after Kaplony 1963, III: fig. 304). Not to same scale.

Consequently, we know rather more about the administration of domains than of estates.

Domains

The oval frames denoting royal domains were once identified as vine-yards, because of the close association of one such foundation of Netjerikhet with wine production. However, it has become clear that they represent a more general type of royal land-holding – often, though by no means exclusively, associated with vineyards (Kaplony 1963, I: 123) – established to support royal activities, especially the king's mortuary cult.

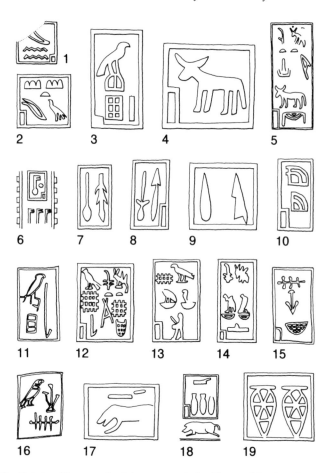

Figure 4.2 Estates. Names of estates connected with provisioning the royal tomb, preserved on Early Dynastic seal-impressions and inscribed stone vessels from Abydos and Saqqara: (1) ḥwt ḥnn (after Emery 1954: 118, fig. 159); (2) ḥwt Zmti-gstw(?) (after Kaplony 1963, III: fig. 182); (3) ḥwt Ḥr-P (after Kaplony 1963, III: fig. 295); (4) ḥwt iḥw (after Petrie 1900: pl. XX.15); (5) ḥwt iḥw-nbw nswt-bity Mr-(p-)bi3 (after Petrie 1900: pl. XXVIII.73); (6) ḥwt (s)nṯr nṯrw(?) (after Kaplony 1963, III: fig. 749); (7) (8) (9) estate of unknown reading, attested in the reigns of Den, Anedjib and Nebra (after Kaplony 1963, III: figs 249, 251, 264); (10) ḥwt ipti(?) (after Petrie 1900: pl. XXVIII.77); (11) ḥwt p-Ḥr-msn (after Petrie 1900: pl. IX.1); (12) ḥwt p-Ḥr-msn nswt-bity Mr-p-bi3 (after Petrie 1900: pl. XXVI.58); (13) ḥwt p-Ḥr[-msn] iri-nbty (after Petrie 1900: pl. XXVIII.72); (14) ḥwt nswt-bity nbti Ḥtp (Kaplony 1963, III: fig. 282); (15) ḥwt z3-ḥ3-nb (after Petrie 1900: pl. IX.2); (16) ḥwt z3-ḥ3-Ḥr (after Lacau and Lauer 1959: pl. 6, no. 27); (17) (18) department responsible for raising (and slaughtering?) pigs (after Petrie 1900: pls XXII.33, XXVI.60); (19) unidentified department denoted by two sealed jars (after Petrie 1900: pl. XXI.29). Not to same scale.

It appears that each king of the Early Dynastic period founded a new domain, the name of which usually expressed an aspect of the god Horus (Kaplony 1963, I: 104).

The earliest attested domain, *Ḥr-sḫnti-ḏw*, 'Horus who advances the mountain (?)', first appears on a sealing from the reign of Djer (Petrie 1901: pl. XVI.124). It was maintained throughout the following reign under the management of the same individual (Amka), and survived into the reign of Den when it was successively the responsibility of Ankhka (Emery 1938: 64, fig. 25, 1949: 75, fig. 37), Medjedka (Emery 1958: pls 80–1) and Hemaka (Emery 1938: 62, fig. 19, 1958: pl. 8.21). For some reason, the tomb of Merneith contained no references to *Ḥr-sḫnti-ḏw*, a fact which is of clear, but unknown, significance (Kaplony 1963, I: 92). A seal-impression from the reign of Djet mentions a second royal domain, *W3ḏ-Ḥr*, 'Horus flourishes' (Petrie 1900: pl. XVIII.5; Emery 1954: 116, fig. 50). Given the striking similarity between this name and the king's Horus name (*W3ḏ*), the domain was probably Djet's own foundation, though it was maintained into the succeeding reign. Throughout its existence, *W3ḏ-Ḥr* was apparently administered by the same official, Sekhemkasedj. The regency of Merneith, early in the reign of Den, saw the foundation of two new domains. The first, *tpi-t-w*, is rarely attested (Petrie 1900: pl. XXI.22); the second, *Ḥr-tpi-ḥt*, 'Horus, first of the corporation (of gods)' (Petrie 1900: pl. XXI.23), continued to flourish throughout Den's majority, being administered by the high official Hemaka (for example, Petrie 1900: pl. XXV.53–6; Emery 1938: 63, figs 21, 23). After the death of Den, each of his successors founded a new domain. The one established by Anedjib was called *Ḥr-sb3-ḥt*, 'Horus, star of the corporation' (Petrie 1900: pl. XXVI.63; Emery 1949: 95, fig. 55); Semerkhet's foundation was named *Ḥr-ḏsr-ḥt*, 'Horus, holy of the corporation' (Petrie 1900: pl. XXVIII.76); Qaa's domain was called *Ḥr-nbw-ḥt*, 'Horus, the gold one of the corporation' (Petrie 1900: pl. XXIX.82–4; Emery 1958: pl. 106.11). Hence, the three foundations of the late First Dynasty seem to have been named according to a convention. A new naming scheme appears to have been introduced at the beginning of the Second Dynasty. Hetepsekhemwy called his domain *Ḥr-ḫʿ-sb3*, 'Horus risen as a star' (Kaplony 1963, III: fig. 281). No domains are attested from the reigns of Nebra and Ninetjer, but this is probably due to the general paucity of inscriptions from the early Second Dynasty. It is highly likely that both these kings established their own domains or, at the very least, maintained the domains founded by their predecessors. The record becomes clear again towards the end of the Second Dynasty. The general non-conformity of Peribsen's reign is reflected in the unusual name given to his domain, *wi3w-iti* (?), 'boats of the sovereign' (Petrie 1901: pl. XXII.178–80). This foundation was maintained by his successor Khasekhemwy (Kaplony 1963, III: fig. 297), who also founded a new domain with a more traditional name, *Ḥr-sb3-b3w*, 'Horus, the star of souls'

(Petrie 1901: pl. XXIII.199–200). Finally, at the beginning of the Third Dynasty, Netjerikhet established a domain by the name of *Ḥr-sb3-ḫnti-pt*, 'Horus, the foremost star of the sky' (Kaplony 1963, III: fig. 304). This was to survive longer than any previous royal foundation: at the end of the Third Dynasty it was administered by Pehernefer (Junker 1939), and it was still in existence in the Nineteenth Dynasty, an amazing 1400 years after Netjerikhet's death (Sethe, in Garstang 1902: 21).

THE ADMINISTRATION OF DOMAINS

Three principal titles were connected with the administration of domains, *ʿd-mr*, *ḥrp* and *ḥri-wd3*. Many, if not all, of the officials delegated to administer royal foundations were probably royal relatives (Malek 1986: 35). The titles *ʿd-mr* and *ḥrp* are first attested in the reign of Djet (Petrie 1900: pls XVIII.6, XIX.8 and 1901: pl. XXXI.8, respectively); *ḥri-wd3* appears in the reign of Den (Petrie 1900: pl. XXIV.47). For some domains, only one title is attested; other domains appear in combination with two or more titles. So it is not entirely clear what distinguished the three offices. Evidence from other areas of the administration suggests that the *ʿd-mr* may have been the administrator with overall control of the domain's land-holdings (since *ʿd-mr* later came to designate a district administrator with a particular geographical responsibility). An exact translation of the title is difficult. Any lasting connection with irrigation would seem to be ruled out by the titles *ʿd-mr zmit*, 'administrator of the desert', and *ʿd-mr ḫ3st*, 'administrator of the hill-country', attested from the reigns of Qaa and Netjerikhet respectively (Gardiner and Peet 1955: 53; Emery 1958: 31, pl. 39; cf. Martin-Pardey 1976: 44). Perhaps by the end of the First Dynasty the title had lost its original meaning and had simply come to designate an administrative position (Martin-Pardey 1976: 44). The *ḥrp* ('controller') may have been in charge of the personnel belonging to and/or employed by the domain. The *ḥri-wd3* may have exercised a more executive power, implementing royal wishes and decrees with regard to the operations of the domain. Towards the end of the Second Dynasty, this distinction of roles seems to have become blurred: no *ḥrp* of a domain is attested after the reign of Peribsen, and the last *ḥri-wd3* of a domain is attested in the reign of Netjerikhet (Kaplony 1963, III: fig. 304). It was the office of *ʿd-mr* which survived throughout the Early Dynastic period.

Several other, more minor, titles connected with domain administration are attested in Early Dynastic inscriptions, particularly from the first-half of the First Dynasty. The title *ḥri-wd3 ḥrpw* is confined to the reign of Den (Petrie 1900: pl. XXIV.47–8, 1901: pl. XX.153; Emery 1958: pls 8.21, 79.16–17), and seems to indicate an official with delegated authority to implement decisions. The exact translation and significance of many other titles remains obscure. For example, the title written with the hieroglyph of a swimming man has been read *nbi* (from the verb 'to swim'), but the meaning of this in the context of domain administration is unclear, unless it involves a pun on the word *nb*, 'lord'. An ingenious, though speculative, suggestion makes a connection between the title *nbi* and the word for 'smelter' (also *nbi*), known from Old Kingdom scenes of metalworkers. If both words share a common derivation, the root meaning of *nbi* may be 'to pour'. In this case, the title may have designated the official who actually filled containers with produce (by pouring) from a given domain (Kaplony 1963, I: 126). A compound title, *ḥrp nbi*, is more common from the reign of Den onwards (for example, Petrie 1901: pl. XIX.146–50). Difficulties also surround the meaning of the title read as *nḥnw* (for example, Petrie 1901: pl. XVI.122) (or *ḥrp nḥnw* in the reign of Den [for example, Petrie 1901: pl. XVIII.142–3]). A connection with the town of Nekhen (Hierakonpolis) seems unlikely, given the contexts in which the title occurs, as does a link with the word *nḥn*, 'fortress'. Rather easier to understand are the pair of titles *ḥri-ib* (Petrie 1901: pl. XIX.153) and *ḥrp ḥri-ib* (for example, Petrie 1901: pl. XVIII.140). They refer to a position 'at the heart of' the system and probably designated senior officials within the administration of domains.

A notable feature of the administration during the reign of Den is the preponderance of titles compounded with the word *ḥrp* 'controller'. Examples already quoted are *ḥrp nbi*, *ḥrp nḥnw* and *ḥrp ḥri-ib*. Whether the appearance of such compound titles indicates administrative reforms cannot be proven, but other evidence suggests that Den's reign was a period of innovation.

By the reign of Peribsen, only the titles *ḥrp*, *ḥrp ḥri-ib*, *ḥri-wdȝ* and *ʿḏ-mr* remained in the context of domain administration (Kaplony 1963, I: 155). Only the last survived into the Third Dynasty. This may suggest a rationalisation of domain administration, possibly by discontinuing some of the ancient (honorific?) titles in favour of a more explicit and streamlined structure.

Estates

Specific estates are attested from the reign of Djet onwards. Some are impossible to identify with certainty; others probably indicate individual localities, specialised production centres, or particular institutions closely associated with the king and his household. The identity of the earliest known estate, *ḥwt ḥnn* (Emery 1954: 118, fig. 159), is unclear, as is the foundation named after King Den, *ḥwt Zmti-gstw*(?) (Emery 1958: pl. 81.36). A seal-impression of Nebra may record an estate in the vicinity of Buto, *ḥwt Ḥr-P* (Kaplony 1963, III: fig. 295). Certainly, Buto was an important centre from Predynastic times and undoubtedly maintained close ideological links with the monarchy throughout the Early Dynastic period. A sealing from the tomb of Merneith mentions *ḥwt iḥw* (Petrie 1900: pl. XX.15), and judging by the much later inscriptions of Metjen and Pehernefer, this may have been the name of a particular locality in the western Delta, perhaps in the vicinity of Kom el-Hisn (Wenke and Brewer 1996: 268). The Delta seems to have been closely associated with cattle rearing – as reflected in the prevalence of cattle amongst the emblems of the Delta nomes – and *ḥwt iḥw* may have been the most important cattle-producing centre of early times. A further connection between the western Delta and cattle rearing may be indicated by the herds depicted on the so-called 'Libyan palette' (Wenke and Brewer 1996: 268). Another estate connected with cattle, 'the estate of the golden cattle of the dual king' (*ḥwt iḥw-nbw nswt-bity Mr-(p-)bi3*) is mentioned on sealings of Anedjib from Abydos (Petrie 1900: pl. XXVIII.73–4). An estate perhaps set up to supply the court with a particular commodity is the foundation called *ḥwt (s)nṯr nṯrw* (?), 'the estate of natron of the gods', mentioned in an inscription from the reign of Ninetjer (Kaplony 1963, III: fig. 749). A further estate of unknown reading is mentioned on sealings of Den and Anedjib, and may still have been in existence during the reign of Nebra (Kaplony 1963, III: figs 249, 251, 264).

A seal-impression from the tomb of Semerkhet makes reference to *ḥwt ipti* (?) (Petrie 1900: pl. XXVIII.77). This may be an estate connected with the queen's household, since the word *ipt* means 'harem palace'. The institution called *ḥwt p-Ḥr-msn* (for example, Lacau and Lauer 1959: pl. 4 no. 21) – also read *ḥwt p-Ḥr-wʿj* (Dreyer *et al.* 1996: 71) – has been identified as the royal palace, perhaps located in Buto for the king as ruler of Lower Egypt (Weill 1961: 135). It is mentioned in inscriptions of the First, Second and Third Dynasties (Lacau and Lauer 1965: 80, no. 216; Dreyer *et al.* 1996: 76, fig. 28, pl. 15.b left, and 72, fig. 25, pl. 14.a). In the reigns of Anedjib and Semerkhet, the estate – perhaps representing the entirety of the palace, its lands and income – bore the king's name: *ḥwt p-Ḥr-msn nswt-bity Mr-p-bi3* and *ḥwt p-Ḥr[-msn] iri-nbty*, respectively (Petrie 1900: pls XXVI.58–60, XXVIII.72). A different, though perhaps related, estate is known from the reign of Hetepsekhemwy at the beginning of the Second Dynasty, once again bearing the king's name: *ḥwt nswt-bity nbty Ḥtp* (Kaplony 1963, III: figs 281–2). The other *ḥwt* closely associated with the king, the *ḥwt z3-ḥ3-nb/ḥwt z3-ḥ3-Ḥr*, appears in inscriptions from the end of the First Dynasty (Petrie 1900: pls IX.1–2, XXX; Lacau and Lauer 1959: pl. 6 nos 26–9; Dreyer *et al.* 1996: 75, pl. 15.b right). It too has been interpreted as the royal residence (Weill 1961: 141), but more likely refers to the royal tomb as a separate institution with its own economic demands and administrative apparatus (Roth 1991: 166–8).

The treasury and its activities

We have seen how Egypt's agricultural resources were exploited by the court through the mechanism of royal foundations. The actual collection of revenue, its storage, processing and redistribution was the responsibility of a separate institution, the treasury (Figure 4.3). This was the government department which directly managed the income of the state, and as such stood at the very centre of the administration. It was the treasury that assessed and levied taxation, filled the government coffers with agricultural produce, and supplied the various branches of the court with revenue to fund their activities and commodities to sustain their employees.

Taxation and collection

Ink inscriptions on pottery vessels from the late Predynastic period make it clear that, right from the beginning of the Egyptian state, taxation was levied separately on the two halves of the country (Figure 4.4). Inscriptions on vessels from the tomb of 'Ka' at Abydos mention either Lower Egyptian or Upper Egyptian revenue (Petrie 1902: pls I–III). A similar division in the collection of produce is attested in the following reigns of Narmer and Aha (Kaplony 1964: figs 1061, 1063; Emery 1939: pls 14 [sic], 20–2). The separate collection of revenue from Upper and Lower Egypt is also indicated by a sealing of Peribsen which mentions the seal-bearer of the Lower Egyptian delivery (*ḥtmw inw-Ḥ3*), probably the individual responsible for the treasury's income from Lower Egypt (Petrie 1901: pl. XXII.184, 186). As well as highlighting the duality which pervaded Egyptian thought, this binary division in the treasury's operations probably reflects geographical and topographical factors. The physical difference between Upper and Lower Egypt would have made the collection of agricultural produce a very different undertaking in each region. In Upper Egypt, where the fields are distributed along the narrow floodplain, gathering revenue could have been achieved by a fleet of barges cruising slowly up- or downstream. By contrast, access to the fields of Lower Egypt, spread throughout the Delta, would have been far more difficult. It is quite likely that central collection points would have been established at strategic locations, probably on the major Nile branches. In short, the collection of revenue by the central treasury would have been most efficiently organised by dividing the country into two halves.

This practice may be reflected in the two different names given to the treasury in the Early Dynastic period. Inscriptions mention either the *pr-ḥḏ*, 'white house', or the *pr-dšr*, 'red house'. The former seems to be the earlier name for the treasury and is first attested early in the reign of Den, on seal-impressions from the tomb of Merneith (Petrie 1900: pls XXII.36, XXIII.40). Towards the end of the First Dynasty, for reasons

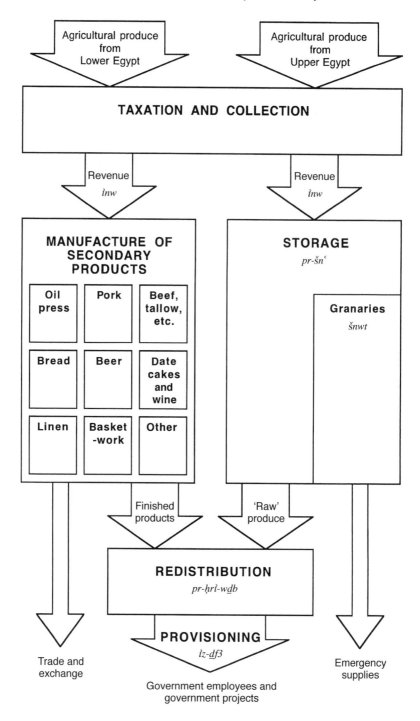

Figure 4.4 Taxation. Ink inscriptions of King 'Ka' on cylinder vessels from his tomb complex at Abydos. They record produce received by the royal treasury through separate taxation of (1) Lower Egypt and (2) Upper Egypt (after Petrie 1902: pls I.2, III.30). These inscriptions provide evidence for the early division of Egypt into two units for administrative purposes.

which are unclear, the name for the treasury was changed to *pr-dšr*. This institution is attested in the reigns of Anedjib (Petrie 1900: pl. XXVII.68), Qaa (Petrie 1900: pls XXIX.85, XXX) and Ninetjer (Lacau and Lauer 1959: pl. 14 no. 70; Kaplony 1963, III: figs 746, 748). With the accession of Sekhemib/Peribsen, the name reverted to *pr-ḥd* (Petrie 1901: pls XXI.167, 169, and XXII.182, 183), only to be changed back to *pr-dšr* under Khasekhemwy (Petrie 1901: pl. XXIII.191, 192, 196). The name remained *pr-dšr* during the reign of Netjerikhet (Kaplony 1963, III: fig. 318), and was changed for the last time under his successor Sekhemkhet to *prwi-ḥd*, 'the two white houses' (Goneim 1957: 14–15), perhaps reflecting an amalgamation of two previously separate institutions. Because the colours white and red are also the colours of the Upper and Lower Egyptian crowns respectively, it is tempting to see the *pr-ḥd* as an Upper Egyptian institution, the *pr-dšr* as its Lower Egyptian counterpart. The two names would then reflect the logical division of the treasury's operations into two halves. However, the two seem never to have coexisted, so the preference given

Figure 4.3 The treasury and its functions. The chart shows the principal operations carried out by the treasury in the Early Dynastic period (based upon information from contemporary sources: seal-impressions, inscribed stone vessels, and the Third Dynasty tomb inscription of Pehernefer).

to one name or the other might reflect the central administration's shifting centre of gravity. The initial change from *pr-ḥd* to *pr-dšr* might indicate a relocation of the state redistributive apparatus to Memphis in the latter part of the First Dynasty. The continued use of the name *pr-dšr* by the kings of the early Second Dynasty certainly complements the location of their tombs at Saqqara and the general Lower Egyptian emphasis of the court at this time. The change of name back to the older *pr-ḥd* under Sekhemib/Peribsen ties in with the Upper Egyptian emphasis of his reign: Peribsen re-adopted Abydos as the site of the royal mortuary complex and he is attested only in Upper Egypt. The final change in nomenclature (to *prwi-ḥd*) under Sekhemkhet possibly indicates an ideological compromise, reconciling the competing traditions of Upper and Lower Egypt in a new, unified institution.

Storage

Inscriptions of the Second Dynasty mention a sub-department of the treasury called the *pr-šnꜥ* (Lacau and Lauer 1959: pl. 18 no. 90; Kaplony 1963, III: fig. 367). The derivation of the word is not altogether clear, but it seems to have been either the department responsible for (corvée?) labour or, more likely perhaps, the department charged with the storage of agricultural produce prior to its redistribution. The *pr-šnꜥ* would then have comprised large-scale storage facilities and would probably have managed the government surpluses held in long-term storage – for example, the 'buffer' stocks of grain – as well as the produce received in the form of taxation and later redistributed.

Cereals were probably the staple crops of Egyptian agriculture in the Early Dynastic period, as in later times, and grain supplies must have lain at the heart of the treasury's operations. The storage of large stocks of grain was a vital necessity, not only to pay the court itself with its hundreds of dependent officials, but also to guard against years with poor harvests. At such times, the emergency supplies held by the government provided the only security for ordinary Egyptians, the vast majority of whom were peasant farmers. The ability of the government to provide a degree of economic security must have brought real benefits to the Egyptian population, and would have been one of the most tangible benefits of a united country with a centrally controlled economy. Curiously, the central government granaries are not explicitly attested before the Third Dynasty, although they must have existed from the very beginning of the Egyptian state, perhaps under a different department of the treasury. They may have been an integral part of the *pr-ḥd/pr-dšr* in the first two dynasties, only to be given separate status at the beginning of the Third Dynasty. Granaries are mentioned on a seal-impression of Sanakht from Beit Khallaf (Garstang 1902: pl. 19.7; Seidlmayer 1996b: pl. 23), while the official Pehernefer was 'overseer of all the king's granaries' (*imi-r3 šnwt nb nt nswt*) at the end of the Third Dynasty (Junker 1939).

Redistribution

Another institution closely connected with the operations of the treasury was the *pr-ḥri-wḏb*, the 'house of redistribution' (sometimes translated 'house of largesse'). This is attested from the reign of Khasekhemwy (Petrie 1901: pl. XXIII.197) and is mentioned quite frequently in official sources of the Third Dynasty (for example, Junker 1939). The *pr-ḥri-wḏb* was probably the department of the treasury directly responsible for the redistribution of agricultural produce to recipients throughout Egypt, including state employees and provincial cults (Gardiner 1938: 85–9; Malek 1986: 35; but note Warburton 1997: 72). Standing at the centre of the state economic apparatus, the *pr-ḥri-wḏb* must have been a key department of the Early Dynastic administration.

Provisioning

An important activity connected with the collection and redistribution of income is attested from the reign of Sekhemib/Peribsen. This is *iz-ḏf3*, the 'provisioning department' (Petrie 1901: pl. XXI.165). It seems to have acted as a constituent department of the treasury, whether the *pr-ḥḏ* under Sekhemib/Peribsen (Petrie 1901: pl. XXI.167, 174, pl. XXII.183) or the *pr-dšr* under his successor Khasekhemwy (Petrie 1901: pl. XXIII.192). A provisioning department of the *pr-nswt* is also attested in the reign of Khasekhemwy (Petrie 1901: pl. XXIII.201), indicating that this administrative innovation was not restricted to the management of state income but was applied equally to the personal economic resources of the king. At the end of the Second and beginning of the Third Dynasty, seal-impressions mention a provisioning department connected with the vineyards of Memphis (Kaplony 1963, III: figs 310, 318).

Manufacture of secondary products

The treasury was not only responsible for the collection, storage and redistribution of income in the form of agricultural produce, it also controlled the manufacture of secondary products from these primary commodities. Products such as oil and meat, bread and beer, were required for the provisioning of the royal household and the court in general. The manufacture of secondary products seems to have been divided amongst a number of specialist departments. Some of these are attested from the First and Second Dynasties. Many more are listed in the tomb inscription of Pehernefer at the end of the Third Dynasty.

The earliest attested specialist department is the oil-press, named on an ebony label of Den from Abydos (Petrie 1900: pl. XV.16). Many of the so-called year labels of First Dynasty kings were originally attached to jars of oil. The oil-press department of the treasury would have undertaken the processing of this valuable commodity. Also from the reign of Den, an unidentified department denoted by two sealed jars is mentioned on several seal-impressions. It probably had some connection with the production of commodities, but it is impossible to be more precise.

A department responsible for raising (and slaughtering?) pigs is mentioned on a sealing from the tomb of Merneith (Petrie 1900: pl. XXII.33) and on another from the reign of Anedjib (Petrie 1900: pl. XXVI.60). A further reference to meat production is a seal-impression from the reign of Peribsen which seems to have been made by the 'seal-bearer of the daily meat ration' (transliteration uncertain) (Petrie 1901: pl. XXII.185). The inscription of Pehernefer mentions a 'house of beef-fat' (*pr-ꜥd*) as a department of the treasury (Junker 1939), perhaps indicating that products such as tallow were the responsibility of a separate operation. Meat must have been a prestigious commodity, beyond the means of many ordinary people. It comes as little of a surprise, therefore, that the government had its own slaughterhouses and that meat production was delegated to a specific department of the treasury.

The specialist departments listed in Pehernefer's tomb inscription (Junker 1939) include those concerned with the production of the primary staples of the ancient Egyptian diet, bread and beer. The manufacture of bread was divided between the millers and the bakers. These tasks were subdivided in turn. The millers were split into at least two different departments, responsible for the milling of different grades of flour: flour to be made into *ḥt3* bread in one case, wheat-grain (*bi*) in another. Two different categories of baker are attested, *rtḥ* bakers and *fsw* bakers, although it is not entirely clear how their functions differed. These two types of baker are named again in the Old Kingdom tomb of Kaninisut at Giza, where they are shown bringing offerings of bread to the tomb owner (Junker 1939). The word *fsw* (or its variant *psj*) is the most common verb associated with bread manufacture (Verhoeven 1984: 85) and seems to have been the general term for 'bake', 'prepare (bread)'; it could refer to the baking of bread directly over a fire or in a mould (Verhoeven 1984: 208). The meaning of the rarer term *rtḥ* is less clear, though a connection with bread used for cultic purposes is possible (Verhoeven 1984: 169). Perhaps the two types of baker mentioned in Pehernefer's inscription were responsible for baking bread for cultic purposes on the one hand and bread for normal domestic consumption on the other. The brewers seem to have been divided on geographical lines into those attached to the Lower Egyptian storage facility (*pr-šnꜥ Mḥw*) and those attached to the Upper Egyptian storage facility (*pr-šnꜥ Hnwt*).

The processing of dates into sweet cakes and/or date wine was the prerogative of a separate department, as was the preparation and manufacture of linen and basketwork. Old Kingdom tomb scenes indicate that flax was an important crop in ancient Egypt, and this is reflected in the careful organisation surrounding the processing of this resource. The raw flax was supervised by one department (*ḥwt mḥ'*), the fulling (washing) of the flax by a second (*ḥwt ḥmwt*), and the final manufacture of linen by a third (*ḥwt šm't*). Basketwork, using the abundant supplies of reeds from the Nile valley, was organised into a further specialist unit (*ḥwt m3t*).

The departments of the treasury attested in the tomb of Pehernefer thus reflect the principal crops of ancient Egypt, and emphasise the importance of bread and beer in the Egyptian diet, even the diet of the court.

Treasury officials

The earliest attested title connected with the treasury is an 'official of the white-house' (*ḥri-' pr-ḥḏ*) early in the reign of Den (Petrie 1900: pls XXII.35, XXIII.40). In the Third Dynasty, the official with similar responsibility was the 'overseer' (*imi-r3 pr-ḥḏ*), a title borne by Nefer, Meri (Weill 1908: 236–42, pl. IV; Helck 1954: 61) and Pehernefer (Junker 1939). Pehernefer also held three other titles connected with the treasury: *iri-ḫt pr-ḥḏ*, *shd iri-ḫt pr-ḥḏ* and *ḥri-sḏ3t pr-ḥḏ*. The first of these seems to indicate merely a functionary of the treasury, the second a higher level of official with a supervisory role over other employees. The third title probably designated the seal-bearer, an important role in ancient Egyptian administration; it was the bearer of the seal who, as the representative of authority, had ultimate responsibility for the daily management of a particular institution. However, the *ḥri-sḏ3t pr-ḥḏ* does not seem to have been at the very top of the treasury hierarchy; this position was occupied by the king's personal representative, the *ḥtmw-bity*, 'royal seal-bearer' (also translated as 'royal chancellor'). This title is sometimes rendered as 'chancellor of the king of Lower Egypt'. Rather than being a geographical designation, however, it is more likely that the word *bity* refers to the secular role of the king as head of state and government (see Chapter 6). Two 'royal seal-bearers' are known from the reign of Den: Setka (Emery 1958: pl. 81.37), and the more famous Hemaka (Emery 1938: 64, fig. 24), whose status is reflected in his huge palace-façade tomb at North Saqqara, equipped with a wealth of grave goods. The pre-eminent position of the *ḥtmw-bity* in the royal administration (Malek 1986: 35) is further illustrated by the fact that the title was borne by Imhotep, famed as Djoser's chief minister and the architect of the Step Pyramid complex. In ancient Egypt, all political authority derived ultimately from the king. Hence, the individual who carried the king's own seal was the representative and agent of the supreme power in the land. The title of *ḥtmw-bity* must therefore have carried considerable symbolic as well as executive authority. A seal-impression from the reign of Peribsen gives a title which may be read as *ḫtmw-nswt* (Petrie 1901: pl. XXI.164). (The proposed reading of this title on a sealing from the Shunet ez-Zebib [Newberry 1909: pl. XXV.XVII] seems rather more doubtful since the '*ḫtmw*' sign looks indistinguishable from an *ankh*.) If so, this could be interpreted as an explicitly Upper Egyptian alternative to the more usual title *ḫtmw-bity* and would provide yet another indication of the emphasis placed upon Upper Egypt and Upper Egyptian titles by Peribsen. (The other possible reading of the title, *ḫtmw Šmˁ*, 'seal-bearer of Upper Egypt', would have similar connotations.) Two further seal-bearers are attested during the reign of Peribsen, a seal-bearer of the daily meat ration and a seal-bearer of the Lower Egyptian delivery (see above), emphasising the important role played by such officials in the Egyptian administrative system.

We know comparatively little about the administration of the state granaries, and what evidence there is comes from the Third Dynasty. A 'controller' (*ḫrp*) of granaries is mentioned on a sealing of the reign of Sanakht from Beit Khallaf (Garstang 1902: pl. 19.7; Seidlmayer 1996b: pl. 23), whilst at the end of the dynasty Pehernefer was in overall control of the central grain stocks in his capacity as 'overseer of all the king's granaries' (*imi-r3 šnwt nb nt nswt*).

The redistributive function of the treasury involved a number of different officials. A sealing from the reign of Khasekhemwy mentions an 'executive of the house of redistribution' (*ḫri-wḏ3 pr-ḥri-wḏb*) who was probably in overall charge (Weill 1908: 102). The other titles come from Third Dynasty sources and seem to indicate different ranks within the department: *zḫ pr-ḥri-wḏb*, a scribal post (Weill 1908: 226); *wḏ-mdw (pr)-ḥri-wḏb*, a title borne by Akhetaa, possibly denoting an official with decision-making authority (Weill 1908: 262–73); *sḥḏ pr-ḥri-wḏb*, a supervisory role, performed by Metjen (Goedicke 1966); and *imi-r3 pr-ḥri-wḏb*, the 'overseer' of the department, a position held by Pehernefer (Junker 1939). The obscure 'estate of life' (*ḥwt ˁnḫ*) seems to have had its own redistributive function at the end of the Third Dynasty: in addition to his many other titles, Akhetaa held the post of *ḥri-wḏb ḥwt ˁnḫ*, 'head of redistribution of the estate of life(?)' (Weill 1908: 262–73). In later periods, the 'house of life' (*pr-ˁnḫ*) was the name given to the temple institution where religious texts were composed and copied, but the Early Dynastic *ḥwt ˁnḫ* probably performed a different role.

The provisioning department would clearly have required a literate bureaucracy to keep detailed accounts of income and outgoings, and a 'scribe of the provisioning department' (*zḫ iz-ḏf3*) is attested from the reign of Peribsen (Petrie 1901: pl. XXI.166).

The specialist departments of the treasury which processed the agricultural produce and manufactured secondary products were each

controlled by an 'overseer' (*imi-r3*), except for the bakers and date proces-
sors who were under the supervision of 'controllers' (*ḫrp*). At the end of
the Third Dynasty, certain vineyards were also administered by Pehernefer
in his capacity as 'controller' (*ḫrp*). In general, the usual title for an official
at the head of a department or operation during the Third Dynasty seems
to have been *imi-r3*, whereas *ḫrp* appears to have been used to refer to
an individual with a supervisory role over other employees.

The pr-nswt

Although in theory all land probably belonged to the king, in practice a
distinction was made between state income and the king's private income.
From the reign of Djet, inscriptions attest, in parallel with the *pr-ḥḏ/
pr-dšr*, a separate department of the administration responsible for the
personal estates and income of the king (Petrie 1900: pl. XXXI.8). This
institution, the *pr-nswt*, was presumably concerned with supporting the
king, the royal family and the royal retinue, as distinct from royal building
projects which were the responsibility of the central government. The *pr-
nswt* was probably under direct royal control (Husson and Valbelle 1992:
29), in contrast to the more outlying royal domains and estates which were
administered on behalf of the king. Unlike these foundations, little is
known about the composition, structure and organisation of the *pr-nswt*.
At the end of the Third Dynasty, the inscription of Metjen mentions a
parallel institution serving the queen mother (*pr-mwt-nswt*) (Goedicke
1966). (Note that a possible identification of the *pr-nswt* as the palace
buildings seems to be ruled out by explicit references to 'the palace' ['ḥ]
in Early Dynastic titles: see below.)

The *pr-nswt* seems to have had a separate administration. Three titles
referring to the *pr-nswt* are known from the Early Dynastic period: 'controller' (*ḫrp*) in the reign of Djet (Petrie 1900: pl. XXXI.8); 'companion'
(*smr*) on the stela of Sabef from the reign of Qaa (Petrie 1900: pl. XXX);
and 'servant/employee' (*ḥm*) in the late Third Dynasty (Weill 1908:
262–73; Goedicke 1966). Both Akhetaa and Metjen bore the last title,
suggesting that it enjoyed a certain status due to its close connection with
the person of the king. Metjen was also a 'servant/employee' (*ḥm*) of the
queen mother's estate.

THE ACTIVITIES OF THE COURT

Royal works

The effective management of royal building projects – mortuary complexes and state-sponsored temple construction – must have required a

substantial administrative apparatus. Unfortunately, very little evidence survives from the Early Dynastic period concerning the organisation and administration of these activities. What sources there are date exclusively to the Third Dynasty, so that we know nothing of how royal construction projects were organised during the first two dynasties. Several individual craftsmen are mentioned in inscriptions of Netjerikhet's reign, including a controller of craftsmen (*ḥrp ḥmww*) (Lacau and Lauer 1965: 64, no.156), an inspector of masons (*sḥd mḏḥw*) (Weill 1908: 180; Kaplony 1963, III: fig. 324) and a royal mason (*mḏḥ nswt*), the last being a member of a turquoise-mining expedition to the Sinai (Gardiner and Peet 1952: pl. I). At the very end of the Third Dynasty Pehernefer bore the title *imi-r3 k3t nb nt nswt*, 'overseer of all the king's works'. This was the office held in the Old Kingdom by the person in charge of royal building activities. Whether a similar position existed in the first two dynasties, or whether the advent of pyramid-building in the Third Dynasty made such a post necessary for the first time, cannot be ascertained from the meagre evidence at our disposal. According to the biographical inscriptions of Old Kingdom overseers of works, the position included responsibility for all projects requiring large resources of materials and/or manpower: royal building projects, the construction of boats and fashioning of large-scale statuary, expeditions to quarry stone, the transport of goods and materials, irrigation works, perhaps even agricultural work (Husson and Valbelle 1992: 42).

Demanding activities such as construction projects and the maintenance of cults required a disciplined and effective work-force, and a specialised administrative mechanism was employed to maximise the efficiency of work teams. This was the rotational *phyle* system, whose origins go back at least as far as the First Dynasty (Roth 1991).

Expeditions, festivals and the royal boat

A development of great significance at the beginning of the Third Dynasty was the organisation of regular mining expeditions to the Sinai, to obtain supplies of turquoise from the area of the Wadi Maghara. Expeditions under Netjerikhet, Sekhemkhet and Sanakht each left a record of their visit, in the form of a rock-cut scene (Gardiner and Peet 1952: pls I, IV). The inscriptions from the reigns of Netjerikhet and Sekhemkhet depict the expedition leader, complete with titles. In both cases the operation was under the control of the *imi-r3 mš'*, 'overseer of the expedition'. An additional member of the Netjerikhet expedition, named as Hemni, was designated as *iri-('3-)'3mwt*, 'keeper of the (door to the) Asiatics'. He therefore seems to have been responsible in some way for the local (Palestinian) inhabitants of the Sinai. Just as the economic exploitation of the Delta through a network of royal foundations seems to have led to the development of a system of regional administration for Lower Egypt, so Egyptian economic involvement in the Sinai and Near East may have underlain the imposition of more direct state control in the desert and border regions of Egypt (see below).

The titles preserved on the stelae of Merka and Sabef from the reign of Qaa (Emery 1958: pl. 39; and Petrie 1900: pl. XXX, respectively) include unique references to certain royal activities which must have been a feature of the Egyptian court throughout the Early Dynastic period. Qaa clearly enjoyed a lengthy reign, and Sabef was charged with overseeing arrangements for the king's Sed-festival (*imi-r3 ḥb-sd*). The responsibility for organising this pre-eminent celebration of kingship would have been assigned to a trusted member of the king's entourage. Sabef's status in this respect is emphasised by his burial within the king's own mortuary complex at Abydos. Merka also performed important duties at court. One of these was *ḥrp wi3-nswt*, 'controller of the royal bark', indicating responsibility for the ship that may have been used by the king on his regular progresses. The character of early kingship seems to have been peripatetic, the monarch travelling throughout Egypt on a regular basis, not only to visit major shrines and take part in important annual festivals but also to reinforce the bonds between ruler and ruled. Royal travel must have played a significant role in the mechanism of early Egyptian administration, and the importance attached to the title 'controller of the royal bark' no doubt reflects this.

Courtly titles

As well as employing distinct bureaucracies for particular activities, such as those listed above, the court seems to have comprised numerous officials with general competence rather than specific duties. We should probably envisage a circle of trusted individuals in the service of the king, whose duties were rather fluid and were assigned according to needs and circumstances. These most influential of state employees were probably royal kinsmen, and the titles they bore expressed their proximity to the king, the ultimate source of all authority. Such titles, which we may call 'courtly', are the most numerous in Early Dynastic inscriptions. They shed some light on the internal workings of the royal household, but rather more on the nature of early Egyptian administration, which emphasised relative status within the hierarchy more than specific responsibilities.

A good example is *iri-p't*. This may have had a specific meaning in the Predynastic period, but by the time it is first attested, in the middle of the First Dynasty (Emery 1958: 60, pl. 83.1), it seems to have designated membership of the ruling élite (*p't*), as opposed to the general populace (*rḥyt*). More specifically, it is likely that the *p't* were royal kinsmen (Baines 1995: 133), for whom the highest echelons of government were reserved until the threshold of the Old Kingdom. On the stela of Merka, from the reign of Qaa (Emery 1958: pl. 39), the title appears in a prominent position, subordinate only to *s(t)m*, indicating the status (and political power?) attached to being an *iri-p't* in the First Dynasty.

Another title with possible Predynastic significance is *iri-Nhn*, 'keeper of Nekhen' (cf. Fischer 1996: 43–5). When Nekhen (Hierakonpolis) was an important centre, playing a pivotal role in the process of state formation, the 'keeper of Nekhen' may have been a prestigious position. By the Early Dynastic period, however, the meaning of the title may have been lost (at least, it is impenetrable to modern scholars), leaving *iri-Nhn* as an honorific designation borne by high officials, for example Nedjemankh in the reign of Netjerikhet (Weill 1908: 180; Kaplony 1963, III: fig. 324). Two possible courtly titles of unknown meaning from the early part of Den's reign are *it*, associated with Ankh-ka and Sekh-ka (Petrie 1900: pls XXI.29, XXII.30; Emery 1958: pls 80–1, 106.4) and *'rp*(?), associated with the latter (Petrie 1900: pl. XXII.30; Emery 1958: pl. 106.4). However, even the reading of the two groups of signs is uncertain, and they may not represent titles at all.

A number of different titles expressed the position of the holder within the circles of power which surrounded the ruler. Merka, at the end of the First Dynasty, was *šms-nswt*, 'a follower of the king' (Emery 1958: pl. 39), while an official of the Second or Third Dynasty was content to call himself *hm-nswt*, 'servant of the king' (Lacau and Lauer 1965: 36, no. 47). A parallel title may be the one borne by the king's sandal-bearer on the Narmer palette and macehead (Winter 1994). In both cases the title may perhaps be read as 'servant of the ruler'. A more exalted position was indicated by the title *hri-tp nswt*, 'chief one of the king', mentioned in inscriptions from the late Second and Third Dynasties (Petrie 1901: pl. XXI.165; Junker 1939; Lacau and Lauer 1965: 33, no. 43). Akhetaa, who lived during the latter half of the Third Dynasty, appears to have been one of the king's innermost circle of advisors, if the meaning of his title 'privy to all the secrets and affairs of the king' (*hri sšt3 nb ht nbt n nswt*) is to be taken at face value (Weill 1908: 262–73). (Note, however, that some commentators have identified *hri-sšt3* as a religious title [cf. Fischer 1996: 45–9 who reads the title *zhy-ntr*].) Pehernefer's title, *hri-sdm*, 'he who has the ear (of the king)' would also seem to indicate a position at the very centre of the court, even though the king is not mentioned explicitly.

Another category of courtly titles makes reference to particular chambers within the palace as a way of indicating proximity to the king. The titles held by some members of the court in present-day Britain may be cited as parallels, for example, 'Lord Chamberlain' (the person having control over many of the royal household's employees). In ancient Egypt, access to the innermost rooms of the palace must have brought with it access to the person of the ruler, considerable prestige which went with this access, and perhaps real influence in the decision-making processes of government. Titles in this category are attested only in the reign of Qaa and in the Third Dynasty, but they must have existed throughout the Early Dynastic period. Two titles are connected with the running of the palace itself (ʿh). The official Merka in the reign of Qaa bore the title ḥrp ʿh, 'controller (perhaps 'comptroller' would be a better English equivalent) of the palace' (Emery 1958: pl. 39). Abneb, who lived in the late Second or early Third Dynasty, held a similar position, imi-r3 ʿh, 'overseer of the palace' (Weill 1908: 220). Within the palace, two chambers seem to have been of particular significance: iz, sometimes translated as 'council chamber', and zh, possibly 'dining-hall' or 'audience chamber'. Thus an imi-iz, 'one who is in the council chamber' (Lacau and Lauer 1965: 16, no. 21), and a smsw-iz, 'elder of the council chamber', are known from the Third Dynasty (Gardiner and Peet 1952: pl. I). At the end of the First Dynasty, Merka, as well as being comptroller of the palace as a whole, was also 'comptroller of the audience chamber' (ḥrp zh); this title was later held by Pehernefer at the end of the Third Dynasty. Merka's contemporary, Sabef, described himself as 'foremost of the audience chamber' (ḥnti-zh), whilst Ankh, an official who lived early in the Third Dynasty, was simply a 'functionary of the audience chamber', (iri-ḥt zh) (Weill 1908: 185).

The vizier

We now come to the position at the very head of the administration, the official closest to the king. At different stages of the Early Dynastic period, this person bore the titles ṯṯ and ṯ3ti z3b ṯ3ti (Figure 4.5). An individual designated as ṯṯ is the earliest attested official of any kind, depicted on the Narmer palette. He walks in front of the king, carrying what appears to be an item of the royal regalia. On the Narmer macehead he appears again, this time standing behind the enthroned king, where he is labelled simply as ṯ. The meaning of the title is uncertain, but the position of the holder *vis-à-vis* the king seems clear enough.

It is tempting to link this title with the one borne by the vizier in later periods: ṯ3ti, or in its fuller form, ṯ3ti z3b ṯ3ti. The vizier stood at the head of the Egyptian administration and was responsible directly to the king for the government of the country. The position was certainly in existence by the beginning of the Third Dynasty. The earliest-known holder of the title was a man named Menka who is mentioned on a number of ink inscriptions from beneath the Step Pyramid (Lacau and Lauer 1965: 1, no. 1). These may date to the middle of the Second Dynasty (Shaw and Nicholson 1995: 15), perhaps to the reign of Ninetjer (Helck 1979). Alternatively, it is possible that the construction of the Step Pyramid, which must have required a degree of administrative organisation and

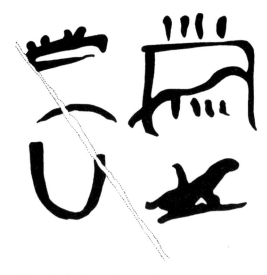

Figure 4.5 The titles of the vizier. The earliest attested reference to the highest administrative office in Egypt, written in ink on a stone vessel from the Step Pyramid complex of Netjerikhet at Saqqara. The inscription, which probably dates to the middle of the Second Dynasty, names the vizier as Menka, and gives the tripartite title associated with the vizierate throughout Egyptian history, *t3iti z3b t3ti* (after Lacau and Lauer 1965: pl. I.3).

sophistication previously unknown in Early Dynastic Egypt, necessitated the creation of a new executive post at the head of the government apparatus, to oversee all its activities and report directly to the king. The viziers of the Third and early Fourth Dynasties seem to have been royal princes, perhaps younger sons removed from the direct line of succession. Only in the reign of Menkaura was the position 'opened up' to a commoner (Husson and Valbelle 1992: 37).

The tripartite title held by a vizier may indicate the threefold nature of his authority. The first element, *t3iti*, emphasises the courtly aspect of the office. The literal meaning of *t3iti* is 'he of the curtain', an epithet reminiscent of positions in the Ottoman court. In Early Dynastic Egypt, it may have carried an ancient significance of which we are unaware. The second element, *z3b*, is usually translated 'noble', and was probably no more than a general designation for an official. Some scholars have interpreted the term as expressing the judicial aspect of the vizierate (Husson and Valbelle 1992: 37); certainly, in later periods the vizier was the highest legal authority in the land under the king, the ultimate court of appeal (barring an appeal to the king himself), and the official who decided important legal cases. The third part of the title, *t3ti*, cannot be translated, but may designate the administrative aspect of the vizier's office. It is perhaps related to the *tt* of Narmer's reign. The three component elements of the title may originally have been separate and distinct (Husson and Valbelle 1992: 36), but it is equally possible that they were used in conjunction from the very beginning, to describe the highest position in the administration.

Perhaps as a further indication of rank, viziers of the Old Kingdom generally bore the additional title *iri-p't*. It may be no coincidence that the two earliest-known holders of the title were buried at North Saqqara, overlooking the seat of Early Dynastic government. It is tempting to identify the owners of all the major tombs at North Saqqara – including S3506 and S3505, each built for an *iri-p't* – as 'proto-viziers'; in other words, the officials at the head of the national administration (cf. Baines 1995: 138).

THE ADMINISTRATION OF THE PROVINCES

State control of the means of production, achieved through the mechanism of royal foundations, gave the court a ready-made network of institutions and administrators by which to exercise political control over the provinces. The system was best developed in the Delta, where the majority of royal foundations were probably located. It is thus in the context of Lower Egypt that the earliest evidence for regional administration is found.

Lower Egypt

At least as early as the middle of the First Dynasty, the Delta seems to have been divided into two for administrative purposes. Sealings from the tomb of Merneith refer, in one case, to the 'fields of the west', in another to the eastern Delta (Petrie 1900: pl. XXIII.37–8; Martin-Pardey 1976: 17). The administrative division of the Delta was apparently maintained until the Third Dynasty – as indicated on a sealing from Beit Khallaf mastaba K5, dated to the reign of Netjerikhet (Garstang 1902: pl. XXVI.8; Weill 1908: 86) – when a widespread reorganisation of regional government seems to have taken place.

The titles most closely connected with provincial administration in Second and Third Dynasty sources are *ḥq3 ḥwt-'3t* and *'d-mr* (Martin-Pardey 1976: 24, 54, 57). Both seem to refer exclusively to localities in Lower Egypt, especially in the western Delta. The connection with the administration of royal domains and estates is clear. Throughout the First Dynasty, the title *'d-mr*, 'administrator', was borne by officials in charge of domains and their produce. Likewise, the other title, *ḥq3 ḥwt-'3t*, 'governor of the great estate', may originally have designated the official responsible for the royal mortuary estate, since this is the likely meaning of *ḥwt-'3t* (Husson and Valbelle 1992: 28). Although *'d-mr* is the usual title for a provincial administrator in the Third Dynasty (for example, in the inscription of Metjen), it may have been replaced by *ḥq3 ḥwt-ʿ3t* in the Old Kingdom when the former title retained purely ranking significance (Martin-Pardey 1976: 43, 54, 45). Since both titles are of great antiquity – *ʿḏ-mr* is first attested in the reign of Djet, while a *ḥwt-ʿ3t* is first mentioned on the stela of Sabef from the reign of Qaa – it is impossible to determine at which point they began to be applied to the sphere of provincial administration, rather than the management of royal landholdings.

Developing, as it did, out of the system of domain administration – with both ideological and functional links to the court – provincial government of Lower Egypt seems to have maintained much closer links with the residence than did the government of the Upper Egyptian regions. During the Early Dynastic period and into the Old Kingdom, the regional administrators of the Delta may have resided at Memphis, rather than in the province(s) for which they had responsibility (Husson and Valbelle 1992: 53). Even though at the end of the Third Dynasty Metjen was both priest of the local god of Letopolis and *ʿḏ-mr* of the Letopolite nome, there does not appear to have been an explicit link between political and priestly office in Lower Egypt (Martin-Pardey 1976: 42).

Upper Egypt

Evidence for the early administration of Upper Egypt is extremely scarce. It has been suggested that the ancient title *iri-Nḫn* was held by the 'governor of the Upper Egyptian regional capital' (Kaplony 1963, I: 450), though there is no evidence to support such an interpretation (Martin-Pardey 1976: 37). In the light of recent evidence from Elephantine, an alternative suggestion, that *iri-Nḫn* was the title of the fortress-commander responsible for guarding Egypt's southern frontier (Martin-Pardey 1976: 38), must also be rejected. None the less, a distinctive pattern of central control – indicated by different titles – seems to have evolved for Upper Egypt in the Early Dynastic period, and aspects of this system may have been inherited from the preceding Predynastic period (Helck 1954: 81).

Possibly the earliest type of local administrator in Upper Egypt was the office of 'mayor' (*ḥ3ti-ʿ*). This title is first attested on a sealing from the tomb of Merneith, where it occurs in conjunction with the name of the official Sekh-ka (Petrie 1900: pl. XXII.32). The title recurs on a Third Dynasty sealing from Beit Khallaf (Kaplony 1963, III: fig. 324), and the overseer of a mining expedition to the Wadi Maghara in the reign of Sekhemkhet also held the title *ḥ3ti-ʿ* (Gardiner and Peet 1952: pl. I). (Exceptionally, the title *ḥ3ti-ʿ* occurs in the context of nome administration in the tomb inscription of Pehernefer; he apparently held the office of 'mayor' of the Busiris nome of Lower Egypt [Martin-Pardey 1976: 40].)

Another title applied in the later Third Dynasty to Upper Egyptian administrators, *ḥq3*, is undoubtedly a very ancient designation of office. In the reign of Den, Setka bore the title *ḥq3* (Emery 1958: pl. 82.38), though a connection with provincial administration is not made explicit. A seal-impression from a Third Dynasty context at Elephantine mentions the governor (*ḥq3*) of a locality called *iti-t3w* (Kaplony 1963, III: figs 282, 285–6; Seidlmayer 1996b: 121) whilst the governor of the island community itself bore the title *imi-r3 3bw*, 'overseer of Elephantine' (Leclant and Clerc 1993: 250; Pätznick, in Kaiser *et al.* 1995: 181 and 182, fig. 29a; Seidlmayer 1996b: 113). During the course of the Third Dynasty, the title *ḥq3* seems to have been superseded by a different administrative designation, *sšm-t3*. This is first attested on a stone vessel from the Step Pyramid galleries (Lacau and Lauer 1965: pl. 28.5) and was the title borne by Metjen in connection with Upper Egyptian regions at the end of the Third Dynasty. The transition from the earlier to the later designation seems to have been gradual, since both titles are attested for the sixteenth Upper Egyptian nome in the Second Dynasty (Martin-Pardey 1976: 63).

In the reign of Netjerikhet, the high official Hesira bore the title *wr mdw Šm'w*, 'greatest of the tens of Upper Egypt'. This may indicate a position in the provincial administration, since in the Sixth Dynasty the same title carried responsibility for conscripting men for corvée labour in the particular districts under the official's control (Wood 1978: 15). Further, it has been suggested that the variation in the lists of titles carved on the relief panels from Hesira's tomb 'might reflect (his) official functions in various geographical districts' (Wood 1978: 20).

The origins of the nome system

As an administrative mechanism, the nome system – the division of Egypt into regional administrative units – allowed the king to appoint trusted officials to various specific duties which were easiest to undertake on a regional basis, such as irrigation and tax assessment (Martin-Pardey 1976: 22). The nomes of Lower Egypt, apparently based on the location of royal domains, probably originated as collection points for agricultural produce destined for the royal treasury (Helck 1954: 80). There is considerable uncertainty about whether the nome system was originally devised for Lower Egypt or for Upper Egypt. Its main purpose was to allow a tighter, more uniform control of the provinces by the state (Martin-Pardey 1976: 28). This would probably have been a greater concern with respect to the regions of Upper Egypt, more distant from the capital and traditionally more independent-minded than the Delta. However, the nome sign itself depicts an area of irrigated land, and this has suggested to some that the system originated in Lower Egypt. The north of the country seems to have lacked any well-defined, pre-existing political structures, and it was therefore more suited to the imposition of a new system of central control by the state (Martin-Pardey 1976: 25). Moreover, the similarities in terminology between the administration of royal domains and the early nome system tend to suggest a direct link between the two.

The division of Egypt into nomes clearly occurred at some point before the beginning of the Third Dynasty (Martin-Pardey 1976: 18). A seal-impression from Abydos dating to the reign of Netjerikhet may show the standard of the eighth Upper Egyptian nome, the Thinite nome (Newberry 1909: pl. XXIII.VIII; Martin-Pardey 1976: 33), suggesting that the system was already in existence. Ink inscriptions on stone vessels from the Step Pyramid complex, plausibly dated to the reign of Ninetjer (Helck 1979: 129), show the sign of the sixteenth Upper Egyptian nome, as does a seal-impression from the tomb of Khasekhemwy. A fragmentary sealing of Sekhemib from the tomb of Peribsen also appears to show the lower part of a nome standard (Petrie 1901: pl. XXI.172). Some scholars have suggested that the nome system was established as a deliberate policy of the early state at the time of Egypt's political unification (Kaiser, quoted in Martin-Pardey 1976: 29; Martin-Pardey 1976: 19), arguing that a system of regional administration would have been essential for the cohesion of the newly unified state (Martin-Pardey 1976: 40). Others have linked the origins of the nome system to the new economic demands created by pyramid-building (Helck, quoted in Martin-Pardey 1976: 30). The latter view may be rejected since the earliest occurrences of nome standards pre-date the beginning of the Third Dynasty, and substantial building projects – which would have required the mobilisation of considerable manpower and resources – were undertaken during the first two dynasties, notably the enclosures of Khasekhemwy at Hierakonpolis and Abydos.

The annals of the Palermo Stone indicate that the biennial 'following of Horus' (*šms-Ḥr*) was an important event in the life of the court. One of its functions may have been as a tour of inspection, allowing officials of the central administration to keep up-to-date records on the agricultural potential of the provinces. However, the 'following of Horus' seems not to have occurred during the reign of Den, and it is likely that an alternative system of tax assessment and economic control would have been required (Martin-Pardey 1976: 33–4). The nome system may therefore have been devised in Den's reign as a substitute. However, in the absence of any firm evidence for the existence of nomes in the First Dynasty, we should probably place the origins of the system somewhere in the Second Dynasty. It is possible that the court's move to Memphis at the beginning of the Second Dynasty – highlighted by the relocation of the royal necropolis from Abydos to Saqqara – necessitated a new mechanism for exercising control over the distant provinces of Upper Egypt. The experience of administering royal domains in the Delta provided a template, and the nome system was devised along the same lines.

Peripheral regions

Administration of the desert regions bordering the Nile valley is first attested in the reign of Qaa. The official Merka was both *'d̲-mr zmit* and *ḥrp zmit*, 'administrator of the desert' and 'controller of the desert' (Emery 1958: pl. 39). One title may have been connected with civil, the other with military administration (Martin-Pardey 1976: 51), though this cannot be confirmed. Both titles also occur in the reign of Netjerikhet, the *'d̲-mr zmit* Nitankh being mentioned in a rock-cut inscription at the turquoise mines of the Wadi Maghara (Gardiner and Peet 1952: pl. I). Clearly, the individual responsible for the desert approaches to the Sinai would have been an important member of a mining expedition. It is possible that Nitankh's position gave him a degree of authority over the Sinai as well. At the end of the Third Dynasty, Pehernefer's sphere of responsibility was defined more precisely as the western desert: one of his titles was *'d̲-mr zmit imntt*, 'administrator of the western desert'. The inscriptions of Metjen and Pehernefer suggest that the locality called *ḥwt iḥt*, possibly Kom el-Hisn, may have been the headquarters of the desert administrator (*'d̲-mr zmit*). This official would have been responsible primarily for the desert region bordering the western Delta (Martin-Pardey 1976: 52), which formed a strategically important buffer zone between Egypt and the Libyan peoples to the west.

The distinction in nomenclature (Husson and Valbelle 1992: 62) between, on the one hand, the low desert fringing the Nile valley (*zmit*) and, on the other, the high desert and foreign lands (*ḫ3st*), must be significant. From an administrative perspective, the low desert – valued as a source of minerals and wild game – could be exploited by means of small-scale expeditions mounted from the Nile valley itself. The desert fringes and their resources could easily have been administered from within Egypt, and the titles attested in the Early Dynastic period seem to be proof of this.

Foreign conquests

By contrast, exploitation and/or administration of the high desert and lands outside Egypt required a more expansionist programme. The imposition of Egyptian control in areas distant from the Nile valley could only be achieved by transplanting the appropriate administrative structures into foreign territory. Such a practice may be attested by the construction of an Egyptian First Dynasty 'Residency' at En Besor in southern Palestine. The only evidence for Egyptian administrative control over neighbouring lands during the Early Dynastic period comes in the form of two seal-impressions from the Shunet ez-Zebib, dated to the reign of Khasekhemwy, which bear the title *imi-r3 ḫ3st*, 'overseer of the foreign land' (Ayrton *et al.* 1904:

pl. IX.9; Newberry 1909: pl. XXII.IV). The 'foreign land' in question is not specified; from later parallels, territory to the east of Egypt – i.e. the Sinai or southern Palestine – was probably indicated. An important piece of supporting evidence in this respect is a fragment of stone relief from the temple area at Hierakonpolis. Also dated to the reign of Khasekhemwy, it lists a number of conquered territories, each name determined by the sign *ḫ3st*, 'foreign land'. It is tempting to link the appearance of the title *imi-r3 ḫ3st* at the end of the Second Dynasty with the start of systematic exploitation of the turquoise reserves in and around Wadi Maghara in the Sinai from the beginning of the Third Dynasty.

Increasing Egyptian involvement in neighbouring areas and the imposition of political control over territory outside the borders of Egypt are important indicators of the court's growing confidence and coercive power. The dynamics of Egypt's foreign relations in the Early Dynastic period are a complex mixture of ideology and practical economics, illuminating some of the problems and priorities which faced Egypt's early rulers. The detailed nature of Egypt's contacts with the outside world is explored in the next chapter.

CONCLUSION: THE EXERCISE OF AUTHORITY IN EARLY DYNASTIC EGYPT

The picture presented above represents no more than isolated pieces of a puzzle. It is unlikely that we will ever understand the precise structure of the Early Dynastic administration, given the limitations of the available evidence (see Figure 4.6 for an educated guess). What is possible at the present time is an investigation of particular aspects of government, as practised by the early Egyptian state. The central theme of this book, the fashioning of ancient Egyptian civilisation by the country's early rulers, requires at least an attempt at explaining one further theme under the heading of administration: how authority was exercised by members of the government apparatus in the first three dynasties. Here, a final category of evidence is invaluable: the careers of prominent individuals.

Individual careers

Amongst the large number of seal-impressions recovered from the First Dynasty royal tombs at Abydos and the contemporary élite burials at North Saqqara, a few high officials are mentioned quite frequently, sometimes at different stages of their career. A tentative reconstruction of these careers can be made, illustrating the opportunities for advancement within the Early Dynastic administration. From the very end of the Third Dynasty, the tomb of Metjen at Saqqara preserved numerous titles held

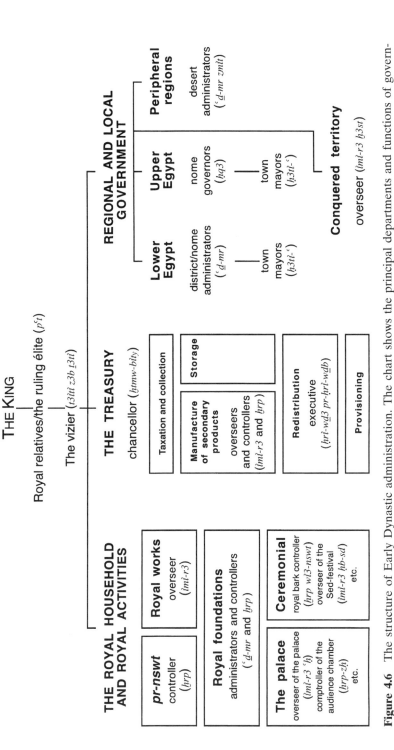

Figure 4.6 The structure of Early Dynastic administration. The chart shows the principal departments and functions of government, together with the titles of some of the major administrative officials (based upon information from contemporary sources: seal-impressions, inscribed stone vessels and Third Dynasty tomb inscriptions).

by its owner during his long career, which probably began in the reign of Huni and came to an end early in the reign of Sneferu. The inscriptions provide valuable information about many aspects of the administration on the threshold of the Old Kingdom.

Amka

The career of Amka (*'m-k3*) seems to have begun in the reign of Djer, spanned the entire reign of his successor, Djet, and continued into the early part of Den's reign, when Egypt was under the regency of Merneith. Seal-impressions naming Amka have been found in the tombs of all three rulers, Djer, Djet and Merneith. The different titles associated with Amka in these three contexts shed some light on his progression through the ranks of the administration. Throughout his career, Amka served in the administration of royal domains. In the reign of Djer, he was already involved in managing the domain called *Hr-shnti-dw*, and held the titles *nbi* and *(hri) nhn(w)* (Petrie 1901: pls XVI.121 and XVI.123, respectively). Amka retained the last of these positions under Djer's successor (Petrie 1900: pl. XIX.10). It was in the regency of Merneith, however, that Amka's career seems to have peaked. In addition to his previous title of *nbi*, now in the variant form *hrp nbi*, he became a mortuary priest (*zhnw-3h*) (Petrie 1900: pl. XX.18) and an administrator (*'d-mr*) (Petrie 1900: pl. XX.15). He finished his career as district administrator (*'d-mr*) of *hwt ihw*, the locality in the western Delta which probably lay in the vicinity of Kom el-Hisn. Hence, he seems to have moved from managing specific royal foundations to a position in the regional administration of the western Delta, the area where most of these foundations were probably situated.

Sekhemkasedj

A second high official whose career spanned more than one reign is Sekhemkasedj (*shm-k3-sd*), almost certainly the owner of tomb S3504 at Saqqara (cf. Kaplony 1963, I: 89). Seal-impressions from the tomb, and from the burial of Djet at Abydos, indicate that it was under this king that Sekhemkasedj began his career, again in the sphere of administering royal domains. At first, he held the title *nhn(w)* (Petrie 1900: pl. XVIII.6, 1901: pl. XVII.129) and a parallel title *nhb* (Petrie 1900: pl. XVIII.6), perhaps connected in some way with the town of Elkab. His principal office, however, was as administrator (*'d-mr*) of Djet's own foundation, the domain *W3d-Hr*. Sekhemkasedj retained this responsibility throughout his career. Indeed, it has even been suggested (Kaplony 1963: 110) that the domain was maintained under Merneith only until Sekhemkasedj died, then to be replaced by a new domain (possibly *Hr-tpi-ht*). During the regency of Merneith, Sekhemkasedj was 'controller' (*ḥrp*) rather than 'administrator' of *W3ḏ-Ḥr* (Emery 1954: 119, fig. 163). He also bore his earlier title *nḫn(w)* in its later variant *ḥrp nḫn(w)* (Emery 1954: 119, fig. 164) and the obscure title *ḥrp nbi* (Emery 1954: 120, fig. 165). In addition to his duties concerning the domain *W3ḏ-Ḥr*, Sekhemkasedj was also connected with a royal estate *ḥwt ḥnn(?)* (Emery 1954: 118, fig. 159), and towards the end of his career achieved the prestigious position of *ꜥḏ-mr* of the domain *Ḥr-sḫnti-ḏw* (Emery 1954: 116 fig. 151), which seems to have been the most important royal foundation of the early First Dynasty.

Hemaka

Although Hemaka (*ḥm3-k3*) served under only one king, namely Den, it is possible to chart something of his career. Kaplony (1963, I: 113) proposed that Hemaka may originally have managed the domain *Ḥr-tpi-ḥt* as both administrator (*ꜥḏ-mr*) and controller (*ḥrp*). Later, he seems to have taken control of the more prestigious domain *Ḥr-sḫnti-ḏw*, in succession to the officials Ankhka and Medjedka. Hemaka then continued to exercise authority with respect to both domains until the end of his career. The peak of Hemaka's achievement must have come with his appointment as royal chancellor (*ḥtmw bity*), the position at the head of the treasury. He seems to have made the leap from a career connected with the management of royal domains to being the king's own seal-bearer and thus the acknowledged representative of royal authority. The size and wealth of Hemaka's tomb at North Saqqara (Emery 1938) is an eloquent testament to the position he achieved by the end of his life.

Metjen

From the disposition of the many titles throughout his tomb chapel, it may be possible to reconstruct something of Metjen's career (Goedicke 1966). Certainly, the latest titles, inscribed on the walls of an unfinished section of the tomb, relate to a temple of Sneferu and a mortuary estate of Huni, both in the Letopolite nome (the second Lower Egyptian nome). The autobiographical inscription contains a rare piece of direct evidence for career progression: Metjen states that he became district administrator (*ꜥḏ-mr*) of the Xoïte nome (the sixth Lower Egyptian nome) after he had been *z3b* and *ḥri-sqr* of the same nome. Whether this represented a common pattern of promotion is, of course, impossible to ascertain without comparative evidence. However, it does indicate that an official employed in the administration of a region could expect to advance within that administration, even as far as the top job.

Merka: a high official of the late First Dynasty

Merka was buried in an élite tomb at North Saqqara, mastaba S3505, in the reign of Qaa, the last king of the First Dynasty. The funerary stela of Merka (Emery 1958: pl. 39) presents the most extensive list of titles held by a single individual in the Early Dynastic period. The combination of administrative, courtly and religious titles tells us something, if not about the precise demarcation of responsibilities within the Early Dynastic government, then about the titles and offices which gave an individual status within the royal court.

Three titles are written larger than the rest and appear directly above Merka's name. We may take these to be the titles considered most important by the deceased himself, and therefore to have indicated most clearly his rank within the highest echelons of the state (Baines 1995: 132–3). Surprisingly, perhaps, two of the three titles are religious: *sm3* and *s(t)m*. The first, usually translated 'stolist', was held in later periods by the priest who clothed the cult statue of a god (Faulkner 1962: 227). Its significance at the end of the First Dynasty is entirely unknown. The *s(t)m* priest was apparently closely connected with the celebration of royal ritual, and the title may additionally have designated the king's son. It was apparently the most important title held by Merka and appears immediately before his name. In other words, despite occupying a number of administrative offices and positions connected with the royal household (detailed below), Merka gained his exceptional status – reflected in the size and sophistication of his tomb, complete with its own funerary chapel – from an ancient religious function strongly associated with the cult of divine kingship. This fact speaks eloquently about the ultimate source of power and authority in Early Dynastic Egypt. That Merka was a member of the royal family is probably indicated by the third title, which appears between *sm3* and *s(t)m*. This is the designation *iri-pʿt*, which marks Merka as a member of the group of royal kinsmen that constituted the ruling élite in the First Dynasty.

Merka's remaining titles are written in two columns, although the rudimentary carving and arrangement of the signs at this early period make precise identification difficult. Religious titles include a possible connection with the cult of Anubis, an obscure reference to the scorpion (a cultic object attested in other Early Dynastic sources), and *ḥm-nṯr Nt*, 'priest of Neith'. The association between the goddess Neith and the royal family is well attested in the First Dynasty (see Chapter 8), and provides yet another indication that Merka was a close member of the king's immediate circle. Specific administrative offices are comparatively few, suggesting – as indicated earlier – that status came from proximity to the king rather than from occupying particular positions within the apparatus of government. Apart from two obscure references to the 'office' (*iz*) and a possible reference to the organisation of *phyles*, Merka's primary administrative function was as 'district administrator of the desert' (*'ḏ-mr zmit*). The sphere of authority of such a position is not known, but it may have entailed responsibility for guarding Egypt's desert frontiers as well as administration of the deserts themselves, their inhabitants and resources (notably stones and minerals). Whether Merka ever carried out such duties in person cannot of course be gauged, but it seems somewhat unlikely that an official based at the capital would have had much direct contact with the desert regions over which he exercised nominal authority. A further title (*ḥrp Wnt*) may indicate administrative responsibility for the region of the Hare-nome, later the fifteenth nome of Upper Egypt, which included the important travertine quarries at Hatnub. It is possible that this combination of regional administrative authority for the desert(s) and the Hare-nome reflects responsibility, above all, for the procurement and supply of raw materials for the stone-cutters of the royal workshops. The other titles held by Merka concern functions within the royal household, once again indicating his membership of the innermost circle of the court. Hence, he was a 'follower of the king' (*šms-nswt*) and 'controller of the royal bark' (*ḥrp wi3-nswt*), the latter being a position which must have been closely involved with royal visits and the periodic 'following of Horus'. As we shall see, these two types of event were important means by which the doctrine of divine kingship was promulgated, and by which newly won political control over the whole of Egypt was maintained and bolstered. The titles 'comptroller of the palace' (*ḥrp 'ḥ*) and 'comptroller of the audience chamber' (*ḥrp zḥ*) may have been purely honorary, or they may point to Merka having effectively controlled access to the person of the king; this would have given him great political influence in a country where the king was the ultimate source of authority. Finally, an apparent reference to singers (*mrwt*) (Emery 1958: 31) cannot be confirmed, since the stela is damaged at this point.

In summary, Merka's titles reflect a society and an administrative system in which the king was at the pinnacle, both ideologically and politically. The stela of Merka adds to the impression that, aside from the departments of government responsible for state and royal income – the treasury and its sub-departments, royal foundations and the *pr-nswt* – Early Dynastic administration was perhaps rather loosely organised, lacking precise demarcation of responsibilities.

CHAPTER FIVE

FOREIGN RELATIONS

—— •◆• ——

Ancient Egyptian civilisation has traditionally been viewed as a civilisation apart. Separated from the rest of the ancient world by the effective natural borders of the eastern and western deserts and the Mediterranean Sea, the Nile valley fostered a distinctive, and in many ways unique, culture. The comparison and contrast of ancient Egypt with its neighbouring civilisation, Mesopotamia, is a familiar theme for ancient historians. However, to the Egyptologists working earlier this century, the surviving archaeological material from the beginnings of Egyptian civilisation suggested much closer contacts between these two great cultures. Particularly striking to archaeologists like Petrie and Emery were the many borrowings from Mesopotamian iconography manifest on the earliest royal objects from Egypt. Coupled with the extraordinary explosion of creativity and organisational skill which seemed to have occurred at the very inception of the Egyptian state, the artistic evidence prompted these scholars to advance the theory of the 'Dynastic race' (Derry 1956; Emery 1961: 39–40). An invasion of people from lands to the east, superior to the indigenous Predynastic Egyptians, was proposed as the driving force behind the foundation of the Egyptian state and the emergence of 'classic' Egyptian civilisation. By the 1970s this theory had been largely discredited, mainly due to the results of subsequent archaeological work at sites dating to the Predynastic period. These demonstrated the long and indigenous development of many of Egyptian civilisation's most distinctive features. Moreover, they proved that the processes of craft specialisation, state formation and artistic formalisation had begun many centuries before the beginning of the First Dynasty, in the emergent territories of Upper Egypt. Over the last twenty years, the intensive investigation of Egypt's origins has enhanced our understanding of these processes immeasurably. Studies have all tended to stress, explicitly or implicitly, the indigenous genius of Egyptian civilisation, eager to claim originality and independence for the achievements of Nile valley culture (cf. Kantor 1965: 12–13).

However, discoveries made within the last few years, particularly at Buto and Abydos, provide tantalising glimpses of a rather different picture of early Egypt. There is a small, but growing body of evidence to suggest that the birth of Egyptian civilisation may, after all, have owed a significant amount to other neighbouring cultures, particularly those of the ancient Near East (see Map 2 for location of sites). In light of this new and immensely exciting evidence, it is perhaps time to begin a reappraisal of early Egypt's place in the ancient world, the extent and intensity of Egyptian interaction with neighbouring cultures, and the influence of those cultures on the development of Egyptian civilisation.

THE NEAR EAST AND EASTERN MEDITERRANEAN

Relations with southern Palestine

There is some evidence for sporadic contacts between Egypt and southern Palestine as early as the Badarian and Naqada I periods, the Chalcolithic in southern Palestine (Prag 1986; Marfoe 1987: 26; Ben-Tor 1991: 3–4; Ward 1991: 13). However, intensive contacts between the two regions do not seem to have begun until later in the Predynastic period. Direct Egyptian involvement in southern Palestine seems to have occurred in two phases, separated by an intervening period of reduced Egyptian activity in the region (Gophna 1992b; Hartung 1994). The first phase occurred during the **EBI**a period in southern Palestine (Hartung 1994: 108–9), which corresponds to the beginning of the Naqada II period in Upper Egypt (Amiran and Gophna 1992). From this time, there is evidence of Egyptian settlers, belonging to the Lower Egyptian cultural sphere (Gophna 1992b: 388–9, fig. 4; Porat 1992: 435; Hartung 1994: 108), at a few sites in southern Palestine: Site H in the Wadi Ghazzeh (Gophna 1990, 1992b), Taur Ikhbeineh (Oren and Yekutieli 1992), Nizzanim (Gophna 1990), Lachish (Gophna 1976, 1992b; Oren and Gilead 1981; Brandl 1992 plus references) and Tel Erani (Weinstein 1984; Kempinski 1992).

From the middle of Naqada II (Naqada IIc) until the end of the Predynastic period (Naqada IIIb/'Dynasty 0') the evidence for an Egyptian presence in southern Palestine is greatly reduced (Hartung 1994: 109–11). A small population may have remained at Taur Ikhbeineh and Tel Erani, but even here the percentage of Egyptian pottery declines markedly compared to the previous phase (Hartung 1994: 109). There is a clear hiatus in the En Besor area between the Egyptian activity at Site H (in EBIa) and the resumption of an Egyptian presence at nearby En Besor (in late EBIb). Interestingly, it is precisely during this period of reduced Egyptian involvement in southern Palestine that imports from the Near East are most numerous in Egyptian contexts, the most dramatic example being the hundreds of imported vessels found in tomb U-j at Abydos. So trade between the two areas was clearly maintained (cf. Amiran 1985). The evidence points to a major realignment of Egyptian–Palestinian contacts during the Naqada II and early Naqada III periods, when the courts of Upper Egypt were expanding their political and economic influence (Hartung 1994).

Colonisation

The very end of the Predynastic period (late EBIb in the Palestinian chronology) witnessed a resumption of direct Egyptian involvement in southern Palestine, but on a much larger scale than before. This development is undoubtedly linked to the process of state formation that was reaching its culmination in Egypt during 'Dynasty 0' (Marfoe 1987: 26). Instead of small-scale trade, perhaps involving middlemen, the Egyptians seem to have engaged in larger, more frequent, state-sponsored expeditions into southern Palestine (Moorey 1987: 43). These were supported by minor way-stations along the north Sinai coast, trading-stations, caravanserais and even permanent settlements in southern Palestine itself (Marfoe 1987: 26; Oren and Yekutieli 1992: 381). This extension of the 'core' into the 'periphery' for a restricted period of time is part of a general phenomenon associated with the rise of early states. The establishment of 'colonies' would clearly have allowed the Egyptians to gather resources and control trade more effectively. More than twenty sites in southern Palestine have produced clear evidence of an Egyptian presence (Brandl 1992; Hartung 1994). This includes pottery and flint tools, made locally from local materials but in a characteristically Egyptian style and using Egyptian techniques (Ben-Tor 1991: 5–6). Buildings constructed in an Egyptian manner – at En Besor (Gophna and Gazit 1985), Afridar (Brandl 1992: 449) and perhaps Tel Maahaz (Gophna 1976: 33; Brandl 1992: 464) – and seal-impressions made locally (Porat 1992) point to an official Egyptian administrative presence at certain sites, presumably acting under orders from a royal court back home (Gophna 1992b: 393). As one leading scholar has commented, 'it is difficult to avoid the conclusion that southern Canaan . . . (in late EBIb) . . . was highly Egyptianized' (Gophna 1992b: 386).

Tel Erani is a key site for understanding Egypt's relations with southern Palestine during the Early Bronze Age. The site has produced a rich assemblage of imported Egyptian and locally made Egyptianising pottery (Weinstein 1984: 61). One vessel fragment was found bearing the incised *serekh* of Narmer. It has been shown that the evidence for destruction layers at Tel Erani, previously interpreted as signs of Egyptian military activity, was illusory (Weinstein 1984: 67). None the less, evidence for Egyptian contacts with the site goes back to the Naqada II period (EBIa–b). The Egyptian pottery at Tel Erani suggests a continuous Egyptian presence from this time until at least the latter part of the First Dynasty.

Another site of key importance is En Besor (Gophna and Gazit 1985; Gophna 1990, 1992a, 1992b). On a low hill overlooking the En Besor springs, Israeli archaeologists excavated a unique brick building, named Building A. It was constructed entirely of mudbrick, without stone foundations, and consisted of several rooms and courtyards covering a total area of some 85 square metres. Some of the walls were preserved up to a height of five courses of mudbricks. Although the bricks were made from the local loess soil, with the addition of large amounts of sand, their dimensions and the pattern in which they were laid have no parallels from contemporary southern Palestine. Rather, they are characteristic of Egyptian mudbrick construction of the Early Dynastic period, in particular the First Dynasty élite tombs at North Saqqara. Furthermore, the building as a whole, which gives the impression of having been built to a preconceived plan, is aligned north–south, as was common in Egyptian building practice (Gophna and Gazit 1985: 9). A faience statuette of a baboon found in a rubbish pit confirms the Egyptian character of the site (Gophna 1992a). From the installations found inside the building – including a large pottery basin sunk into the floor of one room and a quern emplacement in the adjoining room – and from the huge quantities of bread-moulds found scattered throughout the site, it appears that bread and beer were manufactured on the premises (Gophna and Gazit 1985: 12–13). Whilst many of the storage vessels found at the site had been imported from Egypt, the domestic pottery (for cooking, eating and drinking) was all manufactured locally, according to Egyptian ceramic traditions but from locally obtained clays. This indicates that 'the local Egyptian population was large and lived away from their homeland long enough to establish independent pottery workshops, operated by potters trained in the Egyptian tradition' (Porat 1992: 434). Although it may have served as an observation point, Building A lacked any defensive features and could only accommodate about a dozen people. The likeliest explanation for the building's function is that it served as a staging-post on the trade route between Egypt and southern Palestine, providing essential supplies (water, bread and beer) for the passing Egyptian trade caravans. Indeed, the main reason for the location of the facility at En Besor seems to be the local availability of fresh water. The building no doubt afforded the Egyptians control over the springs, which provided 'the richest and most stable perennial water source to be found in the entire southern coastal plain' of Palestine (Gophna and Gazit 1985: 15). Numerous mud-sealings, many of which bear recognisably Egyptian inscriptions, were found in a pit outside the building's main entrance (Gophna and Gazit 1985: 13). They can be dated to the First Dynasty, although there is some disagreement about whether a date early or late in the Dynasty is more probable. The excavator dates the Egyptian presence at En Besor to the very beginning of the First Dynasty (Gophna 1992a). Although several of the sealings can be dated on stylistic grounds to the reign of Aha, partially preserved royal names on others seem to indicate a later date. Three sealings show traces of the names of Djet (no. 42), Den (no. 26) and Anedjib (no. 35) while a fourth (no. 39) may once have included the name of

Semerkhet. A further sealing (no. 46) would seem to offer a more secure example of Anedjib's name (Schulman 1983: 250). As the archaeological stratum associated with the sealings is rather thin, it is unlikely that the building was occupied over a very long period of time. It is therefore possible that the royal names preserved in the sealings do not refer to the reigns themselves, but rather to royal estates or foundations which supplied the building at En Besor with supplies. In any case, the epigraphic evidence from the En Besor sealings indicates that the staging-post was most active during the mid–late First Dynasty (Schulman 1983: 251). The fact that the sealings were made from local clays (the same clays used to make Egyptian-style pottery) is of great importance, as it indicates that Egyptian officials were based at En Besor, marking sealed goods according to standard Egyptian administrative practice.

A similar situation seems to have existed at another site in the northern Negev, Nahal Tillah on the Halif Terrace (Levy *et al.* 1995). Here, at the so-called 'Silo site', large numbers of imported Egyptian vessels have been excavated, including late Predynastic 'Late ware' and Early Dynastic storage jars (Levy *et al.* 1995: 28). A small faience jar and clay seal-impressions confirm the Egyptian nature of the assemblage (Levy *et al.* 1995: 28). A possible public storage area (associated with a circular feature which may have been a silo) (Levy *et al.* 1995: 30) yielded a sherd from an imported Egyptian vessel (Levy *et al.* 1995: 32), incised before firing with the *serekh* of Narmer (Levy *et al.* 1995: 31). The stratum in which the sherd was found has been dated to late EBIb (Levy *et al.* 1995: 29), known from other sites to be contemporary with the reign of Narmer. The Nahal Tillah site may therefore have been another administrative centre for the late Predynastic/Early Dynastic Egyptian presence in southern Palestine, or, at the very least, one of a network of trading sites distributed throughout the region.

The nature of Egypt's involvement in southern Palestine may be gauged from several pieces of evidence. The large number of flint objects recovered from sites showing an Egyptian presence do not include any arrowheads (Ben-Tor 1991: 8). This argues against an Egyptian military presence, suggesting instead that trade was the primary purpose of the settlements. It has been estimated that the number of Egyptians living permanently in southern Palestine during the Early Bronze I period may have reached several hundred (Ben-Tor 1991: 8). The raw materials which they sought probably included honey, wine, bitumen and resin, as well as various coniferous woods (Ben-Tor 1991: 8; Ward 1991: 14–16) with the exception of cedar, the southern limit of which appears to have been Mt. Hermon on the present-day Israeli–Lebanese border (Ward 1991: 14). The apparent intensity of Egyptian activity in southern Palestine in the reign of Narmer – sherds incised with his *serekh* have been found at Tell Arad (Amiran 1974, 1976) and Tel Erani (see above) as well as at Nahal Tillah

– seems to represent the end of the second phase of Egyptian settlement in the region. After the early First Dynasty (EBII) the evidence points to a marked decline in Egypt's contacts with southern Palestine (Hartung 1994: 112). The Egyptian presence at En Besor seems to have been maintained at least until the reign of Anedjib, but contacts with other sites in the region decrease dramatically. The Sinai coastal route to Palestine apparently fell into disuse at the same time, no doubt linked to this reduction in Egyptian activity (Ben-Tor 1991: 5). The growing authority and independence of southern Palestinian cities may have been a factor, whilst an increase in maritime trade may have released the Egyptians from their dependence on southern Palestine as a source of commodities (Brandl 1992: 447–8). The fundamental change in Egyptian relations with southern Palestine mirrors developments in Nubia (see below). Instead of a 'broad border-zone occupied by intermixed Egyptian and native trading-posts and villages' in the northern Sinai and southern Palestine (Seidlmayer 1996b: 113), Egypt seems to have adopted a more exploitative and hostile attitude. This is reflected in military campaigns which are recorded from the beginning of the First Dynasty.

Military activity

Given the lack of any evidence for a military aspect to the late Predynastic and First Dynasty Egyptian presence in southern Palestine, the campaigns launched by Egypt's early rulers perhaps amounted to nothing more than a series of occasional, punitive raids designed to ensure the continued co-operation of the local populace. It has been suggested that the Narmer Palette records a military campaign against Palestine. The determinative accompanying one of the king's slain enemies does indeed bear a close resemblance to a 'desert kite', a stone-walled enclosure used by the nomadic shepherds of southern Palestine. It is possible, therefore, that the campaigns undertaken by the king to secure the borders of his newly unified realm included a skirmish with the people on Egypt's north-eastern border. More certain evidence for Narmer's dealings with Palestine is provided by a fragment of inscribed ivory from his tomb complex at Abydos (B17). It shows a bearded man of Asiatic appearance, wearing a curious pendulous head-dress and a long, dappled robe. The man holds a branch or plant in one hand and is depicted in a stooping posture, perhaps paying homage to the Egyptian king (Petrie 1901: pl. IV.4–5).

There are contemporary inscriptions suggesting military campaigns against 'the Asiatics' by several Early Dynastic kings (Figure 5.1). An ivory label of Den – originally attached to a pair of his sandals – from his tomb at Abydos shows the king smiting a kneeling captive (Amélineau 1899: pl. XXXIII; Spencer 1980: 65, pls 49, 53 [Cat. 460], 1993: 87, fig. 67). The caption can be translated as 'First time of smiting the easterner(s)', though

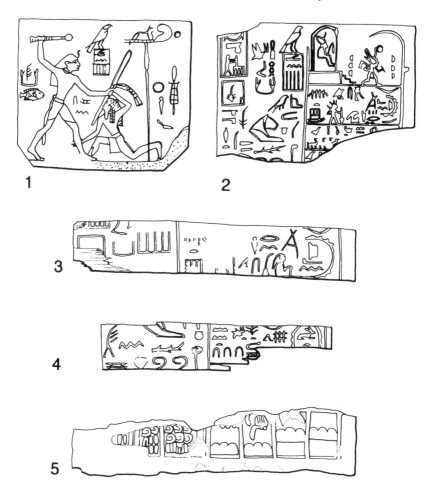

Figure 5.1 Campaigns against southern Palestine. Iconographic evidence for Egyptian aggression (real or ideological) against lands to the north-east: (1) year label of king Den from Abydos, bearing the legend 'First time of smiting the east(erners)' (after Spencer 1980: pl. 53, cat. 460); (2) (3) (4) year labels of Den referring to the destruction of enemy fortresses, presumably in southern Palestine; on the most complete label, the reference to the destruction of a fortress is at the right-hand side of the second register (after Petrie 1900: pl. XV.16–18); (5) fragment of stone relief from a building at Hierakonpolis erected under Khasekhemwy, giving the names of (conquered?) foreign localities (after Quibell and Green 1902: pl. XXIII, bottom). Not to same scale.

the label could record a ritual event rather than an actual campaign. The identification of the conquered enemy is further aided by details of the local landscape which are depicted behind the captive. The sandy, hilly topography confirms the location of the campaign as the arid lands to the north-east of Egypt, in other words the Sinai or southern Palestine. The occurrence of Den's name at En Besor (see above) confirms Egyptian activity in southern Palestine during his reign. Further evidence that Den carried out campaigns against Western Asia is provided by four fragmentary year labels from Abydos (Petrie 1900: pl. XV.16–18, 1902: pl. XI.8). They fall into two pairs of similar or identical inscriptions. Each mentions a fortified oval enclosure, preceded by the sign *wp*, 'open', probably with the meaning 'breach' (cf. Weill 1961: 21). On one type of label, the enclosure is labelled as *wn(t)*, a word which can be translated as 'stronghold' from its occurrence in the Old Kingdom Inscription of Weni (Sethe 1903: 103, line 12; Lichtheim 1975: 20; cf. Weill 1961: 18). Like the *wnwt* destroyed by Weni, the stronghold(s) breached by Den probably lay in northern Sinai or southern Palestine. The other two enclosures, on the second type of label, are named as ʿ*3ʿn* or, more simply, ʿ*3n*. It is tempting to interpret this as the Semitic word 'En/ʿAin: 'well' (Weill 1961: 21), referring to a settlement founded at the site of a spring (for example, En Besor). In each case the enclosure is shown breached on one side, and the hoe depicted next to it probably symbolises destruction. The presence of Palestinian vassals or captives at the Egyptian royal court is again hinted at later in the First Dynasty. An ivory gaming-rod from the tomb of Qaa at Abydos shows a bound Asiatic captive. The hieroglyphs above his head clearly label him as an inhabitant of *Stt* (Syria-Palestine) (Petrie 1900: pl. XII.12–13 = pl. XVII.30).

At the end of the Second Dynasty, sealings of Sekhemib include the epithet *inw ḫ3st*, 'conqueror of a foreign land' (or, alternatively, 'foreign tribute'), suggesting military activity on Egypt's frontiers. A sealing of Peribsen from his tomb at Abydos bears the similar epithet *inw Stt*, 'conqueror/tribute of Setjet'. Whilst Setjet usually signifies Syria-Palestine, the determinative in this case is the town sign, rather than the sign for 'foreign land'. This suggests that Setjet was a locality on Egypt's north-eastern border, possibly Sethroë. The late Second Dynasty witnessed fundamental changes in Egypt's relationship with Palestine. In the reign of Khasekhemwy an official is attested, for the first time, with the title *imi-r(3) ḫ3st*, 'overseer of foreign land(s)'. If this refers to southern Palestine rather than the Sinai (see below), it indicates that a new era had begun in Near Eastern geo-politics. Egypt was now secure enough within its own borders to place its dealings with Palestine on a proper administrative footing.

Imports from Syria-Palestine in the Early Dynastic period

It is likely that the lucrative and important trade with southern Palestine remained a state monopoly throughout the Early Dynastic period. The preservation of such a monopoly may have been one of the factors which contributed to the further centralisation of the state during the first three dynasties (Marfoe 1987: 26–8). An idea of the volume of Early Dynastic trade may be gained from the huge quantities of copper found in some élite and royal burials of the First and Second Dynasties. Tomb S3471 at North Saqqara, dating to the reign of Djer, contained some 700 copper objects, including 75 'ingots' (Marfoe 1987: 26). A smaller but similar hoard was found in the tomb of Khasekhemwy at Abydos. By the Fifth Dynasty, copper had become sufficiently common for a long drain-pipe to be made of the metal for Sahura's funerary complex (Marfoe 1987: 26).

The other main archaeological evidence for trade contact between Egypt and the Near East in the Early Dynastic period consists of a large number of imported Syro-Palestinian vessels found in royal and private tombs, particularly during the mid–late First Dynasty (Adams and Porat 1996). Precise parallels excavated in Israel have helped to confirm the correlation between the First Dynasty in Egypt and the EBII period in Palestine, one of the best-attested chronological connections in Near Eastern archaeology (Bourriau 1981: 128). Imported Syro-Palestinian vessels were first identified in Egypt by Petrie in the royal tombs of Djer, Den and Semerkhet at Abydos, and were thus nicknamed 'Abydos ware'. In fact, this group of foreign pottery comprises three distinct wares. The first, and most common, is a red-polished ware characterised by a drab or brown fabric with gritty mineral inclusions, fired at relatively low temperatures. The second type is a ware with a distinctive metallic ring, produced by high firing; the surface may be plain, burnished, lattice-burnished or combed. The third and rarest ware is of a similar fabric to the red-polished ware, but light-faced or white-slipped, with painted geometric designs in brown or red (Kantor 1965: 15). Painted ware is not found in Egypt before the reign of Den (Adams and Porat 1996: 98), and is most common in contexts dating to the end of the First Dynasty. The first two wares are diagnostic for EBII Palestine, Byblos and other southern Syrian sites. Comparative **petrographic analysis** of vessels from Egypt and the Near East indicates that these wares were probably manu-factured in northern Israel or the Lebanon, in the vicinity of Mt. Hermon (Adams and Porat 1996: 102). Although the light-faced ware also occurs, sporadically, in Phase G of the **Amuq** sites in northern Syria, it too seems to have originated in Palestine, probably in Lower Galilee in the vicinity of Lake Kinneret (Adams and Porat 1996: 104). It seems, therefore, that the combination of pottery types represented by these imports was char-acteristic for Palestine and the Syrian coast, regions which were connected by both land and sea routes to Egypt (Kantor 1965: 16). The appearance of painted ware in Egyptian contexts from the reign of Den onwards may indicate a shift in patterns of trade, with Palestine playing an enhanced role compared to the situation earlier in the First Dynasty.

Imported vessels in Egypt occur in a range of shapes, suggesting that they may have been used to transport a variety of commodities (Bourriau 1981: 128). Oils and aromatic resins were probably amongst the most important trade goods (O'Connor 1987: 33), and a large vessel excavated at Abu Rawash was found to contain a hard black substance, identified as resin (Klasens 1961: 113). Scientific analysis – by gas chromatography/ mass spectrometry – of the contents of vessels from the tomb of Djer indicates that vegetable oils were a major imported commodity. However, one vessel apparently contained resin from a member of the pine family, though it is impossible to identify the species more precisely (Serpico and White 1996). The vast majority of imported Syro-Palestinian pottery comes from sites in Lower Egypt, notably North Saqqara. This is not so surprising, given the greater proximity of northern sites to the Near Eastern trade routes. The few imported vessels from Upper Egypt derive exclusively from the royal burial complexes at Abydos. Obviously, there was no difficulty for the king and the royal court in acquiring imported commodities (especially if foreign trade was a royal monopoly). Altogether, some 124 complete or fragmentary Syro-Palestinian vessels are known from Early Dynastic Egyptian contexts, plus several dozen unrestorable fragments. Two-thirds of the vessels (81) come from tombs dating to the reign of Den. The others range in date from the very early First Dynasty, probably the reign of Narmer (from Abu Rawash tomb 389 [Klasens 1958: 37–8]), to the Second Dynasty, with a particular cluster at the end of the First Dynasty in the reigns of Semerkhet and Qaa (29 vessels). The apparent concentration of imports in the reign of Den is more likely to be a reflection of the large number of élite burials of this date, rather than evidence for an upsurge in trading activity, although the latter possibility cannot be ruled out. Similarly, the paucity of evidence for trade with the Near East after the end of the First Dynasty is probably due, to a large extent, to the relatively small number of élite burials which can be securely dated to the Second and Third Dynasties (Kantor 1965: 17). The single imported vessel from a Second Dynasty tomb at Helwan suggests that trade contacts did continue, albeit perhaps at a reduced level. Egyptian and Egyptianising objects of Second Dynasty date from Ai in southern Palestine provide further evidence for the continuity of trade between the two regions (Kantor 1965: 16), as do the Syro-Palestinian imports found in Old Kingdom contexts.

In addition to the excavated vessels, there is also a limited amount of representational evidence for Palestinian vessels in Early Dynastic Egypt. An ivory fragment from the tomb complex of Narmer at Abydos (B17) depicts a servant carrying on his head a distinctive Palestinian ledge- and loop-handled vessel (Petrie 1901: pl. IIIA.2). Another ivory piece from the royal mortuary complex of Narmer's successor Aha shows a similarly bearded man carrying a loop-handled jar of Palestinian form (Petrie 1901:

pl. IV.6). The other side of this intensive trade is attested at Tell Arad, where large numbers of imported First Dynasty Egyptian vessels have been excavated (Kantor 1965: 16), including a jar-fragment incised with the *serekh* of Narmer (Amiran 1974, 1976).

Changing patterns of trade and the rise of Byblos

Towards the end of the Second Dynasty, the intensity of Egyptian trade with southern Palestine – which had been a continuous feature of Egypt's foreign relations for over half a millennium – seems to have diminished very markedly. This development may be connected with the rise of urban polities in southern Palestine at about the same time. Although the trade in certain commodities, notably copper and bitumen, may have been maintained, evidence for direct Egyptian involvement in southern Palestine during the Old Kingdom is practically non-existent (Ben-Tor 1991: 5). The autobiography of Weni, from the Sixth Dynasty, suggests that punitive raids persisted. These may have been inspired by a desire to maintain access to or control raw materials; certainly, the gathering of booty was an important aspect of such campaigns. However, the formal commercial arrangements which must have characterised Early Dynastic relations had clearly undergone major changes (Marfoe 1987: 26).

The most important factor behind this new pattern of inter-regional contacts is likely to have been the rise of the Lebanese littoral, and in particular the port and hinterland of Byblos, as the new focus of Egypt's trading interests. It is likely that the establishment of regular trade with Byblos made the import of goods from southern Palestine redundant and brought Egyptian ties with the region largely to an end. The Byblos region could now provide Egypt with all the raw materials it required, both those previously obtained from southern Palestine and other products, notably cedar logs. The first definite evidence for Early Dynastic Egyptian contact with Byblos is a fragment of a breccia stone vessel from the area of the Egyptian temple. It is incised with the words *Ḥ'-sḥmwi di 'nḥ*, 'Khasekhemwy, given life', and suggests that some sort of direct contact between the port and Egypt may have been established at the end of the Second Dynasty. Possible support for this view may be provided by the fleet of boats buried adjacent to the Shunet ez-Zebib at Abydos, Khasekhemwy's funerary enclosure, discovered in 1991. Although analysis of the wood has yet to be carried out, it must be at least a possibility that the large quantities of timber involved indicate the beginnings of the timber trade with Byblos.

The first definitely attested use of Lebanese cedar in Egypt is in the construction of Khufu's funerary boats in the Fourth Dynasty at Giza. The earliest surviving inscription referring to cedar from Byblos dates to the reign of Khufu's predecessor Sneferu (Schäfer 1902: 30; Ben-Tor 1991: 4).

The traditional view that cedar was used in Early Dynastic tombs, and indeed in Predynastic burials, cannot be supported, since none of the pieces of wood concerned has been unequivocally identified as Lebanese cedar (Ben-Tor 1991: 4; contra Hoffman 1980: 270). Indeed, it is quite possible that coniferous woods reached Predynastic Egypt from North African or more local sources (Moorey 1987: 41). Precise identification was often impossible, due to the small size and condition of the specimens. In the case of the large beams employed in the construction of the First Dynasty royal tombs at Abydos, the photograph of one plank suggests that the wood was in fact palm (Ben-Tor 1991: 4), which occurred naturally within Egypt. It is probable that most of the early pieces referred to by the excavators as cedar were in fact other coniferous woods (such as fir) which grew in southern Palestine. The existence of Egyptian trade with southern Palestine as early as the Badarian and Naqada I periods makes it likely that coniferous woods were also imported from this region.

As well as the archaeological evidence, there is sound textual evidence that coniferous woods and associated products, such as oils and resins, were imported into Egypt as early as the reign of Aha. Oil from the *mrw*-tree – often translated as 'cedar', but possibly used at this early period to denote Asiatic conifers in general – is mentioned on an alabaster vessel and a label of Aha (Petrie 1901: pl. 10.2; Kaplony 1963: 308; Ward 1991: 14). The third register of this label has been interpreted by one scholar as showing 'the return of a sea-going expedition from Lebanon with a load of the highly desired, coniferous meru wood' (O'Connor 1987: 33–4), although the commodity to which the label was originally attached is more likely to have been the processed *mrw* oil rather than the wood itself. The same oil is also mentioned on a pottery vessel from the Early Dynastic cemetery of Abu Umuri (Kaplony 1964: no. 1065). Later in the First Dynasty, the products of another coniferous tree – ʿš in Egyptian, possibly fir or juniper – are mentioned on stone vessels of Anedjib (Lacau and Lauer 1959: pl. 3.6–7; Kaplony 1963: 306; Ward 1991: 13). The term occurs again on a Second Dynasty stela from Helwan (Saad 1957: 19). A contemporary stela from the same site names another oil or resin obtained from the ʿš-tree, namely *sṯt*. This product is likewise attested on a Third Dynasty stela in Brooklyn (James 1974: 11), while the early Third Dynasty tomb of Hesira at Saqqara mentions both ʿš and *sṯt* oils (H. Altenmüller 1976: 3, 13; Ward 1991: 13).

The virtual abandonment of Egypt's long-standing links with southern Palestine was an important development. The principal reason for such a fundamental change in the pattern of Egyptian foreign trade is likely to have been economic, in particular a 'spiralling interdependence between timber procurement, ship construction and carrying capacity' (Marfoe 1987: 27). Larger ships, capable of undertaking sea voyages, would have provided easier and faster transportation for larger cargoes, compared to overland caravans. It has been estimated that a ship-borne cargo of trade goods could have reached Egypt in half the time required for animal and human porterage. However, the construction of seaworthy ships was only made possible by access to the superior timber of the Byblos hinterland. Thus, once the Egyptians had gained a foothold on the Lebanese littoral, economic factors quickly led to the dominance of this particular trade relationship.

Relations with Libya

Several of the ceremonial palettes from the period of state formation depict slain or captive enemies wearing the penis sheath. In later artistic convention, this piece of clothing was used, *inter alia*, to indicate Libyans. It is possible, therefore, that these palettes record skirmishes between the Egyptians and their western neighbours during the process to forge a unified Egyptian state. A more convincing piece of evidence for Egyptian contact with Libya is the so-called 'Libyan Palette' from the very end of the Predynastic period. The palette seems to record the name *Thnw*, later associated with Libya, below a depiction of booty. This suggests a military campaign against Libya by a late Predynastic ruler, part of a general phenomenon of aggressive activity on and beyond Egypt's borders which characterises the period of state formation. Further support for this interpretation is provided by a small ivory cylinder from Hierakonpolis, dating to the first reign of the First Dynasty. It depicts the catfish element of Narmer's name smiting three registers of bound captives. Under the tail of the catfish a short inscription names *(T3) Thnw*, '(the land of) Libya'. This record of a campaign by Narmer is the earliest-known definite representation of Libyans. In accordance with later practice, they are shown with beards.

After these early contacts of a more or less hostile nature, Egypt seems to have shown little interest in its western neighbour until much later in its history. There is no further, unequivocal evidence for Egypt's relations with Libya during the rest of the Early Dynastic period. Workmen's drawings on the enclosure wall of Sekhemkhet's mortuary complex include a crude figure tentatively identified as a Libyan (Goneim 1957: 2, and 5 fig. 12), but this identification is doubtful.

Long-distance trade contacts

As well as direct contacts of a commercial or military nature with its more immediate neighbours, early Egypt maintained trading contacts with more distant lands. Evidence of long-distance trade is to be found in the wide range of exotic materials buried in wealthy graves of the late Predynastic and Early Dynastic periods. A good example is Tomb 11 at Hierakonpolis

Locality 6 (Adams and Friedman 1992: 334). Dating to Naqada III, the burial contained many examples of prestige materials imported from distant lands. These included lapis lazuli beads from Afghanistan or Iran; small fragments of flanged barrel beads made of silver, probably from eastern Anatolia; garnet from the eastern desert; turquoise from the mines of Sinai; and **obsidian** blades from Ethiopia (or Anatolia). Such a combination of prestige materials in a single grave clearly indicates the wealth of the tomb owner, the economic power of late Predynastic rulers and the well-developed nature of long-distance trade networks in the late fourth millennium BC.

Silver from Anatolia

According to the few analyses which have been conducted, the small number of silver objects from Early Dynastic contexts seem to be made of native Egyptian silver-gold (Prag 1978: 40); that is, gold with a high percentage (as much as 70 per cent) of silver, often referred to as 'electrum' ($\underline{d}^{c}m$). By contrast, the silver from late Predynastic contexts seems to be more pure, with a much lower percentage of gold (Prag 1978: 39), and was, therefore, probably imported from Anatolia. The only major sources of silver in the Near East recognised today are in the Amanus Range (Prag 1978: 40). Situated some 300 kilometres north of Byblos, it was probably this region that Sargon of Akkad referred to as the 'silver mountain', on a tablet set up in the temple Ekur in Nippur (Pritchard 1969: 268).

The largest group of fourth-millennium silver objects (over 200) comes from the *Enéolithique* cemetery at Byblos. Such a concentration of silver at one site suggests that Byblos may have played an important role in the Near Eastern silver trade during the fourth millennium (Prag 1978: 41). The disappearance of imported silver from Egyptian contexts at the beginning of the Early Dynastic period may indicate that the Levantine source of supply had been worked out by this date, causing the trade via Byblos to cease. The new sources further to the north, which had a higher lead content and thus required a more sophisticated technology to extract the silver, seem to have supplied western Anatolia and Mesopotamia in preference to Syria-Palestine and Egypt (Prag 1978: 41). In the Early Dynastic period, therefore, Egypt fell back upon its own reserves of 'white metal', namely the native silver-rich gold ores of the eastern desert.

Obsidian from Anatolia, Arabia and Eritrea

Another material which may have been imported from Anatolia is obsidian, the hard, black, volcanic glass much prized both for blades and for decorative objects. No obsidian occurs within the borders of modern or ancient Egypt. A recent analysis of an obsidian tool from Tell el-Iswid South in the north-eastern Delta suggests that the material itself came from the Taurus Mountains in eastern Anatolia (Nemrut Dag) (Schmidt 1992: 34); Anatolia has been identified as the primary source for the obsidian trade to the Levant, Mesopotamia and Iran in ancient times (Zarins 1990: 509). However, Anatolian obsidian has not been identified in the southern Negev or Sinai, regions known to have been in close contact with Egypt during the late Predynastic and Early Dynastic periods (Zarins 1990: 512). Furthermore, of 16 Egyptian sites with reported obsidian finds, only five are in Lower Egypt (Zarins 1989: 366). Both these factors make it likely that most of the obsidian from early Egyptian contexts derives from the sources closer to the Red Sea. Trace element analysis suggests sources in Arabia and Eritrea, which would have supplied Egypt through coastal exchange and perhaps sea-borne missions down Egypt's Red Sea coast (Zarins 1989: 368).

Obsidian is by no means common in early Egyptian contexts. It may be significant that many pieces were apparently found at Coptos, the town that controlled access to Red Sea trade later in Egypt's history (Zarins 1989: 366). Obsidian was also found in several areas of the Early Dynastic temple at Hierakonpolis, although not all the occurrences can be securely dated to the Early Dynastic period. An obsidian bead was actually found underneath the Narmer Palette in the 'Main Deposit' (Adams and Friedman 1992: 319). Most of the obsidian from Early Dynastic Egypt comes from royal tombs. Three small vases were found in Chamber C of the tomb of Neith-hotep at Naqada (de Morgan 1897: 163, figs 625–7). Tomb B5 at Abydos, also dating to the reign of Aha, contained a serrated object of obsidian, referred to as a 'comb' (Petrie 1901: pl. XXXII.10). Vases and vase fragments were found in the mortuary complexes of Djer and Anedjib at Abydos (Petrie 1901: pl. XLVIII). There seem to be no published examples of obsidian from clear Second or Third Dynasty contexts.

Lapis lazuli from Afghanistan and Iran

The ancient lapis lazuli trade appears to have had more than one supply source (Delmas and Casanova 1990: 504), including mines in the former Soviet Union (Pamir Mountains) and Pakistan (the Chagai Hills on the Pakistan–Iran border), as well as the well-known mines of Sar-i Sang in the Badakhshan province of Afghanistan. Although there is a very faint possibility that there may have been a source of lapis lazuli in the region of the Kharga or Dakhla Oasis, this is unconfirmed (Needler 1984: 311). The sources in Asia remain the most likely origin for the lapis found in Predynastic and Early Dynastic contexts.

The largest object of lapis from early Egypt is the statuette from the Hierakonpolis 'Main Deposit'. It has no parallels in Egypt and may well be of foreign manufacture (Payne 1968: 58; Rice 1990). The Early Dynastic contexts in which lapis has been found include early First Dynasty graves at Tura and Tarkhan, the tomb of Djer at Abydos, and mastaba V at Nazlet Batran. This large tomb is dated by inscription (Petrie 1907: pl. IIIA), by its architecture (Petrie 1907: 5) and by its contents (cf. Petrie 1901: pl. L.153) to the reign of Djet. In addition to the fine toilet objects of gold and ivory, the tomb contained a small but exquisite vase of lapis lazuli (Petrie 1907: 4, pls III, V.3). This represents the last occurrence of lapis in Early Dynastic Egypt, as the long-distance trade seems to have been disrupted early in the First Dynasty (Payne 1968). There is a break in the presence of lapis in Egyptian contexts from after the reign of Djet (contra Rice 1990: 90) and throughout the Second and Third Dynasties. This hiatus in the supply matches a similar disruption in Mesopotamia, from shortly after the beginning of EBI until EBII (Herrmann 1968: 37; Moorey 1987: 39), and may have been the result of political changes in present-day Iran. Lapis lazuli is not attested again in Egypt until the Fourth Dynasty, some 500 years later. The earliest reference to lapis lazuli (ḫsbd) in an inscription is in the early Fourth Dynasty tomb of Rahotep (Petrie 1892: pl. XIII).

The Sinai

Throughout Egyptian history, the northern Sinai coast formed a convenient route from Egypt to southern Palestine. Egypt's contacts with northern Sinai were thus inextricably bound up with the changing pattern of Egyptian–Palestinian relations. Throughout the era of intensive contacts between Egypt and southern Palestine – the late Predynastic period and First Dynasty – northern Sinai must have played an important role. It served as the primary route for the movement of both people and commodities. However, the Egyptian sites along the north Sinai coastal route do not appear to have supported a permanent population, since the pottery was all imported from the Nile valley (Porat 1992: 435) – unlike the situation at sites in southern Palestine itself where, as we have seen, Egyptians made their own pottery from local materials. The storage vessels incised with early royal *serekh*s found at el-Beda in northern Sinai (Clédat 1914) illustrate the region's strategic location on the main trade route between Egypt and the Near East.

By contrast, the more remote and inaccessible southern part of the Sinai peninsula was only of interest to the Egyptians for its mineral resources. The history of Egyptian involvement in southern Sinai is thus essentially the history of Egyptian mining expeditions, beginning only in the Third Dynasty. In the mountains of southern Sinai a network of Palestinian settlements has been excavated, dating to the EBII (First and Second Dynasties in Egypt) (Beit-Arieh 1984). Their material culture shows close links with contemporary sites in southern Palestine, especially Tell Arad. Arad was the largest fortified town in southern Palestine at this time and may well have exercised some degree of control over the southern Sinai settlements. Their primary purpose, it would appear, was to exploit the nearby resources of copper for export. It is striking that none of these EBII settlements shows any signs of Egyptian influence. Egypt therefore seems to have shown little interest in southern Sinai during the First and Second Dynasties. The evidence from southern Sinai makes it unlikely that the First Dynasty Egyptian involvement in Palestine was of an expansionist nature for, in such a situation, the Egyptian authorities would scarcely have allowed the contact between Arad and the copper-mining settlements of southern Sinai to continue uninterrupted (Beit-Arieh 1984: 23).

To date, the earliest evidence of Egyptian involvement in southern Sinai comprises the Third Dynasty rock-cut inscriptions in the Wadi Maghara, the site of turquoise-mining expeditions. It appears that the Egyptians did not venture beyond the immediate sources of turquoise, as there is no evidence of an Egyptian presence or influence at other sites in southern Sinai during the Early Dynastic period (Beit-Arieh 1984: 22–3). Altogether, three kings have left inscriptions at Wadi Maghara: Netjerikhet (Djoser), Sekhemkhet and Sanakht (Gardiner and Peet 1952: pls I, IV; Giveon 1974). It is clear that the main purpose of the Egyptian expeditions was to mine turquoise, a highly valued semi-precious stone used particularly in jewellery. The name given to the Wadi Maghara in later inscriptions is *ḥtyw mfk3t*, 'the turquoise terraces' (Gardiner and Peet 1955: 1). The main stratum of turquoise-bearing rock lay about half-way up the cliff and the workings consisted of galleries with a small opening on the cliff-face (Gardiner and Peet 1955: 20). Expeditions were clearly a royal monopoly, organised along the same lines as military campaigns. The Egyptian word *mšꜥ* may be translated either as 'expedition' or as 'army', depending on the context; it merely denotes an organised body of men.

The rock-cut inscription carved under Netjerikhet is the most informative about the composition and purpose of the Third Dynasty mining expeditions (Gardiner and Peet 1955: 53). As well as depictions of the king, it includes the figure of a man carrying a staff of office and a hand axe. The inscription above his head gives his titles: *imi-r(3) mšꜥ* and *ꜥd-mr ḫ3st*, 'overseer of the expedition' and 'administrator of the foreign land'. It is unclear whether the latter title refers to southern Palestine, southern Sinai or the land beyond Egypt's north-eastern frontier in general. If, in this instance, the title refers to southern Sinai, as the context of the inscription suggests, it indicates that the area was considered to be outside the Egyptian realm, at least for administrative purposes, even though it was accessible to Egyptian mining expeditions. Two columns of text to the left of the figure detail the nature of the 'royal mission' (*wpt nswt*). Although not all the inscription is readable, the end seems to refer to 'this mountain of all minerals'. A smaller figure, accompanied by some illegible signs, follows. Behind this, in turn, are four vertical groups of hieroglyphs, each of which gives the name of a member of the expedition. One individual, called Meri-ib, bore the title 'royal stonemason/ carpenter', giving an indication of the type of craftsmen who accompanied such an expedition to the turquoise mines. The main inscription of Sekhemkhet, a standard scene showing the king smiting a foreign enemy, is also accompanied by a figure labelled as the *imi-r(3) mš^c* (Gardiner and Peet 1955: 52). In addition, he bears a string of titles (*ḥ3ti-^c*, *smr*, . . . *nswt*, *šmsw-iz* and *z3 nswt*), indicating that he was a man of considerable rank with close connections to the royal court. Whether he was in fact a royal son (*z3 nswt*) is not certain, since this title was also used in an honorific sense by some non-royal high officials in the Old Kingdom. Two rock-cut inscriptions of Sanakht show the king in traditional scenes, smiting a captive and accompanied by the standard of Wepwawet (Gardiner and Peet 1955: 54–6). The fragmentary smiting scene, now in the British Museum, includes the earliest-known occurrence of the word *mfk3t*, 'turquoise' (Spencer 1993: 101, fig. 77).

PERIPHERAL REGIONS

Like the Near East and the Sinai, the desert regions bordering the Nile valley also seem to have been a focus of early activity (Figure 5.2). In all probability, the geographical division between the Sinai and Egypt's desert margins, adopted here for convenience, is not one that the Egyptians themselves would have recognised. Indeed, the use of the titles *imi-r3 ḥ3st* and *^cd-mr ḥ3st* may suggest that for the Early Dynastic Egyptians there was only one designation for all the lands beyond their own borders: *ḥ3st*, 'foreign hill-country'. Certainly the Egyptians' interest in the Sinai and the desert margins stemmed from the same consideration: the rich stone and mineral resources which both regions possessed, and which the court required to supply its workshops.

'One might expect that contact between desert and valley was always, if only sporadically, maintained' (Kemp 1983: 118), and there is a surprising amount of evidence for Early Dynastic involvement in the eastern and western deserts. Whilst the geographical limit for rock-cut inscriptions in the western desert appears to be a distance of just 12 miles from the Nile valley, inscriptions in the eastern desert are found 'up to 65 miles from the river, well into the heart of the Red Sea hills' (Hoffman 1980: 243). This indicates a greater intensity of Egyptian activity in the eastern desert, probably accompanied by a greater degree of interaction

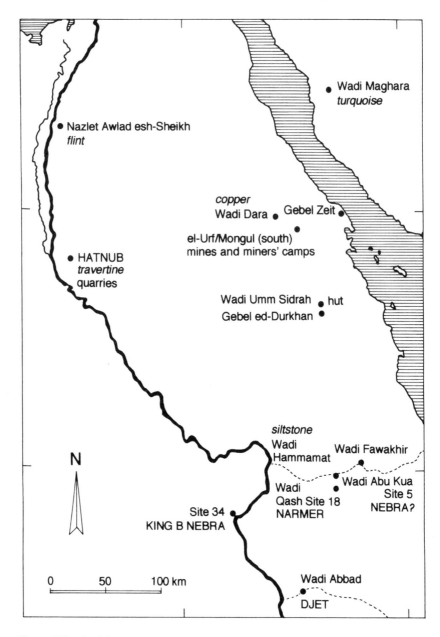

Figure 5.2 Activity in Egypt's desert margins. The map shows the principal sites in the Egyptian deserts where evidence has been found of Early Dynastic activity.

with the indigenous inhabitants of the region. Unfortunately, we know very little about the ancient populations of the desert margins. Scatters of pottery and isolated temporary encampments suggest that the deserts supported groups of semi-nomadic pastoralists, in whose lives and livelihoods cattle played an important part. Their material cultures, as far as they are attested archaeologically, are generally simple and show 'broad overall similarities both to each other and to those of the Nile valley' (Kemp 1983: 116). None the less, it is likely that each group had its own history and identity and that, if more were known about their material cultures, a picture of considerable diversity would emerge (Kemp 1983: 116–17).

The eastern desert

The hills and mountains separating the Nile valley from the Red Sea receive significantly more rainfall than the western desert, especially further south towards Nubia. This gives rise to a number of wells, and enables some of the numerous wadis to support vegetation – even irregular cultivation in the upper reaches of some of the larger wadis. Thus, the eastern desert has, from earliest times, supported a population of nomadic and semi-nomadic pastoralists, with whom the Egyptians – who visited the area frequently on mining and quarrying expeditions – must have come into regular contact.

Records of early Egyptian activity in the eastern desert are found in the form of rock-cut inscriptions. These usually give just the name of the king in whose reign the expedition was mounted. The earliest dated inscription is at Site 18 in the Wadi Qash, a tributary of the Wadi Hammamat almost due east of Qus, half-way between the Nile valley and the Red Sea coast. The *serekh* of Narmer is accompanied by another, tantalisingly empty *serekh* (Winkler 1938: 10, pl. XI.1; Emery 1961: 47, fig. 6). A rock-cut inscription in the Wadi Abbad, east of Elkab, shows the *serekh* of Djet preceded by the *k3* sign (Clère 1938). The inscription is incised on a rock at the junction of the Wadi Miyah and the Wadi Chagab, some 25 kilometres along the Wadi Abbad (Clère 1938: 85, fig. 7) and five kilometres beyond Bir Abbad (Porter and Moss 1951: 321). The Wadi Abbad was one of the principal routes from the Nile valley to the Red Sea, in later times linking Edfu and Berenice (Clère 1938: 92). A third inscription is situated at the mouth of the Wadi Abu Kua (Site 5) within the Wadi Hammamat system, due east of Qift (Winkler 1938: pl. XI.5; Porter and Moss 1951: 328). The meaning of the text is difficult to interpret, but the inscription may include the name of the Second Dynasty king, Nebra. A more extensive inscription in a small wadi north of the Wadi Fawakhir provides a small piece of information about the composition of Egyptian expeditions to the eastern desert. Dated by its orthography to the Early Dynastic period, the inscription depicts a divine bark – of Horus or Sokar – and the accompanying text mentions an overseer of craftsmen. Hence, the expedition which cut this particular inscription was probably engaged in quarrying activity, supervised by a craftsman with experience in stone-cutting (Porter and Moss 1951: 329).

The Wadi Hammamat

The Wadi Hammamat system of the eastern desert was important for two reasons. First, throughout most of Egyptian history it was the main source of siltstone (Lucas 1962: 419–20, who calls the rock 'greywacke'; Aston 1994: 28–32). This was the stone used for cosmetic palettes in the Predynastic period, including the great commemorative palettes created for early Egyptian rulers in celebration of their kingship. Small-scale expeditions to procure supplies of the stone must have been mounted from Upper Egypt as early as the Badarian period, since palettes are a characteristic component of the Badarian funerary repertoire (Brunton and Caton-Thompson 1928: pl. XXI; Spencer 1993: 25). As economic and political power became increasingly concentrated in the hands of a few lineages towards the end of the Predynastic period, missions to the Wadi Hammamat probably came under closer royal control, eventually becoming state-sponsored expeditions in the Early Dynastic period.

Second, the Wadi Hammamat was important as the most direct route between the Nile valley and the Red Sea. From late Predynastic times, this route ran from Qift or Qus to Quseir (Winkler 1938; Baines and Málek 1980: 111). There is still some argument about the likelihood of maritime contacts via the Red Sea between Egypt and other cultures, particularly the early Mesopotamians of Sumer and Susa (Rice 1990). Nevertheless, the Red Sea coast itself was a valuable source of prestige objects for the developing élites of Predynastic Upper Egypt. In particular, Red Sea shells seems to have been imbued with a special symbolic and/or religious importance, as well as being a valued trade commodity (for example, Brunton and Caton-Thompson 1928: 41). Hence, representations of the *Pteroceras* (*Lambis*) shell were carved on the sides of the Coptos colossi, the gigantic sculptures of a fertility god dated to the late Predynastic period (Williams 1988; Payne 1993: 13, pl. IV). Red Sea shells, probably exported from Egypt, have been found in élite contexts elsewhere in the Near East (Moorey, personal communication; cf. Rizkana and Seeher 1989: 117, 125). With the dual attraction of mineral resources and access to the Red Sea, it is not surprising that Egypt's early kings took a keen interest in the Wadi Hammamat, and the royal names carved on rocks are direct evidence for this.

Mines and quarries

STONE

The eastern desert is particularly rich in stone and mineral resources. As we have seen, the focus for stone-quarrying expeditions was undoubtedly the Wadi Hammamat and its associated wadis. None the less, other regions yielded valuable types of stone for various purposes. The travertine quarries at Hatnub in Middle Egypt seem to have been worked in the Early Dynastic period. Some of the incised stone vessels from the Step Pyramid complex bore the name of the site, *Hwt-nbw*, probably indicating the provenance of the material from which they were carved. Also in Middle Egypt, flint deposits were worked to provide the Egyptians with weapons and tools. Large-scale flint workings dating to the Early Dynastic period have been located at Nazlet Awlad esh-Sheikh, on the east bank of the Nile, some 75 kilometres south of the Fayum (Kaiser 1961b; Baines and Málek 1980: 31).

COPPER

The area of Pre-Cambrian formations to the west of Gebel Zeit on the Red Sea coast was exploited for its copper reserves from early times (Abdel Tawab *et al.* 1990). The vicinity of el-Urf/Mongul (south) has produced evidence of mining activity from the beginning of the Early Dynastic period to the early Old Kingdom, including miners' camps and other scattered dwellings. Some vessels could be as early as the end of the Predynastic period or the very beginning of the First Dynasty (Köhler, personal communication), but most of the pottery suggests a First or Second Dynasty date, although a Third Dynasty date is possible. It is significant that some of the pottery from both el-Urf/Mongul (south) and the Wadi Dara (see below) is of marl clay, and must therefore have been brought from Upper Egypt by the mining expeditions (Abdel Tawab *et al.* 1990: 364).

The copper mines of the Wadi Dara were also worked most intensively during the Early Dynastic and Old Kingdom periods. A French survey of Dara West has revealed several Early Dynastic sites (Abdel Tawab *et al.* 1990: 363), of which two have been excavated in detail, a habitation site and a miners' camp (Castel *et al.* 1992; Grimal 1993: 482–8, 1996: 570–2). A thin layer of occupation debris was found on the floor of the habitation site (site 5E), suggesting that the building had been inhabited for only a brief period. The pottery dates the occupation to the Third Dynasty. This is also the case at the nearby miners' camp (site 5A) where finds attest various activities, including cooking, storage of provisions and tools, tool repair and enrichment and storage of the copper ore (malachite). Numerous fragments of malachite were found throughout the camp, but the absence of any slag indicates that smelting took place elsewhere, perhaps on the neighbouring hillside. Another miners' camp in the Wadi Dara (site 3B), consisting of some thirty dry-stone rooms, is more difficult to date but the later strata seem to belong to the Fourth Dynasty. However, earlier activity at the site is indicated by the fact that the rooms are built on earlier mining galleries. Hearths and concentrations of slag on the adjacent terrace indicate the location where the ore was smelted.

The evidence from the copper mines indicates that the greatest intensity of Egyptian activity occurred during the Third Dynasty. This complements the evidence from the Wadi Maghara, Sinai, which attests to turquoise-mining expeditions sponsored by at least three kings of the Third Dynasty. Clearly, the Third Dynasty was a time of great Egyptian interest in the desert regions peripheral to the Nile valley and, more importantly, in the mineral resources of these inhospitable areas. The advances in organisation and centralised administration which must have accompanied the beginning of large-scale pyramid-building seem to have benefited other activities as well. Perhaps, for the first time, long-distance expeditions could be mounted by the royal court to exploit the resources of Egypt's desert borders in a systematic way.

GOLD

The comparative rarity of gold in Early Dynastic graves has led some to suggest that there was little, if any, systematic exploitation of the eastern desert gold reserves at this period (Klemm and Klemm 1994: 193), although grave-robbing could be an alternative explanation. Rather than regular gold-mining expeditions sent from the Nile valley, sporadic finds of gold by the nomadic populations of the eastern desert could have been traded with Egyptians on an *ad hoc* basis. A survey of the gold-bearing regions of the eastern desert has revealed only limited evidence for gold mining in the Predynastic and Early Dynastic periods (Klemm and Klemm 1994: 195, fig. 2). The scattered nature of the sites and the total lack of artefacts suggests that the mines may have been used by the local nomadic populations rather than by Egyptians.

OTHER

Whilst the Egyptians may not have engaged in gold-mining activity in the Early Dynastic period, there is no doubt that they mounted expeditions to the eastern desert in search of other commodities. A single, isolated Early Dynastic hut was discovered in the Wadi Umm Sidrah, near the Roman imperial porphyry mines at Gebel ed-Dukhan (G.W. Murray 1939). Many artefacts were recovered from the hut, including pottery, flint tools, ashes and bone fragments. Five earthenware pot-stands – apparently made from a locally produced fabric – showed signs of careful repair in antiquity, an indication of the value attached to pottery at a site some 160 kilometres from the Nile valley. A small, bag-shaped vessel has been dated to the First or Second Dynasty (G.W. Murray 1939: 38), providing a date for the hut and contents as a whole. The purpose behind such a dwelling is not clear, but is further evidence of the interest shown in Egypt's desert margins in the Early Dynastic period.

The western desert

Early Dynastic Egyptian contact with the western desert seems to have been on two levels. There is evidence for limited mixing of semi-nomadic desert-dwellers and Egyptians, at desert-edge sites in Upper Egypt. Rock-cut inscriptions also attest sporadic expeditions to the western desert, mounted by late Predynastic and Early Dynastic kings.

A desert-edge site to the west of Armant, investigated only summarily, yielded evidence of contact between the inhabitants of the Nile valley and groups of cattle-herding semi-nomads (Kemp 1983: 118). The relationship was possibly a symbiotic one, based upon the exchange of cattle. The site included a cemetery of 76 graves, which seems to indicate that the associated settlement was more than a mere temporary encampment. The pottery from the graves comprised both Egyptian vessels, dated to the Early Dynastic period, and non-Egyptian ripple-burnished ware. Some of the non-Egyptian vessels were decorated with incised patterns of chevrons below the rim. Twenty burials were of oxen, showing the great importance attached to cattle by these people. There were several small camps in the vicinity, indicated by 'scatters of flint tools and sherds with various incised or impressed patterns' (Kemp 1983: 118).

More direct Egyptian involvement in the western desert is illustrated by a number of rock-cut inscriptions on the escarpment of the high desert in the vicinity of Armant. Two separate inscriptions at site 34, on the edge of the limestone plateau, bear an early royal name which has not yet been read convincingly (Winkler 1938: pl. XI.2–3; Wilkinson 1995). The epigraphy of the inscription clearly indicates that the king in question must belong to the very end of the Predynastic period or 'Dynasty 0'. A third inscription, only 12 kilometres away, features the *serekh* of the Second Dynasty king, Nebra (Winkler 1938: 10, pl. XI.4; Emery 1961: 93, fig. 56), indicating that expeditions to the western desert were maintained during the Early Dynastic period. An ongoing survey of the desert roads in the Theban area has discovered a wealth of late Predynastic and Early Dynastic inscriptions; they include the name of a Third Dynasty official, and a large rock-cut scene from the period of state formation (Darnell and Darnell 1997: 26). The latter seems to record a military victory, perhaps one of the key events leading to the political unification of Egypt.

In contrast to the eastern desert, the western desert seems to have had few, if any, resources deemed worthy of exploitation by the ancient Egyptians. Its strategic importance lay in the oases. These fertile pockets of land, which had been settled from Palaeolithic times (Baines and Málek 1980: 187; Hoffman 1980) and which were very much part of the Egyptian realm despite their isolation from the Nile valley, guarded Egypt's frontier with the Libyan peoples to the west (Baines and Málek 1980: 19). References to the *Ṯhnw* from the Early Dynastic period (Hölscher 1955: 12–13), together with the evidence of the so-called 'Libyan Palette', imply hostile relations between Egypt and her western neighbour throughout the late Predynastic to Early Dynastic transition. In such a political climate, the maintenance of Egyptian control of the oases would clearly have been strategically important to Egypt's rulers. Access to the oases was by caravan, leaving the Nile valley at an appropriate point on the west bank. In the New Kingdom, and probably in earlier times too, the most important route through the western desert to the Kharga and Dakhla Oases left the Nile valley at Armant (Baines and Málek 1980: 43). It is possible, therefore, that the early rulers who left their names on the limestone escarpment behind Armant mounted expeditions of one sort or another to the western oases.

The oases

Whilst there is very little material to indicate Early Dynastic Egyptian activity in the oases, evidence from the Old Kingdom may suggest at least limited Egyptian involvement in earlier periods.

Kharga

The southernmost of the western desert oases is the Kharga oasis, which probably lay on the route (called 'the oasis road') from Egypt to Upper Nubia taken by Harkhuf in the Sixth Dynasty. Evidence for Egyptian contact with the Kharga oasis early in the Fourth Dynasty is provided by a complete 'Maidum' bowl, of red-polished ware with a reflexed rim, which was found upturned beside the track at the top of the Matana pass, in the south-east of the Kharga depression (Caton-Thompson 1952: 41, pl. 123.4). The Matana track joins the Bulaq track in the western desert between the oasis and the Nile valley, and reaches the latter in the vicinity of Armant. This ties in with the evidence from the western desert near Armant for Early Dynastic activity in the area. The isolated bowl 'is unlikely to be the unique relic of its kind and period' (Caton-Thompson 1952: 49) in the Kharga oasis and its associated passes. Further surveys may therefore be expected to reveal more evidence for early Egyptian contact with the Kharga oasis.

174

Dakhla

Situated to the north-west of Kharga, the Dakhla oasis was under Egyptian administration from the early Sixth Dynasty at the latest. The town of Balat at the heart of the Dakhla oasis seems to have served as the administrative centre for all the oases. A Canadian expedition found limited evidence for the presence of Egyptians in the Early Dynastic period (Mills 1980: 254). A small cemetery of some 60 graves in the far west of the oasis (32/390-L2) contained a semi-contracted burial of an elderly male (32/390-L2–1) with three intact pottery vessels (a jar and two bowls) (Hope 1980: 288–9, pl. XVII.b, c; Mills 1980: 258). On the basis of parallels from Egypt proper, these have been dated to the Early Dynastic period, although the identification has been described as 'rather tenuous' (Giddy 1987: 166). Even less certain is the attribution of a number of vessels and sherds from a nearby cemetery to the Third Dynasty. Late Old Kingdom parallels are known for all the forms (Giddy 1987: 166–7) and a Sixth Dynasty date is perhaps more likely given the abundant evidence for Egyptian activity in the Dakhla oasis at this period.

NUBIA

Egypt's relations with its southern neighbour were always of a different nature from contacts with the Near East or the desert margins. For the most part, and certainly throughout the Early Dynastic period, no attempt was made to settle those regions on a permanent basis or to incorporate them into the Egyptian realm. Their natural resources – whether foodstuffs, prestige commodities or minerals – were what interested the Egyptians, first and foremost. Though a few 'colony' sites seem to have been established in southern Palestine, they appear to have coexisted peacefully with the indigenous inhabitants. A reciprocal trade relationship between Egyptians and 'Asiatics' would have benefited both sides, and best fits the available evidence for Egyptian–Near Eastern relations in the Early Dynastic period. The desert margins and peripheral regions were visited only sporadically, by expeditions in search of particular materials, usually stones. In contrast to both these areas of Egyptian activity, the land to the south – the Nubian Nile valley – was far more easily accessible, and presented no great geographical difference from the Egyptians' own territory. But for the First Cataract south of Elephantine, the Nubian Nile valley was essentially a continuation of the Egyptian Nile valley, and the Egyptians seem to have seen it as a natural addition to their realm.

Throughout much of Egyptian history, the relationship between Egypt and Nubia was one of subjugator and subjugated, master and servant. Egypt sought to impose both its will and its culture on Nubia, whilst exploiting the country's resources (mineral and human) and controlling access to the lucrative sub-Saharan trade routes; exotic goods from sub-Saharan Africa reached the Mediterranean world via the Nubian 'corridor' (W.Y. Adams 1977; Seidlmayer 1996b: 111). The importance of Nubia to Egypt in the dynastic period stemmed from Nubia's large reserves of gold. It seems likely that Egypt's own sources of gold became exhausted towards the end of the Predynastic period, necessitating the exploitation of new gold-bearing areas. Other imports from Nubia included ebony.

Unlike the Near East and the peripheral regions, Nubia was settled more or less permanently by Egyptians, beginning in the Early Dynastic period. Egyptian contacts with the land to the south stretch far back into the Predynastic period. Although the relationship swiftly became an unequal one, there is some evidence that Lower Nubia was not far behind Egypt in the process of state formation and the race to establish political and economic hegemony over the Nile valley. Had Lower Nubian, rather than Upper Egyptian rulers won that race, the history of north-east Africa would have been very different.

Relations with Lower Nubia

In the early Predynastic period, there was a degree of cultural uniformity throughout Upper Egypt and Lower Nubia. The pottery of Naqada I and the earliest phase of the Lower Nubian A-Group are virtually indistinguishable. Moreover, A-Group sites are found in southernmost Upper Egypt (for example, Kubania) indicating some overlap between the two cultural areas. For the late Predynastic and Early Dynastic periods, the cultural inventory from sites in the Aswan region, especially Elephantine, indicates a contact zone between Egyptian and Nubian cultural areas, rather than a clear boundary (Seidlmayer 1996b: 111). Cultural transfer between Nubia and Egypt is suggested by the cattle burials in the élite cemetery at Hierakonpolis, Locality 6 (Hoffman 1982: 55–6). This practice does not seem to have been indigenous to Predynastic Egypt, but is attested at Qustul in Lower Nubia (Williams 1986: 176). Direct contact between the peoples of Upper Egypt and Lower Nubia in the late Predynastic period may be indicated by a burial from Abusir el-Meleq in northern Upper Egypt. Grave 51b2 was found to be unusual in several respects. It was the only circular grave in the entire cemetery, a shape more characteristic of burials in southern Upper Egypt and Nubia. The grave goods included two black-mouthed jars of Nubian type (Möllers and Scharff 1926: pl. 16.96–7) and a palette of unusual shape (Möllers and Scharff 1926: pl. 33.330), more commonly found in Nubian burials. The excavator concluded that the individual buried in grave 51b2 may have been a Nubian immigrant (Möllers and Scharff 1926: 29; cf. Needler 1984: 224).

176

Graves of the Lower Nubian Terminal A-Group often contain large numbers of imported Egyptian artefacts – particularly pottery and stone vessels – indicating an intensification of trade between Upper Egypt and the emergent complex societies of Lower Nubia towards the end of the Predynastic period (Takamiya 1994). Both regions were actively involved in the process of state formation, and there is clear evidence of a centralised polity in Lower Nubia whose rulers were buried at Qustul. No other cemetery of the Terminal A-Group approaches Qustul Cemetery L in the size or wealth of its burials (O'Connor 1993: 20). Lower Nubia under the Terminal A-Group may therefore be envisaged as a proto-kingdom, comparable to the late Predynastic polities of Upper Egypt (O'Connor 1993: 22). The maces and mace handle from Cemetery 137 near Seyala indicate that the concentration of political power in Lower Nubia had already begun some time earlier (O'Connor 1993: 23).

Egyptian domination

Egyptian expeditions may have ventured into Lower Nubia in late Predynastic times to exploit the diorite quarries 80 kilometres north-west of Toshka. Egypt's attitude towards Nubia certainly became more predatory at the end of the Predynastic period. Sub-Saharan Africa was the source of exotic and prestige goods such as ebony, ostrich eggs, giraffe tails, perhaps incense and unguents. The desire on the part of Upper Egyptian rulers to control trade routes directly, rather than continuing to rely on Lower Nubian middlemen, probably encouraged the Egyptian rulers to mount raids against Lower Nubia. The period of state formation in Egypt was also characterised by territorial expansionism, establishing Egyptian control beyond the borders of the Nile valley. The combination of these two factors prompted Upper Egyptian rulers to launch military expeditions against Lower Nubia towards the end of the Predynastic period, expeditions which were ultimately to result in Egyptian domination of the region and the extirpation of the indigenous A-Group culture.

THE MONUMENTS OF GEBEL SHEIKH SULEIMAN

Just such a campaign is recorded in the famous Gebel Sheikh Suleiman rock-cut inscription (Figure 5.3). The scene was carved on a rock in the Second Cataract region to commemorate an anonymous king of the late Predynastic period/'Dynasty 0'. An empty *serekh* stands at the head of the scene which depicts the aftermath of a battle. Immediately in front of the *serekh* is a prisoner, his arms bound behind his back with a bow, the sign used in later periods to write the name for Nubia (Ta-Sety). In front of the prisoner are three signs, the meaning of which remains uncertain. A pool of water, the hieroglyphic sign for the letter *š*, may indicate

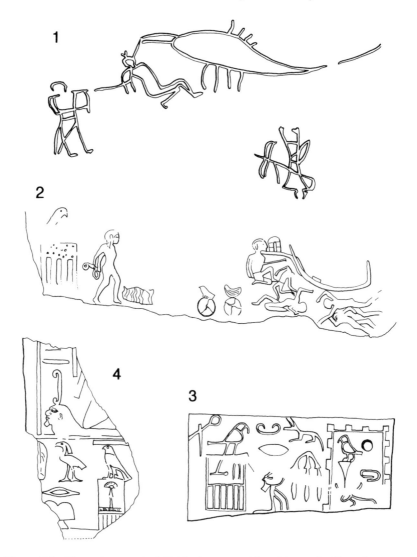

Figure 5.3 Campaigns against Nubia. Iconographic evidence for Egyptian aggression (real or ideological) against its southern neighbour: (1) late Predynastic rock-cut inscription from Gebel Sheikh Suleiman near the Second Cataract, recording a punitive incursion by Egyptians, perhaps under the command of a ruler from Hierakonpolis (after Needler 1967: pl. I, fig. 3); (2) a second rock-cut inscription from Gebel Sheikh Suleiman, recording a subsequent campaign by an Egyptian king of the late Predynastic period (after Murnane 1987: 285, fig. 1A–B); (3) wooden label of Aha from Abydos referring to a campaign against Ta-Sety, the name applied in later periods to Nubia (after Emery 1961: 51, fig. 11); (4) fragmentary limestone stela of Khasekhem from the temple at Hierakonpolis, recording the king's suppression of Nubia; the bow on the head of the prostrate captive identifies him as the representative of subjugated Nubia (the bow was the hieroglyph for (Ta-)Sety, 'Nubia') (after Emery 1961: 100, fig. 64). Not to same scale.

the name of the prisoner or his territory. Two town signs surmounted by birds may also be symbols or names of defeated settlements. The end of the scene shows the prostrate bodies of victims, underneath a high-prowed vessel. This last element probably stands for the ships which bore the Egyptian expedition southwards into Lower Nubia. The whole inscription apparently records an Egyptian military raid into Lower Nubia before the advent of the First Dynasty, setting the scene for similar campaigns in the Early Dynastic period (in the reigns of Aha and Khasekhem).

A second rock-cut inscription at Gebel Sheikh Suleiman, just a short distance away, is also early in date (Needler 1967). The inscription consists of a large scorpion and three human figures (Figure 5.3). One of the figures is a captive, distinguished by an erect feather on his head; his arms are bound behind his back, and he is suspended from a rope, held in the claws of the scorpion. The second figure looks on, brandishing an unidentified weapon; an appendage dangling from the back of his kilt has been interpreted as an animal's tail (after parallels on the Hunters' Palette). The third man shoots with a bow and arrow towards the bound captive; he too appears to wear an animal's tail. There may originally have been further signs between this third figure and the scorpion, but only traces remain which are difficult to delineate. The interpretation of the scene as a whole seems quite clear: the scorpion represents a divine or royal power (other animals are used in this way on late Predynastic objects, such as the catfish which smites a bound captive on an ivory cylinder of Narmer from Hierakonpolis). The two armed men must be followers of this power, whilst the captive is clearly an enemy. The motif of a prisoner being held by a rope is found in other late Predynastic inscriptions, such as the Bull Palette in the Louvre. It seems quite likely that this second inscription at Gebel Sheikh Suleiman records an expedition to the Second Cataract region by a late Predynastic Egyptian ruler, symbolised by the scorpion. The captive identified by a feather on his head may represent a native inhabitant of Lower Nubia. It is possible that the scorpion alludes even more directly to the king (as the catfish does on the ivory cylinder of Narmer). In this case, the inscription would record an expedition of King 'Scorpion' into Nubia during the final stages of Egyptian state formation. Support for this hypothesis may be provided by a stone vessel from Hierakonpolis which is decorated in raised relief with several signs, among them a scorpion and a double-convex bow. One can speculate that this vase may have been commissioned to commemorate a campaign by Scorpion against Nubia, represented by the bow (Needler 1967: 91).

EARLY DYNASTIC MILITARY CAMPAIGNS IN LOWER NUBIA

At the beginning of the First Dynasty the royal cemetery at Qustul was abandoned, indicating that the local rulers had lost power to the invading

Egyptians. The virtual extinction of the Lower Nubian A-Group is traditionally linked to the beginning of Egyptian domination in Nubia. The rulers of a newly unified Egypt seem to have adopted an uncompromising attitude towards their southern neighbours, replacing the previous symbiotic relationship that had existed between Egypt and Lower Nubia, a relationship which greatly benefited the rulers of Qustul in their role as middlemen. Egyptian control may have been less than total at first, requiring follow-up action to keep the local population in check (Figure 5.3). The construction of the fortress on Elephantine at the beginning of the First Dynasty seems to have been part of a new, more aggressive Egyptian policy towards Nubia (Seidlmayer 1996b: 112). As part of its programme to secure and emphasise national unity – to a large extent through ideology – the central government sought to impose political frontiers based upon territorial control, 'in place of former, less clearly delimited ethnic border zones' (Seidlmayer 1996b: 113). The Elephantine fortress may have been used as a springboard for raids into Nubia, such as the punitive campaign recorded on a label of Aha (Petrie 1901: pls III.2 = XI.1). Further military action is attested at the end of the Second Dynasty, in the reign of the Khasekhem (Quibell and Green 1902: pl. LVIII). The increased Egyptian interest in Nubia during the Early Dynastic period may have been connected with changing trade patterns in the Near East. The apparent abandonment of the Egyptian presence in southern Palestine (the 'residency' building at En Besor) at the end of the First Dynasty may have resulted from an Egyptian realisation that exotic goods could be obtained more easily from Nubia.

A permanent Egyptian presence in Lower Nubia

The next phase of Egyptian policy towards Nubia is marked by the establishment of a permanent garrison at Buhen. It must have become apparent to the Egyptians that political control was difficult to maintain without a permanent presence in the conquered territory. It is difficult to establish precisely when the Egyptian settlement at Buhen was founded. Certainly it was in use by the beginning of the Fourth Dynasty. Sneferu used the fortress as a base to launch strikes against Upper Nubia. However, the large size of the mudbricks employed in the lowest courses of the town at Buhen led its excavator to believe that the town was founded in the Second Dynasty (Emery 1963: 117). It is therefore possible that Buhen may have been established as part of Khasekhem's concerted campaign to restore and reinforce Egyptian control over Lower Nubia.

An important piece of evidence may support this interpretation. A rock-cut hieroglyphic inscription on the south face of 'Hill B', behind the Old Kingdom town of Buhen, has been dated to the Early Dynastic period (H.S. Smith 1972). The translation of the inscription presents a number of difficulties. Nevertheless, the large scale of the inscription and its prominent position close to the settlement at Buhen (less than 300 metres from the town enclosure wall) indicate that the inscription is dedicatory in character. It may be no coincidence that the text apparently refers to the two deities later associated with Buhen, namely Horus and Isis. Perhaps it was carved to commemorate the foundation of the Egyptian settlement at Buhen. It provides further evidence for early Egyptian activity in the Second Cataract region: Hill B is only nine kilometres from Gebel Sheikh Suleiman with its early inscriptions.

Relations with Upper Nubia

The status of Upper Nubia in early times and Egypt's relationship with the area south of the Second Cataract are less well-known. Archaeological investigation has been less intensive than in Lower Nubia, and it is to be hoped that future excavations will reveal much more about the early history of the region. Judging by the occasional references in Egyptian texts, Upper Nubia seems to have supported a substantial population during the Old Kingdom, and probably during the preceding Early Dynastic period as well (O'Connor 1993: 27). If the extinction of the indigenous A-Group indicates that Egypt exercised effective control of Lower Nubia from the beginning of the Early Dynastic period, then the raids into Nubia mounted by Early Dynastic kings may have been directed against Upper Nubia in order to maintain Egyptian access to lucrative trade routes (O'Connor 1993: 25). It would certainly have been in Egypt's interests to safeguard its relations with Upper Nubia, since this region was the principal source of many prestige commodities (O'Connor 1993: 27).

Two isolated pieces of evidence suggest a measure of direct contact between Egypt and Upper Nubia towards the end of the Early Dynastic period. The first is an inscribed stone slab from Helwan, dedicated to a man called Sisi (Saad 1957: 46, fig. 32, pl. 27; Fischer 1963: 35, fig. 1). Stylistically, the piece may be dated to the late Second Dynasty or early Third Dynasty. Sisi is shown wearing a series of armlets, a feature which is unknown amongst contemporary representations of the Egyptian male, but which seems to have been a characteristic of Nubians: compare, for example, a scene from the causeway of Sahura's mortuary temple (Fischer 1963: 35, fig. 2). Moreover, Sisi's hair is arranged in a distinctive style, with a series of four twisted locks hanging below shoulder level; a comparable style is found in later representations of Nubians and inhabitants of Punt, for example in the Hatshepsut reliefs at Deir el-Bahri (Fischer 1963: 36, fig. 3). Taken together, these two characteristics strongly suggest that Sisi was a Nubian, most probably from Upper Nubia.

The second piece of evidence argues more convincingly for direct trade relations between Egypt and Upper Nubia. It consists of a peripheral burial in Cemetery 7 at Shellal, just south of Elephantine, on the Egyptian–Nubian border (Fischer 1963; O'Connor 1993: 27). Although the majority of the graves in this cemetery belonged to the A-Group, dating at the very latest to the early First Dynasty, one burial, isolated from the main group, was dated to a later period, probably the Second or Third Dynasty (Fischer 1963: 37). The burial was unquestionably that of a Nubian (O'Connor 1993: 27), and the deceased was clearly a man of some status: he was interred holding two valuable copper objects, and wearing an elaborate gold necklace. Each arm was adorned with a v-shaped armlet of ivory, and in addition he wore a series of smaller bracelets on one wrist. The distinctive v-shaped armlet is of a type never encountered in Lower Nubia, but a very similar object is worn by the (Upper) Nubian represented on the Sahura causeway relief mentioned above (O'Connor 1993: 27). It has been suggested that the individual buried at Shellal was an Upper Nubian trade envoy who died unexpectedly whilst visiting Egypt (O'Connor 1993: 27).

CHAPTER SIX

KINGSHIP

— •◆• —

'From before "history" began, Egyptian society centered on kingship' (Baines 1995: 147). As this quotation makes clear, the central position of kingship in ancient Egyptian culture has long been recognised and acknowledged by Egyptologists (for example, Hoffman 1980: 257). Whilst the enduring achievements of the early Old Kingdom (the Giza pyramids and sphinx) symbolise for many the apogee of royal power, it has become increasingly clear that the roots of Egyptian kingship go back much further, into the Predynastic period. The evidence for growing social stratification and political centralisation during the Predynastic period has been discussed in Chapter 2. The origins of royal iconography, already evident in the Painted Tomb at Hierakonpolis (dating to Naqada II) have now been pushed even further back with the discovery of a painted vessel in a late Naqada I tomb at Abydos. Inasmuch as iconography is the artistic expression of ideology, we can assume that the Upper Egyptian rulers of late Naqada I were already beginning to formulate an ideology of rule. This was developed and elaborated by the Predynastic kings of This, Naqada and Hierakonpolis, and their successors of the period of state formation. The earliest royal monuments, which date from this time, indicate that the late Predynastic kings were already 'charged with the power of divinity' (Frankfort 1948: 34).

By the time Egypt was unified in c. 3100 BC, divine kingship had emerged as a coherent and powerful ideology. Indeed, 'the unification increased the significance of kingship' (Frankfort 1948: 34), promoting the institution from a regional to a national position. The king no longer exercised merely regional authority, shared with a number of other rulers. He was now at the pinnacle of a national government, responsible for the entire land of Egypt and its people. As the sole source of authority, the king symbolised Egypt itself, and was responsible for maintaining and defending the Egyptian way of life. He acted as intermediary between the population and their gods, and was himself the embodiment of the supreme celestial deity, Horus. The ideology of kingship emphasised the power of the king to intercede on his people's behalf, including his ability 'to dominate and further natural processes, especially the inundation' (Frankfort 1948: 58). At its most fundamental, 'kingship in Egypt remained the channel through which the powers of nature flowed into the body politic to bring human endeavor to fruition' (Frankfort 1948: 34).

It fell to the rulers of the Early Dynastic period to exploit this ideology for their own ends: to secure and maintain political and economic control of the country and its resources, to promote kingship as the fulfilment of a divinely ordained model for society (cf. Frankfort 1948: 101), and hence to ensure the survival of kingship as the only acceptable form of government. The ideology of divine kingship was reinforced and promoted by many means, including the king's regalia and titulary, depictions of the ruler and his actions (iconography), and the rituals and ceremonies of the court. By exploring these different aspects of early kingship, we can begin to shed some light on the early development of an institution central to Egyptian civilisation, the nature of the institution itself, the ideology which surrounded it, and the methods by which the Early Dynastic kings successfully utilised this ideology to reinforce their grip on power.

THE FRAMEWORK OF KINGSHIP IN EARLY EGYPT

The king as Horus

The most fundamental aspect of kingship was the ruler's embodiment of Horus, the supreme celestial deity. The king's principal title was the Horus title, 'the simplest and most direct statement regarding the king's nature' (Frankfort 1948: 46). It expressed the notion that Horus was incarnate in the reigning monarch, and the Horus name articulated the particular aspect of Horus that the king wished to stress. Although each new reign might highlight a different facet of the supreme deity, the divine essence of the god which inhabited the body of the reigning king remained unchanged.

The identification of the ruler with Horus, represented by a falcon, is apparent from late Predynastic times, and is given expression on royal monuments and in the *serekh*s of kings from the period of state formation. It is possible that the worship of a celestial falcon god was widespread in Predynastic Egypt since there is evidence for the existence of several falcon cults. As a universal deity, Horus would have been a natural choice to associate with the kingship, since the connection would necessarily have had greater resonance and significance.

The concept of Horus as 'Great(est) god, lord of heaven' is given unique artistic expression in the ivory comb of Djet, from the early First Dynasty. Here, Horus is represented in three forms: the celestial falcon, whose outspread wings form the vault of the sky; the solar deity, a falcon which traverses the sky in the celestial boat; and incarnate in the person of the king (the falcon atop the king's *serekh*). This exceptional work of art is one of the earliest and most concise theological expositions. It expresses the essential elements of the king's association with Horus and the role of Horus as the supreme deity. Moreover, it 'presents concisely and clearly the central tenet binding together ancient Egyptian civilisation, the notion that the king fulfils a role on earth under the protective wings of the celestial falcon in heaven' (Quirke 1992: 21–2).

The dual monarchy

One of the most extraordinary intellectual achievements of Egypt's first kings was the concept of the dual monarchy. From the very beginning of the Egyptian state, official ideology and iconography presented the realm as a union of two halves, the Two Lands. The pervasiveness of such imagery in the ancient Egyptian sources highlights the imagination and creativity of Egypt's early élite. The kings who crafted the Egyptian state from the competing powers of the Predynastic period succeeded in formulating a concept of rule which guaranteed an absolutely pivotal role for the monarchy. The institution of kingship was projected as the sole force which held the country together, and the dual nature of the monarchy was expressed in the king's regalia, in his titulary, and in royal rituals and festivals. This concept – the harmony of opposites, a totality embracing paired contrasts – chimed so effectively with the Egyptian world-view that the institution of kingship acquired what has been called a 'transcendent significance' (Frankfort 1948: 19). This helps to explain the centrality of the institution to Egyptian culture, and its longevity (Frankfort 1948: 15–16). Even when central authority broke down, as it did during the Intermediate Periods, the Egyptians returned unfailingly to the established model of government. The promulgation of such a powerful ideological concept from the very beginning of the Egyptian state effectively masked the political realities of the state formation process, and made a return to the fragmentation of the Predynastic period ideologically inconceivable (cf. Frankfort 1948: 20).

The royal family and the ruling class

The uppermost register of the Scorpion macehead shows a series of standards with a dejected lapwing hanging by a rope from each one. In the hieroglyphic script, the lapwing represented the *rhyt*, the common people of Egypt. Hence, the symbolism of this part of the Scorpion macehead seems clear, if a little uncomfortable to the modern mind: the populace of Egypt is quite literally subject to the divine authority of the king. The significance of the scene may go further, and may illuminate an aspect of ancient Egyptian society which is only barely attested. This is its division into two separate groups, the mass of the populace (*rhyt*) and the ruling class (*p‘t*) (Malek 1986: 34; Baines 1995: 133).

The composition of the *rhyt* is fairly clear from the contexts in which the word is used; it refers to the general population. The significance of the term *p't* is less obvious, though it must refer to the élite, the members of the king's entourage. A high-ranking title borne by officials from the First Dynasty onwards is *iri-p't*, which seems to indicate a 'member of the *p't*'. Although it later became merely an honorific title, marking an individual's illustrious rank within the royal administration, in origin the title seems to have had a more specific sense, designating a member of the ruling class. It is quite likely that the *p't* originally comprised the royal kinsmen who, by virtue of their blood ties to the king, however distant, shared something of the supernatural authority vested in the ruler (Frankfort 1948: 53). The evidence suggests that in early times all the high officials of the central government were royal relations (Malek 1986: 35). This system seems to have broken down during the Old Kingdom when persons of non-royal birth were appointed to important positions within the administration.

The distinction between the populace and the royal kinsmen must have been an important one, dictating how authority was exercised in the Early Dynastic court. The formal separation of the ruling class from the rest of the population provides a valuable insight into the mechanisms of early royal government in Egypt. It appears that access to political power was carefully restricted, to enhance the absolute authority of the kingship and emphasise its supernatural remoteness from the general populace.

ICONOGRAPHY: SYMBOLS OF ROYALTY

Royal regalia

In the Early Dynastic period as in later times, the crowns, sceptres and other elements of royal regalia had a dual role: power and protection. At the most basic level, they served to identify the king and to set him apart from the rest of humanity (Quirke 1990: 10). Moreover, they conveyed his authority, both supernatural (as the gods' representative) and earthly (as head of state and supreme military commander), just as crowns and sceptres do in modern monarchies. They also had an **amuletic** function, to protect the king from danger and from the malign forces which were believed to threaten the cosmos.

Comparatively little has been written about the various items of royal insignia. None the less, it is clear that each object had its own significance and origins. Whilst some of the characteristic royal attributes pre-date the foundation of the Egyptian state, others were added to the developing iconography of divine kingship during the course of the First Dynasty. By the end of the Second Dynasty, royal iconography had been formalised and changed little during the succeeding millennium.

Sceptres and staffs

A sceptre or staff is one of the most widespread and ancient symbols of authority (Figure 6.1). This was certainly true of ancient Egypt, as demonstrated by the hieroglyph for 'nobleman, official' (*sr*) which shows a man carrying a long stave of office in front of him. One of the earliest indications of a hierarchical society comes from the early Predynastic site of el-Omari in Lower Egypt. An otherwise simple grave contained the skeleton of a man, buried with a wooden staff. This has been interpreted as an indication of the dead man's special status within his society. Whether he exercised religious or political authority is less important than the overt recognition of his status by means of a distinctive 'badge of office'. A fragmentary wooden staff, carved to resemble a bundle of reeds, was found in an early First Dynasty mastaba at Saqqara. Similar fragments were recovered from Early Dynastic royal tombs at Abydos (Fischer 1978: 21). As symbols of authority *par excellence*, it is not surprising that staffs were anciently associated with the regalia of Egyptian kingship. A wooden label of Den from Abydos shows the king carrying a long staff, very similar to that shown in the *sr* hieroglyph (Petrie 1900:

Figure 6.1 The staff of office. Fragmentary ivory label of Den from Abydos. The king is wearing the *khat*-head-dress and carries a mace and long staff, the former a symbol of royal authority, the latter a recognised mark of high office in ancient Egypt (after Petrie 1900: pl. XIV.9).

pls X.14, XIV.9). After all, the king was the highest official in the land, the nobleman above all others. His unique position at the head of Egyptian society was usually recognised by more distinctive insignia, reserved for the kingship. An actual example of a royal sceptre was discovered by Petrie in one of the chambers of Khasekhemwy's tomb at Abydos (Petrie 1901: 27, pl. IX.1). The sceptre was fashioned from cylinders of polished sard, decorated with 'double bands of thick gold which encircle the sceptre at every fourth cylinder' (Petrie 1901: 27), the whole held together by a copper rod. Two fragments of the sceptre were found, one 23 inches, the other 5 inches in length. Because of its slender and fragile construction, Petrie concluded that it was 'only just strong enough to carry its own weight', and therefore identified it as a ceremonial, royal sceptre (Petrie 1901: 27).

A variant of the long staff was the *mks*-staff. This is characterised by a nodule approximately half-way down the shaft. In origin a defensive weapon, the *mks*-staff seems later to have assumed 'ceremonial – even priestly – significance' (F.D. Friedman 1995: 20). Stone vessels of Anedjib from Saqqara and Abydos depict a statue of the king holding the *mks*-staff, and these inscriptions are closely paralleled on the northernmost relief panel from beneath the Step Pyramid, where Netjerikhet is shown holding a *mks*-staff (Kemp 1989: 58, fig. 19; F.D. Friedman 1995). In addition to the *mks*-staff and simpler staffs of office, royal iconography of the Early Dynastic period distinguishes two different forms of sceptre, each of which emphasised a particular aspect of the ruler's authority.

THE *HEQA*-SCEPTRE

The symbol of rule with the longest history seems to be the shepherd's crook or *ḥq3*-sceptre. This is entirely appropriate, since the crook symbolised the very concept of rule, and was employed as the hieroglyph for the Egyptian word, 'rule, ruler' (*ḥq3*). The earliest example of a *ḥq3*-sceptre comes from tomb U-547 at Abydos, dated to late Naqada II (Naqada IId). The tomb, a simple pit cut in the desert, contained the upper part of a limestone *ḥq3*-sceptre (Leclant and Clerc 1993: pl. XXIII fig. 26; Dreyer *et al.* 1996). The earliest surviving complete *ḥq3*-sceptre comes from another grave in the same cemetery, tomb U-j (Dreyer 1993b: 11). This was the burial of a late Predynastic ruler of the Thinite region and is unique in several respects. It is by far the largest tomb of its date anywhere in Egypt, suggesting that its owner exercised unrivalled political and economic authority. The status of the deceased is expressed not only in the size and contents of the tomb, but also in the ivory *ḥq3*-sceptre found in the north-eastern chamber. It is clear that the shepherd's crook was already established as a symbol of rule by late Predynastic times, and that it formed part of the ruler's regalia. The earliest representation of a king holding a *ḥq3*-sceptre is a small statuette of Ninetjer (Simpson 1956). As in later times, the king holds the crook across his chest, balancing the **flail** which he holds in the other hand. The symbolism of the *ḥq3*-sceptre is quite easily understood. Metaphorically, the king was the shepherd of his people, guiding and protecting them. In common with some of the other items of royal regalia discussed below, the *ḥq3*-sceptre indicates the pastoralist aspect of Egyptian society. Many of the metaphors of royal authority are derived from the animal kingdom and from the sphere of animal husbandry, emphasising the close interaction between the early Egyptians and their natural environment (cf. Staehelin 1984).

THE *WAS*-SCEPTRE

The second type of sceptre closely associated with kingship is the *w3s*-sceptre (K. Martin 1986b). This is a long staff with a stylised animal's head at one end and two curved prongs at the other. Its origins may well go back to the Predynastic period, although the earliest known representations of the *w3s*-sceptre date to the First Dynasty. An ivory comb of Djet shows two such sceptres supporting the vault of heaven, symbolised by the outspread wings of the celestial falcon. A *w3s*-sceptre, perhaps of ivory (like the *ḥq3*-sceptre from Abydos tomb U-j), was among the hoard of votive objects excavated by Petrie in the early temple at Abydos (Petrie 1903: pl. 2.11). Like the shepherd's crook, the *w3s*-sceptre embodied authority and was used as a hieroglyph to write the word 'dominion' (*w3s*). The *w3s*-sceptre may have had both utilitarian and symbolic value; in origin, it seems to have been used to control animals, although its exact function has not been established beyond doubt. It has been interpreted as a shepherd's staff (Kaplony 1986: 1374), but the shape of the head has suggested to others that the staff may originally have been used to goad donkeys or mules (K. Martin 1986b). A possible connection with snakes has also been mooted. The suggestion that 'the *w3s* prototype as staff or scepter originally may have been a dried bull's penis' (Gordon and Schwabe 1995: 186) seems rather unlikely and has not found general support.

As a symbol of power, the *w3s*-sceptre could be held by deities as well as by the king, and it may have been 'primarily an attribute of the gods' (Fischer 1978: 21). For example, on sealings of Peribsen from Abydos, the god Ash is depicted holding a *w3s*-sceptre (Petrie 1901: pls XXI.176, XXII.178–9). The *w3s*-sceptre is anthropomorphised in reliefs as early as the Third Dynasty. On the Netjerikhet relief panels, *w3s*-sceptres hold fans and one appears to dance (F.D. Friedman 1995). The ivory comb of Djet, already mentioned, illustrates the other symbolic function of the *w3s*-sceptre: as the support of heaven. By extension, the *w3s*-sceptre 'may ... allude to the divine power that supports and protects royal life'

(F.D. Friedman 1995: 26). It is probably true to say that the *w3s*-sceptre symbolised a divine authority, whereas the *ḥq3*-sceptre represented a more secular power and was the pre-eminent symbol of earthly rule.

The flail

The flail has already been mentioned as the usual companion to the crook. However, originally the two items of regalia do not seem to have been so closely connected. The flail appears alone on some of the earliest representations of royal ceremonial, making it one of the most ancient symbols of the office of kingship. The king depicted on the boss-side of the Metropolitan Museum knife handle (dated to the late Predynastic period, Naqada IIIb, *c.* 3100 BC) carries the flail alone (Williams and Logan 1987: fig. 1). A very similar representation occurs on the Narmer macehead from Hierakonpolis, and this king is also shown carrying the flail on his ceremonial palette. A further example from the early First Dynasty is a mud seal-impression from the reign of Djer which shows the king carrying the flail (Petrie 1901: pl. XV.108). To judge from the statuette of Ninetjer, by the Second Dynasty the flail and crook had become associated and were henceforth usually depicted together. The flail is carried by Netjerikhet on his relief panels where it seems to serve as a general 'symbol of authority' (F.D. Friedman 1995: 22). Like the *ḥq3*- and *w3s*-sceptres, the flail seems to have originated in the sphere of animal husbandry. Used to goad livestock, the flail was an obvious symbol of the ruler's coercive power. As shepherd of his flock, the king encouraged his people as well as restraining them; this is the dual symbolism of the flail and crook.

The bull's tail

The influence of the animal world on royal iconography was twofold. As well as holding items of regalia taken from the sphere of animal husbandry – to emphasise his role as shepherd of his people – the king was imbued with the powers of nature, most easily represented in their animal form. Hence, on some of the commemorative palettes from the period of state formation, the king is portrayed as a lion (Battlefield Palette) or as a wild bull (Bull Palette, Narmer Palette). Both animals embodied unrestrained ferocity, and the representation of the ruler as a fierce wild animal conveyed in graphic terms his role as defender of created order and ruthless opponent of the forces of chaos. Soon after the establishment of the Egyptian state, the iconography of kingship underwent a consolidation and codification. In the process, some of the motifs adopted in the late Predynastic period were discarded, particularly those borrowed from contemporary Mesopotamian iconography. This was also the case with overt depictions of the ruler as an animal. We can speculate that, perhaps for theological reasons, it was no longer considered appropriate to represent the king in such a way. Nevertheless, the animal potency of kingship remained important ideologically, and was henceforth expressed in subtler ways. The king's name could incorporate such notions. Hence, the name of the late Predynastic king, 'Scorpion', seems to be an expression of dangerous animal power. In later periods, kings adopted more explicit animal names such as 'Strong Bull'. Indeed, the bull appears to have been the animal most closely associated with the king. The innate power of the bull – its virility and strength – was conveyed by means of a bull's tail, worn by the king suspended from the back of his kilt (Staehelin 1984: 615). The earliest known representation of the bull's tail appears on the Scorpion macehead, and henceforth it became a regular component of royal dress.

Sandals

The Narmer Palette illustrates another element of royal insignia, the king's sandals (cf. Seyfried 1984). As, quite literally, the point of contact between the king and the land over which he ruled, the royal sandals were imbued with a religious importance. They were, therefore, entrusted to a special member of the king's entourage who would have enjoyed intimate access to the king. The sandal-bearer depicted on Narmer's monuments follows close behind his sovereign and is labelled as 'the servant of the ruler'. The king's sandals also had a symbolic role in the eternal struggle between order and chaos. The king's primary task was to crush Egypt's (and creation's) enemies, represented as the inhabitants of neighbouring lands. In later periods, this victory was symbolically achieved by having Egypt's enemies depicted on the king's footstool and on the pavement of the royal palace. Every time the king walked on the pavement or placed his feet on the footstool, the enemies would be conquered by sympathetic magic. In each case, the agent of victory was the king's sandals. This belief finds eloquent expression on a commemorative stela erected by Khasekhem at Hierakonpolis. On it, the king is described as 'effective sandal against the hill-countries'; in other words, a successful conqueror of the forces threatening Egypt and the cosmos.

The uraeus

The earliest depiction of the **uraeus** – the rearing cobra on the king's brow – probably dates to the reign of Den. The scene in question is the famous ivory label which shows the king smiting an enemy captive (Spencer 1993: 87, fig. 67). The king wears a long wig and the uraeus adorns his forehead. A second uraeus appears on the Wepwawet standard which precedes the king. There is some doubt about the label's authenticity (Johnson 1990: 6), but a closely comparable depiction of the king on a fragmentary label from Abydos (Petrie 1900: pls XI.8, XIV.8) tends to support a First Dynasty date. None the less, the inclusion of the uraeus in the royal insignia of this early period is remarkable. Such a feature next appears in the early Third Dynasty, on a relief of Netjerikhet from the Wadi Maghara, Sinai. The adoption of the uraeus into royal iconography seems to be another example of the innovation which characterises the reign of Den.

The symbolic function of the uraeus is clear. The serpent goddess was a potent symbol of 'protection, power and beneficence' (Johnson 1990: 190). Attached to the ruler's brow, the rising cobra spat fire at the king's enemies. The uraeus thus embodied both **apotropaic**, protective power and aggressive intent towards the forces of disorder (K. Martin 1986a). In early royal scenes, the king is often preceded by the standard of the jackal-god Wepwawet, the 'opener of the ways'. As the trail-blazer for the king, Wepwawet may also be accompanied by a uraeus serpent, to provide added protection (Johnson 1990: 53). This is the case on the ivory label of Den and on the Third Dynasty reliefs from the Sinai (Johnson 1990: figs 104–6).

Crowns and head-dresses

Perhaps the most distinctive elements of the royal regalia are the various crowns and head-dresses worn by the king on different occasions. Three crowns are attested in the Early Dynastic period: the red crown, the white crown and the combined 'double crown'. Instead of a crown, the king might wear a cloth head-dress. Two different types figure in Early Dynastic depictions: a long head-dress (*khat*) and an early forerunner of the archetypal *nemes* head-dress.

THE RED CROWN

There is, as yet, no satisfactory explanation for the origin of the two principal crowns, the red and the white (Figures 6.2 and 6.3). Both seem to have originated in Upper Egypt, which saw the first moves towards political centralisation. A sherd from a large black-topped red-ware vessel of late Naqada I date, from the site of Naqada itself, bears a representation of the red crown in relief (Payne 1993: 94, fig. 34.774; Baines 1995: 149, fig. 3.1). Although the red crown is associated in historic times with Lower Egypt, it is generally assumed that it originated as the distinctive headpiece of the Predynastic rulers of Naqada. The colour red was traditionally associated with Seth, the local god of Naqada. The shape of the crown is quite distinctive, but again its symbolic meaning is unknown. The curly protuberance at the front of the crown has been linked with the bee (connected with kingship from at least the middle of the First Dynasty, through the title *nswt-bity*, 'he of the sedge and bee'), and also with goddess Neith, an important Lower Egyptian deity. There is an obscure passage in the Pyramid Texts of Unas which may refer to the curly part of the red crown, but it remains poorly understood.

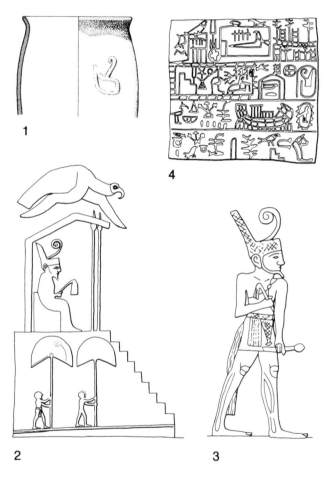

Figure 6.2 The red crown. Early representations of the crown later associated with Lower Egypt: (1) a red crown modelled in relief on a sherd of black-topped red ware from the Predynastic cemetery at Naqada (now in the Ashmolean Museum, Oxford) (after Payne 1993: fig. 34, no. 774); (2) Narmer wearing the red crown, as shown on his ceremonial macehead from Hierakonpolis (after Quibell 1900: pl. XXVIB); (3) Narmer wearing the red crown, as shown on his ceremonial palette from Hierakonpolis (after Kemp 1989: 42, fig. 12); (4) a shrine to the red crown, perhaps located in the north-western Delta, shown on an ivory label of Djer from Abydos (after Emery 1961: 59, fig. 20). Not to same scale.

From the period of state formation onwards, the red crown seems to have symbolised the king's authority in the northern half of his realm. As such, it is worn by Narmer on his ceremonial palette and macehead. It has been suggested that the Scorpion macehead originally showed a figure of the king wearing the red crown to balance the figure in the white crown on the preserved portion (Cialowicz 1991). In this case, the Scorpion macehead would be the earliest example of the king wearing the red crown, pre-dating the Narmer monuments by a short time.

THE WHITE CROWN

The white crown, associated in historic times with Upper Egypt, is first attested later than the red crown, but is directly associated with the ruler somewhat earlier. The earliest known depiction of the white crown is on a ceremonial incense burner from Cemetery L at Qustul in Lower Nubia (Williams 1986: pls 34, 38). Tomb L24 contained a variety of prestige objects, and in all probability belonged to a late Predynastic king of Lower Nubia, contemporary with the ruler buried in Abydos tomb U-j (Naqada IIIa2, *c.* 3150 BC). The Qustul incense burner is a remarkable object of supreme importance for the development of Egyptian royal iconography. The incised scenes around the edge of the object include the representation of a seated ruler, wearing the tall white crown. Evidence of close contacts between the rulers of Qustul and their contemporaries at Hierakonpolis may support the theory that the white crown originated at the latter site. A second, slightly later royal object from Upper Egypt bears a similar representation of a royal figure wearing the white crown. This is the Metropolitan Museum knife handle, mentioned already in connection with the flail. The king holding the flail wears the white crown. Like his counterpart on the Qustul incense burner, he is identified as the ruler by the rosette hieroglyph – also attested on the Scorpion macehead, the Narmer Palette and macehead – in front of his face. Likely to be contemporary with the Metropolitan Museum knife handle is a rock-cut inscription near Aswan which shows a ruler figure (identified as such by the fan-bearer who stands behind him: compare the presence of fan-bearers in attendance upon the king on the Scorpion and Narmer maceheads) wearing a tall, pointed head-dress, probably a schematic rendering of the white crown or a very similar item of regalia (Baines, personal communication).

The Narmer Palette indicates that the white crown was the superior of the two crowns, since the figure of the king wearing the white crown is significantly larger than the figure wearing the red crown. The superiority of the white crown may have derived from its intimate association with the royal line of Hierakonpolis, which played a decisive role in the unification of Egypt. The white crown retained this superiority throughout

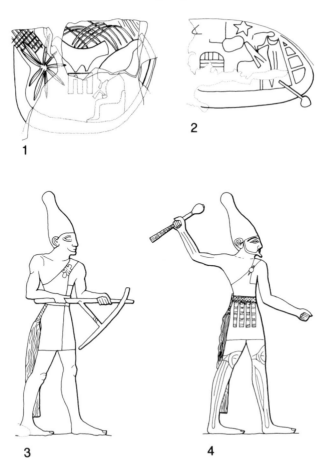

Figure 6.3 The white crown. Early representations of the crown later associated with Upper Egypt: (1) a royal figure wearing the white crown, shown on an incised, decorated incense-burner from tomb 24 in Cemetery L at Qustul, Lower Nubia (after Williams 1986: pl. 34); (2) a late Predynastic Upper Egyptian king wearing the white crown, shown on a carved ivory knife handle of unknown provenance (now in the Metropolitan Museum of Art, New York) (after Williams and Logan 1987: 273, fig. 1); (3) King 'Scorpion' wearing the white crown, as shown on his ceremonial macehead from Hierakonpolis (after Spencer 1993: 56, fig. 36); (4) Narmer wearing the white crown, as shown on his ceremonial palette from Hierakonpolis (after Kemp 1989: 42, fig. 12). Not to same scale.

Egyptian history. More than simple items of regalia, the red and white crowns were imbued with magical significance and were worshipped as cult objects in their own right (see Chapter 8).

THE DOUBLE CROWN

The logical development of combining the red and white crowns into a double crown, symbolising the king's rule of the Two Lands, occurred in the middle of the First Dynasty. A rock-cut inscription of Djet from the western desert apparently shows the falcon atop the king's *serekh* wearing the double crown (Legrain 1903: 221, fig. 7). If the report is accurate, this inscription would represent the earliest known occurrence of the double crown, pre-dating the more famous Abydos label of Den by a generation. The invention of the double crown is usually attributed to the latter king. Two labels of Den show the king in double crown (Petrie 1900: pls X.13 = XIV.7, XI.14 = XV.16). The innovation of the double crown clearly allowed artists to represent the totality of the king's authority in a more compact form, and, as such, marks the increasing sophistication of royal iconography as the First Dynasty progressed.

THE *KHAT-* AND *NEMES-*HEAD-DRESSES

A further innovation in royal iconography seems to have occurred in the reign of Den, namely the appearance of the long head-dress (*ḥȝt*) (contra Eaton-Krauss 1977: 26, n. 38). On the ivory label which shows the 'first time of smiting the east(erner)', the king wears this head-dress, its back-piece reaching half-way down his back. A fragmentary ivory label of the same king from Abydos shows Den wearing the *ḥȝt*, carrying a mace horizontally in one hand and a long staff vertically in the other (Petrie 1900: pls X.14, XIV.9). These are the only depictions of a king from the first two dynasties which show him wearing a head-dress other than one of the crowns. A relief of Netjerikhet from the Wadi Maghara, Sinai, shows the king wearing a 'kerchief' which may be the *ḥȝt*, although the rudimentary rendering 'does not permit positive identification' (Eaton-Krauss 1977: 26, n. 38). The significance of the *khat*-head-dress at this early period is unknown.

The seated statue of Netjerikhet from his **serdab** in the Step Pyramid complex is the earliest example of another royal head-dress, the *nemes*. This was to become the archetypal royal head-covering, surviving in representations of the ruler until the end of pharaonic civilisation. The head-dress as it appears on the statue of Netjerikhet is a forerunner of the classic shape, having large and bulky front **lappet**s with pointed facings. With the appearance of the *nemes*, all the essential elements of the king's regalia had been introduced, and the foundations of royal iconography had been firmly established.

The king smites his enemies

The aforementioned ivory label of Den depicts one of the most characteristic actions of the Egyptian ruler: with his arm upraised, he smites a bound captive cowering at his feet. The instrument of subjugation is the **piriform** mace, a weapon attested archaeologically from the Naqada I period. The mace was a potent symbol of royal power, and could be carried by the king in other situations as part of his insignia of office, as on the fragmentary ivory label of Den mentioned above. None the less, it is in smiting scenes that the mace features most commonly as an attribute of kingship. The motif of the ruler smiting his enemies is of great antiquity. A recently discovered late Naqada I painted pottery vessel from Cemetery U at Abydos shows a royal (?) figure smiting a group of bound captives. This vessel is the very earliest iconographic evidence to date for Egyptian kingship, yet it already presents the motif that characterises depictions of the ruler throughout the succeeding three-and-a-half thousand years. The king smiting his enemies may be regarded as the quintessential royal activity shown in Egyptian iconography. The action emphasised the king's primary duty: to safeguard created order by attacking the forces of disorder (Hall 1986). Just as the barren and hostile deserts which surrounded Egypt represented the antithesis of the fertile Nile valley, so the peoples to the south, west and east of Egypt were cast as embodying the forces that opposed and threatened the Egyptians and their way of life.

Standards on early royal monuments

On many royal monuments from the late Predynastic and Early Dynastic periods, groups of standards are shown accompanying the ruler. The Scorpion and Narmer maceheads and the Narmer Palette each shows a similar group of standards in attendance on the king. Further standards, in other contexts, are depicted on four ceremonial palettes from the period of state formation (the so-called Hunters', Louvre, Battlefield and Libyan palettes).

Forms and contexts

Altogether, ten different standards are attested: an east-sign; the Min (thunderbolt?) symbol; a canine with the *šdšd*-**device**; a second unidentified canine; an ibis; a single or double falcon; a falcon perched on a crescent; the Seth-animal; a curious bag-shaped object; and the desert hieroglyph (Figure 6.4).

Much debate has surrounded the proper identification of the standards, their origins and symbolism. The canine with the *šdšd*-device has been identified as Wepwawet (Kaiser 1960: 122–3), and this would seem to be

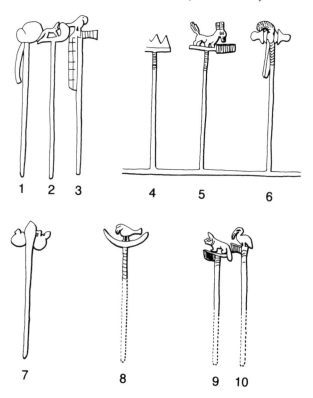

Figure 6.4 Standards on early royal monuments. The ten different types of standard depicted on ceremonial palettes and maceheads of the late Predynastic period and early First Dynasty: (1) placenta; (2) canine and *šdšd*-device; (3) falcon (after Kemp 1989: 42, fig. 12); (4) mountain-sign; (5) Seth-animal; (6) Min-sign (after Spencer 1993: 56, fig. 36); (7) east-sign (after Davis 1992: 94, fig. 28); (8) falcon on crescent (after Spencer 1993: 56, fig. 36); (9) canine; (10) ibis (after Davis 1992: 144, fig. 37). Not to same scale.

confirmed by a Third Dynasty sealing from Beit Khallaf which shows an identical canine standard labelled as Wepwawet (Garstang 1902: pl. VIII.1). The ibis standard may be connected with the god Thoth, although this is by no means certain (Kaiser 1960: 126). The falcon very probably represents the god Horus; the twin falcons, Horus and Seth (Kaiser 1960: 123–4). The falcon on a crescent may represent Anti, the local god of the twelfth Upper Egyptian nome; a similar motif occurs on an elaborate alabaster vessel from the 'Main Deposit' at Hierakonpolis. The bag-shaped sign, later associated with the god Khonsu, was first explained as the royal placenta (Seligman and Murray 1911; Blackman 1916; Frankfort 1948). Other scholars have hesitated to accept this identification (Kaiser 1960: 127), suggesting instead a throne cushion (Helck 1954: 27 n. 99, 37; F.D. Friedman

1995: 4–5) or a variant of the emblem of Nekhen (Posener 1965). However, ethnographic parallels from other **Hamitic** African cultures provide support for the possible deification of the royal placenta in ancient Egypt, and there are convincing etymological reasons for linking Khonsu with the royal placenta. It is possible that the royal placenta was regarded as the king's stillborn twin; it may have been associated with the royal *ka*, the divine essence passed from ruler to ruler which played an important part in Egyptian kingship ideology from the earliest times (Frankfort 1948: 78).

Symbolism and significance

Two separate groups of standards can be distinguished. Those depicted on the late Predynastic palettes and on the upper register of the Scorpion macehead probably represent the most important divine symbols of the period of state formation (Kaiser 1959: 130–1). A second – and for the present study, more informative – group comprises those standards which accompany the person of the king on the Scorpion and Narmer monuments. These are clearly more than a collection of the most important Upper Egyptian deities, since several notable gods and goddesses are missing from the group (for example, Seth, Min and Hathor) (Kaiser 1960: 127). On all three monuments the collection of standards is strikingly similar, suggesting that these particular emblems were closely connected with the king (cf. Frankfort 1948: 92). The following same four standards appear on both monuments of Narmer: two falcons, Wepwawet with the *šdšd*-device, and the royal placenta. Early Dynastic royal monuments after the reign of Narmer show only Wepwawet and the royal placenta. They accompany the figure of a king on a relief block in the Cairo Museum, thought to be from the Early Dynastic temple at Gebelein (W.S. Smith 1949: pl. 30.d), on a relief fragment from the Heliopolis shrine of Netjerikhet (W.S. Smith 1949: fig. 52), and on the same king's relief panels from the Step Pyramid complex (Firth and Quibell 1935: pls 15–17, 40–2).

For the interpretation of these standards later parallels are revealing. In scenes of the Sed-festival from the solar temple of Niuserra (Fifth Dynasty), similar standards are named the *šmsw Ḥr*, 'followers of Horus' (cf. Kaiser 1959: 130), a term also applied to the semi-legendary pre-unification kings in the Turin Canon. For this reason, the standards have been linked with the royal ancestors, and it is true that the worship of ancestors was an important element of kingship from the earliest times (Frankfort 1948: 91). An alternative suggestion is that the group of four standards on the Narmer Palette and macehead were symbols of the Thinite royal house (Frankfort 1948: 93). If the precise origin of the standards eludes us, it none the less seems likely that each symbolised a particular aspect of kingship.

TITLES AND NAMES: EXPRESSIONS OF DIVINE KINGSHIP

One of the most accessible sources for Early Dynastic kingship is the names of the kings themselves (cf. Weill 1961, chapter 18). As in many ancient (and modern) societies, so in ancient Egypt names were full of meaning. They were often selected to express particular beliefs or concerns. This was indeed the case with the kings' names and titles, which were naturally imbued with added religious and/or political significance. Certain concepts are frequently expressed in royal names, such as strength, skill and fecundity (Husson and Valbelle 1992: 20). The king's official titulary may be considered as 'an elaborate statement regarding his divine nature' (Frankfort 1948: 46). Hence, if we can 'translate' or at least interpret Early Dynastic royal names, we should gain important insights into how the early Egyptians regarded the office of kingship, and which aspects of his role a particular king chose to emphasise in the titulary he adopted at his accession (Shaw and Nicholson 1995: 153). As we shall see, two ideas in particular are stressed in the royal titulary: the fact that the king presides over a dual monarchy, and the divine status of the king as the incarnation of Horus (Quirke 1990: 10).

Prior to the development of the fivefold titulary common in later times, kings in the Early Dynastic period bore up to three different names or titles. One of these is attested from the late Predynastic period, others were added during the First Dynasty. The Horus name, written in a rectangular frame or *serekh*, expressed an aspect of the king's nature in his role as the earthly manifestation of the sky god Horus. Many Early Dynastic kings are attested solely by their Horus name, which was the element of the royal titulary most commonly used on monuments and in inscriptions. A second royal title was added in the middle of the First Dynasty. This was *nswt-bity*, 'he of the sedge and bee', a title which expressed the many dualities over which the king exercised rule: Upper and Lower Egypt, the Black Land (cultivation) and the Red Land (desert), the realms of day and night, the natural and the supernatural, and so on (cf. Quirke 1990: 11). The later king lists often referred to rulers by the name that followed this *nswt-bity* title. Towards the end of the First Dynasty, a third title was introduced, first as part of the *nswt-bity* name, and later as a separate title in its own right: *nbty*, the **'Two Ladies'**, referring to the patron deities of Upper and Lower Egypt, the vulture goddess Nekhbet of Elkab and the cobra goddess Wadjet of Buto. The *nbty* title expressed the king's dual role as king of Upper and Lower Egypt. Comparatively few *nbty* names are preserved in contemporary Early Dynastic sources. The origins of a fourth title, the poorly understood 'Golden Horus name', may be traced in royal inscriptions of the First and Third Dynasties, and in the annals of the Palermo Stone. The cartouche, an oval frame which enclosed the king's birth name, first appears at the end of the Third Dynasty.

Attempts to read meaning into the varying use of different titles may be misguided. The composition of the royal titulary seems to have been rather fluid in the Early Dynastic period and early Old Kingdom, not necessarily following the strict rules that modern scholars have tried to discern or even impose (cf. S. Schott 1956). A certain flexibility in practice – even as late as the beginning of the Fourth Dynasty – is indicated by inscriptions of Netjerikhet and Sneferu. For example, a relief fragment from the Heliopolis shrine of Netjerikhet gives the sequence *nswt-bity Ntri-ht* written within the panels of the king's *serekh*, the upper part of which encloses the Horus name, also *Ntri-ht* (S. Schott 1956: 66, fig. 3); whilst a rock-cut inscription of Sneferu from the Wadi Maghara shows the king's *nswt-bity nbty* name (here the same as his Horus name, *Nb-m3't*) and 'Golden Horus' name (*Snfrw*) both enclosed within a cartouche, reserved in later times for the *nswt-bity* name (S. Schott 1956: 64, fig. 1). Clearly, early in the development of the royal titulary, the various elements were, to some extent, interchangeable and could be combined in several different ways. The message that the titulary as a whole conveyed may have been more important than the precise combination or ordering of the various names and epithets.

The Horus title

The primary title was the Horus title. This was adopted by the king at his accession and subsequently used throughout his reign. A modern parallel is the *nengo*, the name adopted at the accession of a Japanese emperor and by which he is always known after his death. Thus, the emperor known in the West by his personal name Hirohito is referred to in Japan as Showa ('radiant harmony'). In much the same way, the personal names of the Early Dynastic Egyptian kings were apparently used very rarely. Instead, contemporary monuments recorded the king's Horus name. This comprised three elements: a phrase or epithet, written within a rectangular panel – representing a section of the palace façade – surmounted by a falcon symbolising the god Horus (cf. Dreyer 1995b: 54, n. 19). The name expressed the close relationship between the king and the celestial deity he embodied. As a celestial deity, Horus was remote yet all-seeing, enfolding within his wings the entire cosmos. A god with such qualities evidently provided Egypt's early kings with a powerful symbol and metaphor for their own earthly rule (Quirke 1990: 21). The *serekh* surmounted by a figure of the god was adopted as a potent symbol of kingship during late Predynastic times. The earliest *serekh*s were empty, the symbol alone conveying the necessary message of royal power. Towards the culmination of the unification process, the king began to write an epithet within the *serekh* (cf. Barta 1990). This epithet expressed a particular aspect of the god Horus immanent in his earthly incarnation, the king (cf. Frankfort 1948: 46). It is likely that the name of the god himself was intended to be read as part of the name as a whole (S. Schott 1956: 56).

Although ancient Egyptian royal names are notoriously difficult to translate – the individual elements comprising a name have been likened to a newspaper banner headline, rather than a grammatically correct sentence – insights into Early Dynastic kingship can be gained from an analysis of the Horus names of the first three dynasties. A survey reveals subtle developments in the type of epithet chosen, and thus in the message conveyed. Changes in the formulation of the Horus name (a Seth-name and a Horus-and-Seth-name are also attested from the late Second Dynasty) must reflect, to some degree, the changing emphasis of Egyptian kingship.

The Horus names of several First Dynasty kings express the aggressive authority of Horus, perhaps reflecting the coercive power of kingship at this early stage of Egyptian statehood. Names like 'Horus the fighter' (Aha), 'Horus the strong' (Djer) or 'arm-raising Horus' (Qaa) call to mind the warlike iconography of the earliest royal monuments from the period of state formation. They emphasise an authority based upon military might and the power of life and death. Amongst First Dynasty Horus names, only Semerkhet, 'companion of the corporation', makes a theological statement, expressing the relationship between Horus and the other principal deities in the Egyptian pantheon. In this respect, it points the way to more sustained efforts at theological exposition in the Third Dynasty.

The emphasis in the Second Dynasty is rather different. Following periods of instability, the first and last kings of the dynasty were each faced with a task of renewal, and this is reflected in their Horus names: 'Horus: the two powers are at peace' (Hetepsekhemwy) and 'Horus and Seth: the two powers have arisen; the two lords are at peace in him' (Khasekhemwy-nebwy-hetep-imef). The other Second Dynasty Horus names express the ideal of kingship in more overtly theological terms: hence names such as 'Horus, lord of the sun' (Nebra), 'Horus of divine nature' (Ninetjer), and especially 'Horus strong-willed, champion of **Maat**' (Sekhemib-perenmaat). This last name is the earliest and most direct expression of the king's principal role: to uphold Maat.

This trend continues into the Third Dynasty when the Horus names describe either the relationship between Horus and the other gods comprising 'the corporation' or the position of Horus as the god most intimately associated with Egyptian kingship. Thus, Horus is both the '(most) divine of the corporation' (Netjerikhet) and the '(most) powerful of the corporation' (Sekhemkhet), and has 'arisen as a *ba*' (Khaba). The king, as the incarnation of Horus, is 'the strong protector' (Sanakht) of mankind and the cosmos, and 'high of the white crown' (Qahedjet), the most exalted item in the royal regalia. The Horus names of the Third

Dynasty kings comprise a miniature theological treatise on Horus, the king, their relationship to each other and to the wider pantheon. In this respect they echo the complex theology of the Pyramid Texts, some of which must date back to the Early Dynastic period.

The 'Two Ladies' title

The title *nbty*, the 'Two Ladies' (Figure 6.5), emphasised the geographical duality of the Egyptian realm, but at the same time the enduring unification of the Two Lands in the person of the king. A similar concept is expressed in a circumlocution for the king found in one of the titles borne by Early Dynastic queens, 'she who sees Horus-and-Seth'. The concept that the king embodied both gods highlights a fundamental role of kingship: the reconciliation of opposites in order to maintain the established order. The *nbty* name emphasised the geographical aspect of this balance.

The *nbty* name itself was written after the images of the two deities, the vulture and cobra. In one instance, on a label of Djet from mastaba S3504 at North Saqqara, the cobra is replaced by the red crown, demonstrating a very early association of the two (Gardiner 1958). Each goddess is depicted resting on a basket (*nb*); the two baskets form a pun on the title itself (*nbty*) (S. Schott 1956: 56). The choice of Nekhbet and Wadjet to symbolise the two halves of the country seems to date back to the immediate aftermath of the unification. Elkab and Buto also represented the very different terrains of the Two Lands: the narrow river valley of Upper Egypt, running through barren desert on either side; and the wide expanses of flat, marshy land in the Delta. It had long been suspected that the towns themselves must have been important localities in the period immediately preceding the unification. Modern excavations have confirmed that this was indeed the case (von der Way 1986, 1987, 1988, 1989, 1991, 1992; Hendrickx 1994).

The concept of the 'Two Ladies' is first met in the reign of Aha. An ebony label from the tomb of Neith-hotep (probably Aha's mother) at Naqada shows the *serekh* of Aha facing a tent-like shrine, enclosing the signs *nbty mn*. There has been considerable debate about the meaning of this group. It may be the name of a king; more plausibly, it may be the name of the shrine itself, 'the Two Ladies endure' (Quirke 1990: 23). In this case, the label attests the existence of the 'Two Ladies', and their close connection with the kingship, from the very beginning of the First Dynasty; but it does not prove the existence of the 'Two Ladies' title at this stage, nor does it have any bearing on the identification of the semi-legendary King Menes.

The element *nbty* first appears as a regular element of the royal titulary in the reign of Semerkhet (the element *nbwy* in Anedjib's titulary may be seen as a precursor [S. Schott 1956: 60]). Many of the Early Dynastic

1

2

Figure 6.5 The Two Ladies. (1) The pairing of the vulture goddess Nekhbet and the cobra goddess Wadjet (known in Egyptian as *nbty*, 'the Two Ladies') is first attested (top) on an ivory label of Aha from the royal tomb at Naqada (after Emery 1961: 50, fig. 10). (2) The pairing of the two goddesses was adopted in the First Dynasty as one of the king's principal titles, as shown here on an ivory year label of Qaa from Abydos (after Petrie 1900: pl. XVII.29). Not to same scale.

kings wrote the titles *nswt-bity* and *nbty* together, followed by a single name which thus served under both headings. An alternative interpretation sees the *nbty* element as part of the *nswt-bity* name, only later becoming a separate title in its own right (Müller 1938: 51; S. Schott 1956; Quirke 1990: 23).

Early Dynastic inscriptions record only a few distinctive *nbty* names; that is, those which differ from the king's *nswt-bity* name. A *nbty* name, *sn*, is attested on a few inscriptions from the reign of Qaa. This may have the meaning 'brother', expressing the king's closeness to the patron goddesses. A recently discovered year label of Qaa from his tomb at Abydos gives an otherwise unattested version of the king's *nbty* name,

204

sḥtp(-nbty), 'the one who pacifies (the Two Ladies)' (Dreyer *et al.* 1996: 74, pl. 14.e). This seems to express the role of the king in placating the gods and in maintaining the harmony of opposites necessary for cosmic order. The Horus Sekhemkhet imitated his illustrious predecessor Netjerikhet in many ways, not least in the choice of his *nbty* name: an ivory plaque, found in one of the subterranean magazines of Sekhemkhet's unfinished step pyramid, is inscribed *nbty ḏsrti(-ꜥnḫ)*. The name *ḏsrti(-ꜥnḫ)* is difficult to translate precisely, but it is clearly connected with the word *ḏsr* and probably refers to the sacred nature of kingship. The word *ḏsr* had added significance in Egyptian, conveying a sense of separateness. This sense that the king is set apart from the rest of humanity was expressed in concrete terms in the location and architecture of the Third Dynasty step pyramid complexes.

The nswt-bity *title*

The *nswt-bity* title was an innovation of Den's reign, one of several important developments which characterise the middle of the First Dynasty. It has been suggested that the adoption of the new title coincided with the first occurrence of the joint ceremony of *ḫꜥt nswt-bity*, 'the appearance of the dual king', recorded on the Palermo Stone in the reign of Den (year x+3) (Godron 1990: 180). The new title took second place in the royal titulary, coming immediately after the king's Horus name. Whereas the Horus name remained the principal means of identifying the reigning king, the *nswt-bity* title and name often seem to have been used in secondary contexts (Quirke 1990: 23). For example, inscriptions referring to buildings or boats named after the king use the *nswt-bity* (or *nswt-bity-nbty*) name.

The name itself followed the title *nswt-bity*, translated literally as 'he of the sedge and bee'. The meaning of the title is complex and many-faceted. In bilingual inscriptions of the Ptolemaic period, the Greek equivalent of *nswt-bity* translates as 'king of Upper and Lower Egypt'. This has remained the traditional translation for *nswt-bity*, even though it is unlikely to have been the original sense. Rather, the recently suggested 'dual king' gives a better approximation of the true meaning (Quirke 1990: 11). The title seems to have stressed the role of the king as the embodiment of all the dualities which made up Egypt and the cosmos according to the Egyptians' world-view. Above all, perhaps, the dual title *nswt-bity* stressed the two different aspects of kingship, the divine and the human. The usual word for 'king' in ancient Egyptian was *nswt*, and this appears to have been the superior designation for the ruler (although it may simply have been an abbreviation of the full title *nswt-bity* [Quirke 1990: 11]). In other contexts, especially administrative, the king might be referred to indirectly as *bity*. For example, the position of 'king's treasurer' was designated by the title *ḫtmw-bity*, not **ḫtmw-nswt*. The *nswt-bity* title 'probably fused two hierarchically ordered words for king and aspects of kingship' (Baines 1995: 127). It seems likely that *nswt*, as the superior title, conveyed the divinity of the king, expressed in his role as the incarnation of Horus and earthly representative of the gods. (It is significant that the Egyptian word for 'kingship' is derived from *nswt*.) By contrast, *bity* may have indicated the king's human aspect, especially his position as head of state and government (Ray 1993: 70; Shaw and Nicholson 1995: 153). The introduction of the *nswt-bity* title marks an important stage in the formulation of kingship ideology. Henceforth, emphasis was firmly placed upon the king's role in binding together Egypt and the cosmos. Harmony of opposites is a theme which was given visual expression in some of the earliest monuments of kingship, particularly the ceremonial palettes from the late Predynastic period. With the introduction of the *nswt-bity* title in the reign of Den, this theme was brought into the royal titulary.

nswt-bity names

After the title *nswt-bity* came a name which may also have been the king's birth name (S. Schott 1956: 76). It was certainly the name by which many kings were known in later annals and king lists. The *nswt-bity* title was often paired with the element *nbty*, after the introduction of the latter in the reign of Semerkhet. Peribsen was the first king to separate the two elements and use the *nswt-bity* title alone once more (S. Schott 1956: 61), on a sealing from Abydos (Petrie 1901: pl. XXII.190).

Den's *nswt-bity* name, *zmti* (S. Schott 1956: 60), appears on many contemporary inscriptions, especially the stone vessels found beneath the Step Pyramid. The name was also used on royal seals, frequently without reference to the king's Horus name. It must, therefore, have had a significance of its own. It means 'the two deserts', referring to the eastern and western deserts which guarded the Nile valley on each side. It reinforces the message of the *nswt-bity* title: that the king's rule extends over the whole of Egypt, east and west as well as north and south. Given the evidence that Den probably conducted a military campaign against the nomadic tribespeople of the eastern desert, his *nswt-bity* name may have had added resonance, proclaiming his intention to subdue Egypt's desert borderlands and bring them under his yoke. An alternative reading of the name is *ḫ3sti*, translated as 'the foreigner' or 'the Sinaitic' (Godron 1990: 21). It has been suggested that Den adopted this secondary name following a military success against the inhabitants of the Sinai, recorded on the ivory label from Abydos (Godron 1990: 180).

The *nswt-bity-nbty* name of Den's successor, the Horus Anedjib, is curious and quite impenetrable: *mr-p-bi3*. For many years, the *nswt-bity-*

nbty name of Semerkhet likewise defied interpretation; but it has now been shown to read *iri-ntr*, 'guardian of the god'. If the *nbty* element is interpreted as forming part of the name, rather than another title, then the name should read *iri-nbty*, 'guardian of the Two Ladies' (Quirke 1990: 23). The name expresses the close relationship between the king and the divine sphere. It also conveys something of the tension inherent in the ideology of divine kingship: the king is separate from the rest of humanity, the interlocutor between people and gods, indeed the gods' representative on earth; but he is still not quite one of the gods, possessing only 'limited divinity' (Quirke 1990: 11). It is the royal **ka**, the divine essence incarnate in the king, which passes unchanged from generation to generation; the king himself cannot escape death. Finally, the *nswt-bity-nbty* name of Hetepsekhemwy (*htp*) is merely an abbreviation of his Horus name.

The gold sign and ring of eternity

Perhaps the most difficult title to interpret satisfactorily is the one which first appears in the Old Kingdom but which clearly has antecedents in the Early Dynastic period. This is the 'Golden Horus' title (cf. S. Schott 1956: 68–73), written with a figure of the god Horus surmounting the hieroglyph for 'gold' (*nbw*). The title seems to have expressed the divinity of the king since, according to Egyptian mythology, the gods' bodies were made of gold. The immunity of this metal from tarnishing, combined with its obvious solar connotations, was no doubt the underlying reason for this association (Quirke 1990: 11). To the Egyptian mind, with its propensity for seeking multiple and intertwined meanings, the 'Golden Horus' title may have had a further significance. The ancient name of Naqada, the cult centre of the god Seth, was Nubt, meaning 'golden (city)'; Seth himself was often described as *nbwty*, 'the one of Nubt' or 'the golden one'. The image of the Horus falcon surmounting the sign for gold may have had the added symbolism of Horus conquering Seth. The title may therefore have expressed the role of the king as champion of Maat and defender of the cosmic order against the forces of chaos.

A fragmentary inscription from the tomb of Den at Abydos shows the king's *serekh* juxtaposed with a vertical group of three signs: a cobra, the gold sign and a ring (Spencer 1993: 87, fig. 66). A similar combination of the gold sign and ring occurs in the titulary of Netjerikhet (Lauer 1939: pl. XVI.1–2; S. Schott 1956: 63). A stone vessel fragment of Khasekhemwy from Abydos shows the group *nbw ht s* in place of the customary *nbwy htp im=f*. The group may, perhaps, be interpreted as the king's 'gold name'. On the Palermo Stone and its associated fragments, it appears that a cartouche and a phrase incorporating the gold sign regularly formed part of the royal titulary, coming between the Horus name of the king and the name of his mother (S. Schott 1956: 71). The entries for Djer, Semerkhet and Ninetjer all show this feature. It may be that the name in the cartouche, at this period and in the reign of Sneferu, is in fact the 'gold name' (S. Schott 1956: 71).

The ring (*šn*) symbolises eternity, and was later elongated to form the cartouche that enclosed the king's birth name (Müller-Winkler 1984). It seems to stress the permanence of Egyptian kingship, the immutability of an institution which was characterised as part of a divinely ordained cosmic order. The earliest cartouche occurs on a fragmentary sealing of the Horus Sanakht from Beit Khallaf (Garstang 1902: pl. XIX.7; Seidlmayer 1996b: pl. 23). Sanakht was probably the penultimate king of the Third Dynasty, and the introduction of the cartouche as a frame enclosing a royal name may have been an innovation of his reign. Although in earlier times the ring seems to have been associated with the king's 'gold name', on the sealing of Sanakht it is likely that the elongated ring – in other words the cartouche – encloses the king's *nswt-bity* name. Certainly, all the examples of a cartouche from the following reign contain the king's *nswt-bity* name. Indeed, this element of the royal titulary seems to have come to prominence at the end of the Third Dynasty.

ROYAL RITUALS AND FESTIVALS: CELEBRATIONS OF KINGSHIP

One of the most enduring ways of reinforcing rule – from the earliest states to the modern world – is through carefully stage-managed ceremonies. The ruler is presented to his people, or a select group of them, in a setting which emphasises his authority, both political and supernatural. This is particularly true of ancient Egypt, where 'kingship is ritual' (Baines 1995: 130). The celebration of periodic festivals not only gave a sense of order and routine to the ritual life of the country, it also guaranteed the institution of kingship regular exposure in a court-controlled setting.

Egypt's Early Dynastic rulers instituted a number of rituals and festivals designed to promote the position of the king and of kingship at the very centre of Egyptian society. The iconography of the Narmer macehead suggests that many aspects of royal ritual and ideology had already been established by the beginning of the First Dynasty. Others may have been innovations of later reigns. All were assimilated into a body of tradition which was presented as eternal and unchanging. The various celebrations took place throughout a king's reign, beginning at his accession and coronation. Regular ritual appearances reinforced his divine status, whilst the legitimacy and efficacy of his rule were renewed later in his reign during the complex Sed-festival.

The accession and coronation

The death of a king was a time of great cosmic danger, since the forces of disorder (both supernatural and human) might take advantage of the transition to disrupt the established order. Whilst in the Middle and New Kingdoms the institution of **co-regency** ensured a smooth succession and reduced the potential for dynastic intrigue, no such mechanism seems to have existed in earlier periods. Certainly, there are hints from the Fourth Dynasty that the succession was not always trouble free. The existence of several royal princes, each with his own powerful position in the administration, must have presented great opportunities for political manoeuvring. As one might expect, the evidence for such events is very limited. None the less, there are intimations of struggle surrounding the succession at certain points in the Early Dynastic period. An ephemeral ruler, perhaps a usurper, called Sneferka is attested at the end of the First Dynasty; the sequence of kings in the middle of the Second Dynasty is still not firmly established, and there may have been a contest for power between two royal factions.

If Egypt was vulnerable to political upheaval at the death of a king, the supernatural dangers were equally great. Since the king was the defender of created order and the conqueror of the forces of chaos, his death represented the temporary victory of those same malign powers. Without its champion, Egypt was in mortal danger from supernatural forces of evil. Hence, the accession of a new king was accompanied by a series of rituals, designed to restore Maat and to reassert Egypt's place at the centre of the cosmos. The ceremonies surrounding a change of reign may be divided into two quite separate events: the accession and the coronation.

According to later sources, the proclamation of a new king – in other words, his accession to the throne – took place at the ideologically propitious moment of sunrise. The dawn of a new day, marking the defeat of darkness by the forces of light, and the rebirth of creation, was an appropriate metaphor for the beginning of a new reign, with its parallel connotations (Frankfort 1948: 148). Indeed, the same verb (h^ci) was used by the Egyptians to denote both the rising of the sun and the public appearance of the king. We have no direct evidence of accession rituals, but we may assume that they were characterised by great solemnity.

By contrast, there is limited evidence for the various ceremonies which marked the coronation of the king. Only after he had completed the necessary ritual acts, on a favourable day in the calendar, was the king possessed of all his powers, and was Egypt once again under the guidance of a divine authority. It is likely that the coronation ceremonies were scheduled for one of the days in the year which marked new beginnings (Frankfort 1948: 104): the first day of the season of winter, when the Nile floodwaters began to recede; the summer and winter solstices; the spring and autumn equinoxes; or New Year's Day itself. In the Early Dynastic period the coronation seems to have consisted of two distinct ceremonies, each of which embodied one of the roles of kingship. Recorded on the Palermo Stone at the beginning of each new reign, these ceremonies were the ritual reunification of the Two Lands and the circuit of the wall at Memphis.

Uniting Upper and Lower Egypt

The precise rituals which characterised the event are not attested. Indeed, 'uniting Upper and Lower Egypt' may represent nothing more than a formal statement of the primary role of the king: the binding force at the centre of Egyptian society. (One interpretation of the Narmer Palette is that it represents this ceremony [Millet 1990: 59].)

The circuit of the wall

The second component of the coronation ceremony involved the king performing a circuit of the wall at Memphis. According to tradition, Memphis – *inb ḥd*, 'the white wall', in Egyptian – had been founded by Menes as his new capital. The city, which was the principal seat of government, stood at the junction of Upper and Lower Egypt, and therefore signified the king's dominion over the Two Lands. By striding or running around the perimeter of the royal capital, the new king asserted his territorial authority and took symbolic possession of his realm and its royal administration. In its emphasis on the territorial aspect of the king's authority, the 'circuit of the wall' was thus akin to one of the main rituals of the Sed-festival (see below).

The appearance of the king

A ceremony which took place at the coronation of at least one Early Dynastic king (probably Netjerikhet) was the ritual 'appearance of the dual king' (*ḫ't nswt-bity*). In contrast to the 'unification of the Two Lands' and the 'circuit of the wall', the ritual appearance of the king was not restricted to his coronation, but took place at other times during a reign. The appearance of the king apparently took one of three forms: the *ḫ't nswt*, 'appearance of the king as *nswt*', the *ḫ't bity*, 'appearance of the king as *bity*', or the combined version *ḫ't nswt-bity*, 'appearance of the dual king (*nswt-bity*)'. We cannot be sure of the ideological difference between these three types of royal appearance. Probably the aspect of kingship being emphasised dictated the name and form of the ceremony, although a geographical distinction cannot be excluded entirely, since one of the characteristics of Egyptian thought was to find multiple meanings in a single word or concept. Given the hints of internal unrest during the middle of Ninetjer's reign, in particular the apparent attack on two (Lower Egyptian?) localities in year 13, the king's subsequent three appearances as *bity* may have been intended to deliver a political message about the extent of his authority.

The ritual appearance of the king would have involved him appearing in public in a carefully managed setting. For the *ḥʿt bity* the king would appear in the red crown, for the *ḥʿt nswt* he would wear the white crown, and for the combined ceremony the double crown would be worn. It is significant in this respect that the earliest occurrence of the *ḥʿt nswt-bity* is an entry on the Palermo Stone which probably falls during the reign of Den. As we have seen, the double crown may have been an innovation of Den's reign, and the combined ritual appearance of the king may have been instituted at the same time. However, the earlier, separate ceremonies were not abandoned altogether: nine years after his appearance as dual king, Den celebrated a ritual appearance as *bity*. This entry on the Palermo Stone is the earliest attestation of the *ḥʿt bity* ceremony; the *ḥʿt nswt* is first recorded somewhat earlier, on the preceding register of the Palermo Stone which may correspond to the reign of Djer.

The 'appearance of the king as *nswt*' is attested only twice on the annals of the Palermo Stone. In both cases, the ceremony seems to have taken place in the king's seventh regnal year. This may be a coincidence, or it may be significant. It is possible that the *ḥʿt nswt* occurred mainly in the early part of a reign. Unfortunately, so little is known about the ceremony that it is impossible to gauge its true importance to the institution of kingship. The 'appearance of the king as *bity*' was celebrated more frequently during the Early Dynastic period. It is possible that the ceremony depicted on the Narmer macehead is the *ḥʿt bity* (Millet 1990: 56). This ritual is attested once during the reign of Den, and no less than four times under Ninetjer. After the latter king's fifteenth year on the throne, he seems to have celebrated the *ḥʿt bity* every other year. The combined ceremony, instituted in the reign of Den, seems to have replaced the two separate ceremonies towards the end of the Second Dynasty. Thus, the lowest register of the Palermo Stone, probably corresponding to the early part of the Third Dynasty, records only 'appearances of the dual king'. One king, possibly Netjerikhet or his immediate successor, celebrated this event three times in his first four years on the throne. The first occurrence, in the king's first regnal year, may represent the actual coronation ceremony; the repetitions of the ritual in successive years were perhaps intended to buttress the power of the new ruler after his predecessor's death. It is possible that the change of dynasty following the death of Khasekhemwy necessitated a greater frequency of royal ritual than usual in the early years of the new reign, to legitimise the king in the eyes of his people and the gods. It is often difficult to identify precisely the royal rituals depicted in Early Dynastic inscriptions. The ritual appearances of the king were probably connected with the Sed-festival. It is noteworthy that the Sed-festival reliefs in the Sun Temple of Niuserra show the distinctive double pavilion associated with the Sed-festival but also the single pavilions for rites specifically associated either with Upper Egypt or with Lower Egypt (Millet 1990: 57).

The Sed-festival

Undoubtedly the pre-eminent festival of divine kingship was the Sed-festival (Hornung and Staehelin 1974). Despite its great antiquity and long survival – its origins reach back into the Predynastic period and it was still celebrated by the Ptolemaic kings – there is surprisingly little explicit evidence for the details of the Sed-festival: where, when and how often it was celebrated, the precise order of events and their symbolic significance. Even the origin of the name is unclear (cf. K. Martin 1984: 782; Gohary 1992: 1–2). The Step Pyramid complex of Netjerikhet is the most informative contemporary source for the form and structure of the Sed-festival in the Early Dynastic period. The various components of the Sed-festival court provided the king with all the necessary spaces and buildings for the eternal celebration of the festival.

Many of the supposed representations of the Sed-festival often quoted for the first three dynasties in fact show other royal ceremonies or even royal statues. None the less, at least two Early Dynastic kings, Den and Qaa, are known to have celebrated a Sed-festival, whilst another, Anedjib, may have done so (Hornung and Staehelin 1974: 86). An ivory statuette of an anonymous First Dynasty king from Abydos shows the ruler wearing the tight-fitting Sed-festival robe. Stone vessel fragments from beneath the Step Pyramid – which may date to the Second Dynasty, perhaps the reign of Ninetjer (Helck 1979) – seem to mention a Sed-festival. Netjerikhet is sometimes said to have celebrated a Sed-festival in his lifetime (F.D. Friedman 1995: 8, quoting Strudwick 1985: 4), but there are no contemporary inscriptions to support this. An ebony label of Den from Abydos (Petrie 1900: pls XI.14, XV.16) is usually cited as an early depiction of the Sed-festival. However, although many of the attributes of the Sed-festival – such as the tight-fitting robe and the king's run between territorial markers – are shown, the absence of the throne-dais with double staircase, an essential element of the Sed-festival, may be decisive. Rather than showing the Sed-festival, the label may depict the ceremony of *ḥ't nswt-bity* (Millet 1990: 56; F.D. Friedman 1995: 7–8). The throne dais with twin staircases is shown on another, fragmentary label of Den from Abydos (Petrie 1900: pl. XIV.12); since his reign is known to have been a long one, it is almost certain that Den celebrated a Sed-festival. At the end of the First Dynasty, Qaa also enjoyed a long reign and apparently celebrated two Sed-festivals: a fragment of a siltstone bowl from beneath the Step Pyramid mentions the king's second Sed-festival (Lacau and Lauer 1959: 12, pl. 8 no. 41).

In later tradition the Sed-festival was celebrated in the king's thirtieth regnal year. For example, on the Rosetta Stone the Egyptian expression *ḥb-sd*, 'Sed-festival', is rendered in Greek as *triakontaeteris* 'thirty-year festival' (Godron 1990: 183). However, there are definite exceptions to this rule from the Dynastic period (Hornung and Staehelin 1974: 54–6). Some kings who are known to have reigned for more than thirty years never, apparently, celebrated a Sed-festival (for example, Senusret III), whilst others (for example, Akhenaten) did so well before their thirtieth regnal year (Gohary 1992). The reasons which lay behind each decision to celebrate the Sed-festival remain obscure, but 'it is unlikely that a mere counting of years was the decisive factor' (Frankfort 1948: 79). The celebration may have depended entirely upon the health of the reigning king (Godron 1990: 184), Sed-festivals celebrated before the thirtieth regnal year representing the actions of elderly or otherwise infirm kings (Gohary 1992: 4).

The Egyptian expression *ḥb-sd* has often been translated as 'jubilee'. As we have seen, this may be inappropriate given the evidence for its somewhat irregular celebration, at least in the early periods of Egyptian history. The significance of the Sed-festival clearly went much deeper than a simple celebration of the king's longevity. In essence, it was a ritual of rejuvenation (Barta 1975; Gohary 1992: 1), by which the powers of the reigning king, both magical and physical, as well as his relationship with the gods and his people, were renewed (Frankfort 1948: 79; K. Martin 1984: 783). The surviving evidence for the Sed-festival from the Early Dynastic period indicates a complex series of rituals whose symbolism goes to the very heart of kingship ideology. The Sed-festival court on the eastern side of the Step Pyramid complex preserves a series of shrines, built in stone but modelled on timber and matting constructions. These temporary structures seem to have been erected at the site of the Sed-festival to house the images of provincial deities (Frankfort 1948: 80). The deities of Upper Egypt assembled on one side of the court, housed in shrines of the quintessential Upper Egyptian type (*pr-wr*). The deities of Lower Egypt gathered on the opposite side of the court, housed in the curved-topped shrines characteristic of Lower Egypt (*pr-nḏr/pr nw*). The various gods and goddesses from important sites throughout Egypt seem to have gathered together to pay homage to the king and to legitimise his authority over the whole of Egypt. For his part, the king probably reciprocated, paying his own homage to these deities, renewing the bond between the kingship and the divine sphere which guaranteed Egypt's continuing prosperity.

Another part of the festival emphasised the king's secular hold on power: the ritual of territorial claim, known as 'encompassing the field'.

Symbolically, it fulfilled much the same function as the circuit of the wall at Memphis, carried out by the king at his coronation (Decker 1992: 34). In the great court which stretches before Netjerikhet's Step Pyramid, and again in the smaller court in front of the 'House of the South', two sets of horseshoe-shaped markers or 'cairns' delimit a ritual 'field'. At Saqqara these markers are arranged in pairs; on other Early Dynastic representations, such as the Narmer macehead and the ebony label of Den, they appear in sets of three. Oriented on a north–south axis, they clearly symbolise the territorial limits of the king's realm, the 'field' between them representing the whole of Egypt (Spencer 1978: 53). Clad in the tight-fitting Sed-festival robe, wearing the red, white or double crown, and carrying a flail in one hand and a baton-like object in the other, the king ran or strode between the two sets of markers, reasserting his claim to the land of Egypt. We know from later references that the baton-like object is the *mks*, a container which held the *imit-pr* (F.D. Friedman 1995: 24). This seems to represent a title deed, expressing the king's legal possession of the territory of Egypt. In origin, the Sed-festival run may also have served to prove the king's continuing physical potency (Decker 1992: 34).

The act of 'encompassing the field' has been interpreted as the central ceremony of the entire festival, since it re-dedicated 'the field' (representing Egypt) to the gods and renewed the legitimacy of the king's rule (Frankfort 1948: 86). However, representations of the Sed-festival, in particular the hieroglyph used to symbolise the event, indicate that another part of the proceedings stood at the symbolic and ritual heart of the celebration. This was the dual enthronement of the king, once as king of Lower Egypt and once as king of Upper Egypt, in the distinctive Sed-festival pavilion (K. Martin 1984: 782). It is this pavilion with twin staircases which forms the hieroglyph for *ḥb-sd*. The base of just such a pavilion has been preserved in the Sed-festival court of the Step Pyramid complex (Plate 6.1). The king would appear twice on the dais, once in the red crown and once in the white crown. For both enthronements, the king wore the long, close-fitting Sed-festival robe. The symbolism of the ritual is unambiguous: it recalled the coronation ceremony and proclaimed the duality of kingship.

In later depictions of the festival (for example, Kaiser 1971), a special building erected near the pavilion served as a robing-room, where the king could change his regalia (Frankfort 1948: 83). The Step Pyramid complex suggests that a number of different buildings were needed during the course of the festival. All were probably light structures of reeds, matting and wooden poles, forming a temporary encampment for the duration of the ceremonies. In addition to, or adjoining, the robing-room, was a festival palace, which provided temporary accommodation for the king. The Step Pyramid complex also comprises two further ceremonial buildings, dubbed the 'House of the North' and the 'House of the South'. They

Plate 6.1   The emblem of the Sed-festival. A throne platform with two staircases, situated at the southern end of the smaller courtyard which lies on the eastern side of the Step Pyramid complex of Netjerikhet at Saqqara (author's photograph). A platform of this kind featured during the ceremonial of the Sed-festival and was used as the hieroglyph for the festival itself.

may represent the buildings in which the king held audiences or received the homage of visiting dignitaries, in his dual capacity as king of Lower Egypt and king of Upper Egypt, respectively. It is likely that members of the royal family and the highest officials of the administration attended the Sed-festival: to reaffirm their bonds of loyalty to the king, to celebrate the rejuvenation of his divine and secular authority, and to witness the renewal of his contract with Egypt and the gods. The architecture of the Step Pyramid complex emphasises the importance of the Sed-festival to Early Dynastic kingship. It also demonstrates that the festival had become firmly established as an integral part of royal ideology at an early period of Egyptian history (K. Martin 1984: 784). The Sed-festival is crucial for our understanding of early kingship, the component rituals illustrating the key features of kingship ideology (Frankfort 1948: 79).

Other rituals

At least three other royal ceremonies are recorded on monuments of the Early Dynastic period, including two from the very dawn of Egyptian history.

Opening the canal

The Scorpion macehead, dating from the end of the Predynastic period, shows the king with a hoe in one hand apparently performing a ritual connected with irrigation. As the conduit for divine beneficence towards the land of Egypt, the king was responsible for the continued fertility of the land and for the success of the annual inundation. The creation and maintenance of irrigation were of crucial importance to Egypt's agricultural productivity. An early First Dynasty slate dish in the Metropolitan Museum of Art, New York, bears an inscription which may also relate to an irrigation ritual: 'the opening of the lake "the striding of the gods" in Memphis' (Hoffman 1980: 313).

Hunting the hippopotamus

It has been suggested (Millet 1990: 58) that the Scorpion macehead originally portrayed a second ceremony, the harpooning of a hippopotamus (Figure 6.6). This is not depicted directly on the surviving portions of the macehead, but may be hinted at by other elements of the decorative scheme, notably the marshland environment and the group of female 'dancers'. In the mythical version of the hippopotamus hunt described on the walls of the Edfu temple, the ritual involves a similar chorus of female musicians. The conjunction of these two rituals – opening the canal and spearing the hippopotamus – occurs in regnal year x+8 of Den on the Palermo Stone. This recorded instance of *stt ḥ3b*, 'spearing the hippopotamus', has been linked with a seal-impression of Den showing the king wrestling with a hippopotamus (Petrie 1901: pl. VII.5–6). Alternatively, the two actions, spearing and wrestling, may be unconnected and may represent two distinct rituals. A more plausible link may be made between the entry on the Palermo Stone and a fragmentary wooden label from Den's tomb at Abydos. This shows a male figure, perhaps the king, thrusting a two-pronged spear into a rounded object which may represent a pool (Petrie 1901: pl. VII.11). In later times, the ritual spearing of a hippopotamus was imbued with powerful ideological connotations.

The earliest depictions of a ritual hippopotamus hunt are to be found on a decorated pottery bowl dated to Naqada I from the cemetery at Mahasna (Ayrton and Loat 1911: pl. XXVII.13), an unprovenanced, incised, siltstone palette of similar date (Asselberghs 1961: pl. XLVI), and a fragment of the painted cloth from a Naqada II grave at Gebelein. All three examples show a hippopotamus being harpooned. Although there is considerable uncertainty about the details of the ritual, there is little doubt about its symbolic significance. The wild hippopotamus is a fierce creature, and must have posed a threat to fishermen and all those travelling the Nile by boat in early times. It was thus cast as an embodiment

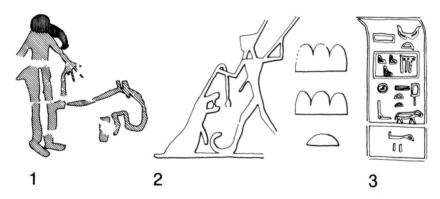

Figure 6.6 Hunting the hippopotamus. Evidence for an obscure royal ritual: (1) a fragment of painted linen from a late Predynastic tomb at Gebelein (now in the Egyptian Museum, Turin) showing a male figure harpooning a hippopotamus; this scene occurs in the context of other ritual activities (after Galassi 1955: 10, fig. 5); (2) seal-impression of Den from Abydos showing (a statue of?) the king spearing a hippopotamus (after Kaplony 1963, III: fig. 364); (3) an entry from the third register of the Palermo Stone, referring to a year in the reign of Den as 'the year of opening the lake "Thrones of the Gods" and hunting the hippopotamus' (after Schäfer 1902: pl. I). Not to same scale.

of the forces of disorder, and in later times associated with the god Seth. The ritual spearing of a hippopotamus, a common theme in the decoration of Old Kingdom private tombs, represented an attack on chaos and struck a blow for the preservation of created order. The ritual doubtless emphasised the paramount role of the king to uphold Maat.

The presentation of tribute

Another commemorative macehead, from the reign of Narmer, has already been mentioned in connection with the 'appearance of the king as *bity*'. The scenes on the macehead also depict another ceremony, namely the reception of tribute. Whether this occurred on a regular basis, or only after a military campaign, cannot be established. The Narmer macehead shows three bound captives being presented to the king. Three captives may represent a simple plurality, since the caption below states, 'captives: 120,000'. The captives appear between the two sets of territorial markers previously encountered in depictions of the Sed-festival. These probably indicate that the ceremony took place in the court of royal appearance, perhaps within the royal palace compound. In addition to the captives, the booty presented to the king comprises 400,000 cattle and 1,422,000 sheep and goats. These figures are scarcely credible, and probably support a symbolic rather than a literal interpretation of the monument as a whole. Be that as it may, it is very likely that the booty of military campaigns was presented to the king in a formal ceremony, which may have resembled, in some respects, the scene on the Narmer macehead.

SPHERES OF ROYAL AUTHORITY

The royal monuments from the period of state formation – the late Predynastic and Early Dynastic palettes and maceheads – are, without doubt, 'crucial sources for early kingship' (Baines 1995: 124). The scenes they carry express and define the role of the king *vis-à-vis* Egypt and the cosmos.

The primary duty of the king was to be the arbiter between the gods and the people of Egypt. Within this overarching role of kingship, there were none the less many other duties to be performed by the ruler. Moreover, the exigencies of government – maintaining political and economic control over the newly unified country – necessitated a whole range of royal activities. These were intended to ensure the continued loyalty of the populace, the continued prestige and appeal of the institution of kingship, and the smooth running of the central administration. As might be expected, the best indications of such activities are to be found, not on monuments, but in documents more closely associated with the apparatus of government.

The evidence: year labels and royal annals

Important insights into early notions of kingship may be gained from a survey of the events considered worthy of record in the royal annals. The annals relating to the Early Dynastic period fall into two groups. First, there are the year labels (Figure 6.7). Second, there are the royal annals, comprising the Palermo Stone and its associated fragments.

The events shown on First Dynasty year labels can be divided into three broad categories, in order of frequency: religious ceremonies, royal visits and scenes of military activity. Uniquely, year labels of Qaa also record the foundation of a religious building and the collection of various timbers, doubtless as raw materials for the royal workshops (Dreyer 1993b: 10; Dreyer *et al.* 1996: 74–5, pl. 14.e). The last type of activity highlights the administrative purpose of year labels; and it is perhaps no surprise, therefore, that the events depicted convey a rather different impression of early kingship from that given by the surviving monuments from the period of state formation. The ceremonial palettes and maceheads are characterised by scenes of aggression and conquest, presenting a picture of the coercive, military aspect of royal power; this is also emphasised in some of the Horus names from the early First Dynasty. By contrast, the year labels concentrate on other royal activities, primarily the king's

Figure 6.7 Year labels. Three First Dynasty labels, originally attached to commodities to record their contents and date: (1) wooden label of Djet from Saqqara (after Gardiner 1958: 38); (2) ivory label of Qaa from Abydos (after Petrie 1901: pl. XII.6); (3) recently discovered label of Qaa from the king's tomb at Abydos (after Dreyer *et al.* 1996: pl. 14.e). Not to same scale.

participation in important religious ceremonies and royal visits to important national shrines. As was mentioned in Chapter 3, in connection with the royal annals, the system of naming a particular year after one or more significant royal events requires, on a purely practical level, that each year be so named at the beginning rather than the end of the twelve-month period: otherwise, it would have been impossible to label accurately commodities received and dispatched during the year. The implications of this fact are enormous: the events 'recorded' on the year labels must have been pre-planned or at least predictable. Scenes of apparent military conquest must, therefore, record an idealised view of events rather than actual campaigns.

A greater range of events is recorded on the Palermo Stone. Like the year labels, the annals include references to religious and royal festivals, royal visits and punitive actions against enemies, but other types of event are mentioned much more frequently. Although they cannot be used as objective sources for ancient Egyptian history (contra Weill 1961; Godron 1990), the annals do nevertheless constitute a rich source of information about early kingship, since every event recorded makes a deliberate statement about the king's role and responsibilities.

The activities recorded

The events recorded on year labels and in the annals primarily reflect the concerns of early kingship and the self-image which the institution sought to project. Within this overall framework, three interwoven strands are discernible, representing three aspects of the king's role: his position at the head of the administration, and the overriding concern of the state for effective government, allowing total control of the country's economic resources; his divine status as the representative of the gods, and his attendant duty to uphold their cults; his role, both ideological and practical, as defender of Egypt from the forces of chaos, real or supernatural.

The following of Horus

By far the most common event recorded for the reigns of Early Dynastic kings on the Palermo Stone is the *šms-Ḥr*, 'following of Horus'. From early in the First Dynasty, this activity seems to have taken place in alternate years. Although there appears to have been a temporary break in the tradition, perhaps during the middle of the First Dynasty, the *šms-Ḥr* was still recorded as a regular event early in the Third Dynasty. Despite a number of alternative interpretations (for example, Kees 1927; Kaiser 1960: 132), the 'following of Horus' is most likely to have been a journey undertaken by the king or his officials at regular intervals for the purpose of tax collection: compare a decree of Pepi I, in which the phrase *šms-Ḥr* can scarcely mean anything other than an official tax-assessment and tax-collection exercise (Sethe 1903: 214; von Beckerath 1980: 52).

It has been suggested that the biennial royal progress allowed the king to exercise his judicial authority, perhaps deciding important legal cases, as well as permitting the detailed assessment and collection of tax revenues. It may be significant that the hieroglyph for *šms*, 'following', used in this context, represents an instrument closely associated with the goddess Mafdet, and which can be interpreted as an executioner's equipment (von Beckerath 1956: 6). The king is likely to have been accompanied by all the senior members of the court during these royal progresses. Hence, the 'following of Horus' would have presented to the Egyptian people their government on a regular basis (von Beckerath 1956: 7). The practice may be interpreted as a key element of the mechanisms of rule developed by Egypt's early kings. It provided a regular forum in which the common people (*rḥyt*) could pay homage, both personal and fiscal, to the ruler and his circle (*pʿt*). Moreover, the biennial royal tour of inspection allowed the government to retain tight central control over the country's economic resources, ensured the regular payment of taxes to the royal treasury – to guarantee the continued functioning of the government apparatus – and reinforced the psychological ties of loyalty felt by the Egyptian populace towards the king.

Royal visits

Royal visits are commonly depicted on the surviving First Dynasty year labels. As befits a country where the primary artery of communication has always been the River Nile, these visits were made by boat. Three year labels record journeys undertaken by the king in the royal bark. Two of these, in the reigns of Aha and Djer, seem to have been to the Delta. The destination of the third, shown in abbreviated form on a year label of Semerkhet, is not identified. An entry for the reign of Den on the third register of the Palermo Stone records a royal visit to Herakleopolis to see the sacred lake of the local god Harsaphes (*ḥri-š=f*, literally 'he who is upon his lake').

A wooden label of Aha from Abydos gives pride of place in the top register to a royal stop-over at the temple of Neith, a goddess with close connections to the First Dynasty royal family. In later times, the main cult centre of Neith was at Saïs in the north-western Delta. The second register of the label shows the shrine of *Ḏbʿwt* at Buto, supporting a Lower Egyptian setting for the events depicted. Of course, whether such a visit ever took place, or whether the label merely depicts an activity considered essential for the king to perform, is impossible to establish. However, the excavation of a substantial Early Dynastic building at Buto which yielded at least one official sealing dated to the reign of Aha makes an actual visit by the king a distinct possibility.

A year label of the following reign seems also to record a royal visit to the same two Delta sites. The right-hand side of the top register shows a cult installation comprising buildings under palm trees either side of a wavy canal. Parallel depictions from later sources confirm Buto as the location for this installation (Bietak 1994). The second register presents a confusing array of signs, but at the right, an oval enclosure containing the red crown may signify a cult centre at Saïs, since the red crown was closely associated with the goddess Neith. The third register clearly shows the royal bark, next to a town identified by a bird. Exactly the same locality may well be depicted in the corresponding register of the Aha year label.

The fact that two consecutive kings of the early First Dynasty chose to record visits (real or symbolic) to the Delta is significant. The homage paid to Neith of Saïs and Wadjet of Buto by Aha and Djer probably indicates the significance of both sites before the unification of Egypt – in the case of Buto, this is confirmed by recent archaeological evidence – and emphasises one of the primary concerns of the early state: the determination to promote national unity through ideology and theology. The incorporation of Wadjet in the royal titulary – as tutelary goddess of the whole of Lower Egypt – and the pious references to Neith in the names of several Early Dynastic queens can be interpreted as two aspects of this programme. A visit by the king in person to the cult centres of the two goddesses would doubtless have served to strengthen the ideological bonds which held Egypt together.

Temple building and the dedication of divine images

A major duty of the king was to construct, beautify and maintain the temples of the gods. He performed this both as their representative and to ensure continued divine favour. In theory, therefore, the king was the ultimate high priest in every temple in the land. Implicitly, all temples were monuments to the king as well as cult centres for the deities to whom they were explicitly dedicated (Quirke 1992: 81). Furthermore, the continual celebration of cult in temples throughout the land was vital for the preservation of cosmic order. Royal involvement in the life of temples could take one of two forms: the foundation and construction of a new temple, accompanied by a complex series of rituals; or a visit to an existing temple. We have seen royal visits to the temples at Saïs and Buto depicted on First Dynasty year labels, and a visit to the sacred lake of Herakleopolis recorded on the Palermo Stone. The royal annals contain several references to temple-building projects, as does a recently discovered year label of Qaa from Abydos. Temple foundation in the Early Dynastic period is dealt with in more detail in Chapter 8. An important royal activity throughout Egyptian history, the Early Dynastic sources show that temple-building was considered a duty of kingship from the earliest times.

After the regular, biennial events – the 'following of Horus' and the census – one of the most frequent activities mentioned on the Palermo Stone is the fashioning or dedication (*ms*) of a divine image. A cult image was the dwelling-place for a deity, the physical embodiment of the divine presence. The creation of a new divine image necessitated the involvement of the king, since he was sole intermediary between the people and their deities, the high priest of every cult. The practice of dedicating divine images is considered in detail in Chapter 8. The year labels and annals give us some idea of the diversity of religious activities undertaken by the king. The emphasis placed upon the religious role of the king in the official record reflects its importance in Early Dynastic Egypt.

222

Military activity

Scenes of the king victorious over his enemies are not particularly common on year labels. Only two, one from the reign of Aha and one from the reign of Den, show events of a militaristic nature. The Aha year label, from Abydos, is incomplete, but seems to record (ritual?) military action against Nubia. The ivory label of Den from Abydos, already discussed, bears the legend *zp tpi sqr i3bt*, 'first time of smiting the east(erners)'. If genuine, the label may record an early punitive raid against Egypt's troublesome north-eastern neighbours (Godron 1990). Four fragmentary year labels of Den hint at military campaigns against Western Asia, as they seem to record the destruction of enemy strongholds (Petrie 1900: pl. XV.16–18, 1902: pl. XI.8).

Like the year labels, the annals of the Palermo Stone make only scant reference to military activity. A single entry on the third register refers to *sqr 'Iwntw*, 'smiting the Bedouin'. The nomadic inhabitants of the eastern or western desert were a persistent irritation to the Egyptian authorities, threatening the economy, stability and cohesion of the new state, and punitive raids were probably mounted at intervals to keep them in check. Whether the reference is to an actual event, or to the theoretical subjugation of Egypt's enemies (a metaphor for containing the forces of chaos), cannot be determined.

More intriguing are the two instances which seem to refer to attacks on specific towns. The third register records an attack on a locality named *wr-k3*, determined by the usual town sign, indicating a settlement within Egypt. This is very significant, since it seems to suggest that a military campaign was mounted against an Egyptian town. It is not unlikely that occasional rebellions within the newly unified country would have taken place during the Early Dynastic period, and it is possible that the Palermo Stone records the royal response to just such an uprising. However, given the strong ideological content of the royal annals, a direct correlation between the written record and historical events cannot be assumed. In the fourth register of the Palermo Stone, similar attacks on two towns are mentioned. In this instance, the localities, whose names may be read as *šm-rʿ* and *h3* ('north'), are shown as rectangular, walled enclosures. It is possible that they represent places outside Egypt, although walled towns are also a feature of Early Dynastic settlement within Egypt. The reign in question is probably that of Ninetjer, and the attack on *šm-rʿ* and *h3* has been associated with the apparent disturbances in the middle of the Second Dynasty.

Whether records of real events or expressions of ideal action, the references to military activity on the Palermo Stone emphasise the coercive power of early kingship. They also testify to the role of the ruler as suppresser of dissent and disorder, whether supernatural or human, from outside or inside his realm.

ARCHITECTURE AS A STATEMENT OF ROYAL POWER

The serekh *and palace-façade*

The *serekh*, enclosing the king's primary name and proclaiming his identity as the incarnation of Horus, has been generally interpreted as depicting a section of the façade of the royal palace. The use of empty *serekh*s during the late Predynastic period shows that the motif alone was a powerful and readily understood symbol of royal authority and ownership. The role of the *serekh* in the early stages of Egyptian kingship not only emphasises the importance of iconography in establishing and propagating royal power, it also indicates the significant part played by architecture in this process (Figure 6.8).

In ancient as in modern times, the king's palace was a powerful symbol of the institution of monarchy and of royal authority. (Compare the use of the term 'pharaoh' – from *pr-ᶜ3*, 'great house' [i.e. the royal palace] – to denote the king himself, from the New Kingdom onwards.) What seems to have made the royal palace a particularly suitable motif for use within the emergent iconography of rule was its distinctive appearance. The architectural style represented in two dimensions by the *serekh* panel is known to Egyptologists as 'palace-façade'. The term denotes a mudbrick building with a series of recessed niches on the exterior walls, forming a decorative façade. Although the style is now best attested in Early Dynastic tombs and mortuary complexes, its connection with the royal palace, long assumed, has been confirmed by the excavation of a monumental First Dynasty gateway, presumably belonging to a royal palace, at Hierakonpolis in Upper Egypt (Weeks 1971–2).

The adoption of niched mudbrick architecture by the ancient Egyptians seems to have occurred in the late Predynastic period. Although the earliest surviving examples of the style date to the early First Dynasty (the Naqada royal tomb and mastaba S3357 at Saqqara, both from the reign of Aha), royal buildings of this appearance must have been in existence several generations earlier, probably as early as Naqada IId (*c.* 3200 BC). Indeed, the two buildings from Aha's reign show considerable sophistication in the decorative use of mudbrick, suggesting that the style was already long-established in Egypt (Frankfort 1941: 334).

Origins

There is little doubt about the foreign origins of the palace-façade style (already noted by Balcz 1930; argued for strongly by Frankfort 1941; for a more cautious interpretation see W.S. Smith 1981: 36; Kaiser 1985b: 32, proposes a Lower Egyptian origin). The similarity between Mesopotamian and Egyptian mudbrick architecture is so close as to make their independent development highly unlikely (Frankfort 1941: 338; Kemp 1975a: 103). As with the adoption of Mesopotamian motifs into Egyptian royal iconography during Naqada II, the process is likely to have involved an imaginative borrowing by the Egyptians from another culture to suit their own purposes: in both cases, the formulation of a repertoire of symbols to embody the ideology of divine kingship. The construction of a large-scale building of exotic appearance must have spoken to its viewers of power and prestige. It must have conveyed not only the economic potential of the ruler, but also a certain amount of awe. None the less, niched mudbrick architecture is unlikely to have been adopted merely for its dramatic impact. As with other borrowings from foreign cultures during the period of state formation and later, the Egyptian attitude seems to have been essentially pragmatic. If a neighbouring civilisation had already developed something for which the Egyptians perceived a need, the Egyptians showed no reticence in adopting it, then modifying and adapting it to suit their own purposes, ultimately creating a distinctive 'Egyptian' tradition.

An expression of élite status

The extent to which the palace-façade style of architecture became closely associated with the king – and thus a symbol of the élite status which derived from access to the royal court – is highlighted by the large First Dynasty mastaba tombs at Saqqara (cf. Kemp 1989: 55). In common with contemporary élite burials at other sites, including Abu Rawash, Tarkhan and Naqada, these large mortuary constructions are decorated with recessed niches on their exterior walls. The architectural style proclaimed the status of the tomb owner, by emphasising his proximity to the ultimate source of power, the king. The élite symbolism of niched architecture was so strong that it was even used for the *internal* walls of a First Dynasty infant burial at Minshat Abu Omar (Kroeper 1992). Although invisible once the tomb had been finished and covered, the power of the architectural style to represent status was clearly undiminished.

The royal burial

The major construction project of each reign in the Early Dynastic period seems to have been the royal mortuary complex. It not only served as the burial place of the ruler, but also 'advertised and embodied the objectives of the ... state' (Hoffman 1980: 267). A monumental tomb symbolised both political power and communal leadership (Hoffman 1980: 335).

The absolute authority of the ruler – his power over life and death – was given literal expression in a particularly chilling aspect of some First

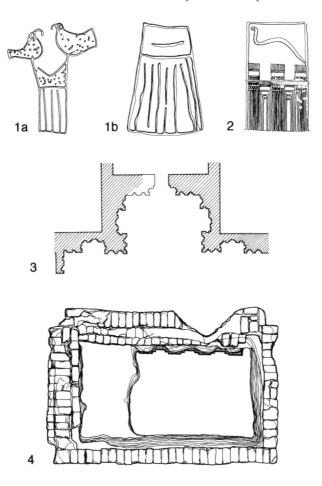

Figure 6.8 Palace-façade architecture, 1. The origins and symbolic applications of an architectural style: (1) early royal *serekh*s, incised on pottery vessels from (a) el-Beda and (b) Tura; the panelled frame represents a section of the façade of the royal palace, and was used to denote royal ownership of the storage jars thus marked (after Kaiser and Dreyer 1982: 263, fig. 14.2, 7); (2) the lower part of the *serekh* carved in relief on the funerary stela of Djet, from Abydos (after Kemp 1989: 38, fig. 10); (3) a monumental gateway of mudbrick, excavated within the early town of Nekhen (Hierakonpolis); the gate is thought to have marked the entrance to an Early Dynastic royal palace, hence confirming the appropriateness of the term 'palace façade' to describe the characteristic niched style of architecture (after Kemp 1989: 40, fig. 11); (4) grave 2275 from the Early Dynastic cemetery at Minshat Abu Omar, north-eastern Delta; three of the internal walls of the grave had been decorated with buttresses and niches in the 'palace façade' style, indicating the symbolic potency of this type of architecture to express status, even when hidden from view (after Kroeper 1992: 135, fig. 7). Not to same scale.

Dynasty royal burials at Abydos. The tombs on the Umm el-Qaab and the accompanying funerary enclosures nearer the cultivation were surrounded by smaller graves, belonging to members of the royal entourage. The household of King Aha – including his wives and other intimate attendants – was buried in a court cemetery, which stretched out from the royal tomb. From an analysis of the surviving skeletal remains, it appears that none of the individuals was older than 25 years, suggesting that the king's retainers followed their royal master to the grave rather swiftly, whether voluntarily or by compulsion (Dreyer 1993b: 11). In subsequent reigns, the royal tomb was surrounded by a ring of subsidiary burials, the distribution of the graves echoing the situation in life. An altogether more absolutist form of rule is expressed in several First Dynasty royal burials, where the mound over the king's tomb also covers the subsidiary burials surrounding the main chamber. Such a feature can only be interpreted as an indication of retainer sacrifice: the members of the king's household were killed (or committed suicide) when their sovereign himself died, so that they might accompany him in death as in life (Hoffman 1980: 275–9). This practice, which – no doubt for practical and economic reasons – was discontinued after the late First Dynasty, must have been a graphic illustration of the ultimate authority of the king, not only during his earthly life but in the hereafter as well. The ideological constraints of the time may have required suicide on the part of retainers. Only the king, as a member of the divine sphere, was guaranteed an afterlife in the company of the gods; others might hope for some share in an afterlife, by 'hanging onto the king's coat-tails' and following him directly to the next world. (Compare the practice in Japan, once widespread, whereby devoted followers of the emperor would commit ritual suicide at his death, in order to follow him into the next world. A number of individuals made this ultimate expression of loyalty as recently as 1991, on the death of Emperor Hirohito.) Be that as it may, the impetus for such a practice in Early Dynastic Egypt is likely to have come from the top downwards: the king required an entourage in the afterlife, and individual servants may have had little or no choice about following him thence.

The funerary enclosures at Abydos and Hierakonpolis were impressive constructions, consciously resembling the royal palace (Plate 6.2). Their visibility was an important aspect of their function. By contrast, the king's actual burial place (the royal tomb) fulfilled a rather different purpose, providing an eternal resting place for the king and the wherewithal for his afterlife. Hence, two conflicting factors affected the appearance and location of the royal tomb, remoteness and visibility. Unlike their Predynastic forebears, whose tombs were located side-by-side with non-royal burials (in Abydos Cemetery U), the kings of the First Dynasty chose to emphasise their unique status, and their separateness from the

Plate 6.2 Palace-façade architecture, 2. The characteristic niched style as applied to the enclosure walls of royal mortuary complexes: (top) the eastern wall of the Shunet ez-Zebib, Khasekhemwy's mudbrick funerary enclosure at Abydos (author's photograph); (bottom) the eastern wall of the step pyramid complex from the following reign (author's photograph).

rest of humanity, by building their tombs in an isolated spot, surrounded in death only by their closest retainers. Whilst the highest officials of the administration were granted the privilege of tombs on the escarpment at North Saqqara, overlooking the Early Dynastic city of Memphis, the First and late Second Dynasty kings chose to be buried in the ancestral royal necropolis of Abydos. Not only did the location of the royal tombs reinforce the legitimacy of the ruling line – by emphasising descent from the Predynastic rulers of This – it also expressed the unique, unrivalled position of the king at the head of Egyptian society.

As 'the principal public statement on the nature of kingship' (Kemp 1989: 53), the royal mortuary complex is of key importance for our understanding of Early Dynastic Egypt. The development of the royal tomb and the sophisticated symbolism of mortuary architecture form the subject of the next chapter.

CHAPTER SEVEN

ROYAL MORTUARY ARCHITECTURE

—— •◆• ——

The most enduring monuments from Early Dynastic Egypt are not the temples of national or provincial deities but the funerary constructions of kings, their relatives and high officials. During the course of the first three dynasties, Egypt's ruling class developed mortuary architecture as a potent expression of authority. Royal building projects necessitated the development of a sophisticated administrative apparatus to organise the human and material resources required. The construction of the king's tomb also fulfilled a number of practical functions, offering the king and his officials an arena in which to demonstrate leadership, providing a focus for the conspicuous consumption of prestige and imported materials, and confirming the legitimacy of the heir to the throne by his participation in the burial of his predecessor (Hoffman 1980: 327–8).

The various elements of a mortuary complex represent a sophisticated symbolic vocabulary, proclaiming the owner's status, embodying the ideology of divine kingship and reflecting contemporary conceptions of the afterlife. Mortuary architecture – especially royal mortuary architecture, which was both more visible and more durable than the burials of ordinary people – is thus a rich source of evidence for Early Dynastic society. This chapter follows the chronological development of royal mortuary architecture, discussing both the changes to the royal tomb over the course of the Early Dynastic period and the symbolism embodied in royal mortuary complexes.

THE MORTUARY COMPLEXES OF THE EARLY DYNASTIC KINGS

Royal funerary monuments of the first three dynasties cluster at two principal sites and comprise two main types of structure. The ancient royal necropolis of Abydos – more specifically, the area known by its modern Arabic name Umm el-Qaab (literally 'mother of pots', from the vast quantities of offering pottery littering the site) – was the focus of royal burials throughout the First Dynasty, and again at the end of the Second Dynasty (Figure 7.1). The necropolis of Saqqara, overlooking the capital city of Memphis, was the favoured location for royal interments during the early part of the Second Dynasty, and became the primary royal burial ground from the beginning of the Third Dynasty (Figure 7.2). There was, thus, an alternation between Abydos and Saqqara during the course of the Early Dynastic period, probably depending upon the political and religious currents of the time. At both sites, but more obviously at Abydos, royal mortuary provision comprised two distinct elements: the tomb itself and an accompanying rectangular enclosure for the celebration of funerary ceremonies and/or the king's mortuary cult. During the First and Second Dynasties, these two elements were geographically separate, but were fused at the beginning of the Third Dynasty, as exemplified in the Step Pyramid complex of Netjerikhet.

The development of the royal tomb reflects both technological and theological advances; the design of the royal mortuary complex has been said to highlight the multiple role of the king as ruler and representative of the gods (Brinks 1979: 157–62). Both symbolic and practical considerations will have affected the planning and construction of the royal tomb, including such factors as axial alignment, symmetry, parallelism, centrality and duality (on the symbolic side), topography, astronomical alignment and technology (on the practical side). Royal mortuary architecture also serves as an index of political change, and not only through the choice of location for the king's tomb. From the reign of Aha onwards, there appears to have been a marked increase in mortuary elaboration, attested by the large mastaba at North Saqqara (S3357), the royal tomb at Naqada, and the greater size of the king's own burial complex at Abydos. This development has been interpreted as reflecting the greater economic and political security brought about by the consolidation of the Egyptian state at the beginning of the First Dynasty (Brinks 1979: 61). Against a background of increased prosperity and more efficient central control of resources, the Early Dynastic kings sought to emphasise their unique position at the head of Egyptian society, above all through the 'monumental scale and distinctive architectural symbolism' of their mortuary constructions (Kemp 1989: 53).

First dynasty

The royal tombs on the Umm el-Qaab

Abydos had been a burial ground for royalty since early Predynastic times, serving the rulers of the Thinite region from at least the Naqada I period (*c.* 3800 BC). According to Manetho, the rulers of the First Dynasty originated from This (Thinis), and their decision to be buried at Abydos, in the ancestral royal necropolis, probably reflects their family ties. The choice of Abydos may have been made for other, equally compelling reasons (Kemp 1966: 19). The site was of great antiquity, and its 'ancient sanctity' would doubtless have conferred an added supernatural legitimacy

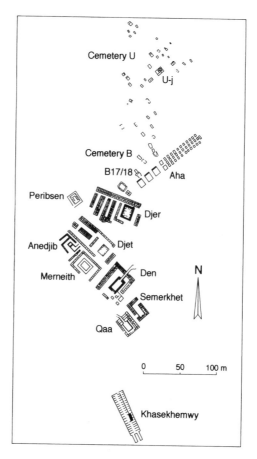

Figure 7.1 The royal cemetery at Abydos. The plan shows the contiguity of the three cemetery areas designated by modern archaeologists as Cemetery U (Predynastic), Cemetery B (late Predynastic to early First Dynasty), and the Umm el-Qaab (First Dynasty) (after Spencer 1993: 76, fig. 53; Dreyer *et al.* 1996: fig.1).

upon those buried there (cf. Kemp 1967: 25). (This may have been the primary reason for the re-adoption of the cemetery by two kings at the end of the Second Dynasty.) Moreover, the site's impressive natural setting – at the foot of a dramatic ridge, and directly aligned with a prominent cleft in the line of hills – may have increased the visual impact of the tombs. Before we look at aspects of individual complexes, and the chronological development over the course of the First Dynasty, it will be useful to describe the general features of a royal tomb on the Umm el-Qaab.

GENERAL FEATURES

At its most basic, each tomb consists of 'a large square pit lined with brick-work' (Petrie 1900: 4). The surrounding chambers – which served as subsidiary burials in late First Dynasty tombs – are often at a higher level than the main burial chamber. In the tombs of Djer and Djet the surrounding rooms open off the central chamber; from the time of Merneith onwards, they surround the burial chamber but do not interconnect. The tombs of the kings from Aha to Anedjib inclusive are accompanied by ranges of smaller, subsidiary burials. These are arranged in rows or blocks, either adjacent to the royal tomb or surrounding it.

Unlike the contemporary mastabas at North Saqqara which emphasised the superstructure, the First Dynasty royal tombs at Abydos seem to have concentrated on the subterranean element. During the early First Dynasty the burial chamber was dug progressively deeper, culminating with the tomb of Den in which the burial chamber is 6 metres below ground level. None the less, the superstructure of the tomb was a symbolically important component. Few, if any, traces of superstructure have survived from the Predynastic royal tombs at Abydos, Hierakonpolis and Naqada; but it has been argued that the superstructure of the First Dynasty royal tombs is likely to have evolved from these earlier burials (Kemp 1989: 53). The appearance of the early First Dynasty tombs remains uncertain, although a simple mound of earth covering the burial chamber seems likely. The existence of any visible superstructure has been doubted (O'Connor 1991: 7, contra Dreyer 1991), although it seems improbable that the tomb would have been entirely unmarked on the surface (cf. Dreyer 1991: 102). The superstructures of the mid- and later First Dynasty tombs (from the reign of Djet onwards) apparently comprised two elements: a hidden tumulus over the burial chamber and a larger mound covering the whole tomb (Dreyer 1991). The hidden tumulus was entirely contained within the grave pit, and was itself covered by the large grave mound. Consequently, it can have fulfilled no architectural purpose and must, therefore, have had a symbolic function. The provision of not one but two tumuli suggests that the symbol of a mound had great importance for the deceased; it may eventually have been regarded as essential for the resurrection of the dead in the grave (Dreyer 1991: 101). As a highly symbolic feature, the hidden tumulus also found its way into the contemporary mastabas at North Saqqara. Several mastabas (for example, S3507 from the reign of Den) were found to contain the remains of a concealed sand and rubble mound covering the burial chamber, completely hidden from view by the rest of the superstructure. As we have seen in Chapter 3, the mound inside Saqqara mastaba S3038, from the reign of Anedjib, had a stepped appearance, foreshadowing the form of the Third Dynasty step pyramids. If the architecture of the élite tombs at North Saqqara kept pace with, and indeed mimicked, the architecture of the royal tombs at Abydos, then the superstructures of the late First Dynasty tombs on the Umm el-Qaab may also have been stepped. This hypothesis receives some support from the iconographic evidence, including the depiction of stepped structures – identified by some as the royal tomb – on inscribed stone bowls of the late First Dynasty. One scholar has gone so far as to suggest that the superstructures of all royal tombs until the beginning of the Fourth Dynasty 'can reasonably be assumed to have been stepped' (Roth 1993: 43–4).

A pair of stelae bearing the name of the royal owner probably stood in front of the tomb, on the east side, although none was found *in situ* (Petrie 1900: 6).

SEQUENCE OF DEVELOPMENT

The sequence of royal tombs from the first half of the First Dynasty shows rapid and dramatic development (cf. Kaiser and Dreyer 1982: 245–60). The tomb complex at the head of the Early Dynastic sequence comprises three elements, two brick-lined chambers (B1 and B2) and an adjacent offering-pit cut into the surface (B0). The complex has been ascribed to a King *Iry-Hor on the basis of seal-impressions and inscribed vessels found in the brick-lined chambers (Kaiser and Dreyer 1982: 232–5; this attribution is disputed by Wilkinson 1993; O'Brien 1996: 131–2). It has been questioned whether the two brick-lined chambers belonged to the same burial, since 'one would have expected ... that if B1 and 2 were parts of the same tomb they would ... have been given the same orientation' (Kemp 1966: 22). This part of the cemetery has suffered greatly from disturbance and mixing of the tomb contents, so that the date and ownership of B0/1/2 must remain in some doubt.

None the less, it seems to have been customary for kings of late 'Dynasty 0' to build a tomb composed of two separate chambers. The adjacent chambers B7 and B9 almost certainly belonged to King 'Ka', probably Narmer's immediate predecessor. Narmer himself combined two chambers in one large pit, producing his double tomb B17/18. Some doubts have been expressed as to whether B17/18 really represents Narmer's tomb. It would seem a rather insignificant monument for so prominent a king, and there are unexplored parts of the Abydos necropolis which might conceal a more impressive tomb. Only by a thorough exploration of the entire Umm el-Qaab can we hope to solve the riddle.

Narmer's successor Aha seems to have reverted to the earlier custom, building his chambers separately, and on a much larger scale (Kemp 1966: 22). His mortuary complex comprises three large chambers (B10, B15 and B19), two smaller pits (B13 and B14) and a series of 34 subsidiary burials (B16), mostly in three parallel rows, spreading eastwards (Petrie 1901:

234

pl. LIX). The graves of retainers which accompany Aha's tomb appear as a new feature in royal mortuary provision, one that was to remain standard at Abydos throughout the First Dynasty. It was once suggested that the westernmost chamber of the Aha complex, B19, may have been built earlier than the other two. Its attribution to an ephemeral successor of Aha is not supported by any inscriptions and has been rejected as 'unconvincing' (Kemp 1966: 22). There seems little doubt that all three chambers, B10/15/19, belong to one and the same complex, given their near identical size and other similarities. The slightly different orientation of chamber B10 may indicate that it was built first (Kaiser and Dreyer 1982: 219). The two chambers to the west of B19 (B13 and B14) show similarities to Narmer's double tomb (B17/18): the northern chamber is smaller than the southern, and contained two post-holes, perhaps from a wooden construction within the pit. Hence, chambers B13 and B14 may represent an earlier stage in Aha's mortuary complex, modelled closely on the tomb of his predecessor. Once the three main chambers had been built, B14 seems to have become the tomb of a person called Benerib (*Bnr-ib*) (Petrie 1901: 5).

To the east of Aha's complex lies a four-chambered tomb, illustrated by Petrie on his cemetery plans but neither numbered nor described by him. Recently designated chamber B50 (Dreyer 1990: 68), the tomb has been re-excavated by the German expedition, which found it to be completely empty, but for a small bone label inscribed with some numerals and a few faience beads. Lack of evidence makes the dating and attribution of B50 impossible. None the less, its orientation, the same as B7/9 and B17/18, may be significant. It may have been the tomb of one of Aha's predecessors; King 'Scorpion' has been suggested as a possible occupant (Dreyer 1990: 71), although the archaeological and historical indications point to him having been buried at Hierakonpolis (Brinks 1979: 148).

Equally mysterious is the adjacent pit, labelled B40 (Dreyer 1990: 70). Discovered beneath a deposit of later offering-pottery, B40 showed no signs of any walling material such as mudbrick. It has been mooted as the tomb of 'Athothis I', a supposed ephemeral successor of Aha (Dreyer 1990: 71).

The tomb complex of Djer, Aha's successor, shows a number of new features. The main burial chamber was provided with a series of recesses, painted red, perhaps early false doors (Petrie 1901: 8). The subsidiary burials – numbering 318, the most of any royal tomb at Abydos – were arranged in two groups. One large block is located to the north-east of the king's tomb, another group surrounds the tomb on all four sides, with a gap to the south-west (Petrie 1901: pls LVIII, LX–LXI).

Many of the subsidiary graves accompanying the tomb of Djet contained crudely inscribed and roughly finished private stelae, giving the name (and sometimes title) of the deceased. In addition, some of the graves were identified by having the names of their occupants 'inscribed in red paint on the walls' (Petrie 1900: 8). The tomb of Djet was the only tomb on the Umm el-Qaab to preserve evidence of the original super-structure. A retaining wall of mudbricks held in place a tumulus of earth which covered the burial chamber (Petrie 1900: 9) but did not rise above the ground surface. Another feature of Djet's burial, unparalleled in the other First Dynasty royal tombs at Abydos, is the presence of ceramic *s3*-signs, which were apparently placed in niches in the burial chamber to provide extra protection for the deceased king (B. Adams 1994).

The tomb of Merneith shows great regularity and precision in its construction. A central burial chamber is surrounded by eight store-rooms, and the whole is encircled by a line of subsidiary graves (Petrie 1900: pl. LXI). As in the tomb of Djer, the ring of subsidiary graves is broken at the south-west corner, providing a direct sight-line between the burial chamber and the cleft in the cliffs behind the Umm el-Qaab. The Egyptians may have believed this cleft to be an entrance to the under-world (Patch 1991: 56–7; cf. R. Friedman 1994: 17).

The tomb of Den was described by Petrie as 'one of the most costly and sumptuous' (Petrie 1900: 11). It shows several unique features, empha-sising Den's reign as a cultural high point of the Early Dynastic period. The burial chamber was paved with slabs of pink granite from Aswan, the largest use of granite until the Step Pyramid complex of Netjerikhet (Petrie 1901: 9). Another innovation is the entrance stairway which gives access to the burial chamber, crossing the east range of subsidiary graves. This must have represented a threat to the security of the burial, and was therefore blocked by a stone 'portcullis' slab. Unique on the Umm el-Qaab is the separate annex with its own staircase, located at the south-west corner of Den's tomb (Petrie 1901: 11; Dreyer 1990: 76–9, figs 7–8). A limestone block in the furthest room strongly indicates a pedestal, perhaps for a statue. Given the proximity of the annex to the king's burial chamber, it is unlikely that such a statue would have been other than of the king himself (Dreyer 1990: 77). This hypothesis leads to an entirely new interpretation of the annex as a whole. The far room may be seen as a forerunner of the *serdab*, housing the statue of the deceased king for his mortuary cult. The staircase leading to the annex has been interpreted as providing not an entrance but an exit for the king's *ka*. The two pits in front of the annex may have been the graves of particularly favoured retainers, or alternatively officials connected in some way with the king's mortuary cult. The orientation of the annex to the south-west is unlikely to have been unintentional, and may be linked to the course of the Great Wadi which connects the Umm el-Qaab and the site of the funerary enclo-sures nearer the cultivation (Dreyer 1990: 78).

The small size and poor, apparently hasty construction of Anedjib's tomb (Petrie 1900: 12) can be explained if it is regarded as an 'emergency burial'

(Kaiser and Dreyer 1982: 251). It is possible that the king died unexpectedly, forcing the rapid completion of a tomb without the necessary time for an elaborate monument. As in the tomb of Den, the entrance stairway approaches the tomb from the east, perhaps oriented to the rising sun.

The tomb of Semerkhet shows a new development: the subsidiary graves are built immediately adjoining the burial chamber, forming a single, unified structure (Petrie 1900: 13, pl. LX). This is of great significance, since 'it would appear probable that the superstructure covered not only the burial chamber but also the subsidiary graves' (Emery 1961: 85). It follows that the occupants of the subsidiary graves must have been buried at the same time as the king himself. Hence, the tomb of Semerkhet seems to represent the first proven instance of retainer sacrifice.

This arrangement was maintained in the tomb of Qaa (Emery 1961: 87; Plate 7.1). Initial excavation of Qaa's tomb suggested 'hasty and defective construction' (Petrie 1900: 14) – many of the bricks seem to have been used before they had dried completely, leading to the collapse of some walls – but recent re-excavation has shown that the monument was built in several phases, apparently over a long period of time (Engel, in Dreyer *et al.* 1996: 57–71). The objects recovered from the tomb of Qaa by Petrie indicate that separate chambers were reserved for different categories of tomb equipment (Hoffman 1980: 272). A new feature is the direction of the entrance stairway, which is now oriented to the north

Plate 7.1   The tomb of Qaa, during re-excavation by the German Archaeological Institute in 1992 (author's photograph).

(Petrie 1900: 4). This foreshadows the Second Dynasty royal tombs at Saqqara and the step pyramid complexes of the Third Dynasty which were aligned to the north.

Funerary enclosures

From the reign of Djer onwards, it has been suggested that the 'twin tomb' of the late Predynastic and early First Dynasty kings was replaced by a single tomb on the Umm el-Qaab, accompanied by a separate funerary enclosure on the low desert nearer the cultivation (Kaiser 1964: 96–102). The internal architecture of the late Predynastic tomb U-j supports the identification of the later enclosures as 'funerary palaces' (Kemp 1966: 16). Their symbolic and architectural similarities with the Step Pyramid enclosure of Netjerikhet (Kaiser 1969) lend added weight to the hypothesis, although other interpretations have been suggested (Lauer 1968: 82–3; Helck 1972). Whilst the long-term function of an enclosure may have been as a focus for the royal mortuary cult (O'Connor 1991: 5, 7) and an arena for the eternal pageantry of kingship (Kaiser 1969: 17), on a more practical level each enclosure may have served to protect the body of the deceased king until all the burial preparations had been completed. The permanent building identified in the south-east corner of Peribsen's and Khasekhemwy's enclosures may have housed the body of the dead king or sheltered his successor during the burial preparations. In addition, the enclosure may have been the location for some of the funeral ceremonies (Kaiser 1969: 18–19).

To date, no enclosure attributable to Narmer or Aha has been located. None the less, the existence of further enclosures on the low desert is quite plausible, given the extensive area of largely unexcavated ground south of the Coptic village, Deir Sitt Damiana. First Dynasty funerary remains have been found over a wider area still, extending to the northwest of the village (Kemp 1966: 15). Since the tomb of Narmer has no subsidiary burials, his funerary enclosure (if he had one) may, likewise, have stood alone. Without the lines of graves such as those that demarcate the enclosures of Djer and Djet, a possible early enclosure would be very difficult to identify archaeologically (Kaiser 1969: 3, n. 3).

It was thought that the great size of the Djer and Djet enclosures precluded their having been permanent constructions of mudbrick (Kaiser 1969: 3), but recent fieldwork has uncovered evidence of a mudbrick wall inside the Djer monument (O'Connor 1989, vindicating Kemp 1966: 15). From the reign of Den, the enclosures were decorated with simple niches on three sides and more elaborate niches on the side facing the cultivation (Lauer 1969: 83, 1988: 5). The middle of the First Dynasty also witnessed a sharp reduction in the size of the monument (cf. Kemp 1966: pl. VIII; Kaiser 1969: 3). Only at the end of the First Dynasty did funerary enclosures once again approach the size of the Djer and Djet monuments: the massive mudbrick walls of Deir Sitt Damiana may incorporate the funerary enclosure of Qaa (Ayrton *et al.* 1904: 2–3; Kaiser 1969: 2). The late First Dynasty seems to have been characterised by a shift in emphasis – and, correspondingly, in expenditure – from the tomb on the Umm el-Qaab to the funerary enclosure nearer the town (Kaiser and Dreyer 1982: 251). The change may reflect a conscious move towards more prominent royal funerary monuments as the visible expressions of divine kingship.

Like the enclosures of Djer and Djet, the structure attributed to Queen Merneith or her son Den (Kaiser 1969: 1–2) is demarcated by lines of subsidiary burials. A deposit of First Dynasty pottery found inside the Merneith/Den enclosure (Kemp 1966: 16–17) suggests that a building once existed here, as in the enclosures of the late Second Dynasty. The so-called 'Western Mastaba' lies immediately adjacent to the Merneith/Den enclosure, and shares the same dimensions and orientation. It is the earliest preserved enclosure to show the two types of niche decoration: simple niches on the north-west, south-west and south-east sides, and a more complex pattern of niches on the north-east wall (Kemp 1966: 14). It provides a model for the reconstruction of the Merneith/Den enclosure although, unlike the latter, it is not provided with any subsidiary burials. This suggests that it dates to the latter part of the First Dynasty, when the practice of subsidiary burials was apparently dying out (Kemp 1966: 15). It has been plausibly attributed to Semerkhet, penultimate king of the First Dynasty. If the Merneith/Den enclosure is attributed to Den and the 'Western Mastaba' to Semerkhet, then the only two rulers of the mid- and late First Dynasty without an identified funerary enclosure would be Merneith and Anedjib. The unique position of the former as queen regent but not monarch in her own right could explain her lack of a funerary enclosure; the absence of an enclosure for Anedjib could be explained by the apparent 'emergency' nature of his tomb (Kaiser and Dreyer 1982: 254, n. 148).

A possible enclosure dated to the reign of Den has been identified at Saqqara, in addition to his putative funerary enclosure at Abydos. A group of graves excavated near the Serapeum (Macramallah 1940) has been interpreted as demarcating a ritual area (Kaiser 1985a). However, the burials are not all contemporary and the rows are not aligned at 90 degrees. The purpose of the feature is unknown, but one suggestion is that it was used for the embalming of the deceased king – assuming that he died at Memphis – before the body was taken south to Abydos for burial. Other similar enclosures of the First Dynasty have not yet come to light at Saqqara, although there are large unexcavated areas in the north-western part of the site, and it is quite possible that others may have existed along or on the edges of the Wadi Abusir. Alternatively, the Den installation could have been used by subsequent kings of the late

First Dynasty, and this could account for the later dating of some of the graves (Kaiser 1985a). The proposal that the graves are subsidiary burials surrounding a large First Dynasty mastaba (Swelim 1991: 392) seems unlikely since resistivity work in the area has uncovered no traces of any structure (Jeffreys and Tavares 1994: 150 and n. 43).

Second dynasty

Saqqara

GALLERY TOMBS

The kings of the early Second Dynasty chose to abandon the ancestral royal cemetery of Abydos in favour of a new location overlooking the capital. This change in location must be significant, but the underlying reasons remain obscure (cf. Roth 1993: 48). Not only did the tombs of the early Second Dynasty kings inaugurate a new royal cemetery, they also present an entirely new conception in royal mortuary architecture, both in terms of their size and layout (Kaiser 1992: 182; cf. Munro 1993: 49). Gone are the lines of subsidiary burials so characteristic of the First Dynasty royal tombs and funerary enclosures at Abydos. The practice of retainer sacrifice seems to have died with Qaa, a short-lived and no doubt wasteful experiment in absolute power. The two Second Dynasty royal tombs at Saqqara identified with certainty now lie beneath the causeway and pyramid of Unas (for example, Spencer 1993: 105, fig. 80). Both tombs comprise a series of galleries, with blocks of store-rooms opening off a central, descending corridor hewn in the bedrock. Sealings found in the western gallery tomb bore the names of Hetepsekhemwy and Nebra. The eastern gallery tomb contained numerous sealings of Ninetjer, third king of the dynasty, identifying him as the probable owner.

The entrance section of the Hetepsekhemwy complex, open to the air after its initial construction, was subsequently covered by large limestone blocks (Munro 1993: 49). The first series of magazines opens off the descending corridor, but access to the second series of magazines is blocked at the bottom of this corridor by a large granite portcullis slab. Three further slabs block the corridor at intervals (Stadelmann 1985: 296). The published plan of the complex (Lauer 1936: 4, fig. 2; Fischer 1961: 46–8, fig. 9; Spencer 1993: 104, fig. 79) 'differs somewhat from the detailed verbal account given by the excavator' (Roth 1993: 43; cf. Barsanti 1902). In particular, the layout of the chambers is 'by no means as regular and right-angled as depicted' (Dodson 1996: 22). In plan, the Hetepsekhemwy complex is very similar to contemporary private tombs (Roth 1993: 44). The suite of rooms at the southern end of the galleries includes a large chamber to the west of the central axis, comparable to the burial chamber in Second Dynasty private tombs, and a more complex group of chambers

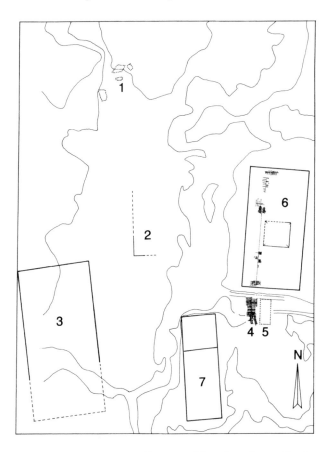

Figure 7.2 The royal cemetery at Saqqara. The plan shows the large number of Early Dynastic features in this part of the Memphite necropolis: (1) a group of graves dating to the reign of Den, possibly outlining a ritual arena; (2) and (3) two large rectangular enclosures of uncertain date (named the Ptah-hotep enclosure and the Gisr el-Mudir, respectively); (4) a set of underground galleries forming the tomb of Hetepsekhemwy and/or Nebra; (5) the location of a second set of underground galleries, forming the tomb of Ninetjer; (6) the Step Pyramid complex of Netjerikhet, incorporating several sets of underground galleries which may represent earlier royal tombs; (7) the unfinished step pyramid complex of Sekhemkhet (after Jeffreys and Tavares 1994: 166, fig. 7; Lauer 1962: pls 6.a, 14.b).

to the east, reminiscent of the bedroom–lavatory–bathroom combination found in private tombs. The layout of the innermost chambers clearly imitates the private apartments of a house (Munro 1993: 49; Roth 1993: 44) and indicates that the tomb was conceived as a house for the *ka* of the deceased.

The Ninetjer galleries follow a similar plan (Kaiser 1992: 180, fig. 4d), although they cover a larger total area. Once again, the rooms do not follow a regular arrangement, perhaps due to the poor quality of the bedrock (Dodson 1996: 22). There remains a small area adjacent to the Unas Causeway where traces of the original superstructure are visible (Munro 1993: 49). The superstructure seems to have comprised two distinct elements. To the north, a platform floored with clay extended over an area some 20 metres deep, covering the outer passages and chambers of the tomb; it may have been used as a setting for funerary ceremonies. To the south, a rock-step may mark the location of a more massive, mastaba superstructure (Leclant and Clerc 1993: 207; Dodson 1996: 22). The rock-cut trench, noted by several writers as a prominent feature in this part of the Saqqara necropolis, may mark the edge of a platform upon which the Second Dynasty royal tombs were built. Two alternative reconstructions have been proposed for the superstructure of Hetepsekhemwy's tomb: either a simple mastaba with sloping walls or a niched mastaba, like the First Dynasty mastabas at North Saqqara. The archaeologist excavating the Ninetjer complex considers it unlikely that the Second Dynasty gallery tombs were covered by large mastaba-like superstructures, because of the immense quantities of material which would have been required for such constructions (Munro 1993: 50), and because little or no trace of massive superstructures has survived. However, it is possible that the superstructures were levelled by Netjerikhet during the construction or enlargement of his Step Pyramid complex, and the material reused (cf. Munro 1993: 48, n. 49). The location of the Step Pyramid complex may indicate that the Second Dynasty superstructures were still standing when Netjerikhet's monument was initially planned. In any case, the Second Dynasty tombs must have been in ruins by the Fifth Dynasty, allowing Unas to level the site for his pyramid complex.

To judge from the inscription on the statue of the priest Hetepdief, the mortuary cult of the first three Second Dynasty kings was celebrated at Saqqara. Nebra's funerary monument must therefore have been located here (Stadelmann 1985: 298). He may have usurped the gallery tomb begun by his predecessor Hetepsekhemwy. Alternatively, a separate mortuary complex adjacent to the Hetepsekhemwy and Ninetjer tombs might have been incorporated into Netjerikhet's grand building scheme. The galleries beneath the Western Massif of the Step Pyramid complex may have been a Second Dynasty royal tomb, given their size and general layout (contra Roth 1993: 43, n. 40). These galleries have been suggested as the tomb of Sened (Dodson 1996: 24) or Khasekhemwy (Stadelmann 1985: 299), but they could equally have been built for Nebra. Recent fieldwork to the west of the Step Pyramid complex has revealed another, possibly royal, Second Dynasty tomb (Giddy 1997a: 28), while the unfinished galleries beneath the North Court of the complex may represent further tombs of this date, incorporated by Netjerikhet into the final phase of his funerary monument.

The precise choice of location for the Second Dynasty royal tombs was probably influenced by the natural topography, in particular a wadi or natural depression running to the south of the Step Pyramid complex (Leclant and Clerc 1994: 381). Although set further back in the desert than the élite tombs at North Saqqara, and therefore invisible from the cultivation to the east, the Second Dynasty royal tombs would have been 'equally, if not more, prominent as viewed from the Abusir valley' (Jeffreys and Tavares 1994: 151). If the Early Dynastic centre of Memphis did indeed lie in the vicinity of Lake Abusir, the sight-line up the Abusir valley would help to explain the location of all the Early Dynastic monuments of western Saqqara, including the possible cultic enclosure of Den, the Second Dynasty royal tombs, and the anonymous rectangular enclosures (Jeffreys and Tavares 1994: 151, 166 fig. 7, 168 fig. 9).

ENCLOSURES

Among the most mysterious monuments in Egypt are the two large, anonymous enclosures to the west of the Netjerikhet and Sekhemkhet complexes (Swelim 1991). Named the Ptahhotep enclosure and the Gisr el-Mudir ('great enclosure'), they are believed by some scholars to be further, unfinished step pyramid enclosures of the Third Dynasty (Wildung 1969a: 136–7; Edwards 1993: 93). However, the Gisr el-Mudir shows no signs of a building at its centre (Mathieson and Tavares 1993: 30), and it would have been extremely difficult and impractical to construct a pyramid once the enclosure wall had been completed (Stadelmann 1985: 305). (Compare the Sekhemkhet complex, where the underground chambers of the pyramid had been finished when the enclosure wall was only six courses high.) The Ptahhotep enclosure, immediately to the west of the Step Pyramid complex, does show a 'large mudbrick rectangular structure' at the centre, 'where there are also fragments of limestone' (Mathieson and Tavares 1993: 28). Unfortunately, the nature of this structure has not been established. It has been plausibly suggested that the Saqqara enclosures were counterparts to the 'funerary enclosures' at Abydos (Stadelmann 1985: 307). In this case, they may have been built to accompany the nearby royal tombs of the Second Dynasty, notably the galleries of Hetepsekhemwy and Ninetjer (Kaiser 1985a: 54, n. 39, for an alternative view). Less plausibly, the Ptahhotep enclosure has been attributed to Khasekhemwy (Stadelmann 1985: 306), although there is no indication that this king ever constructed a funerary monument at Saqqara. A careful survey has found no evidence of a third enclosure to the east of the Gisr el-Mudir (Mathieson and Tavares 1993: 27, contra Stadelmann 1985: 304, n. 28), despite the suggestive aerial photographs of the area (Capart 1930: pl. XIV).

To date, the most intensive investigation has been carried out on the Gisr el-Mudir (Tavares 1995). Although no structure has yet been located with certainty inside the Gisr el-Mudir, fragments of limestone, red quartzite, pink granite and black basalt are strewn over a considerable area in the north-west corner, suggesting that a building may have existed in this part of the enclosure (Mathieson and Tavares 1993: 29–30). Both faces of the west wall are visible, permitting an analysis of the construction technique. The walls seem to have been built with a rubble core, but the corners 'show solid masonry construction' (Mathieson and Tavares 1993: 30). Archive photographs from investigations by the Egyptian Antiquities Organisation show a construction technique reminiscent of Third Dynasty step pyramids, namely 'masonry in two tiers with courses sloping inwards' (Mathieson and Tavares 1993: 29). However, pottery beer-jars found in the fill of the south-west corner of the enclosure have been provisionally dated to the end of the Second/beginning of the Third Dynasty, apparently confirming the early date of the monument (Bettles *et al.* 1995: 3–4). The excavators comment that 'a full investigation of the corners and any possible foundation deposits associated with them may yet prove to be the only way to date more closely the Gisr el-Mudir' (Bettles *et al.* 1995: 3). None the less, the apparent absence of any central structure distinguishes the enclosure from the nearby step pyramid complexes of Netjerikhet and Sekhemkhet. It seems more likely that the Gisr el-Mudir represents an intermediate stage between the mudbrick funerary enclosures of Abydos and the stone step pyramid complexes of the Third Dynasty. The use of stone is certainly cruder and more rudimentary than in the Third Dynasty monuments (cf. Bettles *et al.* 1995: figs 2, 3). A Second Dynasty date would suit such an intermediate type of funerary monument. It is tempting to link the Gisr el-Mudir to one of the Second Dynasty royal tombs in the vicinity; and Ninetjer, as probably the longest reigning king of the dynasty buried at Saqqara, must be a strong candidate for the builder of such an impressive enclosure (cf. Stadelmann 1985). However, it should be acknowledged that there are problems with this hypothesis. The enormous size of the enclosure seems to argue against a Second Dynasty date; and, despite the greater availability of stone at Saqqara, some scholars consider it illogical that a stone enclosure should pre-date the mudbrick enclosures of Peribsen and Khasekhemwy at Abydos (Hendrickx, personal communication).

Abydos

TOMBS

Kings Peribsen and Khasekhemwy at the end of the Second Dynasty chose to be buried amongst their First Dynasty forebears, in the ancestral royal cemetery on the Umm el-Qaab. The reason behind the return to Abydos cannot be ascertained, though internal politics may have played a part

(Kemp 1967: 30; Stadelmann 1985: 295). Judging by the published private and royal tombs at Saqqara and Helwan, a move towards a reduced series of rooms, entered by means of a shaft, seems characteristic of the late Second and early Third Dynasty in the Memphite area. By contrast, the tombs of Peribsen and Khasekhemwy at Abydos appear to have been closely modelled on their First Dynasty antecedents at the same site (Kaiser 1992: 180–1 fig. 4b, e, 183; Roth 1993: 44): their general layout comprises a central burial chamber surrounded by store-rooms.

The tomb of Peribsen reverted to the model of the early First Dynasty (Petrie 1901: pl. LVIII). It is closer in plan to the tombs of Djer and Djet than to the tombs of Den and Qaa, showing a series of small cells surrounding the burial chamber, separated by cross walls. A new feature, however, is a continuous passage surrounding the whole tomb, perhaps designed to safeguard against tomb robbers entering from the side (Petrie 1901: 11).

The tomb of Khasekhemwy is quite different from all the others on the Umm el-Qaab. Its curious, elongated form represents a subsequent extension of the original plan (Kaiser 1992: 183; Giddy 1997b: 28). Much of it was built from newly made bricks which subsequently collapsed. A positive outcome of this poor construction was that the collapsed walls preserved a large number of the original grave goods with which the tomb was furnished. As a result, the tomb of Khasekhemwy yielded a more representative selection of artefacts than the other royal tombs on the Umm el-Qaab (Petrie 1901: 12). A unique feature is the stone-built burial chamber, fashioned from carefully dressed blocks of limestone (Petrie 1901: 13).

FUNERARY ENCLOSURES

Peribsen and Khasekhemwy followed the practice of their First Dynasty predecessors, not only in the choice of location and general layout of their tombs, but also in constructing separate funerary enclosures of mudbrick on the low desert opposite the town of Abydos (Kemp 1966; Kaiser 1969). Unlike the First Dynasty enclosures, those of the late Second Dynasty are not surrounded by lines of subsidiary tombs (Lauer 1988: 5).

The enclosure of Khasekhemwy, known by its Arabic nickname Shunet ez-Zebib (literally, 'Storehouse of Raisins'), is the most prominent ancient building in the northern part of Abydos (Kemp 1989: 53–4, 56 fig. 18A). Its massive mudbrick walls still stand to a great height, testament to the strength and solidity of its construction. Until the recent re-investigation of the Shunet ez-Zebib, the interiors of the Early Dynastic funerary enclosures 'remained generally mysterious and unknown' (O'Connor 1991: 7). The Pennsylvania-Yale Expedition was successful in uncovering a large expanse of the original Second Dynasty mudplaster floor inside the Shunet ez-Zebib. More interesting, a line of angled bricks was all that remained of a destroyed feature in the centre of the enclosure (O'Connor 1991:

9–10, figs 6–7). The angle of the brickwork is suggestive and the excavators reconstruct the feature as 'a large mound made of sand and gravel … covered with a brick skin, of which this brickwork is the lowest and only surviving piece' (O'Connor 1991: 7). Such a mound would have been hidden from general view by the high walls of the enclosure, but immediately visible on entering the building (O'Connor 1991: 8). If this reconstruction is correct, the similarities between the enclosure and the Step Pyramid complex of Netjerikhet become all the more striking (cf. O'Connor 1991: 10, fig. 8). Indeed, in its earliest phase, when the tomb was covered by a simple mastaba (M_1), the Netjerikhet complex was simply 'a larger-scale stone copy of the Khasekhemwy complex' (O'Connor 1991: 8). No feature comparable to the proposed brick-covered mound has yet been found inside any other funerary enclosure at Abydos. The funerary character of the enclosures, and their place at the head of a long tradition of royal mortuary architecture, is emphasised by the discovery of a fleet of funerary boats, buried in special boat graves along-side the Shunet ez-Zebib (see below).

Hierakonpolis

Khasekhemwy built another massive mudbrick enclosure, very similar in size and architecture to the Shunet ez-Zebib, on the edge of the Great Wadi at Hierakonpolis (Clarke, in Quibell and Green 1902: 19–20; Alexanian n.d., 1998). Nicknamed 'the Fort' (because of its massive construction), the monument still stands as a prominent landmark in the area. Decorated fragments of pink granite relief, bearing the king's *serekh*, were found in and around the entrance to the monument (Lansing 1935: 44, fig. 11). The decorative scheme puts particular emphasis on the king, and shows him engaged in ritual activities. This suggests that 'the Fort' was perhaps built as an arena for the celebration and/or commemoration of the royal cult (Alexanian 1998). More specifically, 'the Fort' and its counterparts at Abydos have been interpreted as models of the ʿḥ-nṯr, a building which served as an arena for the celebration of ritual festivals (Arnold 1994: 94, 256–7). There is no indication that Khasekhemwy ever prepared a tomb for himself at Hierakonpolis (contra Dodson 1996: 26), and it remains a mystery why he should have erected two funerary enclosures, one at Abydos and one at Hierakonpolis. He clearly felt a special attachment to the latter site, to judge from the number of monuments and artefacts found there which bear his name.

Third dynasty

The kings of the Third Dynasty made a decisive break with the past, abandoning the ancient royal burial ground of Abydos in favour of the

Memphite necropolis. From the reign of Netjerikhet until the collapse of the Old Kingdom, all royal mortuary complexes were located along the edge of the western desert bordering the Nile valley in the vicinity of the capital. The Step Pyramid of Netjerikhet is the most complete and most impressive mortuary complex of the Third Dynasty. His successor, Sekhemkhet, began an equally ambitious monument nearby, but died leaving it unfinished. Another unfinished step pyramid, dated by its architecture and construction technique to the Third Dynasty, is the 'layer pyramid' at Zawiyet el-Aryan, between Giza and Abusir. It has been attributed to Khaba, on the basis of inscribed stone bowls found in a nearby tomb. The mortuary complex of Sanakht has not been securely identified, though the so-called 'brick pyramid' at Abu Rawash (on the northern edge of the Memphite necropolis) has been suggested as a possible candidate (Dodson 1996: 30). The pyramid presumed to have been built by the last king of the Third Dynasty, Huni, lies far to the south of his predecessors' monuments, at the site of Maidum near the entrance to the Fayum. Begun as a step pyramid, it was converted into a true pyramid at the beginning of the Fourth Dynasty, thus ushering in the distinctive royal mortuary architecture of the Old Kingdom.

The Step Pyramid complex of Netjerikhet

Rather than being a sudden and dramatic innovation, the Step Pyramid complex is more easily understood as the culmination of a long tradition of funerary monuments (Kaiser 1969: 6). Features which remained constant from the reign of Djer in the early First Dynasty include a large enclosed rectangular courtyard with perhaps one permanent building and other temporary structures of wood posts and matting (Kaiser 1969: 16). It is just such lightweight structures that are replicated in the Step Pyramid complex, but this time in stone, built for eternity. The amalgamation of tomb and funerary enclosure represents the most important innovation of Netjerikhet's complex (Kaiser 1969: 16). The Abydos tradition of royal mortuary complexes seems to have had a greater influence on the architecture of the Step Pyramid complex than the design of the nearby Second Dynasty royal tombs (Kaiser 1992: 188–9), although the influence of the Memphite tradition is difficult to gauge without a more accurate knowledge of the monuments concerned. The plan of the Step Pyramid's subterranean galleries – which radiate out from each side of the burial chamber and thus surround it – was followed in subsequent Third Dynasty step pyramids: both Sekhemkhet's step pyramid and the step pyramid at Zawiyet el-Aryan have corridors of store-rooms which branch off the main axis before the burial chamber and encircle it on three sides (Roth 1993: 44; for plans of both substructures, see Lauer 1962: 210, fig. 58). The Step Pyramid complex is just that: a combination of many distinct elements (Lauer 1962: pl. 13), each of which must have had its own symbolism and significance. The lack of contemporary figured or written evidence 'confronts us with a major problem of interpretation' (Kemp 1989: 55); we depend upon earlier and later parallels, especially the funerary enclosures at Abydos, and upon later written sources such as the Pyramid Texts.

THE COMPONENTS OF THE COMPLEX

The complex comprises two principal types of structure: largely dummy buildings, and buildings with 'working' interiors. The difference between the two types of building may reflect either a chronological or a functional distinction (Kaiser 1969 and Lauer 1988, respectively). If the latter, the dummy buildings may have been intended as primarily symbolic, whereas the functional buildings may have been designed for the funeral ceremonies and for the celebration of the king's mortuary cult.

The most prominent feature of the entire complex is the Step Pyramid which covers the burial chamber in the centre of the enclosure. Initially, however, the tomb was covered by a simple mastaba (M_1). This preliminary stage has been attributed to Netjerikhet's presumed predecessor, Sanakht (Lauer 1957: 164); this theory is now disproved by the recent discoveries at Abydos which confirm that Netjerikhet succeeded Khasekhemwy as king. Outside the limits of the mastaba, to the east, lay the galleries which seem to have been intended for the burial of other members of the royal family. The change from a mastaba superstructure to a step pyramid represented a complete change of plan. Construction in horizontal layers of stone was replaced by angled courses of masonry for greater stability, directing the stress inwards towards the centre of the monument. This building technique became the standard one for Third Dynasty step pyramids. At first, a pyramid of four steps (P_1) was built over and around the original mastaba. Subsequently, in a third major change of plan, the pyramid was enlarged to the north and west, and converted into a six-stepped construction (P_2) (Lauer 1988: 6–7). The substructure of the Step Pyramid combines two different elements: galleries approached from above via shafts, and rooms approached from the end via a staircase or sloping corridor (Firth and Quibell 1935, II: pl. 23; Lauer 1962: pl. 14*b*). These may have drawn upon two different traditions, exemplified in the First and Second Dynasty royal tombs at Saqqara and Abydos respectively (Kaiser 1992: 176–85).

Like the pyramid, the entrance colonnade seems to have been built in stages. The earliest section seems to be the small shrine with a niched façade to the south of the main corridor. It has been suggested that the statue base of Netjerikhet bearing the name and titles of Imhotep, discovered south of the southern enclosure wall, was originally dedicated in this shrine (Helck 1972: 97). The shrine may be compared with the small building immediately inside the gateway of the Shunet ez-Zebib and the corresponding building inside Peribsen's funerary enclosure (Kaiser 1969: 9). A theory based upon later religious rituals holds that the shrine was the building in which kingship was passed to the next ruler by his deceased predecessor (or the assembly of royal ancestors) manifest as a white baboon, the *ḥḏ-wr* (Helck 1972: 97).

The 'Great Court' which extends in front of the pyramid to the south seems likely to have replicated a standard element in the Egyptian royal palace: a formal setting for the 'appearance of the king' in which he might take part in important ceremonies, such as the reception of tribute (Kemp 1989: 57–9). A platform at the northern end of the court, against the base of the Step Pyramid (Kemp 1989: 58, fig. 19A), may represent the elevated dais where the king would appear enthroned on the occasion of his ritual appearances and to review the prisoners and booty from foreign campaigns, as depicted, for example, on the Narmer macehead.

A second, smaller courtyard occupies the eastern side of the complex. Dummy shrines line both sides of the court, and a temple (named 'Temple T') lies to the west. The key to understanding this element of the complex is a throne platform with a double staircase in the south of the court. Depicted in First Dynasty inscriptions and later temple reliefs, such a platform was intimately associated with the Sed-festival. Indeed, it became the hieroglyphic determinative for the expression *ḥb-sd*, 'Sed-festival'. This festival has been discussed in Chapter 6. Clearly, the second or 'Sed-festival court' was designed for the eternal celebration of this pre-eminent festival of kingship (Kemp 1989: 61–2). It is unlikely that it was ever used for a real Sed-festival during the king's lifetime (cf. Lauer 1988: 10) since most of the buildings are dummy constructions, filled with rubble.

One of the least understood elements of the complex is the second, miniature tomb built within the southern enclosure wall (Kemp 1989: 55). Designated the 'South Tomb', there is no general consensus on its purpose or symbolism. Parallels have been drawn between the South Tomb and the small satellite pyramids associated with Old Kingdom royal tombs (Lauer 1968: 98; Lehner and Lacovara 1985: 174). The most plausible explanation is that the South Tomb housed the king's *ka*-statue (H. Altenmüller 1972: 3). Certainly, the 'burial chamber' beneath the South Tomb is too small to have contained a coffin of normal proportions. A survey of royal burials from the Early Dynastic period to the New Kingdom suggests that two separate chambers – one for the king's body, the other for his *ka* – was the usual arrangement (H. Altenmüller 1972: 5–6). Support for this hypothesis may be provided by a dismantled canopy-frame found in association with the satellite pyramid of Khafra at Giza. It may be compared with the wooden bier 'found in the T-shaped magazine off the south side of the entrance corridor' of Netjerikhet's South Tomb (Lehner and Lacovara 1985: 174).

Two of the most enigmatic parts of the Step Pyramid complex seem to have been incorporated into the final design at a relatively late stage: the North Court and the so-called 'Western Massif'. The precise purpose of the North Court is difficult to establish, as much of it was left unfinished (H. Altenmüller 1972: 7). One scholar has suggested that the North Court was probably not intended as an open court at all, but rather as a spoil-dump for the adjacent constructions, levelled to form a platform (Lauer 1936: 186). Because it belongs to a later phase in the development of the complex, parallels for its distinctive features have been sought, perhaps misguidedly, in the royal mortuary complexes of the Old Kingdom, rather than in those of the First and Second Dynasties. The strong connection between the royal mortuary cult and the solar cult in the Fifth Dynasty, and the suggestive location of Userkaf's pyramid and mortuary temple next to the North Court, is thought by some to be significant for the interpretation of this element of the Step Pyramid complex (H. Altenmüller 1972: 8–9). In particular, the large platform in the North Court has been interpreted as an early solar platform (H. Altenmüller 1972; Brinks 1979). However, this hypothesis has been firmly rejected by other scholars (for example, Stadelmann 1983: 375). More plausibly, the platform may have been a large altar for the presentation of offerings (Stadelmann 1983: 375–6; Lauer 1988: 8). It may be no coincidence that subterranean store-rooms nearby were found to contain supplies of grain and fruit which might have been intended as offerings. In addition, two rows of poorly built, dummy granaries stood close to the northern enclosure wall. Though 'absurdly narrow' for working granaries (Firth and Quibell 1935, I: 77), they may have been symbolically connected with the North Court platform. A series of galleries beneath the North Court poses further problems of interpretation. The chambers that were found to be ankle-deep in dried fruit and grain (Firth and Quibell 1935, I: v) also yielded seal-impressions of Khasekhemwy and Netjerikhet (Firth and Quibell 1935, I: 141, figs 22, 19–21 respectively). A sealing of Sanakht is mentioned as coming from the same location (Firth and Quibell 1935, I: 8), but this may be a mistake since no further discussion or illustration of the sealing appears. The galleries were divided in two by a small blocking wall, and it was on the face of this wall that the seal-impressions were discovered. Access to the galleries was via two shafts (Lauer 1936: 184, fig. 208). The galleries have no direct relation with the magazines built over them during the last, unfinished phase of the Step Pyramid complex. They could easily have belonged to an earlier (Second Dynasty), unfinished gallery tomb (Stadelmann 1985: 303). A further set of subterranean galleries in the north-west quarter of the North Court comprises four parallel descending corridors which give access to a long, transverse gallery, off which open further chambers (Lauer 1936: 186). The complex may represent another abandoned tomb of the Second Dynasty. Here

Mariette found a travertine offering-table, decorated with lions' heads (Cairo Museum *Catalogue Générale* 1322), although the galleries are unlikely to have been the object's original location. It may have been moved from a nearby temple or offering-place (Firth and Quibell 1935, I: 77). The quality of workmanship suggests that it may have stood in a royal mortuary temple (Stadelmann 1985: 303), strengthening the case for the existence of Second Dynasty royal tombs in the vicinity. The mudbrick remains found under the Western Massif may have been part of such a mortuary temple (Stadelmann 1985: 303). In addition to these two sets of underground chambers, the North Court contains three unfinished stairway tombs of the Third Dynasty which were probably begun before the extension of the Step Pyramid complex northwards, then abandoned after the incorporation of the North Court (Firth and Quibell 1935, I: 77).

As its name suggests, the Western Massif occupies almost the entire western side of the Step Pyramid complex. It comprises three conjoined sections, two outer flat-topped structures (I and III) and a central, arched section (II). With its distinctive superstructure and underground galleries (Lauer 1936: 182, fig. 206, 1962: pl. 14b), the Western Massif seems to form a single, planned building, earlier than the Step Pyramid itself (Stadelmann 1985: 300–1). The initial excavators of the Step Pyramid complex describe the 'elaborate underground galleries' beneath the Western Massif, with 'smaller galleries or chambers at right angles, cut in the soft rock' (Firth and Quibell 1935, I: 17, 71). The similarity to mastaba substructures of the Second and Third Dynasties was noted (Firth and Quibell 1935, I: 71). The entrance to the underground galleries lies to the north. From a descending shaft, further, perpendicular shafts lead directly to the main, central gallery. This, in turn, is linked to two outer galleries by cross-passages. In plan, therefore, the galleries bear a close resemblance to the Hetepsekhemwy galleries. The burial chamber, if there was one, is likely to have lain at the south-west corner of the monument, now inaccessible. Large numbers of stone vessels, apparently uninscribed, were found in the galleries, especially the southern part (Firth and Quibell 1935, I: 17). The dangerous condition of the galleries may have prevented their full exploration (Stadelmann 1985: 302). It is, perhaps, surprising that no seal-impressions were found in the galleries. This could be due to their incomplete exploration, but it is also noteworthy that only a few sealings of Netjerikhet were found in the galleries beneath the Step Pyramid (Stadelmann 1985: 302). It is tempting to see in the Western Massif another Second Dynasty royal tomb, later incorporated by Netjerikhet into his grand plan. In the same way, the superstructures of the Hetepsekhemwy and Ninetjer tombs may well have been 'casualties of Djoser's construction work to the north, since any but the most minimal superstructure ... would have interfered with the construction of his massive enclosure wall'. The presence of large numbers of stone vessels inscribed for Hetepsekhemwy (17) and Ninetjer (13) amongst the funerary provisions of the Step Pyramid complex suggests that 'Djoser apparently had special access to the possessions of these earlier kings'. This would be easily explained if Netjerikhet swept away the superstructures of their tombs and 'appropriated the contents' (Roth 1993: 48, n. 49). (Since the name of Djer occurs on 13 vessels, often associated with a building called *smr-ntrw*, it is possible that this institution, too, lay in the vicinity and 'fell victim to Djoser's workmen' [Roth 1993: 48, n. 49].)

Examination of the topography in the vicinity of the Step Pyramid complex has led one Egyptologist to posit the existence of a 40-metre-wide dry moat, extending around the Step Pyramid complex on all four sides, and doubling back on itself to the south to form the hieroglyph *wsht*, 'broad court' (Swelim 1988). However, only the western and perhaps northern channels can be traced on the ground with any likelihood, and the theory has so far received only limited support (F.D. Friedman 1995: 40–1, fig. 25).

The step pyramid complex of Sekhemkhet

Sekhemkhet began his own step pyramid complex to the south-west of his predecessor's monument (Plate 7.2). The enclosure measures some 500 metres by 200 metres and the pyramid at its centre was planned as a

Plate 7.2 The unfinished step pyramid complex of Sekhemkhet at Saqqara (author's photograph).

seven-stepped structure, in contrast to Netjerikhet's six-stepped pyramid. The construction technique shows notable advances in stone architecture: the enclosure wall uses larger blocks which would have given greater strength and cohesion, as well as allowing economies in the quarrying work; the fine Tura limestone for the outer casing was employed more sparingly than in Netjerikhet's complex. Like the Netjerikhet complex, Sekhemkhet's step pyramid complex seems to have been built in stages. The foundations of an early southern enclosure wall were uncovered, the same distance from the pyramid as the northern enclosure wall. Hence, the complex seems originally to have comprised a rectangle with the step pyramid at its centre (Lauer 1968: 99). The enclosure was subsequently enlarged to the north and south; the southward extension was more restricted due to the more difficult terrain, hence the asymmetry of the complex in its final form (Lauer 1968: 99). Due to limited excavation inside the enclosure, it is unclear how many of the other buildings surrounding the pyramid had been started when work on the complex was abandoned (Edwards 1993: 62). The substructure of the pyramid seems to have been largely completed, even though the monument above ground was abandoned at an early stage. A descending corridor in the north face of the pyramid gives access to the burial chamber, which was roughly hewn into the bedrock and surrounded on three sides by storage magazines. These number 132 in total and open off a transverse east–west corridor with arms extending southwards at both ends (Edwards 1993: 61). The stone sarcophagus discovered in the burial chamber was intact, but contained no body, probably indicating that it was unacceptable to bury a king in an unfinished pyramid. Incidentally, it is the earliest royal stone sarcophagus from Egypt (Edwards 1993: 62).

One element that was finished is the South Tomb. Located closer to the pyramid than in the complex of Netjerikhet (Lauer 1968), the South Tomb was part of the original plan, and seems to have been covered by a small mastaba measuring 60 by 30 cubits (32 by 16 metres) (Lauer 1968: 100).

The 'layer pyramid' at Zawiyet el-Aryan

Another, unfinished step pyramid dated to the Third Dynasty is the so-called 'layer pyramid' at Zawiyet el-Aryan (Dunham 1978: xi). Only the lowest courses of the pyramid's inner core have been preserved, and even the substructure seems to have been left unfinished. The 'layer pyramid' seems to have been planned as a monument of six or seven steps, but work was clearly abandoned at an early stage, judging by the total absence of any funerary equipment (Edwards 1993: 65). The similarities between the Zawiyet el-Aryan pyramid and Sekhemkhet's monument are striking, both in the form of the superstructure and in the overall plan of the subterranean chambers. A date close to the reign of Sekhemkhet seems certain for the 'layer pyramid' (Edwards 1993: 64).

The pyramid at Maidum

Considerable uncertainty surrounds the precise date of the pyramid at Maidum. Its initial stages have generally been attributed to Huni, last king of the Third Dynasty (for example, Wildung 1969a: 135), even though no inscription from the site bears his name. New Kingdom graffiti inside the pyramid itself show that Egyptians of later periods believed Sneferu to have been the builder of the monument (there is no doubt that Sneferu was responsible for the pyramid in its final form) and the fact that several of Sneferu's relatives are buried in nearby mastabas may lend weight to this theory (Edwards 1993: 93). The choice of location is unusual, Maidum lying a considerable distance from the Memphite necropolis which had served Huni's Third Dynasty forebears. The proximity of the Seila pyramid, dated to the early part of Sneferu's reign, may indicate that the Maidum pyramid was also built by this king (Seidlmayer 1996a: 206). However, two pyramids are already known to have been built for Sneferu at Dahshur, and it is perhaps unlikely, although not impossible (Edwards 1993: 95–7), that he could have completed three massive funerary monuments within a single reign. Huni is allotted a reign of identical length (twenty-four years) by the Turin Canon, and would have had ample opportunity to construct an impressive mortuary complex. The fact that the tomb of Metjen, a high official under Huni, was located at Saqqara has suggested to some that the tomb of the king himself lay nearby. However, the tombs of officials seem to have been located at Saqqara throughout the Early Dynastic period, irrespective of changes in the location of the royal tomb (Roth 1993: 50). In the absence of a more plausible candidate – and recent excavations have decisively rejected the Gisr el-Mudir enclosure at Saqqara as an unfinished step pyramid complex of the Third Dynasty (Mathieson and Tavares 1993; Bettles *et al.* 1995) – the pyramid at Maidum, in its initial form, may have been intended as Huni's funerary monument.

Like its predecessors at Saqqara and Zawiyet el-Aryan, the Maidum pyramid was originally planned as a seven-stepped monument. In a second building phase, the pyramid was enlarged to an eight-stepped monument (Petrie 1910; Edwards 1993: 72). A more dramatic change of plan converted the step pyramid into a true pyramid, and it is this innovation, linked with fundamental changes in the Egyptian conception of the afterlife, that has been attributed to Sneferu, first king of the Fourth Dynasty. The courses of masonry used in the two phases of the step pyramid slope inwards towards the centre of the monument, a technique common to all Third Dynasty pyramids (and also shared by the lower half of Sneferu's

'Bent Pyramid' at Dahshur). By contrast, the conversion to a true pyramid used horizontal courses, characteristic of Fourth Dynasty pyramid-building (and used in the upper part of the 'Bent Pyramid' and throughout Sneferu's northern pyramid at Dahshur). Access to the burial chamber, located near ground level beneath the centre of the pyramid, was via a descending corridor leading from an opening in the pyramid's north face. At the end of the corridor, a vertical shaft connected with the burial chamber itself (Edwards 1993: 75). No trace of a sarcophagus was found by the first archaeologist to enter the pyramid in modern times, but the monument is likely to have been robbed in antiquity.

An open causeway led from the pyramid to the valley temple. Due to its location beneath the modern water-table, this part of the complex has not been excavated. By contrast, the mortuary temple on the east side of the pyramid is well preserved. It is entirely devoid of decoration, and the lowest courses of masonry were left undressed, suggesting that the temple was never finished. Two uninscribed, round-topped stelae, presumably intended as funerary stelae, were found inside (Edwards 1993: 76–7). The location of the mortuary temple, to the east of the pyramid, contrasts with earlier Third Dynasty practice – Netjerikhet's mortuary temple lies to the north of his Step Pyramid – and may indicate that it belongs to the latest building phase at Maidum, when the step pyramid was converted to a true pyramid.

THE CHANGING SYMBOLISM OF ROYAL MORTUARY ARCHITECTURE

The form of the royal mortuary complex, its architecture and constituent components provide the best guide available to conceptions of the afterlife in the Early Dynastic period (cf. Edwards 1993: 278). The royal tomb was not simply the repository and final resting place for the body of the king. It was also the means by which the king could participate in the afterlife. The tomb complex provided both the necessary material goods for the eternal sustenance of the royal *ka* – the commodities and other grave goods interred with the king – and, just as importantly, the architectural symbolism to create and foster the right conditions for his rebirth and life in the hereafter. A detailed examination of royal mortuary architecture over the course of the first three dynasties reveals the rich symbolic vocabulary with which it was imbued. Through the prominence of different symbolic elements over time, we can chart the course of afterlife beliefs during the Early Dynastic period. Two symbols emerge as pre-eminent: the primeval mound and the replica royal palace. Each points to a different aspect of royal mortuary ideology.

As we have seen, the superstructures of the royal tombs at Abydos have been reconstructed as simple mounds of sand, held in place by a mudbrick revetment. The symbol of the mound seems to have been so important that a second, hidden tumulus covering the burial chamber became a regular feature of royal tomb architecture. It seems likely that the form of the burial mounds recalled symbolically the primeval mound which first emerged from the floodwaters of chaos at the time of creation (cf. Badawy 1956: 183). The primeval mound was, in later periods at least, a powerful symbol of rebirth and resurrection. Its incorporation into the royal tomb seems to indicate that the resurrection of the dead king was a primary objective, and one which could be assisted magically by the very architecture of the tomb. In the case of the Third Dynasty step pyramids, the symbolism may have been more complex than merely a stepped version of the primeval mound (see below).

From late Predynastic times, concepts of the royal afterlife seem to have given a prominent role to the palace. The architecture of tomb U-j at Abydos (dating to the late Predynastic period, Naqada IIIa2, *c.* 3150 BC) seems to mimic the layout of the royal palace, with interconnecting chambers. The symbolism becomes more explicit from the reign of Djer onwards, when the king's tomb on the Umm el-Qaab was accompanied by a separate funerary enclosure on the low desert. Judging from the Step Pyramid complex of Netjerikhet, the purpose of the enclosure was to provide an arena in which the rituals of kingship could be played out for all eternity. That a replica royal palace was considered an essential element of the royal mortuary complex has important implications for Early Dynastic conceptions of the afterlife. The deduction must be that the afterlife of the king was envisaged, on one level at least, as a continuation of his earthly existence. In death as in life, royal ceremonial was central to the function of the king, and proper provision for its celebration was a necessity in the planning of the royal mortuary complex. The royal tombs of the Second Dynasty at Saqqara emphasise the tomb as a dwelling-place for the king's *ka*. The layout of the innermost chambers consciously imitates the private apartments of a house, and this aspect of the design may have made a separate funerary enclosure redundant (although the anonymous enclosures to the west of the Step Pyramid complex may date to the Second Dynasty).

Certain other aspects of the royal tombs at Abydos hint at the afterlife beliefs of First Dynasty Egyptians. As we have seen, there is a gap in the line of subsidiary burials surrounding some of the royal tombs; in each case, the gap occurs at the south-west corner, aligned with the prominent cleft in the cliffs behind Abydos. Evidence from later periods suggests that the cleft was believed to be an entrance to the underworld; if this belief was current in Early Dynastic times, the gap in the line of subsidiary burials may have been provided to allow the *ka* of the deceased king to travel freely from the tomb to the underworld. A belief in the royal *ka* is also suggested by the separate annex to the south-west of Den's tomb.

In the Third Dynasty step pyramid complexes, this aspect of the design is transmuted into the South Tomb, a second miniaturised tomb to the south of the main pyramid.

The overall orientation of the royal tomb may also be significant. In the tombs of Den and his successor Anedjib, the entrance stairway approaches the burial chamber from the east, perhaps aligned to the rising sun, a powerful symbol of rebirth. The change to a northerly orientation in the tomb of Qaa foreshadows the tombs of the Second Dynasty at Saqqara and the step pyramid complexes of the Third Dynasty. In the last, the northerly orientation may well be connected with the circumpolar stars, identified as the souls of dead kings in the Old Kingdom Pyramid Texts. Seen from the burial chamber, the entrance corridor in the Third Dynasty step pyramids 'would resemble a large ramp which pointed northwards towards the circumpolar stars', providing the means for the king to ascend to the 'astral heaven' (Edwards 1993: 284). It is tempting to speculate that the architecture of Qaa's tomb has a similar significance, indicating that the belief in an astral afterlife for the king was already current at the end of the First Dynasty.

The first unequivocal evidence for a celestial aspect to royal mortuary ideology may be provided by the fleet of funerary boats discovered adjacent to – literally moored alongside – the Shunet ez-Zebib. Their date is still uncertain: the associated pottery suggests the boat burials are contemporary with the Shunet itself, but the stratigraphy of the site seems to indicate an earlier date, perhaps the first half of the First Dynasty. Symbolically, they seem to foreshadow the solar barks buried next to Old Kingdom royal pyramids, although a more prosaic explanation is also possible: that the boats were used to transport the king's body and funerary goods from the Residence at Memphis. Boat burials are attested in connection with First Dynasty private tombs (at Saqqara, Abu Rawash and Helwan), but the boats next to Khasekhemwy's funerary enclosure provide the earliest royal parallel for this practice. Their presence next to the king's most prominent mortuary construction demonstrates their symbolic importance. As well as enjoying an afterlife modelled on his earthly activities (for which a replica royal palace was necessary), the king was apparently considered to participate in some way in the cosmic cycle. Henceforth, the celestial component of the royal afterlife – if it may be called such – was to become increasingly important. By the end of the Third Dynasty, it had completely eclipsed earlier concepts of an afterlife characterised by royal ceremonial. The triumph of the 'celestial model' is emphasised in the symbolic architecture of the Old Kingdom pyramids.

The step pyramid complex of Netjerikhet comprises a multitude of symbolic elements, each of which provides a piece of evidence for contemporary concepts of the royal afterlife. The continuing importance of the replica palace – to provide an arena for royal ritual – is emphasised by the enclosure with its recessed 'palace-façade' decoration. The identity of the various royal rituals which the funerary enclosure was designed to accommodate is hinted at by specific architectural features. The three most important rituals seem to have been the appearance of the king on a raised dais, the Sed-festival, and the ceremony known as 'encompassing the field'. Despite this evidence for increasing sophistication in mortuary ideology, the ancient symbol of the primeval mound was retained. In the earliest phase of the complex, a mastaba covered the king's burial chamber, recalling the superstructures of the First Dynasty tombs at Abydos and their Second Dynasty successors at Saqqara.

The change from mastaba to step pyramid is likely to have been motivated, at least in part, by ideological considerations. As we have seen, the northward orientation of the entire complex – a feature which dates back to the end of the First Dynasty – probably reflects the importance of astral religion. When viewed from Egypt, the stars surrounding the pole-star are never seen to set. For this reason, the Egyptians called them *iḥmw-sk*, 'the ones that know not destruction'. It was the king's wish to ascend to the circumpolar stars, and the Pyramid Texts (Utterances 267 and 619 [§§365 and 1749]) speak of the king doing so by means of a great staircase. The step pyramid may have been designed as just such a staircase, providing the king with a very concrete means of ascending to the sky. (Note that the determinative of the Egyptian verb *'r*, 'to ascend', resembles a step pyramid [Edwards 1993: 281].) Although the Pyramid Texts were only written down in the late Fifth and Sixth Dynasties, their language and content strongly suggest an earlier composition (cf. Edwards 1993: 284). Therefore, it is not entirely inappropriate to use them to illuminate royal mortuary ideology of the Early Dynastic period. It has also been suggested that the step pyramid represented a repetition of the primeval mound symbol, the piling up of mounds, one upon another, intensifying the symbolic assistance in the rebirth of the king.

At the beginning of the Fourth Dynasty, the step pyramid at Maidum was converted into a true pyramid. This conversion represents the end of the distinctive tradition of Early Dynastic mortuary architecture. The purpose of the royal funerary monument – to enable the king to ascend to a celestial afterlife – remained the same, but the symbolism and underlying ideology had changed dramatically. The design of Early Dynastic royal tomb complexes paints a picture of increasing sophistication in royal mortuary ideology, and a growing dominance of celestial, as opposed to earthly, concepts of the afterlife. From simple ideas of rebirth and resurrection, the eternal celebration of royal ritual came to play a central role, reflecting a concept of the afterlife more concerned with the continuation of royal power than with the incorporation of the king in the great rhythm of the universe. As the Early Dynastic period drew to a close, concepts of the royal afterlife underwent a major transformation: at his death, the king was absorbed into the supernatural order, relinquishing his guidance of the ship of state for a place in the celestial bark of the supreme deity.

EXCURSUS: THE ROYAL TOMBS AT ABYDOS: BURIALS OR CENOTAPHS?

Following Petrie's excavations on the Umm el-Qaab, the royal tombs of the First and late Second Dynasty kings were recognised as the burial places of these rulers. The tombs with their accompanying subsidiary burials and pairs of funerary stelae spoke unequivocally of their occupants' royal status. Then, in the two decades following 1936, Emery excavated the Early Dynastic cemetery at North Saqqara with its massive mudbrick mastabas. The impressive size and architecture of the North Saqqara tombs led scholars to question the identification of the smaller tombs on the Umm el-Qaab (Lauer 1957: 156). Emery, in particular, was in no doubt that the North Saqqara mastabas were the true burial places of the First Dynasty kings. He interpreted the tombs on the Umm el-Qaab as southern 'cenotaphs', dummy Upper Egyptian counterparts to the 'true' burials in Lower Egypt, reflecting the duality of Egyptian kingship (Emery 1961). Thus began a protracted scholarly debate over the proper interpretation of the two cemetery areas, the Umm el-Qaab and North Saqqara (cf. Hoffman 1980: 280–7). Since the debate focused on many of the crucial aspects of early royal mortuary architecture, it is of interest and importance for the history of Egyptology and its appreciation of the Early Dynastic period.

The detailed arguments for both sides of the debate have been presented in detail elsewhere (especially Lauer 1957 and Stadelmann 1985 in favour of Saqqara as the royal burial ground; Kemp 1967 and Kaiser 1992 in favour of Abydos), and it is not necessary to rehearse them again here. Recent excavations at Abydos have strengthened the case for identifying this site as the First Dynasty royal necropolis. In particular, Aha's tomb complex on the Umm el-Qaab seems to have been built somewhat later than mastaba S3357 at North Saqqara, to judge from the ceramic evidence. The time-lag between the two tomb complexes argues against the notion that the Saqqara monument is the true burial of the king and the Abydos complex merely his southern cenotaph (Dreyer 1990: 65; cf. Helck 1984b: 394–8). The case for identifying the tombs at Abydos as the true royal burials is increasingly convincing. The combination of tomb and funerary enclosure at Abydos provides a logical ancestry for the Third Dynasty Step Pyramid complex (Kaiser and Dreyer 1982: 259). It is generally accepted that 'the kings were buried at Abydos and that the tombs at Saqqara were for high officials or members of the royal family' (Kemp 1967: 23), although one scholar, in a reversal of Emery's argument, has identified the Saqqara tombs as northern cenotaphs (Hoffman 1980: 287). The belief that the true royal burials of the First and Second Dynasties were located at Saqqara, though steadfastly maintained by a few scholars (principally Lauer 1969, 1988; Brinks 1979; Stadelmann 1987), is now firmly 'a minority view' (O'Connor 1991: 7).

CHAPTER EIGHT

CULTS AND SHRINES

——— •◆• ———

The Early Dynastic tombs and funerary enclosures at Abydos and Saqqara loudly proclaim the concern of the king and his courtiers to provide for themselves in death. However, supernatural assistance and divine intervention were equally necessary in life: Egyptians believed that the daily hazards and periodic disasters which faced them could be prevented, or at least mitigated, by appealing to the gods. This applied just as much to the king, in his fight against the forces of chaos, as it did to the ordinary peasant farmer, concerned for the health of his crops or the survival of his children.

The evidence for Early Dynastic cult – the practices and beliefs that characterised the Egyptians' interaction with the divine sphere – is piecemeal and often difficult to interpret. Yet, with patience, it can be deployed to illuminate many aspects of religion in the first three dynasties. The picture that emerges is one of great complexity and remarkable sophistication. In particular, Egypt's early kings seem to have been adept at using religion for their own ends: to strengthen the bonds which held the country together and to buttress the institution of kingship itself.

The buildings in which early cult was practised ranged from small community shrines to substantial, government-sponsored temples. The difference in scale and elaboration between state and private places of worship emphasises the division in early Egyptian society between the ruling élite and the populace. In religion, as in the other spheres of activity discussed in preceding chapters, the evidence suggests that the concerns of the court were often rather different from those of its subjects.

CULT

Conceptions of god

An attempt to understand ancient Egyptian theology is a difficult enough task for the better-documented periods of dynastic history; for the Early Dynastic period it presents huge problems, not least because of the very limited source material. The names of the deities themselves provide valuable evidence for Egyptian conceptions of the divine, stretching back to the very beginning of the written record (Hornung 1983: 100). Certain deities seem to have had particularly strong local origins; this is sometimes reflected in the name of the deity which may be derived directly from the place which served as the principal cult centre or from a local topographical feature (Hornung 1983: 72). The clearest example is Nekhbet, 'she of Nekheb (Elkab)'; the god of Herakleopolis, *Hri-š=f*, 'He who is upon his lake', is an example of the latter type.

Another informative source for Early Dynastic religious belief is the many personal names of the period that have survived in sealings and other inscriptions (cf. Hornung 1983: 44). Many of these names are theophorous (that is, they include the name of a deity as part of the personal name) and they provide some indication about which cults were popular in the first three dynasties – popular enough, at any rate, to be chosen by parents when naming a child. Moreover, at least 19 Early Dynastic names incorporate the word *ntr*, 'god', referring to an unspecified deity; three female names use the feminine counterpart *ntrt*, 'goddess' (Hornung 1983: 44–9). Of course, in any particular community, 'god' or 'goddess', when unspecified, was probably understood as referring to the local deity. None the less, we should be careful of underestimating the sophistication of Egyptian theology. It seems clear that the general concept of the divine was already well established in the Early Dynastic period.

The embodiment of divine attributes

In religious iconography, the animal chosen to represent a particular deity or aspect of divinity was selected for the qualities (not necessarily beneficial) it embodied. Thus, the great wild cow of the marshes was regarded as an extremely dangerous animal but was also recognised to be aggressively protective towards its offspring. It therefore made an ideal image of protective maternal power, embodied in the early cow goddesses Bat and Hathor. A further idea in Egyptian magic and theology was 'fighting like with like'. Hence, an animal which embodied a particular undesirable characteristic or whose behaviour adversely affected humans was chosen as the image of the deity to guard against such eventualities. For example, in the Predynastic period, when bodies were buried directly in shallow graves with relatively little protection, a common problem (and cause for concern) must have been the digging up of bodies, shortly after burial, by jackals and other wild dogs which lived on the margins of the cultivation. As a result, the jackal was chosen to represent the gods charged with protecting the dead in the necropolis, Khentiamentiu and Anubis (Pinch, personal communication 1995).

Depiction of deities

It has been suggested that Egyptian religion witnessed an evolution during the first two centuries of the third millennium BC, whereby deities were increasingly represented in human form rather than as animals or inanimate totems (Hornung 1983: 105). However, the evidence from the Early Dynastic period seems to indicate a more complex situation, with theriomorphic (in animal form), anthropomorphic (in human form) and 'mixed form' deities all coexisting in religious iconography. Gods such as Anubis, Mafdet and Wepwawet were, in the Early Dynastic period, always depicted in animal form; Min and Ptah were worshipped in human form from the very beginning of Egyptian history. The figures of Bat at the top of the Narmer Palette represent an intermediate stage: although the heads have the ears and horns of a cow, the faces are human. The 'mixed form' so characteristic of Egyptian religion – whereby the deity was shown with a human body and an animal head – is not attested until the early Second Dynasty (Figure 8.1). Incised stone vessels of Hetepsekhemwy and Nebra from the Step Pyramid complex show the cat-headed Bastet standing before the king's cartouche (Lacau and Lauer 1959: pl. 11 nos 57, 58), while sealings of Peribsen from later in the dynasty depict the god Ash with an animal head (Petrie 1901: pl. XXI.176). An undated but

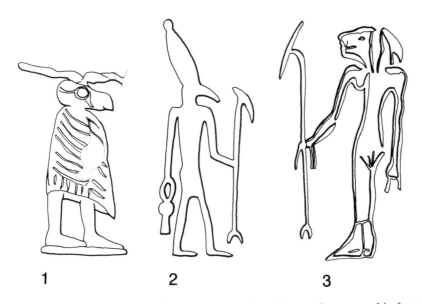

1   **2**   **3**

Figure 8.1 Depictions of deities. Early examples of the anthropomorphic form favoured for Egyptian deities in later periods: (1) an unidentified ram-headed deity from the side of a small, limestone, votive offering in the form of a carrying-chair; the provenance of the object is not known (now in the Kofler-Truniger Collection, Luzern) (after Schlögl 1978: pl. 81b); (2) the god Ash, shown on a seal-impression of Peribsen from Abydos (after Petrie 1901: pl. XXII.179); (3) the goddess Bastet, shown on an incised stone vessel from the Step Pyramid complex of Netjerikhet at Saqqara (after Lacau and Lauer 1959: pl. 11, no. 57). Not to same scale.

clearly Early Dynastic votive offering in the form of a shrine (Schlögl 1978: pls 81a–c) shows two standing figures with 'bird-like heads and ram's horns' (Hornung 1983: 109). In religious texts, deities of 'mixed form' are not described until very late in pharaonic history. Such depictions were clearly an artistic convention, but may not have been a true reflection of how the Egyptians really conceived the appearance of their deities (Pinch, personal communication 1995). Indeed, the determinative used for the name of a god in Early Dynastic inscriptions is usually a simplified human figure (Hornung 1983: 107). One theory holds that the artistic convention of animal-headed deities harks back to Predynastic cultic practices in which priests, wearing animal masks, officiated at religious ceremonies. This hypothesis receives some support from the Predynastic 'Two Dogs Palette' which seems to show a man wearing a dog-like mask and tail performing rites in the midst of a hunt.

Local and national deities

Although most Egyptian gods and goddesses had primary cult centres and are thus ostensibly 'local' deities, some none the less appear to have enjoyed universal, national importance from the very beginning of Egyptian history. We may wonder whether gods such as Khnum and Thoth were in origin local deities or whether, being universal in origin, they subsequently adopted a particular locality as their main cult centre (cf. Hornung 1983: 225). The term *nṯr-niwti*, 'local god', is attested from the Early Dynastic period. A votive statuette of a cloaked anthropomorphic deity in a Swiss private collection (Kofler-Truniger Collection, Luzern) is identified by the inscription *niwti*, 'of the city'. Yet the occurrence of 'local gods' in the Pyramid Texts (for example, §891a) – which were a product of the royal court – indicates that these deities had a degree of national importance (Hornung 1983: 73).

It is important to distinguish between truly local deities, like Bastet and Nekhbet, and the local forms of universal gods such as Horus. The origins of gods like Horus of Nekhen, Horus of Letopolis and Horus the Behdetite are lost in prehistory. One possibility is that they represent an attempt by Egypt's early rulers to integrate disparate centres into a more unified religious framework, local forms of a universal god adopting the heritage of local deities (Hornung 1983: 73). Indeed, some have seen the emergence of the Egyptian pantheon at the beginning of the Early Dynastic period as resulting from the fusion of distinctive regional traditions, mirroring the process of political unification (Baines 1991: 96). However, it is striking that the different deities attested at the beginning of the historic period occupy different niches and perform distinct roles in the overall field of human experience. If a pre-existing plethora of distinctive local deities was successfully moulded into a sophisticated and coherent pantheon, this would represent one of the most outstanding achievements of the Early Dynastic period: a theological unification as impressive as the political unification of the Two Lands. Alternatively, the different deities may not represent separate belief systems with local or regional origins (Quirke 1992: 73). Rather, there may have been a unified religious tradition throughout the Nile valley during the fourth millennium BC, perhaps mirrored in the archaeological record by a unified material culture. If so, this tradition was already characterised by a pantheon of deities which together represented the full complexity of the Egyptians' interaction with their environment. This hypothesis is succinctly summarised by Quirke:

> Despite the local voices for various deities, none of the different forms plays a role external to the pattern found in the pantheon that would be recognised throughout the country. Two forces are at work here, the need to mark off a distinctive form for specifically local worship as an expression of the local community, and the continued membership of a culture, a way of life, common to all living in the Nile Valley ... The interplay of these forces produces the range of the Egyptian pantheon.
>
> (Quirke 1992: 75)

Cult practice

Although we cannot hope to recover the nature of religious ritual, two particular aspects of cult practice are attested in Early Dynastic written sources and a third can be demonstrated by the archaeological record. The first, human sacrifice, may represent a survival of prehistoric practice or alternatively an experiment in absolute power conducted by the first kings of a united Egypt. Although sparsely attested (perhaps reflecting its rarity), it may none the less have continued as a feature of cult practice right down to the Late Period. The second aspect, the role of divine images, seems to have been central to Early Dynastic religion, and was to remain an important component of temple ritual throughout Egyptian history. The same is true of the third aspect of cult practice, the presentation of votive offerings. In this case, the objects themselves have survived, although the forms of worship of which they represent the material component cannot be reconstructed with any certainty.

Human sacrifice

There is a limited amount of evidence to suggest that human sacrifice, in a cultic setting, was practised in the Predynastic period and at the very beginning of the Early Dynastic period (Figure 8.2), albeit, perhaps, on a small scale (cf. Shaw and Nicholson 1995: 134). In common with other unusual aspects of Early Dynastic religion – most notably the reverence shown for the royal placenta – human sacrifice may have belonged to an ancient African substratum of Egyptian culture. We have seen in Chapter 7 that retainer sacrifice seems to have characterised royal burials of the late First Dynasty. As an exercise in absolute power, this particular practice was short-lived and is not attested in Egypt after the First Dynasty. The same does not, however, seem to be true of human sacrifice in a cultic sphere (contra Hoffman 1980: 261). As Egypt's early rulers formulated sophisticated mechanisms of authority, some older, more blatant practices seem to have been replaced; but there is evidence, both archaeological and epigraphic, for the continuation of ritual killings (Schulman 1988; Ritner 1993: 162–3). Although interpretation of the sources is by no means straightforward, a possible distinction may be made between the First Dynasty examples, which suggest the killing of humans as sacrificial victims offered to the gods, and the later occurrences which seem to involve the ceremonial execution of criminals or enemy captives. These latter were apparently carried out in a sacred setting to invoke the supernatural powers in countering the forces of chaos (Willems 1990).

Recent excavations at the Predynastic cemetery of Adaïma have revealed evidence of human sacrifice in burials of the Naqada II period. One body showed signs of the throat having been cut, followed by decapitation (Midant-Reynes *et al.* 1996: 15). Ritual human sacrifice is depicted on a label of Aha from Abydos, and seems to be associated with the 'fashioning' of an *imi-wt* **fetish** (Petrie 1901: pl. III.6). A kneeling figure plunges a sharp weapon into the chest of a prisoner whose hands are tied behind his back, observed by a standing figure of authority with a long staff. A bowl is placed between the assailant and the victim to catch the blood. A similar scene is depicted on a wooden label of Djer from Saqqara, this time associated with the fashioning and dedication of cultic totems (Emery 1961: 59, fig. 21). Since there are no surviving textual references to a ceremony involving sacrifice of this kind, we cannot be sure of the context of the ritual.

On the label of Aha, the scene of human sacrifice is associated with the fashioning of a falcon standard and an *imi-wt* fetish. Both were representative of royal authority; the *imi-wt* fetish was closely associated in later times with Anubis (see below). The religious ceremony associated with ritual killing on the Djer label appears to be more straightforward. It seems to depict the formal presentation of cultic objects to the king. Beneath the sign *ms*, 'fashioning', a line of men parades before the *serekh* of Djer (representing the person of the king), each carrying a different 'totem'. These comprise, on the top register, a ladder-like object (perhaps symbolising the ladder, mentioned in the Pyramid Texts, by which the king ascended to the stars), a **mummiform** figure, a large catfish (which calls to mind the writing of Narmer's Horus name), and a pelican. On the

Figure 8.2 Human sacrifice. Iconographic evidence: (1) a fragmentary label of Aha from Abydos, showing a bound prisoner being sacrificed; an officiant plunges a dagger into the prisoner's breast, while a bowl stands between the two to catch the blood (after Petrie 1901: pl. III.6); (2) a wooden label of Djer from Saqqara, with an identical scene of prisoner sacrifice shown in the top right-hand corner (after Emery 1961: 59, fig. 21). Not to same scale.

second register figures bring a bull standard and a panelled rectangle, perhaps representing the royal *serekh*. The procession of totem-bearers on the top register is followed by a smaller figure carrying a spear.

Divine images

The principal goal of cult practice was to bridge the twin realms of the divine and the human and invoke the presence of the gods on earth in their divine images (Baines 1991: 91; and see also Figure 8.3). The dedication of divine images and statues is well attested in Early Dynastic sources, particularly those dating to the First and Second Dynasties (cf.

Logan 1990: 62). The Egyptian word used to describe the action is *ms*, literally 'to give birth to' and hence 'to fashion'. However, there is some debate about the precise meaning of the phrase in relation to divine images. Some scholars think that the activity thus recorded is the dedication of the image by the king to the god, rather than the manufacture of the image (which would not have been carried out by the king himself, though he would doubtless have commissioned the work). In dedicating the image, possibly by means of the 'opening of the mouth ceremony', the king would have given life to the statue, and the word *ms* may refer to this aspect of the event. Leaving aside the precise significance of the verb *ms*, there is no doubt that the commissioning and dedication of cult images was a major royal activity in the Early Dynastic period (F.D. Friedman 1995: 35). In the annals of the Palermo Stone and its associated fragments, there are some 21 references to the fashioning of divine images in the first two dynasties (Redford 1986: 89). Many First Dynasty labels also record the practice. The creation of cult statues validated the king's own claim to divinity by reinforcing his position as theoretical high priest of every cult and his role as intermediary between gods and humans.

The divine images dedicated by Early Dynastic kings were probably statuettes made from stone or precious metal. The Coptos colossi and a similar stone statue from the early temple at Hierakonpolis represent the earliest surviving cult images of anthropomorphic deities. A number of stone animal sculptures have also survived from the early dynasties, and these are generally assumed to have been cult statues of deities worshipped in animal form. They include a travertine baboon incised with the name of Narmer (perhaps the king who dedicated the image) (E. Schott 1969), a frog of the same material (Cooney and Simpson 1976), and a limestone hippopotamus (Koefoed-Petersen 1951: 4, pl. 1). The Sixth Dynasty gold hawk from the temple of Horus at Hierakonpolis (Quibell and Green 1902: pl. XLVII) indicates that cult statues were also made of precious metals. Unsurprisingly, few have survived from antiquity. Cult statues were probably housed and transported in carrying-chairs (cf. Troy 1986: 79–82). Small model carrying-chairs of glazed composition and stone have been found in deposits of early votive offerings (Kemp 1989: 93, fig. 33); one of these models may represent the carrying-chair as a deity in its own right, named *(r)p(y)t*, 'she of the carrying-chair' (Troy 1986: 80). The Scorpion macehead shows a number of figures on what appear to be sledges; these may also have been divine cult images (Roth 1993: 39, n. 23; cf. Pinch 1993: pls 10, 21b, 24–5). Similar sledge-born figures are shown on a block from the Palace of Apries at Memphis which, although probably of Late Period date (contra Weill 1961: 351), has important iconographic links with Early Dynastic religion (cf. Bietak 1994). Given the general conservatism of religious rituals, we may assume that cult statues were carried in procession, and that the appearances of divine

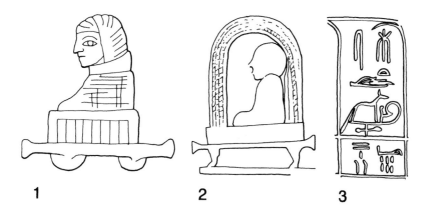

Figure 8.3 Divine images. Representations of cult images from contemporary Early Dynastic sources: (1) female figure on a sledge, possibly a divine image, shown on the Scorpion macehead (after Spencer 1993: 56, fig. 36); (2) female figure in a carrying-shrine, again plausibly identified as a divine image, shown on the Narmer macehead (after Quibell 1900: pl. XXVIB); (3) entry from the third register of the Palermo Stone, referring to a year (in the mid-First Dynasty) as 'the year of dedicating (an image of the god) Sed' (after Schäfer 1902: pl. I). Not to same scale.

images in such circumstances were an important feature of Egyptian cult practice in the Early Dynastic period, as they were in the New Kingdom (Kemp 1989: 185–8). The open plan characteristic of Early Dynastic provincial shrines may be as much practical as symbolic, designed to accommodate this particular aspect of cult practice (Roth 1993: 39).

Votive offerings

From the detailed analysis of Egyptian sources, combined with general observation of contemporary and ancient religious practice, a leading scholar has concluded that individuals visiting a shrine or temple engage in three types of activity: 'prayer, sacrifice, and the dedication of votive offerings' (Pinch 1993: 333). For the Early Dynastic period, there is a complete absence of textual information or elaborate depictions of religious activity; we therefore remain ignorant about the first two categories of private activity, prayer and sacrifice (but, as we have seen, there is limited evidence for human sacrifice at ritual occasions attended by the king). We are slightly better off when it comes to the dedication of votive offerings since, at several sites, the objects themselves have survived. It is likely that visitors to shrines would have routinely brought with them simple offerings of perishable commodities, especially foodstuffs. On certain (perhaps rare?) occasions, however, a visitor would demonstrate particular piety – and/or concern – by donating an object made specifically for this purpose. In the Early Dynastic period, as in later times, these votive offerings were most often made of glazed composition, although stone and pottery examples are known.

Four sites have yielded large numbers of votive objects which, by their style or archaeological context, can be dated to the Early Dynastic period: Abydos, Hierakonpolis, Elephantine and Tell Ibrahim Awad (see below, under individual site headings, for further information about the archaeology of these early shrines). In addition, a fifth, unprovenanced deposit of early votive material was unearthed by illicit digging in the 1940s or 1950s; it is quite possible that this deposit, too, came from Abydos, although other sites, such as Naqada, have also been proposed (Kemp 1989: 79). The date of the material from the first two sites, Abydos and Hierakonpolis, is still the subject of some controversy (Kemp 1968: 153). In particular, the excavation of the Hierakonpolis 'Main Deposit' was carried out without detailed recording, so that the precise archaeological context of the finds cannot now be established (B. Adams 1977). By contrast, the Satet temple at Elephantine and the shrine at Tell Ibrahim Awad have both been excavated in modern times, providing reliable stratigraphic evidence for the date of the votive material (Dreyer 1986; van Haarlem 1995, 1996). This in turn provides an important reference point against which to date comparable objects from Abydos and Hierakonpolis. Hence, although some questions remain, an Early Dynastic date for most of the material can be accepted with some confidence.

In its general character, the votive material from the four sites is substantially similar. Most of the objects are made of glazed composition and depict animal or human figures. Natural pebbles and flint nodules, many in suggestive shapes, also occur (Petrie 1902: pl. IX.195–6), whilst stone and ivory figurines are also represented at all four sites. However, within this broad homogeneity, a few notable distinctions emerge which may be attributable to local customs or preferences. Hence, a distinctive feature of the votive material from Hierakonpolis is the frequency of scorpions and scorpion tails, modelled in faience or stone (Kemp 1989: 75). Two stone vases, also from the 'Main Deposit', were decorated with scorpions in raised relief (Quibell 1900: pls XVII, XXXIII top left, pls XIX.1, XX.1). By contrast, scorpion figurines were not found at Abydos or Elephantine and have not been reported from Tell Ibrahim Awad. It is tempting to make a connection with the late Predynastic king whose ceremonial macehead was found in the same deposit at Hierakonpolis and whose name is read as 'Scorpion'. However, it is perhaps safer to attribute the preponderance of scorpion images at Hierakonpolis to an aspect of the local cult. This particular local allegiance may have been acknowledged in the name chosen by a local ruler. At Elephantine, a common type of votive offering is a small, oval, faience plaque, with the head of an animal (apparently a hedgehog) modelled at one end (Kemp 1989: 73, fig. 24.1). Forty-one examples of this strange object were recovered from the Satet shrine, but the type is not attested at Abydos or Hierakonpolis (although an object from Abydos described as a 'rough mud doll' may be a crude hedgehog plaque [Petrie 1902: 28, pl. XII.264]). Recent excavations at Tell Ibrahim Awad have yielded a few examples of 'hedgehog plaques', but not in the numbers in which they occur at Elephantine. They may therefore represent a local tradition of worship (although the original purpose of these enigmatic objects is lost in the mists of time). The votive material from the early shrines at Hierakonpolis and Elephantine thus hints at local or regional traditions of belief. This is an aspect of Egyptian culture which is difficult to establish in the face of the overwhelming evidence from a court-inspired 'great tradition'. None the less, it appears to be an important feature of early civilisation in the Nile valley, manifest in other classes of small object such as stamp-seals and also in the architecture of local shrines (Kemp 1989: 65–83, 89–91).

Of course, 'a votive offering is not simply an artefact, it is the surviving part of an act of worship' (Pinch 1993: 339). Rituals were probably performed 'to link a votive object with its donor'; and the actual presentation of an offering was, no doubt, accompanied by prayers and perhaps other acts of which no traces have survived. Little is known for certain about who made votive offerings and how they were acquired by donors (Pinch 1993: 326–8). It is dangerous to try and deduce the social status of donors from the quality (or lack of it) of their votive offerings (Pinch 1993: 344). None the less, a key question about shrines and temples at all periods of Egyptian history is the degree of access enjoyed by members of the general population. From the earliest times, state temples are likely to have been off limits to all but temple personnel, the king and his closest officials. Already in the temple enclosure at Hierakonpolis, constructed in the Second or Third Dynasty, we see the architecture of restricted access (see below). To what extent smaller shrines were accessible to members of a local community remains a moot point. Votive offerings are a potentially useful source of information, if it could be established where they were made and what type of person dedicated them. Unfortunately, these questions are difficult to resolve. There is no doubt that royal workshops producing high-quality craft items existed in Egypt from Predynastic times. However, the marked separation between state and private religion, discussed below, makes it unlikely that the small votive offerings found at sites like Elephantine and Tell Ibrahim Awad (both remote from the centres of Early Dynastic political power) were manufactured in royal workshops. Rather, they were probably produced by skilled craftsmen, either working for their own benefit or attached to the local shrine. How they would have been purchased by donors, operating within a barter economy, is difficult to envisage (Pinch 1993: 328). The votive objects from Abydos, Hierakonpolis and Tell Ibrahim

Awad were all found in deposits, representing accumulations of material gathered up and buried at periodic intervals long after it was initially dedicated. Only at Elephantine were votive offerings found *in situ*, on the floor of the Satet shrine. Whether the donors themselves were able to penetrate the inner rooms of the shrine, or whether the offerings were carried there by priests, cannot be established. Evidence from the New Kingdom would favour the latter interpretation, but the situation may well have been different in the Early Dynastic period. To summarise, for the early dynasties many questions about the donation of votive offerings – and about private religious observance in general – must remain unanswered. We cannot be certain, but it is tempting to suggest that Early Dynastic local shrines were used by all members of a community, from the head-man down to the lowliest peasant.

State versus local religion

As for Egyptian religion of later periods, so cult of the Early Dynastic period must be divided into two categories: state and local. Not until the end of the Old Kingdom were local temples systematically 'appropriated' by the state, to be rebuilt and decorated in the formal style of the court as a way, no doubt, of binding the provinces more securely to the king and his government (cf. Kemp 1989: 65–83). Throughout the Early Dynastic period it seems that the religious concerns of the court on the one hand and local communities on the other were entirely separate, and occasionally opposed. Local shrines served local communities, acting as foci for personal piety and probably for acts of collective worship at times of joy or trial. The character of community worship makes it likely that local shrines would have been accessible to the general public, at least as far as the forecourt. By contrast, temples built by and for the state were characterised by their exclusivity. This was emphasised in the architecture, a high enclosure wall restricting access to the temple in its entirety. A clear example of this is the rectangular enclosure-wall built around the temple of Horus at Hierakonpolis. In form it is similar to royal funerary enclosures of the Early Dynastic period, and its construction – effectively rendering the temple 'off limits' to the local population – may be connected with the programme of royal building work undertaken at Hierakonpolis by Khasekhem(wy). Whilst local cult activity was by its nature inclusive, state religion (in which royal cult played a large part) relied upon being exclusive (cf. Baines 1991: 104).

Personnel

Little is known for certain about the personnel involved in Early Dynastic religion, national or local. Specific, if obscure, titles such as *s(t)m* and *sm3* are attested from the First Dynasty (Petrie 1901: pl. X.2; Emery 1958: 31).

The leopard-skin garment worn by the *s(t)m*-priest has led one scholar to speculate that this figure was originally a shaman, practising more intuitive, magical rites, before the institutionalisation of a more 'ordered' religion at the beginning of the First Dynasty (Helck 1984d). There may also have been a connection between the *s(t)m*-priest and the goddess Seshat, who is often depicted wearing the same leopard-skin garment (Wainwright 1941: 37). In later periods, the *s(t)m*-priest officiated at funerals, particularly in the 'opening of the mouth' ceremony (for example, Reeves 1990: 72–3). This connection, together with the high status of the title *s(t)m* in the Early Dynastic period, has led to the suggestion that the holder of the office was the king's eldest son and heir, second only in rank and authority to the monarch himself (Schmitz 1984: 834). Indeed, as the person responsible for intimate royal rituals, the *s(t)m* would very likely have been a close member of the royal family.

A specialist class of funerary priest, *zhnw-3h*, is also attested from the early First Dynasty (Petrie 1900: pl. XVI.119, 1901: pl. XV.111; Emery 1954: 170, fig. 229), responsible for maintaining the mortuary cult of the king (and perhaps also of those of senior members of the royal family). The more general designation for priest, *hm-ntr*, first occurs in the reign of Qaa at the end of the First Dynasty (Emery 1958: 31, pl. 37.9). During the Second Dynasty we meet for the first time the title *hri-hbt*, 'lector-priest' (Amélineau 1902: 144, pl. XXII.8; Lacau and Lauer 1959: pl. 14 no. 70). This in turn implies the formulation of theological texts and a role for the written and spoken word in cult practice. In general, however, the role of myth and dogma in early Egyptian religion was probably restricted, ritual being of primary importance in cult celebration. It has been argued that, prior to the Second Dynasty, the *s(t)m*-priest acted as keeper of ritual texts, but that this role was taken over by the newly created position of 'lector-priest' (Helck 1984d: 106).

Specialised priesthoods serving the major state cults seem to have emerged at the end of the Second and during the Third Dynasties. The title *wr-m3(w)*, literally 'greatest of seers', held in later periods by the High Priest of Ra at Heliopolis but perhaps originally a title relating to astronomical observation, is first attested in the reign of Khasekhemwy (Amélineau 1902: 144, pl. XXII.8); it was subsequently held by Imhotep, chancellor at the court of Netjerikhet. The title held by the High Priest of Horus of Letopolis, *wnr*, first appears at the end of the Third Dynasty (Goedicke 1966), as does the office of *hrp pr-wr*, 'controller of the Per-wer (the national shrine of Upper Egypt)' (Weill 1908: 262–73).

A professional priesthood serving local cults is not attested until the Fifth Dynasty (Hornung 1983: 226). However, there is evidence from the Early Dynastic period for the (part-time) priests of local cults holding important positions within their communities (Seidlmayer 1996b: 118). Thus, an individual named *Nmti-ḥtp*, owner of a large, richly furnished stairway tomb of the late Third Dynasty at Qau (Brunton 1927: pl. 18), is identified as a priest, presumably of the local cult (Seidlmayer 1996b: 118). Temples played an important role in local and national economies from an early period, and it is likely that temple personnel benefited materially, as well as in prestige, from an involvement with the local cult.

Royal cult

The ivory comb of Djet 'presents concisely and clearly the central tenet binding together ancient Egyptian civilisation, the notion that the king fulfils a role on earth under the protective wings of the celestial falcon in heaven' (Quirke 1992: 21–2). The primary role of the king was as arbiter between the gods and the people of Egypt. In return for daily offerings and the celebration of their cult on earth, the gods looked favourably on Egypt and bestowed on the country their divine blessings. The channel of communication in this two-way process was the king. In theory, therefore, the king was the ultimate high priest in every temple in the land: 'all cult in Egypt was royal cult' (Quirke 1992: 81). Implicitly, all temples were monuments to the king as well as cult centres for the deities to whom they were explicitly dedicated (Quirke 1992: 81; cf. Fairman 1958: 76). In discussing royal cult, therefore, a distinction must be made between the cults of deities which were in theory maintained by the king, and worship of the king himself as intermediary between the divine and human realms. The worship of the various gods and goddesses is discussed below. The following discussion focuses on the cult of the king himself.

Royal cult statues

Several depictions of royal statues are known from Early Dynastic sources, indicating that the royal cult was celebrated, at least in part, by means of statuary (Figure 8.4). The earliest certain example dates to the reign of Den (Eaton-Krauss 1984: 89). A seal-impression from Abydos shows three royal figures, each of which stands on a base-line (Kaplony 1963, III: pl. 93, fig. 364; F.D. Friedman 1995: 33, fig. 19b). The accompanying hieroglyphs describe the statues as being made of gold. The manufacture of royal statues from metal is also attested in the late Second Dynasty (see below). On the Den sealing, the first figure wears the white crown and beard, holds a staff and mace, and is in a striding posture. The second figure wears the red crown and beard, and stands in a **papyrus skiff** in the act of harpooning a hippopotamus. It may be compared with two gilded statuettes from the tomb of Tutankhamun; these show the king in a similar posture of harpooning, although the object of the hunt (the hippopotamus) is not shown

(Eaton-Krauss 1984: 90). The third figure on the Den sealing shows the king wearing the red crown and *šndit*-kilt, in the unparalleled posture of wrestling with a hippopotamus. A link has been made between these last two representations and the entry for the reign of Den on the Palermo Stone which records a hippopotamus hunt. A further seal-impression of Den, from the tomb of Hemaka at Saqqara, may also show statues of the king (Emery 1938: 64, fig. 26). Two royal figures are shown in striding or running posture, one wearing the red crown and one the white crown. A ground-line beneath the figures – which does not continue under the animals shown between them – suggests that they are to be interpreted as statues, since human figures on Early Dynastic sealings do not usually stand on a ground-line (Eaton-Krauss 1984: 91). Comparable statues of the king in a striding or running posture are shown in the workshop scenes in the Eighteenth Dynasty tomb of Rekhmira (Davies 1943: pls 36, 37; F.D. Friedman 1995: 33, fig. 19e). A seal-impression from the tomb of Djer may show a similar striding statue (Petrie 1901: pl. V.17), but the rudimentary publication of the sealing makes a certain identification impossible (Eaton-Krauss 1984: 92, n. 484). If proven, the sealing would be the earliest representation of a royal statue, antedating the seal-impressions of Den by two generations.

Six incised stone vessels of Anedjib depict royal statues. Three of these, from Saqqara, bear identical inscriptions, showing a striding figure wearing the red crown, beard and kilt, holding a mace and the *mks*-staff. An inscription from Abydos differs only in that the king wears the white crown. A locality is named in association with the figures, and this probably indicates the cult place where the royal statues were kept. The stone vessels are likely to have belonged to the ritual equipment attached to the royal statue cult (Eaton-Krauss 1984: 93). A rough and partially preserved inscription of Anedjib's reign occurs on a stone vessel fragment from the Step Pyramid complex. It shows a striding figure in the act of harpooning. The head is lost, but, given the parallels from the preceding reign, it almost certainly showed the king (Eaton-Krauss 1984: 94).

The fashioning or dedication of another royal statue is recorded in a well-known entry on the Palermo Stone. The statue depicted the last king of the Second Dynasty and was called *q3-Ḥʿ-shmwi*, 'high is Khasekhemwy'. The inscription states that it was made of copper; it may be compared with the life-size copper statue of Pepi I, found in the temple at Hierakonpolis (Quibell and Green 1902: pls L–LII; Sethe 1914). Some doubt surrounds the identification of the reign in which the statue of Khasekhemwy was commissioned. Some scholars favour Khasekhemwy's successor (for example, Kaiser 1961), but it seems more likely that Khasekhemwy himself had the statue made (W.S. Smith 1971: 147). The royal statues attested from the reigns of Den and Anedjib are examples of kings commissioning statues for their own cults. The creation of large-scale metal sculptures illustrates the technological sophistication of Early Dynastic craftsmen.

Figure 8.4 Royal cult statues. Evidence for the production and dedication of royal sculpture in the Early Dynastic period: (1) seal-impression of Den from Abydos showing three statues of the king engaged in various ritual activities; the accompanying inscription states that the statues were made of gold (after Kaplony 1963, III: fig. 364); (2) (3) inscriptions on stone vessels of Anedjib from the Step Pyramid complex of Netjerikhet; two statues of the king are depicted, one wearing the red crown, the other wearing the white crown (after Lacau and Lauer 1959: planche III.1–2); (4) entry from the fifth register of the Palermo Stone, referring to a year (in the reign of Khasekhemwy or his successor) as 'the year of dedicating the copper statue "high is Khasekhemwy"'; this entry indicates that copper statuary was created long before the well-known images of Pepi I and Merenra found in the temple at Hierakonpolis (after Schäfer 1902: pl. I). Not to same scale.

The six relief panels installed beneath the Step Pyramid and South Tomb of Netjerikhet's mortuary complex may depict royal statues rather than the king himself (F.D. Friedman 1995: 32). The close parallels between one of the panels and the stone vessel inscriptions of Anedjib described above seem to support this hypothesis. A relief fragment of Netjerikhet from Heliopolis, showing the king enthroned and accompanied by three royal ladies, may also depict a royal statue, but this is not certain (Eaton-Krauss 1984: 95).

Buildings of the royal cult

The construction of buildings for the royal cult seems to have been the most important project of each reign, absorbing much of the court's revenue. Hence, the size of the royal mortuary complex offers a guide both to Egypt's prosperity and to the power of the central government to exploit the country's resources. Moreover, the increasing elaboration of royal cult buildings from the Predynastic period onwards is 'one of the most socially, economically and politically sensitive indicators of the rise of the state' (Hoffman 1980: 336). The surviving buildings of the Early Dynastic royal cult are characterised in general by their apparent mortuary nature. The large enclosures of the First and Second Dynasties at Abydos, Saqqara and Hierakonpolis are usually termed 'funerary', and the Step Pyramid complex of Netjerikhet is regarded as having fulfilled a primarily mortuary role. However, the picture may not be so simple. There is evidence from the Old Kingdom to indicate that the royal cult at a pyramid was celebrated during the lifetime of the reigning king. Furthermore, the decoration of Old Kingdom royal 'mortuary' temples does not focus on funerary themes, but on the ritual duties and festivals of kingship, especially the Sed-festival (Seidlmayer 1996b: 122). The same appears to be true of the surviving relief fragments from the Hierakonpolis enclosure of Khasekhemwy, and of the six relief panels from the Step Pyramid complex. It is possible, therefore, that the Netjerikhet complex, and some if not all of its First and Second Dynasty antecedents, was used for the celebration of the royal cult before the king's death.

It has been suggested that the enclosure which occupies one corner of the walled town of Hierakonpolis may have been built by Khasekhem(wy) to serve his royal cult (O'Connor 1992). In this case, it may have been conceived as an institution separate from the local temple of Horus of Nekhen, although occupying the same geographical location (Quirke 1992: 13). There is no doubt that the large mudbrick enclosures built by Khasekhemwy on the low desert at Hierakonpolis and Abydos were connected with the royal cult. They provide an early illustration of the concept that the royal cult was not restricted to one location but could be celebrated throughout the country. Furthermore, it would seem that royal cult centres were not confined to the immediate vicinity of the king's burial (Quirke 1992: 82). The most vivid illustrations of this point are the small step pyramids of the late Third Dynasty (Seidlmayer 1996b). Located at sites throughout Middle and Upper Egypt, all but one of the pyramids seem to have been built in the reign of Huni (Plate 8.1). They 'must have marked the locations of an official cult centered [sic] around the person of the king' (Seidlmayer 1996b: 122). This is confirmed by the objects found at the pyramid of Seila, dated to the following reign of Sneferu: stelae with the king's name, fragments of a shrine, a royal statue

Plate 8.1 Markers of the royal cult. Four of a series of small step pyramids erected throughout the Nile valley at the end of the Third Dynasty: (top left) Zawiyet el-Meitin, on the east bank of the Nile just south of the modern city of Minya; (top right) Abydos south, also known as Sinki; (bottom left) Tukh, just north of Naqada; (bottom right) el-Kula, just north of Hierakonpolis (author's photographs).

and an offering-table (Leclant and Clerc 1988: pl. 32; Edwards 1993: 69; Seidlmayer 1996b: 122). The distribution of royal cult centres of this type throughout the country seems to be linked to the exploitation of agricultural resources. There may originally have been a small step pyramid in each nome: the location of the three southernmost pyramids certainly suggests such a distribution. They would therefore have represented 'a project of mapping the royal cult across the country' (Seidlmayer 1996b: 124). The small step pyramids may be seen as the predecessors of the funerary estates depicted in procession in the temple of Sneferu's Bent Pyramid at Dahshur, and of the nome-**triad**s from the valley temple of Menkaura. The small step pyramids belong to a time when the economic system characteristic of the Old Kingdom was being devised. 'Constructing these monuments throughout the country could have served to make explicit and intelligible the ideological background to the economic demands of the state on a local level' (Seidlmayer 1996b: 124). The monuments of Huni's reign emphasise that the royal cult, through its political and economic influence, was central to the unity of Egypt.

The situation on the island of Elephantine is particularly revealing about the religious programme and priorities of the Early Dynastic court.

The investment of resources in a monument of the royal cult – a small step pyramid and an adjoining administrative complex – stands in marked contrast to the official neglect of the local shrine. Indeed, the state-sponsored construction of a fortress at the beginning of the Early Dynastic period showed flagrant contempt for local religious practice, encroaching as it did on the small community shrine nearby. 'The failure of the central authorities to care for this sanctuary was clearly not a matter of lacking funds, but of a completely different ideological background' (Seidlmayer 1996b: 122). The name of the complex adjacent to the small step pyramid at Elephantine was *sšd-nswt-Ḥwi*, '(the palace) diadem of King Huni'. This may be connected with *ḥb-sšd*, 'the festival of the diadem', which figures among the coronation rites of Shepseskaf as recorded on the Palermo Stone. Like the cult at royal 'funerary' monuments, the royal cult practised at Elephantine seems also to have been connected with festivals of kingship (Seidlmayer 1996b: 122–4).

Royal ancestors

Reverence for the royal ancestors, well attested in later periods (for example, the New Kingdom king lists at Karnak and Abydos), may already have played an important role in Early Dynastic theology. In particular, the role of royal ancestors in legitimising a new king seems to have been recognised by Netjerikhet who, according to later tradition (the Turin Canon) was the founder of a new dynastic line, and whose connection with the kings of the First and Second Dynasties may have been tenuous. His appropriation of the stores of stone vessels collected by royal predecessors to furnish his own burial may be interpreted in this light as 'a retrospective acknowledgement of the pharaonic monarchy' (F.D. Friedman 1995: 10, quoting Redford 1986: 134).

Corpus of deities attested in the Early Dynastic period

Throughout the course of Egyptian civilisation, unnamed deities are notoriously difficult to identify. The phenomenon of the 'interchangeability of attributes' makes secure identification difficult, even if the iconography seems to point unambiguously to a particular god or goddess (Pinch, personal communication 1995). The identification of the deities listed below is reasonably certain in all but six cases, these being denoted with a question mark (?). (See Figure 8.5 for a map showing the location of cults.)

Anti

Depicted as a falcon in a bark, Anti was a local god of Middle Egypt, worshipped on the east bank of the Nile, especially in the Badari region.

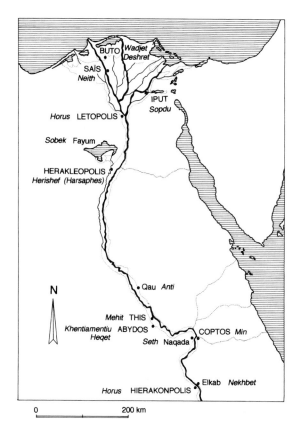

Figure 8.5 Early Dynastic cult dedications. The map shows the location of cult centres associated with particular deities, as attested in contemporary sources. Capitals denote ancient place names.

The deity was known to classical authors as Antaeus, and his cult centre, Qau, as Antaeopolis. A copper ewer from a wealthy late Second Dynasty grave at Badari, grave 429, bore the incised inscription *ḥm-nṯr ꜥnti-ḥtp*, 'the priest Anti-hotep' (Brunton 1927: pl. XVIII.10). This theophorous name is probably the earliest mention of the god Anti, and indicates the reverence shown to the deity in the Badari region from an early period.

Anubis

The fashioning or dedication of a divine image of a jackal is recorded as a salient event on a label of Aha from Abydos. The jackal deity in question is generally assumed to be Anubis, god of the desert necropolis, and he figures prominently in First Dynasty royal inscriptions. The dedication of his image was apparently repeated in subsequent reigns of the First Dynasty: the Palermo Stone records an occurrence in the penultimate regnal year of an unidentified First Dynasty king, and in year 8 of a subsequent First Dynasty ruler. The distinctive standard of Anubis appears on a sealing of Djer from Abydos (Petrie 1901: pl. XV.108), whilst a stone vessel fragment from the same king's tomb is incised with the figure of Anubis (Petrie 1902: pl. IV.8). From the end of the First Dynasty, a jackal deity is depicted on a sealing from the tomb of Qaa (Petrie 1900: pl. XXIX.86), and a recumbent jackal appears on the stela of Sabef, an official buried in one of the tomb's subsidiary graves (Petrie 1900: pl. XXX; cf. Weill 1961, chapter 8). The figure of Anubis also appears on a private First Dynasty stela excavated by Amélineau in 1895 (Petrie 1900: pl. XXXII.17).

The *imi-wt* fetish, closely associated in later times with Anubis, occurs not infrequently on Early Dynastic sealings. One scholar has suggested that the fetish played an important role during formal appearances of the king in public, and that a new fetish would have been fashioned to commemorate significant royal events, especially the foundation or dedication of a temple (Logan 1990: 69). The hypothesis that the fetish was associated with ritual killings (Logan 1990: 69) is based upon a single piece of evidence, a wooden label of Aha from Abydos, and must remain unproven.

Anubis should not be confused with another jackal god, Wepwawet (perhaps the same as Sed).

Apis (Hap)

In later periods the Apis bull was identified with Ptah, but it is possible that Apis was originally a separate deity. According to later tradition, the cult of Apis was established by Menes (cf. Simpson 1957; Logan 1990: 64), although the earliest known reference to the Apis bull occurs somewhat later, in the reign of Den. His regnal year x+12 on the Palermo Stone is identified by the 'running of the Apis'. This festival also took place in year 2 of Semerkhet (preserved on the main Cairo fragment of the annals), in the reign of Qaa (recorded on two year labels from Abydos: Leclant and Clerc 1992: pl. XXVIII, fig. 35; Dreyer *et al.* 1996: 75) and in years x+4 and x+10 of the Second Dynasty king, Ninetjer.

An ebony label of Aha from Abydos which records a royal visit to the Delta also depicts, in the second register, a bull within an enclosure (Petrie 1901: pl. IIIA.5). The bull is not named, and it may be the Apis bull, but a connection with a bull cult at Buto (von der Way 1989: 285) is perhaps more plausible, given the nearby location of the other shrines shown on the label.

Ash

Probably a protector deity connected with royal estates, Ash appears to have been particularly important at the end of the Second Dynasty (for example, Petrie 1901: pl. XXII.179). Ash is depicted on a number of sealings from the reigns of Peribsen and Khasekhemwy. On sealings of Peribsen and Sekhemib the god may be shown wearing the white crown, and is sometimes depicted with the head of the Seth-animal, suggesting that there may have been a connection – perhaps an early example of **syncretism** – between the two gods.

Bastet

Closely associated in later times with the site of Bubastis in the Delta (ancient Egyptian *B3st*), the cat goddess Bastet may none the less have had a separate origin, since her name is written from the earliest times with the ointment jar (which also had the sound value *b3st* in ancient Egyptian). The name Bastet may therefore mean 'she of the ointment jar' rather than 'she of Bubastis' (Shaw and Nicholson 1995: 50). Bastet assumed a degree of prominence in the early Second Dynasty, though for what reason remains unclear. The figure of the goddess appears on inscribed stone vessels of both Hetepsekhemwy and Nebra (Lacau and Lauer 1959: pl. 11, nos 57, 58). An inscription from the following reign of Ninetjer names the phyle of priests responsible for the provisioning of Bastet (in other words, for maintaining her cult): *s3 df3w B3stt* (Lacau and Lauer 1959: pl. 13, nos 63–6). At the end of the Second Dynasty, a priest of Bastet (and servant of Sobek) is mentioned on an incised stone vessel from the tomb of Khasekhemwy (Amélineau 1902: pl. XXII.1). In Utterance 508 (§1111) of the Pyramid Texts, Bastet appears as the king's mother, but we cannot be sure if she was identified as such in the Early Dynastic period.

Bat/Hathor

Bat is a rather obscure goddess whose cult centre seems to have been in the seventh Upper Egyptian nome, near the town of Hu. A Predynastic palette from Girza shows a celestial cow goddess, her head surrounded by stars. This object indicates that the worship of a female protective deity with astral connotations, perhaps already identified as Bat, was a feature of Egyptian religion from at least the middle of the fourth millennium BC (Hornung 1983: 103). A very similar representation may be seen on the rim of a diorite bowl from Hierakonpolis, dated to the late Predynastic period or early First Dynasty (Burgess and Arkell 1958; Fischer 1962). The best-known representations of Bat occur on the Narmer Palette (cf.

Baines 1991: 104). A celestial goddess with a human face and the ears and horns of a cow appears both at the top of the palette and on the king's belt. (At least one author identifies the goddess on Narmer's belt as Hathor, based upon Utterance 335 (§546) in the Pyramid Texts which states that 'the "apron" of the king comes from Hathor' [Troy 1986: 54].) Another Early Dynastic representation of Bat occurs on a limestone model of a carrying shrine, from a deposit of early votive objects. The figure of Bat is recessed within the front of the shrine (Schlögl 1978: 27, pls 81.a–c). A gold amulet from the Early Dynastic cemetery at Naga ed-Deir (grave N 1532) shows a bull with the Bat-fetish and an *ankh* pendant hanging from its neck (Reisner 1908: pl. 6; Fischer 1962: 12). The Bat-fetish is also depicted on the ivory inlays of a box from Abu Rawash (Klasens 1958: 53–4, fig. 20(y), pl. 59; Fischer 1962: 13, n. 45), whilst an ivory from the tomb of Semerkhet at Abydos is decorated with two heads of Bat, very similar to those shown at the top of the Narmer Palette (Petrie 1900: pl. XXVII.71).

The name of Bat seems to be a feminine form of the word *b3*, 'soul'. In Utterance 506 (§1095) of the Pyramid Texts, the king identifies himself with 'Bat with her two faces'; the Texts also contain several references to the 'great wild cow' as the king's mother, for example Utterance 675 (§2003). The 'great wild cow' was later regarded as a manifestation of Hathor; and, indeed, there are strong connections between Bat and Hathor, even though they probably had separate origins. Both goddesses probably served a protective function (F.D. Friedman 1995: 3); Bat is sometimes described as a particular manifestation of Hathor; Hathor eventually supplanted Bat as the local deity of Hu; and the two goddesses share very similar iconography. These similarities have led to some confusion in the minds of modern scholars. Thus, the Bat-fetish, although sometimes accompanied, and hence identified, by its phonetic complement, is often referred to as the 'Hathor emblem', 'on the basis of the later and abundant evidence for its identification with that goddess' (Fischer 1962: 11). There is no explicit reference to Hathor before the Fourth Dynasty, although the temple of Hathor at Gebelein apparently received royal patronage at the end of the Second Dynasty. It seems likely that, in this area, Egyptian theology was characterised by 'a common substratum of ideas which lent the two goddesses a somewhat similar character' (Fischer 1962: 12).

Hathor's name ('house of Horus') 'proclaimed motherhood as her principal function' (Frankfort 1948: 171), so it is not surprising that the Egyptians portrayed her as a cow: there are parallels in other African, particularly Hamitic, cultures in which the cow is a powerful mother-image (Frankfort 1948: 173–4).

Deshret (the red crown)

A shrine or enclosure dedicated to the red crown is shown on a year label of Djer from Abydos (Amélineau 1904: pl. XV.19; Emery 1961: 59, fig. 20). The label seems to record a royal visit to the Delta, and a device in the top register probably indicates a sacred complex at Buto (see below). It is very likely that the shrine to the red crown – a symbol closely associated with Lower Egypt since the unification of the country – would have been located in the Delta. A connection between the red crown and Wadjet, the serpent goddess of Buto and tutelary goddess of Lower Egypt, is suggested by an ivory label of Djet from mastaba S3504 at Saqqara (Emery 1954: pl. XXXVb). In the writing of the 'Two Ladies', the usual serpent is replaced by a red crown (cf. Gardiner 1958). We may perhaps conclude that the shrine to the red crown of Lower Egypt was located within the temple of Wadjet at Buto.

Geb

The earth god Geb is shown in human form on a relief fragment from a limestone chapel of Netjerikhet from Heliopolis (now in Turin). It has been suggested that the original decoration showed all nine members of the Heliopolitan ennead, since the figure of Seth is also preserved (cf. Baines 1991: 96). However, it is also possible that the shrine was dedicated to the 'corporation' (*ḥt*), an earlier grouping of gods, referred to in the names of Semerkhet, Netjerikhet and Sekhemkhet; the corporation may have been superseded by the Heliopolitan ennead when solar theology rose to prominence towards the end of the Third Dynasty (Hornung 1983: 222). Originally, both groupings probably symbolised the gods in their 'indefinite plurality': in Egyptian writing, three represented the plural concept, three times three (making an ennead) a plural of pluralities (Hornung 1983: 222). As one of the Heliopolitan ennead and as an earth god from the time of creation, Geb features prominently in the Pyramid Texts (for example in the 'Cannibal Hymn' Utterances 273–4 [§§393–414]). The king himself is identified with Geb in Utterance 599 (§1645).

Harsaphes

The ram god Harsaphes (*Ḥri-š=f* in Egyptian) may have originated as a primitive fertility god (cf. B. Altenmüller 1977), but is better attested in historic times as the local god of Herakleopolis. The Palermo Stone records a visit by Den in his regnal year x+9 to Herakleopolis; in the same year the king also visited the temple of a ram deity, and it is tempting to identify this as the local god of Herakleopolis, Harsaphes. An inscribed stone vessel fragment of Den from his tomb at Abydos may refer to the same event: it shows an ornate sanctuary with a ram inside, and a shrine topped by a bucranium (Petrie 1901: pl. VII.8–9). A connection with the royal cult has been posited for Harsaphes, particularly given the Egyptian name for Herakleopolis, *Nn-nswt* (B. Altenmüller 1977).

Hedjet (the white crown)

A chapel of the white crown (or, less plausibly, an estate named after the white crown) is named on an inscribed stone vessel of Hetepsekhemwy from the Step Pyramid complex (Lacau and Lauer 1959: pl. 11, no. 55). An institution by the same name is mentioned on a vessel of Ninetjer (Lacau and Lauer 1959: pl. 16, no. 78), suggesting a special reverence towards the white crown by the kings of the early Second Dynasty. One possible interpretation is that homage to Upper Egypt and its iconography may have been stressed following the relocation of the royal necropolis to Saqqara at the beginning of the Second Dynasty, and the concomitant loosening of ties between the kingship and Upper Egypt. It has been suggested that the inscriptions of Hetepsekhemwy and Ninetjer refer to shrines set up at the Residence in Memphis (R. Friedman 1994: 422, quoting Kaplony 1963). In origin, the white crown may have been particularly closely associated with the Predynastic rulers of Hierakonpolis. The local god of Hierakonpolis, Horus of Nekhen, was customarily depicted as an archaic falcon, often wearing the white crown (B. Adams 1977).

Hedjwer

The baboon deity named *ḥd-wr*, 'the Great White', is first attested unequivocally on an ivory label of Semerkhet from Abydos (Petrie 1900: pl. XII.1 = pl. XVII.26). However, a baboon statue from the reign of Narmer (E. Schott 1969) may represent the same deity, as may the figure of an enthroned baboon shown before a statue of Den on a seal-impression from Saqqara (Kaplony 1963, III: fig. 211; F.D. Friedman 1995: 33, fig. 19c). One scholar has suggested that the royal ancestors – in whose presence the king took possession of the symbols of rule at the beginning of his reign and again at the beginning of the Sed-festival – were manifest as a white baboon (Helck 1952: 75, 1972: 97; cf. Kemp 1989: 60, fig. 20). The middle relief panel of Netjerikhet from beneath his Step Pyramid shows the king standing at the *(ʿḥ-)ḥd wrw*, 'the white shrine of the great ones' (an alternative reading is *wrw ʿḥ-ḥd*, 'the great ones of the white shrine') (F.D. Friedman 1995: 24). The *wrw*, 'great ones', are determined by the figure of a large, squatting baboon. If Helck's interpretation is correct, 'the plurality of ancestors denoted by the baboon may be handing over rulership to Djoser, as signified by the testament he holds' (F.D. Friedman 1995: 26).

It is possible that the baboons of glazed composition and stone, frequently deposited as votive offerings in early shrines, were connected with Hedjwer, although other baboon deities are known to have existed. References to a baboon deity, sometimes explicitly identified as Hedjwer, are common in the Early Dynastic period and Pyramid Texts, but are rare in subsequent periods (Kaplony 1977).

Heqet

The frog goddess Heqet was associated with fertility and childbirth. This connection probably derived from the myriad tadpoles which a frog produces, a fact which also led to the tadpole being used as the hieroglyph for one-hundred-thousand. Heqet is mentioned only once in the Pyramid Texts, but her cult seems to have been popular in the Early Dynastic period (Cooney and Simpson 1976: 205–7). Two high-status individuals (including a royal prince) buried at Helwan in the Second Dynasty bore theophorous names compounded with Heqet, indicating that her cult was active at the time (Saad 1957: 7–10, pls III, IV [nos 2, 3]). The Early Dynastic stela of Wepemnofret (now at Berkeley) also mentions Heqet. A large travertine statuette of a frog in the Cleveland Museum of Arts (CMA 76.5) may be an early cult image of Heqet (Cooney and Simpson 1976). One of only a few surviving examples of large-scale stone animal sculpture from the late Predynastic and Early Dynastic periods, it has been tentatively dated to the reign of Narmer, largely on the basis of stylistic parallels with the baboon statue in Berlin. Although acquired on the art market and unprovenanced, the frog statuette may have come from Abydos where there seems to have been a particular emphasis on the cult of Heqet: small frog figurines were found in the votive deposits underneath the Abydos temple (Petrie 1903: pls X.214, 227, XI.240, 245; cf. Dreyer 1986: pls 32.170–2, 61.d, i, 62.i), and the goddess Heqet is shown in her shrine in the temple of Seti I (Cooney and Simpson 1976: 207, fig. 12).

Horus

Perhaps originally a sky god, Horus became the deity most intimately associated with the kingship from the late Predynastic period onwards (cf. Hayes 1953: 29, fig. 22; Williams 1986: pls 33, 34). It is difficult to be sure exactly how the Egyptians envisaged the relationship between Horus and the king (Hornung 1983: 192), but the adoption of Horus as the supreme royal title suggests that the Egyptians 'found in the soaring falcon their perfect metaphor for majesty' (Quirke 1992: 21).

Falcon deities were worshipped at several sites in Egypt. Whilst they are usually regarded as local gods of independent origin, it is equally possible that 'they were predynastic differentiations of one and the same deity', regarded as the supreme god by Egyptians in general (Frankfort 1948: 39–40). Perhaps the most important cult centre of Horus in Early Dynastic times was Hierakonpolis. Even in later dynastic times the cult image of the local god, Horus of Nekhen, was depicted as an archaic falcon, apparently emphasising the antiquity of the Horus cult at the site. The association of Horus with the kingship may reflect the importance of Hierakonpolis as a centre of Predynastic political power.

A distinctive form of Horus attested by name from the early Third Dynasty is *Ḥr-Bḥdti*, 'Horus the Behdetite'. The northernmost relief panel under the Step Pyramid shows the king, wearing the white crown, 'standing in the Upper Egyptian shrine of Horus the Behdetite' (Kemp 1989: 58, fig. 19; F.D. Friedman 1995: 18). The corresponding panel from the South Tomb gives this same name to the falcon hovering over the king and holding an *ankh* (F.D. Friedman 1995: 20). In origin, the word *bḥdt* means 'throne seat', and *bḥdti* may mean 'he of the throne seat' (Otto 1975; F.D. Friedman 1995: 18). Hence, there may have been a special connection between Horus the Behdetite and kingship. Although Behdet was later identified with Tell el-Balamun in the northern Delta (Gardiner 1944) or with Edfu in southern Upper Egypt, 'in Djoser's day the Behdetite may not have been associated with a fixed locality, possibly being understood more generally as a protective power of the king' (F.D. Friedman 1995: 20; cf. Kemp 1989: 41).

The middle relief panel from the South Tomb mentions another distinct form of Horus: *Ḥr Ḫm*, 'Horus of Letopolis'. It is significant that this panel is the only one on which the king wears the red crown, and the accompanying inscription uses the archetypal Lower Egyptian shrine as the determinative for the cult-place of Horus of Letopolis. The god 'had important royal associations in the early Old Kingdom' (F.D. Friedman 1995: 36), various aspects of his insignia being depicted on the funerary furniture of Queen Hetep-heres.

Iat/Iamet

On the Palermo Stone, the fifth regnal year of an unidentified First Dynasty king is denoted by the fashioning or dedication of a divine image of Iamet. Iat/Iamet (the reading of the name is uncertain) is also mentioned in the Pyramid Texts, and she was possibly a milk goddess, responsible for nourishing and nursing the king (Helck 1980).

Isis (?)

The *tyet*-girdle associated with Isis is attested as early as the First Dynasty. An amulet of this shape made of glazed composition was found in an Early Dynastic tomb at Helwan. However, unambiguous references to Isis by name do not appear until the Fifth Dynasty (in the Pyramid Texts of Unas). The throne-sign used to write the name of Isis occurs on a sealing of Peribsen (Petrie 1901: pl. XXI.176), but it is unclear whether the goddess herself is meant. An Early Dynastic rock-cut inscription on Hill B near Buhen may mention Isis (H.S. Smith 1972: 59–60).

Khentiamentiu

The god of the Abydos necropolis, 'the Foremost of the Westerners', is named on the necropolis seals of Den (Dreyer 1987) and Qaa (Dreyer *et al.* 1996: 72, fig. 25). It is likely that the first temple at Abydos, founded in the late Predynastic period, was dedicated to Khentiamentiu (perhaps already an epithet used as a euphemism for Osiris). The temple retained this dedication throughout the Old Kingdom (a stela set up in the temple refers to statues of Pepi II 'in the temple of Khentiamentiu' [O'Connor 1992: 89]), only becoming a cult centre dedicated explicitly to Osiris in the First Intermediate Period.

Khnum

A ram deity, possibly Khnum, is one of the elements composing a personal name on a private stela from Abydos dating to the reign of Djer (Petrie 1901: pl. XXVI.62) and one from the following reign of Djet (Petrie 1902: pl. XIII.151). Another theophorous personal name, read as Khnum-hotep, occurs on a sealing from the tomb of Merneith (Petrie 1900: pl. XXIII.42). Numerous inscribed stone vessels from the galleries beneath the Step Pyramid bear the personal name Iy-en-khnum (Lacau and Lauer 1965: 3–8, pls 2–9 [nos 2–8]) and this individual probably lived during the reign of Ninetjer (Kahl 1994: 880; Faltings and Köhler 1996: 100, n. 52). An even closer devotion to the god is expressed in the personal name *Hnmw-it(=i)*, 'Khnum is (my) father', inscribed on another stone vessel from the Step Pyramid hoard (Lacau and Lauer 1965: 49, pl. 29.3 [no. 95]). An incomplete First Dynasty plaque of glazed composition from the early temple at Abydos shows a ram holding a *was*-sceptre. The figure is accompanied by a complex jumble of hieroglyphs, the interpretation of which is difficult, but the ram may be Khnum (Petrie 1903: pls I, V.36).

Mafdet

A stone vessel fragment from the tomb of Den at Abydos shows the fetish of the feline goddess Mafdet (Petrie 1901: pl. VII.7). Possibly from the same reign, another inscribed stone vessel shows Mafdet as a lioness, though clearly identified by name; the left-hand fragment was found in the tomb of Den at Abydos (Petrie 1901: pl. VII.10), but the right-hand fragment was found in the neighbouring tomb of Semerkhet (Petrie 1900: pl. VII.4). (For the two fragments joined see O'Connor 1987: 35, fig. 14.) A fragmentary sealing from the tomb of Den also shows the fetish of Mafdet (Petrie 1900: pl. XXXII.39). The importance of the goddess in the reign of Den is emphasised by an entry for this king on the Palermo Stone: one of the eponymous events of Den's year x+13 is the fashioning or dedication of a divine image of Mafdet (see Figure 8.6 for all these illustrations). Since an image of Seshat was dedicated in the same year, there may have been a connection between the two goddesses, though this is by no means certain.

In the Pyramid Texts, Mafdet is referred to as a killer of snakes (Utterance 295 [§438]) (Gardiner 1938: 89), and more particularly as the

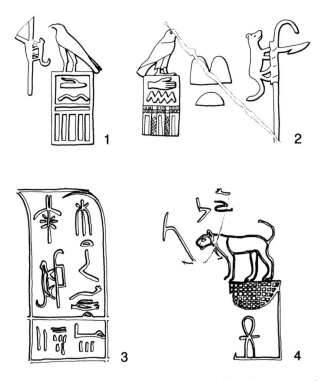

Figure 8.6 The goddess Mafdet. Represented as a feline, Mafdet may have acted as guardian of the king in the palace. Her cult appears to have enjoyed particular prominence during the reign of Den: (1) seal-impression of Den from Abydos, showing the fetish of Mafdet (after Petrie 1900: pl. XXXII.39); (2) relief inscription on a stone vessel from the tomb of Den at Abydos, showing the fetish of the goddess Mafdet (after Petrie 1901: pl. VII.7); (3) entry from the third register of the Palermo Stone, referring to a year in the reign of Den as 'the year of dedicating an image of Mafdet' (after Schäfer 1902: pl. I); (4) inscription depicting and naming Mafdet, on a stone vessel from Abydos, dating to the reign of Den (after Petrie 1900: pl. VII.4; Petrie 1901: pl. VII.10). Not to same scale.

protectress and avenger of the king (Utterance 297 [§440–1]). The points of the harpoon with which the king decapitates his adversaries are likened to 'the claws of Mafdet' (Utterance 519 [§1212]). Mafdet may have held a special place in the sphere of kingship during the Early Dynastic period, perhaps responsible for the purely physical well-being of the king (Westendorf 1966: 131–5). As *nbt ḥwt 'nḫ*, 'mistress of the estate (or mansion) of life', Mafdet may have been considered as the protecting power of the royal court. In the Early Dynastic period the 'Estate of Life' may have designated the living-quarters of the royal palace (Gardiner 1938: 89), or perhaps more specifically 'the royal eating and food storage areas', and Mafdet may have been embodied in the cats which probably protected these facilities against snakes and vermin (O'Connor 1987: 35). Another suggestion is that Mafdet was originally a tamed big cat (possibly a leopard used for hunting) who escorted the ruler, protecting him and at the same time symbolising his silent power and strength (Westendorf 1966: 131–5). The fetish of Mafdet shows execution equipment, and the goddess is thus regarded as a manifestation of judicial authority (Lurker 1980: 79). The connection may be that, as the deity symbolic of royal power, she led rebels to their execution.

Mehit

A deity associated with Hierakonpolis and (primarily) This (Emery 1961: 125), Mehit is depicted as a recumbent lioness with three bent poles projecting from her back. Mehit occurs on a number of Early Dynastic sealings (for example, Petrie 1901: pl. XVI.116), always preceding a depiction of the archetypal Upper Egyptian shrine, the *pr-wr*. Mehit may have been a general protector deity, associated with holy places. It is quite possible that, like Horus the Behdetite, the lioness goddess later identified as Mehit was not, at first, attached to a particular locality.

Min

The colossal statues of a fertility god found in the temple at Coptos indicate that the cult of the deity later named as Min was important from Predynastic times (Payne 1993; cf. Kemp 1989: 81, fig. 28; Dreyer 1995b). Although in origin a local deity of Coptos (which always remained the god's principal cult centre), Min probably enjoyed a national significance from an early period. The tradition in the Late Period that Min ruled Egypt at the beginning of history – a myth which linked Min with the first 'historic' King Menes – may preserve echoes of the god's importance during the period of state formation (Hornung 1983: 108). The 'thunderbolt' symbol of Min, also attested from the Predynastic period, occurs on the Scorpion macehead, on a divine standard. Two such symbols are depicted flanking the head of Bat on a decorated ivory plaque from Early Dynastic Cemetery 300 at Abu Rawash (Klasens 1958: 50, fig. 20(y), 53, pl. XXV). The symbol is also shown on a private stela from the reign of Djer (Petrie 1901: pl. XXVI.68) and on a sealing from the tomb of Merneith at Abydos (Petrie 1901: pl. XVII.135). It has been suggested that, like other prominent deities, Min may originally have been a god associated with the celestial realm, in this case the phenomenon of thunder (Wainwright 1941: 30). The Palermo Stone records the fashioning or dedication of an image of Min as the eponymous event of year 7 of an unidentified First Dynasty king. An identical entry is given for year 6 of Semerkhet (on the main Cairo fragment), and for year 3 of an unidentified Third Dynasty king. A fragment of a slate bowl from the tomb of Khasekhemwy is inscribed in ink with the figure of Min (Petrie 1902: pl. III.48). Identical inscriptions were found in the galleries beneath the Step Pyramid, indicating that both sets of funerary provisions were drawn from the same source (Lacau and Lauer 1965: pl. 15.1–5). The full text gives the legend *pr Mnw*, 'estate of Min', showing that the cult of Min was flourishing and in receipt of royal patronage at the end of the Second Dynasty.

Neith

Neith was a warlike goddess whose name perhaps means 'the terrifying one'. Her symbol, the crossed arrows, occurs as early as the Predynastic period, and Neith was clearly an important deity at the very beginning of the Early Dynastic period, with a 'dominant role at the royal court' (Hornung 1983: 71). 'Neith' is thus a common element in the theophorous names of Early Dynastic queens (cf. Weill 1961, chapter 13), notably Neith-hotep (the wife of Narmer), Herneith (possibly a wife of Djet) and Merneith (the mother of Den and regent during his minority). Personal names incorporating the name of Neith are also common amongst the retainers buried in the subsidiary graves surrounding the royal tombs at Abydos from the reign of Djer (Petrie 1900: pl. XXXI.9 [tomb Z], 10 [tomb W51], 11 [tomb W58], 20 [tomb T], pl. XXII.14). A label of Aha seems to record a royal visit to the shrine of Neith. This was probably located at Saïs in the north-western Delta, the principal cult centre of Neith in historic times (Petrie 1901: pl. IIIA.5). (The inscription of Wadj-hor-resne, recording the restoration of the temple of Neith at Saïs during the Persian period, speaks of the antiquity of the temple and its cult [Lichtheim 1980: 36–41].) One of Merka's numerous titles was *ḥm-nṯr Nt*, 'priest of Neith'. The reverence shown to the cult of Neith by the early kings of Egypt and their wives may reflect the importance of the Delta, and of Saïs in particular, in the process of state formation.

Neith clearly remained important during the Second Dynasty. An inscribed stone bowl from the Step Pyramid complex shows the figure of the goddess in front of the *serekh* of Ninetjer, with an estate of Nebra also named (Lacau and Lauer 1959: 14, pl. 16 no. 77). A Second Dynasty princess bore the name Neith-hotep (Lacau and Lauer 1959: pl. 21, no. 112), while a phyle (or more likely, perhaps, its head priest) was called *ḥm Nt*, 'servant of Neith' (Lacau and Lauer 1959: 17, pl. 21 no. 116).

Nekhbet

The name Nekhbet simply means 'she of Elkab', and the main cult centre of the goddess was located at this site in southern Upper Egypt. However, from the very beginning of Egyptian history, Nekhbet assumed an additional, national importance as tutelary goddess of the whole of Upper Egypt. Depicted as a vulture, Nekhbet joined the cobra goddess of Buto, Wadjet, to form the 'Two Ladies', divine protectresses of the Two Lands. The balance of opposites which Nekhbet and Wadjet embodied led to the inclusion of the 'Two Ladies' in the formal titulary of the king, from at least the reign of Semerkhet. The earliest surviving depiction of the 'Two Ladies' occurs somewhat earlier, on the celebrated ebony label from the tomb of Neith-hotep at Naqada, dating to the reign of Aha. Rock-cut inscriptions of Qaa near Elkab also show the figure of Nekhbet, and there is a reference to the goddess on the Palermo Stone in regnal year x+14 of Ninetjer. The incorporation of various important local deities (such as Nekhbet, Wadjet and Seth) into early royal titulary and iconography seems to have been one of the means by which the unity of the new state was promoted on a psychological level. It thus forms a key component of the mechanisms of rule developed by Egypt's Early Dynastic rulers.

Osiris (?)

Although the god Osiris is not attested by name until the Fifth Dynasty Pyramid Texts, the probable antiquity of many of these texts makes it not unlikely that he was recognised at an earlier period, perhaps under the name Khentiamentiu. A central element of the later Osiris myth, the pairing of Horus and Seth, is attested from the middle of the First Dynasty, 'antedating the first attestations of Osiris by six centuries or more' (Quirke 1992: 61). It may be significant that two ivory objects in the form of the *djed*-**pillar**, later one of the emblems associated with Osiris, were found amongst the grave goods in a First Dynasty tomb at Helwan (Saad 1947: 27, pl. XIV.b).

Ptah

Later revered as the god of craftsmen, Ptah was always closely associated with the royal capital, Memphis. Manetho records that Menes, the legendary first king of Egypt, built a temple to Ptah at Memphis, but it is possible that a local cult of Ptah existed in the area before the beginning of the First Dynasty. The first definite attestation of Ptah is on a travertine bowl from tomb 231 at Tarkhan, dated to the middle of the First Dynasty, possibly the reign of Den (Petrie *et al.* 1913: 12, 22, pls III.1, XXXVII). The figure of the god in his shrine is accompanied by the name 'Ptah', making the identification certain. A sculptor named Peh-en-Ptah is mentioned on a stone vessel from the tomb of Peribsen at Abydos (Amélineau 1905: pl. L.2) and on several similar vessels from the Step Pyramid complex at Saqqara (Lacau and Lauer 1959: pl. 25, nos 140–5).

Ra (?)

An ivory comb of Djet from Abydos shows a pair of outstretched wings and above them a falcon in a bark. This is the first known representation of a deity travelling across the sky in a bark, a common image in later religious iconography (cf. Hornung 1983: 227). It may be assumed that the falcon represents a cosmic deity, and more specifically the sun god 'since the sun is the principal heavenly body that moves across the heavens' (Quirke 1992: 22). However, in the first two dynasties it is possible that the word *r*ᶜ was used to denote the sun as an object rather than the name of a deity. Hence, the name of the Second Dynasty king may be read as Nebra, 'Lord of the sun', rather than Raneb, 'Ra is (my) lord' (Quirke 1992: 22). Otherwise, the earliest depiction of the solar disc in a context where it may symbolise a deity is on a sealing of Peribsen from Abydos. Here, the sun disc appears above the Seth-animal, possibly suggesting an association between the two gods, perhaps even an early example of syncretism (Petrie 1901: pl. XXI.176).

A growing emphasis on Ra as the central deity associated with divine kingship is apparent during the Third Dynasty (cf. Quirke 1992: 62). Imhotep, legendary architect of the Step Pyramid complex and chancellor in the reign of Netjerikhet, bore the title *wr-m3(w)*, 'greatest of seers', held from the Old Kingdom onwards by the High Priest of Ra at Heliopolis. The construction of a decorated shrine at Heliopolis by Netjerikhet also suggests growing royal interest in the cult centre of Ra. The name of Hesira, a high official of the same reign, seems to indicate that the cult of Ra had already attained some prominence (Wood 1978: 15).

Satet (?)

Satet was worshipped from an early period as the local goddess of Elephantine. The early shrine on Elephantine, which dates back to the late Predynastic period, is assumed to have been dedicated to Satet from its foundation. This assumption is made on the basis of evidence from later periods, but cannot be proven. It may be significant that in Utterance 439 (§812) of the Pyramid Texts the king is identified with Satet.

Sed

The fashioning or dedication of a divine image of Sed is recorded on the Palermo Stone in regnal year x+11 of Den. The name of the god is determined by 'a wolf or wild dog on a divine standard with a protuberance at the foot (the *šdšd*-device) and a mace across the shaft' (Brovarski 1984a). Since the same standard is sometimes shown accompanying the king in representations of the Sed-festival, one author suggested a possible connection between the festival and the god (M.A. Murray 1904: 34). The same standard is also commonly identified with Wepwawet in later periods. Hence, it is possible that Sed and Wepwawet are the same god, Wepwawet being originally an epithet of Sed but later becoming the main name by which the deity was known (Brovarski 1984a).

Seshat

Seshat was the goddess associated with temple foundation ceremonies – in which record-keeping and measurement were important (Wainwright 1941) – and as such is attested several times in Early Dynastic sources. A temple foundation ceremony involving a priest of Seshat is recorded on the Palermo Stone for year x+7 of Den's reign. A granite block of Khasekhemwy from the temple area at Hierakonpolis shows the king 'stretching the cord', assisted by Seshat (Engelbach 1934). A similar scene appears on a relief block from the temple of Hathor at Gebelein, dated stylistically to the late Second or early Third Dynasty (W.S. Smith 1949: pl. 30). A fragment of a diorite cup from beneath the Step Pyramid gives a theophorous name which may be compounded with the goddess Seshat (Lacau and Lauer 1959: 17, pl. 21 no. 115).

Seth

The local god of Naqada, Seth was closely associated with the king from the period of state formation. The link between Horus and Seth in the person of the reigning king is made explicit in the title borne by First Dynasty queens, 'she who sees Horus-and-Seth' (Petrie 1901: pl. XXVII.129). The exotic and probably mythical Seth-animal is first attested on the Scorpion macehead, surmounting one of the divine standards from which lapwings hang. Here, it may symbolise either a provincial deity or an aspect of royal power. The Seth-animal may also be depicted, together with sheep, on a First Dynasty pottery vessel (Habachi 1939: 770; te Velde 1967: 15). Seth is named on a private stela from a subsidiary grave surrounding the tomb of Djer at Abydos (Petrie 1901: pl. XXVII.96); whilst a First Dynasty travertine bowl purchased in Qena bears a crudely incised inscription mentioning a festival of Seth (Fitzwilliam Museum E.3.1901).

For reasons which remain unclear, Seth attained particular prominence in the late Second Dynasty, temporarily replacing, then joining, Horus as the god atop the royal *serekh*. The importance of Seth in the reign of Peribsen is also reflected in a sealing of the king from Abydos (Petrie 1901: pl. XXII.190). This refers to a god named 'the golden one' or, perhaps more likely, 'he of Nubt (Naqada)', the usual epithet of Seth in historic times. Seth seems to have been adopted by Peribsen as his personal deity, and this close connection is emphasised in the wording of the inscription: 'He of Nubt has handed over (?) the Two Lands to his son, the dual king Peribsen'. The Horus Sekhemib-Perenmaat (perhaps the same king as the Seth Peribsen) also seems to have expressed a close connection with the god Seth. A stone vessel fragment in the British Museum (BM 52862) shows the lower part of the *serekh* of Sekhemib-Perenmaat and also the lower part of a divine figure (Spencer 1980: 42, pls 24, 26 [cat. 277]). The figure can probably be identified as Seth by a parallel fragment on which the figure of Seth is fully preserved and further identified by the accompanying label, 'he of Nubt' (Spencer 1980: 42, pl. 26 [cat. 278]). The entries for Peribsen's predecessor on the main Cairo fragment of the annals apparently included references to Seth, including an estate or temple of the god (hand copy by I.E.S. Edwards in the Library of the Faculty of Oriental Studies, Cambridge University). A late Second Dynasty inscribed stone slab from Helwan belonged to a royal priest called *Nfr-Stš*, 'Seth is beautiful' (Saad 1957: 51–3, pl. XXX [no. 25]). This is further evidence for the popularity of Seth at the time.

Shu (?)

The name of Shu, a sky deity and a member of the Heliopolitan ennead of gods, was restored by Sethe (W.S. Smith 1949: 133–4) from the fragments of a decorated shrine built by Netjerikhet at Heliopolis. Otherwise, Shu is not attested until the Pyramid Texts of the late Fifth Dynasty.

Sobek

The crocodile god Sobek was originally a water and fertility deity, and his principal early cult centre seems to have been in the Fayum (Brovarski 1984b). On a seal-impression from Tarkhan grave 414, dated to the reign of Narmer, a shrine topped by a bucranium is depicted together with crocodiles (Petrie *et al.* 1913: pl. II.4). A shrine of this form was later associated with the cult centre of Sobek at Medinet el-Fayum (ancient

Shedet/Krokodilopolis) and is used in the Pyramid Texts as a determinative for this locality (Brovarski 1984b). The proximity of Tarkhan to the Fayum tends to support the identification, although another crocodile god is later attested from the area of Akhmim (Fischer 1968: 4, n. 14); and a shrine surmounted by a bucranium is not peculiar to the Fayum (Brovarski 1984b: n. 7) since it also appears to denote a cult centre at Herakleopolis (Petrie 1901: pl. VII.8). Facing the shrine on the Tarkhan sealing is the figure of a crocodile on a divine perch with two projections issuing from its back. These may be ostrich feathers, a divine attribute in Early Dynastic times (Petrie *et al.* 1913: 22; cf. Petrie 1900: pls XXIX.86, XXX). A fragmentary sealing from subsidiary tomb W33 at Abydos, dating to the reign of Djet, shows several crocodiles, but they are not identified explicitly as representations of Sobek (Petrie 1900: pl. XXXII.40). An inscription on a stone vessel from the Step Pyramid complex refers to *ḥm Sbk*, 'servant of Sobek' (Lacau and Lauer 1959: 17, pl. 22 no. 117), and the same name or title occurs on an incised stone vessel from the tomb of Khasekhemwy (Amélineau 1902: pl. XXII.1). A sealing from the Shunet ez-Zebib also mentions Sobek, though the context is unclear (Newberry 1909: pls XXV, XVIII).

Sokar (?)

Perhaps originally an earth and fertility god, Sokar became a mortuary deity because his cult centre was near the Memphite necropolis (Lurker 1980: 113). It is possible that his festival was already celebrated during the First Dynasty, since several sources record a ritual involving a divine bark (see below, under 'Religious festivals').

Sopdu

In later periods, Sopdu bears the epithet 'lord of the east', and it has been suggested that his cult originated in the Sinai (Godron 1990: 163). The festival of Sopdu is recorded in year 7 of Semerkhet, on the main Cairo fragment of the annals. An inscribed stone bowl from Helwan, bearing the *serekh* of the same king, names Sopdu (Saad 1969: pl. 32). The god is also attested in the early Second Dynasty: a sealing from the tomb of Hetepsekhemwy at Saqqara names a priest (*iri-ḫt*) of Sopdu, Per-neb. The inscription also mentions the unidentified town of Iput, likely to be a cult centre of Sopdu, probably in the eastern Delta (Maspero 1902: 189, type no. 5). Stone vase inscriptions from beneath the step pyramid likewise mention Iput, in conjunction with another priest (*ḥm-nṯr*) called Per-en-ka (Lacau and Lauer 1959: 18, pl. 22 nos 121, 122). A third priest of Sopdu is mentioned in a more-or-less contemporary, fragmentary inscription found by Amélineau at Abydos (Weill 1908: 196, no. 2; cf. Giveon 1984:

1107). A plumed figure depicted on a wooden label of Den has been identified as Sopdu (Godron 1990: 58), though this interpretation has not
received general acceptance.

Thoth

The fashioning or dedication of a cult image of an ibis deity – perhaps,
though not necessarily, Thoth – is an event attested in three consecutive
reigns of the First Dynasty. Year x+3 of the reign of Djer, on the Cairo
fragment of the annals, records the dedication of such an image, as does a
label of the succeeding king, Djet, from Saqqara (Emery 1954: fig. 105). A
fragmentary label of Den from Abydos (Petrie 1900: pl. XIV.12) also seems
to record the dedication of an ibis statue. The existence in Predynastic times
of an ibis cult is confirmed by the depiction of an ibis standard on at least
two late Predynastic palettes (Kaiser 1959: 122–5). Thoth certainly plays a
significant role in the Pyramid Texts (for example, Utterance 210
[§§126–130]), not least as scribe of the gods.

Wadjet

The Lower Egyptian counterpart to Nekhbet was Wadjet, a cobra goddess
whose principal cult centre was at Buto. Utterance 601 (§1671) of the
Pyramid Texts associates Wadjet more precisely with Dep, one of the twin
cities which comprised ancient Buto. As we have seen, the earliest depiction of the 'Two Ladies' is on the ebony label of Aha from Naqada.
A sealing of Khasekhemwy from Abydos depicts a female figure holding
an *ankh* in one hand and a large *w3ḏ*-sign in the other; she has been
identified as an anthropomorphic representation of Wadjet (Petrie 1901:
pl. XXIII.192).

Wepwawet

The jackal deity Wepwawet was, in later periods, the local god of Asyut,
but probably played a more general role in Early Dynastic religion. In
contrast to Anubis and Khentiamentiu who are usually depicted as recumbent jackals, Wepwawet is usually portrayed in a standing position (Logan
1990: 64). A jackal standard is a common element in Early Dynastic royal
iconography, where it is shown accompanying the king in religious rituals,
royal processions and military expeditions. Amongst other Early Dynastic
depictions of Wepwawet are sealings of Djer from Abydos (Petrie 1901:
pl. XV.108, 109), a sealing from the tomb of Merneith (Petrie 1901:
pl. XVII.135) and an ivory label of Den from Abydos (Spencer 1980: 65,
pls 49, 53, 1993: 87, fig. 67). A fragmentary sealing from the tomb of Den,
on which the king is depicted performing an unidentified ceremony, shows

what seems to be the standard of Wepwawet (Petrie 1900: pl. XXXII.39). The standing jackal may originally have been known as Sed, gaining the epithet Wepwawet, 'opener of the ways', in the Third Dynasty (F.D. Friedman 1995: 5, citing a seal-impression from Beit Khallaf [Garstang 1902: pl. VIII.1]). As the name indicates, Wepwawet 'opened the ways' before the king, not only those in life but also the ways to the necropolis (Johnson 1990: 53). Wepwawet was 'leader of the gods' and is sometimes shown accompanied by the warlike rearing cobra (Johnson 1990: 53). One scholar suggested that Wepwawet may have had a particular connection with the first-born son of the king (Frankfort 1948: 71), whilst in the Pyramid Texts, Wepwawet appears as a manifestation of the living king (F.D. Friedman 1995: 20).

Other unnamed cultic objects attested in the Early Dynastic period

HIPPOPOTAMUS

A sealing of Den from Abydos shows the king wrestling with a hippopotamus (Petrie 1901: pl. VII.5–6), and the ritual harpooning of a hippopotamus is recorded as the salient event of Den's regnal year x+8 on the Palermo Stone (cf. Millet 1990: 58). The apparent prominence of the hippopotamus in Den's reign is hard to explain, and there is no evidence that the later association between the hippopotamus and Seth was current in the Early Dynastic period. More plausibly, perhaps, the hippopotamus may have represented in more general terms the untamed and aggressive forces of nature which it was the king's duty, as upholder of the cosmic order, to control and suppress. A large limestone statue of a hippopotamus in Copenhagen (Ny Carlsberg Glyptothek) dates to the Early Dynastic period (Koefoed-Petersen 1951: 4, pl. 1). Its size and material suggest that it was a cult statue. A similar stone statue is in the Athens Museum (Cooney and Simpson 1976: 203). Both examples emphasise the early importance of hippopotamus cults. Several smaller hippopotamus figurines of glazed composition or pottery have been found in deposits of early votive objects (van Haarlem 1996: 34, pl. 2). The hippopotamus is likely to have been viewed with awe in early times because of the threat it posed to fishermen and people crossing the Nile. The dedication of hippopotamus figurines in provincial temples may have been acts of propitiation, designed to guard against such a threat.

PELICAN

One of the cult objects carried in procession on a label of Djer from Saqqara is clearly a pelican (Emery 1938: 35, fig. 8, pls 17.A, 18.A, 1961: 59, fig. 21). The references to pelicans in the Pyramid Texts may be significant in this regard, emphasising that the bird had a cultic symbolism in early times. No fewer than four separate Utterances (226, 293, 383, 387 [§§226, 435, 671, 680]) refer to 'the Majesty of the Pelican'. Utterance 254 (§278) mentions two different pelicans: 'The *hnt*-pelican will prophesy, the *psdt*-pelican will go up'. Utterance 318 (§511) states that 'The pelican is the king's mother', suggesting that there may have been a connection between the pelican and the royal cult.

ROYAL PLACENTA (?)

One of the divine standards which frequently accompany the king on early royal monuments apparently shows the (royal) placenta (Seligman and Murray 1911; Blackman 1916: 199; Rice 1990: 109–10, 271–2). Ethnographic parallels for the worship of the royal placenta have been cited amongst the Baganda people of Uganda; the élite of this tribe are Hamitic in origin, and therefore supposedly share elements of a common Hamitic belief-system with the ancient Egyptians (Seligman and Murray 1911; Blackman 1916).

SCORPION

The frequent occurrence of the scorpion motif in royal contexts of the late Predynastic period (notably a rock-cut inscription at Gebel Sheikh Suleiman) makes it likely that the animal held a special cultic significance for Egypt's rulers during the period of state formation. It may have been a potent symbol of royal aggression. The relief decoration of a stone vase from the temple at Hierakonpolis includes scorpions, whilst model scorpions of glazed composition and stone have been found in a number of early votive deposits, notably Hierakonpolis itself (Quibell 1900: pls XVIII.15, 16, XX.10, XXII.4). On the northernmost relief panel beneath the Step Pyramid, a scorpion is depicted behind the king, presumably in a protective position. The attributes of the scorpion defy explanation, particularly the cylinder seals with which it appears to be equipped (F.D. Friedman 1995: 19 fig. 12, 21, n. 107, cf. 38 fig. 23). The scorpion standing on a ring depicted on the stela of Merka – from tomb S3505 at North Saqqara, dating to the reign of Qaa (Emery 1958: pl. 39) – has been interpreted as the earliest attestation of the scorpion goddess Selket/Serket (von Känel 1984; followed by Shaw and Nicholson 1995: 262). However, given the similarities between the Merka scorpion and examples on the Netjerikhet relief panels, the identification of the First Dynasty scorpion as an unnamed cultic object seems more plausible, especially as Selket is not attested by name until the Pyramid Texts of the late Fifth Dynasty.

URAEUS

The earliest representation of the royal uraeus adorning the brow of the king is on an ivory label of Den from Abydos showing the king smiting a foreign captive. The Wepwawet standard which accompanies the king also has a uraeus in front of the jackal deity (Johnson 1990: 40). (Note, however, that the authenticity of this label has been questioned [Johnson 1990: 6]. If it is not genuine, the earliest definite occurrence of the uraeus would be in the rock-cut scene of Netjerikhet in the Wadi Maghara, Sinai [Gardiner and Peet 1952: pl. I, 1955].)

Summary list of deities and cult objects attested in the Early Dynastic period

Anti, Anubis, Apis (Hap), Ash, Bastet, Bat/Hathor, Deshret (the red crown), Geb, Harsaphes, Hedjet (the white crown), Hedjwer, Heqet, Horus, Iat/Iamet, Isis (?), Khentiamentiu, Khnum, Mafdet, Mehit, Min, Neith, Nekhbet, Osiris (?), Ptah, Ra (?), Satet (?), Sed, Seshat, Seth, Shu (?), Sobek, Sokar (?), Sopdu, Thoth, Wadjet, Wepwawet, hippopotamus, pelican, royal placenta (?), scorpion, uraeus.

Religious festivals

The eponymous event chosen to identify a particular regnal year in the Early Dynastic royal annals was often a religious festival, suggesting both that such festivals were common at this period and that they were of great importance in the life of the court (cf. Emery 1961: 127). Apart from festivals of kingship, like the Sed-festival and coronation rituals, five other festivals are attested. Two of them are known from later periods, whilst the precise significance of the other three eludes us.

The running of the Apis bull

The running of the Apis bull took place at Memphis. The festival is recorded in regnal year x+12 of Den, year 2 of Semerkhet, and in two years (x+4 and x+10) of Ninetjer's reign. In addition, the running of the Apis is shown on a sealing of Den, and is recorded on two year labels of Qaa from Abydos. The event could evidently take place more than once in a reign, since the fourth register of the Palermo Stone records the second occasion of the running of the Apis.

ḏt

The Palermo Stone records this obscure festival as the principal event of Den's regnal year x+5. It was also celebrated in year x+14 of Ninetjer, and may perhaps have been connected in some way with the goddess Nekhbet, who is also mentioned for this year. The Djet festival seems to have been a recurrent event, since the second occasion of its celebration is recorded in the annals.

dw3-Ḥr-pt

'The adoration of the celestial Horus' is another obscure festival mentioned in the royal annals for year x+8 of the reign of Ninetjer.

The festival of Sokar (?)

A label of Qaa from Abydos records the third occasion of a festival involving a divine bark (Dreyer *et al.* 1996: 75), a celebration also attested on the Palermo Stone in year 5 of an unidentified First Dynasty king, year x+6 of Den, and years x+6 and x+12 of Ninetjer (see Figure 8.7). In later times, the most prominent festival involving a divine bark was that of Sokar, god of the Memphite necropolis. A stone, perhaps a cultic image of the deity, was 'dragged across the fields in a barque [sic] fixed to a sledge' (Lurker 1980: 113). A relief fragment from the Step Pyramid complex which shows the king pulling a bark may depict the same festival (Firth and Quibell 1935, II: pl. 109.1; W.S. Smith 1949: 137). The festival mentioned on the Palermo Stone was first read as the 'Festival of Sokar' by Schäfer (1902), and this interpretation has been widely accepted. However, the form of the bark shown on the Palermo Stone is not the characteristic Henu-bark associated with Sokar (Anthes 1957: 78). Rather, it belongs to a group of divine barks which includes the Maaty-bark and the *šms-Ḥr*-boat of the king. None the less, the Pyramid Texts make an explicit connection between Sokar and the Maaty-bark, so the festival recorded in the annals may indeed be a festival of Sokar (Gaballa and Kitchen 1969: 14). In the reign of Ninetjer, the Sokar festival seems to have been celebrated at regular intervals of six years (but note O'Mara 1996: 204). In subsequent dynasties, the festival may have become annual, since its celebration was no longer a distinctive enough event to be used for dating purposes (Gaballa and Kitchen 1969: 15–17).

The earliest depiction of a bark resembling the Henu-bark of Sokar appears on the Naqada label of Aha. However, the boat, shown in the first register, appears to sail on water, unlike the Sokar-bark which was drawn on a sledge. The device representing the king's name which appears behind the boat holds a hoe; this group of signs may record an agricultural rite, perhaps 'ancestral to (or related to) the later *ḥbs-t3* and performed by the king at a Sokar festival' (Gaballa and Kitchen 1969: 18).

dšr

Another festival in which a boat played a major role was the otherwise unknown *dšr*-festival (the name is followed by a boat determinative). This is recorded just once, in an entry on the Palermo Stone corresponding to the early First Dynasty. The frequent depiction of boats on contemporary labels emphasises the importance of boats and/or a riverine setting for Early Dynastic rituals. This is not surprising in a country where the river was the principal geographical feature, source of life, means of transport and artery of communication.

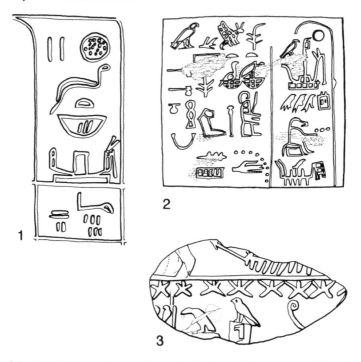

Figure 8.7 Festivals involving a divine bark. Several important religious festivals seem to have involved a sacred boat: (1) entry from the second register of the Palermo Stone, referring to a year in the early First Dynasty as 'the year of the second occasion of the Djet-festival'; the hieroglyphic determinative suggests that this festival involved a boat (after Schäfer 1902: pl. I); (2) ivory year label of Semerkhet from Abydos, referring to the regular royal progress by boat (the 'following of Horus') and another ritual denoted by a divine boat (bottom right-hand corner) (after Petrie 1900: pl. XVII.26); (3) a relief block from the Step Pyramid complex of Netjerikhet showing the king dragging a boat, perhaps during the Sokar festival (after Firth and Quibell 1935, II: pl. 109.1). Not to same scale.

SHRINES

Upper Egyptian and Lower Egyptian architectural styles

The earliest shrines must have been light-weight structures, built from wooden posts and reed matting. This became fossilised as the 'ideal type' for temple architecture, and as such was repeated in the more permanent medium of stone throughout Egyptian history until the very end of pharaonic civilisation (Kemp 1989: 91–105). An actual example of such a building has been excavated on the low desert at Hierakonpolis, the post-holes demarcating an irregular, oval-shaped enclosure (R. Friedman 1996). The temple seems to have been provided with flag-poles, confirming the accuracy of representations on early labels and seal-impressions (for example, Petrie 1901: pls IIIA.5, X.2). The latter typically show shrines of the 'Sarifenbau' type; that is, reed structures resembling those built by the Marsh Arabs of southern Iraq up to modern times (Petrie 1901: pl. XVI.114, 116, 117; Kuhlmann 1996). In Egyptian texts from the Third Dynasty onwards, a shrine of this form is used as the determinative for *pr-wr*, the ancestral and archetypal shrine of Upper Egypt (Arnold 1982). By contrast, the Lower Egyptian shrine, the *pr-nw* or *pr-nḏr*, is depicted as a more solid construction with a rounded or pitched roof. Examples of both types may be seen, translated into stone, lining the Sed-festival court of Netjerikhet's Step Pyramid complex. The origin of the two distinctive types of architecture is lost in the mists of time. The post-and-matting temple excavated at Hierakonpolis seems to prove the existence of shrines of classic Upper Egyptian type in Predynastic Upper Egypt, while the Narmer macehead and early First Dynasty labels depict shrines of the Lower Egyptian type in a probable Lower Egyptian context. So, the iconographic distinction between Upper and Lower Egyptian shrine types may have some basis in prehistory, rather than merely reflecting the Egyptian obsession with duality.

State versus local temples

The few Early Dynastic shrines and temples that have survived and been excavated seem to be distinguished as state or local shrines by their architecture and decoration (or lack of decoration).

Kemp (1989) has classified Egyptian temples according to the 'formality' of their architecture; that is, how far their design corresponds to the ideal of temple architecture propounded by the royal court. The local shrines at Elephantine and Medamud are described as 'pre-formal' and are characterised by their 'openness'. They may be compared with the iconographic evidence from early inscriptions which 'suggests that the barriers at the temple entrance were largely symbolic: only a small picket gate was shown in front of archaic temples' (Roth 1993: 39). As we have seen, an open plan may have suited the nature of early cultic activity, which seems to have put great emphasis on the carrying of divine standards and cult statues in procession. Only when provincial temples were rebuilt by the state at the end of the Old Kingdom did their architecture become 'formal', reflecting the stylistic dictates of the court.

O'Connor (1992) has put forward an alternative hypothesis; that is, that at least some Early Dynastic provincial temples were large and formal structures, the result of court initiatives. He argues that the chief Old Kingdom temple at sites such as Medamud, Elephantine, Hierakonpolis and Abydos has not yet been located and excavated; and that the temples at these sites discussed by Kemp, characterised as 'pre-formal', are minor, peripheral establishments (O'Connor 1992: 84, 89). However, this argument seems difficult to sustain, since extensive excavation on the island of Elephantine has markedly failed to produce any evidence for another temple of the Early Dynastic period or Old Kingdom besides the local shrine of Satet (Seidlmayer 1996b: 116–17). Here, then, and probably at other sites as well, 'the negative evidence for state sponsored temple construction ... is very real' (Seidlmayer 1996b: 118).

Temples in the provinces which show signs of state activity or royal involvement seem, on the whole, to be confined to sites connected with the emergence and ideology of kingship or sites with royal residences nearby (Seidlmayer 1996b: 116). Moreover, royal interest in selected provincial shrines seems to have been confined to the First and Second Dynasties (Seidlmayer 1996b: 118–19). In the Third Dynasty, there seems to have been almost no court involvement outside important state cult centres like Heliopolis (although it must be acknowledged that the Third Dynasty represents a relatively short period of time, and that our evidence for internal developments is sparse).

Together with the royal funerary establishments, state shrines in the provinces seem to have formed elements in a network of Early Dynastic court culture. They bound the provinces to the central administration both ideologically and economically, and in this respect may be seen as an early example of the administrative apparatus employed so effectively in Old Kingdom Egypt and New Kingdom Nubia. On the other hand, 'the rôle of the local cults as foci of personal loyalty and as an expression of the collective identity of the local communities must be regarded as a genuine element of Egyptian provincial culture' (Seidlmayer 1996b: 118).

Local temples and shrines seem to have been devoid of relief decoration. They were probably built entirely from mudbrick, the monumental use of stone apparently being a royal monopoly in the Early Dynastic period. By contrast, temples founded or 'usurped' by the state were either entirely stone built, or, more commonly, embellished with stone elements. These were carved with relief scenes depicting the rituals of kingship, especially temple foundation ceremonies and the Sed-festival. This essential difference between local and state temples has been summarised as follows:

> Evidently, state interests were pursued independently, without acknowledging the temples in their rôle as indigenous organisational and ideological nuclei of the local communities, and these shrines were not the places the kings chose to display their relationship to the local gods as a tenet basic to their ruling ideology. Consequently, it was felt unnecessary to adorn the provincial sanctuaries with carved and inscribed architectural elements which would have offered the possibility to express such a doctrine in visible and lasting form.
>
> (Seidlmayer 1996b: 119)

Temple building

An entry on the Palermo Stone for the reign of Den records the erection (‘ḥ‘) of an unspecified temple (ḥwt-nṯr), whilst a label of Qaa from Abydos (Dreyer *et al.* 1996: 75) is unique amongst year labels of the First Dynasty in that it mentions a building project: the foundation of a building called q3w-nṯrw. The annals suggest that the foundation of a new religious building usually comprised a more elaborate sequence of events. Three different ceremonies – perhaps stages in the process – are recorded on the Palermo Stone for the same temple swt-nṯrw, 'thrones of the gods', during the reign of Den. The first ceremony seems to have been designated by the word ḥ3, perhaps indicating the initial decision to found a new temple and perhaps the first planning phase (Erman and Grapow 1929: 8, definition 4). However, the main Cairo fragment of the royal annals seems to challenge this interpretation since it apparently records a *second* 'planning' of the *same* building smr-nṯrw in the one reign. The term ḥ3 may instead refer to a ritual circuit of the building, performed by the king (Gaballa and Kitchen 1969: 15; F.D. Friedman 1995: 14). The annals also record the crucial ceremony of pḏ-šs, 'stretching the cord', which is customarily shown in temple foundation scenes, such as the relief block from the Early Dynastic temple at Gebelein and the door-jamb of Khasekhemwy from Hierakonpolis. The stretching of the cord represented the formal laying out of the temple, and accompanied the sanctification of the land on which the temple was to be built. A subsequent phase, wpt-š, 'opening of the (sacred) lake', is recorded for the temple 'thrones of the gods'. For this building, the three ceremonies are recorded for consecutive years. This indicates, perhaps, that the temple was not a particularly large one, since the construction of a major building might be expected to have taken considerably longer. Apparently, it was not necessary to accomplish (or to record) all three ceremonies for every new temple. Early in the First Dynasty, only one ceremony (*ḥ3*) is mentioned for a temple called *smr-nṯrw*, 'companion of the gods', whilst in the early Third Dynasty the stretching of the cord seems to have been the initial ceremony in the foundation of the temple *qbḥ-nṯrw*, 'refreshment of the gods'.

Early Dynastic shrines

The evidence for early temples is both epigraphic and archaeological (Figure 8.8). Two distinct religious precincts at Buto, a complex with palm trees and the shrine of *Db'wt*, are well attested in Early Dynastic inscriptions – and throughout Egyptian history – but have not been located at the site itself. Excavations in the main temple area have not, so far, revealed any material older than the New Kingdom. Likewise, the important shrine of Neith at Saïs is known to have existed in the Early Dynastic period but still awaits discovery and excavation. Some early provincial shrines, like those at Tell Ibrahim Awad, Badari, Armant and Elephantine, do not merit a mention in the written record but are known through their surviving archaeological remains, which indicate very modest structures (Kemp 1995: 688). In the case of important cult centres such as Heliopolis, Abydos and Hierakonpolis, discoveries through excavation have confirmed the epigraphic evidence for the importance of these sites at an early period of Egyptian history.

Elephantine

'Elephantine is the only site in Egypt where, thanks to a lucky combination of circumstances, the development of a provincial sanctuary can be followed from protodynastic times onwards' (Seidlmayer 1996b: 115). The earliest shrine on the island of Elephantine has been uniquely preserved, thanks to its unusual location. It was situated in a natural niche between a group of large boulders, to the north of the early settlement. Successive rebuildings and enlargements required more space, and so filled in the site of the early shrine, building over the top of the boulders. The structure of the Early Dynastic temple and many of the votive objects deposited there survived (Dreyer 1986; Kemp 1989: 69–74).

The first structure to be built comprised two small mudbrick chambers, which appear to have been designed to protect and shield the sanctuary holding the cult image. This was presumably housed at the very back of

Figure 8.8 Early Dynastic shrines and temples. The map shows the sites at which Early Dynastic religious buildings are known to have existed, based upon archaeological and/or inscriptional evidence. Capitals denote ancient place names.

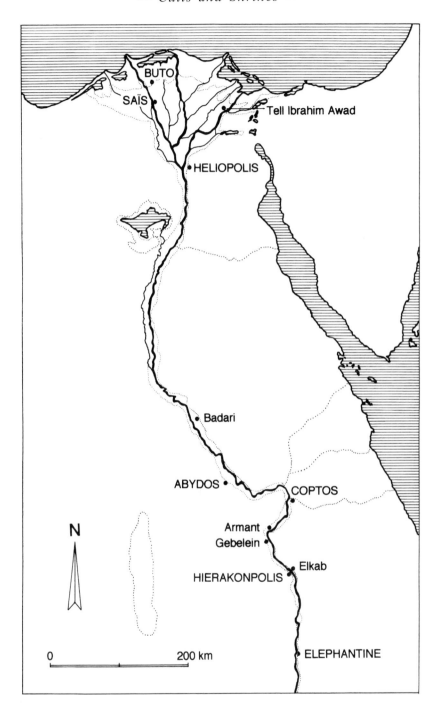

BUTO

SAÏS

Tell Ibrahim Awad

HELIOPOLIS

Badari

ABYDOS

COPTOS

Armant
Gebelein

Elkab

HIERAKONPOLIS

N

0   200 km

ELEPHANTINE

the niche, directly between two of the boulders. In front of these two small rooms, a courtyard, possibly roofed, was created by enclosing the space with further brick walls (Kemp 1989: 70, fig. 23). Although Pre-dynastic pottery was found within the shrine, the small mudbrick buildings which formed the earliest shrine seem to date to the Early Dynastic period (Kemp 1989: 69). During the first half of the First Dynasty, modifications to the adjacent fortress impinged directly upon the shrine, restricting the space in the forecourt. As a result, the entrance to the shrine had to be moved to the north. A subsequent strengthening of the fortified wall further reduced the area of the shrine forecourt. Indeed, the actions of the Early Dynastic state showed wilful disregard for local religious prac-tices, and the community shrine was entirely neglected by the court in favour of a royal cult installation on the southern part of the island (Seidlmayer 1996b: 115). Towards the end of the Second Dynasty, the expansion of the town led to the abandonment of the inner fortifications. This allowed the shrine to expand once again, regaining its former extent. Further expansion of the sacred enclosure took place during the Third Dynasty and early Old Kingdom (Kaiser *et al.* 1988: 135–82; Ziermann 1993).

A large collection of votive material was recovered from the floor of the shrine. Many of the pieces may be dated to the Early Dynastic period (Dreyer 1986: 59–153; Kemp 1989: 72, 73 fig. 24). Figurines of animals and humans in glazed composition form the most numerous group of objects. Animals represented include baboons, frogs and crocodiles. A particularly common type of votive offering consists of an oval-shaped faience plaque with the stylised head of a hedgehog at one end; 41 exam-ples of this strange object have been recovered from the shrine. None of the objects gives an indication of the deity worshipped in the shrine. In later times, the sanctuary is known to have been dedicated to Satet, local goddess of Elephantine, but it is possible that the Predynastic and Early Dynastic periods witnessed cultic practices of a more general nature. These may have focused in particular on the phenomenon of the annual inundation (Husson and Valbelle 1992: 94) since, according to later beliefs, the waters of the inundation were believed to well up from a subterranean cavern beneath Elephantine.

Elkab

The temple at Elkab, presumably dedicated to the local goddess Nekhbet, received royal patronage at the end of the Second Dynasty, in the form of a stone building erected by Khasekhemwy. A carved granite block bearing the king's name was found during excavations at the beginning of the twentieth century but was subsequently lost (Sayce and Clarke 1905: 239). Two additional fragments showing human figures in low relief were found at the same time, but their present whereabouts are also unknown. Further, uninscribed granite blocks still standing in the same spot, just inside the northern corner of the Great Wall, confirm the location of the building (Hendrickx and Huyge 1989: 13), in all probability a small shrine or temple.

The results of archaeological investigation in the main temple area indicate that a sacred building stood there from Early Dynastic times. On the site of the existing temple ruins, excavations failed to reveal any domestic settlement material later than the Early Dynastic period, suggesting that the site was demarcated as a sacred area prior to the Old Kingdom (Sayce and Clarke 1905: 262). Being on a slight elevation, the temple site would have been prominent above the surrounding area (Sayce and Clarke 1905: 262), and therefore ideally suited to a sacred role.

Hierakonpolis

The early twentieth-century excavators of Hierakonpolis found the remains of a circular mound in the centre of the large rectangular enclosure within the walled town of Nekhen (Quibell 1900: 6, pl. IV; Quibell and Green 1902: pl. LXXII). A revetment of rough sandstone blocks enclosed a mound of clean desert sand. This structure has been dated to the Early Dynastic period (Hoffman 1980: 131; Kemp 1989: 75) and probably served as the foundation for a temple, which, like its predecessor on the low desert plain, is likely to have been a reed-and-post shrine. The revetment itself probably symbolised the primeval mound, upon which, according to Egyptian mythology, the falcon Horus had first alighted. A pavement of compacted earth, reinforced by rough sandstone blocks in the areas of greatest wear, extended from the base of the mound on all sides, but especially to the south-east (Quibell and Green 1902: 7). There were also the remains of rough limestone column bases or pedestals for statues, the exact function of which is not clear (Quibell and Green 1902: 8; cf. B. Adams 1977). Excavations in 1969 confirmed that the stone revetment enclosing the mound of clean sand and the associated paved area date to the period of state formation. The remains of a door socket suggested that 'access to the platform had been controlled by a gate or door' (Hoffman 1980: 131). Two parallel wall trenches and three postholes indicated the existence of a building some 2 metres by 1.5 metres, either contemporary with the pavement or slightly earlier. It is tempting to identify the building as an early shrine made of posts and reed matting, perhaps even the *pr-wr*, the archetypal shrine of Upper Egypt (Hoffman 1980: 132).

The temple of Horus was the location of the famous 'Main Deposit', a collection of votive objects probably buried some time in the New Kingdom: not only did the deposit lie immediately beneath an early New

Kingdom temple, it even contained an Eighteenth Dynasty **scarab** and sherd (Kemp 1968: 155). This makes accurate dating of uninscribed objects from the 'Main Deposit' extremely difficult (cf. B. Adams 1977). The most important early objects, the commemorative palettes and maceheads, bear witness to the patronage bestowed on the cult of Horus by the first kings of Egypt. The fact that kings like 'Scorpion' and Narmer dedicated such important artefacts in the temple emphasises the pre-eminence of the local god, Horus of Nekhen, as the deity intimately associated with divine kingship. Long after Hierakonpolis had lost its status as a centre of political importance, the presence of a temple to the supreme god of kingship ensured continued royal patronage: a number of stone elements with the name of Khasekhem(wy) probably derive from a temple or shrine, perhaps situated on the circular mound. One block shows a temple foundation scene (Engelbach 1934). The construction of houses during the Second and Third Dynasties apparently encroached upon the earlier temple, 'leaving the mound rising above the new accumulation' (Quibell and Green 1902: 8).

Outside the rectangular enclosure, Green found a large limestone statue, much worn and damaged, but recognisably early in style and comparable to the colossi from Coptos (Quibell and Green 1902: 15). The statue is cylindrical in form and represents a man wearing a long, off-the-shoulder cloak. The figure's left arm is held horizontally across the chest, while the right arm, greatly elongated, hangs close to the side of the body. The right fist was perforated, perhaps to hold a mace or other object, as seems to have been the case with the Coptos colossi (Kemp 1989: 81, fig. 28). The figure was evidently shown in the characteristic semi-striding position typical of later representations, with the left leg slightly advanced. The knees are crudely indicated, again a feature found in the Coptos colossi. An identification of the statue has not been established, but the piece clearly indicates the importance of the temple at Hierakonpolis at the very beginning of Egyptian history.

In a radical reinterpretation of the early monumental architecture at Nekhen, the large rectangular enclosure has been dated to the First Dynasty by its architecture and comparisons with the funerary enclosures at Abydos (O'Connor 1992: 85). Despite stratigraphic evidence that the circular revetment supporting the temple mound pre-dates the enclosure wall by a considerable period of time, O'Connor prefers to see the two structures as roughly contemporary. He interprets the enclosure as a royal cult complex (cf. Roth 1993: 39) and the Early Dynastic palace gateway as the entrance to a second, adjacent enclosure. A mound of sand is reconstructed within this second, purely hypothetical enclosure, based upon traces of sand found during the course of very limited test excavations (O'Connor 1992: 87). Despite the lack of supporting evidence, O'Connor's arguments do emphasise two important points: the similarity in layout between the temple of

Hierakonpolis and a royal ritual precinct (Seidlmayer 1996b: 117), and the way in which royal interest in the temple of Horus at Nekhen at the end of the Second Dynasty changed the nature of the temple, and in all probability the nature of worship at Hierakonpolis. The construction of an enclosure wall around the early temple probably served to exclude persons of insufficient status. The Early Dynastic state embellished the shrine of the god of kingship with new stone buildings, but the price was restricted access. The temple-building activity attested for the reign of Khasekhemwy at Gebelein, Elkab and Hierakonpolis clearly indicates considerable royal interest in the provincial temples of Upper Egypt. This development may be connected with the beginning of the nome system of provincial administration, and perhaps reflects a programme to consolidate central government control of the national economy through the institution of local temples. Seal-impressions of the Second or Third Dynasty from the temple precinct at Elkab mention an 'inspector of the granary of Elkab' (van de Walle 1954) and illustrate the economic importance of local temples in the Early Dynastic period as storage centres for agricultural produce (Seidlmayer 1996b: 118). The fruits of increased state control of the economy can be seen in the reign of Khasekhemwy's successor: the construction of Netjerikhet's Step Pyramid complex represents an unprecedented marshalling of the country's resources, channelled into a project of the royal court.

On the low desert to the west of the town of Nekhen, the large ceremonial centre dating back to early Naqada II (R. Friedman 1996) apparently remained in use up to the beginning of the First Dynasty.

Gebelein

A limestone block with relief decoration from the temple of Hathor at Gebelein indicates the existence of an Early Dynastic shrine at the site (Curto 1953; Galassi 1955: 64–85). The block, now in Turin, was found during Schiaparelli's excavations in 1910 (Curto 1953: 105; Donadoni Roveri 1990: 24). An unprovenanced companion piece in the Cairo Museum has been attributed to the Gebelein temple, in view of the close similarity of the limestone as well as the style of the relief (W.S. Smith 1949: 137, pl. 30).

The temple of Hathor was situated on the northern edge of the southern hill at Gebelein (Donadoni Roveri 1990: 23, fig. 3.1). Unfortunately, Schiaparelli's excavations were very poorly documented, so further information about the early Hathor temple or the exact circumstances in which the decorated block was discovered is lacking (Donadoni Roveri 1990: 23–4).

The Gebelein reliefs undoubtedly date to the late Second or early Third Dynasty, although a more exact dating is difficult. Similarities to the Heliopolis reliefs from the reign of Netjerikhet suggest an early Third Dynasty date (W.S. Smith 1949: 137). However, the Turin block shows slight peculiarities in style, which may simply reflect its provincial origin or may indicate an earlier, Second Dynasty date (W.S. Smith 1949: 137–8; cf. Seidlmayer 1996b: 116). Both blocks apparently depict a temple foundation ceremony, perhaps the foundation of the Hathor temple itself. On the Turin block the striding figure of the king carries a bundle of four staves in his right hand. On the Cairo companion piece he is shown driving these stakes into the ground. The closest parallel for this subject matter is the granite block of Khasekhemwy from Hierakonpolis, suggesting that the Gebelein blocks, too, date from the late Second Dynasty. In common with the surviving fragments of relief decoration from Khasekhemwy's other buildings in Upper Egypt, the Gebelein block in Turin alludes to the festivals and ritual activities of divine kingship. A figure below the king wears a curious wig and holds the tail of the king's leopard-skin garment, details which are paralleled in Fifth Dynasty scenes of the Sed-festival (W.S. Smith 1949: 137). A boat associated with the ceremonial progress of the king, the *šms-Ḥr*, is also depicted.

The reason why a king of the late Second Dynasty should have founded or re-founded a temple at Gebelein remains something of a mystery. The site clearly supported a flourishing community in the late Predynastic period, but it does not seem to have played a particularly important part in the process of state formation, neither does it emerge as a major Early Dynastic centre. The temple at Gebelein was dedicated, at least in later times, to Hathor, one of the mythical divine ancestors of the king, and this connection with the royal cult has been suggested to account for court interest in the site (Seidlmayer 1996b: 116). However, as we have seen, Hathor – as distinct from Bat – is not directly attested until the Fourth Dynasty and, in any case, there were probably other early cult centres of Hathor besides Gebelein. Rather, Khasekhemwy's involvement at Gebelein seems to be part of a pattern of royal building at provincial shrines in southern Upper Egypt.

Armant

A temple foundation deposit dating to the threshold of the Early Dynastic period was discovered during excavations in the west forecourt of the later temple at Armant (McEuen and Myers 1940: 29). The deposit comprised the remains of two large Early Dynastic pottery vessels, some sand and squeezes of mud. These last may be accounted for by the fact that an early temple would almost certainly have been constructed of mudbrick (McEuen and Myers 1940: 29). However, no walls were discovered, indicating that the early temple was probably swept away during later building activity.

Coptos

The temple at Coptos was excavated by Petrie at the end of the nineteenth century (Petrie 1896). From the published report, it is difficult to establish the size or relative location of the earliest building. Nevertheless, several large-scale stone sculptures, including the famous Coptos colossi (Payne 1993: 12–13, pls I–IV, V.a, b; Dreyer 1995b), indicate that a temple probably stood at the site from the late Predynastic period. The three colossi themselves 'lay beneath the thick sand bed of the Ptolemaic temple' (Petrie 1896: 7). It was not possible to date them precisely by stratigraphic means, but on art historical grounds they have been assigned to the late Predynastic period or early First Dynasty. The carvings on the side of the colossi include the saws of sawfish – an alternative suggestion interprets these motifs as branches or fronds of foliage (Dreyer 1995b: 51) – and *Pteroceras* (*Lambis*) shells, emphasising the close connection between Coptos and the Red Sea. The early importance of Coptos derived from its strategic location at the head of the Wadi Hammamat, which served as the principal route between the Nile valley and the Red Sea coast.

Other large stone sculptures found by Petrie at Coptos confirm the existence of a late Predynastic temple at the site. These included the figure of a bird, probably an archaic falcon (Petrie 1896: pl. V.6), and three lions (Petrie 1896: pl. V). Particularly significant for the dating of the animal sculptures is the mention of 'New Race' (in other words, Predynastic) pottery which was found at the same level (Petrie 1896: 7). The bird and lions were crudely finished by hammering (Petrie 1896: 8) and belong to a class of large-scale animal sculpture from the period of state formation. They seem to confirm that the Egyptians of the late Predynastic period already worshipped deities as large cult statues erected in temples.

Abydos

Excavations at the beginning of the twentieth century uncovered substantial material from an early shrine within the later temple of Osiris at Abydos (Petrie 1902). Two aspects of the archaeological evidence are worth discussing separately: the architectural remains of the shrine itself, and the deposits of votive objects, many of which may date to the Early Dynastic period.

THE EARLY TEMPLE BUILDINGS

Petrie's excavations revealed a jumble of walls, representing numerous building phases of the early temple, dedicated to the local jackal god Khentiamentiu. The lowest walls probably belonged to temple buildings of the Early Dynastic period (Kemp 1975b: 30). Royal patronage of the temple can certainly be traced back to the beginning of the First Dynasty. A fragment from a vase of glazed composition decorated with the *serekh* of Aha was found by Petrie adjacent to a pit of votive objects. It is also possible that several of the large ceremonial palettes from the late Predynastic period – including the so-called Battlefield, Libyan, Hunters' and Bull palettes – were found in the temple area at Abydos, and this would take royal patronage of the site even further back (Sayce 1898: 99; Legge 1900: 130, 133, footnote).

Petrie published plans of the temple buildings over the course of the first three dynasties and he offered a reconstruction of the temple's development (Petrie 1903: 7–9 and pls L–LI). The early history of the Abydos temple area was re-examined in detail by Kemp (1968). He found that the effect of Petrie's stratigraphic assumptions had been to date many of the walls too early. Furthermore, the complex mass of isolated wall fragments poses great problems for reconstructing complete buildings and for establishing the relative date of the numerous building phases. The earliest temple building (Kemp's building H) seems to date to the Old Kingdom, although it overlay walls and sand beds which probably belonged to an earlier building, one perhaps as old as the First Dynasty (Kemp 1968: 150). The discovery of small twists of burnt clay beneath building H supports its identification as the early temple, since similar objects were discovered in an apparently Early Dynastic deposit beneath the New Kingdom temple at Armant (Mond and Myers 1940: 29). Based upon comparisons with the large rectangular enclosure at Nekhen, the existence of a royal cult enclosure at Abydos has been proposed (O'Connor 1992: 89). However, it is hard to see why a complex of this kind would have been located within the early town when the immediately adjacent area of low desert was the chosen location for several such enclosures.

DEPOSITS OF VOTIVE MATERIAL

Three deposits of Early Dynastic votive objects were found by Petrie in the temple area at Abydos. The most important collection of votive material came from a pit designated chamber M69. The floor of chamber M69 was covered with a thick mat of organic matter; embedded within this layer were the votive objects, comprising ivory and faience figurines, and numerous beads (Petrie 1903: 23). Two further deposits of discarded votive objects (M64, M65 and M89) were discovered nearby (Petrie 1903: 26–7). The majority of the material from these pits was dated to the early First Dynasty on the basis of similar material from the Hierakonpolis 'Main Deposit'.

However, a re-examination of the complex stratigraphy in the Abydos temple area has shown that chamber M64 probably dates to the early New Kingdom, while chamber M69 could have been dug at any time from the Old Kingdom to the Eighteenth Dynasty (Kemp 1968: 153). However, while not all the objects are necessarily Early Dynastic, some of the votive material discarded in these pits is clearly early in style, such as the ivory lion 'gaming pieces'.

Similar votive material was found scattered within the temple area itself (Petrie 1903: 28). Particularly important is the group of human heads, modelled in clay. One of the pottery heads looks distinctly Asiatic (Petrie 1903: pl. XI.257), whilst the appearance of another (Petrie 1903: pl. XI.260) has attracted comment from several scholars (for example, Rice 1990). It is very un-Egyptian in style, and the head-dress, in the form of a turban, is reminiscent of depictions of Sumerian deities. The figure has been identified as a Mesopotamian, but whether human or divine is not known. The presence of such an object in the early temple at Abydos raises fundamental questions about Egypt's early relations with its eastern neighbours, and the extent to which early religious iconography was influenced from abroad.

Badari

There is some evidence for the existence of an Early Dynastic shrine at Badari, on a finger of low desert called Spur 3. Underneath mudbrick walls of the Old or Middle Kingdom and New Kingdom, identified as successive phases of a small local temple, there was a stratum of Early Dynastic debris which itself overlay some unidentified late Predynastic or Early Dynastic mudbrick structures (Brunton 1927: 18–19). Four objects found *in situ* provide the best indications that an Early Dynastic shrine did exist on the site of the later temple. A finely finished cup of deep blue glazed composition, very similar in form to a copper example found in the tomb of Khasekhemwy at Abydos, may have been donated as a votive object at an Early Dynastic shrine (Brunton 1927: pl. XX.61). The temple area also yielded the upper part of a pottery figurine, depicting a bearded man with a broad face and a curious, shoulder-length wig (Brunton 1927: pl. XXI.3). In general style, the figurine is reminiscent of similar objects found in the Early Dynastic temple at Hierakonpolis. A siltstone falcon of archaic appearance (Brunton 1927: pl. XX.63) quite possibly represents an Early Dynastic cult object (cf. Brunton 1927: 17). Anti, the local god of the Badari region – who is attested from at least the Second Dynasty – was worshipped in the form of a falcon, and it is possible that the siltstone statue was an image of the god. Finally, a bird's head, in pink pottery with 'little lumps of pottery added to represent the eyes' (Brunton 1927: 17), was also found in the temple area (Brunton 1927: pl. XX.62). Although difficult to date, it may be Early Dynastic and can also be interpreted as a votive offering to the local falcon god.

Heliopolis

Fragments of limestone relief from a small shrine were found within the ancient enclosure at Heliopolis (Weill 1911–12: 9); they are now in the Egyptian Museum in Turin (W.S. Smith 1949: 133–7, figs 48–53). The building from which the reliefs came was badly destroyed but it was probably a small shrine. The decoration appears to be connected with the celebration of a Sed-festival and may also have shown the Heliopolitan ennead, the group of nine gods involved in the Heliopolitan creation myth. Two fragments bear the name of the king, Netjerikhet. Another fragment shows the king seated with the ladies of his family gathered around his feet (W.S. Smith 1949: 133, fig. 48). The women are shown as tiny figures, two (the king's daughter and the queen) in front of the king's legs, and a third (whose name is illegible) behind with her arm around his leg. An unpublished fragment from the Heliopolis shrine shows

> the seated king with clenched hands held to his breast, one of them grasping two staves and the other perhaps the flail. A small atten-dant places his hand on the king's elbow. This would appear to be the scene where the king is seated on the Heb-Sed throne while one of the officiants arranges his dress.
>
> (W.S. Smith 1949: 136)

A fragment of fine limestone relief in the Cairo Museum may also have come from the same shrine at Heliopolis (W.S. Smith 1949: 136). On one side the king wears the tight-fitting garment associated with the Sed-festival, on the other side he wears the red crown. The beginning of royal patronage in the temple area at Heliopolis suggests official support for the local solar cult, which subsequently became the major state cult in the Fourth Dynasty.

Tell Ibrahim Awad

The site of Tell Ibrahim Awad in the north-eastern Delta has been the focus of excavations since the late 1980s (van den Brink 1992b). In the last few seasons, a number of deposits of pottery and votive objects have been found beneath the foundations of the Middle Kingdom temple (van Haarlem 1995, 1996). The deposits of offering-pottery probably date to the late Old Kingdom or early First Intermediate Period, but the non-ceramic material is likely to be rather earlier. Some of the small votive objects of glazed composition, ivory and stone have close parallels from the Satet temple at Elephantine, suggesting that the Tell Ibrahim Awad objects are also Early Dynastic in date (van Haarlem 1995: 46). The largest deposit of votive material, discovered in 1996, comprised some 212 items. Unique objects included an oryx of glazed composition, a diorite palette and the figure of a dwarf made from cornelian. In total, the number of early votive objects recovered so far from Tell Ibrahim Awad equals the collection from Elephantine. Moreover, Tell Ibrahim Awad is the only documented site north of Abydos where such material has been found to date. Excavations in 1996 reached the deepest temple strata, just above the water-table. They have been dated preliminarily to the end of the Early Dynastic period or early Old Kingdom, and must represent the building where the votive objects were originally dedicated (van Haarlem 1996: 32). Tell Ibrahim Awad is the only example of an Early Dynastic provincial shrine yet excavated in the Delta.

Buto

Excavations in the late 1980s at the site of Tell el-Fara'in/Buto in the north-western Delta have revealed mudbrick buildings of the Early Dynastic period which may have served a cultic purpose (von der Way 1993: 288–9). The complex which dominates the Early Dynastic level excavated so far consists of a labyrinth of corridors and interconnecting rooms (von der Way 1996). At the heart of the building lie two rooms; in one of these a limestone platform stood against one wall. Its original function remains a mystery, although the excavator suggested that it may have supported a throne or statue (von der Way 1992: 7). The peculiar layout of the building as a whole would seem to indicate that it served a special purpose, perhaps as a royal residence or a building associated with the royal cult. An adjacent building, dated to the reign of Narmer, may also have served a sacred purpose. In front of a simple, rectangular building, a large pottery vessel had been sunk into the ground. On the inside of the vessel two stylised bull figures had been marked in the wet clay (von der Way 1989: 295, fig. 12.1–2), giving rise to the suggestion that the vessel was perhaps a feeding trough for a divine bull worshipped at Buto (see Figure 8.9). A wooden label of Aha from Abydos offers possible confirmation for this theory. The label apparently records the king's visit to important Delta shrines (Petrie 1901: pl. IIIA.5; Emery 1961: fig. 12). The second register depicts a round-topped sanctuary surmounted by a bird, almost certainly the shrine at Buto known as *Ḏbʿwt* (see below, and Figure 8.10). In front of this shrine is a bull inside an enclosure. If the same location applies to both shrine and bull, it suggests the worship of a sacred bull at Buto in the early First Dynasty.

The motif of a shrine with a rounded or pitched roof surmounted by a bird, depicted on the Aha label, is first attested on the Narmer macehead from Hierakonpolis (Quibell 1900: pl. XXVIB). Here, the shrine is shown behind the enthroned king. The fact that Narmer is shown wearing the red crown may be significant, perhaps indicating that the event depicted took place in Lower Egypt (Millet 1990: 54, 56). A bone label

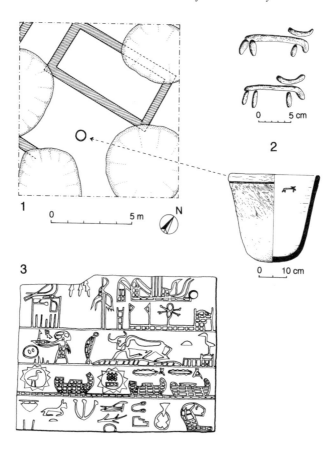

Figure 8.9 Early cult at Buto, 1: the sacred bull. Indications of a bull cult prac-tised at Buto in the Early Dynastic period: (1) a rectangular mudbrick building, excavated by the German Archaeological Institute expedition to Tell el-Fara'in/ Buto in 1988; in front of the building, which dates to the very beginning of the First Dynasty, a large pottery basin had been sunk into the floor (after von der Way 1989: 284, fig. 7.b); (2) the pottery basin was incised on the interior with two schematic bulls, giving rise to speculation that it may have served as the feeding trough of a sacred bull kept at Buto (after von der Way 1989: 295, fig. 12.1–2); (3) wooden label of Aha from Abydos recording a royal visit to the north-western Delta; the enclosure with a bull may refer to a sacred precinct at Buto, if the heron-topped building next to it represents the Djebaut shrine (after Emery 1961: 52, fig. 12). Not to same scale.

from the late Predynastic tomb U-j at Abydos shows a similar motif, consisting of a rectangular, panelled building with a flat roof, surmounted by a long-beaked bird, possibly a heron (Dreyer 1993a: pl. 7.j). An iden-tical label was excavated in the tomb of Aha (Petrie 1901: pl. III.12). In an entry on the Palermo Stone for the reign of Userkaf, a hieroglyph showing a heron on a perch is used as the determinative for the place-name *Ḏbʿwt* (Schäfer 1902: 34). This locality is mentioned in the Pyramid Texts, and has been securely identified as a sacred area in the vicinity of Buto (Gauthier 1929: 127; Erman and Grapow 1931: 567; Faulkner 1969: 327). It is perhaps noteworthy that the same heron-on-a-perch hieroglyph (Gardiner 1957: sign-list G32) is also used as an **ideogram** or determinative in the verb *bʿḥi*, 'to be inundated'. This may have an ancient connection with the marshy, inundated nature of the land around Buto. The significance of the bird shown atop the shrine is not clear, but possibly the sanctuary at *Ḏbʿwt* was dedicated to the worship of a heron deity.

A second feature of the sacred landscape at *Ḏbʿwt*/Buto recorded on early inscriptions was a complex comprising buildings and palm trees either side of a wavy canal (Bietak 1994, plus references). Two identical labels of Djer, one from Abydos (Amélineau 1904: pl. XV.19; Legge 1907:

Figure 8.10 Early cult at Buto, 2: the Djebaut shrine. Depictions of the distinctive shrine surmounted by the figure of a heron: (1) bone label from tomb U-j at Abydos, dating to the late Predynastic period (after Dreyer 1993: pl. 14.j); (2) similar label from the tomb of Aha at Abydos (after Petrie 1901: pl. III.12); (3) the shrine as shown on the ceremonial macehead of Narmer from Hierakonpolis (after Quibell 1900: pl. XXVIB); (4) detail from a label of Aha recording a royal visit to the north-western Delta (after Petrie 1901: pl. X.2); (5) the name of the Djebaut shrine as recorded on the Palermo Stone, in an entry for the reign of Userkaf (after Schäfer 1902: 34). Not to same scale.

319

no. 4 [Berlin 18.026]) and one from Saqqara (Quibell 1923: 6, pl. XI.2–3; cf. Weill 1961: 351), record the visit of the king to this place. The same locality is shown on relief fragments from a number of Old Kingdom royal monuments, in conjunction with the heron standard of *Db'wt*, whilst a virtually identical scene from the Palace of Apries at Memphis (Petrie 1909: 8–11, pl. VI; Mogensen 1930: pl. CII; cf. Weill 1961: 351) clearly identifies the locality as *Db'wt*. Judging from similar scenes in Old Kingdom private tombs and the New Kingdom Theban tomb of Rekhmira, it is possible that a palm tree was originally planted *in front of* each shrine, and that the apparent alternation of shrines and palm trees on the Djer labels simply reflects the conventions of Egyptian artistic representation (Bietak 1994: 3). Several different interpretations have been offered for the buildings and palm trees at Buto: chapels, house-burials or temporary buildings erected for a specific royal occasion (Wallert 1962: 114–28; H. Altenmüller 1975; Bietak 1994: 5). The discovery of tree pits in front of an Early Dynastic mastaba at North Saqqara (Emery 1949: 73) and the excavation of similar pits in front of late Middle Kingdom tombs at Tell ed-Daba tend to favour the interpretation of the Buto complex as a sacred cemetery, perhaps the burial place of the Predynastic rulers of Buto (Bietak 1994).

Excavations at Buto have proved the site's importance from early Predynastic times. The attention paid by Early Dynastic kings, especially those of the early First Dynasty, to the various sacred precincts at Buto suggests that the site may have played a key role in the process of state formation, and that due reverence for its temples was an important part of the programme designed to cement and strengthen the unity of Egypt.

Saïs

A label of Aha apparently records a visit by the king to the shrine of Neith (Petrie 1901: pl. IIIA.5; Emery 1961: fig. 12). Since the other motifs on the label suggest a Delta location, it is likely that the cult centre of Neith was already located at Saïs in the north-western Delta. This was the site of a major temple to Neith in later periods of Egyptian history (cf. Lichtheim 1980: 36–41), although no evidence for an Early Dynastic building has yet come to light from Saïs itself. (Presumably, the Early Dynastic levels now lie beneath the water-table, as they do at nearby Buto.)

PART III

THE DIVERSITY OF LOCAL EXPERIENCE

CHAPTER NINE

THE RISE OF URBANISM

—— •◆• ——

Egypt during the first three dynasties was not the monolithic state the royal court may have wished it to be: there was significant local and regional variation. The pace and character of urbanism is one of the areas in which this variation is most discernible.

An urban centre may be defined as 'a geographical and cultural central place exercising regional political control, with a relatively large and dense population, a complex division of labour, and internal social stratification' (Hoffman *et al.* 1986: 175). The migration of people from small, scattered villages to larger, more densely populated settlements marks a fundamental change in the nature of society (Kemp 1995: 687). Urbanism – the concentration of population in such settlements – is an important stage in the structural evolution of a state (cf. Hoffman 1980: 310), reflecting the 'interaction between central organisation and local communities' (Seidlmayer 1996b: 127). Consequently, urbanism is one of the defining characteristics of complex societies, and of early states in particular. The process of state formation in Egypt seems to have been accompanied by the nucleation of settlements in several areas of Upper Egypt (Kemp 1977; F.A. Hassan 1988: 161). The process is directly attested by the rapid expansion of certain settlements, and is also reflected in the mortuary record by the simultaneous abandonment of several small cemeteries in a single region. The best evidence for these phenomena comes from the Abydos region, Naqada and Hierakonpolis.

When calculating changes in the size of ancient populations it is important to consider settlement density as well as settlement area. For example, at Hierakonpolis tightly packed houses excavated within the walled town enclosure suggest a high density of settlement during the Early Dynastic period; this is likely to have offset any reduction in settlement area during the period of state formation (contra Trigger 1985: 348). The evidence from all areas of Egypt points towards a process of permanent, if gradual, urbanisation (contra Janssen 1978: 216). It is likely that the majority of the population – who were farmers, then as now – 'remained dispersed in hamlets and small villages' (Trigger 1985: 348); but, in the light of significant recent excavations, Egypt, even early Egypt, can no longer be considered 'a civilisation without cities' (Wilson 1960).

FACTORS INFLUENCING URBANISM

The factors affecting the beginning of urbanism are likely to have been several, and to have varied according to local conditions (Trigger 1972, 1985), especially the 'political, cultural and regional setting' (Seidlmayer 1996b: 126). The growth of large towns in Upper Egypt at the end of the Predynastic period may have been partly for defensive reasons (Trigger 1984: 103), although it doubtless facilitated central control of the population by state authorities (Seidlmayer 1996b: 113). The nucleation of settlement at Hierakonpolis may have been the result of climatic and/or ecological factors (Hoffman 1976: 41). What is clear is that urbanism both reflected, and was made possible by, the large-scale changes which took place within Egyptian society during the Predynastic period. Increasing social stratification, the production of agricultural surpluses and the redistribution of these resources by the local élite enabled a section of the population to become engaged in full-time non-agricultural activity. The trend of craft specialisation was undoubtedly fostered by the demands of the élite and ultimately encompassed the development of writing and the growth of a literate scribal class engaged in administration. No longer tied to the land, a significant section of society could now benefit from living and working in a more compact form of settlement. Such a move would have been particularly advantageous to a nascent administration, allowing for more effective central storage of agricultural produce. Even after the unification of Egypt, local aristocracies – such as are attested, perhaps, by the élite First Dynasty mastabas at Tarkhan and the Third Dynasty mastabas at Beit Khallaf – may have continued to exert significant influence over their communities, and this factor should also be borne in mind when considering early urbanisation (Kemp, personal communication). Furthermore, the role of cult centres in the beginnings of urbanism should not be overlooked (Trigger 1972: 590–1; Hoffman 1980: 307–8). The site of a local shrine would have provided a natural focus for activity, particularly if the local élite depended upon intimate association with the supernatural to maintain its authority. The archaeological evidence at Hierakonpolis suggests that the location of an important shrine was one of the factors responsible for the growth of the early town (Hoffman 1980: 307).

Regional differences

Fundamental though it was, urbanism did not take place simultaneously in all regions of Egypt (Kemp 1977: 196, 198). It appears to have begun in Upper Egypt, where socio-economic change had been most rapid and where the process of state formation was initiated. Hence, the earliest domestic mudbrick architecture has been found at Hierakonpolis and Naqada (Petrie and Quibell 1896; Weeks 1971–2), the leading centres of

Predynastic Upper Egypt. Based upon the available evidence, the settlement pattern in Middle Egypt seems to have been less affected by changes in late Predynastic society. However, this apparent situation may reflect the poor preservation of archaeological sites in Middle Egypt – due to geological factors, encroachment of sand dunes from the western desert, and the movement of the Nile channel – rather than the true extent of urban development in the region. Throughout the Nile valley, the major settlements appear to have been located on the west bank of the river. The apparent absence of significant sites from the west bank in Middle Egypt has undoubtedly influenced our view of the region; it may have been more flourishing in ancient times than the surviving evidence suggests. Indeed, until the dates of foundation of important later centres like Hermopolis and Herakleopolis have been established, we will remain ignorant of early urbanism in Middle Egypt. A reference to Herakleopolis on the Palermo Stone, in an entry dating to the reign of Den, suggests that the town may have been founded before the First Dynasty. On the east bank of the Nile, in the Matmar–Qau region, there is little evidence for the growth of urban centres until the Old Kingdom, when administrative developments connected with the royal court resulted in the growth of el-Etmania (O'Connor 1972: 93–4). The **demography** of the Memphite region was undoubtedly dominated by the foundation of Memphis itself, marking the imposition of central authority and control by the new national administration. There is increasing evidence that urbanism was well advanced in the Delta in late Predynastic times (contra Janssen 1978: 216). Recent excavations have demonstrated the importance of sites like Buto and Mendes in the Predynastic period (see below), whilst other centres such as Saïs and Bubastis are likely to have been significant before the incorporation of the Delta into a unified kingdom (Kaiser 1986: 1071). The appearance of mudbrick architecture in Delta settlements (van den Brink 1989; Wilkinson 1996b: 95) is likely to mark a fundamental change in the structure of Lower Egyptian society (von der Way 1993: 96) and probably indicates the incorporation of the region into an expanding Upper Egyptian polity. 'From this moment the spread of urbanism in the north could well have been closely parallel to that in Upper Egypt' (Kemp 1995: 687). The variable pace of urbanisation in different regions of the country emphasises the importance of local factors in the process of state formation (Wilkinson 1996b: 86–90).

Topographical and ecological factors

The most favoured location for settlements in Egypt, in ancient times as today, would have been the floodplain of the Nile. The river provided not only supplies of fresh water but also the most efficient means of transport and communication within the country (O'Connor 1972: 79). However, the alluvium was prone to inundation, and it would therefore have been preferable to locate settlements on raised areas of land, beyond the reach of the floodwaters. In Upper Egypt, Predynastic settlements developed on isolated hillocks or abandoned levees within the floodplain, or on the margins of the low desert. The majority of early settlements which were located within the floodplain now lie under deposits of alluvium, and are covered either by fields or by modern towns and villages. As a result, few settlements have been excavated in Egypt, compared to the numerous cemeteries which lie along the desert edge and which are therefore much more accessible to archaeologists. In the earlier phases of the Predynastic period, marginal settlements at a number of sites, notably Hierakonpolis, spread back into the desert, following the edges of major wadis until the limits of cultivation were reached (Hoffman 1980: 148). These desert-edge communities would have depended largely upon herding, the savannahs of the now arid low desert providing pasturage for flocks. The desiccation of these pasturages following the end of the Neolithic subpluvial, accompanied by a change to agriculture as the principal subsistence base, probably led to the widespread relocation of settlements to the floodplain. This may account for the demise of Maadi towards the end of the Naqada II period (see Chapter 10). The settlements that remained at the edge of the cultivation are likely to have been 'functionally rather specialized' (O'Connor 1972: 79; cf. R. Friedman 1994: 322), perhaps serving as administrative or symbolic centres, like Naqada South Town. However, with very few exceptions, it is such desert-edge settlements that have been studied in detail. It is important to remember this bias in the evidence when examining early urbanism in Egypt. We must admit that, to date, our picture of urban development is far from complete. Within the general setting of the Nile valley, the first urban centres seem to have developed in locations 'favored by their overseas trading possibilities and by their economic hinterlands' (Bietak 1979: 129). Chapter 10 explores the role of geographical and ecological factors in the growth of important regional centres. A settlement located at a strategic point in the course of the Nile – such as a natural constriction of the valley (for example, Memphis), or an intersection between the river and desert routes (perhaps the early town of This) – would have been in a position to control trade, and to function as an entrepôt for goods.

FUNCTIONS OF EARLY TOWNS

The centralising tendencies of the early Egyptian state, especially the redistributive economy which funded state projects, were doubtless important influences on the beginnings of urbanism in the Nile valley. They may also have had a direct effect on the character of early towns. Many of the earliest urban centres were surrounded by a large mudbrick wall, defining and restricting the area of dense habitation (Elephantine, Hierakonpolis and Naqada are all examples). The defensive role of town enclosure walls may have extended beyond protecting the inhabitants from aggressively jealous marauders. Walls may also have been intended to control access to and provide security for the administrative and economic centres located within early towns (Trigger 1985: 348). A redistributive economy must have required a network of centralised storage facilities where agricultural produce could be collected for redistribution to the population, a proportion being retained as buffer stocks and some being channelled to the central treasury. These storage facilities would have required adequate protection, and are likely to have been located within towns. The evidence from Naqada South Town points to the settlement having served just such a purpose (see below). It has even been suggested that regional urban centres were not primarily concentrations of population but, rather, state foundations serving as locations for shrines and convenient nodes for the operation of the central administration. If so, the inhabitants of early Egyptian towns may have been principally state officials, craftsmen employed by the royal workshops, and priests: in other words, specialists not engaged in agriculture (Trigger 1985: 348). As the Early Dynastic period progressed, the increasing economic demands made by the royal court on the country as a whole – to fund increasingly elaborate building projects – resulted in a widespread process of urbanisation, urban centres eventually functioning as 'the backbone of Egypt's political and administrative organisation' (Seidlmayer 1996b: 127). State interference, if it may be characterised as such, was also manifest in another area: the foundation of planned settlements. These are well attested from the Old and Middle Kingdoms, but state activity was also important in the foundation or growth of earlier towns, such as Elephantine. By contrast, settlements like Hierakonpolis owed their existence more to local and/or regional socio-economic developments (Seidlmayer 1996b: 127).

THE EVIDENCE FOR EARLY URBANISM

Comparatively few settlements have been systematically excavated in Egypt. This state of affairs is the result of two main factors. First, the changing aims of archaeology and ancient history have influenced, to a considerable degree, the types of site investigated. Until the latter half of the twentieth century, the primary aim of archaeologists working in Egypt was often the acquisition of artefacts for museums and private collections. These were to be found in abundance in the numerous cemeteries of all ages which lie along the desert edge. Archaeological activity was therefore primarily focused on cemeteries, and on the visible monuments of pharaonic Egypt: royal tombs and temples. An important exception was the work of Myers at Armant, unfortunately cut short by outside circumstances. The excavation of tombs and temples suited an age of scholarship which viewed Egyptian history from the perspective of the royal court. Social and economic history, an attempt to understand the experience of ordinary Egyptians in antiquity, has become a major academic concern only in the last thirty or so years. As a result, interest in Egyptian settlements – which constitute the primary source of evidence for economic and social history, administrative hierarchies, patterns of socioeconomic organisation, and the daily life of the general population – has increased dramatically, and excavations are now underway at several settlements from various periods of Egyptian history. Second, the location of settlements in Egypt has hindered their archaeological exploration. As we have seen, the majority of ancient towns and villages will have been located in the floodplain, at sites which are now inaccessible due to modern land-use activities, the accumulation of alluvium, or changes in the course of the Nile. These factors limit the number of settlement sites which are readily accessible to scientific investigation (although the Dutch East Delta Survey revealed a large number of Old Kingdom settlements lying beneath the fields, not far below the surface). Furthermore, the earliest settlement levels of sites in the alluvial floodplain lie close to or beneath the water-table. Excavation of such sites is virtually impossible without pumping equipment (Mendes is a recent exception). This has been used to great effect at Buto in the north-western Delta, and we may expect other settlement sites lying below the water-table to be excavated in the future (for example, the Early Dynastic city of Memphis).

In the absence of sufficient direct evidence for urbanism, scholars have often turned to the cemetery record (O'Connor 1972: 80; Mortensen 1991). The location of a cemetery provides a reasonable, though by no means infallible, guide to the location of its accompanying settlement. Likewise, the size of a cemetery gives an indication of the size of settlement it served; the distribution of cemeteries has been used to reconstruct settlement patterns in various regions and at various periods (for example, Patch 1991; Seidlmayer 1996b: fig. 2). The conspectus of sites presented below draws upon both types of evidence for early urbanism: actual settlement material, most of it excavated in recent years, and Early Dynastic cemeteries for which the accompanying settlement has not yet been located or excavated.

Elephantine

Excavations on the island of Elephantine have revealed a continuous picture of urban development from Predynastic times. In the Predynastic and Early Dynastic periods, the southern part of the island was divided into two, at least during the annual inundation. The settlement was located in the centre of the eastern island. The earliest habitation is now dated to the end of Naqada II, although a few isolated finds of earlier material out of context may indicate that the settlement had already begun at the beginning of Naqada II (Seidlmayer 1996b: 111). The arrangement of post-holes suggests an open settlement of reed huts (cf. Leclant and Clerc 1994: 430). The original extent of the Predynastic settlement is hard to gauge, since only limited areas have been excavated. The settlement may have been restricted to the northern part of the island, with a cemetery occupying the southern part; but it is also possible that the early village may have been much larger (Ziermann 1993: 14–15; Seidlmayer 1996b: 111). The habitation area certainly extended eastwards towards the river bank, where it overlooked the main navigation route through the First Cataract area. The first mudbrick buildings were constructed on Elephantine at the very end of the Predynastic period ('Dynasty 0'). Also at this time, industrial activity is attested: an oven with pieces of slag and traces of copper indicates that metalworking took place within the Predynastic settlement (Leclant and Clerc 1994: 430).

The unification of Egypt at the end of the Predynastic period, accompanied by the imposition of a national government apparatus on the whole country, marked a decisive turning-point in the history of Elephantine. At the beginning of the First Dynasty, probably as the direct result of royal policy, a fortress was built on the island. Its strategic location was clearly designed to facilitate control of river traffic on the main river branch and the monitoring of activity in the area of cultivable land on the east bank of the Nile, the site of modern Aswan (Ziermann 1993: 32, fig. 12; Seidlmayer 1996b: 112). Moreover, the prominence of the building would have emphasised to the local inhabitants and to passing traffic the omnipotence of the central, royal government. The fortress seems to have been built as part of a change in Egyptian policy towards Nubia, a policy which now became hostile and exploitative. Certainly, the construction did not benefit the local community nor did it take account of local sensibilities. Neither the existing settlement nor its shrine was included within the fortifications; the fortress was erected in the optimum location, with scant regard for the pre-existing buildings (Seidlmayer 1996b: 112). When the fortification was strengthened and extended during the first half of the First Dynasty, the new wall ran so close to the forecourt of the local shrine that the shrine's entrance had to be moved. As the result of a subsequent strengthening of the wall, the shrine forecourt had to be further reduced in size. The adverse impact of the fortification programme on the religious life of the local community paints a none-too-beneficent picture of the early state. The construction of the fortress on Elephantine illustrates the political dominance of the royal court after the unification of Egypt.

At the beginning of the Second Dynasty the settlement and shrine, which had previously been unenclosed, were fortified by means of a double wall connecting with the bastion of the fortress. This new town wall and the outer section of the fortifications were strengthened several times over the succeeding decades. Eventually, towards the end of the Second Dynasty, the expansion of the town led to the abandonment of the inner fortifications. This allowed the shrine to expand once again, regaining its former extent. Early in the Third Dynasty the walls of the old fortress, now surrounded by habitations, were levelled to form a continuous settlement area. None the less, a sealing of the governor of Elephantine from the reign of Sekhemkhet gives the town the determinative of a fortress, indicating that Elephantine was still viewed as a fortified settlement, at least by the central government who had built the fortifications in the first place (Pätznick, in Kaiser *et al.* 1995: 181; Seidlmayer 1996b: 113).

Until the middle of the Third Dynasty, settlement activity was confined to the eastern island. This was to change with the construction of a large complex of buildings on the northern granite ridge of the western island some time during or after the reign of Netjerikhet (Seidlmayer 1996a, 1996b: 120–4). The complex was enlarged and reinforced during a series of building phases. Late in the Third Dynasty, the courtyard area between the northern and southern granite ridges was filled and levelled, to support a new building. This development connected the original building complex on the northern ridge to the small step pyramid constructed on the southern ridge in the reign of Huni. The size and construction of the entire complex distinguish it from other contemporary buildings on Elephantine, and mark it out as an official, state-sponsored project (Seidlmayer 1996b: 120). This is confirmed by the associated finds, especially seal-impressions. Most significant is a sealing from a papyrus roll giving the title of the 'royal seal-bearer of the *pr-nswt*' from the reign of Sanakht. Even if this official was not himself based at Elephantine, the consultation of a court document on the island indicates that the Third Dynasty complex was associated with the royal domain. Other sealings indicate that food distribution operations were carried out on the site, confirmed by the vast quantities of bread-moulds and beer-jars recovered. The excavator concludes that the building was an administrative centre connected with the royal estate and notes that it was located 'in a convenient place near the river and in the vicinity of the cultivable alluvial land accumulating to the north' (Seidlmayer 1996b: 121). It is quite likely that the complex on the eastern island at Elephantine was connected with a fundamental restructuring of the administration under the last king(s) of the Third Dynasty, a development which paved the way for the unprecedented harnessing of resources evident in the pyramid-building of the Fourth Dynasty. Elephantine is thus a key site for the rise of the Egyptian state and it bears witness to the changes which marked the transition from the Early Dynastic period to the Old Kingdom.

Elkab

The significance of Elkab from the period of state formation onwards is demonstrated both archaeologically and iconographically: by the numerous graves of the late Predynastic and Early Dynastic periods; and by the adoption, at the very beginning of the Early Dynastic period, of the local deity (Nekhbet) as the tutelary goddess of Upper Egypt and, later, as an element of the royal titulary (Vandersleyen 1971: 35).

Excavations at the turn of the century (Quibell 1898b; Sayce and Clarke 1905; Clarke 1921), and by successive Belgian missions since the 1940s (Vermeersch 1970; Vandersleyen 1971; Huyge 1984; Hendrickx and Huyge 1989; Hendrickx 1993) have revealed several settlement and cemetery areas (Figure 9.1). The ancient site of Elkab is mostly contained within a large rectangular enclosure wall of mudbrick, named the Great Wall by the early excavators. Within this outer enclosure are situated a smaller, walled temple enclosure and the partial remains of a curved, double wall (Hendrickx and Huyge 1989: pl. II) which may have enclosed the early town (Vermeersch 1970: 32–3). The double wall must originally have demarcated a roughly circular area, conforming to the hieroglyph for 'town'. Because of the northward movement of the river channel since ancient times, the south-western half of the ancient town has been eroded and is now lost. However, there is some evidence that the town extended westwards beyond the limits of the Great Wall. At the end of the nineteenth century, there was 'ample evidence of habitations, outside and westward of the western line of the Great Walls' (Clarke 1921: 56). A few years later, a section of the curved double wall and large amounts of ancient pottery could be seen exposed in the Nile bank (Sayce and Clarke 1905: 263; Clarke 1921: 56).

The location of the large, late Predynastic (Naqada III) cemetery (Hendrickx 1993) – which would have lain outside the settlement – indicates that the early town lay in the south-west corner of the later, rectangular enclosure wall. The limited amount of archaeological material excavated within the curved double walls seems to confirm this area as the heart of the ancient town. The only architectural evidence consists of small mudbrick constructions. The floor of one chamber was covered with sherds of Early Dynastic pottery, and a large jar had been sunk into the ground. Numerous flint objects found here provide further evidence of early occupation (Vermeersch 1970). Similar material (pottery, flints, fragments of stone vessels), some of it dating back to the Predynastic period, was excavated at the beginning of the twentieth century in a trench to the east of the temples (Sayce and Clarke 1905: 259). This location would correspond to the edge of the probable ancient town-site. Unfortunately, more extensive evidence of the early occupation at Elkab is unlikely to be forthcoming, since it appears that much of the site was thoroughly

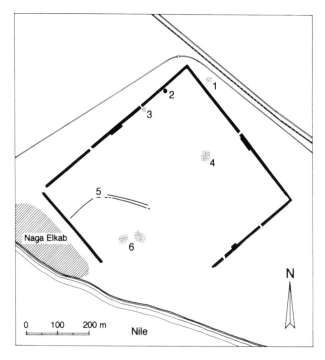

Figure 9.1 Elkab. Confirmed Early Dynastic features within and around the later rectangular town wall (after Hendrickx and Huyge 1989: 10–14, pl. II). Key: 1 possible location of a Predynastic cemetery; 2 building of Khasekhemwy; 3 Early Dynastic tombs; 4 late Predynastic cemetery; 5 double wall, enclosing the early town; 6 excavated areas of the Early Dynastic town.

levelled at the end of the Early Dynastic period or perhaps during the Old Kingdom, for the construction or reconstruction of the temple compound (Vermeersch 1970: 33; Vandersleyen 1971: 35). Moreover, a substantial town mound within the curved double walls, noted in an early century account, was removed by sebakh diggers in the nineteenth century (Clarke 1921: 56–61). On the spot where the temple now stands, excavations failed to reveal any domestic settlement material later than the Early Dynastic period. This fact suggests that the site was regarded as holy from an early period (Sayce and Clarke 1905: 262). However, domestic vessels ('ash-jars') of Predynastic date indicate that the site was probably not sanctified until after the formation of the Egyptian state (Sayce and Clarke 1905: 262–3).

There is only limited datable evidence of Early Dynastic activity in the Elkab region. One of the stairway tombs (No. 6) excavated at the end of the nineteenth century just outside the north-western side of the Great Wall contained a rectangular stone palette, characteristic of the early First

Dynasty (Quibell 1898). From the end of the First Dynasty there are two rock-cut inscriptions of Qaa (Huyge 1984). Both show the royal *serekh* facing a figure of the local goddess Nekhbet. One inscription is carved on a rock in the Wadi Hellal, the other at a site some 12 kilometres downstream. A small steatite plaque bearing the name of the Second Dynasty king Nebra was reported to have come from another of the stairway tombs (No. 2) (Quibell 1898b). The existence of a stone building of the late Second Dynasty, just inside the northern corner of the Great Wall, is indicated by a number of granite blocks, one of which (now lost) bore the name of Khasekhemwy.

There are several cemeteries of the Predynastic and Early Dynastic periods at Elkab. The principal Predynastic cemetery, dating to the period of state formation (Naqada III), lies within the Great Wall and seems to have formed part of a more extensive cemetery, the original extent of which is difficult to establish (Hendrickx and Huyge 1989: 12 (24); Hendrickx 1993). Tombs of the Early Dynastic period are somewhat better represented at Elkab. In particular, the existence of several high-status burials indicates the early importance of the town. A group of small mastabas dating to the Second and Third Dynasties was excavated adjacent to the inside north-western edge of the Great Wall, close to the granite blocks of Khasekhemwy (Sayce and Clarke 1905: 239; Hendrickx and Huyge 1989: 12). Although thoroughly plundered, the burials seem to have belonged to a larger cemetery comprising also some early Old Kingdom mastabas (Sayce and Clarke 1905: 242). There are sketchy reports of further Early Dynastic graves having been uncovered in the elevated part of the enclosure north of the temple; and there were apparently a few early burials within the mainly Middle Kingdom cemetery to the east of the temple area (Sayce and Clarke 1905: 246).

Hierakonpolis

Excavations at Hierakonpolis since the end of the nineteenth century have revealed much of the site's history. Towards the end of the Predynastic period (Naqada III), the newly founded town of Nekhen, situated at the edge of the cultivation, swiftly became the main regional centre of population, replacing the more scattered desert settlements characteristic of the earlier Predynastic period (Hoffman 1976: 41; Kemp 1977: 198). Previously extensive, these had declined to an area of just 2 hectares by the beginning of the Early Dynastic period (Hoffman *et al.* 1986). This marked contraction of settlement seems to have been part of a more widespread phenomenon associated with the rise of urbanism (Kemp 1989). The town of Nekhen had not, however, been founded on a virgin site: deep soundings indicate an unbroken sequence of settlement material, dating back to the Badarian period, beneath the Early Dynastic and Old

Kingdom town (Hoffman 1987). Moreover, Predynastic burials were found within the town enclosure (Quibell and Green 1902: 2).

At the beginning of the Early Dynastic period, with the inauguration of the new capital city at Memphis, Hierakonpolis was relegated to the status of a mere provincial capital. Nevertheless, the close involvement of Hierakonpolis in the process of state formation and the strong ideological links between the local god Horus and kingship ensured the town's continuing importance. This is most spectacularly attested by the excavation of part of a large building, interpreted as a royal palace, in the centre of Nekhen (Weeks 1971–2). A monumental gateway, decorated with elaborate niches, provides the first example of this distinctive architectural style in a secular building, and seems to confirm the validity of the term 'palace façade'. The Early Dynastic date of the gateway is confirmed by the fact that Old Kingdom houses were built over it (B. Adams 1977). Three seal-impressions found within the gateway have been dated to the late Second or early Third Dynasty, although the elaborate nature of the niche decoration suggests a First Dynasty date. Behind the gateway lay an assortment of residential and administrative buildings, including a number of store-rooms, although it is not certain if these constructions are contemporary with the palace itself. Reasons for identifying the gateway as part of a palace include its location within an urban area, its monumental size, and the elaborate nature of its external appearance (Weeks 1971–2: 31; see O'Connor 1992 for an alternative interpretation).

At some point during the Early Dynastic period or early Old Kingdom, a rectangular town wall was built around Nekhen (Kemp 1989: 39). Comparisons with other sites support an Early Dynastic date for the wall, whilst clay-sealings of Netjerikhet and Khaba found within some of the houses indicate Early Dynastic occupation. Within the town enclosure, the buildings were tightly packed and the town must have had a high population density. It also seems to have been characterised by functional patterning, with different quarters for different activities. This indicates a degree of town planning, whether conscious or unconscious (Bietak 1979: 108). Although the walled town of Nekhen became the main centre of population from the beginning of the Early Dynastic period – a potsherd incised with the *serekh* of Narmer was found within the town area (Garstang 1907: pl. 3.1; B. Adams 1995: 124) – some settlement endured in two 'outliers' until the early Old Kingdom (B. Adams 1977). Hierakonpolis remained an important town into the early Old Kingdom, but declined thereafter following the establishment of Edfu as the new regional population centre (Kemp 1989).

In contrast to the abundant settlement remains, graves of the Early Dynastic period are comparatively few at Hierakonpolis. This serves as a useful caveat, highlighting the disparity which can exist between settlement and cemetery evidence. The 'Fort Cemetery', which seems to have served as the burial ground for the majority of the local population during the later Predynastic period (B. Adams 1987), probably continued in this role during the First Dynasty. Surface surveys of the areas adjacent to the 'Fort' 'have indicated that the cemetery extended well beyond the walls' (B. Adams 1987: 177), and it is to the north of the structure that the Early Dynastic burials are probably located. Some Early Dynastic mastabas were in fact excavated in this area at the turn of the nineteenth century (Quibell and Green 1902: 25–6, pl. LXXIII; R. Friedman 1994: 386).

Edfu

Although there is no incontrovertible evidence of Early Dynastic occupation at Edfu, a number of oval graves, completely plundered but none the less thought to be early, were excavated in the 1930s (Bruyère 1937; Kemp 1977). Edfu occupies a natural elevation within the floodplain, and one might expect such an attractive location to have enticed settlers from an early period (Kemp 1977). The earliest pottery from the town enclosure appears to date to the late Old Kingdom. However, the type of construction seen in the inner of the two concentric enclosure walls – 'two near-vertical layers of brick' – recalls the stone architecture of the Third Dynasty step pyramids (Kemp 1977). Hence, it is possible that the early walled town at Edfu was already established by the beginning of the Old Kingdom. Similar layering of brick walls is found at Elephantine and Elkab (Kemp, personal communication), perhaps confirming a Third Dynasty date for Edfu.

Gebelein

Like the modern Arabic name, the ancient name of Gebelein, *'Inrty*, reflects the topography of the site: two hills, rising parallel to the Nile. The smaller, southern hill was the location for the temple of Hathor which was founded before the end of the Second Dynasty. The larger, northern hill seems to have been the site of the main settlement, with the adjacent desert serving as a burial ground (Donadoni Roveri 1990: 23, fig. 3.1).

There are strong indications that Gebelein was an important site during the Predynastic period, and that it remained so into the Early Dynastic period. A rich and extensive cemetery spanning the whole of the Predynastic period was situated in the desert to the north of the settlement. The wealth of the cemetery made it the focus of grave-robbing at the end of the nineteenth century, but subsequent, sporadic excavations yielded numerous artefacts. One of the graves contained a unique painted cloth dating to Naqada II (Galassi 1955: 5–42). The presence of such a prestige artefact suggests that late Predynastic Gebelein was a flourishing community with advanced social stratification. A layer of ash on the northern spurs of the northern hill represents the only remains of the Predynastic settlement (Donadoni Roveri 1990: 23).

Even though no Early Dynastic settlement remains have been excavated at Gebelein, the continued existence of the community is indicated by the cemeteries in the vicinity. An Early Dynastic necropolis covered the ash layer on the northern hill. In the earlier burials, bodies were wrapped in mats or baskets; later graves contained pottery or wooden coffins. Several rectangular graves, dated to the First Dynasty, indicate the presence of another Early Dynastic cemetery nearby, but it has never been excavated (Donadoni Roveri 1990: 25).

Armant

There is limited evidence for a settlement at Armant in the late Predynastic period (Mond and Myers 1940: 1). The earliest material found *in situ* was some Naqada III pottery, although it is possible that the town was founded somewhat earlier. A temple foundation deposit dating to the very end of the Predynastic period or early First Dynasty was excavated in the west forecourt of the later temple. The only evidence for Early Dynastic habitation was some fragments of pottery and stone vessels (Mond and Myers 1940: 2). As at Abydos and Hierakonpolis, small villages on the desert edge at Armant seem not to have survived into the Early Dynastic period. It is likely that their populations were absorbed into a new town in late Predynastic times (Kemp 1977: 192; cf. Ginter and Kozlowski 1994).

Naqada

A similar phenomenon is attested at Naqada, where the small communities in the immediate vicinity of the larger town were apparently abandoned during the period of state formation (Lamberg-Karlovsky and Sabloff 1979: 132). At the same time, the surviving settlement (the South Town), its population probably swelled by an influx from the surrounding villages, was enclosed by thick mudbrick walls (Kemp 1977: 198, 1989: 35–6; Lamberg-Karlovsky and Sabloff 1979: 132). The South Town remained the main regional focus of population throughout the late Predynastic period and into the First Dynasty, probably serving an administrative and perhaps symbolic function (R. Friedman 1994: 287, 322).

Until recently, it was generally accepted that the settlement had been abandoned at the beginning of the First Dynasty in favour of Nubt, the historic town located a little to the north. However, an Italian expedition to Naqada in the 1980s found a particularly high frequency of 'Late'-ware pottery in the northern part of the South Town. The preliminary results were tested by means of a systematic collection of surface sherds over the entire site. This survey confirmed the hypothesis that the northern and north-western parts of the South Town continued to be inhabited into the Early Dynastic period (Barocas *et al.* 1989: 300). Moreover, the internal development of the settlement has been traced by looking at the distribution of ceramic types. It seems that the whole area was occupied during the Naqada II period, the town gradually shifting from the western side of the site towards the edge of the cultivation during the course of the Predynastic period. The inhabited area shrunk to the north and north-western parts of the town during the period of state formation. There is also some evidence for later dynastic occupation in the south-eastern part of the site, although the main centre of population in the region in dynastic times was the town of Nubt (Barocas *et al.* 1989: 300).

Mud seal-impressions provided further evidence for Early Dynastic occupation of the South Town and attest continuing activity at Naqada on the part of the royal administration after the unification of Egypt. Two sealings show rows of animals, characteristic of the reign of Aha (Dreyer, personal communication). The Italian excavations discovered some 300 clay-sealings in total, some of them used to close jars, others still attached to pieces of string or wooden pegs. Most of the seals have been interpreted as door-locking devices (R. Friedman 1994: 313). The combination of substantial mudbrick architecture and doors that were closed with seals suggests the existence of an administrative centre at Naqada South Town (R. Friedman 1994: 37). The botanical remains from the site support this interpretation, indicating that substantial grain processing took place in the town (R. Friedman 1994: 322). The South Town may therefore have served as a centralised food storage facility as well as an administrative centre for the surrounding region. The importance of Naqada in the reign of Aha is further emphasised by the presence of two royal tombs to the south of the settlement (Kemp 1967: 24–5, footnote), one of them probably constructed for Aha's mother Neith-hotep. The élite tombs were apparently accompanied by one or more Early Dynastic cemeteries (R. Friedman 1994: 286–7), probably accommodating the burials of the local First Dynasty officials. Preparations for the burial of Neith-hotep no doubt involved agents of the central government, and the sealings from the South Town certainly suggest official involvement at Naqada.

Dendera

Although the earliest settlement material from Dendera dates to the Old Kingdom, the presence of a few Early Dynastic burials in the adjacent cemetery suggests that the town may have already been in existence at an earlier period. A group of fifteen Early Dynastic burials was excavated at the centre of the main cemetery, due south of the Temple of Hathor. Although several of the graves were devoid of any objects, many others contained pottery vessels, and two burials in particular yielded material which is undoubtedly Early Dynastic (Fischer 1968; Slater 1974). The small number of Early Dynastic burials at Dendera probably indicates that the town itself was small at this period. However, it is possible that the Early Dynastic cemetery was originally somewhat more extensive, since the excavated tombs were located in a wadi, and other graves in the vicinity may have been washed away. Moreover, it has been suggested that two mastabas (numbers 5: 981 and 8: 111) adjacent to an early Old Kingdom tomb group may in fact be Early Dynastic. One of them was found to contain a cylinder vessel fragment with an incised decorative band below the rim, characteristic of the Early Dynastic period (Slater 1974).

Abydos

The early town at Abydos, situated within the later temple enclosure of Osiris, was mapped and partially excavated at the beginning of the twentieth century (Garstang 1901: pl. XXXVII; Petrie 1902; Kemp 1968, 1989: 77–9). Remains of walls and settlement debris were found beneath the present ground level on, and adjacent to, the surviving town mound (the Kom es-Sultan). In addition, the early town may have extended further to the south-west. Houses of the Early Dynastic period were excavated outside the area of the early temple; some contained seal-impressions which may be dated by their style to the First and Second Dynasties (Petrie 1903: 31, pl. XVI.1–7, 8–11, 14). A nearby cemetery of the early First Dynasty, Cemetery M, undoubtedly served the early town (Petrie 1902: 14–15). The fact that the graves lie within the inhabited area suggests that the settlement may not have been walled at the beginning of the First Dynasty. A town wall *was* constructed at some subsequent period, perhaps during the Second Dynasty, although an accurate dating is difficult (Kemp 1977: 189).

With the exception of the élite Cemetery U, the Predynastic cemeteries at Abydos are rather limited in extent, and this suggests that a substantial town was not founded until the very end of the Predynastic period (Kemp 1975b: 30). The earliest occupation level can be dated to the period of state formation (Naqada IIIa2) (Petrie 1902: 22; Kemp 1977: 189; Wilkinson 1993a: 218–19), contemporary with the royal burial in tomb U-j.

The early settlement at Abydos has been the focus of recent archaeological activity. A preliminary survey of the town in 1976 (Kemp 1977) was followed three years later by test excavations, carried out by the Pennsylvania-Yale Expedition. These greatly increased the available data, indicating that the Early Dynastic–Old Kingdom settlement extended over an area of at least 5.6 hectares, probably more (O'Connor 1990: 7). In the southern part of the site, excavation revealed the corner of a massive mud-brick enclosure of the Early Dynastic period. It may have surrounded an early palace or temple, perhaps comparable to the Early Dynastic palace gateway excavated at Hierakonpolis (Weeks 1971–2), but in the Old Kingdom it was incorporated into a residential complex (O'Connor 1990: 8, map 8: 8, figs 6–7, pl. 3). Once again, this seems to emphasise the close connection between Abydos and the royal court in the Early Dynastic period.

Memphis

According to later Egyptian tradition, the city of Memphis was founded by Menes, legendary unifier and first king of Egypt, when he diverted the course of the Nile (Lloyd 1988: 6–13). If we identify Menes as the historical Narmer (or his successor Aha), the earliest settlement at Memphis should date to the beginning of the First Dynasty. However, as we shall see in the next chapter, it is possible that the settlement was founded rather earlier, towards the end of the Naqada II period. Certainly, the earliest graves at Helwan – the necropolis which served Early Dynastic Memphis as its main burial ground – pre-date the beginning of the First Dynasty (Wilkinson 1993a: 209–10; cf. Saad 1947: 111–12, pl. LX), suggesting that the city, too, was founded before the reign of Narmer. Recent survey work and an extensive series of drill cores carried out by the Egypt Exploration Society's Survey of Memphis have revealed the position of the Nile channel in Predynastic/Early Dynastic times, and have pin-pointed the most likely location for the early city of Memphis (Giddy and Jeffreys 1991: 6; Jeffreys and Tavares 1994). Drill cores taken in 1996 yielded cultural material from this location – at the foot of the North Saqqara escarpment, immediately to the east of the First Dynasty élite cemetery – including pottery sherds, shell fragments and a piece of blue frit. The material is concentrated in a layer between 4.5 and 5.5 metres below the surface. Preliminary examination of the pottery sherds suggests an Early Dynastic date, and it is hoped that future seasons of excavation will be successful in revealing areas of Early Dynastic Memphis.

Giza

Excavations around the Menkaura pyramid complex uncovered settlement material, including flints and pottery, dating to the Predynastic and Early Dynastic periods. It seems that a small settlement which had stood on the site was removed to allow the construction of the pyramid complex, and that the debris from this settlement was then dumped in the area of desert to the south (Bietak 1979: 114, 142, n. 35).

The eastern Delta

Recent surveys in the eastern Delta have revealed numerous sites with late Predynastic and/or Early Dynastic material (Kroeper 1989). Although most of the evidence is funerary, the settlement pattern can be deduced from the distribution of cemeteries. It seems to have been characterised by small villages occupying sites elevated above the floodplain, particularly *geziras* or 'turtle-backs'. The importance of foreign trade during the period of state formation is shown by the large number of sites in the north-eastern Delta, along the trade route to southern Palestine. Interestingly, there is very little evidence for settlement in this area from the early Old Kingdom. It may be that when foreign trade became a monopoly of the royal court after the foundation of the Egyptian state, the settlements which had grown up along the major trade route were suddenly deprived of their economic role. With all foreign trade now organised centrally, there may have been little incentive to settle an otherwise marginal area such as the north-eastern Delta (Bietak 1979). However, elsewhere in the Delta, settlements with Old Kingdom material are comparatively widespread, suggesting that the Delta was probably quite densely settled from the very beginning of Egyptian history (Wenke 1989). The ongoing excavations at Tell el-Fara'in (Buto) and Tell er-Ruba (Mendes) have revealed significant activity at both sites during the Predynastic period. It is therefore quite likely that most, if not all, of the major Old Kingdom population centres in the Delta had been inhabited at an earlier period.

Bubastis

A single Early Dynastic tomb was discovered at Tell Basta, indicating that there was a settlement in this area from early times. The importance of Bubastis in the Old Kingdom already suggested that the site was a much earlier foundation. The prominence of the goddess Bastet in inscriptions of the early Second Dynasty may provide additional evidence for this. A further inscription may indicate that Bubastis was already an important settlement at the end of the Predynastic period: a bone label from tomb U-j at Abydos (Dreyer 1993a: pl. 7.i) is incised with two hieroglyphs, the saddlebill stork *b3* (Houlihan 1986: 23–4) and the throne *st*. This may represent an early writing of the place-name *B3st*, 'Bubastis' (cf. Sethe 1906: 432; Gauthier 1925: 5).

Tell el-Iswid

Two soundings made at Tell el-Iswid (south) revealed settlement material dating from the late Predynastic and Early Dynastic periods. The Early Dynastic material is characterised by mudbrick architecture. A silo, querns and stone pounders indicate that the settlement was probably a farming community. The site seems to have been abandoned at some point in the Early Dynastic period (van den Brink 1989). This development may have been part of a wider change in the settlement pattern of the Delta, perhaps connected with the establishment of royal and temple estates in Lower Egypt towards the end of the Third Dynasty.

Minshat Abu Omar

Excavations at Minshat Abu Omar, in the north-eastern corner of the Delta, have revealed an extensive cemetery spanning the late Predynastic period and First Dynasty (Kroeper and Wildung 1985, 1994; Kroeper 1988). Soundings produced evidence of settlement in the area from early Neolithic times, although the later Predynastic and Early Dynastic settlement has not been securely located. The importance of the site in the late Predynastic period appears to have been the result of its strategic geographical location. It lay near the coast, on the Pelusiac branch of the Nile, and at the Egyptian end of the principal overland trade route to southern Palestine. It was thus ideally located for both maritime and overland trade with the Near East, an activity which flourished during the late Predynastic period. Imported Palestinian pottery in some of the burials bears witness to the active trade engaged in by the Predynastic and Early Dynastic inhabitants of the Minshat area. The reasons for the abandonment of the site are unclear. Perhaps a change in the position of the Pelusiac branch removed the strategic benefits of the site. Alternatively, a rise in sea level may have made the low-lying area uninhabitable (Kroeper and Wildung 1985: 98). The creation of a royal monopoly in foreign trade may also have played a part, denying the inhabitants of Minshat Abu Omar their principal livelihood.

Mendes

The two mounds of Tell er-Ruba and Tell Timai comprise the ancient site of Mendes (Brewer and Wenke 1992: 193); the earliest settlement seems to have been restricted to Tell er-Ruba (Wenke and Brewer 1996: 267, fig. 2). In Early Dynastic times the site almost certainly lay on a major Nile branch, providing efficient communication both with the rest of Egypt and with the Mediterranean Sea (Bietak 1975: 110). It is possible that Mendes was a major trading-post in the late Predynastic and Early Dynastic periods, connecting Egypt with the eastern Mediterranean littoral and southern Palestine via both sea and land routes (Brewer and Wenke 1992: 193). Mendes is first attested in an inscription dating to the reign of Djer, when it was known under the name 'npt (Brewer and Wenke 1992: 193).

Excavations in the 1960s revealed Early Dynastic levels in a limited area within the temple enclosure. A number of Early Dynastic graves were uncovered, and although grave goods were scarce, the pottery from the surrounding stratum was dated to the First or Second Dynasty. Similar early pottery was also encountered to the north of a nearby tomb. An Early Dynastic vessel was found at the level of the ground water, in the earliest stratum excavated (Hansen 1967: 16).

During recent fieldwork two trial trenches revealed Early Dynastic remains (Brewer and Wenke 1992), including a vaulted brick structure which may be the remains of a tomb, and a mudbrick structure and hearths, possibly the remains of domestic buildings. Further excavation uncovered 'a series of compacted clay living floors' (R. Friedman 1992: 204). The deepest levels, sampled by means of an auger, yielded crude chaff-tempered pottery of simple shapes, perhaps comparable to the Predynastic domestic pottery from Buto (Brewer and Wenke 1992: 194). This evidence indicates that Mendes, too, was already inhabited in the Predynastic period. From the evidence gained thus far, the excavators conclude that Mendes 'was an extensive community' in the Early Dynastic period. They estimate that at this time the settlement covered much of the later temple area (Brewer and Wenke 1992: 196).

Buto

The site of Buto (modern Tell el-Fara'in) probably owed its importance in Predynastic and Early Dynastic times to a strategic location. Geological surveys of the region have shown that the town lay not only on a major Nile branch, but also on or near the coast (Wunderlich 1988). Buto may have served as a major port and entrepôt for trade between Predynastic Egypt and the eastern Mediterranean basin (Wenke and Brewer 1996: 270). Excavations at Tell el-Fara'in/Buto since 1985 have revealed a continuous settlement sequence from late Naqada I to the end of the Early Dynastic period (von der Way 1986, 1987, 1988, 1989, 1992; Faltings and Köhler 1996). The earliest levels lack any mudbrick architecture; buildings seem to have been matting and post structures, of which only the post-holes have survived (Faltings and Köhler 1996). The period of state formation (Naqada III) is marked at Buto by the adoption of a new ceramic repertoire, signalling a change in technology, production and distribution (Köhler 1992). This coincides with the appearance of the first mudbrick buildings. The special nature of the Early Dynastic complex (see Chapter 8) may also be reflected in some of the unusual forms of pottery found within its walls. These include small, rough pots and bag-shaped jars pierced after firing with one or two holes (Köhler 1992: 19, fig. 7). The original function of both types is far from clear. The importance of Buto in the Early Dynastic period is also apparent from contemporary inscriptions. First Dynasty year labels suggest that more than one Early Dynastic king visited Buto. The town later came to symbolise Lower Egypt as a whole, just as Hierakonpolis came to represent Upper Egypt

(Wilson 1955). The involvement of officials from the central administration is attested by clay seal-impressions found within the Early Dynastic building (Kaplony 1992). These give the names of various administrative departments, and the titles of officials, including Iy-en-khnum, also named on inscribed stone vessels from beneath the Step Pyramid at Saqqara.

CHAPTER TEN

THE REGIONS OF EGYPT

—— •◆• ——

As we have seen, the scale and pace of urban development in Early Dynastic Egypt depended to a large extent on local factors, economic, political, ecological and topographic. To appreciate the full complexity of local variation, it is important to consider the evidence from a regional perspective. The geographic location of settlement sites, their hinterlands and economic resources, and their relationships with neighbouring settlements all provide valuable evidence for the nature of provincial life in ancient Egypt (cf. Bietak 1979: 133). The dominance not only of particular sites but also of certain regions during the period of state formation and the following Early Dynastic period can be understood by looking at the distribution of natural resources along the Nile valley.

'Nature may often set the stage for history' (Seidlmayer 1996b: 108), and the regions with an advantageous resource base – ideally a combination of agricultural potential, access to minerals, and a strategic position allowing control of trade or transport routes – emerged as the main centres of power in the late Predynastic period. The foundation of the Egyptian state brought overtly political factors into play, occasionally overriding local conditions – as in the case of Elephantine – to promote the development of a particular location as an outpost of central government control. The foundation of the new national capital at Memphis propelled the surrounding region to prominence far beyond that which it had enjoyed before the First Dynasty. As the Early Dynastic period progressed and the court established ever more effective mechanisms for controlling the national economy, some of the older centres of influence lost out to newer state foundations. The history of the regions of Egypt during the late fourth and early third millenniums BC therefore reflects the complex interplay of a host of factors, local, regional and national. As Egypt headed towards the centralised state characteristic of the Old Kingdom, the success or failure of a particular region in attaining or maintaining prominence depended to an ever greater degree on the priorities of the court. In the Early Dynastic period, as in later phases of Egyptian history, regional development is thus an instructive barometer of central authority.

THE FIRST CATARACT REGION

Southernmost Upper Egypt was always a border zone, separating the Egyptian and Nubian spheres of political and cultural influence. In the late Predynastic period, settlements of the Nubian A-Group are attested as far north as Kubania, some 18 kilometres north of Aswan. Moreover, pottery of Nubian origin, or made by potters working in the Nubian tradition, seems to have been relatively common in late Predynastic Egyptian contexts in southernmost Upper Egypt, suggesting close cultural links between the First Cataract region and Nubia (Needler 1984: 224). The earliest pottery assemblage from the settlement on Elephantine is predominantly Egyptian, but does include some A-Group Nubian material (Seidlmayer 1996b: 111). Trade between Egypt and Nubia is well attested in the late Predynastic and Early Dynastic periods (Takamiya 1994), and there is also evidence – in the cattle burials at Hierakonpolis (Hoffman 1982; B. Adams 1996) and Qustul, and the shared iconography of early kingship at both sites (Williams 1986, 1987) – for deeper cultural exchange between the late Predynastic polities of Upper Egypt and Lower Nubia.

Regional settlement and the resource base

Although occupying an important strategic position at Egypt's southern boundary, and able to control the lucrative trade with Nubia and sub-Saharan Africa, the First Cataract region lacked the agricultural base associated with other important Upper Egyptian centres. The strip of cultivable land is extremely narrow in this part of the Nile valley, and early settlers took advantage of slight broadenings of the valley in desert embayments and wadi mouths. The distribution of late Predynastic cemeteries indicates that the region was characterised by a series of small villages, strung out along the river's edge at intervals of about 6 kilometres (Seidlmayer 1996b: 113, plus references, 114, fig. 2). This pattern of settlement seems to have been seriously disrupted by the activities of the state on Elephantine at the very beginning of the Early Dynastic period, especially the construction of a fortress to guard Egypt's southern frontier (Seidlmayer 1996b: 113). Hence, it was Elephantine that dominated the region both economically and politically from the early First Dynasty. It is probably no coincidence that Elephantine lies close to the largest area of cultivable land in the region. This lay on the east bank, in the area now occupied by the modern city of Aswan. The islands of the First Cataract could have supported limited cultivation, but other sources of food seem to have been more important in the local subsistence economy. Hunting in the adjacent desert areas would have provided game, whilst animal bones from the settlement on Elephantine indicate that fish formed a significant element in the local diet (von den Driesch 1986; Katzmann 1990).

The riches of the First Cataract region 'did not lie in bread but in stone' (Seidlmayer 1996b: 111). The granite outcrops which form such a prominent feature of the local topography were exploited in early times; the earliest monumental use of pink granite is the lining of Den's burial chamber at Abydos. Various other crystalline rocks are available in the vicinity, and these were valued for stone vessel manufacture, an important craft activity in late Predynastic times. Stone vessels played a key part in the conspicuous consumption favoured by growing élites, and as the source of the necessary raw materials the First Cataract region must have been important. The combination of this factor and Elephantine's strategic location for trade and defence guaranteed central interest – and interference – in the region from the very beginning of the Egyptian state.

Elephantine and the early state

An easily defended location, together with the factors outlined above, made Elephantine a natural focus for early settlement. Probably from Predynastic times, the island served as an entrepôt for prestige goods coming from sub-Saharan Africa via Nubia (Seidlmayer 1996b: 111). Because Egyptian access to these trade routes was reinforced by sporadic punitive campaigns against indigenous groups (Needler 1967; Murnane 1987), Elephantine acquired a strategic importance as well (Seidlmayer 1996b: 111). The site 'gained its character as a town through the functions it took over on the national level' (Seidlmayer 1996b: 127). The construction of a fortress on the island at the beginning of the First Dynasty must have had a profound effect on the local community. The foundation, in the Third Dynasty, of an administrative complex tied to the royal estate probably had a significant impact on the local economy. However, despite heavy-handed state interference, 'the local community retained the informal layout of the village and remained devoted to its temple as its ideological and organisational nucleus' (Seidlmayer 1996b: 127).

THE HIERAKONPOLIS REGION

The growth of the Hierakonpolis region during the Predynastic period has been the focus of much research and is fairly well understood. By contrast, the subsequent history of this part of Egypt during the Early Dynastic period is still rather obscure, although significant contributions have been made in recent years (notably Hoffman *et al.* 1986). By combining the information derived from excavations at Elkab and Hierakonpolis, we can begin to sketch a picture of development for this part of southern Upper Egypt during the first three dynasties (Figure 10.1). Although the fates of the two sites were intertwined, the importance

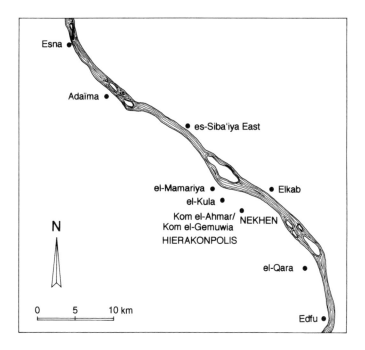

Figure 10.1   Map of the Hierakonpolis region showing sites mentioned in the text
(after Needler 1984: map 3). Capitals denote ancient place names.

of each derives from a particular set of ecological and economic factors.
Lying some 15 kilometres to the south of Hierakonpolis, on the west bank,
the town of Edfu grew up during the Old Kingdom, eventually eclipsing
Hierakonpolis as the main regional centre. The history of southern Upper
Egypt during the Early Dynastic period and early Old Kingdom can be
charted in the varying fortunes of these three sites.

The resource base

To the south of the Hierakonpolis region, at Gebel es-Silsila, the cliffs of
the Nubian sandstone formation come close to the river, forming a
pronounced constriction. South of this point, the more resistant nature of
the rock causes the river to flow in a much narrower floodplain, greatly
reducing the strip of cultivable land along the banks of the Nile.
Hierakonpolis thus represents the southernmost point of agricultural
productivity in Egypt (Bard 1987: 90). However, the growth of the region
during the Predynastic period resulted from a combination of advantages,
strategic as well as agricultural.

In addition to an unusually large area of fertile floodplain (Fairservis
1971–2: 10), the Hierakonpolis region offered other ecological advantages

which made it particularly attractive for early settlement. In Predynastic times, the wide expanse of what is now low desert would have been less arid savannah, capable of supporting game as well as providing pasturage for livestock. The combination of arable and grazing land was clearly advantageous, and 'the existence of a now defunct Nile channel close to the edge of the desert may have attracted settlers to an array of closely spaced ecozones' (R. Friedman 1994: 388–9; cf. Hoffman *et al.* 1986: 178). The presence of abundant fuel, desert clays and suitable locations for kilns favoured the development of large-scale pottery production (Hoffman 1984: 237), an industry which reached industrial proportions as early as the Naqada I period. Hierakonpolis seems also to have developed as an important entrepôt for prestige goods imported from Nubia and the African hinterland, especially elephant ivory, ebony and gold (cf. Bard 1987: 90–1). During the period of state formation, Hierakonpolis was a centre of production and distribution for Egyptian goods found in Lower Nubian A-Group graves, including the pottery known as 'Late-ware' or 'Hard orange ware' (Takamiya 1994; B. Adams 1995: 21). Finally, the site of Hierakonpolis lies opposite the head of a major wadi system, the Wadi Abbad, which gave access to the mineral resources of the eastern desert, including gold-bearing rocks which were probably exploited in Predynastic times. This factor may have been a key one for the early importance of Hierakonpolis (Trigger, in Trigger *et al.* 1983: 39; R. Friedman 1994: 389). Hierakonpolis thus had the agricultural base to support a substantial population, and the concentration of resources to produce a regular surplus. This in turn enabled craft specialisation. Ready access to raw materials and favourable sites for pottery manufacture provided further support for local industry; access to markets and a strategic location astride an important trade route encouraged economic activity.

In sharp contrast to the situation on the west bank, the strip of cultivable land in the vicinity of Elkab is extremely narrow. The present course of the Nile is probably not very different from that in ancient times. Then, as now, the town of Elkab seems to have been situated on the river's edge. As a result, control of river traffic – rather than access to a large area of fertile floodplain – was one of the keys to the site's prosperity. Moreover, the location of Elkab at the mouth of the Wadi Hellal permitted control of land routes as well (Hendrickx 1994: 10). Elkab must therefore have been an important communications and transport node from Predynastic times. The Wadi Hellal also gave access to the wider wadi system of the eastern desert with its gold-bearing rocks. Gold was certainly dispatched via Elkab during historic times (Hendrickx 1994: 10, quoting Helck 1975: 126); whilst soda, also mined in the vicinity (Hendrickx 1994: 10, quoting Lucas 1962: 192–8), provided a further mineral resource. Whatever the benefits of raw materials and a strategic location, a site can enjoy little long-term viability without at least some agricultural potential.

Although lacking in alluvial arable land, the population of Elkab did have access to grazing land, in the Wadi Hellal. The wadi appears to have supported limited pasturage as late as the end of the Old Kingdom, indicating that rainfall must have been considerably higher in ancient times. A savanna-type environment probably extended several kilometres along the wadi, providing hunting grounds. Rock drawings, some of which are likely to be Predynastic, show some of the game which lived in the area and which the local population hunted (Hendrickx 1994: 10). Like its neighbour over the river, Elkab benefited from the twin blessings of a resource base (though with the emphasis on minerals rather than agricultural land) and a strategic location.

Changing patterns of settlement

The pattern of Predynastic settlement in and around Hierakonpolis is relatively well-established. Due to its unique combination of advantages, Hierakonpolis itself seems to have been the focus of regional settlement. No doubt a buoyant local economy and the presence of a ceremonial centre attracted people from the surrounding region. Although there has been no systematic survey of the Hierakonpolis region beyond the limits of the American expedition's concession, visits by members of the expedition to nearby desert-edge sites, local knowledge and an earlier archaeological-geological survey (Kaiser 1961b) all indicate that Hierakonpolis is the only significant Predynastic settlement in the area (Hoffman 1984: 236). However, de Morgan's survey of the region in 1906–7 and 1907–8 revealed at least 20 Predynastic and/or Early Dynastic sites between Esna and Gebel es-Silsila (Needler 1984; Bard 1987: 81). This suggests that southern Upper Egypt was quite extensively settled during the Predynastic period (cf. Bard 1987: 81), and subsequently experienced a nucleation of settlement at the beginning of the Early Dynastic period (in common with other regions of Egypt).

Adaïma was the largest site excavated by de Morgan, and is now the focus of ongoing excavations (Midant-Reynes *et al.* 1990, 1992, 1996). The cemetery was used continuously from late Naqada I to the beginning of the First Dynasty (Midant-Reynes *et al.* 1992: 141); continued activity into the Early Dynastic period is attested by the lithic assemblage, in particular a fragment of a large, bifacially ripple-flaked, flint knife (Needler 1984: 83). On the east bank of the Nile, 12 kilometres north of Elkab, de Morgan reported a heavily plundered cemetery at es-Siba'iya East which seems to have remained in use throughout much of the Early Dynastic period (Needler 1984: 146). Indeed, a nearby children's cemetery, largely unexplored, can be dated by its associated pottery to the middle of the First Dynasty. Only 5 kilometres north of Nekhen, a very large cemetery of over 200 graves was excavated at el-Mamariya (Needler 1984: 90). It seems to have comprised two distinct areas: an earlier one dating to the Predynastic period (Naqada I–II) (Needler 1984: 91), and a later one spanning the end of the First Dynasty and the Second Dynasty. In the southern part of the Hierakonpolis region, 7 kilometres north of Edfu, de Morgan excavated an Early Dynastic cemetery of about 100 tombs at el-Qara. His notebooks also mention a settlement at this site, but no investigations were made (Needler 1984: 122).

It is difficult to draw reliable conclusions from the published results of de Morgan's survey and excavations, but if the site of Adaïma may be taken as typical of the region as a whole, it would appear that many communities which had flourished during the Predynastic period were subsequently abandoned in the aftermath of state formation: a phenomenon which marks the rise of urbanism. As Nekhen and Elkab emerged as leading centres of economic activity and population, many smaller village communities in the vicinity seem to have succumbed to the inevitable pressures. A few, such as es-Siba'iya East and el-Qara must have retained enough local advantages to survive. The settlement at el-Mamariya may actually have benefited from its proximity to Nekhen; the local population may have been able to take some part in the increased economic activity which was now concentrated within its neighbouring town.

During the late Naqada II and throughout the Naqada III periods the Hierakonpolis region witnessed a progressive shift of settlement away from the Great Wadi and towards the floodplain (B. Adams 1995). The town of Nekhen continued to grow during the First Dynasty; the site as a whole witnessed renewed royal patronage at the end of the Second Dynasty. Occupation of the walled town and its two outliers seems to have persisted into the early Old Kingdom (B. Adams 1995: 64), and Nekhen may have continued during this period as 'an important manufacturing and trading centre for copper and, possibly, gold' (Hoffman *et al.* 1986). The settled area at Elkab seems to have remained fairly static during the late Predynastic and Early Dynastic periods (cf. Hendrickx and Huyge 1989: pl. II). Strategic considerations, which lay behind the location of the early town, probably prevented any significant shift of the settled area.

THE NAQADA REGION

Whilst the Hierakonpolis region seems to have been at the forefront of state formation, another site has emerged as the leading Upper Egyptian centre in earlier Predynastic times. This is Naqada, located on the west bank of the Nile, opposite the entrance to the Wadi Hammamat. The wadi, 'one of the relatively few direct and well watered accesses to the

Red Sea coast' (R. Friedman 1994: 286), afforded easy access to the gold reserves of the eastern desert. Moreover, the bend in the Nile as it flows through the Naqada region 'brings the river closer to the Red Sea than at any other point in its course' (R. Friedman 1994: 286). Both these geographic factors would have made Naqada (and Coptos, on the opposite bank of the Nile) an ideal centre for the Predynastic gold trade. After the early First Dynasty the major focus of population moved northwards to a new location, the town of Nubt. During the course of the Early Dynastic period, this too declined in importance, as Naqada was relegated to a position of provincial obscurity. The eclipse of Naqada was accompanied by the rise of Dendera, some 25 kilometres to the north, and perhaps of Thebes, a similar distance to the south. This is probably no coincidence, and may be part of a more widespread phenomenon in which the role of provincial capital was transferred from the traditional centre – in many cases an important Predynastic settlement – to a new town (Kemp 1989).

Coptos, Hu and the rise of Dendera

Just why Naqada – rather than Coptos, located directly at the mouth of the Wadi Hammamat – came to dominate the surrounding region in the Predynastic period is not clear. It is a curious fact that all the most important centres of late Predynastic and Early Dynastic Upper Egypt were located on the west bank of the river (with the possible exception of Elephantine, an island in the Nile). Whether this is pure coincidence, or whether the west bank had a natural advantage, is difficult to say. In Upper Egypt today, the expanse of floodplain is wider on the west bank than on the east bank, but this may not have been the case in the fourth millennium BC. The Coptos colossi indicate that this site was an important cult centre from late Predynastic times, and the symbols carved on these statues suggest that Coptos was a centre of long-distance trade in artefacts from the Red Sea coast; but it never seems to have become a major regional focus of population. At the beginning of the Old Kingdom, both Coptos and the neighbouring site of Hu/Abadiya (cf. Williams 1986: 176) were displaced as important provincial centres by Dendera: the titles borne by the early Fourth Dynasty administrators of Dendera refer to a grouping of three adjacent districts, Coptos, Dendera and Hu (Fischer 1968). The centralisation of power which seems to have occurred at the beginning of the Old Kingdom – and which is most spectacularly attested by the pyramids of the Fourth Dynasty – was achieved partly by means of a fundamental reorganisation of economic and administrative structures. The evidence from sites such as Dendera suggests that another plank of this programme was a conscious policy to integrate the provinces of Upper Egypt by removing the reins of power from the hands of the traditional ruling families (which may have retained significant influence over their communities during the Early Dynastic period). Centres such as Hierakonpolis, Naqada, Coptos and Hu had risen to great prominence during the Predynastic period. Following the formation of the Egyptian state, regional capitals would have served as key nodes in the national administrative apparatus. The transfer of this role from traditional centres to new towns would have been an effective means of bypassing pre-existing regional power structures and exerting central control.

Smaller communities

A re-examination of the evidence has shown that, far from being isolated centres within an otherwise sparsely populated region, Naqada and Coptos were surrounded by an extensive network of smaller communities, all of which seem to have benefited from the region's economic and political advantages (R. Friedman 1994: 345, fig. 8.1; contra Patch 1991: 353). Although settlement remains have only been identified at a few sites – Coptos, Naqada North Town and South Town, and Khattara – a larger number of cemeteries have been excavated in the Naqada region, pointing to a relatively dense settlement pattern. On the east bank of the Nile, the most significant site published to date is the Predynastic burial ground at Khozam, 25 kilometres south of Coptos (Hendrickx 1992). Here, a series of cemeteries seems to have been strung out along the desert edge, comprising many hundreds of burials ranging in date from the Badarian or Naqada I period to the threshold of the First Dynasty. The general picture at Khozam seems to parallel that in other regions of Upper Egypt: a series of small cemeteries spanned the entire duration of the Predynastic period, only to be abandoned at the beginning of the Early Dynastic period when the regional population moved to fewer, densely packed settlements, in this case Naqada and Coptos.

THE ABYDOS REGION

The Abydos region (Figure 10.2) was at the heart of the state formation process, and the demographic changes which took place here during the first three dynasties reflect the wider political developments affecting the nation as a whole. A detailed archaeological survey of the Abydos region (Patch 1991) has indicated that the local south-east quadrant of the region was always lightly settled; by contrast, settlements were more numerous in the north-east quadrant and along the entire west bank of the region (O'Connor 1990: 6). By the Old Kingdom at the latest, settlement clustered around two major centres, Abydos itself and This, the regional capital.

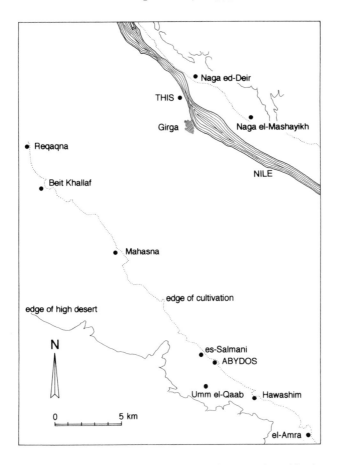

Figure 10.2 Map of the Abydos region showing sites mentioned in the text (after Wilkinson 1993a: fig. 22). Capitals denote ancient place names.

The resource base

'Abydos today is the richest agricultural zone in Upper Egypt, and presumably agriculture was the basis of its wealth in Predynastic times' (Bard 1987: 90). Moreover, it has been suggested that herding and the exploitation of large stands of timber may have been important elements in the regional economy (O'Connor 1990: 6). However, the capacity to produce a food surplus is, on its own, not enough to explain the rise to prominence of the Abydos region during the Predynastic period. A similar advantage must have been shared by other stretches of the Nile valley which did not develop a central place on the scale of Abydos/This (Bard 1987: 90–1). The Abydos region seems to have benefited from a strategic location for trade. Abydos itself lies closer to the oases of the western desert than any other site in the Nile valley. It is possible that the Abydos region acted as an entrepôt for prestige materials (such as elephant ivory, hard stones for vessels and beads, and ochre) entering the Nile valley from the western desert (Bard 1987: 90).

The town and cemeteries of This

'The history and functions of Abydos cannot be understood without reference to Thinis' (O'Connor 1990: 6). Ironically, the principal settlement in the Abydos region during the Predynastic and Early Dynastic periods has not been located by archaeologists. The town probably lay close to, if not directly beneath, the modern town of Girga. An inscribed statue fragment which mentions Thinis is said to have been found at the nearby site of el-Birba, a little to the west; this may help to identify the precise whereabouts of the ancient settlement (Brovarski 1986: 475, 481 n. 2). If the burials at Naga ed-Deir may be taken as a guide – the cemetery probably served This as its main burial ground – the town seems to have existed from at least the Naqada I period. It assumed a greater significance during the late Predynastic period, as the presumed capital of one of the three Upper Egyptian polities, Naqada and Hierakonpolis being the other two. The political and economic power wielded by the late Predynastic Thinite kings must have brought the town itself prosperity and importance on a truly national scale. However, the victorious Thinite kings of the First Dynasty chose to found a new national capital at the junction of Upper and Lower Egypt: Memphis. The town of This probably drew some benefit from its close contacts with the court, but it was to be denied a role as the pre-eminent city of the newly unified state. Instead, it was relegated to the position of a regional capital.

To judge from the cemeteries at Naga ed-Deir, the population of This seems to have remained relatively stable throughout the Predynastic and Early Dynastic periods. None the less, the changes in settlement and cemetery patterns which affected the region as a whole – like many other parts of Egypt – during the period of state formation may not have bypassed the regional capital entirely. Hence, towards the end of Naqada II, and for reasons which remain unclear, Naga ed-Deir was apparently abandoned in favour of an alternative burial site. Graves from the late Predynastic period (late Naqada II) and from the period of state formation (Naqada III/'Dynasty 0') are notable by their scarcity (cf. Brovarski 1982: 300). It seems fairly certain that a substantial population remained in the area (despite arguments to the contrary [Patch 1991: 309]), since Naga ed-Deir saw renewed use as a major cemetery in the Early Dynastic period and Old Kingdom.

With the advent of the Third Dynasty, the Abydos region lost the special role it had enjoyed as the ancestral home and burial place of the First and

Second Dynasty kings. However, the local rulers – possibly the lineal descendants of the First Dynasty kings – evidently continued to exercise considerable authority at a regional level. The economic power of the Thinite governors, derived from their control of one of the most fertile and prosperous stretches of the Nile valley, was expressed in their funerary monuments: a series of huge mudbrick mastaba tombs was erected on the low desert at Beit Khallaf, to the west of This and directly opposite Naga ed-Deir. The scale of Beit Khallaf mastabas K1 and K2, dated by seal-impressions to the reigns of Netjerikhet and Sanakht, is quite unparalleled at any other contemporary provincial site. Smaller mastabas, probably belonging to lesser officials of the regional administration, are located at the nearby cemetery of Reqaqna. The evidence from the Thinite area for the continuing strength of local identity after the foundation of the Egyptian state provides an important balance to the outward appearance of centralised control promoted by the royal court. The distribution of cemeteries in the Thinite area during the Early Dynastic period mirrors the picture in the Memphite region: the local élite were buried in tombs on the western desert edge, while the lesser officials and the majority of the local population were interred in a separate cemetery on the east bank of the Nile.

Settlement nucleation and the early town at Abydos

The temporary abandonment of the cemetery at Naga ed-Deir reflects the demographic changes which affected many parts of the country during the period of state formation. More striking evidence comes from the vicinity of Abydos itself. Many of the cemeteries close to Abydos – including es-Salmani (el-Sayed 1979) and Hawashim on the west bank, and Naga el-Mashayikh on the east bank – were abandoned at the end of the Predynastic period, indicating that a nucleation of settlement took place (Kemp 1977: 189). This phenomenon seems to have had an impact even upon the previously stable communities of Mahasna and el-Amra. Both apparently suffered an irreversible decline in their fortunes at the beginning of the Early Dynastic period (Wilkinson 1993a: 220–1). The foundation of the town at Abydos can be dated to Naqada III (*c.* 3150 BC) and was probably closely bound up with the process of state formation. The town is likely to have attracted the populations of scattered villages, lured by the economic and physical security which a town provided, as well as by potentially greater employment opportunities. The continued prosperity of the Abydos region in the Early Dynastic period is demonstrated at Abydos itself: the town expanded throughout the first six dynasties, and the temple seems to have undergone several rebuilding phases (cf. Kemp 1968: 150).

THE BADARI REGION

In Middle Egypt, the wide alluvial plain on the east bank of the Nile is demarcated by the line of steep limestone cliffs which approach closest to the river near Matmar in the north and el-Etmania in the south (O'Connor 1972: 91). Between these two points the cliffs recede, forming a large embayment. The fertile floodplain is considerably wider in this part of Nile valley than further south, giving the Badari region a high agricultural yield (Wilson 1955: 217) and enabling it to support a relatively large population. However, the region possessed no other particular advantages. Certainly, it was not strategically located for either internal or external trade. This function was dominated by Asyut, to the north, which was situated at a constriction of the Nile valley, ideal for controlling riverine traffic (O'Connor 1972: 91–2). The lack of access to trade routes may have been a major reason why the processes of social stratification and state formation did not progress as far or as fast in the Badari region as in some of the communities further south (Bard 1987: 90–1). The nucleation of settlement seen in other regions of Egypt during the period of state formation is not apparent in the Badari region. Only in the Old Kingdom did a regional capital of any size develop at el-Etmania (O'Connor 1972), perhaps connected with the establishment of royal estates in the area (Jacquet-Gordon 1962: 130–1).

The size and distribution of cemeteries in the Badari region (Holmes and Friedman 1989) suggest both a shift in the centre of population and a change in the settlement pattern at the end of the Predynastic period. Whilst the principal Predynastic settlements were located in the northern part of the region, in particular Matmar, Mostagedda and Hemamia (Brunton 1937, 1948), the Early Dynastic population seems to have been concentrated in the southern area between Hemamia and el-Etmania (O'Connor 1972: 91). The abandonment of the settlement at Hemamia towards the end of the Naqada II period (Brunton and Caton-Thompson 1928: 78) probably reflects a more general settlement shift from the desert edge to the floodplain, perhaps connected with intensified basin irrigation (Kemp 1977: 197). The burial rate for the Badari region in the Early Dynastic period, as reflected in the number of excavated graves, is extremely low, especially by comparison with the preceding Predynastic period (O'Connor 1972: 86). It has been suggested that this reflects a low population (O'Connor 1972: 92–3), but other factors may be responsible. It is quite possible, for instance, that the number of recorded Early Dynastic burials in the Badari region does not accurately reflect the original mortuary population. Furthermore, evidence from the Memphite region indicates that the widespread encroachment of desert dunes towards the end of the Old Kingdom affected settlement on the west bank of the Nile (Jeffreys and Tavares 1994); if this phenomenon was repeated in Middle Egypt, it is likely that Predynastic and Early Dynastic settlements on the west bank – and perhaps their accompanying cemeteries – were abandoned in the face of the advancing dunes, and now lie buried several metres below the present ground surface. This could account for the apparent absence of early remains on the west bank from the entrance to the Fayum southwards to the Abydos region.

At Matmar, there is a continuous burial record from a period of some two millenniums, from Naqada I to the Old Kingdom (Brunton 1948: 29–40). The process of state formation appears to have had little effect upon the community at Matmar. In all probability a small farming village without the network of trading contacts enjoyed by other centres, Matmar illustrates the remarkable stability of the rural Egyptian population over long periods of time. Whilst major centres of political and economic importance were clearly affected by changing circumstances, smaller settlements inhabited largely by subsistence farmers were less prone to national forces. The cemeteries at Mostagedda probably served a village which was inhabited continuously throughout the Predynastic Period (Brunton 1937). The burial record does not extend into the Early Dynastic period, but it is possible that some ancient cemeteries have been destroyed by modern building or grave-digging. In the Early Dynastic period the Badari region was characterised by a series of small settlements, reflecting its remoteness from the centres of economic and political power. The Second and Third Dynasty stairway tombs near Badari suggest that a local élite was able to benefit from the region's agricultural wealth and general prosperity. However, the region as a whole remained insignificant in national terms.

THE MEMPHITE REGION

The apex of the Nile Delta emerges as a crucial region from the very beginning of Egyptian history (Figure 10.3). It was here that the early kings of a united Egypt chose to establish their capital city, the centre of the administrative apparatus created to supervise and control the new nation state. However, Memphis was certainly not founded in a virgin location, nor was the choice of location arbitrary. Three localities displaying the ceramic assemblage characteristic of the Predynastic northern tradition have been excavated along a short stretch of the Nile's east bank, perhaps indicating that there was a significant density of settlement in the Memphite region in the early Predynastic period.

The sudden demise of Maadi in the latter part of Naqada II raises important questions; the most plausible explanation would appear to lie in the changes in climate, ecology and subsistence patterns which seem to have occurred throughout Egypt at this time. The desiccation of the desert savannahs following the end of the Neolithic subpluvial was accompanied by a change to agriculture as the principal subsistence base. The decline in the importance of herding and the deterioration of the previously advantageous desert-edge ecosystem seem to have led to the widespread relocation of settlements to the floodplain. The alluvium now offered the most attractive environment for human activity, which was based almost entirely on agriculture. Maadi, situated on the low desert with easy access to the now arid pasturages, was no longer an attractive location for a local population of farmers. It is likely that this population moved to a new settlement in the floodplain, and the site later occupied by the city of Memphis would be an obvious candidate.

At the beginning of the Early Dynastic period incipient urbanism – and in particular the establishment of Memphis as the national capital

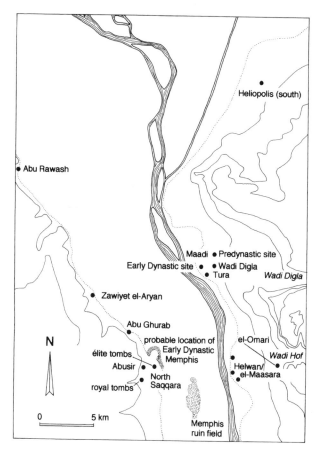

Figure 10.3 Map of the Memphite region showing sites mentioned in the text (after Jeffreys and Tavares 1994: 161, fig. 1).

– seems to have had a major impact on the smaller, surrounding settlements. The growth of Memphis as the dominant population centre of the region, and changes in local topography – caused by the eastward movement of the Nile channel and the rising height of the river's floodplain – emerge as the major factors affecting settlement and cemetery distribution in the Memphis region during the Early Dynastic period.

The early city of Memphis

It would not be surprising if future excavations revealed that the city of Memphis had indeed come into existence during the late Naqada II period. Isolated stone palettes found in the vicinity of Abusir (Kaiser 1964: 106–7) strongly suggest a late Predynastic presence and, as we have seen in Chapter 9, the earliest graves at Helwan pre-date the beginning of the First Dynasty, the traditional date for the foundation of Memphis.

A strategic location

The choice of Memphis by Egypt's first kings as their new national capital reflects the site's strategic importance. First, and most obvious, the apex of the Delta was a politically opportune location for the state's administrative centre, standing at the 'balance of the Two Lands' (a later appellation for Memphis) and offering ready access to both parts of the country. The older, Predynastic centres of power, This and Hierakonpolis, were too remote from the vast expanse of the Delta which had been incorporated into the unified state. Only a city within easy reach of both the Nile valley to the south and the more spread out, difficult terrain to the north could provide the necessary political control that the rulers of Early Dynastic Egypt required.

Second, the region of Memphis must have served as an important node for transport and communications, even before the unification of Egypt. The region probably acted as a conduit for much, if not all, of the riverine trade between northern and southern Egypt. Moreover, commodities (such as wine, precious oils and metals) imported from the Near East by the royal courts of Predynastic Upper Egypt would have been channelled through the Memphite region on their way south. In short, therefore, the site of Memphis offered the rulers of the Early Dynastic period an ideal location for controlling internal trade within their realm, an essential requirement for a state-directed, redistributive economy. Equally important for the national administration was the ability to control communications within Egypt. The Nile provided the easiest and quickest artery of communication, and the national capital was, again, ideally located in this respect. Recent geological surveys of the Memphite region have revealed much about its topography in ancient times. It appears that the

location of Memphis may have been even more advantageous for controlling trade, transport and communications than was previously appreciated.
Surveys and drill cores have shown that the level of the Nile floodplain
has steadily risen over the last five millenniums (Jeffreys and Tavares
1994: 157–8). When the floodplain was much lower, as it would have been
in Predynastic and Early Dynastic times, the outwash fans of the Wadi
Hof and Wadi Digla would have been much more prominent features on
the east bank. The fan associated with the Wadi Hof extended a significant way into the Nile floodplain, forming a constriction in the vicinity of
Memphis. The valley may have narrowed at this point to a mere 3 kilometres (Jeffreys and Tavares 1994: 158), making it the ideal place for
controlling river traffic.

Third, the Memphite region seems to have been favourably located for
the control not only of riverine trade, but also of desert trade routes (cf.
Jeffreys and Tavares 1994: 158). The two outwash fans already mentioned
gave access to extensive wadi systems of the eastern desert. In Predynastic
times, the Wadi Digla may have served as a trade route between the
Memphite region and the Near East, to judge from the unusual concentration of foreign artefacts found in the Predynastic settlement of Maadi.
Access to, and control of, trade routes between Egypt and the Near East
seems to have been a preoccupation of Egypt's rulers during the period
of state formation. The desire to monopolise foreign trade may have been
one of the primary factors behind the political unification of Egypt. The
foundation of the national capital at the junction of an important trade
route with the Nile valley is not likely to have been accidental. Moreover,
the Wadis Hof and Digla provided the Memphite region with accessible
desert pasturage. As we have already seen in the cases of Hierakonpolis
and Elkab, the combination of desert pasturage and alluvial arable land
in the same area was a particularly attractive one for early settlement;
this combination no doubt contributed to the prosperity of the Memphite
region from early Predynastic times.

The settlement and cemeteries of Memphis in the
Early Dynastic period

The extensive Early Dynastic cemeteries of North Saqqara/Abusir (on the
west bank) and Helwan/el-Maasara (on the east bank) are eloquent testi-
mony to the size of early Memphis and to the wealth of its highest officials.
The élite mastabas strung out along the edge of the escarpment at North
Saqqara are impressive funerary constructions (Emery 1949, 1954, 1958).
A cemetery of poorer graves was excavated by Bonnet (1928) a little to
the north, near the modern village of Abusir, and more recent investigations by the Egyptian Antiquities Organisation have uncovered further
Early Dynastic graves in this area (Leclant and Clerc 1992: 242, 1993: 200,

1994: 376). It is now clear that both cemetery areas in fact comprise a single, large burial ground which served the early city of Memphis. Over on the east bank of the river, and directly opposite the élite cemetery of North Saqqara, the huge necropolis of Helwan (more precisely, el-Maasara) represents the largest Early Dynastic burial ground anywhere in Egypt (Saad 1947, 1951; Wilkinson 1996a). Helwan clearly served as the capital's second cemetery during the first three dynasties. The sheer number of burials indicates a considerable Early Dynastic population, including a large administrative class.

Drill cores taken by the Egypt Exploration Society's Survey of Memphis have revealed deposits of Early Dynastic material concentrated in a band running along the base of the North Saqqara escarpment (Giddy and Jeffreys 1991). Here, it seems, was the core of the early city, and such a location fits well with the distribution of cemeteries in the vicinity: the Early Dynastic city would have stood directly between its two principal cemeteries, North Saqqara and Helwan. The inhabited area also seems to have spread northwards, occupying an area close to the modern village of Abusir. This probably reflects the location of the Nile channel in ancient times, which evidently flowed quite close to the edge of the Saqqara escarpment, providing only a thin strip of land on its western bank for cultivation and settlement (Jeffreys and Tavares 1994: 155–7). Hence, the early city of Memphis would have extended as a ribbon development along the river's edge, and evidently in a northerly direction. Towards the end of the Third Dynasty, the eastward progression of the river channel and the steady rise in the height of the floodplain seem to have caused the centre of population to shift southwards. The Abusir Wadi continued to serve as a burial ground, but the main access route to the necropolis seems to have been further south, and entered from the plateau from the east (Jeffreys and Tavares 1994: 159). The élite cemetery of North Saqqara, so closely linked to the early city, was abandoned, and high-status burials were constructed further south, closer to the Step Pyramid enclosure of Netjerikhet.

The foundation and growth of Memphis: regional effects

The foundation of Memphis, and its growth to become the largest concentration of population and employment in the region, might be expected to have had profound effects upon the demography of the surrounding area. However, the degree to which these developments affected individual communities seems to have depended very much upon local factors. Thus, some communities were dealt a fatal blow by the rise of Memphis; others, perhaps with greater natural advantages, survived and prospered.

The repercussions were certainly felt as far afield as Tarkhan. Having been an important centre during the period of state formation ('Dynasty

0'), Tarkhan subsequently declined to a provincial backwater by the end of the First Dynasty. It is probable that, by the middle of the First Dynasty or so, Memphis had become the largest city in Egypt. Hence, whilst there is no evidence to support Petrie's suggestion that the Tarkhan settlement was actually 'the temporary capital of the dynastic people, before the founding of Memphis' (Petrie 1914: 1), his linkage of the growth of Memphis with the decline of Tarkhan is probably a valid one. The rise of Memphis and the huge expansion of the cemetery at Helwan seem to have had little effect, however, on the community at Tura. This was probably a direct successor of the Predynastic settlement at Maadi, since the two sites are only 1 kilometre apart. The area's ecological and strategic advantages (discussed above) were clearly attractive to settlement. Such local factors seem to have enabled the community to survive and prosper even after the growth of Memphis: the burial record at Tura continues unbroken throughout 'Dynasty 0' and the Early Dynastic period, with some of the wealthiest graves dating to the First Dynasty. Also largely unaffected was the community at Abu Rawash, at the northern end of the Memphite necropolis. The sequence of Early Dynastic cemeteries continues unbroken, the number of interments undiminished, throughout 'Dynasty 0', the First and Second Dynasties. At Zawiyet el-Aryan, nearer Memphis, the picture is very different. The foundation and growth of the new capital appears to have dealt the small community a fatal blow, the number of burials in the cemetery showing a dramatic decline after the beginning of the First Dynasty (although the burial rate increases again slightly towards the end of the First Dynasty; and a similar temporary resurgence of local activity may also be reflected in the First Dynasty élite mastabas at Tarkhan [Wilkinson 1993a: 211]).

THE DELTA

Recent survey and excavation have revealed that the Delta was a flourishing area in Predynastic and Early Dynastic times (van den Brink 1992c; Wilkinson 1996b: 91–6). Wherever intensive surveys have been conducted, numerous early sites have been discovered, often in quite dense concentrations (Wenke and Brewer 1996: 271). In terms of landscape, resources and factors affecting early settlement, the Delta presents a very different picture from the Nile valley south of Memphis (Wenke and Brewer 1996: 271).

Geography and trade seem to have been particularly influential in the development of the Delta. Sites raised above the low-lying floodplain were favoured for early settlement; in practice this meant the levees of Nile branches and *geziras*. The latter seem to be concentrated in the eastern Delta, giving this region an advantage. The most striking feature of the Delta, apart from the flatness of the terrain, is the network of branching waterways which divides the land into natural pockets. This would have acted as something of a barrier to east–west communication, although settlements located on the main Nile branches would have enjoyed easy access both to the Nile valley upstream and to the Mediterranean Sea. The proximity of the Delta to Egypt's Near Eastern neighbours – especially Syria-Palestine – gave the region a leading role in foreign trade. As trade in prestige commodities intensified during the period of state formation, sites in the Delta which controlled or channelled such trade were able to reap the benefits. The very existence of some communities, such as Minshat Abu Omar in the north-eastern Delta, seems to have been based on trade with Palestine (Kroeper and Wildung 1985: 97–8). As a result of geographical and economic factors, then, the most important early settlements in the Delta seem to have grown up on major Nile branches, often close to the Mediterranean coast, or at focal points on Near Eastern trade routes. This helps to explain the prominence of sites like Buto, Saïs and Mendes, as well as Minshat Abu Omar. In general, early sites are concentrated in the north-eastern Delta and along the western Nile branches. By contrast, the central Delta seems to have been rather sparsely populated in the Early Dynastic period (Wenke and Brewer 1996: 272).

After the unification of Egypt, the policies of the state towards Lower Egypt became primary determinants of regional development. Large areas of fertile and productive agricultural land made the Delta an attractive location for the foundation of royal domains and estates, which the Early Dynastic kings established to provide for their mortuary cults and to support the royal household (Wilkinson 1996b: 96). The efficient exploitation of the Delta's natural resources also required a network of strategically located collection points, where agricultural produce could be gathered for distribution to the central treasury. This factor probably had a significant impact on the settlement pattern of the Delta in the Old Kingdom. The policies of the central government affected Delta communities in other ways as well. From the beginning of the First Dynasty, foreign trade may have become a royal monopoly. For a site like Minshat Abu Omar, the 'nationalisation' of trade would have removed its key advantage and the basis for its prosperity. On another level, the court was keen to promote and defend the territorial integrity of the state, partly through the explicit demarcation of national frontiers. It seems likely that certain Delta sites were chosen to act as strategic border posts by the Early Dynastic government, perhaps giving some settlements a new *raison d'être*. Buto and Kom el-Hisn may have performed such a role with respect to the western Delta, guarding the Egyptian state against infiltration by Libyan peoples (Wenke and Brewer 1996). As part of the intensive program of royal propaganda launched by Egypt's early kings, important Delta sites were visited by the king. He may have had residences at the more important locations, and there are inscriptions which suggest a royal palace at Buto in the Early Dynastic period (*ḥwt p-Ḥr-msn*, attested on seal-impressions and inscribed stone vessels). The presence of a royal residence would naturally have boosted the importance of a local community, and this is another way in which the state may have influenced the development of Delta sites. Hence, the history of the Delta during the late Predynastic and Early Dynastic periods reflects the interplay of a combination of factors, geographical, economic and political. These can be seen at work more closely in the most intensively studied region of the Delta.

The north-eastern Delta

The north-eastern Delta has emerged as an area of substantial early activity (Kroeper 1989), as attested by the concentration of élite objects found at sites in the region (Clédat 1914; Leclant 1952: 244; Fischer 1958, 1963) and confirmed by the excavation of numerous settlement and cemetery sites.

In the western Delta, before the end of the fifth millennium, the landscape seems to have been free from the effects of the inundation, making it more attractive for Neolithic settlement. However, from at least the beginning of the fourth millennium, climatic and geological conditions in the western Delta changed significantly, necessitating the removal of settlements to higher ground. This seems to have tilted the balance in favour of the eastern Delta as the more favourable area for settlement (Andres and Wunderlich 1992: 164). The widespread presence of 'turtle-backs' or *geziras* in the eastern Delta offered attractive locations for villages and their accompanying cemeteries. It is noteworthy that all of the eastern Delta archaeological sites investigated in recent years are located on *geziras*, including Tell Ibrahim Awad (van den Brink 1992b), Tell el-Farkha (Chlodnicki *et al.* 1992) and Minshat Abu Omar (Krzyzaniak 1992). At a time when contacts between Egypt and the Near East were intensifying, the added attraction of access to trade routes helps to explain the concentration of late Predynastic and Early Dynastic sites in the eastern Delta revealed by recent excavations (Bard 1987; but note the comments of Chlodnicki *et al.* 1992: 183).

Following the unification of Egypt, some communities in the eastern Delta continued to flourish for as long as the court maintained intensive contacts with southern Palestine. However, by the beginning of the Second Dynasty, a realignment of trading relations, combined with a possible change in the course of the main eastern Nile branch, removed the strategic advantages of these communities. A rise in sea level may also have contributed, making the low-lying areas uninhabitable (Kroeper and Wildung 1985: 98). The abandonment of the cemetery at Minshat Abu Omar by the end of the Second Dynasty at the latest mirrors the decline of the region as a whole. The administrative structure imposed by the First Dynasty kings on the Delta seems to have treated it as 'unclaimed land', ripe for appropriation by the court for the foundation of royal estates (Wilkinson 1996b: 96). In contrast with sites in the central and western Delta which retained their importance throughout the Early Dynastic period and beyond, the erstwhile important Predynastic centres of the eastern Delta were either abandoned entirely or declined to become distant provincial backwaters. Not until the late Middle Kingdom was the eastern Delta once again to occupy a central position in Egyptian political and economic life.

EPILOGUE

—— •◆• ——

Early Dynastic Egypt has come of age. It can no longer be regarded as an obscure transition, bridging the gap between the beguiling Predynastic period and the spectacular Old Kingdom. The Early Dynastic period deserves to be treated in its own right as a major stage of ancient Egyptian civilisation; not just any stage, but the formative one. As we have seen, most of the key features which, for us, define ancient Egyptian civilisation were initially developed by the ruling élite of the Early Dynastic period. The mechanisms of rule which remained at the heart of Egyptian government for some three thousand years had their origin in the first three dynasties. They were formulated in response to the enormous challenge of ruling the world's first nation state. Their particular character suited not only the geography of Egypt but also the Egyptian psyche. Whether administrative structures, foreign relations, the ideology of divine kingship, royal mortuary architecture or the practice of religion, the solutions adopted by Egypt's early rulers to the problem of establishing authority moulded their country and profoundly influenced its subsequent development. Away from the interests and influence of the court, however, local communities and the regions had their own concerns. Such factors were equally important for the character of life in the Nile valley and for the trajectory of Egyptian history.

After more than a century of interest in the earliest period of Egyptian history, we can now attempt to answer the question, 'what came before the pyramids?' The body of evidence for Early Dynastic Egypt is considerable (if complex) and growing all the time. Every year, new information from excavations and scholarly studies is enhancing our understanding of Egypt's early civilisation. The picture is far from complete, but it is certain that in future years many more pieces of the puzzle will fall into place.

GLOSSARY

—— ·◆· ——

From the outset, it has been the author's intention to make this book as accessible as possible to non-Egyptologists. Specialist and technical vocabulary has therefore been kept to a minimum. However, in the interests of accuracy and conciseness it has proved necessary to retain some terms which may be unfamiliar to readers from outside the field of Egyptology. Such terms fall into two broad categories: specialist words and phrases which are confined to the study of ancient Egypt, and terms which are in general usage but which have a specific, sometimes different, meaning to Egyptologists. For the sake of clarity, both types of term have been included in the following glossary. It is important to understand that certain words and phrases will be used in slightly different ways by different authors. The glossary below explains the meaning of terms *as they are used in the current work*. The first instance of each glossary entry in the text has been marked in bold.

A-group *(n.)* The indigenous *Neolithic* culture of Lower Nubia which flourished in the second half of the fourth millennium BC.

amuletic *(adj.)* Possessing the magical, protective power of an amulet (a small object worn about the person to protect its wearer from malign forces).

Amuq *(n.)* A plain in coastal northern Syria; also used to describe the cultural sequence of this region during the fourth and early third millenniums BC.

annals *(n.)* Records of the reigns of the *Early Dynastic* period and early Old Kingdom, compiled at a later date and inscribed on blocks of stone which would originally have been set up in a temple context. Several fragments of ancient annals stones have survived, notably the *Palermo Stone* and the associated Cairo fragment. When complete, they would have recorded the major events of each king's reign – from the beginning of the First Dynasty to the middle of the Fifth – in a year-by-year format.

apotropaic *(adj.)* Able to ward off evil.

Archaic *(adj.)* Term used to denote the first two dynasties as a period of Egyptian history; now often replaced by *Early Dynastic*.

Asiatic *(n. and adj.)* An inhabitant of the lands to the north-east of Egypt (present-day Sinai, Israel, Jordan, Lebanon and Syria). Its pejorative tone accurately reflects the usage of the parallel ancient Egyptian term ˤ3m.

bark *(n.)* The sacred or ritual boat of a king or deity.

breccia *(n.)* Technically 'red and white limestone breccia'; a rock with white inclusions in an orange-red matrix, favoured for stone vessels and small sculptures in the *Early Dynastic* period.

cartouche *(n.)* In ancient Egyptian inscriptions, the elongated oval frame used to enclose certain royal names from the end of the Third Dynasty.

cenotaph *(n.)* A tomb or other monument built for purely symbolic purposes.

ceramic *(adj.)* Referring to pottery.

ceramicist *(n.)* A specialist who studies (ancient Egyptian) pottery.

Chalcolithic *(n. and adj.)* Literally 'copper stone age'; an archaeological period applied to the Near East; the transitional stage between the end of the *Neolithic* and the beginning of the Early Bronze Age (*EBI*) when copper and stone tools were both in use; its dating varies from region to region, but in the Levant it roughly corresponds to *c.* 4000–3600 BC, equivalent to the Badarian and Naqada I periods in Upper Egypt.

co-regency *(n.)* A constitutional practice whereby a king's successor (usually his eldest surviving son) would be crowned during his predecessor's (father's) lifetime, and the two monarchs would reign jointly for a period. The practice was designed to ensure a smooth transition of power from one reign to the next.

corvée labour *(n.)* The administrative and economic system whereby agricultural workers (the bulk of the population in ancient Egypt) gave their labour to the state during the annual *inundation* in return for the use of the land – which in theory belonged to the king – the rest of the year; this system allowed the state to mobilise the huge resources of manpower needed to build royal monuments such as the pyramids.

cosmological *(adj.)* Referring to speculation about the composition and workings of the universe (cosmology).

cursive *(adj.)* Describing inscriptions written in ink with a running hand, the individual signs more hastily executed than monumental hieroglyphs.

cylinder seal *(n.)* A cylindrical piece of stone (or occasionally wood), carved with an inscription, often identifying ownership; to seal an item, the cylinder would be rolled over a sealing of wet clay, making an impression of the original inscription.

cylinder vessel *(n.)* A cylindrical jar, up to about 30 centimetres in height, usually made from *marl clay* pottery and fired to a pale cream colour, probably in imitation of stone. Cylinder vessels of stone, usually *travertine*, are also known. Pottery cylinder vessels were manufactured in large numbers during the late *Predynastic* to *Early Dynastic* transition. The pattern of the incised decorative band around the shoulder changed over time, making cylinder vessels a good chronological indicator.

demography *(n.)* The study of population, especially its distribution.

diorite *(n.)* A hard, igneous rock, dark with lighter mottles, obtained principally from the western desert, and used for stone vessels and statuary.

djed-pillar *(n.)* An ancient *fetish* of unknown origin, associated with the god Ptah and, later, with Osiris, god of the dead; used as the hieroglyphic sign for 'stability', the symbol may represent a leafless tree or a notched stick; sometimes called the 'backbone of Osiris'.

dolomite *(n.)* A variety of limestone composed of calcium and magnesium carbonate, used for stone vessels.

domain *(n.)* A royal foundation, comprising an area of agricultural land together with its livestock and workforce; established to provide income for a king's mortuary cult.

double crown *(n.)* In Egyptian *iconography*, the crown formed by combining the separate *red crown* and *white crown*.

'Dynasty 0' *(n.)* Term coined to describe the late *Predynastic* kings who ruled over part or all of Egypt before the beginning of the First Dynasty. The use of the word 'dynasty' is misleading since the rulers before Narmer probably belonged to a variety of royal houses, some of them perhaps reigning concurrently in different parts of the country.

Early Dynastic *(adj.)* Term applied to the first major phase of Egyptian history, comprising the first two or (in this book) three dynasties; increasingly favoured as an alternative to the term *Archaic*.

EBI *(n. and adj.)* Early Bronze Age I. An archaeological period (divided into an earlier phase EBIa and a later phase EBIb) applied to the Near East, c. 3600–3000 BC; it follows the *Chalcolithic*, and corresponds to the Naqada II and Naqada III periods in Egypt.

EBII *(n. and adj.)* Early Bronze Age II. An archaeological period applied to the Near East, c. 3000–2700 BC; it follows the EBI.

ennead *(n.)* A group of nine deities, particularly those associated with the creation myth of Heliopolis (Atum, Shu, Tefnut, Geb, Nut, Osiris, Isis, Seth and Nephthys).

entrepôt *(n.)* A location which acts as a collection and processing centre for incoming commodities, especially trade goods.

epigraphy *(n.)* The study, style or technique of ancient inscriptions.

epithet *(n.)* A descriptive word or phrase, often applied to a god.

eponymous *(adj.)* Giving its name to something. (For example, in the royal *annals*, each year is designated by one or more particular eponymous events.)

fetish *(n.)* A symbol or totem associated with a deity and believed to contain or invoke the supernatural power associated with that deity.

flail *(n.)* A short rod with two or more pendant strips or strings of beads attached to it; perhaps originally a shepherd's whip for goading his flock, the flail became part of the royal insignia from late *Predynastic* times.

funerary enclosure   *(n.)* At Abydos, Hierakonpolis and Saqqara, a large, rectangular court, either surrounded by solid walls of mudbrick or masonry, or delineated by lines of graves; an enclosure was probably intended to serve as a focus for the mortuary cult of the king who built it (although other purposes have been suggested), and is likely to have been provided with additional structures inside, either temporary or permanent; funerary enclosures are sometimes called 'funerary palaces'.

gezira   *(n.)* Arabic name for a low, sandy hill, rising above the Nile flood-plain; such features, also called 'turtle-backs', are particularly common in the eastern Nile Delta where they provided suitable locations for early settlement.

glazed composition   *(n. and adj.)* A more accurate term than 'faience', used to describe the glassy material – composed of crushed quartz with small amounts of lime, plant ash or natron, and colouring agent – from which *votive* offerings and other small objects were made throughout Egyptian history.

Hamitic   *(adj.)* Belonging to the grouping of north African languages or cultures which includes, amongst others, ancient Egyptian and Berber.

hierarchical scaling   *(n.)* A system used in ancient Egyptian art to indicate the relative status of human figures, whereby the larger the figure, the greater its importance.

Horus   *(n.)* An ancient sky god, depicted as a falcon (in later periods as a human figure with the head of a falcon). Horus was closely associated with kingship from the earliest period of recorded history; according to ancient Egyptian ideology, the king was the earthly incarnation of Horus; the image of Horus atop the king's principal name (*serekh*) proclaimed this identity.

iconography   *(n.)* A system of symbols and motifs used in a consistent way, above all to express notions of theology and ideology.

ideogram   *(n.)* A hieroglyphic sign that stands for a concept or a whole word rather than a letter or syllable.

inundation   *(n.)* Before the construction of the Aswan dams in modern times, the annual flooding of the River Nile which renewed the fertility of the land; the floodwaters rose in July and receded again in September.

ka   *(n.)* Ancient Egyptian term for the creative life-force which survived the physical death of a person and required sustenance in the afterlife; the royal *ka* was the divine essence of kingship which passed at the death of a king directly to his successor, inhabiting his body and giving him the supernatural powers associated with the ruler.

king list   *(n.)* A list compiled in ancient times recording the names and order of succession of Egyptian kings, sometimes with additional information about reign lengths and salient events; with the possible exception of the *Turin Canon*, king lists were not intended as objective historical documents, but were compiled to promote a particular view of kingship, stressing the unbroken line of rulers from the beginning of time; hence, foreign kings and others who were viewed by posterity as illegitimate were excluded from the king lists at Abydos, Karnak and Saqqara.

label *(n.)* A small rectangular piece of wood, bone or ivory, inscribed with characters and attached to an object by means of a piece of string threaded through a hole in one corner of the label. The inscription might denote the quantity, provenance, ownership or contents of the object. More elaborate *year labels* carried additional information about the date of the labelled object.

lappet *(n.)* A flap or pendulous side-piece of a wig.

Lower Egypt *(n.)* The northern part of the Egyptian Nile valley together with the Nile Delta, from the Fayum entrance in the south to the Mediterranean Sea; it includes the *Memphite* region.

Maat *(n.)* Ancient Egyptian for 'truth, justice'. The concept of correct behaviour and cosmic order which it was the king's primary duty to uphold and defend against the forces of chaos. In later periods, Maat was characterised as a goddess in her own right.

macehead *(n.)* The solid end of a mace, conical, disc-shaped or *piriform*, perforated by a hole for the shaft; made from clay or, more frequently, stone, maceheads were potent symbols of authority in late *Predynastic* and *Early Dynastic* Egypt; ceremonial maceheads were made as vehicles of *iconography*, but were not intended for practical use.

magazine *(n.)* A store-room.

magnetometry *(n.)* A method of remote sensing using a device (magnetometer) that detects buried features by the slight distortions they produce in the earth's magnetic field.

'Main Deposit' *(n.)* Name given to a large collection of *votive* objects unearthed at Hierakonpolis at the end of the nineteenth century in circumstances which remain unclear; many of the objects date to the period of *unification*, including the famous Scorpion *macehead* and Narmer *Palette*; other artefacts may be somewhat later in date.

marl clay *(n.)* Calcareous clay used to make pottery which is generally finer, harder and less porous than pottery made from alluvial Nile clay; the production of marl clay pots, centred around Qena in Upper Egypt, required more advanced *ceramic* technology and its inception marks an important stage in the process of cultural development during the late *Predynastic* period.

mastaba *(n.)* Arabic for 'bench'. Name given to a tomb with a rectangular superstructure whose walls slope slightly inwards; in the *Early Dynastic* period mastabas were constructed for both royal and private individuals; the external walls of mastabas were often decorated in the '*palace façade*' style.

Memphite *(adj.)* Belonging to the city or region of Memphis, the capital of ancient Egypt from the beginning of the First Dynasty.

Menes *(name)* According to later Egyptian tradition (including the New Kingdom *king lists*), the first king of Egypt; credited by Herodotus with diverting the course of the Nile and founding the city of Memphis; Menes may be a semi-legendary figure, or may be a conflation of more than one king; he has been identified both with Narmer and with his successor Aha.

Middle Egypt *(n.)* A rather imprecise geographical term, applied to the stretch of the Nile valley between the entrance to the Fayum and the *Thinite* region; corresponds to northernmost *Upper Egypt*.

mummiform *(adj.)* Shaped like a mummy; that is, a human figure tightly wrapped in bandages.

Naqada culture *(n.)* Modern name given to the *Predynastic* cultural tradition of Upper Egypt, after the important settlement and cemeteries at Naqada, north of Luxor.

necropolis *(n.)* A large burial ground, often comprising several cemeteries or distinct cemetery areas.

Neolithic *(n. and adj.)* 'New Stone Age'. An archaeological period, characterised by the use of stone tools and the replacement of hunting and gathering by agriculture as the primary means of subsistence; the Neolithic is followed in the Near East by the *Chalcolithic* and *EBI*, in Egypt by the *Predynastic* period.

Neolithic subpluvial *(n.)* A geological period of increased rainfall over Egypt; its end, *c.* 3300 BC, was marked by the desiccation of the desert savanna and a probable influx of population into the Nile valley.

nome *(n.)* A province and administrative division of Egypt; Upper Egypt was divided into 22 nomes, Lower Egypt into 20; the origins of the nome system probably go back to the First Dynasty, and the system was fully developed in the early Old Kingdom.

nswt-bíty *(n.)* Ancient Egyptian for 'he of the sedge and bee'. Title borne by Egyptian kings, to express the many dualities over which they ruled; often translated 'King of Upper and Lower Egypt', though 'dual king' is perhaps more accurate.

obsidian *(n.)* A hard, black volcanic glass, used to make sharp cutting blades and for inlays.

'palace-façade' *(adj.)* A style of architectural decoration – used predominantly on tombs of the *Early Dynastic* period – whereby alternating recessed niches and buttresses give a panelled appearance to the façade of a building; the motif is believed to have imitated the external appearance of the early royal palace.

Palermo Stone *(n.)* Name given to the largest surviving fragment of an ancient *annals* stone, now housed in the Archaeological Museum in Palermo.

palette *(n.)* A flat piece of siltstone, designed for grinding mineral pigments to make cosmetics; carved in a wide variety of shapes, palettes are one of the most distinctive types of artefact from *Predynastic* Egypt; during the period of state formation, elaborate ceremonial palettes were decorated with complex scenes; most famous of such objects is the Narmer Palette.

papyrus skiff *(n.)* A lightweight boat made from papyrus reeds, used by the ancient Egyptians especially for fishing and hunting birds in marshland environments.

petrographic analysis *(n.)* The scientific technique of examining thin sections of pottery or rock under magnification to determine the mineral composition and hence, often, the provenance of the sample.

phyle *(n.)* A team of workers which served with other teams on a rotational basis in the service of the royal palace or mortuary cult.

piriform *(adj.)* Pear-shaped, usually applied to *maceheads*.

polity *(n.)* A territory under unified political control; applied to the kingdoms which came into existence before the *unification* of Egypt at the end of the fourth millennium BC.

pr-nswt *(n.)* Ancient Egyptian for 'king's estate'. A separate department of the administration responsible for the personal estates and income of the king; it was presumably concerned with supporting the king, the royal family and the royal retinue, and was probably under direct royal control.

Predynastic *(adj.)* Term applied to the period of Egyptian prehistory ending with the *unification* of Egypt and the advent of the First Dynasty, *c.* 3050 BC; the beginning of the Predynastic period is not so easily defined, but is often taken to coincide with the appearance of the *Neolithic* Badarian culture in northern Upper Egypt; in the Predynastic sequence of *Upper Egypt*, the Badarian is followed by three major phases of the *Naqada culture*; before *c.* 3200 BC, the Predynastic period in *Lower Egypt* is characterised by a sequence of several indigenous material cultures .

raised relief *(n.)* A technique of decoration, usually applied to walls, whereby the background is cut away, leaving the figures and/or texts raised above the surrounding surface.

red crown *(n.)* The head-dress worn by the king in his capacity as ruler of Lower Egypt, though perhaps of Upper Egyptian origin; called *dšrt* ('the red one') in ancient Egyptian, the crown has a low front and a tall back projection with a coil protruding forwards from it.

register *(n.)* In ancient Egyptian art, one of a series of horizontal compartments or strips into which scenes were divided.

resistivity *(n.)* A method of remote sensing that detects buried features by passing an electrical current through the soil and measuring changes in conductivity; such changes can be caused by the differential retention of groundwater that distinguishes built features from their surroundings.

rosette/palmette *(n.)* A symbol found on royal monuments from the period of *unification*, resembling a flower with six or seven petals, or a crown of palm leaves viewed from above; it is thought to have signified the ruler.

scarab *(n.)* The dung-beetle, viewed by the ancient Egyptians as a manifestation of the sun god; amulets and seals in the form of scarabs were popular from the end of the Old Kingdom onwards.

šdšd-device *(n.)* From the ancient Egyptian word, an unidentified bag- or balloon-shaped object of unknown origin which is often shown attached to the front of the standard of the jackal god Wepwawet.

Sed-festival *(n.)* The pre-eminent festival of kingship which served to renew and rejuvenate the king's powers through a series of highly symbolic rituals.

sequence dating system *(n.)* A system developed by the British archaeologist Sir Flinders Petrie for assigning relative dates to *Predynastic* graves, largely by means of their pottery; the system was based upon the study of pots from the cemeteries at Naqada, Ballas and Diospolis Parva; it relied on several assumptions, notably that graves containing similar types of pottery are close in date, and that certain classes of pottery – especially *cylinder vessels* and their forerunners, wavy-handled jars – underwent gradual but continuous stylistic change.

serdab *(n.)* Arabic for 'cellar'. The room in a *mastaba* tomb where a statue of the deceased was placed to act as a resting place for the *ka*; the room was often provided with 'eye-holes', giving the *ka* access to the statue and allowing the statue to 'look out'; the earliest *serdab* is in the Step Pyramid complex of Netjerikhet, from the beginning of the Third Dynasty.

serekh *(n.)* Ancient Egyptian word for the rectangular device, representing a section of the royal *palace-façade*, which served as a frame enclosing the king's *Horus* name; the *serekh* is usually surmounted by the figure of a falcon.

Seth-animal *(n.)* The mysterious dog-like animal with a long snout, square-ended ears and upright, forked tail which embodied and signified the god Seth; it has been variously identified as an anteater, pig, dog or wild ass, but probably represents a composite or entirely mythical creature.

sherd *(n.)* A piece of broken pottery.

Shunet ez-Zebib *(n.)* Arabic for 'storehouse of raisins'. Nickname given to the massive *funerary enclosure* of mudbrick built for the last king of the Second Dynasty, Khasekhemwy, at Abydos.

siltstone *(n.)* A very fine-grained, green-grey rock, used especially for the manufacture of elaborate stone vessels in the *Early Dynastic* period (erroneously called 'slate', 'schist' or 'greywacke' by earlier authors); the main source of this rock was the Wadi Hammamat in the eastern desert.

social stratification *(n.)* The division of a community into a hierarchy of social classes, based upon differences in status; the presence of social stratification is generally taken as an indication that a society is becoming increasingly complex and is moving towards state formation.

stela (plural stelae) *(n.)* A slab of stone or (less often) wood, usually rectangular with a rounded top, bearing inscriptions and/or figurative scenes; stelae served funerary, *votive* and commemorative purposes, and could also be erected as boundary markers.

stratigraphic *(adj.)* Relating to the sequence of layers (strata), their order and significance (stratigraphy), on an archaeological site.

subsidiary burial *(n.)* A small grave, usually one of a group, accompanying the tomb of a king or high official, or a royal *funerary enclosure*; the servants and retainers interred in subsidiary burials would accompany their master or mistress into the afterlife to continue their service.

syncretism *(n.)* The identification or fusion of two (or more) deities to produce a compound deity incorporating attributes from both (or all) its 'parent' gods; an example of early syncretism is the close identification of the goddesses Bat and Hathor.

Syria-Palestine *(n.)* Geographical term applied by Egyptologists to the area of the Near East comprising the modern countries of Israel, Lebanon, Syria and western Jordan.

tell *(n.)* Arabic for 'hill', 'mound'. An archaeological site, especially in the Nile Delta, where the accumulation of cultural material over centuries has resulted in a mound visible above the surrounding area.

Thinite *(adj.)* Belonging to the city or royal house of This/Thinis, capital of the Abydos region from *Predynastic* times and ancestral home of the First and Second Dynasties.

titulary *(n.)* The collected titles and names borne by a king, comprising a number of separate and distinctive elements; *Early Dynastic* royal titularies comprised the *Horus* title (written with the *serekh*), 'Two Ladies' title, *nswt-bíty* title and the 'Golden Horus' title; the name which followed the last of these came to be written in a *cartouche*.

transliteration *(n.)* The rendition into the Roman alphabet (with some additional special signs and accents) of ancient Egyptian words, using a standard system; this allows ancient Egyptian words to be written when a hieroglyphic font is not available, and to be 'pronounced' following certain conventions:

3   stands for a sound which occurs in Hebrew and Arabic but not in English, a little like the glottal stop; conventionally pronounced like the *a* in 'c*a*r'

i̯   another sound common in Hebrew and Arabic but not in English; like the English *y*; conventionally pronounced like the *i* in 'b*i*t'

ʿ   stands for the equivalent of the Hebrew and Arabic letter *ayin*, not found in English; a guttural sound made in the back of the throat; conventionally pronounced like the *a* in 'c*a*r', so difficult to distinguish in 'spoken ancient Egyptian' from *3*

ḥ   an aspirated, emphatic *h*; often pronounced like a normal *h*

ḫ   like the *ch* in Scottish 'lo*ch*' and conventionally pronounced as such

ẖ   rather softer than *ḫ*, more like the *ch* in German 'i*ch*'; sometimes pronounced more like the *ch* in 'chaos'

š   stands for a single letter corresponding to *sh* as in *sh*ip; pronounced *sh*

q   a guttural *k* sound made in the back of the throat; often pronounced like a normal *k*

ṯ   usually said to represent the sound *ch* as in 'chair', and conventionally pronounced as such; but perhaps more like *ty*, as in 'mee*t you*'

ḏ   usually said to represent the sound *j* as in '*j*am', and conventionally pronounced as such; but perhaps more like *dy*, as in 'fee*d you*'

    To assist pronunciation of ancient Egyptian words in transliteration a neutral vowel (*e* as in b*e*d) is generally inserted between adjacent consonants, while *w* – when it occurs in the middle or at the end of a word – is pronounced like the *u* in r*u*ne. Hence, *pr-nswt* is pronounced per-nesut.

travertine   *(n. and adj.)* The yellowish or white translucent stone, technically calcium carbonate, often called 'Egyptian alabaster'; it was mined at Hatnub in northern Upper Egypt and was widely used for stone vessel manufacture.

triad   *(n.)* A statue comprising a group of three figures.

tumulus   *(n.)* A low, rounded artificial mound.

Turin Canon   *(n.)* Name given to a fragmentary papyrus, now in the Egyptian Museum in Turin, inscribed with a *king list* compiled in the reign of Ramesses II (*c.* 1279–1213 BC); unlike other king lists, the Turin Canon seems to have aimed at completeness.

'Two Ladies'   *(n.)* Translation of the ancient Egyptian word *nbty*, referring to the two protector deities of *Upper Egypt* and *Lower Egypt*: the vulture goddess Nekhbet of Elkab, and the cobra goddess Wadjet of Buto; from the late First Dynasty, the 'Two Ladies' formed one of the king's titles, expressing the geographical duality of his rule; some *Early Dynastic* kings bore a distinctive 'Two Ladies' name, written after this title.

Umm el-Qaab *(n.)* Arabic for 'mother of pots' (from the huge quantities of later offering-pottery which still litter the site). The name given by Egyptologists to the desert cemetery at Abydos in Upper Egypt where the kings of the First Dynasty and the last two kings of the Second Dynasty were buried.

unification *(n.)* Term applied to the formation of the ancient Egyptian state, *c.* 3100 BC; a lengthy and gradual process rather than a single, swift event, unification involved the coalescence of a number of territories to form a single country from the Mediterranean coast to the First Cataract at Elephantine.

Upper Egypt *(n.)* The southern half of the Egyptian Nile valley, from the Fayum entrance in the north to Elephantine in the south; the northernmost stretch, north of the *Thinite* region, is sometimes called *Middle Egypt.*

uraeus *(n.)* The figure of a rearing cobra which adorned the brow of the king to give him magical protection; in *Early Dynastic* inscriptions, the uraeus also appears on the standard of the jackal god Wepwawet.

vizier *(n.)* Name given by Egyptologists to the person at the head of the ancient Egyptian administration who bore the title(s) (*t3tti z3b*) *t3ti*; the position entailed judicial as well as political authority.

votive *(adj.)* Donated to express or reinforce a wish or prayer.

wadi *(n.)* A dry valley, often marking the course of a torrent during rare rainstorms.

white crown *(n.)* The head-dress worn by the king in his capacity as ruler of Upper Egypt; called *ḥdt* ('the white one') in ancient Egyptian, the crown is tall and conical in shape with a bulbous tip.

year label *(n.)* An elaborate type of *label*, on which specific events are depicted in order to identify the year and hence date the attached commodity; year labels provide much of our evidence for *Early Dynastic* history; year labels are also referred to by the German term *Jahrestäfelchen.*

BIBLIOGRAPHY

———— •◆• ————

ABBREVIATIONS OF SERIES AND PERIODICALS

ÄA	Ägyptologische Abhandlungen.
Ägypten und Levante	*Ägypten und Levante. Zeitschrift für Ägyptische Archäologie und deren Nachbargebiete.*
AJA	*American Journal of Archaeology.*
Antike Welt	*Antike Welt. Zeitschrift für Archäologie und Kulturgeschichte.*
ASAE	*Annales du Service des Antiquités de l'Egypte.*
Atiqot	*Atiqot* (Israel Department of Antiquities).
AVDAIK	Archäologische Veröffentlichungen, Deutsches Archäologisches Institut, Abteilung Kairo.
BASOR	*Bulletin of the American Schools of Oriental Research.*
Biblical Archaeologist	*Biblical Archaeologist.* Perspectives on the Ancient World from Mesopotamia to the Mediterranean.
BIFAO	*Bulletin de l'Institut Français d'Archéologie Orientale.*
CdE	*Chronique d'Égypte.*
CRAIBL	*Comptes Rendus à l'Academie des Inscriptions et Belles-Lettres.*
Egyptian Archaeology	*Egyptian Archaeology.* The Bulletin of the Egypt Exploration Society.
Eretz-Israel	*Eretz-Israel.* Archaeological, Historical and Geographical studies.
Expedition	*Expedition.* The Bulletin of the University Museum of the University of Pennsylvania.
Geographical Journal	(Royal Geographical Society).
GM	*Göttinger Miszellen.* Beiträge zur Ägyptologischen Diskussion.
HÄB	Hildesheimer Ägyptologische Beiträge.
IEJ	*Israel Exploration Journal.*
Iraq	(British School of Archaeology in Iraq).
JARCE	*Journal of the American Research Center in Egypt.*
JEA	*Journal of Egyptian Archaeology.*
JNES	*Journal of Near Eastern Studies.*
JSSEA	*Journal of the Society for the Study of Egyptian Antiquities.*
Kêmi	*Kêmi.* Revue de Philologie et d'Archéologie Égyptiennes et Coptes.
KMT	*KMT.* A Modern Journal of Ancient Egypt.
LÄ	Lexikon der Ägyptologie. (Vol. I: eds W. Helck and E. Otto; Vols II–VII: eds W. Helck and W. Westendorf).
Levant	*Levant.* Journal of the British School of Archaeology in Jerusalem.

— Bibliography —

Man	Man. A Monthly Record of Anthropological Science (Royal Anthropological Institute).
MÄS	Münchner Ägyptologische Studien.
MDAIK	Mitteilungen des Deutschen Archäologischen Instituts, Abteilung Kairo.
Nyame Akuma	Nyame Akuma. Bulletin of the Society of African Archaeologists.
OMRO	Oudheidkundige Mededeelingen uit het Rijksmuseum van Oudheden te Leiden.
Orientalia	Orientalia, Nova Series.
PSBA	Proceedings of the Society of Biblical Archaeology.
RdE	Revue d'Égyptologie.
SAK	Studien zur Altägyptischen Kultur.
Science	(American Association for the Advancement of Science).
Sphinx	Sphinx. Revue Critique Embrassant le Domaine Entier de l'Égyptologie.
ZÄS	Zeitschrift für Ägyptische Sprache und Altertumskunde.

Abdel Tawab, M., Castel, G. and Pouit, G. (1990) 'Archéo-géologie des anciennes mines de cuivre et d'or des régions el-Urf/Mongul-Sud et Dara-Ouest', *BIFAO* 90: 359–64, figs 1–18.

Adams, B. (1977) 'Hierakonpolis', *LÄ* II: 1182–6.

—— (1987) *The Fort Cemetery at Hierakonpolis*, London: Kegan Paul International. Studies in Egyptology.

—— (1994) 'Possible *s3*-signs from the tomb of Djet (Uadji)', *JEA* 80: 183–7.

—— (1995) *Ancient Nekhen. Garstang in the City of Hierakonpolis*, New Malden: Sia Publishing. Egyptian Studies Association Publication No. 3.

—— (1996) 'Elite graves at Hierakonpolis', in J. Spencer (ed.) *Aspects of Early Egypt*, 1–15, pls 1, 5a. London: British Museum Press.

Adams, B. and Friedman, R.F. (1992) 'Imports and influences in the Predynastic and Protodynastic settlement and funerary assemblages at Hierakonpolis', in E.C.M. van den Brink (ed.) *The Nile Delta in Transition: 4th–3rd millennium BC*, 317–38. Tel Aviv: van den Brink.

Adams, B. and Porat, N. (1996) 'Imported pottery with potmarks from Abydos', in J. Spencer (ed.) *Aspects of Early Egypt*, 98–107, pls 16–21. London: British Museum Press.

Adams, W.Y. (1977) *Nubia, Corridor to Africa*, London: Allen Lane.

—— (1985) 'Doubts about the "Lost Pharaohs"', *JNES* 44: 185–92.

Aldred, C. (1965) *Egypt to the End of the Old Kingdom*, London: Thames and Hudson. Library of the early civilizations.

Alexanian, N. (n.d.) 'The excavation of the MMA-Egyptian Expedition at the so-called "fort" at Hierakonpolis in 1935: The relief-decoration of King Khasekhemui', manuscript on file with the author.

—— (1998) 'Die Reliefdekoration des Chasechemui aus dem sogennanten *Fort* in Hierakonpolis', in N. Grimal (ed.)*Les Critères de Datation Stylistiques à l'Ancien Empire*, 1–21, pls 1–8. Cairo: IFAO. Bibliotheque d'Etude 120.

Algaze, G. (1993) *The Uruk World System. The Dynamics of Expansion of Early Mesopotamian Civilization*, Chicago and London: University of Chicago Press.

Altenmüller, B. (1977) 'Harsaphes', *LÄ* II: 1015–18.

Altenmüller, H. (1972) 'Bemerkungen zur frühen und späten Bauphase des Djoserbezirkes in Saqqara', *MDAIK* 28: 1–12.

—— (1975) 'Butisches Begräbnis', *LÄ* I: 887.

—— (1976) 'Das Ölmagazin im Grab der Hesire in Saqqara (QS 2045)', *SAK* 4: 1–26.

Amélineau, E. (1899) *Les Nouvelles Fouilles d'Abydos 1895–1896*, Paris: Ernest Leroux.

—— (1902) *Les Nouvelles Fouilles d'Abydos. Seconde Campagne 1896–1897*, Paris: Ernest Leroux.

—— (1904) *Les Nouvelles Fouilles d'Abydos 1897–1898*, Paris: Ernest Leroux.

—— (1905) *Les Nouvelles Fouilles d'Abydos 1897–1898 (Deuxième Partie)*, Paris: Ernest Leroux.

Amiran, R. (1974) 'An Egyptian jar fragment with the name of Narmer from Arad', *IEJ* 24: 4–12.

—— (1976) 'The Narmer jar fragment from Arad: an addendum', *IEJ* 26: 45–6.

—— (1978) *Early Arad: The Chalcolithic Settlement and Early Bronze Age City. I. First–Fifth Seasons of Excavations, 1962–1966*, Jerusalem: Israel Exploration Society. Judean Desert Studies 2.

—— (1985) 'Canaanite merchants in tombs of the Early Bronze Age I at Azor', *Atiqot* (English Series) 17: 190–2.

Amiran, R. and Gophna, R. (1992) 'The correlation between Lower Egypt and southern Canaan during the EB I Period', in E.C.M. van den Brink (ed.) *The Nile Delta in Transition: 4th–3rd Millennium BC*, 357–60. Tel Aviv: van den Brink.

Anderson, W. (1992) 'Badarian burials: evidence of social inequality in Middle Egypt during the early Predynastic era', *JARCE* 29: 51–66.

Andres, W. and Wunderlich, J. (1992) 'Environmental conditions for early settlement at Minshat Abu Omar, eastern Nile Delta, Egypt', in E.C.M. van den Brink (ed.) *The Nile Delta in Transition: 4th–3rd Millennium BC*, 157–66. Tel Aviv: van den Brink.

Anthes, R. (1957) 'Die Sonnenboote in den Pyramidentexten', *ZÄS* 82: 77–89.

Arkell, A.J. (1956) 'Stone bowls of Kha'ba (Third Dynasty)', *JEA* 42: 116.

—— (1958) 'Stone bowls of Kha'ba (Third Dynasty)', *JEA* 44: 120.

Arnold, D. (1982) 'Per-wer II', *LÄ* IV: 934–5.

—— (1994) *Lexikon der Ägyptischen Baukunst*, Zürich: Artemis.

Asselberghs, H. (1961) *Chaos en beheersing. Documenten uit Aeneolithisch Egypte*, Leiden: E.J. Brill.

Aston, B.G. (1994) *Ancient Egyptian Stone Vessels: Materials and Forms*, Heidelberg: Heidelberger Orientverlag. Studien zur Archäologie und Geschichte Altägyptens 5.

Ayrton, E.R. and Loat, W.L.S. (1911) *Pre-Dynastic Cemetery at El Mahasna*, London: Egypt Exploration Fund. Memoir 31.

Ayrton, E.R., Currely, C.T. and Weigall, A.E.P. (1904) *Abydos, Part III*, London: Egypt Exploration Fund.

Badawy, A. (1956) 'The ideology of the superstructure of the mastaba-tomb in Egypt', *JNES* 15: 180–3.

Baines, J. (1991) 'Egyptian myth and discourse: myth, gods and the early written and iconographic record', *JNES* 50: 81–105.

—— (1995) 'Origins of Egyptian kingship', in D. O'Connor and D. Silverman (eds) *Ancient Egyptian Kingship*, 95–156. Leiden: E.J. Brill.

Baines, J. and Málek, J. (1980) *Atlas of Ancient Egypt*, Oxford: Phaidon.

Balcz, H. (1930) 'Die altägyptische Wandgliederung', *Mitteilungen des Deutschen Instituts für Ägyptische Altertumskunde in Kairo* (later *MDAIK*) 1: 38–92.

Balty, J.-C., de Meulenaere, H., Homès-Fredericq, D., Limme, L., Strybol, J. and vanden Berghe, L. (1988) *Musées Royaux d'Art et d'Histoire Bruxelles, Antiquité*, Brussels: Musea Nostra.

Bard, K.A. (1987) 'The geography of excavated Predynastic sites and the rise of complex society', *JARCE* 24: 81–93.

—— (1988) 'A quantitative analysis of the Predynastic burials in Armant Cemetery 1400–1500', *JEA* 74: 39–55.

—— (1992) 'Towards an interpretation of the role of ideology in the evolution of complex society in Egypt', *Journal of Anthropological Archaeology* 11: 1–24.

—— (1994) *From Farmers to Pharaohs. Mortuary Evidence for the Rise of Complex Society*, Sheffield: Sheffield Academic Press.

Bard, K.A. and Carneiro, R.L. (1989) 'Patterns of Predynastic settlement location, social evolution and the circumscription theory', *Cahiers de Recherches de l'Institut de Papyrologie et d'Egyptologie de Lille* 11: 15–23.

Barguet, P. (1953) *La Stèle de la Famine, à Séhel*, Cairo: IFAO. Bibliothèque d'Étude 24.

Barocas, C., Fattovich, R. and Tosi, M. (1989) 'The Oriental Institute of Naples expedition to Petrie's South Town (Upper Egypt), 1977–1983: an interim report', in L. Krzyzaniak and M. Kobusiewicz (eds) *Late Prehistory of the Nile Basin and the Sahara*, 295–301. Poznan: Poznan Archaeological Museum. Studies in African Archaeology 2.

Barsanti, A. (1902) 'Fouilles autour de la pyramide d'Ounas (1901–1902)', *ASAE* 3: 182–4.

Barta, W. (1975) *Untersuchungen zur Göttlichkeit des regierenden Königs*, Munich and Berlin: Bruno Hessling. MÄS 32.

—— (1981) 'Die Chronologie der 1. bis 5. Dynastie nach den Angaben des rekonstruierten Annalensteins', *ZÄS* 108: 23–33.

—— (1990) 'Der Palasthorustitel und seine Vorläufer in der Frühzeit', *GM* 117/118: 55–9.

Baumgartel, E.J. (1970) *Petrie's Naqada Excavation: A Supplement*, London: Quaritch.

—— (1975) 'Some remarks on the origins of the titles of the Archaic Egyptian kings', *JEA* 61: 28–32.

Beckerath, J. von (1956) '*Šmšj-Ḥw* in der Ägyptischen Vor- und Frühzeit', *MDAIK* 14: 1–10.

—— (1980) 'Horusgeleit', *LÄ* III: 51–2.

Behrmann, A. (1989) *Das Nilpferd in der Vorstellungswelt der alten Ägypter*, I, Frankfurt: Peter Lang. Europäische Hochschulschriften, Reihe XXXVIII (Archäologie), Band 22.

Beit-Arieh, I. (1984) 'New evidence on the relations between Canaan and Egypt during the Proto-Dynastic period', *IEJ* 34: 20–3.

Bell, B. (1970) 'The oldest records of the Nile floods', *Geographical Journal* 136: 569–73.

Ben-Tor, A. (1991) 'New light on the relations between Egypt and southern Palestine during the Early Bronze Age', *Tel Aviv* 11: 11–19; and *BASOR* 281: 3–10.

Bettles, E., Clarke, J., Dittmer, J., Duhig, C., Ikram, S., Mathieson, I., Smith, H. and Tavares, A. (1995) *National Museums of Scotland Saqqara Project Report 1995*, Edinburgh: National Museums of Scotland.

Bietak, M. (1975) *Tell el-Dabʻa*, II. *Der Fundort im Rahmen einer archäologisch-geographischen Untersuchung über das agyptische Ostdelta*, Vienna: Verlag der Österreichischen Akademie der Wissenschaften. Denkschrift der Gesamtakademie 4.

—— (1979) 'Urban archaeology and the "town problem" in Ancient Egypt', in K. Weeks (ed.) *Egyptology and the Social Sciences*, 97–144. Cairo: The American University in Cairo Press.

—— (1994) 'Zu den heiligen Bezirken mit Palmen in Buto und Sais – Ein archä-ologischer Befund aus dem mittleren Reich', in M. Bietak, J. Holaubek, H. Mukarovsky, and H. Satzinger (eds) *Zwischen den beiden Ewigkeiten. Festschrift Gertrud Thausing*, 1–18. Vienna: Eigenverlag des Institutes für Ägyptologie der Universität Wien.

Blackman, A.M. (1916) 'Some remarks on an emblem upon the head of an ancient Egyptian birth-goddess', *JEA* 3: 199–206.

Boehmer, R.M. (1974) 'Orientalische Einflüsse auf verzierten Messergriffen aus dem prädynastischen Ägypten', *Archäologische Mitteilungen aus Iran* 7: 15–40.

Bonnet, H. (1928) *Ein frühgeschichtliches Gräberfeld bei Abusir*, Leipzig: J.C. Hinrichs. Veröffentlichungen der Ernst von Sieglin Expedition in Ägypten 4.

Borchardt, L. (1898) 'Das Grab des Menes', *ZÄS* 36: 87–105.

—— (1917) *Die Annalen und die zeitliche Festlegung des alten Reiches der ägyptischen Geschichte*, Berlin: von Behrend. Quellen und Forschungen zur Zeitbestimmung der Ägyptischen Geschichte 1.

Bourriau, J. (1981) *Umm el-Qa'ab. Pottery from the Nile Valley Before the Arab Conquest*, Cambridge: Fitzwilliam Museum.

Brandl, B. (1992) 'Evidence for Egyptian colonization of the southern coastal plain and lowlands of Canaan during the Early Bronze I Period', in E.C.M. van den Brink (ed.) *The Nile Delta in Transition: 4th–3rd Millennium BC*, 441–76. Tel Aviv: van den Brink.

Brewer, D.J. and Wenke, R.J. (1992) 'Transitional late Predynastic–Early Dynastic occupations at Mendes: a preliminary report', in E.C.M. van den Brink (ed.) *The Nile Delta in Transition: 4th–3rd Millennium BC*, 191–8. Tel Aviv: van den Brink.

Brink, E.C.M. van den (1989) 'A transitional Late Predynastic–Early Dynastic settlement site in the north-eastern Nile Delta', *MDAIK* 45: 55–108.

—— (1992a) 'Preface and short introduction', in E.C.M. van den Brink (ed.) *The Nile Delta in Transition: 4th–3rd Millennium BC*, vi–viii. Tel Aviv: van den Brink.

—— (1992b) 'Preliminary report on the excavations at Tell Ibrahim Awad, seasons 1988–1990', in E.C.M. van den Brink (ed.) *The Nile Delta in Transition: 4th–3rd Millennium BC*, 43–68. Tel Aviv: van den Brink.

—— (1996) 'The incised *serekh* signs of Dynasties 0–1. Part I: complete vessels', in J. Spencer (ed.) *Aspects of Early Egypt*, 140–58, pls 24–32. London: British Museum Press.

—— (in preparation) 'The *serekh* signs of Dynasties 0–1. Part II: fragments'.

Brink, E.C.M. van den (ed.) (1988) *The Archaeology of the Nile Delta. Problems and Priorities*, Amsterdam: Netherlands Foundation for Archaeological Research in Egypt.

—— (ed.) (1992) *The Nile Delta in Transition: 4th–3rd Millennium BC*, Tel Aviv: van den Brink.

Brinks, J. (1979) *Die Entwicklung der königlichen Grabanlagen des Alten Reiches*, Hildesheim: Gerstenberg. HÄB 10.

Brovarski, E.J. (1982) 'Naga (Nag')-ed-Dêr', *LÄ* IV: 296–317.

—— (1984a) 'Sed', *LÄ* V: 779–80.

—— (1984b) 'Sobek', *LÄ* V: 995–1031.

—— (1986) 'Thinis', *LÄ* VI: 475–86.

Brunton, G. (1927) *Qau and Badari* I, London: British School of Archaeology in Egypt and Quaritch.

—— (1937) *Mostagedda and the Tasian Culture (British Museum Expedition to Middle Egypt, first and second years 1928, 1929)*, London: Quaritch.

—— (1948) *Matmar (British Museum Expedition to Middle Egypt 1929–1931)*, London: Quaritch.

Brunton, G. and Caton-Thompson, G. (1928) *The Badarian Civilisation and Predynastic Remains Near Badari*, London: British School of Archaeology in Egypt.

Bruyère, B. (1937) *Tell Edfou*, Cairo: IFAO. Fouilles franco-polonaises, Rapports 1.

Burgess, E.M. and Arkell, A.J. (1958) 'The reconstruction of the Hathor bowl', *JEA* 44: 6–11.

Capart, J. (1930) *Memphis à l'Ombre des Pyramides*, Brussels: Fondation Egyptologique Reine Elisabeth.

Carneiro, R.L. (1970) 'A theory of the origin of the state', *Science* 169: 733–8.

Case, H. and Payne, J.C. (1962) 'Tomb 100: the decorated tomb at Hierakonpolis', *JEA* 48: 5–18.

Castel, G., Mathieu, B., Hélal, H., Abdallah, T. and Hawary, M. el- (1992) 'Les mines de cuivre du Ouadi Dara. Rapport préliminaire sur les travaux de la saison 1991', *BIFAO* 92: 51–65.

Caton-Thompson, G. (1952) *Kharga Oasis in Prehistory*, London: University of London/The Athlone Press.

Cénival, J.L. de (1965) 'Un nouveau fragment de la pierre de Palerme', *Bulletin de la Société Française d'Egyptologie* 44: 13–17.

Chlodnicki, M., Fattovich, R. and Salvatori, S. (1992) 'The Nile Delta in transition: a view from Tell el-Farkha', in E.C.M. van den Brink (ed.) *The Nile Delta in Transition: 4th–3rd Millennium BC*, 171–90. Tel Aviv: van den Brink.

Cialowicz, K.M. (1991) *Les Têtes de Massues des Périodes Prédynastique et Archaïque Dans la Vallée du Nil*, Krakow: Uniwersytet Jagiellonski.

Clarke, E.S. (1921) 'El-Kâb and the Great Wall', *JEA* 7: 54–79.

Clédat, J. (1914) 'Les vases de El-Béda', *ASAE* 13: 115–21.

Clère, J.-J. (1938) 'Un graffito du roi Djet dans le désert arabique', *ASAE* 38: 85–93.

Cohen, R. (1978) 'State origins: a reappraisal', in H.J.M. Claessen and P. Skalník (eds) *The Early State*, 31–75. The Hague: Mouton.

Cooney, J.D. and Simpson, W.K. (1976) 'An Early Dynastic statue of the goddess Heqat', *Bulletin of the Cleveland Museum of Arts* 63: 202–9.

Curto, S. (1953) 'Nota su un rilievo proveniente da Gebelèn nel Museo Egizio di Torino', *Aegyptus (Rivista Italiana di Egittologia e di Papirologia)* 33: 105–24.

Daressy, G. (1905) 'Un édifice archaïque à Nezlet Batran', *ASAE* 6: 99–106.

—— (1916) 'La pierre de Palerme et la chronologie de l'Ancien Empire', *BIFAO* 12: 161–214.

Darnell, D. and Darnell, J. (1997) 'Exploring the "narrow doors" of the Theban desert', *Egyptian Archaeology* 10: 24–6.

Davies, N. de G. (1943) *The Tomb of Rekh-mi-re' at Thebes*, 2 volumes, New York: The Metropolitan Museum of Art.

Davis, W. (1989) *The Canonical Tradition in Ancient Egyptian Art*, Cambridge: Cambridge University Press. Cambridge New Art History and Criticism.

—— (1992) *Masking the Blow: The Scene of Representation in Late Prehistoric Egyptian Art*, Berkeley, CA: University of California Press.

Debono, F. and Mortensen, B. (1988) *The Predynastic Cemetery at Heliopolis*, Mainz am Rhein: von Zabern. AVDAIK 63.

—— (1990) *El Omari. A Neolithic Settlement and Other Sites in the Vicinity of Wadi Hof, Helwan*, Mainz am Rhein: von Zabern. AVDAIK 82.

Decker, W. (1992) *Sports and Games of Ancient Egypt*, trans. A. Guttmann, New Haven and London: Yale University Press.

Delmas, A.B. and Casanova, M. (1990) 'The lapis lazuli sources in the ancient East', in M. Taddei (ed.) *South Asian Archaeology 1987*, I (*Proceedings of the Ninth International Conference of the Association of South Asian Archaeologists in Western Europe*), 493–505. Rome: Istituto Italiano per il medio ed estremo oriente. Serie Orientale Roma 66, 1.

Derry, D.E. (1956) 'The Dynastic race in Egypt', *JEA* 42: 80–6.

Dodson, A. (1996) 'The mysterious 2nd Dynasty', *KMT* 7, 2: 19–31.

Donadoni Roveri, A.M. (1990) 'Gebelein', in G. Robins (ed.) *Beyond the Pyramids: Egyptian Regional Art From the Museo Egizio, Turin*, 23–9. Atlanta: Emory University Museum of Art and Archaeology.

Dreyer, G. (1981) 'Ein frühdynastisches Königsfigürchen aus Elephantine', *MDAIK* 37 (Festschrift Habachi): 123–4, pl. 16.

—— (1986) *Elephantine VIII. Der Tempel der Satet*, Mainz am Rhein: von Zabern. AUDAIK 39.

—— (1987) 'Ein Siegel der frühzeitlichen Königsnekropole von Abydos', *MDAIK* 43: 33–43.

—— (1990) 'Umm el-Qaab. Nachuntersuchungen im frühzeitlichen Königs-friedhof. 3/4 Vorbericht', *MDAIK* 46: 53–90.

—— (1991) 'Zur Rekonstruktion der Oberbauten der Königsgräber der 1. Dynastie in Abydos', *MDAIK* 47 (Festschrift Kaiser): 93–104.

—— (1992a) 'Horus Krokodil, ein Gegenkönig der Dynastie 0', in R. Friedman and B. Adams (eds) *The Followers of Horus. Studies Dedicated to Michael Allen Hoffman*, 259–63. Oxford: Oxbow. Monograph 20. Egyptian Studies Association Publication No. 2.

—— (1992b) 'Recent discoveries at Abydos Cemetery U', in E.C.M. van den Brink (ed.) *The Nile Delta in Transition: 4th–3rd Millennium BC*, 293–9. Tel Aviv: van den Brink.

—— (1993a) 'Umm el-Qaab. Nachuntersuchungen im frühzeitlichen Königs-friedhof. 5/6 Vorbericht', *MDAIK* 49: 23–62.

—— (1993b) 'A hundred years at Abydos', *Egyptian Archaeology* 3: 10–12.

—— (1995a) 'Recent activities of the German Institute of Archaeology in Egypt', unpublished paper delivered at the Seventh International Congress of Egyptologists, Cambridge, 3 September 1995. (To be published in the Proceedings of the Seventh ICE.).

—— (1995b) 'Die Datierung der Min-Statuen aus Koptos', in Deutsches Archä-ologisches Institut Abteilung Kairo, *Kunst des Alten Reiches: Symposium im Deutschen Archäologischen Institut Kairo am 29 und 30 Oktober 1991*, 49–56, pls 9–13. Mainz am Rhein: von Zabern. DAIK Sonderschrift 28.

—— (1996) 'Ein Tongefäss mit Frauenfiguren. Ein Neufund aus Abydos', *Antike Welt* 27, 3: 242.

Dreyer, G. and Kaiser, W. (1980) 'Zu den kleinen Stufenpyramiden Ober- und Mittelägyptens', *MDAIK* 36: 43–59.

Dreyer, G. and Swelim, N. (1982) 'Die kleine Stufenpyramide von Abydos-Süd (Sinki), Grabungsbericht', *MDAIK* 38: 83–93.

Dreyer, G., Engel, E.-M., Hartung, U., Hikade, T., Köhler, E.C. and Pumpen-meier, F. (1996) 'Umm el-Qaab. Nachuntersuchungen im Frühzeitlichen Königsfriedhof. 7/8 Vorbericht', *MDAIK* 52: 11–81.

Driesch, A. von den (1986) *Fische im alten Ägypten: eine osteoarchäologische Untersuchung*, Munich: Kanzler. Documenta Naturae 34.

Dunham, D. (1978) *Zawiyet el-Aryan. The Cemeteries Adjacent to the Layer Pyramid*, Boston: Museum of Fine Arts.

Eaton-Krauss, M. (1977) 'The *khat* headdress to the end of the Amarna period', *SAK* 5: 21–39.

—— (1984) *The Representations of Statuary in Private Tombs of the Old Kingdom*, Wiesbaden: Harrassowitz. ÄA 39.

Edwards, I.E.S. (1971) 'The Early Dynastic period in Egypt', in I.E.S. Edwards, C.J. Gadd and N.G.L. Hammond (eds) *The Cambridge Ancient History*, 3rd edition, Volume I, Part 2, *Early History of the Middle East*, 1–70. Cambridge: Cambridge University Press.

—— (1993) *The Pyramids of Egypt*, 5th edition, Harmondsworth: Penguin Books.

Emery, W.B. (1938) *Excavations at Saqqara. The Tomb of Hemaka*, Cairo: Government Press.

—— (1939) *Excavations at Saqqara 1937–1938. Hor-Aha*, Cairo: Government Press.

—— (1949) *Great Tombs of the First Dynasty*, I, Cairo: Government Press.

—— (1954) *Great Tombs of the First Dynasty*, II, London: Egypt Exploration Society.

—— (1958) *Great Tombs of the First Dynasty*, III, London: Egypt Exploration Society.

—— (1961) *Archaic Egypt*, Harmondsworth: Penguin.

—— (1963) 'Egypt Exploration Society. Preliminary report on the excavations at Buhen, 1962', *Kush* 11: 116–20.

—— (1965) 'Preliminary report on the excavations at North Saqqâra 1964–5', *JEA* 51: 3–8, pls II–V.

—— (1968) 'Tomb 3070 at Saqqâra', *JEA* 54: 11–13, pls II–III.

—— (1970) 'Preliminary report on the excavations at North Saqqâra, 1968–9', *JEA* 56: 5–11, pls II–XX.

Engelbach, R. (1934) 'A foundation scene of the Second Dynasty', *JEA* 20: 183–4.

Erman, A. (1890) *Die Märchen des Papyrus Westcar, I. Einleitung und Commentar*, Berlin: W. Spemann. Königliche Museen zu Berlin, Mittheilungen aus den Orientalischen Sammlungen V.

Erman, A. and Grapow, H. (eds) (1929) *Wörterbuch der ägyptischen Sprache*, Band 3, Leipzig: J.C. Hinrichs.

—— (1931) *Wörterbuch der ägyptischen Sprache*, Band 5, Leipzig: J.C. Hinrichs.

Fairman, H.W. (1958) 'The kingship rituals of Egypt', in S.H. Hooke (ed.) *Myth, Ritual, and Kingship. Essays on the Theory and Practice of Kingship in the Ancient Near East and in Israel*, 74–104. Oxford: Oxford University Press at the Clarendon Press.

Fairservis, W.A. (1971–2) 'Preliminary report on the first two seasons at Hierakonpolis', *JARCE* 9: 7–27, 67–8.

—— (1991) 'A revised view of the Na'rmr palette', *JARCE* 28: 1–20.

Faltings, D. and Köhler, E.C. (1996) 'Vorbericht über die Ausgrabungen des DAI in Tell el-Fara'in/Buto 1993 bis 1995', *MDAIK* 52: 87–114.

Faulkner, R.O. (1962) *A Concise Dictionary of Middle Egyptian*, Oxford: Griffith Institute.

—— (1969) *The Ancient Egyptian Pyramid Texts*, Oxford: Oxford University Press.

Firth, C.M. and Quibell, J.E. (1935) *The Step Pyramid* (2 volumes), Cairo: IFAO.

Fischer, H.G. (1958) 'A fragment of late Predynastic Egyptian relief from the eastern Delta', *Artibus Asiae* 21: 64–88.

—— (1961) 'An Egyptian royal stela of the Second Dynasty', *Artibus Asiae* 24: 45–56.

—— (1962) 'The cult and nome of the goddess Bat', *JARCE* 1: 7–18.

—— (1963) 'Varia Aegyptiaca', *JARCE* 2: 17–51.

—— (1968) *Dendera in the Third Millennium BC Down to the Theban Domination of Upper Egypt*, Locust Valley, NY: J.J. Augustin.

—— (1978) 'Notes on sticks and staves in ancient Egypt', *Metropolitan Museum Journal* 13: 5–32.

—— (1996) *Varia Nova*, New York: The Metropolitan Museum of Art. Egyptian Studies 3.

Frankfort, H. (1941) 'The origin of monumental architecture in Egypt', *American Journal of Semitic Languages and Literatures* (later *JNES*) 58: 329–58.

—— (1948) *Kingship and the Gods*, Chicago: University of Chicago Press.

Friedman, F.D. (1995) 'The underground relief panels of King Djoser at the Step Pyramid complex', *JARCE* 32: 1–42.

Friedman, R. (1992) 'The Early Dynastic and transitional pottery of Mendes: the 1990 season', in E.C.M. van den Brink (ed.) *The Nile Delta in Transition: 4th–3rd Millennium BC*, 199–205. Tel Aviv: van den Brink.

—— (1994) 'Predynastic settlement ceramics of Upper Egypt: a comparative study of the ceramics of Hemamieh, Nagada, and Hierakonpolis', unpublished doctoral thesis, University of California at Berkeley.

—— (1996) 'The ceremonial centre at Hierakonpolis Locality HK29A', in J. Spencer (ed.) *Aspects of Early Egypt*, 16–35. London: British Museum Press.

Gaballa, G.A. and Kitchen, K.A. (1969) 'The festival of Sokar', *Orientalia* 38: 1–76.

Galassi, G. (1955) 'L'arte del più antico Egitto nel Museo di Torino', *Rivista dell'Istituto Nazionale d'Archeologia e Storia dell'Arte* New Series 4: 5–94.

Gardiner, A.H. (1938) 'The Mansion of Life and the Master of the King's Largess', *JEA* 24: 83–91.

—— (1944) 'Horus the Behdetite', *JEA* 30: 23–60.

—— (1946) 'The instruction addressed to Kagemni and his brethren', *JEA* 32: 71–4, pl. XIV.

—— (1957) *Egyptian Grammar* (3rd edition, revised), Oxford: Griffith Institute.

—— (1958) 'The personal name of King Serpent', *JEA* 44: 38–9.

—— (1959) *The Royal Canon of Turin*, Oxford: Griffith Institute.

—— (1961) *Egypt of the Pharaohs*, Oxford: Oxford University Press at the Clarendon Press.

Gardiner, A.H. and Peet, T.E. (1952) *The Inscriptions of Sinai*, I, 2nd edition, revised and augmented by J. Černý, London: Egypt Exploration Society.

—— (1955) *The Inscriptions of Sinai*, II, edited by J. Černý, London: Egypt Exploration Society. Memoir 45.

Garstang, J. (1901) *El Arabah*, London: Quaritch. Egyptian Research Account Memoir 6.

—— (1902) *Mahâsna and Bêt Khallâf*, London: Quaritch. Egyptian Research Account Memoir 7.

—— (1904) *Tombs of the Third Egyptian Dynasty at Reqâqnah and Bêt Khallâf*, Westminster: Archibald Constable and Co.

—— (1907) 'Excavations at Hierakonpolis, at Esna, and in Nubia', *ASAE* 8: 132–48.

Gauthier, H. (1914) 'Quatre fragments nouveaux de la pierre de Palerme au musée du Caire', *CRAIBL* 1914: 489–96.

—— (1925) *Dictionnaire des Noms Géographiques Contenus Dans les Textes Hiéroglyphiques*, tome 2ᵐᵉ, Cairo: IFAO.

—— (1929) *Dictionnaire des Noms Géographiques Contenus Dans les Textes Hiéroglyphiques*, tome 6, Cairo: IFAO.

Giddy, L.L. (1987) *Egyptian Oases. Bahariya, Dakhla, Farafra and Kharga During Pharaonic Times*, Warminster: Aris and Phillips.

—— (1996) 'Digging diary 1995–1996', *Egyptian Archaeology* 9: 27–30.

—— (1997a) 'Digging diary 1996', *Egyptian Archaeology* 10: 27–30.

—— (1997b) 'Digging diary 1996–1997', *Egyptian Archaeology* 11: 25–8.

Giddy, L.L. and Jeffreys, D.G. (1991) 'Memphis 1990', *JEA* 77: 1–6.

Ginter, B. and Kozlowski, J.K. (1994) *Predynastic Settlement Near Armant*, Heidelberg: Heidelberger Orientverlag. Studien zur Archäologie und Geschichte Altägyptens 6.

Giveon, R. (1974) 'A second relief of Sekhemkhet in Sinai', *BASOR* 216: 17–20.

—— (1984) 'Sopdu', *LÄ* V: 1107–10.

Godron, G. (1990) *Etudes sur l'Horus Den et Quelques Problèmes de l'Egypte Archaïque*, Geneva: Patrick Cramer. Cahiers d'Orientalisme 19.

Goedicke, H. (1956a) 'King *Ḥwḏf3?*', *JEA* 42: 50–3.

—— (1956b) 'The pharaoh *Ny-Śwtḥ*', *ZÄS* 81: 14–15.

—— (1966) 'Die Laufbahn des *Mṯn*', *MDAIK* 21: 1–71.

—— (1984) 'Sechemchet', *LÄ* V: 776–7.

Gohary, J. (1992) *Akhenaten's Sed-festival at Karnak*, London and New York: Kegan Paul International. Studies in Egyptology.

Goneim, Z. (1957) *Horus Sekhem-khet. The Unfinished Step Pyramid*, Cairo: IFAO.

Gophna, R. (1976) 'Egyptian immigration into southern Canaan during the First Dynasty?', *Tel Aviv* 3: 31–7.

—— (1990) 'The Early Bronze I settlement at 'En Besor Oasis', *IEJ* 40: 1–11.

—— (1992a) 'A faience statuette from 'En Besor', *Eretz-Israel* 23: 45–7.

—— (1992b) 'The contacts between 'En Besor Oasis, southern Canaan, and Egypt during the late Predynastic and the threshold of the First Dynasty; a further assessment', in E.C.M. van den Brink (ed.) *The Nile Delta in Transition: 4th–3rd Millennium BC*, 385–94. Tel Aviv: van den Brink.

Gophna, R. and Gazit, D. (1985) 'The First Dynasty Egyptian residency at 'En Besor', *Tel Aviv* 12: 9–16.

Gordon, A.A. and Schwabe, C.W. (1995) 'The Egyptian *w3s*-scepter and its modern analogues: uses as symbols of divine power and authority', *JARCE* 32: 185–96.

Grdseloff, B. (1944) 'Notes d'épigraphie archaïque', *ASAE* 44: 279–302.

Grimal, N. (1992) *A History of Ancient Egypt*, trans. I. Shaw, Oxford: Blackwell.

—— (1993) 'Travaux de l'Institut Français d'Archéologie Orientale en 1992–1993', *BIFAO* 93: 425–519.

—— (1996) 'Travaux de l'Institut Français d'Archéologie Orientale en 1995–1996', *BIFAO* 96: 489–617.

Haarlem, W.M. van (1995) 'Temple deposits at Tell Ibrahim Awad – a preliminary report', *GM* 148: 45–52.

—— (1996) 'Temple deposits at Tell Ibrahim Awad II – an update', *GM* 154: 31–4.

Habachi, L. (1939) 'A First Dynasty cemetery at Abydos', *ASAE* 39: 767–74.

Habachi, L. and Kaiser, W. (1985) 'Ein Friedhof der Maadikultur bei es-Saff', *MDAIK* 41: 43–6.

Hall, E.S. (1986) *The Pharaoh Smites His Enemies*, Berlin: Bruno Hessling. MÄS 44.

Hansen, D.P. (1967) 'The excavations at Tell el Rub'a', *JARCE* 6: 5–16.

Hartung, U. (1994) 'Bemerkungen zur Chronologie der Beziehungen Ägyptens zu Südkanaan in spätprädynastischer Zeit', *MDAIK* 50: 107–13.

Hassan, F.A. (1988) 'The Predynastic of Egypt', *Journal of World Prehistory* 2, 2: 135–85.

—— (1995) 'Egypt in the prehistory of northeast Africa', in J.M. Sasson (ed.) *Civilizations of the Ancient Near East*, volume II, 665–78. New York: Charles Scribner's Sons.

Hassan, S. (1938) 'Excavations at Saqqara 1937–1938', *ASAE* 38: 503–21.

Hawass, Z. (1994) 'A fragmentary monument of Djoser from Saqqara', *JEA* 80: 45–56.

Hayes, W.C. (1953) *The Scepter of Egypt*, Part I, New York: The Metropolitan Museum of Art.

Helck, W. (1952) 'Die Herkunft des abydenischen Osirisrituals', *Archiv Orientální* 20: 72–85.

—— (1954) *Untersuchungen zu den Beamtentiteln des ägyptischen alten Reiches*, Glückstadt: J.J. Augustin Verlag. Ägyptologische Forschungen 18.

—— (1970) 'Zwei Einzelprobleme der thinitischen Chronologie', *MDAIK* 26: 83–5.

—— (1972) 'Zu den "Talbezirken" in Abydos', *MDAIK* 28: 95–9.

—— (1974) 'Bemerkungen zum Annalenstein', *MDAIK* 30: 31–5.

—— (1975) *Wirtschaftsgeschichte des alten Ägypten im 3. und 2. Jahrtausend vor Chr*, Leiden/Köln: E.J. Brill. Handbuch der Orientalistik.

—— (1979) 'Die Datierung der Gefäßaufschriften der Djoserpyramide', *ZÄS* 106: 120–32.

—— (1980) 'Iat', *LÄ* III: 114.

—— (1982) 'Palermostein', *LÄ* IV: 652–4.

—— (1984a) 'Sanakht', *LÄ* V: 375–6.

—— (1984b) 'Saqqara, Nekropolen der 1.–3. Dyn.', *LÄ* V: 387–400.

—— (1984c) 'Sened', *LÄ* V: 849.

—— (1984d) 'Schamane und Zauberer', in *Mélanges Adolphe Gutbub*, 103–8. Montpellier: Institut d'Égyptologie, Université Paul Valéry Montpellier III. Publications de la Recherche.

Hendrickx, S. (1992) 'The Predynastic cemeteries at Khozam', in R. Friedman and B. Adams (eds) *The Followers of Horus. Studies Dedicated to Michael Allen Hoffman*, 199–201. Oxford: Oxbow. Monograph 20. Egyptian Studies Association Publication No. 2.

—— (1993) 'Relative chronology of the Naqada culture', unpublished paper delivered at the British Museum Colloquium on 'Early Egypt', London, 22 July 1993. Manuscript on file with the author.

—— (1994) *Elkab* V. *The Naqada III cemetery*, Brussels: Musées Royaux d'Art et d'Histoire, Comité des Fouilles Belges en Egypte.

Hendrickx, S. and Huyge, D. (1989) *Elkab IV. Topographie. Fascicule 2: Inventaire des Sites Archéologiques*, Brussels: Fondation Egyptologique Reine Elisabeth.

Herrmann, G. (1968) 'Lapis lazuli: the early phases of its trade', *Iraq* 30: 21–57.

Hoffman, M.A. (1976) 'The city of the hawk: seat of Egypt's ancient civilization', *Expedition* 18, 3: 32–41.

—— (1980) *Egypt Before the Pharaohs*, London: Routledge and Kegan Paul.

—— (1982) *The Predynastic of Hierakonpolis – An Interim Report*, Giza and Macomb, Illinois: Cairo University Herbarium and Western Illinois University. Egyptian Studies Association Publication No. 1.

—— (1984) 'Predynastic cultural ecology and patterns of settlement in Upper Egypt as viewed from Hierakonpolis', in L. Krzyzaniak and M. Kobusiewicz (eds) *Origin and Early Development of Food-Producing Cultures in North-Eastern Africa*, 235–45. Poznan: Poznan Archaeological Museum. Studies in African Archaeology 1.

—— (1987) 'A regional perspective of the Predynastic cemeteries of Hierakonpolis', in B. Adams, *The Fort Cemetery at Hierakonpolis*, 187–94. London: Kegan Paul International. Studies in Egyptology.

Hoffman, M.A., Hamroush, H.A. and Allen, R.O. (1986) 'A model of urban development for the Hierakonpolis region from Predynastic through Old Kingdom times', *JARCE* 23: 175–87.

Holmes, D.L. and Friedman, R.F. (1989) 'The Badari region revisited', *Nyame Akuma* 31: 15–19.

Hölscher, U. (1912) *Das Grabdenkmal des Königs Chephren*, Leipzig: J.C. Hinrichs.

Hölscher, W. (1955) *Libyer und Ägypter. Beiträge zur Ethnologie und Geschichte libyscher Völkerschaften nach den altägyptischen Quellen*, Glückstadt: Verlag J.J. Augustin. Ägyptologische Forschungen 4.

Hope, C.A. (1980) 'Dakhleh Oasis Project – report on the study of the pottery and kilns', *JSSEA* 10: 283–313.

Hornung, E. (1983) *Conceptions of God in Ancient Egypt. The One and the Many*, trans. J. Baines, London: Routledge and Kegan Paul.

Hornung, E. and Staehelin, E. (1974) *Studien zum Sedfest*, Basel/Geneva: Ägyptologisches Seminar der Universität Basel/Centre d'études orientales de l'Université de Genève. Aegyptiaca Helvetica 1.

Houlihan, P.F. (1986) *The Birds of Ancient Egypt*, Warminster: Aris and Phillips.

Husson, G. and Valbelle, D. (1992) *L'État et les Institutions en Egypte: des Premiers Pharaons aux Empereurs Romains*, Paris: Armand Colin.

Huyge, D. (1984) 'Horus Qa-a in the Elkab area, Upper Egypt', *Orientalia Lovaniensia Periodica* 15: 5–9.

Jacquet-Gordon, H. (1962) *Les Noms de Domaines Funéraires sous l'Ancien Empire*, Cairo: IFAO.

James, T.G.H. (1974) *Corpus of Hieroglyphic Inscriptions in the Brooklyn Museum, I. From Dynasty I to the End of Dynasty XVIII*, Brooklyn, NY: The Brooklyn Museum.

Janssen, J.J. (1978) 'The early state in ancient Egypt', in H.J.M. Claessen and P. Skalník (eds) *The Early State*, 213–34. The Hague: Mouton.

Jeffreys, D. and Tavares, A. (1994) 'The historic landscape of Early Dynastic Memphis', *MDAIK* 50: 143–73.

Jéquier, G. (1911) *Le Papyrus Prisse et Ses Variantes*, Paris: Librairie Paul Geuthner.

Johnson, S.B. (1990) *The Cobra Goddess of Ancient Egypt. Predynastic, Early Dynastic, and Old Kingdom Periods*, London and New York: Kegan Paul International. Studies in Egyptology.

Junker, H. (1912) *Bericht über die Grabungen der kaiserl. Akademie der Wissenschaften in Wien auf dem Friedhof in Turah. Winter 1909–1910*, Vienna: Alfred Hölder. Denkschriften der Kaiserlichen Akademie der Wissenschaften in Wien, Philosophisch-Historische Klasse 56.

—— (1939) 'Phrnfr', *ZÄS* 75: 63–84.

Kahl, J. (1994) *Das System der ägyptischen Hieroglyphenschrift in der 0.–3. Dynastie*, Wiesbaden: Harrassowitz. Göttinger Orientforschungen. IV. Reihe Ägypten. Band 29.

Kaiser, W. (1956) 'Stand und Probleme der ägyptische Vorgeschichtsforschung', *ZÄS* 81: 87–109.

—— (1957) 'Zur inneren Chronologie der Naqadakultur', *Archaeologia Geographica* 6: 69–77, pls 15–26.

—— (1958) 'Zur vorgeschichtlichen Bedeutung von Hierakonpolis', *MDAIK* 16 (Festschrift Junker): 183–92.

—— (1959) 'Einige Bemerkungen zur ägyptischen Frühzeit. I', *ZÄS* 84: 119–32.

—— (1960) 'Einige Bemerkungen zur ägyptischen Frühzeit. I (Forts.)', *ZÄS* 85: 118–37.

—— (1961a) 'Einige Bemerkungen zur ägyptischen Frühzeit. II', *ZÄS* 86: 39–61.

—— (1961b) 'Bericht über eine archäologisch-geologische Felduntersuchung', *MDAIK* 17: 1–53.

—— (1964) 'Einige Bemerkungen zur ägyptischen Frühzeit. III', *ZÄS* 91: 36–125.

—— (1969) 'Zu den königlichen Talbezirken der 1. und 2. Dynastie in Abydos und zur Baugeschichte des Djoser-Grabmals', *MDAIK* 25: 1–21.

—— (1971) 'Die kleine Hebseddarstellungen im Sonnenheiligtum des Neuserre', *Beiträge zur Ägyptischen Bauforschung und Altertumskunde* 12 (Festschrift Ricke): 87–105.

—— (1985a) 'Ein Kultbezirk des Königs Den in Sakkara', *MDAIK* 39: 61–87.

—— (1985b) 'Zu Entwicklung und Vorformen der frühzeitlichen Gräber mit reich gegliederter Oberbaufassade', in *Mélanges Mokhtar* II, 25–38. Cairo: IFAO. Bibliothèque d'Etude 97.

—— (1986) 'Vor- und Frühgeschichte', *LÄ* VI: 1069–76.

—— (1987) 'Zum Friedhof der Naqada-kultur von Minshat Abu Omar', *ASAE* 71: 119–26.

—— (1990) 'Zur Entstehung der gesamtägyptischen Staates', *MDAIK* 46: 287–99.

—— (1991) 'Zur Nennung von Sened und Peribsen in Sakkara B3', *GM* 122: 49–55.

—— (1992) 'Zur unterirdischen Anlage der Djoserpyramide und ihrer entwicklungsgeschichtlichen Einordnung', in I. Grammer-Wallert and W. Helck (eds) *Gegengabe: Festschrift für Emma Brunner-Traut*, 167–190. Tübingen: Attempto Verlag.

Kaiser, W. and Dreyer, G. (1982) 'Umm el-Qaab. Nachuntersuchungen im frühzeitlichen Königsfriedhof. 2. Vorbericht', *MDAIK* 38: 211–69.

Kaiser, W. and Grossmann, P. (1979) 'Umm el-Qaab. Nachuntersuchungen im frühzeitlichen Königsfriedhof. 1. Vorbericht', *MDAIK* 35: 155–63, pls 31–2.

Kaiser, W., Avila, R., Dreyer, G., Jaritz, H., Rösing, F.W. and Seidlmayer, S. (1982) 'Stadt und Tempel von Elephantine. 9./10. Grabungsbericht', *MDAIK* 38: 271–345.

Kaiser, W., Dreyer, G., Jaritz, H., Krekeler, A., Schläger, T. and Ziermann, M. (1987) 'Stadt und Tempel von Elephantine. 13./14. Grabungsbericht', *MDAIK* 43: 75–114.

Kaiser, W., Dreyer, G., Jaritz, H., Krekeler, A., Lindemann, J., von Pilgrim C., Seidlmayer, S. and Ziermann, M. (1988) 'Stadt und Tempel von Elephantine. 15./16. Grabungsbericht', *MDAIK* 44: 135–82.

Kaiser, W., Becker, P., Bommas, M., Hoffmann, F., Jaritz, H., Müntel, S., Pätznick, J.-P. and Ziermann, M. (1995) 'Stadt und Tempel von Elephantine. 21./22. Grabungsbericht', *MDAIK* 51: 99–187.

Känel, F. von (1984) 'Selqet', *LÄ* V: 830–3.

Kantor, H.J. (1965) 'The relative chronology of Egypt and its foreign correlations before the late Bronze Age', in R.W. Ehrich (ed.) *Chronologies in Old World Archaeology*, 1–46. Chicago: University of Chicago Press.

Kaplony, P. (1958) 'Sechs Königsname der 1. Dynastie in neuer Deutung', *Orientalia Suecana* 7: 54–69.

—— (1962) 'Gottespalast und Götterfestungen in der ägyptischen Frühzeit', *ZÄS* 88: 5–16.

—— (1963) *Die Inschriften der ägyptischen Frühzeit*, (3 vols.), Wiesbaden: Harrassowitz. ÄA 8.

—— (1964) *Die Inschriften der ägyptischen Frühzeit, Supplement*, Wiesbaden: Harrassowitz. ÄA 9.

—— (1965) 'Bemerkungen zu einigen Steingefäßen mit archaischen Königsnamen', *MDAIK* 20: 1–46.

—— (1966) *Kleine Beiträge zu den Inschriften der ägyptischen Frühzeit*, Wiesbaden: Harrassowitz. ÄA 15.

—— (1977) 'Hedjwer', *LÄ* II: 1078–80.

—— (1986) 'Zepter', *LÄ* VI: 1373–89.

—— (1992) 'Archäische Siegel und Siegelabrollungen aus dem Delta: die Arbeit an den Siegeln von Buto', in E.C.M. van den Brink (ed.) *The Nile Delta in Transition: 4th–3rd Millennium BC*, 23–30. Tel Aviv: van den Brink.

Katzmann, L. (1990) 'Tierknochenfunde aus Elephantine in Oberägypten (Grabungsjahre 1976 bis 1986/87): Vögel, Reptilien, Fische und Mollusken', unpublished doctoral thesis, University of Munich.

Kees, H. (1927) 'Zum Ursprung der sogenannte Horusdiener', *Nachrichten von der Gesellschaft der Wissenschaften in Göttingen, Philologisch-Historische Klasse, aus dem Jahre 1927*: 196–207.

Kemp, B.J. (1966) 'Abydos and the royal tombs of the First Dynasty', *JEA* 52: 13–22.

—— (1967) 'The Egyptian 1st Dynasty royal cemetery', *Antiquity* 41: 22–32.

—— (1968) 'The Osiris temple at Abydos', *MDAIK* 23: 138–55.

—— (1973) 'Photographs of the decorated tomb at Hierakonpolis', *JEA* 59: 36–43.

—— (1975a) 'Architektur der Frühzeit', in C. Vandersleyen (ed.) *Das alte Ägypten*, 99–112. Berlin: Propyläen Verlag. Propyläen Kunstgeschichte 15.

—— (1975b) 'Abydos', *LÄ* I: 28–41.

—— (1977) 'The early development of towns in Egypt', *Antiquity* 51: 185–200.

—— (1983) 'Old Kingdom, Middle Kingdom and Second Intermediate Period, c. 2686–1552 BC', in B.G. Trigger, B.J. Kemp. D. O'Connor, and A.B. Lloyd, *Ancient Egypt: A Social History*, 71–182. Cambridge: Cambridge University Press.

—— (1989) *Ancient Egypt. Anatomy of a Civilization*, London and New York: Routledge.

—— (1995) 'Unification and urbanization of ancient Egypt', in J.M. Sasson (ed.) *Civilizations of the Ancient Near East*, volume II, 679–90. New York: Charles Scribner's Sons.

Kempinski, A. (1992) 'Reflections on the role of the Egyptians in the Shefelah of Palestine in the light of recent soundings at Tel Erani', in E.C.M. van den Brink (ed.) *The Nile Delta in Transition: 4th–3rd Millennium BC*, 419–25. Tel Aviv: van den Brink.

Klasens, A. (1957) 'The excavations of the Leiden Museum of Antiquities at Abu-Roash. Report of the first season: 1957. Part I', *OMRO* 38: 58–68.

—— (1958) 'The excavations of the Leiden Museum of Antiquities at Abu-Roash. Report of the second season: 1958. Part I', *OMRO* 39: 32–55.

—— (1959) 'The excavations of the Leiden Museum of Antiquities at Abu-Roash. Report of the second season: 1958. Part II', *OMRO* 40: 41–61.

—— (1960) 'The excavations of the Leiden Museum of Antiquities at Abu-Roash. Report of the third season: 1959. Part I', *OMRO* 41: 69–94.

—— (1961) 'The excavations of the Leiden Museum of Antiquities at Abu-Roash. Report of the third season: 1959. Part II. Cemetery M', *OMRO* 42: 108–28.

Klemm, R. and Klemm, D.D. (1994) 'Chronologischer Abriß der antiken Goldgewinnung in der Ostwüste Ägyptens', *MDAIK* 50: 189–222.

Koefoed-Petersen, O. (1951) *Egyptian Sculpture in the Ny Carlsberg Glyptothek*, Copenhagen: Bianoc Lunos Bogtrykkeri.

Köhler, E.C. (1992) 'The Pre- and Early Dynastic pottery of Tell el-Fara'in (Buto)', in E.C.M. van den Brink (ed.) *The Nile Delta in Transition: 4th–3rd Millennium BC*, 11–22. Tel Aviv: van den Brink.

—— (1993) 'Tell el-Fara'in-Buto: Die Keramik der Schichten III bis VI. Untersuchungen zur Töpfereiproduktion einer frühen Siedlung des Nildeltas', unpublished doctoral thesis, University of Heidelberg.

—— (1995) 'The state of research on late Predynastic Egypt: new evidence for the development of the Pharaonic state', *GM* 147: 79–92.

Kroeper, K. (1988) 'The excavations of the Munich East-Delta Expedition in Minshat Abu Omar', in E.C.M. van den Brink (ed.) *The Archaeology of the Nile Delta: Problems and Priorities*, 11–46. Amsterdam: Netherlands Foundation for Archaeological Research in Egypt.

—— (1989) 'Settlement in the Nile Delta to the end of the Old Kingdom', unpublished doctoral thesis, Uniwersytet Warszawski Wydzial Historcyczny.

—— (1992) 'Tombs of the elite in Minshat Abu Omar', in E.C.M. van den Brink (ed.) *The Nile Delta in Transition: 4th–3rd Millennium BC*, 127–50. Tel Aviv: van den Brink.

—— (1996) 'Minshat Abu Omar – burials with palettes', in J. Spencer (ed.) *Aspects of Early Egypt*, 70–91. London: British Museum Press.

Kroeper, K. and Wildung, D. (1985) *Minshat Abu Omar. Münchner Ostdelta-Expedition Vorbericht 1978–1984*, Munich: Staatliche Sammlung Ägyptischer Kunst. Schriften aus der Ägyptischen Sammlung 3.

—— (1994) *Minshat Abu Omar. Ein vor- und frühgeschichtlicher Friedhof im Nildelta*, I, Mainz am Rhein: von Zabern.

Krzyzaniak, L. (1992) 'Again on the earliest settlement at Minshat Abu Omar', in E.C.M. van den Brink (ed.) *The Nile Delta in Transition: 4th–3rd Millennium BC*, 151–5. Tel Aviv: van den Brink.

Kuhlmann, K.P. (1996) 'Serif-style architecture and the design of the Archaic Egyptian palace ("Königszelt")', in M. Bietak (ed.) *Haus und Palast im alten Ägypten/House and Palace in Ancient Egypt*, 117–37. Vienna: Verlag der Österreichischen Akademie der Wissenschaften. Untersuchungen der Zweigstelle Kairo des Österreichischen Archäologischen Institutes, Band XIV.

Lacau, P. and Lauer, J.-P. (1959) *La Pyramide à Degrés* IV. *Inscriptions Gravées sur les Vases*, Cairo: IFAO.

—— (1965) *La Pyramide à Degrés* V. *Inscriptions à l'Encre sur les Vases*, Cairo: IFAO.

Lamberg-Karlovsky, C.C. and Sabloff, J.A. (1979) *Ancient Civilizations: The Near East and Mesoamerica*, Menlo Park, California: Benjamin/Cummings Publishing Co.

Lansing, A. (1935) 'The Museum's excavation at Hierakonpolis', *Supplement to the Bulletin of the Metropolitan Museum of Art* 30, 11: 37–45.

Lauer, J.-P. (1936) *Fouilles à Saqqarah. La Pyramide à Degrés*, I–II. *L'Architecture*, Cairo: IFAO.

—— (1939) *Fouilles à Saqqarah. La Pyramide à Degrés*, III. *Compléments*, Cairo: IFAO.

—— (1957) 'Evolution de la tombe royale égyptienne jusqu'à la pyramide à degrés', *MDAIK* 15 (Festschrift Junker): 148–65.

—— (1962) *Histoire Monumentale des Pyramides d'Egypte*, I. *Les Pyramides à Degrés (IIIe Dynastie)*, Cairo: IFAO. Bibliothèque d'Etude 39.

—— (1966) 'Quelques remarques sur la Ire Dynastie', *BIFAO* 64: 169–84.

—— (1968) 'Découverte du tombeau sud de l'Horus Sekhem-khet dans son complexe funéraire à Saqqarah', *RdE* 20: 97–107.

—— (1969) 'A propos des vestiges des murs à redans encadrés par les "tombs of the courtiers" et des "forts" d'Abydos', *MDAIK* 25: 79–84.

—— (1976) *Saqqara. The Royal Cemetery of Memphis. Excavations and Discoveries Since 1850*, London: Thames and Hudson.

—— (1988) 'Sur certaines modifications et extensions apportées au complexe funéraire de Djoser au cours de son règne', in J. Baines, T.G.H. James, A. Leahy and A.F. Shore (eds) *Pyramid Studies and Other Essays Presented to I.E.S. Edwards*, 5–11. London: Egypt Exploration Society.

Leclant, J. (1952) 'Fouilles et travaux en Égypte, 1950–1951, Part 2', *Orientalia* 21: 233–49.

Leclant, J. and Clerc, G. (1988) 'Fouilles et travaux en Égypte et au Soudan, 1986–1987', *Orientalia* 57: 307–404, pls VI–LXXI.

—— (1992) 'Fouilles et travaux en Égypte et au Soudan, 1990–1991', *Orientalia* 61: 214–322.

—— (1993) 'Fouilles et travaux en Égypte et au Soudan, 1991–1992', *Orientalia* 62: 175–295.

—— (1994) 'Fouilles et travaux en Égypte et au Soudan, 1992–1993', *Orientalia* 63: 345–473.

Legge, F. (1900) 'The carved slates from Hieraconpolis and elsewhere', *PSBA* 22: 125–39.

—— (1907) 'The tablets of Negadah and Abydos', *PSBA* 29: 18–24, 70–3, 101–6, 150–4, and plates.

Legrain, G. (1903) 'Notes d'inspection', *ASAE* 4: 193–226.

Lehner, M. and Lacovara, P. (1985) 'An enigmatic object explained', *JEA* 71: 169–74.

Lesko, L.H. (1988) 'Seila 1981', *JARCE* 25: 215–35.

Levy, T.E., Brink, E.C.M. van den, Goren, Y. and Alon, D. (1995) 'New light on King Narmer and the Protodynastic Egyptian presence in Canaan', *Biblical Archaeologist* 58, 1: 25–35.

Lichtheim, M. (1975) *Ancient Egyptian Literature. Volume I: The Old and Middle Kingdoms*, Berkeley, CA: University of California Press.

—— (1980) *Ancient Egyptian Literature. Volume III: The Late Period*, Berkeley: University of California Press.

Lloyd, A.B. (1988) *Herodotus Book II. Commentary 99–182*, Leiden: E.J. Brill. Études Préliminaires aux Religions Orientales dans l'Empire Romain.

Logan, T.J. (1990) 'The origins of the *Jmy-wt* fetish', *JARCE* 27: 61–9.

Lucas, A. (1962) *Ancient Egyptian Materials and Industries*, 4th edition, revised and enlarged by J.R. Harris, London: Edward Arnold.

Lurker, M. (1980) *The Gods and Symbols of Ancient Egypt. An Illustrated Dictionary*, London: Thames and Hudson.

Mace, A.C. (1909) *The Early Dynastic Cemeteries of Naga-ed-Dêr*, II, Leipzig: J.C. Hinrichs.

McEuen, R.E. and Myers, O.H. (1940) 'Two sondages', in R. Mond and O.H. Myers, *Temples of Armant*, text volume, London: Egypt Exploration Society.

Macramallah, R. (1940) *Un Cimetière Archaïque de la Classe Moyenne du Peuple à Saqqarah*, Cairo: Imprimerie Nationale.

Malek, J. (1986) *In the Shadow of the Pyramids. Egypt During the Old Kingdom*, London: Orbis.

Marfoe, L. (1987) 'Cedar forest to silver mountain: social change and the development of long-distance trade in early Near Eastern societies', in M. Rowlands, M. Larsen and K. Kristiansen (eds) *Centre and Periphery in the Ancient World*, 25–35. Cambridge: Cambridge University Press. New Directions in Archaeology.

Martin, G.T. (1979) *The Tomb of Hetepka and Other Reliefs and Inscriptions From the Sacred Animal Necropolis, North Saqqâra 1964–1973*, London: Egypt Exploration Society. Texts from excavations, fourth memoir.

Martin, K. (1984) 'Sedfest', *LÄ* V: 782–90.

—— (1986a) 'Uräus', *LÄ* VI: 864–8.

—— (1986b) 'Was-Zepter', *LÄ* VI: 1152–4.

Martin-Pardey, E. (1976) *Untersuchungen zur ägyptischen Provinzialverwaltung bis zum Ende des Alten Reiches*, Hildesheim: Gerstenberg. HÄB 1.

Maspero, M.G. (1902) 'Note sur les objets recueillis sous la pyramide d'Ounas', *ASAE* 3: 185–90.

Massoulard, E. (1949) *Préhistoire et Protohistoire d'Égypte*, Paris: Institut d'Ethnologie. Travaux et mémoires 53.

Mathieson, I.J. and Tavares, A. (1993) 'Preliminary report on the National Museums of Scotland Saqqara Survey Project, 1990–91', *JEA* 79: 17–31.

Meltzer, E.S. (1972) 'Horus *dn* "cutter," "severer (of heads)"?', *JNES* 31: 338–9.

Midant-Reynes, B., Buchez, N., Hesse, A. and Lechevalier, C. (1990) 'Le site prédynastique d'Adaïma. Rapport préliminaire de la campagne de fouilles 1989', *BIFAO* 90: 247–58.

Midant-Reynes, B., Buchez, N., Crubezy, E., Janin, T. and Hendrickx, S. (1992) 'Le site prédynastique d'Adaïma. Rapport préliminaire de la troisième campagne de fouille, 1991', *BIFAO* 92: 133–46.

Midant-Reynes, B., Crubezy, E. and Janin, T. (1996) 'The Predynastic site of Adaïma', *Egyptian Archaeology* 9: 13–15.

Millet, N.B. (1990) 'The Narmer macehead and related objects', *JARCE* 27: 53–9.

Mills, A.J. (1980) 'Dakhleh Oasis Project – report on the second season of survey, September–December, 1979', *JSSEA* 10: 251–82.

Mogensen, M. (1930) *La Glyptothèque Ny Carlsberg. La Collection Égyptienne*, Copenhagen: Levin and Munksgaard.

Möllers, G. and Scharff, A. (1926) *Die archaeologischen Ergebnisse des vorgeschichtlichen Gräberfeldes von Abusir el-Meleq*, Leipzig: J.C. Hinrichs.

Mond, R.L. and Myers, O.H. (1937) *Cemeteries of Armant*, I, London: Egypt Exploration Society.

—— (1940) *Temples of Armant. A Preliminary Survey*, London: Egypt Exploration Society.

Montet, P. (1928) 'Notes et documents pour servir à l'histoire des relations entre l'ancienne Égypte et la Syrie, II. Nouvelles traces des Égyptiens à Byblos', *Kêmi* 1: 83–93.

—— (1938) 'Tombeaux de la Ière et de la IVe dynasties à Abou-Roach', *Kêmi* 7: 11–69, pls I–XIV.

—— (1946) 'Tombeaux de la Ière et de la IVe dynasties à Abou-Roach. Deuxième partie: inventaire des objets', *Kêmi* 8: 157–223, pls I–XIV.

Moorey, P.R.S. (1987) 'On tracking cultural transfers in prehistory: the case of Egypt and lower Mesopotamia in the fourth millennium BC', in M. Rowlands, M. Larsen and K. Kristiansen (eds) *Centre and Periphery in the Ancient World*, 36–46. Cambridge: Cambridge University Press. New Directions in Archaeology.

Morgan J. de (1896) *Recherches sur les Origines de l'Egypte*, I. *L'Age de la Pierre et les Métaux*, Paris: Ernest Leroux.

—— (1897) *Recherches sur les Origines de l'Egypte*, II. *Ethnographie Préhistorique et Tombeau Royale de Négadah*, Paris: Ernest Leroux.

Mortensen, B. (1991) 'Change in the settlement pattern and population in the beginning of the historical period', *Ägypten und Levante* 2: 11–37.

Müller, H. (1938) *Die formale Entwicklung der Titulatur der ägyptischen Könige*, Glückstadt: J.J. Augustin. Ägyptologische Forschungen 7.

Müller-Winkler, C. (1984) 'Schen-Ring', *LÄ* V: 577–9.

Munro, P. (1993) 'Report on the work of the Joint Archaeological Mission Free University Berlin/University of Hannover during their 12th campaign (15th March until 14th May, 1992) at Saqqâra', *Discussions in Egyptology* 26: 47–58.

Murnane, W.J. (1987) 'The Gebel Sheikh Suleiman monument: epigraphic remarks', *JNES* 46: 282–5.

Murray, G.W. (1939) 'An Archaic hut in Wādi Umm Sidrah', *JEA* 25: 38–9, pls VIII–IX.

Murray, M.A. (1904) *The Osireion at Abydos*, London: Quaritch.

Needler, W. (1956) 'A flint knife of King Djer', *JEA* 42: 41–4.

—— (1967) 'A rock-drawing on Gebel Sheikh Suliman (near Wadi Halfa) showing a scorpion and human figures', *JARCE* 6: 87–92.

—— (1984) *Predynastic and Archaic Egypt in the Brooklyn Museum*, Brooklyn: Brooklyn Museum.

Newberry, P.E. (1909) 'Impressions of seals from Abydos', *Annals of Archaeology and Anthropology* 2: 130, pls XXII–XXV.

O'Brien, A. (1996) 'The serekh as an aspect of the iconography of early kingship', *JARCE* 33: 123–38.

O'Connor, D. (1972) 'A regional population in Egypt to circa 600 BC', in B. Spooner (ed.) *Population Growth: Anthropological Implications*, 78–100. Cambridge, MA: The MIT Press.

—— (1987) 'The earliest pharaohs and the University Museum. Old and new excavations: 1900–1987', *Expedition* 29, 1: 27–39.

—— (1989) 'New funerary enclosures, (*Talbezirke*) of the Early Dynastic Period', *JARCE* 26: 51–86.

—— (1990) Unpublished, untitled project proposal for excavation of the early settlement at North Abydos. Manuscript on file with the author (courtesy of B.J. Kemp).

—— (1991) 'Boat graves and pyramid origins. New discoveries at Abydos, Egypt', *Expedition* 33, 3: 5–17.

—— (1992) 'The status of early Egyptian temples: an alternative theory', in R. Friedman and B. Adams (eds) *The Followers of Horus. Studies Dedicated to Michael Allen Hoffman*, 83–98. Oxford: Oxbow. Monograph 20. Egyptian Studies Association Publication No. 2.

—— (1993) *Ancient Nubia: Egypt's Rival in Africa*, Philadelphia: University Museum, University of Pennsylvania.

—— (1995) 'The earliest royal boat graves', *Egyptian Archaeology* 6: 3–7.

O'Mara, P.F. (1979) *The Palermo Stone and the Archaic Kings of Egypt*, La Canada, CA: Paulette. Studies in the structural archaeology of ancient Egypt.

—— (1996) 'Was there an Old Kingdom historiography? Is it datable?', *Orientalia* 65: 197–208.

Oren, E.D. and Gilead, I. (1981) 'Chalcolithic sites in northwestern Sinai', *Tel Aviv* 8: 25–44.

Oren, E.D. and Yekutieli, Y. (1992) 'Taur Ikhbenieh – earliest evidence for Egyptian interconnections', in E.C.M. van den Brink (ed.) *The Nile Delta in Transition: 4th–3rd Millennium BC*, 361–84. Tel Aviv: van den Brink.

Otto, E. (1975) 'Behedeti', *LÄ* I: 683.

Patch, D.C. (1991) 'The origin and early development of urbanism in ancient Egypt: a regional study', unpublished doctoral thesis, University of Pennsylvania.

Payne, J.C. (1968) 'Lapis lazuli in early Egypt', *Iraq* 30: 58–61.

—— (1973) 'Tomb 100. The decorated tomb at Hierakonpolis confirmed', *JEA* 59: 31–5.

—— (1993) *Catalogue of the Predynastic Egyptian Collection in the Ashmolean Museum*, Oxford: Clarendon Press.

Petrie, W.M.F. (1892) *Medum*, London: David Nutt.

—— (1896) *Koptos*, London: Quaritch.

—— (1900) *Royal Tombs of the First Dynasty*, I, London: Egypt Exploration Fund. Memoir 18.

—— (1901) *Royal Tombs of the Earliest Dynasties*, II, London: Egypt Exploration Fund. Memoir 21.

—— (1902) *Abydos*, I, London: Egypt Exploration Fund. Memoir 22.

—— (1903) *Abydos*, II, London: Egypt Exploration Fund. Memoir 23.

—— (1907) *Gizeh and Rifeh*, London: School of Archaeology in Egypt/Quaritch.

—— (1909) *Memphis, II. The Palace of Apries*, London: School of Archaeology in Egypt/Quaritch.

—— (1910) *Meidum and Memphis, III*, London: School of Archaeology in Egypt/Quaritch.

—— (1914) *Tarkhan, II*, London: School of Archaeology in Egypt/Quaritch.

—— (1925) *Tombs of the Courtiers and Oxyrhynkhos*, London: British School of Archaeology in Egypt.

—— (1939) *The Making of Egypt*, London: The Sheldon Press.

—— (1953) *Ceremonial Slate Palettes, Corpus of Proto-Dynastic Pottery*, London: British School of Egyptian Archaeology.

Petrie, W.M.F. and Quibell, J.E. (1896) *Naqada and Ballas*, London: Quaritch.

Petrie, W.M.F., Wainwright, G.A. and Gardiner, A.H. (1913) *Tarkhan, I and Memphis, V*, London: School of Archaeology in Egypt/Quaritch.

Pinch, G. (1993) *Votive Offerings to Hathor*, Oxford: Griffith Institute.

Porat, N. (1992) 'An Egyptian colony in southern Palestine during the late Predynastic–Early Dynastic period', in E.C.M. van den Brink (ed.) *The Nile Delta in Transition: 4th–3rd Millennium BC*, 433–40. Tel Aviv: van den Brink.

Porter, B. and Moss, R.L.B. (1937) *Topographical Bibliography of Ancient Egyptian Hieroglyphic Texts, Reliefs, and Paintings, V. Upper Egypt: Sites*, Oxford: Oxford University Press at the Clarendon Press.

—— (1951) *Topographical Bibliography of Ancient Egyptian Hieroglyphic Texts, Reliefs, and Paintings, VII. Nubia, the Deserts, and Outside Egypt*, Oxford: Oxford University Press at the Clarendon Press.

—— (1974) *Topographical Bibliography of Ancient Egyptian Hieroglyphic Texts, Reliefs, and Paintings, III. Memphis*, 2nd edition revised and augmented by J. Málek, Oxford: Oxford University Press at the Clarendon Press.

Posener, G. (1965) 'Brèves communications', *RdE* 17: 193–5.

Postgate, N., Wang, T. and Wilkinson, T. (1995) 'The evidence for early writing: utilitarian or ceremonial?', *Antiquity* 69: 459–80.

Prag, K. (1978) 'Silver in the Levant in the fourth millennium BC', in R. Moorey and P. Parr (eds) *Archaeology in the Levant. Essays for Kathleen Kenyon*, 36–45. Warminster: Aris and Phillips.

—— (1986) 'Byblos and Egypt in the fourth millennium BC', *Levant* 18: 59–74.

Pritchard, J.B. (ed.) (1969) *Ancient Near Eastern Texts Relating to the Old Testament*, 3rd edition with supplement, Princeton, New Jersey: Princeton University Press.

Quibell, J.E. (1898a) 'Slate palette from Hieraconpolis', *ZÄS* 36: 81–4.

—— (1898b) *El Kab*, London: Quaritch.

—— (1900) *Hierakonpolis, I*, London: Quaritch.

—— (1904–5) *Catalogue Général des Antiquités Égyptiennes du Musée du Caire. Nos 11001–12000 et 14001–14754. Archaic Objects*, 2 volumes, Cairo: IFAO.

—— (1913) *Excavations at Saqqara (1911–1912). The Tomb of Hesy*, Cairo: IFAO.

—— (1923) *Excavations at Saqqara (1912–1914). Archaic Mastabas*, Cairo: IFAO.

Quibell, J.E. and Green, F.W. (1902) *Hierakonpolis, II*, London: Quaritch.

Quirke, S. (1990) *Who Were the Pharaohs? A History of Their Names With a List of Cartouches*, London: British Museum Press.

—— (1992) *Ancient Egyptian Religion*, London: British Museum Press.

Quirke, S. and Spencer, J. (eds) (1992) *The British Museum Book of Ancient Egypt*, London: British Museum Press.

Randall-MacIver, D. and Mace, A.C. (1902) *El Amrah and Abydos, 1899–1901*, London: Egypt Exploration Fund.

Ray, J.D. (1993) 'The Pharaohs and their court', in J. Malek (ed.) *Egypt. Ancient Culture, Modern Land*, 69–77. Sydney: Weldon Russell. Cradles of Civilization.

Redford, D.B. (1986) *King-Lists, Annals and Day-Books. A Contribution to the Study of the Egyptian Sense of History*, Mississauga, Ontario: Benben Publications. Society for the Study of Egyptian Antiquities Publication 4.

Reeves, N. (1990) *The Complete Tutankhamun. The King, the Tomb, the Royal Treasure*, London: Thames and Hudson.

Reisner, G.A. (1908) *The Early Dynastic Cemeteries of Naga-ed-Dêr*, I, Leipzig: J.C. Hinrichs.

—— (1931) *Mycerinus. The Temples of the Third Pyramid at Giza*, Cambridge, MA: Harvard University Press.

Renfrew, A.C. and Bahn, P. (1991) *Archaeology: Theories, Methods, and Practice*, London: Thames and Hudson.

Ricci, S. (1917) 'La table de Palerme', *CRAIBL* 1917: 107–15.

Rice, M. (1990) *Egypt's Making. The Origins of Ancient Egypt 5000–2000 BC*, London: Routledge.

Ritner, R.K. (1993) *The Mechanisms of Ancient Egyptian Magical Practice*, Chicago: The Oriental Institute of the University of Chicago. Studies in Ancient Oriental Civilization 54.

Rizkana, I. and Seeher, J. (1989) *Maadi III. The Non-Lithic Small Finds and the Structural Remains of the Predynastic Settlement*, Mainz am Rhein: von Zabern. AVDAIK 80.

—— (1990) *Maadi IV. The Predynastic Cemeteries of Maadi and Wadi Digla*, Mainz am Rhein: von Zabern. AVDAIK 81.

Roth, A.M. (1991) *Egyptian Phyles in the Old Kingdom. The Evolution of a System of Social Organization*, Chicago: The Oriental Institute of the University of Chicago. Studies in Ancient Oriental Civilization 48.

—— (1993) 'Social change in the Fourth Dynasty: the spatial organization of pyramids, tombs, and cemeteries', *JARCE* 30: 33–55.

—— (1995) 'Buried pyramids: symbolic shapes and spaces in Old Kingdom mortuary architecture', in C. Eyre (ed.) *Seventh International Congress of Egyptologists, Cambridge, 3–9 September 1995. Abstracts of Papers*, 154–5. Oxford: Oxbow for International Association of Egyptologists.

Rowlands, M., Larsen, M. and Kristiansen, K. (eds) (1987) *Centre and Periphery in the Ancient World*, Cambridge: Cambridge University Press. New Directions in Archaeology.

Saad, Z.Y. (1947) *Royal Excavations at Saqqara and Helwan (1941–1945)*, Cairo: IFAO. Supplément aux Annales du Service des Antiquités de l'Egypte, Cahier 3.

—— (1951) *Royal Excavations at Helwan*, Cairo: IFAO. Supplément aux Annales du Service des Antiquités de l'Egypte, Cahier 14.

—— (1957) *Ceiling Stelae in Second Dynasty Tombs from the Excavations at Helwan*, Cairo: IFAO. Supplément aux Annales du Service des Antiquités de l'Egypte, Cahier 21.

—— (1969) *The Excavations at Helwan: Art and Civilization in the First and Second Egyptian Dynasties*, Norman, Oklahoma: University of Oklahoma Press.

Sayce, A.H. (1898) 'The beginnings of Egyptian monarchy', *PSBA* 20: 96–101.

Sayce, A.H. and Clarke, E. S. (1905) 'Report on certain excavations made at El-Kab during the years 1901, 1902, 1903, 1904', *ASAE* 6: 239–72.

Sayed, A. el- (1979) 'A prehistoric cemetery in the Abydos area', *MDAIK* 35: 249–301.

Schäfer, H. (1902) *Ein Bruchstück altägyptischer Annalen*, Berlin: Verlag der Königliche Akademie der Wissenschaften.

Schlögl, H. (ed.) (1978) *Le Don du Nil. Art Égyptien dans les Collections Suisses*, Basel: Société de Banque Suisse.

Schmidt, K. (1992) 'Tell el-Fara'in/Buto and El-Tell el-Iswid (South): the lithic industries from the Chalcolithic to the early Old Kingdom', in E.C.M. van den Brink (ed.) *The Nile Delta in Transition: 4th–3rd Millennium BC*, 31–41. Tel Aviv: van den Brink.

Schmitz, B. (1984) 'Sem(priester)', *LÄ* V: 833–6.

Schott, E. (1969) 'Die Sockelinschrift des Narmeraffen', *RdE* 21: 77–83.

Schott, S. (1956) 'Zur Krönungstitulatur der Pyramidenzeit', *Nachrichten der Akademie der Wissenschaften in Göttingen, Philologisch-Historische Klasse, aus dem Jahre 1956*, 55–79.

Schulman, A.R. (1980) 'More seal impressions from 'En Besor', *Atiqot* (English series) 14: 17–33.

—— (1983) 'On the dating of Egyptian seal impressions from 'En Besor', *JSSEA* 13, 4: 249–51.

—— (1988) *Ceremonial Execution and Public Rewards. Some Historical Scenes on New Kingdom Private Stelae*, Freiburg/Göttingen: Universitätsverlag/ Vandenhoeck and Ruprecht. Orbis Biblicus et Orientalis 75.

Seidlmayer, S.J. (1988) 'Funerärer Aufwand und soziale Ungleichheit: eine methodische Anmerkung zum Problem der Rekonstruktion der gesell- schaftlichen Gliederung aus Friedhofsfunden', *GM* 104: 25–51.

—— (1996a) 'Die staatliche Anlage der 3. Dyn. in der Nordweststadt von Elephantine. Archäologische und historische Probleme', in M. Bietak (ed.) *Haus und Palast im alten Ägypten/House and Palace in Ancient Egypt*, 195–214. Vienna: Verlag der Österreichischen Akademie der Wissenschaften. Denk- schriften der Gesamtakademie. Untersuchungen der Zweigstelle Kairo des Österreichischen Archäologischen Institutes, Band XIV.

—— (1996b) 'Town and state in the early Old Kingdom. A view from Elephantine', in J. Spencer (ed.) *Aspects of Early Egypt*, 108–27, pls 22–3. London: British Museum Press.

Seligman, C.G. and Murray, M.A. (1911) 'Note upon an early Egyptian standard', *Man* 11: 163–71.

Serpico, M. and White, R. (1996) 'A report on the analysis of the contents of a cache of jars from the tomb of Djer', in J. Spencer (ed.) *Aspects of Early Egypt*, 128–39. London: British Museum Press.

Service, E.R. (1975) *Origins of the State and Civilization: The Process of Cultural Evolution*, New York and London: W.W. Norton.

Sethe, K. (1903) *Urkunden des alten Reichs*, I, Leipzig: J.C. Hinrichs.

—— (1906) *Urkunden der 18. Dynastie*, II. *Historisch-biographische Urkunden aus der Zeit der Könige Thutmosis' I und II*, Leipzig: J.C. Hinrichs.

—— (1914) 'Hitherto unnoticed evidence regarding copper works of art of the oldest period of Egyptian history', *JEA* 1: 233–6.

Seyfried, K.-J. (1984) 'Sandale', *LÄ* V: 379–82.

Shaw, I. and Nicholson, P. (1995) *The British Museum Dictionary of Ancient Egypt*, London: British Museum Press.

Simpson, W.K. (1956) 'A statuette of King Nineter', *JEA* 42: 45–9.

—— (1957) 'A running of the Apis in the reign of Aha', *Orientalia* 26: 139–42.

Slater, R. (1974) 'The archaeology of Dendereh in the First Intermediate Period', unpublished doctoral thesis, University of Pennsylvania.

Smith, H.S. (1971) 'Walter Bryan Emery' (obituary), *JEA* 57: 190–201.

—— (1972) 'The rock inscriptions of Buhen', *JEA* 58: 43–82.

—— (1992) 'The making of Egypt: a review of the influence of Susa and Sumer on Upper Egypt and Lower Nubia in the 4th millennium BC', in R. Friedman and B. Adams (eds) *The Followers of Horus. Studies Dedicated to Michael Allen*

Hoffman, 235–46. Oxford: Oxbow. Monograph 20. Egyptian Studies Association Publication No. 2.

Smith, W.S. (1949) *A History of Egyptian Sculpture and Painting in the Old Kingdom*, London: Oxford University Press (for the Museum of Fine Arts, Boston).

—— (1971) 'The Old Kingdom in Egypt and the beginning of the First Intermediate Period', in I.E.S. Edwards, C.J. Gadd and N.G.L. Hammond (eds) *The Cambridge Ancient History*, 3rd edition, Volume I Part 2 (Early history of the Middle East), 145–207. Cambridge: Cambridge University Press.

—— (1981) *The Art and Architecture of Ancient Egypt*, 2nd revised edition with additions by W.K. Simpson, New Haven, CT and London: Yale University Press. Pelican History of Art.

Spencer, A.J. (1978) 'Two enigmatic hieroglyphs and their relation to the Sed-Festival', *JEA* 64: 52–5.

—— (1980) *Catalogue of Egyptian Antiquities in the British Museum*, V. *Early Dynastic Objects*, London: British Museum Publications.

—— (1993) *Early Egypt: The Rise of Civilisation in the Nile Valley*, London: British Museum Press.

Spencer, A.J. (ed.) (1996) *Aspects of Early Egypt*, London: British Museum Press.

Stadelmann, R. (1983) 'Das vermeintliche Sonnenheiligtum im Norden des Djoserbezirkes', *ASAE* 69: 373–8.

—— (1984) 'Saujet el-Arjan', *LÄ* IV: 495–7.

—— (1985) 'Die Oberbauten der Königsgräber der 2. Dynastie in Sakkara', in *Mélanges Mokhtar* II, 295–307. Cairo: IFAO. Bibliothèque d'Etude 97.

—— (1987) 'Königinnengrab und Pyramidenbezirke im alten Reich', *ASAE* 71: 251–60.

Staehelin, E. (1984) 'Ornat', *LÄ* V: 613–18.

Strudwick, N. (1985) *The Administration of Egypt in the Old Kingdom. The Highest Titles and Their Holders*, London: Kegan Paul International. Studies in Egyptology.

Swelim, N. (1988) 'The dry moat of the Netjerykhet complex', in J. Baines, T.G.H. James, A. Leahy and A.F. Shore (eds) *Pyramid Studies and Other Essays Presented to I.E.S. Edwards*, 12–22. London: Egypt Exploration Society.

—— (1991) 'Some remarks on the great rectangular monuments of Middle Saqqara', *MDAIK* 47 (Festschrift Kaiser): 389–402.

Takamiya, I. (1994) 'Egyptian pottery in A-Group cemeteries, Nubia: towards an understanding of pottery production and distribution in pre-dynastic and early-dynastic Egypt', unpublished M.Phil. thesis, University of Cambridge.

Tavares, A. (1995) 'The National Museum of Scotland Saqqara Survey Project', unpublished paper delivered at the Seventh International Congress of Egyptologists, Cambridge, September 1995.

Teissier, B. (1987) 'Glyptic evidence for a connection between Iran, Syro-Palestine and Egypt in the fourth and third millennia', *Iran* 25: 27–53.

Trigger, B.G. (1972) 'Determinants of urban growth in pre-industrial societies', in P.J. Ucko, R. Tringham and G.W. Dimbleby (eds) *Man, Settlement and Urbanism*, 575–99. London: Duckworth.

—— (1984) 'The mainlines of socio-economic development in dynastic Egypt to the end of the Old Kingdom', in L. Krzyzaniak and M. Kobusiewicz (eds) *Origin and Early Development of Food-Producing Cultures in North-Eastern Africa*, 101–48. Poznan: Poznan Archaeological Museum. Studies in African Archaeology 2.

—— (1985) 'The evolution of pre-industrial cities: a multi-linear perspective', in F. Geus and F. Thill (eds) *Mélanges Offerts à Jean Vercoutter*, 343–53. Paris: Éditions Recherche sue les Civilisations.

Trigger, B.G., Kemp, B.J., O'Connor, D. and Lloyd, A.B. (1983) *Ancient Egypt. A Social History*, Cambridge: Cambridge University Press.

Troy, L. (1986) *Patterns of Queenship in Ancient Egyptian Myth and History*, Uppsala: University of Uppsala. Acta Universitatis Upsaliensis. Boreas. Uppsala Studies in Ancient Mediterranean and Near Eastern Civilizations 14.

Vandersleyen, C. (1971) 'Les fouilles belges d'Elkab (Haute Egypte)', *Revue des Archéologues et Historiens d'Art de Louvain* 4: 25–38.

Vandier, J. (1968) 'Une stèle égyptienne portant un nouveau nom royal de la troisième dynastie', *CRAIBL* 1968: 16–22.

Velde, H. te (1967) *Seth, God of Confusion*, Leiden: E.J. Brill.

Verhoeven, U. (1984) *Grillen, kochen, backen im Alltag und im Ritual Altägyptens. Ein lexikographischer Beitrag*, Brussels: Fondation Égyptologique Reine Élisabeth. Rites Égyptiens IV.

Vermeersch, P.M. (1970) 'Elkab 1966–1969. Le secteur archaïque', *CdE* 45: 32–4.

Vigneau, A. (ed.) (1935) *Encyclopédie Photographique de l'Art: Les Antiquités Égyptiennes du Musée du Louvre*, vol. 1, no. 1, Paris: Tel.

Wainwright, G.A. (1941) 'Seshat and the pharaoh', *JEA* 26: 30–40.

Walle, B. van de (1954) 'Empreintes de sceaux archaïques', in *Fouilles de El Kab. Documents*, Livraison III, 91–8. Brussels: Fondation Égyptologique Reine Elisabeth, Parc du Cinquantenaire.

Wallert, I. (1962) *Die Palmen im alten Ägypten*, Berlin: Bruno Hessling. MÄS 1.

Warburton, D.A. (1997) *State and Economy in Ancient Egypt. Fiscal Vocabulary of the New Kingdom*, Fribourg/Göttingen: University Press Fribourg/ Vandenhoeck and Ruprecht. Orbis Biblicus et Orientalis 151.

Ward, W.A. (1969) 'The supposed Asiatic campaign of Narmer', *Mélanges de l'Université Saint-Joseph* 45: 205–21.

—— (1991) 'Early contacts between Egypt, Canaan, and Sinai: remarks on the paper by Amnon Ben-Tor', *BASOR* 281: 11–26.

Way, T. von der (1984) 'Untersuchungen des Deutschen Archäologischen Instituts Kairo im nördlichen Delta zwischen Disûq und Tida', *MDAIK* 40: 297–328, pls 37–9.

—— (1986) 'Tell el-Fara'in – Buto. 1. Bericht', *MDAIK* 42: 191–212.

—— (1987) 'Tell el-Fara'in – Buto. 2. Bericht', *MDAIK* 43: 241–57.

—— (1988) 'Tell el-Fara'in – Buto. 3. Bericht', *MDAIK* 44: 283–306.

—— (1989) 'Tell el-Fara'in – Buto. 4. Bericht', *MDAIK* 45: 275–307.

—— (1991) 'Die Grabungen in Buto und die Reichseinigung', *MDAIK* 47 (Festschrift Kaiser): 419–24.

—— (1992) 'Excavations at Tell el-Fara'in/Buto in 1987–1989', in E.C.M. van den Brink (ed.) *The Nile Delta in Transition: 4th–3rd Millennium BC*, 1–10. Tel Aviv: van den Brink.

—— (1993) *Untersuchungen zur Spätvor- und Frühgeschichte Unterägyptens*, Heidelberg: Heidelberger Orientverlag. Studien zur Archäologie und Geschichte Altägyptens 8.

—— (1996) 'Early Dynastic architecture at Tell el-Fara'în-Buto', in M. Bietak (ed.) *Haus und Palast im alten Ägypten/House and Palace in Ancient Egypt*, 247–52. Vienna: Verlag der Österreichischen Akademie der Wissenschaften. Denkschriften der Gesamtakademie. Untersuchungen der Zweigstelle Kairo des Österreichischen Archäologischen Institutes, Band XIV.

Way, T. von der and Schmidt, K. (1985) 'Bericht über den Fortgang der Untersuchungen im Raum Tell el-Fara'in/Buto', *MDAIK* 41: 269–91.

Weeks, K.R. (1971–2) 'Preliminary report on the first two seasons at Hierakonpolis. Part II: the Early Dynastic palace', *JARCE* 9: 29–33.

Weill, R. (1908) *Les Origines de l'Egypte Pharaonique, 1ᵉʳᵉ Partie. La IIᵉ et la IIIᵉ Dynasties*, Paris: Ernest Leroux.

—— (1911–12) 'Monuments nouveaux des premières dynasties', *Sphinx* 15: 1–35.

—— (1961) *Recherches sur la Iʳᵉ Dynastie et les Temps Prépharaoniques*, Cairo: IFAO. Bibliothèque d'Etude 38.

Weinstein, J.M. (1984) 'The significance of Tell Areini for Egyptian-Palestinian relations at the beginning of the Bronze Age', *BASOR* 256: 63.

Wenke, R.J. (1989) 'Egypt: origins of complex societies', *Annual Review of Anthropology* 18: 129–55.

—— (1991) 'The evolution of early Egyptian civilization: issues and evidence', *Journal of World Prehistory* 5, 3: 279–329.

Wenke, R.J. and Brewer, D.J. (1996) 'The Archaic–Old Kingdom Delta: the evidence from Mendes and Kom El-Hisn', in M. Bietak (ed.) *Haus und Palast im alten Ägypten/House and Palace in Ancient Egypt*, 265–85. Vienna: Verlag der Österreichischen Akademie der Wissenschaften. Denkschriften der Gesamtakademie. Untersuchungen der Zweigstelle Kairo des Österreichischen Archäologischen Institutes, Band XIV.

Westendorf, W. (1966) 'Beiträge aus und zu den medizinischen Texten, I. Mafdet, die Herrin des Lebenshauses, und Seth, groß an Lebenskraft', *ZÄS* 92: 128–43.

Whitehouse, H. (1987) 'King Den in Oxford', *Oxford Journal of Archaeology* 6: 257–67.

Wildung, D. (1969a) 'Zur Deutung der Pyramide von Medum', *RdE* 21: 135–45.

—— (1969b) *Die Rolle ägyptischer Könige im Bewußtsein ihrer Nachwelt*, I, Berlin: Bruno Hessling. MÄS 17.

—— (1981) *Ägypten vor den Pyramiden. Münchner Ausgrabungen in Ägypten*, Mainz am Rhein: von Zabern.

Wilkinson, T.A.H. (1993a) 'Egypt in transition: Predynastic–Early Dynastic chronology and the effects of state formation', unpublished doctoral thesis, University of Cambridge.

—— (1993b) 'The identification of Tomb B1 at Abydos: refuting the existence of a king *Ro/*Iry-Hor', *JEA* 79: 241–3.

—— (1995) 'A new king in the western desert', *JEA* 81: 205–10.

—— (1996a) 'A re-examination of the Early Dynastic necropolis at Helwan', *MDAIK* 52: 337–54.

—— (1996b) *State Formation in Egypt: Chronology and Society*, Oxford: Tempus Reparatum. BAR International Series 651. Cambridge Monographs in African Archaeology 40.

Willems, H. (1990) 'Crime, cult and capital punishment (Mo'alla inscription 8)', *JEA* 76: 27–54.

Williams, B.B. (1986) *Excavations Between Abu Simbel and the Sudan Frontier. The A-Group Royal Cemetery at Qustul: Cemetery L*, Chicago: The Oriental Institute of the University of Chicago. Oriental Institute Nubian Expedition III.

—— (1987) 'Forebears of Menes in Nubia: myth or reality?', *JNES* 46: 15–26.

—— (1988) 'Narmer and the Coptos colossi', *JARCE* 25: 35–59.

Williams, B.B. and Logan, T.J. (1987) 'The Metropolitan Museum knife handle and aspects of pharaonic imagery before Narmer', *JNES* 46: 253–80.

Wilson, J.A. (1955) 'Buto and Hierakonpolis in the geography of Egypt', *JNES* 14: 209–36.

—— (1960) 'Egypt through the New Kingdom. Civilization without cities', in C.H. Kraeling and R.M. Adams (eds) *City Invincible*, 124–64. Chicago: The University of Chicago Press.

Winkler, H.A. (1938) *Rock-Drawings of Southern Upper Egypt*, I, London: Egypt Exploration Society.

Winter, E. (1994) 'Wer steht hinter Narmer', in M. Bietak, J. Holaubek, H. Mukarovsky and H. Satzinger (eds) *Zwischen den beiden Ewigkeiten. Festschrift Gertrud Thausing*, 279–90. Vienna: Eigenverlag des Institutes für Ägyptologie der Universität Wien.

Wittfogel, K. (1957) *Oriental Despotism. A Comparative Study of Total Power*, New Haven: Yale University Press.

Wood, W. (1978) 'A reconstruction of the reliefs of Hesy-Re', *JARCE* 15: 9–24.

—— (1987) 'The Archaic stone tombs at Helwan', *JEA* 73: 59–70.

Wright, H.T. and Johnson, G. (1975) 'Population, exchange and early state formation in southwestern Iran', *American Anthropologist* 77: 267–89.

Wunderlich, J. (1988) 'Investigations on the development of the western Nile Delta in Holocene times', in E.C.M. van den Brink (ed.) *The Archaeology of the Nile Delta: Problems and Priorities*, 251–7. Amsterdam: Netherlands Foundation for Archaeological Research in Egypt.

Yadin, Y. (1955) 'The earliest record of Egypt's military penetration into Asia?', *IEJ* 5: 1–16.

Zarins, J. (1989) 'Ancient Egypt and the Red Sea trade: the case for obsidian in the Predynastic and Archaic periods', in A. Leonard and B.B. Williams (eds) *Essays in Ancient Civilization Presented to Helene J. Kantor*, 339–68. Chicago: The Oriental Institute of the University of Chicago. Studies in Ancient Oriental Civilization 47.

—— (1990) 'Obsidian and the Red Sea trade: prehistoric aspects', in M. Taddei (ed.) *South Asian Archaeology 1987*, I (*Proceedings of the Ninth International Conference of the Association of South Asian Archaeologists in Western Europe*), 507–41. Rome: Istituto Italiano per il Medio ed Estremo Oriente. Serie Orientale Roma 66, 1.

Ziermann, M. (1993) *Elephantine XVI. Befestigungsanlagen und Stadtentwicklung in der Frühzeit und im frühen alten Reich*, Mainz am Rhein: von Zabern. AVDAIK 87.

INDEX

— ◆ —

Page numbers in bold refer to figures.